DEC 1 4 1999 DATE			

Also by BERYL ROWLAND:

Blind Beasts: Chaucer's Animal World, 1971

Animals with Human Faces, 1973

Birds with Human Souls, 1978

*Chaucer and Middle English Studies in Honour of
Rossell Hope Robbins*, 1975
Edited by Beryl Rowland

COMPANION TO
chaucer
STUDIES
REVISED EDITION

EDITED BY
BERYL ROWLAND
YORK UNIVERSITY, TORONTO

New York   Oxford
OXFORD UNIVERSITY PRESS
1979

First edition of *Companion to Chaucer Studies*,
© Oxford University Press (Canadian Branch) 1968

Printed in the United States of America

printing, last digit: 10

Library of Congress Cataloging in Publication Data

Rowland, Beryl.
  Companion to Chaucer studies.

  Includes bibliographies and index.
  1.   Chaucer, Geoffrey, d. 1400—Criticism and interpretation.   2.   Chaucer, Geoffrey, d. 1400—Criticism
and interpretation—History.   I.   Title.
PR1924.R68   1979   821'.1   78-14542
ISBN 0-19-502489-3

Preface

The *Companion to Chaucer Studies* has been devised to help students when they confront the formidable mass of Chaucerian scholarship. In particular, it endeavors to give those possessing limited library facilities some idea of the critical background that seems essential for an appreciation of Chaucer's poetry at any but a superficial level. Perhaps it may also prove useful and stimulating to those already familiar with Chaucer scholarship.

Each chapter, specially commissioned by the Oxford University Press, is subjective and an entity to itself; the writer reviews the scholarship that he considers to be the most significant and offers his own opinion on the topic. There is no attempt to standardize approaches. Conflicting views, diverse considerations of the same critical material have been welcomed.

The first edition of the *Companion to Chaucer Studies* reviewed scholarship up to 1968; the present edition advances it to 1978. There is good reason for this updating. In the last ten years, more than one thousand articles and nearly forty books on Chaucer and his poetry have been published. The scholars in the *Companion* review this material selectively, bearing in mind that the student of Chaucer needs to be aware of the best that has been said. Two new chapters have been included in this second edition: "Chaucer, the Church, and Religion" by Robert W. Ackerman and "The *Legend of Good Women*" by John H. Fisher.

This edition appears at a time of unprecedented industry in Chaucer studies. A journal important to Chaucerians, *The Chaucer Review*, edited by Robert W. Frank, Jr., has published some twenty papers annually since 1968. After ten years of preparation, the *Chaucer Variorum*, under the general editorship of Paul G. Ruggiers, has produced its first volume, a facsimile of the Hengwrt manuscript, containing a transcription of the text and a comparison of variant readings from the Ellesmere manuscript, and will shortly publish *The Variorum Commentary on Chaucer's Minor Poems*, edited by George B. Pace and Alfred David. *The Chaucer Library*, under Robert E. Lewis and his committee, has begun publication of its classical and medieval works, so edited from medieval manuscripts as to provide texts most closely resembling those that Chaucer used. The first volume, *The Medieval Achilleid of Statius*, edited by Paul M. Clogan, will be followed by *De Miseria Condicionis Humane*, edited by Robert E. Lewis, and by Nicholas of Lynne's *Kalendarium*, edited by Sigmund Eisner. In addition, major scholars of our time, Albert C. Baugh, Derek S. Brewer, E. Talbot Donaldson, John H. Fisher, and Robert A. Pratt have provided texts with superb notes, and F. N. Robinson's famous edition, revised in 1957, is in the process of being updated. Indicative of the present enthusiasm for Chaucer studies is the formation of the New Chaucer Society with a newsletter, annual conference, and yearbook.

An important reason for Chaucer's perennial appeal is his ability to make his audience *work*. Throughout his literary career Chaucer is obsessed with an audience that is fictive, varied, unpredictable, independent of time and place. Again and again he looks for a response in readers capable of making sound critical judgments, of sharing the emotional experience of the poem, and of sympathizing with the poet's difficulties of composition. He may address them directly, describing how they should react and warning them against errors of judgment. On other occasions he may present his material equivocally, offer inadequate or conflicting opinions, or portray protagonists and their actions from many and even contradictory points of view, thereby forcing upon the audience an ingenious kind of indepth participation. Every poem carries some kind of address to the audience and eventually that audience, whether past or present, is compelled to realize its responsibilities as critic or interpreter.

Contemporary critics can help us to respond to the demands that Chaucer makes upon us. They bring to the study of

Chaucer's works scholarly techniques, more comprehensive, objective, and scientific than were employed in the past; while they recognize that the values of their own age may influence their appreciation of his art, they examine the poetry in the perspective of Chaucer's period with a new awareness of medieval culture. Yet their function is not only to inform us but to sharpen us for the challenge. Over the centuries Chaucer continues to speak to us, urging us to realize the imaginative and creative role which he offers us. We too must be active critics, expressing independent opinions on his poetry, and making up our own minds.

B.R.

York University, Toronto
December 1978

Contents

COMPANION
TO
chaucer
STUDIES

ONE

ALBERT C. BAUGH

Chaucer the Man

There are two Chaucers, as we all know, or two aspects of the man. There is Chaucer the civil servant, who has left abundant traces in the records, and Chaucer the poet, the creator of *Troilus and Criseyde* and the *Canterbury Tales* as well as various minor poems, which are minor only by comparison with his two master works. (There is also the image of himself which he projects in a number of the poems.) That the two men are the same is perhaps incapable of proof, but the eagle in the *House of Fame* calls him "Geffrey" and alludes to his portly figure. He is busy all day with his reckonings, going home at night to bury himself in another book. This last seems to fit the Geoffrey Chaucer who, we believe, was at the time Comptroller of the Customs. Even the portliness of the poet is alluded to elsewhere and is confirmed by Hoccleve's portrait and other representations. The Man of Law refers to the many tales "Chaucer" has told. The Geoffrey Chaucer of the records appoints another poet, John Gower, his attorney. Much other circumstantial evidence, together with the fact that no other Geoffrey Chaucer is known, leads to the reasonable belief that civil servant and poet were one man. So far as I know the identity has never seriously been questioned.

It is surprising how much we know of a fourteenth-century

Englishman who was neither a great noble like John of Gaunt nor an important public figure. Chaucer's name occurs in, or is associated with, nearly 500 contemporary documents. These were gradually turned up by students between Speght and Sir Harris Nicolas until Frederick J. Furnivall and the professionals whose help he was able to enlist (W. D. Selby, E. A. Bond, R. E. G. Kirk, and his son E. F. Kirk) produced the collection known as *Life-Records of Chaucer*. These volumes, together with the collection of references and allusions published by Caroline F. E. Spurgeon under the title *Five Hundred Years of Chaucer Criticism and Allusion*, have had to serve us until quite recently. And they have served us very well, enabling us to dissipate the legends with which early biographies of the poet were disfigured and to describe a career which in its main outlines will not be substantially altered. In the course of the present century more than 200 books and articles have been published on Chaucer's life. Many of these have been of the first importance, such as A. A. Kern's dissertation on Chaucer's ancestry and J. R. Hulbert's on his official life. Others have thrown light on special episodes. Of particular importance at the time was the article by Samuel Moore, "Studies in the Life-Records of Chaucer," because it brought to bear on several incidents in Chaucer's career parallel records concerning friends and contemporaries in the same offices or circumstances. It is naturally impossible to mention separately most of these books and articles, but they are easily found in the bibliographies of Hammond, Griffith, Crawford, Wells, and the appropriate section of the *CBEL*.

The largest addition, from a documentary point of view, to our knowledge of Chaucer's life has resulted from the project conceived by J. M. Manly and Edith Rickert, supported mainly by generous grants over a period of ten years (1927-37) from the General Education Board. The project as it developed amounted to a systematic search, by a team of professional record searchers directed by Lilian J. Redstone, of all classes of fourteenth-century records which might conceivably contain references to the poet. Some of the individual finds were published in occasional communications to the *Times Literary Supplement* and elsewhere, but the task of combining the old and new material and preparing it for the press had scarcely begun at the time of Miss Rickert's death in 1938. Manly was then completely occupied with finishing their joint undertaking, *The Text of the Canterbury Tales.* His own death followed two months after this monumental eight-volume work was published, and the life-records long lay in manuscript. That they have now appeared is due to the unselfish devotion of Martin M. Crow and Clair C. Olson, both former students of Manly and Rickert, who undertook in 1950 to edit the material for publication. The result is a handsome volume of 629 pages, *Chaucer Life-Records,* that will be for years to come the point of departure of any work on the poet's biography.

The history of this great project is given in succinct form in the preface to the volume and with additional details in "Materials for a New Edition of the Chaucer Life-Records" by Crow. Although the published volume contains every document now known which concerns Chaucer directly and a number of collateral documents, it is important to remember that the requirements of the publisher made necessary a considerable reduction (about a third) in the size of the volume originally contemplated. In the preliminary draft completed in 1941 by Miss Redstone the manuscript amounted to 2932 pages in longhand. Most of the material on the ancestry of Chaucer collected by Vincent B. Redstone over a period of forty years in a half-dozen voluminous notebooks (now at the University of Chicago) had to be omitted. This is as it should be, since the first purpose of the volume is to give us the life-records of Chaucer himself; but this material is of great interest and it is good to know that a book on Chaucer's ancestry, completed by Miss Redstone and her father, will eventually be published, it is hoped, as a supplement to the *Life-Records.* In the meantime students of Chaucer should remember that a number of the omitted documents are included in the Chaucer Society collection and that the book (really four separate parts) resulting from the efforts of Furnivall and his collaborators retains its usefulness.

Some idea of the contribution which the new *Chaucer Life-Records* makes to our knowledge of Chaucer's life and the advance which it represents over the older collection must be given. In the mere number of documents printed the new collection nearly doubles the size of the Chaucer Society volume. That volume contained 299 numbered items. The chronological list of documents in the new volume runs to 493. A few of these do not contain the Chaucer name but have to do with the offices which he held. On the other hand Kirk's total includes a number concerning earlier representatives of the Chaucer family, which are not reprinted. It must be admitted, however, that the most important facts of Chaucer's life were established by Kirk's collection and that most of the records subsequently found only sharpen the biographical picture. As the editors note, much of the new material had been published before, especially by Manly and Rickert, who rightly felt that it was of immediate interest to students of Chaucer and should be communicated to them as promptly as circumstances justified. When they delayed, it was because of puzzling details in a new document which they hoped might be cleared up by further search. For it must be realized that many fourteenth-century records cannot be understood, can sometimes be actually misunderstood, when considered out of their administrative and procedural context. As Miss Redstone wrote, "The chancery clerks, law clerks, exchequer clerks and others from whose writings the records are drawn had no biographical intentions, and their documents, even in their own day, were comprehensible only by men of their own kind" (quoted in the preface to *Chaucer Life-Records*, pp. xii-xiii). An important part of the material collected by Miss Redstone and her co-workers consisted of documents not about Chaucer himself but about his associates and contemporaries in offices and situations like his. The bulk of this material could not be printed *in extenso*, but it is the basis of the commentary, prepared by Miss Redstone, which accompanies many of the Chaucer documents. This commentary has been ably condensed (and supplemented) by Crow and Olson. It provides an indispensable background against which a particular document is to be viewed. The editors deserve the greatest credit for the way in which they have carried out this laborious task, incorporating the results of Chaucerian scholarship during the twenty-five years since Miss Redstone prepared her first draft and bringing the whole treatment up to date.

One other feature of the new volume will certainly be generally approved. It is the organization of the documents on a subject basis. Thus there are thirty-one chapters, each devoted to a single episode or aspect of Chaucer's career, e.g. "Chaucer's Capture in the Campaign of 1359-60," "Chaucer's Journeys," "Philippa Chaucer, Wife of Geoffrey Chaucer." Not so much violence is done to chronology as might be expected, since the chapters follow a natural time sequence and the items under each are presented chronologically. A list of all the published documents in chronological order is included in an appendix.

The biography that emerges is of course quite different from the legend-encrusted accounts that prevailed in the seventeenth and eighteenth centuries. Certain features of these accounts persisted down to the middle of the nineteenth century. Their gradual elimination can be followed in the lecture by Olson listed in the bibliography of this chapter. What is now known from the records that have survived need not be repeated here. It is familiar to all students of the poet, and can be found well summarized in recent editions of his work, such as Robinson's, and elsewhere. A new full-length biography, which will make use of the large amount of collateral material excluded from the *Chaucer Life-Records*, is in preparation by the editors of that volume.

Some questions naturally still remain. The exact date of the poet's birth is not known, present opinion varying from 1340, which sorts well with the testimony of the Scrope-Grosvenor suit and is a convenient round number, to 1343-5, which seems to some to be more in keeping with the age of the poet writing the *Book of the Duchess* and his apparent youth at the time the Countess of Ulster provides him with garments and spending money in 1357. Correspondence on the subject in the *TLS* (1957) is inconclusive, but the communication of G. D. G. Hall (June 28) is helpful. Some discussions such as that of George Williams (*A New View*) seem to be special pleading to support a theory. Again, we know nothing about Chaucer's schooling. Edith Rickert's suggestion that he went to the almonry school of St. Paul's rests on slight grounds, though there is nothing inherently improbable in it. Whether he once attended one of the Inns of Court is still debated. It was urged by Edith Rickert, accepted by Manly (*New Light*), but rejected by Tout, that great student of medieval administrative history. The evidence has most recently been reexamined by D. S. Bland, who concludes that it is an attractive possibility, but no more than a plausible theory.

One thing that recommends the theory to some is that, if true, it would explain what Chaucer was doing at least part of the time between 1360 and 1366, a blank period in our knowledge. At the end of this period we find him married. We would like to know the date of his marriage, to be sure of the exact family relationship of his wife, to have a convincing explanation of *Pan'* in *Philippa Pan'*, in what seems to be the earliest reference to her. The explanation *Panetaria* still crops up in books and essays of less than scholarly quality, in spite of Manly's finding that pantry mistresses were always men. Haldeen Braddy proposes to interpret it as "daughter of Panneto." Manly's suggestion (*New Light*) that Philippa was possibly a Pandolf is shown by Margaret Galway (*N&Q*, 1957) to rest on incorrect or doubtful identification of Pullesdon in the Countess of Ulster's accounts, where an unnamed groom is paid 12*d* for escorting her damoiselle Philippa Pan' from Pullesdon to Hatfield. Galway opts for Pudleston, co. Hereford, which was in the possession of the Mortimers and other connections of Lionel and his wife. This, of course, throws no light on the meaning of Pan' or the identification of Philippa, and Galway's speculations on how she happened to be in "Pullesdon" are unconvincing. In another article (*MLR*, 1960) she makes the plausible suggestion that Philippa and Geoffrey were both in the service of Elizabeth's infant daughter

Philippa of Eltham, and that the mark after the name Pan, usually represented by an apostrophe, is in reality only a small dot and not necessarily a sign of abbreviation. Since Sir Payne de Roet usually appears in the records as Panetto or Paon(net), the use of Pan' in the Countess of Ulster's records may have been for the purpose of distinguishing Philippa Pan' from Philippa of Eltham. We thus come back to Braddy's interpretation mentioned above.

Of Chaucer's various missions abroad the records are often tantalizingly vague. "On secret negotiations of the king" tells us very little, but our information on the mission to Lombardy in 1378 is a little more explicit. He and Edward de Berkeley, each with a company of men and horses, were sent to confer with Bernabò Visconti and Sir John Hawkwood on matters touching the "expedicionem guerre Regis." New documents brought forward by Haldeen Braddy (*MLN*, 1933), Manly (*ibid.*, 1934), and Robert A. Pratt (*ELH*, 1949) make clear various details of the mission.

One of the most distressing incidents of Chaucer's life, by no means fully understood, is the Cecilia Chaumpaigne affair. On May 1, 1380 she released Chaucer from all her rights of action against him "de raptu meo." P. R. Watts has examined the evidence from the point of view of a modern lawyer, but seems to take insufficiently into account medieval accusations of *raptus* for other offenses as well as the felony. T.F.T. Plucknet's comments on Watts's article are a useful corrective, since they are by a historian of English law. But he, too, believed that Cecilia was seduced by Chaucer, though the offense was not rape. It would be well if the episode were studied in the light of other contemporary actions based on the charge of "raptus."

During the last generation or so we have learned somewhat more about the poet's children, especially about Thomas Chaucer, who in the first third of the fifteenth century was a rich and important person. The beginning of our fuller understanding was Martin Ruud's monograph on him. This was supplemented by an extensive body of records collected by Kirk and intended for a companion volume to the Chaucer Society's *Life-Records* of the poet, but for some reason it was not issued. Kirk's collection was found by the present writer and published with additions. Later a most important document was printed by Manly (*TLS*, 1933) concerning a lawsuit during the poet's lifetime in which the son is named "Thomas Chaucer, esquire, son of Geoffrey Chaucer, esquire." This satisfies most scholars, but there are a few who cannot believe that so powerful a magnate could have been the son of the poet. They therefore suggest that Philippa Chaucer was one of John of Gaunt's mistresses and that John of Gaunt was the real father. The theory was urged by Russell Krauss in "Chaucerian Problems," vigorously refuted by Manly (*RES*, 1934), and revived with no new evidence by George Williams (*A New View*). Kittredge's question whether the "little Lewis, my son" for whom Chaucer wrote *A Treatise on the Astrolabe* in 1391 was Lewis Chaucer or Lewis Clifford (*MP*, 1917) seems to be answered by Manly's finding Lewis and Thomas Chaucer associated in 1403 in the garrison of the royal castle of Carmarthen (*TLS*, 1928). Finally, Thomas Chaucer's daughter Alice, who by her third marriage became Duchess of Suffolk, is treated fully by Marjorie Anderson. Concerning Chaucer's daughters there is more uncertainty, but it seems likely that the Elizabeth who was admitted to Barking as a nun in 1381, and in connection with whose admission John of Gaunt paid over £51, was the poet's daughter. Likewise, Manly's conjecture that the Agnes Chaucer who was one of the damsels in waiting, along with Joan Swynford, at the coronation of Henry IV was also a daughter of the poet is not improbable, and there are certain *a priori* reasons for accepting it.

That new discoveries are still possible is suggested by our recently learning that Chaucer on one of his earliest missions was sent to Spain. The document which tells us this has been in print since 1890, but because Chaucer's name was wrongly transcribed it escaped notice until 1955, when its proper identification was suggested by Suzanne Honoré-Duvergé. It is a safe-conduct issued February 22, 1366, by the king of Navarre to "Geffroy de

Chauserre escuier englois en sa compaignie trois compaignons avec leurs varlez chevaux et bens quelconques troussez ou a trousser en males ou dehors pour aler venir demorer se remuer conversser et retorner par tout ou il lui playra par touz noz villes forteresses pors passages et destroiz tant de jour que de nuit . . . ." It was to be valid until Pentecost (May 24). The document is of great interest both because we learn from it for the first time that Chaucer was in Spain and because it falls within the period 1360-6, albeit at the end of that period, which had hitherto been a complete blank in our knowledge of the poet. The nature of Chaucer's mission, I believe, is misunderstood by Honoré-Duvergé; I have discussed the matter at length in "The Background of Chaucer's Mission to Spain."

Not only do we know much about the poet's life but, what is even more remarkable, we may feel confident that we may form a just idea of his appearance. We have first of all the representation painted at the instance of Thomas Hoccleve which appears in manuscripts of his *Regement of Princes* and the fine miniature in the Ellesmere MS. of the *Canterbury Tales*, which is even earlier, and we have a number of later portraits in oil which seem to preserve an authentic tradition. Several of these are described and reproduced in Spielmann's *The Portraits of Geoffrey Chaucer*. The Harvard portrait is reproduced in color as the frontispiece of Manly's *Some New Light on Chaucer*. The Plimpton portrait is reproduced and discussed by Reginald Call. Of more derivative character are the many engravings, in connection with which the article by George L. Lam and Warren H. Smith may be consulted. And not to be overlooked is the handsome full-page illumination at the beginning of the manuscript of *Troilus and Criseyde* in the Corpus Christi College, Cambridge, library, which represents Chaucer reading his poem to a noble and aristocratic audience in the open air. Identifications of some of the personages are suggested by Margaret Galway (*MLR*, 1949). All of the portraits of Chaucer are sufficiently alike in showing a man in later life, of a ruddy complexion, fair-haired, with a forked beard and drooping mustache, somewhat portly, to justify the belief that they bear a close resemblance to the Chaucer of real life, and the playful allusions in the poetry—of the eagle in the *House of Fame* and the Host in the *Prologue to Sir Thopas* ("this were a popet in an arm t'enbrace")—confirm the corpulence observable in the portraits.

It is inevitable that students and readers of Chaucer should speculate about the kind of man he was, and should try to discover what his attitudes were toward the questions that were occupying men's minds, where his sympathies lay, and what were the predominating qualities of his temperament and disposition. These things can only be a matter of inference. From the fact that he was sent on a good many missions abroad, some of them of a delicate kind (like the negotiations for the marriage of the young Richard to the daughter of the French king), one may argue that he possessed tact, urbanity, responsibility and other appropriate attributes. This is what E. P. Kuhl does in "Why Was Chaucer Sent to Milan in 1378?" ending up with a list of qualities which the most accomplished diplomat can hardly possess in their entirety. Chaucer was doubtless possessed of many of them, and for some that he lists (humor, gaiety, the ability to see the funny side of higher things, the artful jest . . . suavity, etc.) the inference is reinforced by the impression derived from his poetry, if indeed they are not derived in the first place from the poetry. C. E. Lawrence's "The Personality of Geoffrey Chaucer" is frankly an attempt to discover the poet's personality from his writings. It is a popular article, and the author is cheerfully unembarrassed by the findings of modern scholarship, but when he says Chaucer's thought "never was mean or petty, as even Wordsworth's could be, for the reason that Geoffrey Chaucer was not a vain man" most of us will agree with him. It is when we undertake to conclude what Chaucer's opinion was on any particular topic that disagreements are pretty certain to arise. For example, those who accept Kittredge's view of the "Marriage Group" as a dramatically integrated segment of the *Canterbury Tales* are most likely also to believe with him that the Franklin's solution is what Chaucer thought about marriage, a solution which was ahead of his time. This is questioned by Donald R. Howard in "The Conclusion of the Marriage Group." There have been similar attempts to define Chaucer's position on various other matters, though the dangers and limitations of drawing autobiographical inferences from a poet's works have been stressed by George Kane. Chaucer's stand on questions of contemporary politics and religion is discussed by Roger S. Loomis in "Was Chaucer a Laodicean?" and "Was Chaucer a Free Thinker?" The conclusion reached in the former is that Chaucer may naturally have been restrained in the expression of his political opinions by his dependence upon the court and his own relations with the persons involved, but that on more than one occasion he made it clear on which side he stood; in the latter, that while heterodox opinions and skeptical ideas crop up in his poems, Chaucer was doubtless a devout and orthodox Christian. This is also the general opinion. As E. P. Kuhl puts it in "Chaucer and the Church," there is no reason to think that Geoffrey Chaucer's views on the church differed from those of his intimate acquaintances and his king. In "Chaucer the Patriot" Kuhl draws his conclusions not from the poetry, but from Chaucer's relations with his contemporaries in the Customs. I have not been able to see Naozo Ueno's *The Religious View of Chaucer in His Italian Period* (Tokyo, 1958). Also representing inferences from the poet's writings are "Chaucer and the Common People" by Howard Patch, and "Chaucer's Sense of History" by Morton W. Bloomfield.

No one can question the fact that a very real personality emerges from Chaucer's poetry. Every reader feels that he is in the presence of a genial and urbane man, endlessly intrigued by the life about him, interested in people of all kinds, amused at their foibles and weaknesses, tolerant outwardly even of the vicious. It is popular of late to try to distinguish between the Chaucer who is one of the characters in a poem and Chaucer the poet. The attempt is at least as old as Lüdeke's monograph (1928) on the function of the narrator in Chaucer's poetry. We have long known that the representation of the character who tells the story in the first person is not to be taken in all respects at its face value. Chaucer's eight years' sickness in the *Book of the Duchess* was long ago shown by Sypherd to be a convention of allegorical love visions and not necessarily autobiographical. And when the dreamer is represented as naive or obtuse, as in the *Book of the Duchess* or the *House of Fame*, we have never ourselves been so naive as to believe that the writer of the poem was also naive or obtuse. Nevertheless, the game of separating the two is currently popular, and the ways in which poet and *persona* are differentiated have been explained in numerous articles, e.g. James R. Kreuzer, "The Dreamer in the *Book of the Duchess*," Charles A. Owen, Jr., "The Role of the Narrator in the *Parlement of Foules*," Robert M. Jordan, "The Narrator in Chaucer's *Troilus*," Dorothy Bethurum, "Chaucer's Point of View as Narrator in the Love Poems," and David M. Bevington, "The Obtuse Narrator in Chaucer's *House of Fame*," to name a few in the order of their appearance. An exception to the poet-*persona* approach is J. Burke Severs' treatment of Chaucer's self-portrait in the *Book of the Duchess*.

It is in the *Canterbury Tales*, where the poet is also one of the pilgrims and at the same time the reporter of all that happens, that the idea of discriminating between the two roles seems to have enjoyed the greatest vogue. Marchette Chute in her *Geoffrey Chaucer of England* observed that the narrator was as much Chaucer's literary creation as any other pilgrim, and the implications of this fact have been explored in a number of articles. Again it must suffice to mention a representative selection, in roughly the order of their appearance: Ben Kimpel, "The Narrator of the *Canterbury Tales*," Edgar H. Duncan, "Narrator's Points of View in the Portrait-sketches, Prologue to the *Canterbury Tales*," Ralph Baldwin's chapter "The Poet and the Pilgrim" in his *The Unity of the Canterbury Tales*, E. Talbot Donaldson, "Chaucer the Pilgrim," Rosemary Woolf, "Chaucer as a Satirist in the General Prologue to the *Canterbury Tales*," John M. Major, "The Personality of Chaucer the Pilgrim." Not all of these scholars are convinced of a sharp cleavage. Kimpel and

Major in particular express reservations or raise dissenting voices.

There is no harm in being reminded that when Chaucer appears in any of his poems he is just as much a creation of the poet as the eagle or the Prioress or the Cook. If, as Manly tried to show, he based his description of some of the pilgrims on actual people whom he had known or observed in real life, he was doing only what poets and novelists and dramatists have always done. But whereas we cannot be certain that Thomas Pynchbek was the prototype of the Man of Law, there can be no doubt about the identity of the narrator who joined the "wel nine and twenty" other pilgrims at the Tabard Inn. And just as we need not suppose that the Man of Law corresponds in all respects with the real Sergeant of the Law whom Chaucer was thinking of, so we need not believe that every characteristic attributed to the pilgrim-narrator, or the "I" of other poems, is a faithful reflection of the poet himself. In most descriptions some features are heightened, some suppressed. Chaucer may, for reasons of discretion, have portrayed some of the pilgrims in the *Canterbury Tales* as recognizable without being legally identifiable. For other reasons he may have represented himself as slow-witted, inexpert in love, or slightly ridiculous.

The most important of these reasons is the nature of literary publications in the fourteenth century. A modern writer addressing a public he will never see, speaking to it through the impersonal medium of print, may assume an attitude toward his audience that an after-dinner speaker cannot. Every one knows, but we are inclined to forget, that Chaucer read his poetry aloud to assembled audiences at the court, as indeed we see him doing in the beautiful Corpus Christi College, Cambridge, manuscript of the *Troilus* already mentioned. Those in the audience would be his friends and acquaintances. An air of pomposity or self-importance would have evoked a sneer; an incident or situation in which he might appear slightly ridiculous would provoke good-natured laughter or a smile. Can we suppose that Chaucer, as he wrote, would have forgotten for a moment that he would eventually have to stand up and read what he was writing to an audience that might either smile or snicker? He was not only a good storyteller, but he also had the knack, to use Grandgent's phrase, of "getting a laugh." In trying to recover the personality of Chaucer, therefore, we must distinguish between what has a good chance of being real and what is almost certainly fictitious, introduced for humorous or dramatic effect. When on various occasions he makes fun of his figure, as in the *House of Fame*, 574, and most explicitly in Harry Baily's words,

> He in the waast is shape as wel as I;
> This were a popet in an arm t'enbrace
> For any womman, smal and fair of face . . .
> (*Prol to Thop*, 700-2)

we can hardly doubt his corpulence or his sense of humor. On the other hand, the Host's other comments, which imply a shy person riding on the edge of the company ("approche neer") and always staring on the ground, are contradicted by the *General Prologue*—

> And shortly, whan the sonne was to reste,
> So hadde I spoken with hem everichon
> That I was of hir felaweshipe anon
>
> (30-2)

—as well as by the easy affability of his conversation with the Monk ("and I seyde his opinioun was good," *Gen Prol*, 183). It is clear that at this point he is assuming a pose suitable to the occasion, one that is in keeping with his forthcoming performance, and, when that performance is abruptly cut short, with the tone of injured innocence which he assumes in response to the Host's remarks. All this is obvious enough (as is much of the criticism that calls it forth), but it needs to be said from time to time. It has been well said by B. H. Bronson:

> It is a current fashion, not to say a fad, to discuss the *persona* in works of fiction, and of late there has been a rash of talk about Chaucer's *persona*, meaning the "I" in his poetry. I have little hesitation in saying that nine-tenths of this talk is misguided and palpably mistaken. . . . Lip service is paid from time to time to

the knowledge that Chaucer wrote for oral delivery, but this
primary fact is continually lost sight of or ignored by those who
write on the *persona*, and its implications are seldom fully
realized. (pp. 25-6)

The reader should also ponder the remarks of Donald R. Howard
in "Chaucer the Man."

The two sides of Chaucer the man—public servant and poet
—emerge quite clearly from the accumulated scholarship of the
last two centuries. That the picture has undergone changes was
to have been expected. One thing is obvious. Chaucer, like Shakespeare later, was a busy man of affairs. The positions he filled
and the missions on which he was sent were laborious ones. It
must often have been very difficult for him to find the time for
reading, which he so much loved—"On bokes for to rede I me
delyte" (*Prol LGW*, 30)—and still more the quiet necessary for
writing. Much of his poetry must have been written in such
intervals as he was able to salvage from a busy, active life. That
he had the urge to write goes without saying. That his storytelling gifts were appreciated can hardly be doubted, and may
have reinforced the urge, for it is natural to want to do what one
knows one does well. That his success was due in an important
measure to the personality that shines through every page of his
poetry is altogether likely. It is this personality that marks him
off from most other Middle English poets, indeed from most
other English poets of any age.

* * * * *

Since the above essay was written a few points concerning
Chaucer's life and personal characteristics have been clarified.
Mlle. d'Ardenne has emphasized the qualities of temperament
and attitude that mark Chaucer as an Englishman, thus redress-
ing an imbalance created by those who have mainly stressed his
indebtedness to French and to other foreign sources. The occasion for Chaucer's mission to Spain in 1366 has been discussed
independently by Thomas J. Garbáty and the present writer in

articles published within a few months of each other. Both contest the opinion accepted, perhaps tacitly, in *Chaucer Life-Records* that Chaucer's purpose was to join forces with Henry de Trastamara in Trastamara's effort to drive Pedro, his half-brother, from the throne of Castile. It is more likely that Chaucer's mission was to detach the bands under Sir Hugh Calveley, Sir Matthew Gournay, and other Englishmen from Trastamara's forces. Edward III was bound by the treaty of 1362 to help the Castilian king *toto posse*, and the participation of these leaders was in violation of the treaty. The English had everything to lose and nothing to gain if Henry de Trastamara succeeded in wresting the throne from Pedro the Cruel. The English (and Edward III in particular) were unwavering in their support of Pedro. Near the end of his life Chaucer received a cluster of small grants from Richard II and Henry IV which have been puzzling to scholars, not because he received them but because of the dates of the patents and their confirmations. The matter has been cleared up in two articles by Sumner Ferris (see bibliography). Ferris offers a plausible explanation of the October thirteenth dates and shows that the proper order of the grants, some of which were predated, is established by the order of the entries in the Patent Rolls. The new evidence requires a change of a few months in the date assigned to the poet's *Complaint to His Empty Purse*.

BIBLIOGRAPHY

Anderson, Marjorie. "Alice Chaucer and Her Husbands." *PMLA*, 60 (1945), 24-47.

Ardenne, S.R.T.O.d'. "Chaucer the Englishman." In *Chaucer und seine Zeit: Symposion für Walter F. Schirmer*. Ed. Arno Esch. Tübingen: M. Niemeyer, 1968, pp. 47-54.

Baldwin, Ralph. *The Unity of the 'Canterbury Tales.'* Anglistica, 5. Copenhagen: Rosenkilde og Bagger, 1955.

Baugh, Albert C. "Kirk's Life Records of Thomas Chaucer." *PMLA*, 47 (1932), 461-515.

————. "The Background of Chaucer's Mission to Spain." In *Chaucer und seine Zeit: Symposion für Walter F. Schirmer*, pp. 55-69.

Bethurum, Dorothy. "Chaucer's Point of View as Narrator in the Love Poems." *PMLA*, 74 (1959), 511-20.

Bevington, David M. "The Obtuse Narrator in Chaucer's *House of Fame*." *Speculum*, 36 (1961), 288-98.

Bland, D.S. "Chaucer and the Inns of Court: A Reexamination." *ES*, 33 (1952), 145-55.

Bloomfield, Morton W. "Chaucer's Sense of History." *JEGP*, 51 (1952), 301-13.

Braddy, Haldeen. "New Documentary Evidence Concerning Chaucer's Mission to Lombardy." *MLN*, 48 (1933), 507-11.

————. "Chaucer's Philippa, Daughter of Panneto." *MLN*, 64 (1949), 342-43.

Bronson, Bertrand H. *In Search of Chaucer*. Toronto: Univ. of Toronto Press, 1960.

Call, Reginald. "The Plimpton Chaucer and Other Problems of Chaucerian Portraiture." *Speculum*, 22 (1947), 135-44.

Chute, Marchette. *Geoffrey Chaucer of England*. New York: Dutton, 1946.

Crow, M.M. "Materials for a New Edition of the Chaucer Life-Records." *Univ. of Texas: Studies in English*, 31 (1952), 1-12.

————, and Clair C. Olson, eds. *Chaucer Life-Records*. Oxford: Clarendon Press, 1966.

Donaldson, E. Talbot. "Chaucer the Pilgrim." *PMLA*, 69 (1954), 928-36.

Duncan, Edgar H. "Narrator's Points of View in the Portrait-sketches, Prologue to the *Canterbury Tales*." In *Essays in Honor of Walter Clyde Curry*. Foreword by Hardin Craig. Nashville, Tenn.: Vanderbilt Univ. Press, 1955, pp. 77-101.

Emerson, O.F. "Chaucer's Testimony as to His Age." *MP*, 11 (1913), 117-25.

Ferris, Sumner. "The Date of Chaucer's Final Annuity and of the *Complaint to His Empty Purse*." *MP*, 65 (1967), 45-52.

————. "Chaucer, Richard II, Henry IV, and 13 October." In *Chaucer and Middle English Studies: In Honour of Rossell Hope Robbins.* Ed. Beryl Rowland. London: Allen & Unwin, 1974, pp. 210-17.

Galway, Margaret. "The 'Troilus' Frontispiece." *MLR,* 44 (1949), 161-77.

————. " 'Pullesdon' in the Life-Records of Chaucer." *N&Q,* 202 (1957), 371-74.

————. "Philippa Pan; Philippa Chaucer." *MLR,* 60 (1960), 481-87.

Garbáty, Thomas J. "Chaucer in Spain, 1366: Soldier of Fortune or Agent of the Crown?" *ELN,* 5 (1967), 81-87.

Honoré-Duvergé, Suzanne. "Chaucer en Espagne? (1366)." In *Recueil de Travaux offert à M. Clovis Brunel.* Paris: Société l'École des Chartes, 1955. II, 9-13.

Howard, Donald R. "The Conclusion of the Marriage Group: Chaucer and the Human Condition." *MP,* 57 (1960), 223-32.

————. "Chaucer the Man." *PMLA,* 80 (1965), 337-43.

Hulbert, J.R. *Chaucer's Official Life. 1912.* Rpt. New York: Pantheon, 1970.

Jordan, Robert M. "The Narrator in Chaucer's *Troilus.*" *ELH,* 25 (1958), 237-57.

Kane, George. *The Autobiographical Fallacy in Chaucer and Langland Studies.* London: H.K. Lewis, 1965.

Kern, Alfred A. *The Ancestry of Chaucer.* Diss. Johns Hopkins, 1906.

Kimpel, Ben. "The Narrator of the *Canterbury Tales.*" *ELH,* 20 (1953), 77-86.

Kittredge, G.L. "Lewis Chaucer or Lewis Clifford." *MP,* 14 (1917), 513-18.

Krauss, Russell. "Chaucerian Problems." In *Three Chaucer Studies.* Ed. Carleton Brown. 1932. Rpt. Folcroft, Pa.: Folcroft Press, 1973, pp. 9-182.

Kreuzer, James R. "The Dreamer in the *Book of the Duchess.*" *PMLA,* 66 (1951), 543-47.

Kuhl, E.P. "Chaucer and the Church." *MLN,* 40 (1925), 321-38.

————. "Chaucer the Patriot." *PQ*, 25 (1946), 277-80.

————. "Why Was Chaucer Sent to Milan in 1378?" *MLN*, 62 (1947), 42-44.

Lam, George L., and Warren H. Smith. "George Vertue's Contributions to Chaucerian Iconography." *MLQ*, 5 (1944), 303-22.

Lawrence, C.E. "The Personality of Geoffrey Chaucer." *QR*, 242 (1924), 315-33.

Loomis, Roger Sherman. "Was Chaucer a Laodicean?" In *Essays and Studies in Honor of Carleton Brown*. New York: New York Univ. Press, 1940, pp. 129-48.

————. "Was Chaucer a Free Thinker?" In *Studies in Medieval Literature*. Ed. MacEdward Leach. Philadelphia: Univ. of Pennsylvania Press, 1961, pp. 21-44.

Lüdeke, H. *Die Funktionen des Erzählers in Chaucers epischer Dichtung*. Studien zur englischen Philologie, 72. Halle, 1928.

Major, John M. "The Personality of Chaucer the Pilgrim." *PMLA*, 75 (1960), 160-62.

Manly, John Matthews. *Some New Light on Chaucer*. 1926. Rpt. New York: P. Smith, 1952.

————. "Litel Lowis My Sone." *TLS*, June 7, 1928, p. 430.

————. "Thomas Chaucer Son of Geoffrey." *TLS*, Aug. 3, 1933, p. 525.

————. "Chaucer's Mission to Lombardy." *MLN*, 49 (1934), 209-16.

————. "Three Recent Chaucer Studies." *RES*, 10 (1934), 257-72.

Moore, Samuel. "Studies in the Life-Records of Chaucer." *Anglia*, 37 (1913), 1-26.

Olson, Clair C. *The Emerging Biography of a Poet*. Stockton, Ca.: Third Annual College of the Pacific Research Lecture, 1953.

Owen, Charles A., Jr. "The Role of the Narrator in the *Parlement of Foules*." *CE*, 14 (1953), 264-69.

Patch, Howard Rollin. "Chaucer and the Common People." *JEGP*, 29 (1930), 376-84.

Plucknet, T.F.T. "Chaucer's Escapade." *Law Qu. Rev.*, 64 (1948), 33-36.

Pratt, R.A. "Geoffrey Chaucer, Esq., and Sir John Hawkwood." *ELH*, 16 (1949), 188-93.

Rickert, Edith. "Was Chaucer a Student at the Inner Temple?" In *Manly Anniversary Studies*. 1923. Rpt. New York: Books for Libraries, 1968, pp. 20-31.

———. "Chaucer at School." *MP*, 29 (1932), 257-74.

Rickert, Margaret. "The Ellesmere Portrait of Chaucer." In *The Text of the Canterbury Tales*. Ed. John Matthews Manly and Edith Rickert. Chicago: Univ. of Chicago Press, 1940. I, 587-90.

Ruud, Martin B. *Thomas Chaucer*. Research Pub. of the Univ. of Minnesota: Stud. in Lang. and Lit., No. 9. Minneapolis, 1926.

Selby, W.D., et al. *Life-Records of Chaucer*. Chaucer Soc., 2nd ser., Nos. 12, 14, 21, 32. London: Trübner, 1875-1900.

Severs, J .Burke. "Chaucer's Self-Portrait in the *Book of the Duchess*." *PQ*, 43 (1964), 27-39.

Spielmann, M.H. *The Portraits of Geoffrey Chaucer*. Chaucer Soc., 2nd ser., No. 31. London: Trübner, 1900.

Spurgeon, Caroline F.E. *Five Hundred Years of Chaucer Criticism and Allusion, 1357-1900*. 2nd ed. 3 vols. 1925. Rpt. New York: Russell & Russell, 1961.

Stewart, George R. "The Moral Chaucer." *Essays in Criticism: Univ. of Calif. Pub. in English*, 1 (1929), 89-109.

Sypherd, W.O. "Chaucer's Eight Years' Sickness." *MLN*, 20 (1905), 240-43.

Tout, Thomas F. "Literature and Learning in the English Civil Service in the Fourteenth Century." *Speculum*, 4 (1929), 365-89.

Watts, P.R. "The Strange Case of Geoffrey Chaucer and Cecilia Chaumpaigne." *Law Qu. Rev.*, 63 (1947), 491-515.

Woolf, Rosemary. "Chaucer as a Satirist in the General Prologue to the *Canterbury Tales*." *CritQ*, 1 (1959), 150-57.

TWO

ROBERT W. ACKERMAN

Chaucer, the Church, and Religion

Commentators and biographers have been perennially interested in the attitudes toward the Church and religion expressed or implied in the Works of Chaucer, as Kuhl observed long ago. So all-encompassing was the Christian culture of the Middle Ages that, for poets at least, a purely secular treatment of most subjects was nearly impossible. A very large part of the Chaucer canon bears out this truism, but the fullest reflections of Church life and Christian thought are to be found in the *Canterbury Tales* and in several of the short poems, such as "An ABC," "Fortune," "Truth," and "Gentilesse." Moreover, *Troilus and Criseyde* and the love-visions, the *Book of the Duchess*, the *House of Fame*, and the *Parliament of Fowls*, despite their allegorical or ancient settings and their indebtedness, direct or indirect, to classical sources, are shot through with Christian references and Christian thought.

Drawing mainly on the *Canterbury Tales*, but sometimes also on *Jack Upland* and other attacks on the Church once attributed to Chaucer, early writers, including John Foxe, in about 1570, Reginald Scot, 1584, John Milton, 1641, Thomas Hyde, 1674, and Thomas Warton, 1782, praise the poet for his fearless and clear-sighted castigation of religious abuses. Other comments in the same vein are cited in Caroline Spurgeon's anthology of Chaucer allusions. Perhaps the most eloquent of all these statements appears in Warton's *History of English Poetry*. Chaucer, apart from his excellence, says Warton, quite understandably became a favorite in a court "which laid the foundations for the reformation of religion," for he opened "the eyes of the people to the absurdities of popery." He cautions, however, that Foxe the martyrologist may go too far in asserting that Chaucer "proved the pope to be the anti-christ of the apocalypse."

In Caroline Spurgeon's words, "he [Chaucer] was annexed by the Reformers, not without reason, as a kind of forerunner and a sharer of their opinions with regard to Rome, as evidenced by his keen satirical exposure of the religious orders of his time." Of course, along with fuller understanding of the religious attitudes that prevailed in late medieval England came the realization that Chaucer's decidedly unflattering portraits of friars, monks, nuns, canons, and of such ecclesiastical hirelings as the Summoner and Pardoner, and also his obvious scorn for priests who threatened delinquency in tithing with excommunication, are no more than echoes of complaints about abuses that had long been voiced by the most devout Churchmen. At the same time, his presumed Wyclifite or Lollard sympathies, inferred from his associations with the family of John of Gaunt, his acquaintance with several "Lollard knights," such as Sir John Clifford, and his depiction of the country Parson, who "Cristes gospel trewely wolde preche," came to be discounted. At least by the beginning of the present century, the view of Chaucer as a man well within the bounds of orthodoxy gained wide acceptance, as stated by Kittredge and others. Struck by the poet's air of free inquiry and his occasional irreverence, a few critics, like Tatlock, tended to claim Chaucer as a religious skeptic or as perhaps a "Laodicean," that is, one given to lightly-held opinions. Such possibilities have been explored and mainly dismissed by Mary Edith Thomas, Loomis, and Wagenknecht.

The assumption that we may ascribe to Chaucer the man the attitudes and points of view embodied in his pictures of the ecclesiastical pilgrims and in other passages in the Works may be detected in some of the commentators. The popular biographer, Marchette Chute, in spite of a generally careful attitude in this respect, claims that, with the growing tendency toward realism in his poetry, Chaucer moved further and further away from "the ideal teachings of his religion." As would be expected, however, no satisfactory evidence as to personal views may be found in the body of life-records compiled by Crow and Olson, unless one is willing to credit Thomas Gascoigne's few remarks on this subject as based on special knowledge of the poet. A timely warning against such "autobiographical fallacies" in Chaucer and Langland studies has been issued by Kane. Whatever is set down in the writings is competent testimony to Chaucer's awareness of, sensitivity to, and sometimes delight in religious views, controversies, and superstitions of his day, but it must remain uncertain evidence as to his innermost beliefs and articles of faith.

The reflections of the fourteenth-century religious scene in the Works must, naturally, be glossed and interpreted with the help of the best modern historians. Flick has remarked that greater social changes overtook England in Chaucer's age than in any other century prior to the nineteenth. The more fundamental of these changes resulted from such exigencies and catastrophes as the Black Death, the Hundred Years' War, the Peasants' Revolt, and the rapid dismantling of the feudal order and the growth of a money economy. But the convulsions that rocked the Church of the late Middle Ages produced almost equally important consequences. The first shock was Pope Clement V's removal of the Pontiff's court from Rome to the French city of Avignon in 1309 where the head of Western Christendom was to remain for seven decades. This so-called "Babylonian Captivity," during which seven popes in succession were subject to the direct influence of French rulers, intensified long-standing

English resistance to Papal provisions to bishropics and other benefices and to the levying of Papal taxes in the kingdom, as McKisack and Flick explain.

The return of the Papacy to Rome under Gregory XI in 1378 was the signal for the election in Avignon, chiefly by French cardinals, of a rival, Clement VII, and from that date until 1417 the Church was split into two, and, for a very brief period, into three, warring camps. France and her allies, such as Scotland, acknowledged the Avignonese popes, whereas England's allegiance was, predictably, to Rome. The Great Western Schism of 1378 to 1417, most authoritatively treated by Delaruelle and Labande, led to political disclocations and, in McKisack's opinion, was responsible for the prolongation of the Hundred Years' War. One significant reaction in England was the enactment of statutes that made the ecclesiastical establishment in that country much more firmly answerable to the state. The day had passed when Pope Innocent III's likening of the *sacerdotium* to the sun and the *regnum* to the moon could be considered even remotely symbolic of the relationship of Papacy and hierarchy to national states.

Despite the existence of a Papal schism, which certainly helped produce conditions favorable to the flourishing of heresies like that of Wyclif, the religious faith of the people at large seems to have been only slightly disturbed, according to Pantin, Deanesly, and McKisack. The extremely low rate of literacy, the restricted horizons of the masses, and the sheer weight of age-old habituation to religious institutions are probably responsible for this phenomenon. Moreover, the worsening conflicts between the Papacy and the rising nationalist states, particularly England, took place at the level of Curia and Crown, far above the heads of the folk.

Geoffrey Chaucer, given his position in the royal court, his diplomatic missions to France, Italy, and Flanders during the period 1360 to 1381, and his service as Knight of the Shire in 1386, had extraordinary opportunities to learn about and even to observe some of the effects of the Papal "residence" in Avignon and, after 1378, of the Great Schism. Nevertheless, not an allusion to the "Babylonian Captivity," the "sinful city of Avignon," the Great Schism, or to any pope later than Innocent III (1198-1216) appears in the Works. One may argue, of course, that such topics would not come naturally to a court poet whose interests centered on depicting human foibles and idiosyncrasies rather than on social classes and social problems and much of whose work consisted of the retelling of "olde stories." Similar reasons have been given for his apparent indifference to events of his own day, especially to the Peasants' Revolt and to the terrible ravages of the Black Death, although a few references to social unrest and to plague are to be noted in, for example, the *Clerk's Tale* and the *Pardoner's Tale*. Patch quotes older historians, such as G. G. Coulton, to the effect that, whereas Langland cries out in anger over social conditions, Chaucer, seeing mainly a merry England, looks on and smiles. Of passing interest in this connection is that, in *Piers Plowman*, the literary work of the period which beyond all others would be expected to denounce evils stemming from a divided Church, Avignon is mentioned only once by name. In his edition of this work, Skeat remarks that the rarity of such allusions may be the result of caution on the poet's part. Perhaps, too, both Langland and Chaucer were content to leave polemics on such great issues to ecclesiastical writers of tracts. On the other hand, neither shows the slightest hesitancy about representing, each in his own way, the serious hostility between the secular clergy and the orders of friars and also other subjects of controversy well summarized by Pantin.

Chaucer's disregard of popes, anti-popes, cardinals, legates, and other high officers of the Western Church extended to his treatment of the upper hierarchy of the Church in England. His one reference to a fourteenth-century Archbishop of Canterbury is to Thomas Bradwardine, a distinguished scholar whose consecration as primate preceded his death in 1349 by only a few weeks. Moreover, Chaucer's sole interest was with Bradwardine's contribution to the predestination-freewill debates of the time. He found no occasion to allude to an Archbishop of York or to the bishops of any of the seventeen dioceses of the kingdom. The terms "pope," "bishop," and "prelate" occur here and there in the Works in reference to otherwise unidentified dignitaries, but, as in *Troilus and Criseyde* and the *Romance of the Rose*, these are often of a pagan rather than of the Christian religion.

With respect to Church life, reflections of which are found mainly in the *Canterbury Tales*, the focus is steadily on the less exalted clerics, secular and regular, and also on the minor officials of the Church establishment who would have been more or less familiar figures to the common people even in rural parishes. The seculars include the exemplary "Persoun of a toun," the "Nonnes Preest," probably the confessor for the Prioress's convent, and chantry priests, mentioned only indirectly. The latter were clerics whose primary occupation was the celebration of Masses in chantry chapels for deceased relatives of affluent persons. The Parson was too ethical to seek such a sinecure in London churches. The several clerks, at least some of whom were undoubtedly in minor orders, such as lector or acolyte, would likewise be classified as seculars, and these would include the Clerk of Oxford, "Hende" Nicholas and Absolon in the *Miller's Tale*, and the two lecherous students in the *Reeve's Tale*. The Monk, the lady Prioress, her nun-chaplain, Friar Huberd, the friar in the *Summoner's Tale*, the monk in the *Shipman's Tale*, and the Canon in the *Canon's Yeoman's Tale* would all be regular clergy. Mrs. Hamilton has suggested that the alchemist was very likely a Canon Regular of St. Augustine, and she has also advanced the case for considering the Pardoner as a Canon of Rounceval Chapel in Charing Cross. The status of the Pardoner, however, remains most doubtful in the light of his confession that his relics and probably his pardons are bogus.

A pilgrimage, as commentators have noted, would be especially attractive to persons in the service of religion. Nevertheless, the fact that one-third of the Canterbury wayfarers and no small number of the characters in the tales they relate are either clerics or lay servants of the Church is worthy of note. Such a concentration would not have surprised Chaucer's original audiences, as one must conclude upon inquiring into the population by classes of fourteenth-century England. As analyzed by Russell, the Poll Tax Returns of 1377 show some 8,000 holders of religious benefices, 11,000 monks, friars, nuns, and canons in the 800 religious houses and cathedral chapters, and approximately 16,000 unbeneficed, or ecclesiastically unattached, clerks. Allowance would also have to be made for an indefinite number of unrecorded hermits, recluses, and the like. The members of the secular hierarchy and of the religious orders taken together with the clerks must have comprised a proportion of the total population, estimated to have sunk to about 2,200,000 after the visitations of the Black Death, many times greater than the totality of clergy of all religions would represent in the population of modern England. The large numbers of clergy and their rather even distribution throughout the kingdom should have insured a high degree of familiarity between Churchmen and laity of all walks of life.

Because of this contact, Chaucer could assume a general awareness of the enmity between secular priests in their parishes and the mendicant orders. Knowles and Pantin report that complaints of encroachments of friars on the rights of local priests gave rise to a decree by an early thirteenth-century Council requiring all Christians to make confession at least once annually to their own parish priests, thus discriminating against friar-priests in the role of confessors. The antipathy engendered by such developments is evident in Chaucer's sardonic comments about Friar Huberd, in the Wife of Bath's labeling of mendicants as incubi, and in the tale of the greedy friar related by the Summoner. A discussion of the reasons for this popular attitude is provided by Williams.

Even though his first audiences were largely made up, we assume, of ladies and gentlemen of cosmopolitan background, Chaucer could reasonably impute to them much of the same schooling in religion as he had acquired in the Church of St. Martin's Vintry. Before so homogeneous a group, he could scarcely have felt obliged to enter into great detail about most aspects of religious life. He alludes to the Mass a number of times, but only rarely do the requirements of his narrative lead him to mention specific features. His satire of the Wife of Bath's love of ostentation offers one such occasion, for she is said to become angered if any parishioner dared precede her down the aisle to the chancel with his Mass-penny. Again, the Summoner, in the course of his feud with the Friar, gives us a vignette of a church in Yorkshire in which a friar-preacher exhorts the people to buy trentals, that is, series of thirty Masses for the deliverance of souls from purgatory. These they should buy from a community of frairs rather than from "possessioners," or monastic priests, noted for squandering Mass fees on extravagant living, or from a simple parish priest, who could sing but one Mass a day.

More often discussed is the portrait of the Pardoner, who could read a "lessoun" or "storie" and, best of all, sing the "offertorie." Here, "lessoun" has been equated with the "lectio" or reading from Scripture or a saint's life forming an element in the daily office, and "storie" with a series of such readings. "Offertorie" is the offertory verse which the priest sings after the Creed and before beginning the Canon of the Mass. Since the Pardoner is never said to be a priest, the offertory reference may be merely a jibe at his avarice, not to be taken literally. The fact that he is represented as preaching after the offertory rather than before, in accordance with the standard order of the Mass, causes difficulty. A note in Robinson's edition suggests that the sermon, or sales pitch, was meant to be an accompaniment to the bidding prayer, following the offertory. Recently, Miller and Bosse have argued that not only the offertory but also the "lessoun" and "storie" are to be associated with the Mass: "lessoun" being identified with the epistle and "storie" with the Gospel. This would place all three of the Pardoner's liturgical performances within the context of the Mass although it leaves to one side how a person, never said to be a priest, could have sung the offertory. The authors of this article further call attention to an analogy between a Mass perverted by the Pardoner's hypocrisy and the devil's sacrifice to which the rioters' carousing is likened in the exemplum of the Pardoner's sermon.

Allusions to the Divine or Canonical Office, the official daily prayer of the Church from an early date, as explained by Salmon and Knowles, are surprisingly few. In the *Summoner's Tale*, Chaucer speaks of the "divine servyce" celebrated in "hooly houses," and he once or twice refers collectively to the hours which clerics were obliged to read daily in their breviaries as "thynges" or "matyns and hooly thynges." Of the eight individual hours, he mentions five by name, although by his day the term "prime," designating the mid-morning service, had come commonly to indicate a time of the day. The "belle of laudes," which in the *Miller's Tale* awakens Alisoun and Nicholas at about three in the morning after an exhausting night, must have been rung at a nearby monastery since in parish churches public celebration of the hours was generally restricted to Saturday vespers and Sunday matins. And in the *Reeve's Tale*, one of the students makes a crude jest having to do with compline as the bed-time office.

An abridged version of the Divine Office, the Little Office of the Virgin Mary, was commonly used in nunneries, and, in the opinion of Sister Mary Madeleva, was the service which the Prioress "entuned in hir nose ful semely." Sister Mary goes on to note that, since a religious while traveling would never have sung or recited the office audibly, Chaucer could not have known that it was sung "through the nose" in her conventual choir unless he had at one time been admitted to a cloister where he could hear the nuns at their office. She further finds in the prologues of both the Prioress and her Nun paraphrases of the morning office of Our Lady. Chaucer, she concludes, must have acquired a special familiarity with that form of daily prayer, a possibility about which Brown has also written.

The exact meaning of other terms pertaining to the liturgy

or hagiography, such as "passioun," "miracle," and "legende," appearing occasionally in Chaucer, has been investigated by Strom. Also of some value in this general connection are older essays by Mossé and Sister M. Bonaventure McKenna.

Even before the publication of two important books by G. R. Owst in 1926 and in 1933, medieval preaching and its possible connections with Chaucer were studied by Chapman and others. Sermons, including the Parson's, figure in the *Canterbury Tales*, and references to preachers and preaching appear elsewhere in the Works, as in the *Romance of the Rose*. In this last-named work, a translation, it should be remembered, friar-preachers are ironically said to be "goode men alle." Attempts have been made to show structural conformity of certain tales to sermons of the day and also to show that Chaucer borrowed figures of speech and proverbs from preachers. Studies of this sort, as Wenzel has argued, are generally less convincing than the more vigorous inquiries into analogues, and of these Pratt's adducing of parallels between images and figures in the friar's lecture to old Thomas in the *Canon Yeoman's Tale* and passages in the popular *Communiloquium* of John of Wales is perhaps the best.

The greater frequency of preaching in the late Middle Ages as compared with at least the earlier part of the thirteenth century was prompted by efforts to comply with the legislation of the Third and Fourth Lateran Councils of 1179 and 1215 respectively. These reforming councils promulgated measures intended to improve the morals and religious knowledge of clergy and laity alike. Priests having the cure of souls were theoretically required to preach sermons several times annually on the rudiments of the faith, but, as Robertson has found, the custom of frequent preaching was especially slow to develop in England. The establishment of private, auricular confession, not hitherto a settled practice of the Church, also provided an opportunity for instruction of the laity, for the confessor was enjoined, in the interests of securing a full confession, to question his penitent closely with respect to his understanding of the Creed, the

Pater noster, the Commandments, the sacraments, the works of mercy and the vices and virtues.

Because the clergy, at least in the country parishes, were generally poorly educated, a number of prelates provided "constitutions," spelling out the new canons for the guidance of their clergy. The constitutions were supplemented by priests' manuals, such as Archbishop Thoresby's *Catechism* (1357). Further, the instructional program of six points or so associated with the confessor's interrogation of penitents, provided the basis for an astonishing production of lengthy tracts in the vernacular dating from the thirteenth century. Ostensibly written for the layman who knew no Latin, these monitory works seem also to have served the clergy as handbooks of pastoral theology as well. They were well adapted to such a purpose since their writers took pains to illustrate the treatment of doctrine by a lavish use of allegory, metaphor, and exempla. Thus, we find in them "trees" of life, of righteousness, of the sins and virtues, and the like, and also the representation of sin as lesions of the body. Examples include *The Mirror of Holy Church*, originally written in Latin by St. Edmund Rich (d. 1240), Robert of Brunne's *Handlyng Synne* (1303), basically a translation from the French, and the famous *Ayenbite of Inwit* (1340), another work with a series of antecedents. Pantin has provided an excellent systematic treatment of these manuals and treatises.

As the present writer has noted, the didactic works just mentioned probably give us the clearest available understanding of the content of parochial Christianity, the community of belief to which the poets of the late Middle Ages could appeal with confidence. As such, they may well deserve more attention as literary sources than they have hitherto been accorded. Chaucer's *Parson's Tale* may properly be considered among the doctrinal tracts since it combines a "sermon" on the sacrament of penance with a long discourse on the sins, together with their remedies. Kate Petersen's and Germaine Dempster's essays on the *Parson's Tale* identify Chaucer's main sources as treatises by

Pennafort and Peraldus, but Kellogg and others have expressed reservations.

Including the *Parson's Tale* and the *Romance of the Rose*, both translations, Chaucer's writings are full of references, most of them casual in nature, to points of doctrine: the sacraments, the Creed, the Pater noster, the seven sins, excommunication, and the like. Penance seems to be the sacrament figuring most often in the *Canterbury Tales* in allusions to "shrift," the "confiteor," and "shrift-father." In the *Book of the Duchess* appears the phrase, "shryfte wythoute repentaunce," conveying the important warning that absolution without contrition and repentance is of no avail. Direct references to the Eucharist are confined to the *Parson's Tale* and the *Romance of the Rose*, and one of these in the latter work is expanded with the observation that the required annual communion must be preceded by confession to one's own parish priest. The suggestion that an original literary use of sacramental confession is to be seen in the Canon's Yeoman's long and rueful disclosure of his service in the "cursed craft" of alchemy has been recently developed by Ryan. Whereas the Wife of Bath and the Pardoner both acknowledge their sins, they do so in a boastful, unrepentant spirit. In contrast, the Yeoman is terrified of hell-fire, and for this reason his outburst partakes of more of the nature of a true confession.

Conventional references to saints are numerous in many of the Works, some anachronistic invocations occurring in *Troilus and Criseyde*. Gerould counts more than forty such saints in Chaucer's "calendar," and he seeks to explain Harry Bailey's absurd corruptions of several saints' names. Ruth Cline points out the appropriateness of the saints by whom certain of the pilgrims swear.

In contrast, Chaucer's Biblical references are scarcely of a perfunctory, conventional nature. More than seventy Old and New Testament personages are named in the Works, sometimes with additional matter that indicates the poet's knowledge of their context. Magoun provides impressive evidence of Chaucer's acquaintance with the Biblical and ancient world, and his use of Scripture is treated by a number of critics, including Bennett, Grace Landrum, Elliott, and Coghill. In an unpublished dissertation, Johnson counters Grace Landrum's position as to the availability of the Vulgate Bible to Chaucer with the argument that many of the scriptural passages were readily to be found in the French *Bible Historiale*, an exemplum book, and Pope Innocent III's *De contemptu mundi*, the last-named well known to Chaucer. Robertson describes the Wife of Bath, the Friar in the *Summoner's Tale*, and the Parson as exegetes on the grounds of their dealing more or less learnedly with patristic commentary. Utley has written about Chaucer and exegetical knowledge, and Howard finds some hints of Biblical commentary in *Troilus and Criseyde*. Margaret Deanesly's book on the Lollard Bible contains valuable information as to the extent of Biblical knowledge in the fourteenth century.

The attitudes toward the Church and its teachings and the reflections of religious life so far considered tend to fall within the scope of popular Christianity. Above this level, an awareness of the theological debates of the period is suggested from time to time, being typically introduced by expressions such as "in scole is great altercacioun...and greet disputisoun." But, contrary to his usual fondness for name-dropping, Chaucer mentions only a few philosophers and theologians, chief among whom are Aristotle, Plato, Avicenna, Averroes, St. Augustine, St. Gregory the Great, and, as the sole representative of his own century, Bradwardine. He allows the Pardoner some inkling of the philosophical issue of universals and an acquaintance with a current question about Eucharistic theory when he puts the terms "substance" and "accident" in the Pardoner's mouth, and a similar use of these terms occurs elsewhere. Yet, the only philosophical and theological matters figuring at all importantly in the Works are those inspired directly by *The Consolation of Philosophy*, the sixth-century work of Boethius which profoundly affected religious thought and literary expression throughout the Middle Ages and into the Renaissance, and which was translated by King Alfred and Jean de Meun as well as by Chaucer. Boethian wisdom, indeed, is sprinkled broadside throughout Chaucer's poetry, and sometimes one encounters direct quotations from his own *Boece*, but of greater moment are the several key ideas of Boethius to which he returns again and again and which are deeply seated in his literary perceptions.

When exception is made for such fairly literal renderings of passages from the *Consolation* as "The Former Age," one finds the densest concentration of Boethius in the *Knight's Tale* and *Troilus and Criseyde*. The Boethian material in both, it should be added, was included without benefit of the sources. In Jefferson's phrase, he was "afire" with Boethius when composing the two poems. Beyond that, one may justly say that Chaucer was indebted to the *Consolation* vastly more than to any other single book for the ordering of his general ideas and also for the way in which he gave expression of those ideas.

Patch's survey of the influence of the *Consolation* has not been surpassed. Schmidt-Kohl expounds the neo-Platonic basis of the work, and Courcelle, in the course of discussing the literary tradition, describes a number of the medieval manuscripts containing "iconographical" drawings. Huppé and Robertson's discussion of Chaucer's allegories offers useful insights into literary applications of Boethianism, and Héraucourt studies the Boethian origin of Chaucer's "terminology of values," including "sovrayn blisfulnesse," "parfyt felicitee," and "gentiless." Recent scholarship on Chaucer's *Boece* and his reliance on the *Consolation* is extensive and may be only sketchily noted here. The most helpful studies include those by Stroud, Meech, Bloomfield, James Cline, F. Anne Payne, Gerhard, and Gallagher.

Within the past twenty-five years, several critics, notably Ralph Baldwin, have maintained that we must understand the *Canterbury Tales* as an allegorical or anagogical pilgrimage of the soul to the heavenly Jerusalem, "a rehearsal for death and the judgment." Elsewhere in the present book, Robert M. Jordan and Charles A. Owen, Jr. present some of the difficulties inherent in an exegetical reading of this kind, yet it retains its attractiveness for many. In his perceptive treatment of the poet's relationship to fourteenth-century religious life and philosophy, Geoffrey Shepherd observes that, even though fully aware of these aspects of his times, Chaucer habitually declines to pass judgment or to voice his own religious and philosophical views. Shepherd rounds out his discussion with especially enlightening remarks about Bradwardine and Wyclif.

Even if we stop short of accepting the thesis that the journey to Canterbury is by intention a spiritual pilgrimage at the deeper level, we may conclude that Chaucer's Works are in the mainstream of the Christian culture of the late Middle Ages. The Chaucer canon includes no didactic allegories or pious treatises like the *Livre de Seyntz Medicines* of Henry, first Duke of Lancaster, or the "Merita Missae" ascribed to John Lydgate, yet the spacious world depicted in his poetry, even when the setting is ancient Thebes or Troy, functions under the benign providence of God as interpreted by Boethius.

BIBLIOGRAPHY

Ackerman, Robert W. "*The Debate of the Body and the Soul* and Parochial Christianity." *Speculum*, 37 (1962), 541-65.

Baldwin, Ralph. *The Unity of the 'Canterbury Tales'*. Anglistica, 5. Copenhagen: Rosenkilde og Bagger, 1955.

Baldwin, Summerfield. *The Organization of Medieval Christianity*. Berkshire Studies in European History. New York: Holt, 1929.

Bennett, H.S. *Chaucer and the Fifteenth Century*. Oxford History of English Literature, II, pt. 1. Oxford: Oxford Univ. Press, 1947.

Bloomfield, Morton W. "Distance and Predestination in *Troilus and Criseyde*." *PMLA*, 72 (1957), 14-26.

Boyd, Beverly. *Chaucer and the Liturgy*. Philadelphia: Dorrance, 1967.

Brown, Carleton. "Chaucer and the Hours of the Blessed Virgin." *MLN*, 30 (1915), 231-32.

Capes, W.W. *The English Church in the Fourteenth and Fifteenth Centuries*. A History of the English Church, vol. 3. London: Macmillan, 1900.

Chapman, C.O. "Chaucer on Preachers and Preaching." *PMLA*, 44 (1929), 179-85.

Chute, Marchette. *Geoffrey Chaucer of England*. New York: Dutton, 1958.

Cline, James M. "Chaucer and Jean de Meun: *De Consolatione Philosophiae*." *ELH*, 3 (1936), 170-81.

Cline, Ruth. "Four Chaucer Saints." *MLN*, 60 (1945), 480-82.

Coghill, Nevill. *The Poet Chaucer*. London: Oxford: Oxford Univ. Press, 1949.

Courcelle, Pierre. *La Consolation de Philosophie dans la tradition littéraire. Antécédents et posterité de Boèce*. Études augustiennes. Paris: Centre de Recherche scientifique, 1967.

Crow, M.M., and C.C. Olson, eds. *Chaucer Life Records*. London: Oxford Univ. Press, 1966.

Curry, Walter Clyde. "Destiny in Chaucer's *Troilus*." *PMLA*, 45 (1930), 129-68.

Deanesly, Margaret. *The Lollard Bible and other Medieval Biblical Versions*. Cambridge: Cambridge Univ. Press, 1920.

————. *A History of the Medieval Church, 590-1500*. London: Methuen, 1925.

Delaruelle, E., and E. Labande. *L'Église au temps du Grand Schisme et de la crise conciliaire (1378-1449)*. 2 vols. Paris: Bloud and Gay, 1962, 1964.

Dempster, Germaine. "The *Parson's Tale*." In *Sources and Analogues of Chaucer's Canterbury Tales*. Ed. W.F. Bryan and Germaine Dempster. 1941. Rpt. New York: Humanities Press, 1958, pp. 723-60.

Elliott, Ralph W.V. "Chaucer's Reading." In *Chaucer's Mind and Art*. Ed. A.C. Cawley. New York: Barnes and Noble, 1969, pp. 46-68.

Flick, Alexander Clarence. *The Decline of the Medieval Church*. 2 vols. New York: Burt Franklin, 1967.

Gallagher, Joseph E. "Theology and Intention in Chaucer's *Troilus*." *ChauR*, 7 (1972), 44-46.

Gallick, Susan. "A Look at Chaucer and His Preachers." *Speculum*, 50 (1975), 456-76.

Gerould, G.H. *Chaucerian Essays*. Princeton: Princeton Univ. Press, 1952.

Hall, Donald J. *English Medieval Pilgrimage*. London: Routledge and Kegan Paul, 1965.

Hamilton, Marie P. "The Clerical Status of Chaucer's Alchemist." *Speculum*, 16 (1941), 103-8.

————. "The Credentials of Chaucer's Pardoner." *JEGP*, 40 (1941), 48-72.

Héraucourt, Will. *Die Wertwelt Chaucers: die Wertwelt einer Zeitwende*. Heidelberg: Carl Winter, 1939.

Howard, Donald R. *The Three Temptations*. Princeton: Princeton Univ. Press, 1966.

Huppé, Bernard F., and D.W. Robertson, Jr. *Fruyt and Chaf: Studies in Chaucer's Allegories*. Princeton: Princeton Univ. Press, 1963.

Hussey, Maurice, A.C. Spearing, and James Winny. *An Introduction to Chaucer*. Cambridge: Cambridge Univ. Press, 1965.

Jefferson, Bernard L. *Chaucer and the Consolation of Philosophy of Boethius*. Princeton: Princeton Univ. Press, 1917.

Johnson, Dudley R. "Chaucer and the Bible." Diss. Yale, 1941.

Joseph, Gerhard. "The Gifts of Nature, Fortune, and Grace in the *Physician's, Pardoner's* and *Parson's Tales*." ChauR, 9 (1975), 237-45.

Kane, George. *The Autobiographical Fallacy in Chaucer and Langland Studies*. London: Chambers Memorial Lecture, 1965.

Kellogg, Alfred L., et al. *Chaucer, Langland, Arthur: Essays in Middle English Literature*. New Brunswick: Rutgers Univ. Press, 1972.

Knowles, Dom David. *The Monastic Order in England. A History of its Development from the Times of St. Dunstan to the Fourth Lateran Council, 940-1216*. 2nd ed. Cambridge: Cambridge Univ. Press, 1966.

Kuhl, E.P. "Chaucer and the Church." *MLN*, 40 (1925), 321-38.

Landrum, Grace W. "Chaucer's Use of the Vulgate." *PMLA*, 39 (1924), 75-100.

Loomis, Roger Sherman. "Was Chaucer a Laodicean?" In *Essays and Studies in Honor of Carleton Brown*. New York: New York Univ. Press, 1940, pp. 129-48.

————. "Was Chaucer a Free-Thinker?" In *Studies in Medieval Literature in Honor of Professor Albert Croll Baugh*. Ed. Mac-Edward Leach. Philadelphia: Univ. of Pennsylvania Press, 1961, pp. 21-44.

McKenna, Sister M. Bonaventure. "Liturgy of the *Canterbury Tales*." *Catholic Educational Review*, 35 (1937), 474-80.

McKisack, May. *The Fourteenth Century, 1307-1399*. The Oxford History of England, vol. 5. Oxford: Clarendon Press, 1959.

Madeleva, Sister Mary. *Chaucer's Nuns and Other Essays*. New York: Appleton, 1927.

Magoun, Francis P., Jr. "Chaucer's Ancient and Biblical World." *MS*, 15 (1953), 107-36.

Maxfield, Ezra K. "Chaucer and Religious Reform." *PMLA*, 39 (1924), 64-74.

Meech, Sanford B. *Design in Chaucer's Troilus. 1959*. Rpt. New York: Greenwood Press, 1970.

Miller, Clarence H., and Roberta Bux Bosse. "Chaucer's Pardoner and the Mass." *ChauR*, 6 (1971), 171-84.

Moorman, J.R.H. *A History of the Church in England*. London: Adam and Charles Black, 1953.

————. *Church Life in England in the Thirteenth Century*. Cambridge: Cambridge Univ. Press, 1955.

Mossé, Fernand. "Chaucer et la liturgie." *Revue Germanique*, 14 (1923), 283-89.

Oberman, Heiko A. "Fourteenth-Century Religious Thought: A Premature Profile." *Speculum*, 53 (1978), 80-93.

Olson, Claire C. *The Emerging Biography of a Poet*. Stockton: Ca.: Third Annual College of the Pacific Research Lecture, 1953.

————, and M.M. Crow, eds. *Chaucer's World*. Compiled by Edith Rickert. New York: Columbia Univ. Press, 1948.

Owst, G.R. *Preaching in Medieval England*. 1926. Rpt. New York: Russell & Russell, 1965.

————. *Literature and the Pulpit in Medieval England*. 1933. Rev. 2nd ed. Oxford: Blackwell, 1961.

Pantin, W.A. *The English Church in the Fourteenth Century*. Notre Dame, Ind.: Univ. of Notre Dame Press, 1962.

Patch, Howard Rollin. *The Tradition of Boethius: A Study of His Importance in Medieval Culture*. New York: Oxford Univ. Press, 1935.

Payne, F. Anne. "Foreknowledge and Free Will: Three Theories in the *Nun's Priest's Tale*." *ChauR*, 10 (1975), 201-19.

Peterson, Kate O. *The Sources of the Parson's Tale*. Boston: Ginn, 1901.

Pfander, Homer G. *The Popular Sermon of the Medieval Friar in England*. Diss. New York Univ., 1937.

Powicke, Sir Maurice. *The Thirteenth Century, 1216-1307*. The Oxford History of England, vol. 4. Oxford: Clarendon Press, 1954.

Pratt, R.A. "Chaucer and the Hand that Fed Him." *Speculum*, 41 (1966), 619-42.

Quinn, Esther C. "Religion in Chaucer's *Canterbury Tales*: A Study in Language and Structure." In *Geoffrey Chaucer: A Collection of Original Articles*. Ed. George Economou. New York: McGraw-Hill, 1975, pp. 55-73.

Robertson, D.W., Jr. "The Frequency of Preaching in Thirteenth-Century England." *Speculum*, 24 (1949), 376-88.

————. *A Preface to Chaucer*. Princeton: Princeton Univ. Press, 1962.

Ruggiers, Paul G. *The Art of the Canterbury Tales*. Madison: Univ. of Wisconsin Press, 1965.

Russell, Josiah Cox. *British Medieval Population*. Albuquerque: Univ. of New Mexico Press, 1948.

―――. "The Clerical Population of Medieval England." *Traditio*, 2 (1944), 177-212.

Ryan, Lawrence V. "The Canon's Yeoman's Desperate Confession." *ChauR*, 8 (1974), 297-310.

Salmon, Dom Pierre. *The Breviary through the Centuries*. Trans. Sister David Mary. Collegeville: Liturgical Press, 1962.

Schmidt-Kohl, Volker. *Die neoplatonische Seelenlehre in der Consolatio Philosophiae des Boethius*. Beiträge zur klassischen Philologie, 16 (1965).

Shepherd, Geoffrey. "Religion and Philosophy in Chaucer." In *Writers and Their Background: Geoffrey Chaucer*. Ed. D.S. Brewer. London: Bell, 1974, pp. 262-89.

Skeat, Walter W., ed. *Piers the Plowman*. 2 vols. London: Oxford Univ. Press, 1924.

Spurgeon, Caroline F.E. *Five Hundred Years of Chaucer Criticism and Allusion, 1357-1900*. 2nd ed. 3 vols. 1925. Rpt. New York: Russell & Russell, 1961.

Strohm, Paul. "*Passioun, Lyf, Miracle, Legende*: Some Generic Terms in Middle English Hagiographic Narrative." *ChauR*, 10 (1975), 62-76, 154-71.

Stroud, Theodore. "Boethius' Influence on Chaucer's *Troilus*." *MP*, 49 (1951), 1-9.

Tatlock, J.S.P. "Chaucer and Wyclif." *MP*, 14 (1916), 257-68.

Thomas, Mary Edith. *Medieval Skepticism and Chaucer*. New York: William Frederick Press, 1950.

Utley, Francis L. "Chaucer and Patristic Exegesis." In *Chaucer's Mind and Art*. Ed. A.C. Cawley. New York: Barnes and Noble, 1969, pp. 69-85.

Wagenknecht, Edward. *The Personality of Chaucer*. Norman: Univ. of Oklahoma Press, 1968.

Wenzel, Siegfried. "Chaucer and the Language of Contemporary Preaching." *SP*, 73 (1976), 138-61.

Williams, Arnold. "Chaucer and the Friars." *Speculum*, 28 (1953), 499-513.

Young, Karl. "Chaucer and the Liturgy." *MLN*, 30 (1915), 97-99.

THREE

ROBERT O. PAYNE

Chaucer and the Art of Rhetoric

The first problem with medieval rhetoric is to discover what it was—or how many different things it was. In the universities of the late twelfth and thirteenth centuries, *rhetorica* was a set portion of a tightly organized curriculum—the second of the three courses of the *trivium*, which were intended to perfect the student's writing, speaking, and thinking in the Latin language. But the textbooks written by the leading teachers of rhetoric in these universities were usually analyses of the art of writing poetry, and in their titles *rhetorica* and *poetica* were more or less interchangeable words. As the preaching orders began to emerge into prominence, in the later medieval church, new and different treatises were written in which rhetoric appeared as an ordered and codified system of pulpit oratory, the *ars praedicandi*. And concurrent with these three ran still another fairly common medieval usage in which a "rhetor" was a sort of highly trained and highly placed private secretary, skilled in writing elaborate formal letters, that is, in the *ars dictandi*.

Still, it is possible to discern a related pair of concerns fundamental to all of these diverse "rhetorics": an elegant and orderly style and the use of language to persuade. And it is principally in these that the composition of a poem and a diplomatic epistle approach each other. This proximation is not our main interest here, but it can tell us something about medieval aesthetics which is of central importance: poetry (like the other arts) belonged among the practical uses of knowledge—practical in the sense that it is an orderly application of knowledge to produce a predictable result. What distinguished poetry then, from other such arts and disciplines? Principally, that the surface materials of poetry are lies and illusions, its effects emotional rather than rational. In medieval academic theory only the ends of poetry— the service of truth—could justify its imaginative and irrational means, and only the maintenance of systematic and categorical order among its means could keep them from getting out of hand. In much of the medieval discussion of poetry, there is a clear (sometimes quite puritanical) implication that if men were as reasonable and clear-sighted as they ought to be, logic would be the only necessary form of persuasion. That is pretty much what Aristotle had said at the beginning of his slightly apologetic justification for his *Rhetoric*, and although he offered a significantly different rationale for poetry, the medieval schoolmen simply did not see any difference, and in general they considered poetry and most other non-logical forms of persuasion as kinds of *rhetorica*. Outside the academy and among the poets, Dante defined a poem as a piece of rhetoric set to music, and he called "regular poets" those who wrote by the rule of the school treatises on rhetoric; Chaucer praised Petrarch, and was in turn praised by Deschamps and Lydgate, as a greater "rhetor."

The earlier "monumental" survey investigations of medieval intellectual life by modern scholars, studies like Rashdall's *The Universities of Europe in the Middle Ages* (1895) and Paetow's less broad *The Arts Course in Medieval Universities* (1910), were not especially concerned with literary studies, either by medieval or by modern students. Rather, they surveyed the whole academic structure of medieval education, or some major part of it, in which the theoretical and practical study of rhetoric and poetry occupied a relatively minor position. It was not until the mid-1920's that Edmond Faral and C. S. Baldwin, in rapid succession, published detailed, book-length studies of medieval rhetorical-poetic doctrine, taken by itself as an important phase in the history of criticism and literary theory rather than as a minor part of the medieval university curriculum. It is really with these two books that modern study of medieval rhetoric as an element in medieval poetic practice begins.

Faral's *Les arts poétiques du XIIᵉ et du XIIIᵉ siècle* (1924) and Baldwin's *Medieval Rhetoric and Poetic* (1928) are strikingly different in a variety of ways, although their differences are rarely matters of primary historical data. They reveal, right at the beginning of the scholarly investigation of the subject, two quite different evaluations of the net aesthetic worth of the rhetorical poetic—evaluations which have continued to influence the response of subsequent scholars and critics. The conclusion is inescapable as one reads Faral's work that he saw the medieval rhetoricians sympathetically as men developing a viable literary aesthetic and one on the whole understandable to modern theorists, even though parts of its theoretical substructure were never adequately worked out and many (perhaps most) of their assumptions about language and psychology are assumptions we no longer care to make. Baldwin, on the other hand, was openly hostile to what he saw as an inexcusable despoiling of the fine old rhetoric of Aristotle or Cicero and the fine old poetics of Aristotle or Horace in order to blend (or mangle) them into a sterile hybrid. Faral says little directly, but implies clearly that he thought it probable that academic rhetoric-poetics had heavily influenced medieval Latin poetry and to some extent medieval French poetry. Baldwin scoffs at the very idea that real poetry could have been written on the bastard principles described in the school texts, although he is willing to admit that some of the schoolmen wrote something in Latin which they called poetry and which does exemplify the principles of the school texts. Faral finds the rhetorical texts intrinsically interesting as poetic theory, and in some parts intrinsically sound, whether or not they ever influenced any poetic practice; Baldwin finds it a somewhat distasteful historical necessity to study them as records of a curious turn of the academic mind at its most perverse, cloistered, and ineffectual. Yet Baldwin and Faral are in complete agreement about what the medieval rhetoricians literally said!

The difficulty lies precisely in what the school rhetoricians literally said. Theirs was a doctrine as rigidly systematic and categorical as they could make it. Starting from the orthodox position that poetry aimed to cause an emotional acceptance of reasonable truths which it was not the poet's business to invent or discover, Geoffrey of Vinsauf, Jean de Garlande, and their colleagues proceeded at once to the kinds of ordered language which they thought would produce such effects. Consequently, great sections of their treatises consist of tedious, often superficial, and sometimes far-fetched catalogues of figures of speech and patterns—from meter to metaphor—in which words can be artfully arranged. Nearly always, the rhetorical theorists seem to assume that an author will be working from a prior source, and therefore what little they have to say about overall structure (*dispositio*) is concerned with ways of stripping out what is no longer efficacious (*abbreviatio*) and fitting in newly effective language (*amplificatio*). Poetry's business was to persuade, but to persuade through the emotions aroused by figures and images rather than through the rational convictions of logic. Hence, so the rhetorical theorists apparently reasoned, the proper business of poet and critic, and the distinguishing quality of the craft of poetry, is the artful ordering of words: style or diction or, in the rhetoricians' jargon, *elocutio*.

Chaucer, like many other late medieval poets, repeatedly expresses his sense of the practical immediacy of these theoretical problems. Not only are all his poems reconstructions of prior sources, rebuilt stylistically to create new effects; all of them as well incorporate (usually at the opening and closing) quite overt discussion of the 'rhetorical' principles outlined in the preceding paragraph. These expressions of Chaucer's consciousness of the relations of his poetry to a generally persuasive enterprise are so omnipresent (and variously ironic) that a safely representative quotation is hard to choose, especially if one intends it to illustrate what is in fact a changing and highly complex response by Chaucer to the demands such theory seemed to make upon him. But occasionally he does startle even his most sympathetic modern critics with an old-fashioned rationale for his general procedures, drawn almost *verbatim* from the school rhetorics:

> But soth is, though I kan nat tellen al,
> As kan myn auctour, of his excellence,
> Yet have I seyd, and God toforn, and shal
> In every thyng, al holy his sentence;
> And if that ich, at Loves reverence,
> Have any word in eched for the beste,
> Doth therwithal right as youreselven leste.
>
> For myne wordes, heere and every part,
> I speke hem alle under correccioun
> Of yow that felyng han in loves art,
> And putte it al in youre discrecioun
> To encresse or maken dymynucioun
> Of my langage, and that I yow biseche.
>
> (*Tr*, III, 1324-36)

Following his "auctour" with a certified general faithfulness, Chaucer still claims for himself the rhetor's time-honored privilege—or obligation—to select the most useful "sentence" (which is what the medieval rhetoricians could still make of the Ciceronian *inventio*), and to decorate it attractively and instructively. We should view his art in approximately the same way as he viewed his sources. As he has "seyd . . . al holy his [source's] sentence," still edging in such language as will assert his own version of the reverence due to Love, so we are to take Chaucer's language under the same rhetorical rules of application, testing it against our own emotional experience (and vice versa?) to see what *abbreviatio* (dymynucioun) or *amplificatio* (encresse) might yet sharpen its point or broaden its pertinence. At least in Chaucer's view, the rhetorical process did not stop with a particular definitive persuasion, but was rather a continuing interaction among what one man could see, what he could make others see, and how they in turn could repeat and amplify that seeing.

Partly, that view of things simply reflects the pedagogical concern of the school rhetoricians. Their first job as academics was to teach and explore the uses of language (principally Latin) insofar as they might conduce to persuasion. But partly, the school rhetorics also reflect a position—a group of decisions about answers to some of the primary questions which have troubled literary theorists since before Plato's time. A critic who shares Faral's relatively neo-classical view of poetry as a conscious, technical, fairly rational art is likely to see a good deal in common between what he judges to be the best qualities of the best medieval poetry and the categories and catalogues of the rhetoricians. One with Baldwin's romantic emphasis on the individual expressiveness, the originality, the emotional personality of poetry will often feel that the rhetoricians were not talking about poetry at all, and will seldom be able to relate the qualities of what he considers good poetry to what the rhetoricians did talk about.

All these considerations are pertinent to the work of J. M. Manly, Traugott Naunin, and two or three others who make up the first group of investigators of Chaucer's poetry in relation to medieval rhetoric. Naunin's *Der Einfluss der mittelalterlichen Rhetorik auf Chaucers Dichtung* (1929) takes the most extreme stand, but he differs from the others mainly in the degree of vehemence with which he asserts that medieval rhetoric is essentially a mechanical and superficial system of analysis. Both Manly and Naunin, followed a few years later by Marie P. Hamilton and Florence Teager, seem to agree that the way to measure the relationship between Chaucer's poetry and the thirteenth-century school texts is to count and categorize the schemes and figures in the poetry which correspond to labels and definitions in the texts. Manly, in "Chaucer and the Rhetoricians" (1926), can thus even calculate numerically the "percentages of rhetoric" in various of Chaucer's poems, by which he apparently means the

ratio of figures of speech for which he could find labels and
definitions in the school rhetorics to the total amount of language
employed in the poem. Naunin eschews such arithmetical precision, but provides endless tables and lists of Chaucer's rhetorical
figures, arranged by type. Both scholars agree that the only possible "influence" of rhetoric on his poetry must have been in the
models for certain figures provided by such books as Geoffrey
of Vinsauf's *Summa de coloribus rhetoricis* (a catalogue of the
"colors" or figures), since what little else the schoolmen had to
say about poetry could never have been taken seriously by a
writer of Chaucer's wit, perception, and intelligence. Further,
both Manly and Naunin seem to operate from the assumption
that rhetorical "influences" are only those elements of style which
derive from specific rhetorical precepts as set forth in the textbooks. On such grounds, Manly argues that Chaucer is breaking
away from rhetorical influence whenever the rhetoricians'
"colors" function as effective parts of a poem. Naunin refuses
to count as "colors of rhetoric" any of Chaucer's common figures
such as metaphor or simile, even though the rhetorical texts
regularly list and define them, because Chaucer cannot be assumed to have learned about them solely from those textbooks.

There can be little doubt that Manly and Naunin saw something
of the truth—and again Chaucer himself can, in his occasional
frustrated exasperation, anticipate their desiccant analyses of
what traditional academic theory was able to contribute to his
poetry:

> For wel I wot that folk han here-beforn
> Of makyng ropen, and lad awey the corn;
> And I come after, glenynge here and there,
> And am ful glad if I may fynde an ere
> Of any goodly word that they han left.
>
> (*Prol LGW*, G, 61-5)

Chaucer is probably as close here as anywhere to the assessment
of rhetorical poetics that Manly and Naunin imply: the hack
versifier, his imagination and insight atrophied, picking his
laborious way between the lines of his peers and betters in search

of an occasional simile which can be re-pointed and dressed up in a witty new *allegoria*, perhaps even doubly tin-plated in some syntactical scheme such as *anaphora* or *polysyndeton*.

And it should not surprise us to find that some of Chaucer's most polished and charming *tours de force* can be made to yield to the analytical terminology of the school rhetorics, as Naunin's catalogues, especially, show. Nor need such poetry appear stiff and textbookish just because it can be described in the vocabulary of thirteenth-century stylistic analysis. For instance, we are rightly accustomed to remarking the direct colloquial ease with which Chaucer leads into the *Book of the Duchess*:

> I have gret wonder, be this lyght,
> How that I lyve, for day ne nyght
> I may nat slepe wel nygh noght;
> I have so many an ydel thoght,
> Purely for defaute of slep,
> That, by my trouthe, I take no kep
> Of nothing, how hyt cometh or gooth,
> Ne me nys nothyng leef nor looth.
> Al is ylyche good to me—
> Joye or sorowe, wherso hyt be—
> For I have felynge in nothyng,
> But, as yt were, a mased thyng,
> Alway in poynt to falle a-doun;
> For sorwful ymagynacioun
> Ys alway hooly in my mynde.

We may fail to notice that this is also a textbook-formula opening: the sententious proverb about sleeplessness is elaborated in an *exclamatio* (address to the reader) built on the hoary "modesty topos" ("I'm not really up to this job"), developing into a half-line pattern of *contentio* (balanced opposites) in "how hyt cometh or gooth," "nothyng leef nor looth," "joye or sorowe."

One reason for noting such procedures in his poetry is that every now and again Chaucer himself laughs aloud over his own awareness of them. In "The dayes honour, and the hevenes yë,/ The nyghtes foo—al this clepe I the sonne—" (*Tr*, II, 904-5), the three *traductiones* ("conceited" metaphors) are piled up in parallel structures (*frequentatio*) on the same syntactical scheme (the dayes—the hevenes—the nyghtes: *polysyndeton*) within the crowded compass of a line and a half. This is too much for even so involved a sentimentalist as the narrator of *Troilus and Criseyde*, so the technical trip-wire explodes the effect: "al this clepe I the sonne—," and we are left laughing at what looks like all that can be done with the stylistic prescriptions of Geoffrey of Vinsauf and his confreres.

The work of Manly and Naunin gave us a fairly unified initial interpretation: Chaucer had read at least one or two of the principal rhetoric texts and had made discernible use of them, but only superficially. The surface rhetorical cast of much of his poetry, they felt, is a kind of historical accident, a partly inescapable function of the time in which he lived and wrote; what makes his poetry survive his time is never any quality that has much to do with medieval rhetoric.

Interestingly enough, Manly and Naunin disagree notably about the sources of Chaucer's greatness, so that even though they share a negative assessment of the rhetorical poetic, they find very different sorts of fault with it. For Manly, Chaucer's greatness was defined by his journalistic aptitude for setting down in words the exact likenesses of men and women he knew and the events in which they participated. The suggestion that Chaucer may have "merely imagined" something is to Manly an aspersion upon his poetry. Consequently, Manly sees Chaucer's poetic career as a constant struggle to record photographically the exact historical truth, in the face of the constant distracting pressures of literary tradition toward generalization, stylization, conventionalization—imagination. Now, however much one may damn the rhetoricians for their artificial sterilities, there is no escaping their insistence that poetry's whole business is with generalizations through the means of stylization and conventionalization. Like most thoughtful medieval men, they were interested in the immediate particulars of history mainly because they could be interpreted or reordered into general patterns. So

Manly, by his own lights, was quite right to judge Chaucer's quality by his movement away from the aesthetic implied in the rhetorical treatises. But at the same time—if only because of his absolute historical commitment—Manly could see that some, or even many, of the rhetoricians' observations about techniques of style need not be confined to poetry alone but could be used as well by a journalist, historian, romancer, or Sunday-school moralist. Since, according to Manly, the rhetoricians could make no satisfactory connection between their elaborately explicated systems of means and the almost unexplored ends poetry was supposed to serve, then a bright and well-read poet like Chaucer could easily adapt any or all of their means to whatever ends he might choose. In a way, although he himself never makes the distinction in these terms, Manly assesses the rhetorical tradition finally as one of those peripheral, but important, artificial cultural forces which affect the external structure of literary language, but neither express accurately any primary aesthetic concerns nor persuade anyone to any real aesthetic purpose.

Naunin's is a very different assessment of Chaucer's accomplishment, and therefore of the kind and extent of rhetorical influence in his work. Probably nearly no one—casual reader of Chaucer or professional critic—has ever been much affected by Naunin's obscure doctoral dissertation of forty years ago, but it does express a point of view which underlies much modern historical criticism. Simply stated, Naunin's is the position of a long line of post-Romantic critics for whom the norm of quality is difference. What counts is to be moving, to break the shackles of the old, to approximate what is to us contemporary. For Naunin in 1929 what seemed most convincingly contemporary was a genially comic skepticism toward established values. He, like D. W. Robertson, Jr., B. F. Huppé, R. E. Kaske, and a few other critics of the fifties and sixties, sees the normal literary world of Chaucer's time as whole and entire unto itself, fixed by its own inner historical necessity and scarcely comprehensible to any subsequent age. But to Naunin, the incomprehensibly fixed and inviolable conventions of medieval literature were wrong, and Chaucer (or any other medieval poet) was "good" to the extent that he saw through their pretenses and rejected them in favor of whatever he could anticipate of the "modern" attitude of humorous rational skepticism.

So Naunin will diligently catalogue the *exclamatio* (narrator's apostrophe to the reader), *allegoria* (personification of God's will put into action), *frequentatio* (multiplication of metaphors with the same referent), and even the metaphor itself (*traductio*) in a passage like

> But O Fortune, executrice of wyrdes,
> O influences of thise hevenes hye!
> Soth is, that under God ye ben oure hierdes,
> Though to us bestes ben the causes wrie.
> (*Tr*, III, 617-20)

But he will simply have nothing at all to say about whether this sequence of very deliberately stylized language is like or unlike the superficially similar sequence in *Troilus*, II, 904-5. He has already assumed that the geometry of such patterning is a function of Chaucer's accidental historical location and has nothing to do with his unique poetic intention or accomplishment.

Nevertheless, Naunin took medieval rhetorical poetic more seriously than Manly did, and he rejected it more absolutely. He saw the schoolmen as expressing the binding literary fashions of an age; Manly saw them as tabulating some of the linguistic and stylistic determinants of a small, esoteric group. Manly wished to find a norm for the measurement of Chaucer's success completely outside the rhetorical poetic, and he was relatively unconcerned whether the rhetoricians' tables of 'colors' can be illustrated from Chaucer's work. Naunin wished to verify Chaucer's greatness against some expressed and operative standard of his own age which Chaucer was able to reject and thus measure up to a "modern" critical standard.

Finally, what C. S. Baldwin, Manly, Naunin, and the few others in the early thirties who interested themselves in the rhetorical question all had in common was the conviction that the school rhetoric simply never raised or attempted to resolve any fundamental aesthetic questions. No matter how differently the individual investigators might define a "fundamental aesthetic question," only Faral, the one who had worked most intensively with the actual documents, was able to maintain a conviction that the rhetoricians ever addressed themselves to such questions. The consensus by the mid-1930's, when the question of Chaucer and the rhetoricians was more or less shelved for the next fifteen or twenty years, was that Chaucer may have learned some debatable proportion of superficial stylistic gambitry from this academic tradition so far removed from the vital currents of late medieval vernacular literature. Future investigation of the subject seemed unlikely to exceed squibs in *Notes and Queries*, in which alert graduate students would intermittently identify hitherto overlooked polysyndetons in the *House of Fame*.

But again, as when the whole subject had first been opened by Faral and Baldwin, two important and controversial books, published in quick succession, precipitated a major change. Neither book addressed itself specifically to the subject of Chaucer's poetry; neither was more than tangentially engaged with late medieval school rhetoric. But what both did was to force us to reconsider the substructure of implication which might underlie such cultural phenomena as the school rhetorics, and consequently to question Baldwin's and Manly's and Naunin's too-easy dismissal of their aesthetic pretensions. Rosemond Tuve's *Elizabethan and Metaphysical Imagery* (1947) seriously advanced, for the first time since Faral, the proposition that the rhetorical poetic not only might be taken seriously by historical scholars, but in fact might have been taken seriously by good contemporary poets. No matter that Tuve's concern was with sixteenth- and early seventeenth-century rhetoric and the great Renaissance English lyrists from Sidney through Donne and Marvell. The rhetorical theory her book analyzed was essentially unchanged from that of Geoffrey of Vinsauf and Jean de Garlande in the early thirteenth century. And whether she was right or wrong in her explications of the Elizabethan and Jacobean poets, she persuaded even her opponents to take Renaissance school rhetoric seriously as a theory of poetry.

Ernst Robert Curtius' *Europäische Literatur und lateinisches Mittelalter* (1948) has probably been even more hotly debated among historians than Rosemond Tuve's book was among literary critics. But again, even if finally we decide to accept none of Curtius' answers, we are now committed to considering the questions he raised, and these are different from and more basic than the questions raised earlier about medieval academic rhetoric.

Like Tuve, Curtius takes the academic procedures of the era he studies as antecedently neither good nor bad, but simply as expressions of the problems most apt to have engaged the best contemporary minds. And as Curtius sees it, the two great concerns of medieval academia were what could be salvaged from fallen Rome, and how it could be reconciled with reborn Christian Europe. Medieval rhetoric—like the other *artes* in the university curriculum—is taken then to express a specifically medieval Christian attitude toward an area of human knowledge which pagan antiquity had previously, though incompletely, explored. It is here particularly that Curtius' way of seeing leads us to definitions and conclusions far removed from those of the earlier investigators of rhetorical influences. Curtius does not make any very detailed analysis of academic rhetoric, and he has nothing at all to say about its effects on Chaucer, but it is clear that he would be little interested in the question of which particular figures in Chaucer's poetry are there because Chaucer had read Geoffrey of Vinsauf. Rather, medieval rhetorical doctrine and Chaucer's poetry should *both* be taken as expressions of the medieval idea of poetry, and we should interest ourselves in the ways in which they do and do not correspond. Like Faral, Curtius does think it possible to see a real and fairly fully detailed theory of literature in the school teachings; perhaps even more strongly than Faral, Curtius feels that most medieval poetry possesses dominant characteristics indicative of values similar to the ones catalogued in the theoretical treatises.

In 1950, Dorothy Everett published her Gollancz Memorial Lecture "Some Reflections on Chaucer's 'Art Poetical'," a short and very interesting reconsideration of the old, negative attitude toward rhetorical theory and Chaucer's involvement with it. This pamphlet is the first announcement of what has since developed into a full-scale reinvestigation. Everett's principal argument is that we should look more carefully at what Chaucer says and does about his craft, and in a sense she also asks that we approach the questions Manly had raised with less of Naunin's hostility and more in the spirit of Tuve or Curtius. Five years later, Ralph Baldwin attempted something very like what Everett had called for, but limited his study to the *Canterbury Tales*.

Baldwin's *The Unity of the Canterbury Tales* is a small book and much of what it suggests is not worked out in detail, but it is a significant contribution. Baldwin's point of departure is that the operative poetic in the *Canterbury Tales* is the rhetorical poetic; indeed, he finds the unity of the tales precisely in their commitment to moral demonstration by means of the attractive persuasions of an ordered poetic style. It no longer seems to matter very much how many or few of the schemes and tropes and "colors" can be tabulated in Chaucer's verses. What does matter, in Baldwin's study, is that Chaucer seems, in the *Canterbury Tales*, to share the rhetoricians' notions of what poetry should do and how it should do it—of the relationships between intention, form, and effect.

Of course, we need not agree that moral persuasion is the main business of poetry in order to recognize that to most of us now in the sixties the various romanticisms and naturalisms underlying much of the criticism of the twenties no longer seem self-evidently valid. Not only in Chaucer studies, nor only in criticism of earlier literature, but frequently even in very contemporary poetry, artificiality, stylization, and traditionalism have come to take on quite positive values, and it would seem naive to most of us to make any one particular literary style the norm of quality. Much of the best work on Chaucer in recent years has had the effect of making us more comfortable with the various conven-

tions his poetry commands, and with the various stylistic form-
alities it assumes.

In all the discussion of Chaucer's connections with the orthodox
academic view of poetry, however, no one had made any systematic examination of everything Chaucer says and does in his
works from which we might infer his own theory of poetry. As
early as 1924, Whitney H. Wells had taken a first step in his
article "Chaucer as a Literary Critic," and Everett suggested in
her Gollancz Memorial Lecture several things which a full-scale
study of Chaucer's ideas about poetry would have to take into
account. But in the main, the various assertions about Chaucer's
poetic tenets and intentions had been more-or-less impressionistic
generalizations.

In 1963, Robert O. Payne attempted in *The Key of Remembrance: A Study of Chaucer's Poetics* to provide the complete
and detailed study previously lacking. At the same time, Payne
produced probably the most favorable discussion of the school
rhetorics since Faral's and argued that nearly all of Chaucer's
own critical and theoretical vocabulary either derives from that
academic tradition or expresses ways of thinking closely similar
to those of the school rhetoricians. Still, *The Key of Remembrance*
does not try to show us a Chaucer who simply and consistently
carried out the rhetoricians' instructions to write moral truth in
the attractive guise of poetic fictions. Rather, Payne finds,
Chaucer was himself profoundly interested in the problems of
the nature of poetry and its techniques and he expressed in his
poems—especially in the *Prologue to the Legend of Good
Women*—a great deal of serious independent thought about the
questions which had been central to nearly all Christian considerations of poetry and rhetoric from Augustine's time to his
own. The new dimension in Chaucer's own perspective, then,
is his constant awareness that mortal men (whether poets or
readers) really cannot do what the rhetorical poetic required of
them, although what it required of them is surely to be taken
as the ideal toward which they must aspire. "Sentence and

solas" were for Chaucer the necessary and adequate aims for
poetry, and he knew as well as Sidney, Milton, or Eliot that
no man attempts to provide them in his work unless he thinks
he knows what he is doing. But he also knew as well as Swift
and Sterne that for even the best of men, what one thinks he
is doing is never quite exactly what he is doing. The school
rhetoricians themselves had advised poets to remake the great
works of the past in order to correct and reactivate them where
they had failed or not aged well. Chaucer shared the rhetoricians' attitude toward past literature: "And if that olde bokes
weren aweye, / Yloren were of remembrance the keye" (*Prol
LGW*, 25-6). Chaucer can look down the centuries ahead (just
as he can look back over the centuries behind to Ovid or Virgil)
and see the combination of his inadequacies and our ignorance
producing the same sort of failure. But neither he nor we willed
the failure; no one has to be "wrong" for it to occur. Language
changes, and the fact that we know it will not prevent it.
Individual perception varies, but no man can fully correct his
own perceptions even though he knows the general rule. Time
and change are the conditions under which fallen men must
learn about eternity and permanence.

Medieval rhetoricians had charged poets with the burden of
adjusting language so that it would make men's emotions serve
their reason. But if men are in fact fallen (and we can hardly
take Chaucer to have believed otherwise), then neither language
nor emotion nor human reason is perfectly reliable and the
poet is inevitably going to find himself exactly where the
dreamer-poet in the *Prologue to the Legend of Good Women*
found himself: on trial for having produced effects he didn't
intend—perhaps even to the detriment of the very effects he
did intend. What Payne finally asks the modern reader of
Chaucer to do is to treat Chaucer rather as Chaucer treated the
great ancient poets he is shown reading in his self-portraits.
We must try to see him as he is limited by his own time, place,
and person, precisely in order to see how he engages in his own

time, place, and person most of the poetic issues we are still concerned with, however differently we may express them in our own times, places, and persons.

Payne's book presents in several ways a continuation and expansion of the sense of the validity of the theoretical concerns of medieval rhetoric which Faral had felt and which Curtius subsequently tried to rehabilitate against the dominantly neo-romantic tendencies of much criticism in the twenties and thirties. However, a group of articles by James J. Murphy, beginning with "The Earliest Teaching of Rhetoric at Oxford" (1960) and coming forward to "A New Look at Chaucer and the Rhetoricians" (1964), has raised again something like the old Manly question of the purely historical transmission of the influence of the school rhetorics. Where Faral, Tuve, Curtius, and Payne have been concerned with similarities and dissimi-larities between theory and practice, largely regardless of specific channels of transmission, Murphy has reopened—with some new evidence—the question of what specific new sources and agencies of conveyance may have influenced Chaucer or Gower or (presumably) any particular late medieval English poet. In general, Murphy argues that the sort of teaching of rhetoric Faral had defined never took a very strong hold in the English universities and certainly had not done so by the time of Gower and Chaucer, and in fact that a passage in Book VII of Gower's Confessio Amantis is "the first discussion of rhetoric in the English language."

Yet surely we need not have a local English academic tradi-tion to account for the rhetorical cast of the theoretical vocabulary of poets so sophisticated and cosmopolitan as Chaucer, the Gawain poet, and Gower. And surely Chaucer (in HF, PF, and Prol LGW) had already given extended consideration to most of the basic tenets of the academic rhetorics well before the Con-fessio was written. Still, it is useful to be reminded that by Gower's time the specific continuity of the tradition was frag-mented and diffused and that Gower's attempt to summarize a specific source (Geoffrey of Vinsauf) and a specific school discipline is neither very successful nor very like Chaucer's imaginative penetration to the vital aesthetic issues entangled in the pedantry and superficiality of the school texts. What we must be careful of, however, is the historicist's fallacy lurking under Murphy's argument: that if most of his English contemporaries were not very informed or perceptive about rhetorical doctrine, then Chaucer probably couldn't have been either. Gower, we might remember, also didn't know anything about Boccaccio.

In effect, what has happened during the past twenty years or so is that nearly all the questions scholars of the twenties had raised about the school rhetorics and medieval poetic theory and practice have been reopened, although our major indebtedness for the materials with which to pursue these studies is still to Edmond Faral and C. S. Baldwin. But the negative prejudices of Manly and Naunin, and their consequent location of the effects of rhetorical influence on Chaucer solely in superficial stylistic devices, have all but disappeared. Ralph Baldwin and Robert O. Payne take the school rhetorics to be one form of expression of medieval ideas about poetry, and make general analytical comparisons between them and Chaucer's poetry. Both find Chaucer closer to the rhetoricians in his primary assumptions about his art than in the surface details of his style. Even James J. Murphy's recent attempts to discount the rhetorical influence on fourteenth-century English poets by arguing the weakness of the tradition in the English schools has about it none of the old aura of trying to clear Chaucer's work of a damaging aspersion. Finally, Payne is even able to argue that the school rhetorics, by raising questions about the correlation of language with truth and volatile human emotion, were at least one factor in the evolution of that complex ironic perspective which has for so long seemed to modern readers distinctively Chaucerian.

* * * * *

Since 1968, activity in the study of medieval rhetoric and Chaucer's relations with it has increased notably in quality as well as in quantity. Not only have we had recently a spate of new editions and translations of medieval rhetorical texts, we have also had the first new interpretative history of medieval rhetoric since C. S. Baldwin's.

To take the latter first, James J. Murphy's *Rhetoric in the Middle Ages* gives us a welcome new objective but sympathetic start on understanding the transformation of classical rhetorical theory in the minds of medieval Christian preachers, poets, and professional clerks. Working from better texts than Faral had and with a more sensitive critical perception than Baldwin's, Murphy writes a clear, simple narrative account of the history of medieval rhetoric which is not only factually reliable, but also particularly illuminating for students of medieval literature. Readers of Chaucer will want to pay especially close attention to part two, chapter four: "Ars Poetriae; Preceptive Grammar, or the Rhetoric of Verse Writing." That chapter, together with Douglas Kelly's "The Scope of the Treatment of Composition in the Twelfth- and Thirteenth-Century Arts of Poetry," provides an exceptionally challenging attempt to take medieval rhetoric seriously without surrendering our own literary judgments.

To return to texts and translations, there have been several in the past decade that are of use to beginning Chaucerians. To save space here, it may serve to mention one broad, general introductory collection and a translation with commentary on the rhetorical text Chaucer knew best. *Readings in Medieval Rhetoric*, edited by Joseph M. Miller, Michael H. Prosser and Thomas W. Benson, offers good, accurate translations of extracts from a usefully varied group of medieval rhetorical texts, so that beginning literary historians can quickly acquire a usable sense of what medieval rhetorical theory was like. And Ernest Gallo's *The Poetria Nova and Its Sources in Early Rhetorical Doctrine* gives a convenient parallel-text translation of Geoffrey of Vinsauf's influential work, as well as a succinct résumé of its sources in late classical and early medieval doctrine.

There has also been a gratifyingly steady stream of discussion (sometimes fairly heated) of how to apply our increasing understanding of medieval rhetoric to Chaucer's poetry. The revised bibliography below reflects much of that discourse. To offer an evaluative generalization in lieu of closer comments, nearly all of it seems informed, provocative, and worth arguing over. Especially notable are Judson B. Allen's *The Friar as Critic*, for its too brief but often perceptive sketches of the intellectual milieu in which late medieval literary theory developed; R. W. Frank, Jr.'s "*Troilus and Criseyde*: The Art of Amplification," for its demonstration of how easily now we can convert the categories of medieval rhetoric to the purposes of modern criticism; and Glending Olson's "Deschamps' *Art de dictier* and Chaucer's Literary Environment," for its incisive questioning of the supposed limits of medieval literary theory.

BIBLIOGRAPHY

Allen, Judson B. *The Friar as Critic*. Nashville: Vanderbilt Univ. Press, 1971.

Allen, Robert J. "A Recurring Motif in Chaucer's *House of Fame*." *JEGP*, 55 (1956), 393-405.

Atkins, J.W.H. *English Literary Criticism: The Medieval Phase*. 1943. Rpt. Gloucester, Mass.: P. Smith, 1961.

Baldwin, C.S. *Medieval Rhetoric and Poetic*. 1928. Rpt. Gloucester, Mass.: P. Smith, 1959.

Baldwin, Ralph. *The Unity of the 'Canterbury Tales'*. Anglistica, 5. Copenhagen: Rosenkilde og Bagger, 1955.

Beck, Richard J. "Educational Expectation and Rhetorical Result in *The Canterbury Tales*." *ES*, 44 (1963), 241-53.

Boughner, Daniel C. "Elements of Epic Grandeur in the *Troilus*." *ELH*, 6 (1939), 200-10.

Clogan, Paul M. "The Figural Style and Meaning of *The Second Nun's Prologue and Tale*." *M&H*, NS 3 (1972), 213-40.

Craig, Hardin. "From Gorgias to Troilus." In *Studies in Medieval Literature in Honor of Professor A.C. Baugh.* Ed. MacEdward Leach. Philadelphia: Univ. of Pennsylvania Press, 1961, pp. 97-107.

Curtius, E.R. *Europäische Literatur und lateinisches Mittelalter.* Bern, 1948. Trans. W.R. Trask. *European Literature and the Latin Middle Ages.* New York: Pantheon Books, 1953.

Everett, Dorothy. "Some Reflections on Chaucer's 'Art Poetical'." *PBA,* 36 (1950). Rpt. In *Essays on Middle English Literature.* Ed. P.M. Kean. Oxford: Clarendon Press, 1955, pp. 149-74.

Faral, Edmond. *Les arts poétiques du XIIe et du XIIIe siècle.* 1924. Rpt. Paris: E. Champion, 1958.

Fisher, John H. "The Three Styles of Fragment 1 of the *Canterbury Tales.*" *ChauR,* 8 (1973), 119-27.

Frank, R.W. Jr. "*Troilus and Criseyde:* The Art of Amplification." In *Medieval Literature and Folklore Studies: Essays in Honor of Francis Lee Utley.* Ed. Jerome Mandel and Bruce A. Rosenberg. New Brunswick, N.J.: Rutgers Univ. Press, 1970, pp. 155-71.

Gallo, Ernest. *The Poetria Nova and Its Sources in Early Rhetorical Doctrine.* The Hague: Mouton, 1971.

Glunz, H.H. *Die Literarästhetik des europäischen Mittelalters: Wolfram, Rosenroman, Chaucer, Dante.* Bochum: Pöppinhaus, 1937.

Halm, Carl Felix. *Rhetores latini minores.* Leipzig: Teubner, 1863.

Hamilton, Marie P. "Notes on Chaucer and the Rhetoricians." *PMLA,* 47 (1932), 403-9.

Harrington, David V. "Chaucer's *Man of Law's Tale:* Rhetoric and Emotion." *MSpr,* 61 (1967), 353-62.

Harrison, Benjamin S. "Medieval Rhetoric in the *Book of the Duchess.*" *PMLA,* 49 (1934), 428-42.

————. "The Rhetorical Inconsistency of Chaucer's Franklin." *SP,* 32 (1935), 55-61.

Kelly, Douglas: "The Scope of the Treatment of Composition in the Twelfth- and Thirteenth-Century Arts of Poetry." *Speculum,* 41 (1966), 261-78.

Knight, Stephen. "Rhetoric and Poetry in the *Franklin's Tale.*" *ChauR,* 4 (1970), 14-30.

Koban, Charles. "Hearing Chaucer Out: The Art of Persuasion in the *Wife of Bath's Tale.*" *ChauR,* 5 (1971), 225-39.

Kopp, Jane Baltzell. "The New Poetics." In *Three Medieval Rhetorical Arts.* Ed. J.J. Murphy. Berkeley: Univ. of California Press, 1971, pp. 29-108.

Koretsky, Allen C. "Chaucer's Use of the Apostrophe in *Troilus and Criseyde.*" *ChauR,* 4 (1970), 81-84.

McKeon, Richard. "Rhetoric in the Middle Ages." *Speculum,* 17 (1942), 1-32.

Manly, John Matthews. "Chaucer and the Rhetoricians." *PBA,* 12 (1926).

Merrill, Thomas F. "Wrath and Rhetoric in *The Summoner's Tale.*" *TSLL,* 4 (1962), 341-50.

Miller Joseph M., Michael H. Prosser, and Thomas W. Benson, eds. *Readings in Medieval Rhetoric.* Bloomington: Indiana Univ. Press, 1973.

Mossé, Fernand. "Chaucer et le 'métier' de l'écrivain." *EA,* 7 (1954), 394-401.

Mroczkowski, Przemyslaw. "*The Friar's Tale* and Its Pulpit Background." In *English Studies Today.* Ed. G.A. Bonnard, 2 (1961), 107-20.

Murphy, James J. "The Earliest Teaching of Rhetoric at Oxford." *SM,* 27 (1960), 345-47.

———. "The Arts of Discourse, 1050-1400." *MS,* 23 (1961), 194-205.

———. "John Gower's *Confessio Amantis* and the First Discussion of Rhetoric in the English Language." *PQ,* 41 (1962), 401-11.

———. "A New Look at Chaucer and the Rhetoricians." *RES,* 15 (1964), 1-20.

———, ed. *Three Medieval Rhetorical Arts.* Berkeley: Univ of California Press, 1971.

———. *Rhetoric in the Middle Ages.* Berkeley: Univ. of California Press, 1974.

————, ed. *Medieval Eloquence*. Berkeley: Univ. of California Press, 1978.

Naunin, Traugott. *Der Einfluss der mittelalterlichen Rhetorik auf Chaucers Dichtung*. Diss. Bonn, 1929.

Nist, John. "Chaucer's Apostrophic Mode in the *Canterbury Tales*." *TSL*, 15 (1970), 85-98.

Olson, Glending L. "Deschamps' *Art de dictier* and Chaucer's Literary Environment." *Speculum*, 48 (1973), 714-23.

Paetow, J.L. *The Arts Course at Medieval Universities, with Especial Reference to Grammar and Rhetoric*. Univ. of Illinois Studies, 3, No. 7. 1910. Rpt. New York: Irvington, n.d.

Payne, Robert O. *The Key of Remembrance: A Study of Chaucer's Poetics*. 1963. Rpt. Westport, Conn.: Greenwood Press, 1973.

————. "Chaucer's Realization of himself as Rhetor." In *Medieval Eloquence*. Berkeley: Univ. of California Press, 1978.

Shain, Charles E. "Pulpit Rhetoric in Three Canterbury Tales." *MLN*, 70 (1955), 235-45.

Simmons, J.S. "The Place of the Poet in Chaucer's *House of Fame*." *MLQ*, 27 (1966), 125-35.

Teager, Florence E. "Chaucer's Eagle and the Rhetorical Colors." *PMLA*, 47 (1932), 410-18.

Tuve, Rosemond. *Elizabethan and Metaphysical Imagery: Renaissance Poetic and Twentieth-Century Critics*. Chicago: Univ. of Chicago Press, 1947.

Wells, Whitney H. "Chaucer as a Literary Critic." *MLN*, 39 (1924), 255-68.

FOUR

TAUNO F. MUSTANOJA

Chaucer's Prosody

Prosody is language in the hands of the poet. Sounds, syllables, words, and even silences are woven into a texture of rhythmic patterns to serve the purposes of artistic expression.

The systematic study of Chaucer's prosody began in the nineteenth century, with the pioneer publications of Francis James Child, Jakob Schipper, and Bernhard Ten Brink. Since then special studies have kept appearing, though not at a very fast rate. There has been no drastic change in the scholarly approach, but the shift of emphasis from language to literature in the English departments of British and American universities in the 1920's and 1930's, together with the present-day vogue for free verse, has had a certain modifying effect on the scansion of Chaucer's poetry.

Chaucer's language, the London speech of the late fourteenth century, is too different from the English of today to be made accessible to the modern reader simply by modernizing the spelling and punctuation, as has been done with Shakespeare. Chaucer's language cannot be modernized, it must be translated; and translations, however good, are inevitably poor substitutes for the original diction. A reader who wishes to enjoy Chaucer's art to the full must read him in the original, which means that he has to understand the peculiarities of the poet's language. To help him, illuminating brief accounts of Chaucer's pronunciation, grammar, and versification are included in most editions of his poems. For a more profound understanding of Chaucer's language, however, one has to consult books of a more detailed character.

Books on the history of the English language keep pouring out, but the best general description of linguistic conditions in Chaucer's time is still Baugh's *History of the English Language*. Another good general treatment of the linguistic background is Brunner's *Die englische Sprache*. The works of Kaluza, Wright, Jordan, Wyld, and Luick on historical phonology, or on both phonology and morphology, have served generations of philologists and are still valuable or even standard. There are some more recent books intended mainly for the non-specialist, such as Brunner's *Outline of Middle English Grammar* and Mossé's *Handbook*—where syntactical aspects are also considered, Moore's *Historical Outlines* (revised by Marckwardt), which devotes a chapter to Chaucer's language, and Berndt's *Einführung*. Special discussions of syntax are Mustanoja's *Middle English Syntax*, where Chaucer receives a great deal of attention, and Visser's very comprehensive *Historical Syntax*.

On pp. 464-509 of her *Chaucer: A Bibliographical Manual* Eleanor Hammond prints useful comments on a number of special studies in Chaucer's language. The most important of those which deal with his sounds and inflections were written by Ten Brink and Wild. The second edition of Ten Brink's work, from which the English translation was made, was revised much less extensively than the third, in which, for example, the author's theory of "hovering vowels" ("schwebende Vokale") was omitted altogether. Ten Brink has been justly criticized for his eagerness to emend manuscript readings; yet his book is still considered the standard guide to Chaucer's language and versification. A useful practical book for beginners is Kökeritz's *Guide to Chaucer's Pronunciation*. Chaucer's morphemic structures have been examined recently by Fisiak through the structural approach. Mersand, using mainly the statistical method, finds that the ratio of Romance loanwords in the longer works ranges between approximately 22 and 51 per cent. Karpf's illuminating study of some syntactical aspects has been recently supplemented by Kerkhof, and Margaret Schlauch, in "Chaucer's Colloquial English," notes that Chaucer makes members of all social classes use colloquial expressions and that he uses them himself in many expository passages. Gertrud Sauerbrey's doctoral dissertation, based on Wilhelm Wundt's doctrines, would probably be useful to those interested in the psychological and stylistic background of Chaucer's linguistic usage.

Ten Brink's book retains its standard value among the special studies of Chaucer's versification in spite of the fact that some of his opinions have been shown to be inaccurate or even erroneous and that he has been accused—though not always justly—of being too rigid in his metrical principles. Schipper's *History of English Versification* is a translation of his *Grundriss der englischen Metrik*, an abridgment of *Englische Metrik*. Many of Schipper's details are in need of revision, but Hammond's violent attack in her *Chaucer* ("Schipper subjects the verse of Chaucer to a most mechanical and obdurate analysis . . . fruitless line-dissection . . . the entire basis of Schipper's work is questionable . . . " pp. 477-8) is less than just. Hammond herself, however, particularly in her *English Verse between Chaucer and Surrey*, proves to be a prosodist of great sensitiveness. In the first volume of his *History of English Prosody* Saintsbury has some good observations on Chaucer's technique, but one cannot avoid the impression that his real strength lies in his treatment of the later periods. Kaluza's *Short History of English Versification* is still a useful general guide for students of English poetry, and so are the more recent books of Egerton Smith, Enid Hamer, and Joseph Raith. Verrier's very technical *Essai* is concerned mainly with rhythm. Baum's *Chaucer's Verse* is a sensitively written and highly informative account of Chaucer's versification, although the general plan seems to be somewhat lacking in clarity and some quotations from Chaucer's works can be interpreted in more than one way.

The basis of meter is rhythm. Rhythm is a fundamental element in the dance, called "the mother of the arts," and indeed in all forms of art. As understood in the present context, rhythm is characterized by the recurrence of certain prominent linguistic features at perceptibly regular intervals.

In the classical poetry of Greece and Rome the meter was quantitative, based essentially on an alternation of long and short vowels. Romance poetry, on the other hand, is fundamentally syllabic in character, i.e. the rhythmic effect is achieved by the occurrence of a fixed number of syllables in a line. In Germanic poetry the prominent element is usually an accent of intensity ("dynamic accent" or "stress"). This is naturally to be connected with the replacement of the Indo-European musical accent, based predominantly on pitch, by an accent of intensity in primitive Germanic.

Whether the rhythm of English poetry is accentual (i.e. characterized by variations in stress) or syllabic, or both, or whether quantity plays a part in it is a much-debated question. Illuminating reviews of varying opinions are included in Omond's *English Metrists* and Evelyn Scholl's "English Metre Once More." To mention only a few typical views, Hamer on pp. 2-3 thinks that "in English the most important and easily perceptible movement occurs in a quality which may be best called stress, and it is on this quality that the rhythm of verse is founded." J. Thompson agrees, but quotes a poem by Marianne Moore as an example of verse where the metrical structure is based on the number of syllables alone, without regard to their degree of stress (p. 5). Verrier connects the rhythm of English poetry with duration when he emphasizes the fact that the interval between two noticeable increases in intensity is a division of time, a simple duration—"une division du temps, une simple durée" (*Essai*, I, 146). According to Sonnenschein, rhythm is based "not upon accent but upon the duration of the foot" (p. 105).

Our idea of the scansion of early poetry is inevitably inferential. We have no means of telling exactly what it sounded like when it was recited. There is good reason to assume that the differences between the various rhythmic bases were not nearly so clear-cut as many prosodic theorists seem to believe. Thus accentuation has undoubtedly been a contributory feature in the early metric systems defined as quantitative, and although the accent must have been a predominantly musical one, an intrinsic connection is demonstrable between the musical accent and stress. It was a shift of preponderance from the musical to the dynamic quality in the accent that brought the quantitative system in Latin versification to an end—with the result that from the fourth century onwards Latin poetry has been accentual. Another fact worth consideration is that strongly stressed syllables tend to be longer than lightly stressed ("unstressed") ones. Schramm, for example, noticed that when English tetrameter poetry is read aloud the accented syllables are, on the average, almost twice as long as the unaccented ones. More recently, Fry has called attention to the fact that in evaluations of syllabic stress duration appears to be an even more decisive factor than intensity.

The Old English system of versification was based on alliteration and a fixed number of stresses in a line. In Middle English it was replaced by a new system. The primary source of this new versification was the French system, which was syllabic, though the influence of accentual Latin poetry must have been considerable. From the beginning the new English system was made to conform to the native tradition of accentuation, with the result that its meter was both syllabic and accentual, but the rhythm depended essentially on the number of stressed syllables; the number of unstressed syllables was of less consequence and was therefore liable to some variation.

That stress was a more important element in the English verse of Chaucer's time than the number of syllables is borne out in a striking way by the metrical "irregularities" of the French poetry written or copied in England. Romance scholars are accustomed to look down on Anglo-Norman versification as a debased form of the strictly syllabic meters of continental French verse. They fail to see that the poets and scribes, living in an English-speaking community as they did, shared the phonetic and accentual habits of their environment and measured their lines by the number of stresses and not of syllables. Hence the ease with which English poets wrote macaronic verses like "Máiden móder mílde / Oiéz cel óreysoún."

The conflict between the normal rhythm of speech and the requirements of meter has intrigued generations of metrists. Malof discusses it under what he calls "the tension exploited by English rhythms." "On the most general level" this is "the tension between the continual influx of foreign patterns and the natural gravitation toward native English speech characteristics." The result is "a compromise recorded in scansion." Stein, taking meter to be an ideal rhythmic pattern, refers to the meter-language conflict as a clash of "the ideal" with "the natural." "Metre gives us two kinds of satisfaction," says Hamer, "that of repeated rhythmic pattern, which we hear in our minds, and that of the expressive modulations, which we actually hear" (pp. 7-8; by modulations she means departures from the basic rhythm). Baum in *Chaucer's Verse* finds that "the beauty of a line is its modulation away from the fixity of meter" (p. 126, n. 7).

Chaucer's greatness as a metrical artist is seen in the easy flexibility with which he resolves the conflict between his meter and the natural prose rhythm of living speech. In this he is superior to all his contemporaries, English and French alike. Clashes between the word-stress and the metrical stress do occur in his verse (e.g., *feláwe, singínge* [:*singe*], *whylóm*), but not very often, and with the sentence-stress this hardly ever happens. Joerden finds that Chaucer's metrical modulations never give the impression of being mere emergency measures (p. 55). Schlauch in "Chaucer's Colloquial English" feels that the collo-quialisms which Chaucer inserts into his narrative "contribute to the sense of happy ease and flowingness which were characteristic of [his] poetry in all its periods." The matter is also touched upon by Everett in "Chaucer's 'Good Ear'."

Chaucer's linguistic technique in reconciling the rhythm of normal speech with his meters deserves a brief mention. A valuable comprehensive treatment of the subject is Bihl's fifty-year-old monograph, where he discusses the accentuation of native and Romance words, the inflections, word-formation, and syntax. Unfortunately, the modifying effect of the meter has not been taken sufficiently into account in all studies dealing with Chaucer's linguistic usage. To mention only one example of this, the variation *softely/softe* in "And up he roos, and softely he wente / Unto the cradel . . . / And baar it softe unto his beddes heed" (*RvT*, 4211-13), clearly due to metrical considerations, is ascribed by Heuer on p. 118 simply to "syntactical competition," which explains nothing.

It is impossible in this context to give an idea of the multiplicity of devices which Chaucer resorts to as metrical aids, from aphetic forms like *corden* (alternating with *acorden*) to the presence or absence of the article ("Alla kyng," "Alla the kyng") or of *to* before an infinitive ("bygynneth sprynge," "bigan to sprynge"). There is the periphrastic use of the verb *gin* (e.g., "he goth hym hom, and gan ful sone sende / For Pandarus," *Tr*, v, 1667), discussed by Funke, Beschorner, and Smyser (who calls it "a concession—perhaps even Chaucer's greatest concession to the popular"). Chaucer's use of this verb is metrical in such instances. Another favorite of his was "the pleonastic *that*" (*whan that, which that*, etc.). Bihl (pp. 189-94 and 204-16) and Eitle (pp. 4-8 and *passim*) describe it correctly as a convenient rhythmical device, while in a recent article by Kirsti Kivimaa its character is obscured by an indiscriminate application of syntactical and metrical criteria.

Did Chaucer write his poems to be read or heard? In the well-known miniature in the manuscript in Corpus Christi College, Cambridge, described by Brusendorff on pp. 19-23, he is represented as reading his poems to an aristocratic audience. Ruth Crosby in "Chaucer and the Custom of Oral Delivery" believes that he wrote primarily for a listening public. But it is tantalizing that we do not know how he scanned his poems. "Chaucer speaks to us," Baum says in *Chaucer's Verse*, "not always distinctly, across the interval of nearly six centuries" (p. 52). And, he adds, "when the now eminent Chaucerians read him aloud each goes his own way." Spearing's recommendation is perhaps typical of the attitudes prevailing in many, perhaps most—perhaps all—English departments today: "In reading Chaucer aloud, it is probably better not to attempt a mechanical division into feet and stressed and unstressed syllables, but simply to follow the natural rhythm of each phrase as it might be spoken, while at the same time keeping in mind the basic x / x / x / x / x / pattern. Like other English poets, Chaucer produces some of his most effective verse by playing off the actual rhythms of speech against the 'ideal' pattern of metrical regularity: the expectation of regularity is built up so that it may be defeated as well as fulfilled" (p. 101).

A question of great significance for the scansion of Chaucer's poetry is whether the unstressed final -e is to be sounded or not. The matter has received a great deal of scholarly attention ever since the publication of Child's pioneer study in 1863. All the treatments of historical phonology mentioned at the beginning of the present chapter include a discussion of it. According to the testimony of the surviving texts, this -e was disappearing or perhaps had disappeared from the colloquial spoken language by the time Chaucer wrote his works. Friederici, who studied the language of contemporary London documents, found it impossible to say whether the final -e was pronounced in London at that time, but, calling attention to a rapid increase in the use of the inorganic -e in the first decades of the fifteenth century, he implied that not every trace of the organic -e had disappeared before that time (pp. 72-3). Charlotte Babcock noticed that apocope of -e was much commoner in Chaucer's early and late works than in those written near the middle of his career and also that he retained the -e more often in Romance than in native nouns and in the weak adjective more often than in any other part of speech. Ruth McJimsey, concerned with -e in Chaucer's monosyllabic nouns, considers Chaucer's linguistic practice remarkably flexible and believes that in disregarding many grammatically justifiable -e's Chaucer was linguistically nearer the fifteenth century than earlier studies indicate and that he used -e largely to indicate the length of the preceding syllable.

The present vogue for free verse, based not on meter but on cadence, so characteristic of our age of prose, appears to have influenced many recent discussions on Chaucer's versification. It may, perhaps, have been responsible for Southworth's article "Chaucer's Final -e in Rhyme," in which he complained that "the generally accepted hypothesis of pronunciation on the basis of historical grammar" is "unduly hampered by exceptions and exceptions to exceptions," so that "at the present time only about 20 per cent of [Chaucer's] final -e's are pronounced." The evidence collected by Southworth suggested that Chaucer's -e was inorganic and that "we need not pronounce, and probably should not pronounce final -e in rhyme."

This was directly opposite to the prevailing view that -e (-es, -ed, -en, -er) is always pronounced at the end of a line. Southworth's article provoked a reply from Donaldson, who found that according to historical grammar the -e was pronounced except in elision and when apocope was required by the meter. Southworth, counting the nouns and verbs where -e was not pronounced, included the instances of elision in his count and arrived at the ratio of 3.5 silent to 1 pronounced -e; Donaldson, excluding the elided instances, arrived at the virtually reverse ratio of nearly 3 pronounced to 1 silent -e. In his carefully argued article Donaldson adduced evidence of various kinds to support his view that -e was also pronounced in rhyme. Donaldson agreed with the prevailing view that Chaucer, from the choice offered him by common speech or by poetic convention or both, used the forms that fitted his requirements. Even if the final -e had ceased to be pronounced in London, Chaucer frequently chose to sound it in his verse.

Southworth, unpersuaded, replied in "Chaucer's Final -e, Continued" (to which Donaldson appended a brief final reply) and in two monographs, *Verses of Cadence* and *The Prosody of Chaucer and his Followers*. In the article, as before, he refused

to accept "Child's assumption about final *-e* as a proved fact."
In the monographs he abandons the whole idea that the iambic
pentameter is the basis of Chaucer's prosody. He is convinced
that Chaucer's prosody is based on cadence and not on meter:
"Chaucer brought the rhythmical tradition to its greatest pitch
of perfection"; in his diction "the movement is that of *Piers
Plowman, Sir Gawayn,* Gower, and others—it is the movement
of a highly developed English speech" (*Verses of Cadence,*
pp. 90-1). It is unfortunate that, as Baum observes, Southworth
has not made the meaning of the term "rhythmical" entirely clear.
In *Chaucer's Verse,* p. 126, in an appendix, Baum subjects Southworth's views to sharp criticism. Southworth states that he has
based his theory on C. S. Lewis' article "The Fifteenth-Century
Heroic Line"; but Lewis clearly points out that "there are hun-
dreds of lines in Chaucer that demand pure decasyllabic reading
. . . and the pleasure which not a few generations have now had
in Chaucer thus read is strong, though not conclusive, evidence
that they have read him correctly" (p. 38). It might also be remarked that as a convention or ornament of style the final *-e*
was used a long time after Chaucer. Licklider notes its occurrence
in Hawes's and Wyatt's poetry (pp. 225-8) and Bihl in Surrey's
(p. 20); there is also a brief note on Hawes's usage by Frankis.
Southworth's attack on the traditional scansion of Chaucer's verse
elicited an article from Christophersen, who doubts the irregu-
larity of two lines in the *General Prologue.* He suggests that in
line 49 *cristendom* is disyllabic (*cris[t]dom*) and that *seint* in line
173 ("seint Maure") is stressed.

In Chaucer's prose, discussed by Schlauch in "Chaucer's Prose
Rhythms" and more recently in "The Art of Chaucer's Prose,"
the rhythm was influenced by the long tradition of cadenced
Latin prose. As pointed out in the former article, in his prose "the
frequency of cadence and other rhythmical devices is related to
the total subject matter and to the intended audience of a given
text."

Chaucer's two principal types of line are the four-stress line
(or four-beat, short, octosyllabic, or iambic tetrameter line, as it

is alternatively called) and the five-stress (or five-beat, heroic, decasyllabic, or iambic pentameter) line. The older of the two, perhaps the earliest foreign type in English poetry, is the four-stress line, used only in couplet form. There has been, however, some divergence of opinion regarding its provenance. Schipper, on p. 183 of his *History*, regards it simply as an imitation of the French *vers décasyllabe*, made known in England by Anglo-Norman poets. Ten Brink agrees, but thinks that the influence of the closely related native line seen in *The Proverbs of Alfred* and *King Horn* is to be taken into consideration (p. 108). Charlton Lewis emphasizes the vitality of the native tradition; he does believe that the line borrowed its number of stresses from the Latin, but the syllabic character—so far as it was imported at all—came in only gradually through the French (pp. 94-8). The more recent opinion seems to favor the view that the four-stress line represents a fusion of the native and French traditions, though some scholars tend to emphasize the native, some the French element. Illuminating statements are to be found in Hamer, p. 25, Malof, p. 591, and Baum's *Chaucer's Verse*, pp. 27-8.

Although Ten Brink admits that the structure of Chaucer's four-stress line does not essentially differ from that of his predecessors (p. 168), yet he (p. 184) and Schipper (*History*, p. 187) emphasize Chaucer's technical superiority, seen particularly in his skilful use of enjambement. This opinion has been shared by all subsequent Chaucerians. Crow, who compared the metrical properties of *The Harrowing of Hell*, *Cursor Mundi*, and Chaucer's *House of Fame*, shows how Chaucer turned the pounding rhythm of the popular rhymers into a more refined, smoothly flowing diction, how he surpassed his predecessors in the use of metrical licence and developed his verse into a vehicle of subtle shades of meaning (p. 63). Alden (p. 166) and E. Thompson are likewise impressed by the flexibility which Chaucer gave to the short couplet. Clemen emphasizes Chaucer's remarkable freedom in the use of the couplet in comparison with his French models and Gower (p. 63), though he has a feeling that in the *House of Fame* Chaucer is still experimenting with techniques of poetic expression (p. 120). Shannon, on the other hand, finds that Chaucer is a more accomplished metrist in the *House of Fame* than in the *Book of the Duchess*.

According to Lounsbury, Chaucer learned early to recognize the insufficiency of the four-stress line: "It could be easy and animated; but volume, sonorousness, majesty . . . it could rarely, if ever, attain" (III, 301). To the poet himself the four-stress line was "light and lewed" (*HF*, 1096). In fact it was the line of five stresses that became his favorite in his mature poetry. He used it not only in the heroic couplets of the *Canterbury Tales* and the *Legend of Good Women* but also in his stanzaic poetry with varying rhyme-schemes. It is found occasionally in earlier Middle English poetry, but he was the first to make extensive and varied use of it.

It appears first in his *Complaint unto Pity*, obviously a work of the "French" period, and it is tempting to think that he modeled it on the *décasyllabe*. Indeed, Schipper, on p. 209 of his *History*, takes it to be simply an imitation of the French line. Ten Brink, however, while he admits that it is primarily derived from the French type, points out that Chaucer did not become thoroughly acquainted with it until he visited Italy (pp. 173-4); and Maynard shares this view (pp. 67-8, 80, and 82). Hammond in her *Chaucer* emphasizes the poet's debt to the hendecasyllabic line of Dante and Boccaccio (p. 478). Charlton Lewis rejects the whole idea of foreign influence. The line, he says, cannot go back to French models based solely on counting syllables (pp. 98-9). Alden doubts the validity of Lewis' arguments; he admits, however, that "the genius of English verse was not so averse to the formation of a decasyllabic five-stress line as to make it a serious innovation" (p. 179). Thomas, on pp. 89-92, and Licklider, on p. 27, agree with Ten Brink but take the native tradition into account. Southworth, in *Verses of Cadence*, denies any influence of the French *décasyllabe* or the Italian *endecasillabo*, being convinced of the "rhythmical" quality of Chaucer's prosody (pp. 32-54). C. S. Lewis, likewise emphasizing the absence of rhythm (in the English sense) from the French decasyllabic verse, argues that Chaucer's five-stress line contained a native element which went back to a variant of the Old English four-stress line and that it was this element that became dominant in the meter of his followers.

There is something very mechanical about the view that Chaucer's five-stress line could not be modeled on the French type because the latter was based on counting syllables. The transformation on English soil of the syllabic meter of continental French poetry into an accentual meter was a process which must have been quite automatic, as Alden points out on p. 179. This assumption is strongly supported by the metrical "defects" in the Anglo-Norman copies of continental French poems. There is every reason to believe that Chaucer's five-stress line, like the four-stress one, owes its existence to a fusion of Romance and native elements.

"Iambic" is the term used by most prosodists to describe the general rhythm of Chaucer's line. The question of how far he admitted trisyllabic feet—with two successive unstressed syllables—has been much debated. Ten Brink does not admit such feet (pp. 170, 175-6). Bischoff, analyzing thousands of lines, concluded that Chaucer used them only at a caesural pause. Eckhardt, who revised Ten Brink's book, doubts the complete absence of trisyllabic feet (pp. 139, n., and 170, n.). Saintsbury, like many others, is convinced that there are a good many of them in Chaucer's poetry (I, 171). The question seems to be very much dependent on whether elision and slurring are admitted. In Manly's opinion "slurring is a better way of dealing with groups of two unstressed syllables between stresses than is the usual mode of suppressing one of them" (CT, p. 127), while Baum in Chaucer's Verse believes that "once the trisyllabic foot is admitted among the other variations from a strict iambic pattern, the freer and richer becomes Chaucer's versification and the closer it comes to the practice of modern poets" (p. 21).

Chaucer occasionally reverses the order of the stressed and unstressed syllables within his iambic foot, a phenomenon generally known as "inversion" or "trochaic substitution." Every now and then he omits the unstressed syllable at the beginning of the line, as in "Twenty bookes, clad in blak or reed" (*Gen Prol*, 294), with the result that a four-stress line comes to have only seven syllables and the five-stress one only nine. Nineteenth-century metrists tended to ascribe such "headless" lines to scribal blunders or, when they had to admit that they were intentional, considered them as structurally deficient. Ten Brink admitted the practice in Chaucer's four-stress but not in his five-stress verse, where he considered it a scribal error. Freudenberger, on the other hand, found that it was no less common in Chaucer's five-stress than in his four-stress line. Seeberger has called attention to its occurrence in the Middle High German courtly epic, particularly in Heinrich von Veldeke and Hartmann von Aue (p. 13). Present-day opinion considers headless lines as a fully legitimate feature in Chaucer's technique of versification.

In the opening line of *The General Prologue* Manly's scansion "Whán that Áprill . . . " has generally superseded the traditional "Whan thát Aprílle . . . ." However, Evans, after a careful re-examination of the manuscript readings, doubts the validity of Manly's evidence and suggests that Chaucer read the line as a regular decasyllable, possibly with a trochaic substitution in the first foot ("Whán that / Apríll / e"), as Skeat did (vi, lxxxviii-ix).

In a recent article Halle and Keyser, dissatisfied with "the strict interpretation of the iambic pentameter line" and the many "allowable deviations" from that metrical standard, propose a new set of rules for Chaucer's five-stress line. It has the appearance of being logical, precise, and so comprehensive that it covers both the basic principle and all the poetic "liberties and licences." In practice, however, the superiority of the new formulation does not seem to be so clear, to judge from the demonstration given by the authors: it requires a complicated terminology and gives the impression of being rather rigid. Its usefulness will have to be proved in actual practice; all that one can say at present is that it will probably satisfy the needs of linguists better than those of students of literature. The latter, for example, will hardly agree that metrical tension, i.e. a conflict between metrical regularity and the rhythm of normal speech (cf. above, pp. 70 and 72), is simply a difference in complexity, as the authors define it on p. 198. The empirically-oriented philologist, used to full documentation, is certainly puzzled by the sweeping hypothesis that "the Romance stress rule" has dominated the accentuation of simple English words since Middle English, supported as it is by no other evidence than a footnote reference to a forthcoming treatise.

A pause within a line is a powerful regulator of poetic rhythm. Not very much has been written about Chaucer's pauses since the detailed study of Bischoff, who had occasion to believe that Chaucer did not use trisyllabic feet outside the so-called epic caesura. Baum, in *Chaucer's Verse*, devotes a few pages to the subject (pp. 73-7). Oras, although he deals primarily with later periods, includes a brief but illuminating discussion of Chaucer's practice. "From the very beginning Chaucer avoids falling into the French extreme of an absolutely obligatory fourth-position caesura." Italian verse, Oras thinks, in which the arrangement of pauses was freer, may well have influenced Chaucer; but "here, too, Chaucer was certainly far from being a mere docile imitator: his ratios for even pauses are lower in his later patterns than those of the Italian poets" (p. 7). Oras illustrates his point by a number of graphs for several of Chaucer's works in five-stress verse and for Guillaume de Machaut, Eustache Deschamps, Petrarch, and Boccaccio.

A number of special studies of Chaucer's rhymes have been published since the time of Schipper and Ten Brink. Vockrodt attempted to determine the chronology of the works on the basis of their rhymes, but had to admit that the results obtained by that method had only a relative value. Frieshammer compared Chaucer's rhyme-words with the words of his prose; but the dialectal differences revealed by his study have significance only when the verse and prose were written by the same scribe. Chaucer generally distinguished in his rhyme between the open and the close long *o*, but he sometimes rhymed them with each other (*do : fro*, etc.). Bowen has collected such *o*-rhymes from Chaucer's

works. Correcting Ten Brink, Langhans found in his study of
stressed *e* in rhyme that Chaucer did not rhyme a short *e* with a
long one except in a very few cases and that he observed the
quantity of the long *e* as a rule, though he occasionally did make
the open and close varieties rhyme with each other. Tatlock has
a brief note on the subject ("Chaucer's *Dremes* : *Lemes*") and
two on what he chooses to call "hermaphrodite rhyme," i.e.
rhyming a masculine line with a feminine one. Buck thinks that
since most of the 480 feminine rhymes (as against the 380
masculine ones) of the *General Prologue* have a final -*e*, Chaucer
had at his disposal a metrical device which no poet has had since
and that it is this metrical device that is responsible for part of
the unique flavor of Chaucer's rhymes. Mersand shows on p. 78
that the ratio of Romance rhyme-words in Chaucer's longer
works varies approximately from 30 to 40 per cent, and he has
a few other interesting observations on the subject.

In 1964 Michio Masui published an impressive book-size study
of Chaucer's rhyme-words, devoting 266 pages to matters of
syntax and word-formation and 33 to semantic and stylistic
features. He called attention to a conflict between the natural
rhythm of speech and the rhyme which parallels that caused by
the meter (see p. 70 above), and he showed that Chaucer tended
to use archaic, unusual, and dialectal words and phrases and
exclamatory expressions of various kinds at the end of the line
and to resort to many other syntactical arrangements. There are
two appendices listing the rhyme-words in the *Canterbury Tales*
and *Troilus and Criseyde*. The elaborate metrical structure of
Anelida and Arcite, to whose internal rhyme Masui devotes
several pages (222-6), has also been analyzed by Green, who
agrees with Lounsbury (III, 309) that the poem contains "daring
experiments in versification."

Ten Brink's opinion that alliteration never plays such an
essential role in the literary form of Chaucer's poetry as rhyme
does (p. 189) is probably justified. On the other hand, Chaucer
made such extensive use of stereotyped alliterative phrases in
his poetry that one has reason to suspect that he took a keener

interest in the native tradition than early Chaucerians were willing to admit. In two of his battle-scenes (*KnT*, 2601 ff., and *LGW*, 635 ff.) the wording and rhythm come particularly close to those of contemporary alliterative romances. To Stuart Robertson the passage from the *Knight's Tale* sounds like Old English poetry: "Is it not significant . . . that in this battle-scene one may hear, surging to the surface through the alien iambic metre, the echoes of the rhythm of Maldon and Brunanburh?" R. M. Smith quotes parallels from *Ipomedon* and *Partonope,* but the connection with the alliterative romances was established as far back as the late nineteenth century. The studies in Chaucer's alliterative element made at that time by Lindner, McClumpha, and Petzold are still useful. Everett calls attention to "Flemere of feendes // out of hym and here" (*MLT*, 460), which occurs in a prayer: "If this line were met with out of its context, one's first thought would probably be that it came from some Middle English poem in alliterative verse" (p. 139).

In the early part of his poetic career Chaucer obviously enjoyed exploring the possibilities provided by enjambement, or a run-on line, as the phenomenon is also called. In his later works he employed it more sparingly and in a more natural way. Malone, convinced that the G-version of the *Prologue to the Legend of Good Women* is a revision of the F-version, points out that the three enjambements of F are not to be found in G and concludes that Chaucer "seems to have looked upon a run-on line as metrically inferior" (p. 88). Masui has a detailed discussion on the subject (pp. 192-218), and it is dealt with in a 70-page doctoral dissertation by Klee, who believes that he can distinguish four chronological groups of Chaucer's works according to the quality and frequency of their run-on lines.

In the rather few special treatments of Chaucer's stanzaic forms published since the end of the nineteenth century the stanza of seven five-stress lines rhyming *ababbcc*—the rhyme royal or Chaucerian stanza—has naturally attracted more attention than any other type. In spite of its earlier occurrence in French and Provençal poetry it has always been connected with Chaucer because of his decisive role in developing it into one of the favorite stanza-types of English poetry. Maynard, who devotes a considerable part of a monograph to this stanzaic type, traces it back to the French *ballade*. He calls attention to the fact that in none of his ballades does Chaucer observe all the rules of the ballade structure and that the seven-line ballade (instead of the normal type of eight lines), with and without an envoy, was common in France at the time and that Guillaume de Machaut and Eustache Deschamps used it as a variant type. Chaucer developed his rhyme royal from the decasyllabic seven-line ballade stanza rhyming *ababbcc* by freeing it from the restrictions of the ballade form, just as he applied the French ballade octave to the verse of *An A B C* and the *Monk's Tale*. When Chaucer came to know Dante and Boccaccio he learned to use the seven-line stanza with greater freedom, but the Italian influence does not extend beyond that. He did experiment with *terza rima*, but only once, in *A Complaint to his Lady*; he did not use it in his borrowings from the *Divine Comedy*, nor did he use *ottava rima* in *Troilus and Criseyde*, nor the sonnet form when he translated Petrarch's "S'amor non è" (*Tr*, I, 400-20). Maynard derives the term "rhyme royal" from *chant royal* through "royal ballade," as suggested by Helen Cohen (*The Ballade*, p. 265). *Chant royal* as a model for "rhyme royal" was suggested by Guest as far back as 1838 (II, 359).

Ten Brink splits the Chaucerian (rhyme royal) stanza into three parts (*ab ab bcc*) and believes that Chaucer often, though not pedantically, observed this tripartition. Egerton Smith disagrees: "Chaucer, if he divided the stanza at all, did so at whatever point suited him best" (p. 244). Cowling believes that the Chaucerian stanza is bipartite—that there is usually somewhere what he calls a half-pause dividing the stanza into two parts. The commonest type of stanza is one consisting of a quatrain and a tercet (*abab bcc*), but other types, like *aba bbcc*, also occur. Cowling believes that these structural features make it possible to recognize two chronological groups of Chaucer's poems in rhyme royal, one from 1372 to 1380 and the other from 1380 or 1381 to the period of the *Canterbury Tales*. Cowling's test is criticized by Julia Lineberger, to whom it appears to be "as subjective, perhaps even more subjective than any test it aspires to supersede." Robinson also finds Cowling's results "very uncertain" (p. 642).

In a brief note Watson corrects the persistent belief among literary historians that it was Wyatt who first introduced *terza rima* into English poetry. It was, as all Chaucerians know, used by Chaucer in his *Complaint to his Lady*. Manly in "The Stanza-Forms of *Sir Thopas*" does not believe that the variations in the verse form of the *Tale of Sir Topas* are due to a desire on Chaucer's part to satirize the techniques of the popular romances or to illustrate the various meters found in them. He suggests that in varying the stanzaic forms of *Sir Thopas*—which is not a bitter satire but a good-humored burlesque—Chaucer wished to communicate to his audience a vivid sense of his own frolicsome mood.

One small point remains to be mentioned. The single line has been generally found to provide a convenient basis for analyzing the structure of Chaucer's poetry—as of any metrical poetry. The soundness of this practice has been questioned, however, by some prosodists, especially by Hammond in her *English Verse between Chaucer and Surrey*, pp. 17 ff. Convinced that "Chaucer is a master of the larger speech-unit which his narrative key requires, and no man working in his key has ever done better," she emphasizes the fact that "Chaucer understood the shift of weight from line to line" (pp. 18-19). This, of course, in no way diminishes the value of the one-line principle; it only implies that a line must be seen on occasion as part of a larger unit of several lines.

To sum up: owing to various influences there is now somewhat more freedom in reading Chaucer's poetry aloud than some fifty years ago. The strict metrical principles described by Schipper and Ten Brink have been criticized, at times even sharply, but those who have criticized them have not been able to propose a better system. The set of rules suggested recently by Halle and

Keyser has certain advantages, such as the division of the five-stress line into ten positions instead of ten syllables; but, taken as a whole, it is largely a rewording of the traditional view of Chaucer's five-stress line, and one wonders how useful it will prove in the practical analysis of Chaucer's versification. Nor do the principles of punctuation in the surviving manuscript copies seem a promising basis for the study of Chaucer's prosody, despite Southworth's gallant effort to show that they are. We do not really know the principles behind the highly varying systems of punctuation and have no objective means of finding out which of those systems—if any—could be assumed to represent Chaucer's own idea of the scansion of his poetry. Generations of modern readers have enjoyed reading Chaucer in the traditional way outlined in the nineteenth century, and will probably continue to read him along the same lines at least for some time to come.

*   *   *   *   *

Since 1968 there have been some indications of a growing or at least sustained interest in Chaucer's prosody. Eliason's, Elliott's and Davis's studies contain illuminating observations on prosodic matters. Marina Tarlinskaya has examined statistically the syllabic and accentual structure of the line in Middle English verse. Halle and Keyser's book on English stress has a section devoted to their metrical theory.

A study of the line structure of the *Book of the Duchess* has convinced Malone that it and that of *CT* are based on the native tradition. Ian Robinson, strongly influenced by Southworth (though critical of some of his claims), sees Chaucer's five-stress lines as "balanced pentameters," i.e., pentameters working not only in feet but in half-lines, as in alliterative poetry. According to Robinson the practice of sounding the *-e*'s, particularly those in rhyme, makes Chaucer's poetry sound artificial and second-rate; they are to be sounded only if to do so helps its expressiveness. This has elicited a rejoinder from Samuels, who points out that Chaucer wrote not in the colloquial London English of his time, in which -*e* no longer survived, but in a more formal and conservative register, in which -*e* still had a specific grammatical distribution. Davis is somewhat more reconciled to Robinson's view: in most places inside the line where -*e* is justified by historical grammar it is sounded, but in a good many it is not. Chaucer did not generally rhyme together words with and without it; yet, if regularly sounded in rhyme, -*e* seems to hamper the easy flow of informal language.

Stanley, in *Stanza and Ictus*, finds that in *Troilus* "the last line of the rhyme-royal stanza and within that line the metrically stressed syllable preceding the caesura are positions of special and pivotal emphasis," and Adams, in his study of assonance, points out that Chaucer used this device for binding lines together and for various other rhetorical and structural purposes.

BIBLIOGRAPHY

Adams, Percy G. "Chaucer's Assonance." *JEGP*, 71 (1972), 527-39.

Alden, Raymond M. *English Verse: Specimens Illustrating Its Principles and History*. 1904. Rpt. New York: AMS Press, 1929.

Babcock, Charlotte R. "A Study of the Metrical Use of the Inflectional *e* in Middle English, with Particular Reference to Chaucer and Lydgate." *PMLA*, 29 (1914), 59-92.

Baugh, Albert C. *A History of the English Language*. 2nd ed. New York: Appleton-Century-Crofts, 1957.

Baum, Paull F. *The Principles of English Versification*. 1922. Rpt. Hamden, Ct.: Shoe String, 1969.

―――. *Chaucer's Verse*. Durham, N.C.: Duke Univ. Press, 1961.

Berndt, Rolf. *Einführung in das Studium des Mittelenglischen, unter Zugrundelegung des Prologs der "Canterbury Tales."* Halle, 1960.

Beschorner, Franz. *Verbale Reime bei Chaucer*. Studien zur englischen Philologie, 60. Halle, 1920.

Bihl, Josef. *Die Wirkungen des Rhythmus in der Sprache von Chaucer und Gower*. AF, 50. Heidelberg, 1916.

Bischoff, Otto. "Über zweisilbige Senkung und epische Caesur bei Chaucer." *ESt*, 24 (1898), 353-92, and 25 (1898), 339-98. (Pt. I also publ. as a Königsberg diss., 1897.)

Bowen, Edwin W. "Confusion between ǫ and ō in Chaucer's Rimes." *ESt*, 20 (1895), 341-44.

Brink, Ten. See under Ten Brink.

Brunner, Karl. *Die englische Sprache.* 2 vols. 2nd ed. Tübingen: M. Niemeyer, 1960-1962.

————. *An Outline of Middle English Grammar.* Trans. G. Johnston. Cambridge, Mass.: Harvard Univ. Press, 1963.

Brusendorff, Aage. *The Chaucer Tradition.* London: Oxford Univ. Press, 1925.

Buck, Howard. "Chaucer's Use of Feminine Rhyme." *MP*, 26 (1928), 13-14.

Child, Francis J. "Observations on the Language of Chaucer." *Memoirs of the American Academy of Arts and Sciences*, NS, 8, 2 (1863), 445-502.

Christophersen, Paul. "The Scansion of Two Lines in Chaucer." Supplement to *ES*, 45 (1964), 146-50.

Clemen, Wolfgang. *Chaucer's Early Poetry.* Trans. C.A.M. Sym. London: Methuen, 1963.

Cohen, Helen L. *The Ballade.* New York: Columbia Univ. Press, 1915.

————. *Lyric Forms from France.* New York: Harcourt, Brace, 1922.

Cowling, G.H. "A Note on Chaucer's Stanza." *RES*, 2 (1926), 311-17.

Crosby, Ruth. "Chaucer and the Custom of Oral Delivery." *Speculum*, 13 (1938), 413-32.

Crow, Charles L. *Zur Geschichte des kurzen Reimpaars im Mittelenglischen* [*Harrowing of Hell, Cursor Mundi*, Chaucer's *House of Fame*]. Diss. Göttingen, 1892.

Davis, Norman. "Chaucer and Fourteenth-Century English." In *Geoffrey Chaucer.* Ed. D.S. Brewer. London: Bell, 1974, pp. 58-84.

Donaldson, E. Talbot. "Chaucer's Final -*e*." *PMLA*, 63 (1948), 1101-24, and 64 (1949), 609 (reply to Southworth).

Eckhardt, E. See under Ten Brink.

Eitle, Hermann. *Die Satzverknüpfung bei Chaucer. AF,* 44. Heidelberg, 1914.

Eliason, Norman E. *The Language of Chaucer's Poetry: An Appraisal of the Verse, Style and Structure.* Anglistica, 17. Copenhagen: Rosenkilde og Bagger, 1972.

Elliott, Ralph W.V. *Chaucer's English.* London: Deutsch, 1974.

Evans, Robert O. "Whan that Aprill(e)?" *N&Q,* 202 (1957), 234-37.

Everett, Dorothy. "Chaucer's 'Good Ear'." *RES,* 23 (1947), 201-8. Rpt. In *Essays on Middle English Literature.* Ed. P.M. Kean. Oxford: Clarendon Press, 1955, pp. 139-48.

Fisiak, Jacek. *Morphemic Structure of Chaucer's English.* Alabama Linguistic and Philological Series, 10. University, Ala.: Univ of Alabama Press, 1965.

Frankis, P.J. "The Syllabic Value of Final *-es* in English Versification about 1500." *N&Q,* 212 (1967), 11-12.

French, Robert D. *A Chaucer Handbook.* 2nd ed. New York: Appleton-Century-Crofts, 1947.

Freudenberger, Markus. *Über das Fehlen des Auftakts in Chaucers heroischem Verse.* Diss. Erlangen, 1889.

Friederici, Hans. *Der Lautstand Londons um 1400.* Forschungen zur englischen Philologie, 6. Jena, 1937. Also diss. Jena, 1937 (part only).

Frieshammer, Johann. *Die sprachliche Form der Chaucerschen Prosa, ihr Verhältnis zur Reimtechnik des Dichters sowie zur Sprache der älteren Londoner Urkunden.* Studien zur englischen Philologie, 42. Halle, 1910.

Fry, Dennis B. "Duration and Intensity as Physical Correlates of Linguistic Stress." *JAS,* 27 (1955), 765-68.

Funke, Otto. "Die Fügung *ginnen* mit dem Infinitiv im Mittelenglischen." *ESt,* 56 (1922), 1-27.

Green, A. Wigfall. "Meter and Rhyme in Chaucer's *Anelida and Arcite.*" *UMSE,* 2 (1961), 55-63.

Guest, Edwin. *A History of English Rhythms.* 2 vols. London, 1838. Rev. 2nd ed. W.W. Skeat. 1882. Rpt. New York: Haskell House, 1968.

Halle, Morris, and Samuel J. Keyser. "Chaucer and the Study of Prosody." *CE,* 28 (1966), 187-219.

————. *English Stress: Its Form, Its Growth, and Its Role in Verse.* New York: Harper & Row, 1971.

Hamer, Enid. *The Metres of English Poetry.* 1930. 4th ed. London: Methuen, 1958.

Hammond, Eleanor P. *Chaucer: A Bibliographical Manual.* 1908. Rpt. New York: P. Smith, 1933.

————. *English Verse between Chaucer and Surrey.* 1927. Rpt. New York: Octagon Books, 1965.

Hampel, Ernst. *Die Silbenmessung in Chaucer's fünftaktigem Verse.* Pt. I. Diss. Halle, 1898.

Heuer, Hermann. *Studien zur syntaktischen und stilistischen Funktion des Adverbs bei Chaucer und im Rosenroman. AF,* 75. Heidelberg, 1932.

Joerden, Otto. *Das Verhältnis von Wort-, Satz- und Vers-Akzent in Chaucers Canterbury Tales.* Studien zur englischen Philologie, 55. Halle, 1915. Also diss. Göttingen, 1914.

Jordan, Richard. *Handbuch der mittelenglischen Grammatik, I: Lautlehre.* Rev. 2nd ed. H.C. Matthes. Germanische Bibliothek, I, 1, No. 13. 1934. Rpt. Trans. Eugene J. Crook. The Hague: Mouton, 1974.

Kaluza, Max. *Historische Grammatik der englischen Sprache.* 2 vols. 2nd ed. Berlin: E. Felber, 1906-7.

————. *A Short History of English Versification.* Trans. A.C. Dunstan. 1911. Rpt. Folcroft, Pa.: Folcroft, 1973.

Karpf, Fritz. *Studien zur Syntax in den Werken Geoffrey Chaucers,* I. Wiener Beiträge zur englischen Philologie, 55. Vienna, 1930.

Kerkhof, J. *Studies in the Language of Geoffrey Chaucer.* Leidse Germanistische en Anglistische Reeks van de Rijksuniversiteit te Leiden, 5. Leyden: Leyden Univ. Press, 1966.

Kittredge, G.L. *Observations on the Language of Chaucer's Troilus.* Chaucer Soc., 2nd ser., No. 28. London, 1894. Also in Harvard Studies and Notes in Philology and Literature, 3. Boston, 1902.

Kivimaa, Kirsti. "The Pleonastic *That* in Relative and Interrogative Constructions in Chaucer's Verse," *Commentationes Humanarum Litterarum, Societas Scientiarum Fennica,* 41, 1 (Helsinki, 1966), 1-39.

———. "Clauses in Chaucer Introduced by Conjunctions with Appended *That." Commentationes Humanarum Litterarum, Societas Scientiarum Fennica,* 43, 1 (Helsinki, 1968), 1-75.

Klee, Friedrich. *Das Enjambement bei Chaucer.* Diss. Halle, 1913.

Kluge, F. See under Ten Brink.

Kökeritz, Helge. *A Guide to Chaucer's Pronunciation.* New Haven, Conn.: Whitlock, 1954.

Langhans, Viktor. "Der Reimvokal *e* bei Chaucer." *Anglia,* 45 (1921), 221-82, 297-392.

Lewis, C.S. "The Fifteenth-Century Heroic Line." *E&S,* 24 (1938), 28-41.

Lewis, Charlton M. *The Foreign Sources of English Versification with Special Reference to the So-called Iambic Lines of Eight or Ten Syllables.* Yale Studies in English, 1. Halle, 1898. Also Diss. Yale, 1898. Rpt. Folcroft, Pa.: Folcroft, 1969.

Licklider, Albert H. *Chapters on the Metric of the Chaucerian Tradition. Diss. Johns Hopkins, 1907.* Baltimore: Johns Hopkins Univ. Press, 1910.

Lindner, Felix. "Alliteration in Chaucer's *Canterbury Tales," Jahrbuch für romanische und englische Sprache und Literatur,* 14 (1875), 311-55. Also in *Essays on Chaucer, His Words and Works.* Chaucer Soc., 2nd ser., No. 16, pt. iii. London: Trübner, 1876, pp. 197-226.

Lineberger, Julia E. "An Examination of Professor Cowling's New Metrical Test," *MLN,* 42 (1927), 229-31.

Lounsbury, T.R. *Studies in Chaucer: His Life and Writings.* 3 vols. 1892. Rpt. New York: Russell & Russell, 1962.

Luick, Karl. *Historische Grammatik der englischen Sprache*, 1. Leipzig, 1921-40. Rpt. Oxford: Blackwell, 1964.

McClumpha, Charles F. *The Alliteration of Chaucer*. Diss. Leipzig, 1888. Rpt. Folcroft, Pa.: Folcroft, 1974.

McJimsey, Ruth B. *Chaucer's Irregular '-e'; a Demonstration among Monosyllabic Nouns of the Exceptions to Grammatical and Metrical Harmony*. New York: R. West, 1942.

Malof, Joseph. "The Native Rhythm of English Meters." *TSLL*, 5 (1964), 580-94.

Malone, Kemp. *Chapters on Chaucer*. Baltimore: Johns Hopkins Univ. Press, 1951.

———. "Chaucer's *Book of the Duchess*: a Metrical study." In *Chaucer und seine Zeit: Symposion für Walter Schirmer*. Ed. Arno Esch. Tübingen: M. Niemeyer, 1968, pp. 71-95.

Manly, John Matthews. "The Stanza-Forms of *Sir Thopas*." *MP*, 8 (1910), 141-44.

———, ed. *Canterbury Tales*. New York: Holt, 1928.

Marckwardt, Albert H. See under Moore, Samuel.

Masui, Michio. *The Structure of Chaucer's Rime Words: An Exploration into the Poetic Language of Chaucer*. Tokyo: Kankyusha, 1964.

Matthes, H.C. See under Jordan, Richard.

Maynard, Theodore. *The Connection between the Ballade, Chaucer's Modification of It, Rime Royal, and the Spenserian Stanza*. Diss. Catholic Univ. of America, 1934.

Mersand, Joseph. *Chaucer's Romance Vocabulary*. 1937. Rpt. New York: Kennikat Press, 1968.

Moore, Samuel. *Historical Outlines of English Sounds and Inflections*. Rev. by Albert H. Marckwardt. Ann Arbor: G. Wahr, 1951.

Mossé, Fernand. *A Handbook of Middle English*. Trans. James A. Walker. Baltimore: Johns Hopkins Univ. Press, 1952.

Mustanoja, Tauno F. *A Middle English Syntax*, I: *Parts of Speech*. Mémoires de la Société Néophilologique de Helsinki, 23. Helsinki, 1960.

————. "Verbal Rhyming in Chaucer." In *Chaucer and Middle English Studies in Honour of Rossell Hope Robbins*. Ed. Beryl Rowland. London: Allen & Unwin, 1974. Kent, Ohio: Kent State Univ. Press. 1974, pp. 104-10.

Omond, T.S. *English Metrists of the Eighteenth and Nineteenth Centuries*. London: Frowde, 1907.

Oras, Ants. *Pause Patterns in Elizabethan and Jacobean Drama: An Experiment in Prosody*. Univ. of Florida Monographs: Humanities, 3. Gainesville: Univ. of Florida Press, 1960.

Owen, Charles A., Jr. "Thy Drasty Rymyng. . . ." *SP*, 63 (1966), 533-64.

Petzold, Ernst. *Über Alliteration in den Werken Chaucers, mit Ausschluss der Canterbury Tales*. Diss. Marburg, 1889.

Raith, Joseph. *Englische Metrik*. Munich: M. Hueber, 1962.

Rarick, Louise. "Ten-syllable Lines in English Poetry." *NM*, 75 (1974), 66-73.

Robertson, Stuart. "Old English Verse in Chaucer." *MLN*, 42 (1928), 234-36.

Robinson, F.N., ed. *The Works of Geoffrey Chaucer*. 2nd ed. Boston: Houghton Mifflin, 1957.

Robinson, Ian. *Chaucer's Prosody: A Study of the Middle English Verse Tradition*. London: Cambridge Univ. Press, 1971.

Saintsbury, George. *A History of English Prosody from the Twelfth Century to the Present Day*. 3 vols. 1906-10. Rpt. New York: Russell & Russell, 1961.

Samuels, M.L. "Chaucerian Final -*e*." *N&Q*, NS, 29 (1972), 445-48.

Sauerbrey, Gertrud. *Die innere Sprachform bei Chaucer*. Diss. Halle, 1917.

Schipper, Jakob. *Englische Metrik in historischer und systematischer Entwickelung dargestellt*. 2 parts in 3 vols. Bonn: 1881-88.

————. *A History of English Versification*. 1910 (ed. cit.). Rpt. New York: AMS Press, 1971.

Schlauch, Margaret. "Chaucer's Prose Rhythms." *PMLA*, 65 (1950), 568-89.

————. "Chaucer's Colloquial English: Its Structural Traits." *PMLA*, 67 (1952), 1103-16.

————. "The Art of Chaucer's Prose." In *Chaucer and Chaucerians: Critical Studies in Middle English literature*. Ed. D.S. Brewer. London: Nelson, 1966, pp. 140-63.

Scholl, Evelyn H. "English Metre Once More." *PMLA*, 63 (1948), 293-326.

Schramm, Wilbur L. "Time and Intensity in English Tetrameter Verse." *PQ*, 13 (1934), 65-71.

Seeberger, Alfred. *Fehlende Auftakt und fehlende Senkung nach der Cäsur in der Chaucerschule*. Diss. Munich, 1911.

Shannon, E.F. "Chaucer's Use of Octosyllabic Verse in the *Book of the Duchess* and the *House of Fame*." *JEGP*, 12 (1913), 277-94.

Skeat, Walter W., ed. *The Complete Works of Geoffrey Chaucer*. 7 vols. 1894-97. Rpt. London: Oxford Univ. Press, 1960.

————, ed. See under Guest, Edwin.

Smith, Egerton. *Principles of English Prosody*. 1923. Rpt. Westport, Conn.: Greenwood Press, 1970.

Smith, Roland M. "Three Notes on the Knight's Tale." *MLN*, 51 (1936), 320-22.

Smyser, Hamilton M. "Chaucer's Use of *Gin* and *Do*." *Speculum*, 42 (1967), 68-83.

Sonnenschein, E.A. *What Is Rhythm?* Oxford: Blackwell, 1925.

Southworth, James G. "Chaucer's Final -*e* in Rhyme." *PMLA*, 62 (1947), 910-35, and 64 (1949), 601-10.

————. *Verses of Cadence: An Introduction to the Prosody of Chaucer and His Followers*. Oxford: Blackwell, 1954.

————. *The Prosody of Chaucer and His Followers: Supplementary Chapters to "Verses of Cadence."* Oxford: Blackwell, 1962.

Spearing, A.C. "Chaucer's Language." In *An Introduction to Chaucer*. By M. Hussey, A.C. Spearing, and J. Winny. London: Cambridge Univ. Press, 1965, pp. 89-114.

Stanley, E.G. "Stanza and Ictus: Chaucer's Emphasis in *Troilus and Criseyde.*" In *Chaucer und seine Zeit: Symposion für Walter Schirmer.* Ed. Arno Esch Tübingen: M. Niemeyer, 1968, p. 123-48.

———. "The Use of Bob-Lines in Sir Thopas." In *Studies Presented to Tauno F. Mustanoja.* NM ,73 (1972), 417-26.

Stein, Arnold. "A Note on Meter." *KR,* 18 (1956), 451-60.

Sudo, Jun. "Some Specific Rime-Units in Chaucer." *SELit* (Tokyo), 45 (1969), 221-36.

Tarlinskaya, Marina. "The Syllabic Structure and Meter of English Verse from the Thirteenth through the Nineteenth Century." *Lang&S,* 6 (1973), 249-72.

Tatlock, J.S.P. "Chaucer's Dremes: Lemes." *MLN,* 20 (1905), 126.

———. "The Hermaphrodite Rhyme.' *MLN,* 32 (1917), 373.

———. "Hermaphrodite Rhyme." *SatR,* 9 (1932), 161.

Ten Brink, Bernhard. *The Language and Metre of Chaucer.* Trans. M.B. Smith. From rev. 2nd ed. by F. Kluge. London: Macmillan, 1901.

———. *Chaucer's Sprache und Verskunst.* Rev. 3rd ed. by E. Eckhardt. Leipzig: C.H. Tauchnitz, 1920 (ed. cit.).

Thomas, Walter. *Le décasyllabe roman et sa fortune en Europe.* Travaux et Mémoires de l'Université de Lille, nouv. série, I, 4. Lille, 1904.

Thompson, Elbert N. "The Octosyllabic Couplet." *PQ,* 18 (1939), 257-68.

Thompson, John. *The Founding of English Metre.* New York: Columbia Univ. Press, 1961.

Verrier, Paul. *Essai sur les principes de la métrique anglaise.* 3 vols. Paris, 1909-10.

Visser, F. Th. *An Historical Syntax of the English Language,* I-III. Leyden: E.J. Brill, 1963-73.

Vockrodt, Gustav. *Reimtechnik bei Chaucer als mittel zur chronologischen Bestimmung seiner im Reimpaar geschriebenen Werke.* Diss. Halle, 1914.

Watson, Melvin R. "Wyatt, Chaucer, and *Terza Rima.*" *MLN,* 68 (1953), 124-25.

Wild, Friedrich. *Die sprachlichen Eigentümlichkeiten der wichtigeren Chaucer-Handschriften und die Sprache Chaucers.* Wiener Beiträge zur englischen Philologie, 44. Vienna, 1915.

Wright, Joseph, and Elizabeth M. Wright. *An Elementary Middle English Grammar.* 1924. 2nd ed. Oxford: Clarendon, 1928.

Wyld, Henry C. *A Short History of English.* 3rd ed. London: Murray, 1927.

FIVE

ROBERT M. JORDAN

Chaucerian Narrative

Chaucer is acknowledged to be primarily a narrative poet, that is, one who tells stories. "Narrative" in this traditional generic sense, differentiated from lyric and drama, has yielded some useful classifications but few significant critical insights. In recent years Chaucerian scholars have begun to reexamine the concept of narrative and have associated it with mode of presentation rather than with genre. The result has been a renewed attentiveness to principles of rhetoric, particularly those concerned with invention and disposition. A closely allied interest in Chaucer's uses of style has developed, and the study of rhetoric and stylistics has been accompanied by increased interest in poetics, or poetic theory. I wish to survey recent developments in these three areas under the general rubric "Chaucerian narrative." Though other chapters of this volume will offer more detailed coverage of one or more of these topics, I am hopeful that the larger view proposed here will have a usefulness of its own.

The most salient feature of the new view of Chaucerian narrative is its attentiveness to the palpabilities of the text. While earlier commentary concentrated on the depicted life of the fiction, recent studies have looked more closely at the process of illusion-making itself, in effect discriminating between the scene that emerges in the reader's mind and the verbal texture and organizational patterns of the text which evokes that scene. The earlier view is represented by Kittredge's well-known pronouncement that the Canterbury pilgrimage is "a Human Comedy, and . . . the stories are merely long speeches expressing, directly or indirectly, the characters of the several persons" (pp. 154-5). In this view "people," speaking and moving, enact a continuous living "drama." On the other hand, recent commentary, as characterized by this passage from B. H. Bronson's *In Search of Chaucer*, looks not only at "life" but at art, and sees "rapid shifts of stylistic level, the apparent sacrifice of achieved effects, the reversals of mood and tone, the abrupt stoppage of narrative momentum, the commingling of colloquial and artificial diction, the breathtaking incorporation of the whole range of language into the working texture of the verse" (p. 22). This rich variety —not to say clashing incongruity—of narrative elements was not of serious interest to the generation of critics who saw the *Canterbury Tales*, as Lowes did, as "an organic whole, and that whole . . . essentially dramatic" (p. 164).

The shift of critical attention from the road to Canterbury (and the streets of Troy) to the "working texture of the verse" has opened new avenues of approach to the understanding of Chaucerian narrative. Among many books on Chaucer in recent years, two seem to me particularly noteworthy for their grasp of the subtle and complex interplay of elements—historical, aesthetic, and literary—which make Chaucerian narrative both of its own time and of all time. Wolfgang Clemen's *Der junge Chaucer: Grundlagen und Entwicklung seiner Dichtung* appeared in 1938 and was revised and translated in 1963 as *Chaucer's Early Poetry*. Charles Muscatine in *Chaucer and the French Tradition* (1957) shares with Clemen a keen sense of the differences, as well as the relationships, between mode and matter in Chaucer's poetry, and thereby helps to establish criteria for the differing methods of historical and critical appraisal. Indeed, the strength of both these works derives from the combination of discerning analytical powers and a firm command of theoretical principles. Muscatine points out, for example, that "the tradition of the Troy *story* does not coincide with the tradition of *style* in which Chaucer writes the *Troilus*" (p. 5). This fundamental distinction, now widely appreciated, underlies the shift of large segments of scholarly attention from source-study to style-study, though it by no means denies the historical dimensions of style. Muscatine's study of the French roots of Chaucer's literary styles illustrates perhaps even more explicitly than does Clemen's study of Chaucer's early poetry the importance of the critical principle that the study of Chaucer requires a balance of historical and analytic emphases. The following is Clemen's formulation of that principle:

> The "historical approach" cannot of course claim to be the only gateway to an artistic appreciation of the individual poems. For what determines the artistic impact of a poem and of its individual themes is not their earlier development, provenance and historical limitations, but the entire verbal shaping and composition, the way in which each part is linked to the whole, how one item follows on from another and how certain images and impressions are awakened thereby . . . . Every poem has . . . two aspects; it does not exist purely in isolation as an individual work of art; it also represents a stage in its creator's development as an artist and in the course of literature. Every work of art is thus permeated with tendencies and trends that lead backwards and forwards beyond its own individual limits. (p. 5)

The major difference between the historicism of Clemen and Muscatine and that of earlier studies—as represented by *Sources and Analogues*—is the emphasis on mode, both of composition and of verbal expression, as distinct from the earlier emphasis on subject matter and vocabulary. Muscatine's primary concern is verbal expression, while Clemen is more concerned with the larger structural elements of poetic composition. The two are not mutually exclusive, however, and Muscatine arrives at some provocative comments on the "Gothic" principle of juxtaposition of structural elements (pp. 128-9, 167-9), while Clemen is always sensitive to verbal nuance and stylistic variation.

Another important recent contribution to a structural and stylistic approach to Chaucerian narrative is Robert O. Payne's *The Key of Remembrance: A Study of Chaucer's Poetics* (1963). As do Clemen and Muscatine, Payne stresses Chaucer's artistry, his mastery of a diversity of literary styles and structures and of the attitudes and meanings which such materials convey. Payne's study of the interplay of rhetoric and poetics in the development of a theory of literary composition in the Middle Ages goes a long way toward exonerating medieval rhetorical theory and practice from charges of sterility and superficiality. Payne clarifies the relationship between a rhetorical poetic and the operative forces in the structure of a poem, as distinct from a different kind of poetic which is concerned with effects in the reader or with psychological processes in the author. By stressing the seriousness of the medieval rhetoricians' concern with the structural patterns of a literary composition, Payne establishes a firm basis for the study of medieval narrative in terms appropriate to it. He goes on to demonstrate Chaucer's overt and pervasive consciousness of the aesthetic implications and problems of the rhetorical poetic, using in particular the *Prologue to the Legend of Good Women* as a complex demonstration of Chaucer's artistic self-consciousness. Payne's sensitive and tightly reasoned argument moves through the dream visions, touches on the *Canterbury Tales*, and culminates in an extensive study of *Troilus*, which displays with impressive force the variety and profundity of expression achieved by Chaucer within a poetic which emphasizes the disposition of structural elements and the labor of style.

In his notable effort to refine the terms of generic criticism, Northrop Frye has centered on a question which has loomed large in recent Chaucer criticism. Frye defines the "radical of presentation," or authorial role *vis-à-vis* reader or audience, as the characteristic which differentiates the two major forms of narrative: (1) "epos," such as the epic, in which the radical of presentation is oral address to a present audience, and (2) "fiction," such as the novel, in which the radical of presentation is the printed page addressed to an absent reader (pp. 246-51).

Chaucer's historical position in an age of script—between ages of oral and printed literature—made available to him two "radicals of presentation," and, as recent commentary has begun to make clear, he used both at the same time.

The literary implications of this "transitional" situation have been effectively highlighted by Scholes and Kellogg in their comprehensive study *The Nature of Narrative*. Taking informed account of the nature and importance of oral tradition, the authors recognize in the storytelling art of the late Middle Ages a crucial transition in form as the "orator" of traditional tales is displaced by the "narrator" of written fictions:

> The sudden acquisition by medieval narrative artists of the new role of authorship found them unprepared and somewhat ill at ease. Like all authors they attempted to "refine themselves out of existence." The most natural course was found to be a fairly straightforward imitation of a teller reciting his story to an audience. But even this emergency measure opened the Pandora's box of irony, giving such masters as Chaucer . . . new fields to conquer. (p. 55)

The box is still open. One of the liveliest concerns of recent commentary has been Chaucer's management of the authorial role in his narratives. Prior to Donaldson's important contribution, a major difference of interpretation existed between those who, like Kittredge and Lowes, read Chaucer as "fiction" in Frye's sense—that is, as a "modern novel"—or even as "drama"—and those who, like Bronson in "Chaucer's Art," Ruth Crosby, and Mary Giffin, stressed the social circumstances of oral delivery. Donaldson's "Chaucer the Pilgrim" changed the course of the controversy by impressively arguing the palpability of the narrator-role and its function as a literary device within the narrative controlled by the author. As such it is causally related to traditional conditions of oral presentation, yet artistically independent of any specific time and place of presentation. Donaldson stresses the difference between verisimilitude and truth, the former being an artistic effect which is meaningful only so long as we distinguish it from the latter. Chaucer the pilgrim-reporter is a means of establishing verisimilitude, but to the discerning eye it is sufficiently off the mark of autobiographical truth to produce a pervasive comic-ironic effect. Donaldson argues that the pilgrim *persona* is "the chief agent by which the poet achieves his wonderfully complex, ironic, comic, serious vision of a world which is but a devious and confused, infinitely various pilgrimage to a certain shrine" (p. 929).

The appearance of Wayne Booth's *The Rhetoric of Fiction* has lent enormous theoretical support not only to Donaldson's argument but to the whole approach to Chaucerian narrative we have been surveying. Seen against the background illuminated by Booth's sweeping erudition and critical sophistication, Chaucer's use of the first-person singular narrator is readily recognized as one of a vast range of possible rhetorical strategies which have been used by narrative artists in all tongues in all eras. Booth excludes from his study both social and psychological considerations and casts an intense light on the ample area of the narrating voice and its many possible deployments as the author's inescapable, always audible medium for controlling the reader's response. He teaches us how to name the many types of narrating voice for which the old vocabulary of "first person," "omniscient," and similar terms are much too broad and clumsy. We see, for example, that whether the narrating voice speaks in the first or the third person, important questions remain to be determined, such as the extent to which the narrator participates in the action, the extent to which he displays (shows) or summarizes (tells) the action, the nature of his commentary—whether merely ornamental, or rhetorically purposeful but detached from the action, or integral to the dramatic structure—the control of distance, the management of moral suasion, indirect, straight, or ironic. All of these and more are the possibilities mediated by the voice the author projects and fixes in the language of his narrative. The entryway to understanding of a text is therefore the "rhetoric" of its presentation, and, as Booth makes clear, "the author cannot choose to avoid rhetoric; he can choose only the kind of rhetoric he will employ" (p. 149).

Among Chaucerians the rhetorical approach to narrative and narrating personae has elicited some notable opposition. Although the differences of opinion seem less than fundamental, the controversy has produced some sensitive and illuminating commentary. The principal concern, as voiced with particular force by Bertrand Bronson in *In Search of Chaucer* (pp. 25-31, 66, 67) and Donald Howard in "Chaucer the Man," is that an excessively formalistic criticism, developing around the concept of a "fictional Chaucer" separated from the real Chaucer, destroys our sense of the presence of Chaucer the man in his poetry. Thus Bronson derides "the schizoid notion of two Chaucers, so named, presented simultaneously, one a puppet, the other the living, speaking poet, with attitudes and intelligences radically different from each other's . . ." (p. 28). For Bronson the decisive consideration is the circumstances of oral delivery. He visualizes Chaucer as an "adroit master of ceremonies presenting events" (p. 31), and on occasion presenting himself, usually with an ironic and engaging self-mockery which would fool no one in his audience into either taking him literally or into believing he is talking about someone else. Howard makes the similar point that the narrating persona and all the "devices" associated with him are of interest to us precisely because "everywhere *in* and *behind* them lies Chaucer the man" (p. 337). Of course it would be foolish to contest this point, but the fact that it even needed to be articulated seems to indicate the heart of the problem: no critical approach is any better than the critic who uses it. Certainly any "rhetorical" critic who does not regard as axiomatic the truth pointed out by Howard is undeserving of serious attention, though there may indeed be instances when a certain amount of labeling and counting can provide important data for thoughtful interpretive criticism, as in Lüdeke's *Die Funktionen des Erzählers* and Bloomfield's "Distance and Predestination." On the other hand—and this, I think, is the basic critical assumption of the rhetorical approach —the most reliable available means we have for apprehending "the man" and his feeling for life is the text of his poetry. What we know about Chaucer's audiences and about the traditions and varying practices of oral delivery can reveal some of the conditions which gave rise to certain verbal and structural characteristics in the poetry. But in reading Chaucer we must respond to what we, with our sharpest vision, find in the text, including authorial (or disguised authorial) intrusions, the tone in which they are embodied, their relative prominence, their effect on aesthetic distancing, on pacing, on governing attitude and moral perspective. What we thus discern may not correspond with what any given auditor (or reader) or social class contemporary with Chaucer might have discerned there. There would have been good listeners (or readers) in Chaucer's time as there are good and bad readers now, and Chaucer, like any other poet in any age, was writing for those able to understand. Payne has made the point, in his discussion of *Troilus,* that "the kinds of roles Chaucer creates for his narrators almost necessarily imply complementary roles for an audience which is nearly as much a created fiction within or around the poem as the narrator is" (p. 228). The narrating voice identifies the poem's enduring audience, which is not confined to particular social occasions. It includes all of us who can discern the tonal variations of civilized literary discourse.

A pioneering effort in sustained stylistic analysis of Chaucer's narrative art was Ralph Baldwin's *The Unity of the Canterbury Tales* (1955), a work very uneven in its mixture of rhetoric and symbolism but valuable precisely because of its eclecticism. Baldwin brought to bear upon the *Canterbury Tales* some of the insights of Romance stylistics—as represented by the work of Curtius, Hatzfeld, Singleton, and others—and some of the techniques of exegetical symbolism. At a time when the "roadside drama" conception of the *Canterbury Tales* was proving less and less able to answer the important questions about Chaucer's narrative art, and yet was the only available theory of the whole, Baldwin attempted to "unify" the *Canterbury Tales* in a new way. Romance stylistics provided the conceptual basis for viewing the whole as a structural deployment of narrative elements, defined and differentiated according to rhetorical purpose. Thus the *General Prologue*—itself composed of introduction, "clause," and conclusion—is the introduction to the totally conceived, though fragmentarily realized, *Canterbury Tales*. The *General Prologue* establishes the time, setting, characters, and—most important for Baldwin's analysis—the symbolic direction for the total narrative. Baldwin convincingly argues the Christian overtones of the Canterbury pilgrimage, which point that journey inevitably to its conclusion in the *Parson's Prologue and Tale*: "The Parson declares that he, as priest, as one who has charge of souls, wishes to show them on this journey, 'in this viage,' the 'wey,' of that perfect and glorious pilgrimage that is called the heavenly Jerusalem . . . " (p. 91). The Parson thus replaces the Host ultimately as docent, "because this is the function of a priest, not an innkeeper, and all the pilgrims to Canterbury in becoming pilgrims to the Heavenly Jerusalem must take the *wey* or *via* of Penitence . . . ," by which means the destination of the pilgrimage becomes "not so much the Canterbury shrine as the Parson's Tale, because it unfolds the *wey* to Him who is the way, the truth, and the light" (pp. 92-3).

Attractive and important as Baldwin's interpretation is, it falls short of demonstrating the unity of the *Canterbury Tales*. It demonstrates the unity and the generative power of the framing idea of pilgrimage, as firmly embodied in the pillar-like beginning and concluding fragments of the total poem, and as activated to a limited extent by the pilgrims introduced in the *General Prologue*. But it fails to account satisfactorily for that disproportionately large body of recalcitrant materials, the tales themselves. The Achilles heel in Baldwin's argument is symbolism, which has brought low many another critic facing similar problems. Injudicious extension of the possibilities—not to say the imperatives—of symbolic interpretation leads Baldwin to make more extravagant claims for unity than he is able (or willing) to substantiate (see Jordan, pp. 111-31). It is a venial indiscretion to read the Parson's sermon-like treatise on Penitence as a matrix in which each of the pilgrims recognizes, faces, and struggles with his own sinful nature (pp. 101-5), but for Baldwin this is the step that leads to crippling vitiation of his attempt to unify the *Tales*. The mortal struggle for salvation which he sees as the unifying principle of the poem is a product of his own imagination —given some clear Christian signs in the text; it is not presented by Chaucer as a realized narration, neither as psychomachia nor as drama. What Chaucer presents as the conclusion of his poem is a very lengthy treatise—not even a narrative—which by virtue of its bulk alone challenges the literary impact of the Parson's dramatic prologue to salvation. The critic who reads the *Parson's Tale* as drama is not reading what Chaucer wrote. In Baldwin's interpretation, as in other instances of symbolic enthusiasm, the hard facts of Chaucer's poem are sacrificed to the all-subsuming truths of Christian doctrine. Not only the "tale" told by the Parson, but all the other tales are thus lumped within the drama of the Canterbury framework and *in toto* spiritualized as manifestations of the sinfulness of the pilgrim-tellers, the salvation of whom thus becomes the culminating unification of Chaucer's poem. The most that can be claimed for Baldwin's theory of unity —which is a good deal—is that it is frame-deep. For the rest he falls back upon assumptions about the dramatic relationships of tales and tellers which, particularly in the light of recent improvements in the tools of criticism, are highly questionable. Perhaps if Baldwin had examined the tales with the same attentiveness to details of voice and perspective which distinguishes his study of the *General Prologue* and frame, he would have recognized the limitations of his unitary hypothesis.

The major problems confronting Chaucerians today are problems of narrative, not of drama. The most compelling testimony to the subtlety of Chaucer's narrative art is the fact that we find it so easy to acquiesce in the fiction, as though the poems were not narrated as works of literary art but simply reproduced, in direct presentation, either from historical sources, as in *Troilus*, or, as in the *Canterbury Tales*, from the personal experience of the worried eyewitness who begs us not to hold him responsible for the words of his fellow pilgrims (*Gen Prol*, 715-46; *Prol MillT*, 3167-84). Such a response indicates a confusion not only between art and life but also between reading and criticism. Literary art is always concerned with the problem of rendering illusion credible, and as readers we become immersed in the fiction. Criticism, on the other hand, must be concerned with understanding the artistic means employed to achieve credibility, and as critics we are necessarily withdrawn from the fiction. With a poet like Chaucer it is not always easy to tell where illusion begins and ends, since Chaucer is so intrigued with the aesthetic and philosophical implications of illusion. For Chaucerians a perceptive and useful definition of the problem has been provided by Morton Bloomfield's article, "Authenticating Realism and the Realism of Chaucer." Bloomfield discusses Chaucer's use of "authenticating" devices to establish the persuasiveness of his fictions—the dream situation in the vision poems, past history in *Troilus*, and the frame in the *Canterbury Tales*. But Bloomfield is also aware—and shows that Chaucer was too—of the limits of authentication: " . . . all authenticating devices not only authenticate but also call attention to the need for authentication and hence to the inauthenticity of the work of art" (p. 340). Thus he can suggest some of the implications of Chaucer's management of levels of realism and point out that "the dialectic between real and unreal is handled in a masterly fashion and creates one of the fascinations of the *Canterbury Tales*" (p. 357). This kind of attentiveness to Chaucer's variously manifested sense of the nature and limitations of his poetic art underlies Bloomfield's essay on "Distance and Predestination in *Troilus and Criseyde*," which is complemented by Donaldson's "The Ending of Chaucer's *Troilus*" (see Jordan, pp. 61-110).

In an important essay on Chaucer's "art poetical" Dorothy Everett has shown how the teachings and practices of medieval rhetoric affected in a fundamental way not only the language, diction, and verbal style of Chaucer's art, but also its narrative organization and structure. Everett argues that Chaucer's practice in shaping and deploying the parts of his narratives is an imaginative, creative application of the rhetorical device of *interpretatio*. Geoffrey of Vinsauf lists *interpretatio* as the first means of amplification, and writes of it, "let the same thing be covered in many forms; be various and yet the same." Although the rhetoricians did not discuss the principle beyond its verbal applications, Everett suggests that Chaucer followed it in the disposition of larger elements of narrative structure. Her brief discussion of the *Book of the Duchess* illustrates Chaucer's use of "parallelism" in narrative structure, a practice—by no means exclusive to Chaucer among medieval storytellers—which consists in a repetition of the same incident with some variation in detail. In the *Book of the Duchess* Chaucer achieves a richness of amplification by placing together two stories of the loss of a loved one and the lover's grief: both the Ceyx and Alcyone story —in which a wife mourns the loss of her husband—and the story of the Black Knight—in which the knight mourns his lady —convey literary parallels of the grief of John of Gaunt for the Duchess Blanche. More complex effects of this kind are achieved by Chaucer in other works, some of which Everett illustrates briefly.

Parallelism of this kind, as Everett points out, has certain disadvantages, such as a tendency toward shapelessness. Narrative structures composed in this way—based on the coordinate ordering of more or less fixed units of narrative—are particularly difficult to contain within the strictures of modern novelistic theory. A narrative composed according to the additive, repetitive principle of "letting the same thing be covered in many forms" is bound to be uncongenial to the expectations and criteria of a literary aesthetic which values economy, relevance, and organic unity of effect. The structural principles of juxtaposition and parallelism produce a form of narrative more expository than dramatic, more inclined to "tell" than to "show," as Booth's terms would describe it. Further contribution to the "non-organic" character of Chaucer's art is provided by the Chaucerian narrators, with their irrepressible tendency to intrude, to break the illusion, to broadcast, even celebrate, transitions, divisions, and other overt signs of "making" in the narrative.

In a notably reasonable study, *The Art of the Canterbury Tales* (1965), Paul Ruggiers has examined both the total form and several of the tales it comprises. His discussion of the total form (pp. 3-50) elucidates the complex narrative situation in which a vital dramatic framework of pilgrimage not only informs but also interacts with a series of tales told by the pilgrims. Ruggiers follows Baldwin (to whom, unfortunately, he does not allude) in emphasizing both the narrative shape and the metaphorical overtones provided by the form and the substance of the pilgrimage. He is not deceived, however, into the easy assumption that tales and tellers flow into an organic unity of Salvation. He apprehends the aesthetic problem posed by the structure of the two-pillared frame of pilgrimage and the "great middle" of tales, but in seeking solutions he tends to shift from the structural and aesthetic considerations established in the opening chapters on the total form to thematic and generic issues in the study of individual tales. To the extent that Ruggiers' strong effort divides thus into two parts, we may be compelled to the troublesome conclusion that the *Canterbury Tales* is more than one poem.

The task facing students of Chaucerian narrative is to render a just account of an art whose aesthetic bases are not readily accessible in the vocabulary of modern criticism. The commentary I have noted in this brief survey, plus much that I have been forced to leave unexamined—such as Brenner and McCall on *Troilus*, Cunningham on the *General Prologue*, Joselyn on the *Nun's Priest's Tale*, Shumaker on the Wife of Bath—indicates the direction of this effort. Emphasis falls principally upon a revaluation of rhetoric and an expansion of our understanding of Chaucer's "rhetorical poetic," the end of which is to arrive at a just appreciation of the aesthetic possibilities of a highly manipulative art. Intrinsic to such a study is the growing realization that what Chaucer confronts with such virtuosity and skill is not only the materials of his art but also the attitudes and assumptions they represent—philosophical and spiritual as well as aesthetic and literary.

In the closing paragraphs of this survey I should like to draw attention to some works of extra-Chaucerian and extra-literary scholarship which I think hold particular promise for enlarging our understanding of Chaucer. Among the landmarks of modern criticism Erich Auerbach's *Mimesis* holds a prominent and secure place, yet allusions to it and signs of its influence are surprisingly rare among Chaucer studies. Though Auerbach has nothing to say about Chaucer, his firm grasp of the philology of style and the rhetoric of structure, and his profound understanding of the expressive relationship between both of these literary phenomena and fundamental human concerns of attitude and value, make *Mimesis* a provocative study for Chaucerians interested in the structure of narrative. Especially valuable are chapters 5, 7, 8, and 9 on the *Chanson de Roland*, the *Mystère d'Adam*, Dante, and Boccaccio, in which Auerbach displays exemplary techniques for discerning and interpreting narrative structure and verbal style in a variety of medieval texts. Vinaver on medieval romance and Nykrog on fabliaux are similarly peripheral yet fundamentally relevant to Chaucerian narrative.

Art historians such as Gombrich, Hauser, de Bruyne, Wölfflin, and Panofsky have been notably successful in discriminating between reality and realisms—a distinction which has caused considerable difficulty among Chaucerians. In *Art and Illusion* Gombrich has persuasively argued the thesis that there is no such thing as "neutral naturalism" and has shown how significant a part is played by the received concept, or artistic convention, in the work of Villard d'Honnecourt and other artists of the Gothic period. Hauser has propounded in *The Social History of Art* some thoughtful generalizations on the characteristics of Gothic in the forms of life and the forms of art in the late Middle Ages.

Particularly interesting for students of literary art is Panofsky's *tour de force*, *Gothic Architecture and Scholasticism*, which develops a detailed analogy between cathedral and treatise as

Gothic forms of aesthetic structure. This study makes available to students of the verbal arts the carefully worked out taxonomy of the art historian. On the Gothic itself, and its intellectual bases in Platonic number science and Christian symbolism, Otto von Simson's *The Gothic Cathedral* is a valuable guide.

The most comprehensive and detailed study of medieval aesthetics in general is Edgar de Bruyne's *Études d'esthétique médiévale*, which traces throughout the Middle Ages the continuity of antique principles of order and their Christian modifications. Robertson's *A Preface to Chaucer*, which is the first book on Chaucer to deal extensively with the non-literary art of the Middle Ages, is in part a corrective to what Robertson regards as failure on de Bruyne's part to pay sufficient attention to St. Augustine's role in medieval aesthetics. Since Robertson associates medieval aesthetics with Augustinian exegetics, his concern is understandable. However, the basis of this concern is questionable. Robertson seems to regard aesthetics as exclusively a thematic consideration, concerning the Christian interpretation of substantive signs within a text—words, images, characters, etc. —as "icons" of *caritas* or *cupiditas*. But iconography of this kind, whether applied to church sculpture or literary texts, was in the Middle Ages as now a matter of doctrinal interpretation rather than aesthetic analysis. The latter was concerned with form rather than content or theme, and as de Bruyne and others have shown, the Middle Ages discriminated sharply between form and content. Form was governed by aesthetic considerations, which were defined for the Middle Ages in the quantitative terminology of the ubiquitous passage from Scripture describing God's creation of the world: "Thou hast ordered all things in measure and number and weight" (Wisdom, xi, 20). Although balance and proportion are not prominent features of Chaucerian narrative, sufficient evidence has accumulated in recent years to suggest that for Chaucer writing was a compositional art, in which the poet stood as a master of his materials, ordering them according to principles that seemed right and good to him. A major task confronting Chaucerians today is to elucidate those principles.

*　*　*　*　*

From the numerous studies of Chaucerian narrative since 1968 I have tried to select those which seem most germane to the view of narrative I proposed in 1968, and of these I have space to discuss only the more theoretical and broadly applicable, others being noted in the bibliography.

Josipovici's study of prose fiction places Chaucer in a broad aesthetic and literary context, and it articulates a theoretical framework which embraces much recent commentary. Unlike post-Renaissance authors of narratives of "social realism" (i.e., novels) and in a narrower sense unlike Dante and Langland, Chaucer is self-consciously a maker of fictions who simultaneously is "keenly aware of the folly of such an activity for one who is also concerned with truth" (p. 82). Similarly Stevens proposes that "modernist" attributes of disjunction and multiplicity are a better guide to Chaucer's medievalism than are the presuppositions of "realist" criticism. Also viewing Chaucer primarily as a maker of fictions rather than a depicter of life, Burlin stresses "the dynamic interplay of the fictive matter with the control of the shaper" (p. 150). The text thus becomes the vital nexus in which the elements of narrative converge and variously interact: depicted world, mediating narrator, and audience or reader.

Miskimin devotes a chapter to "Self-impersonation: The Chaucerian Poetic 'I'," and reveals multiple personalities giving rise to multiple perspectives. This protean role is the subject of extensive attention in Burlin, Howard, and David. In other studies of the narrator, Donner makes a general survey while Garbáty concentrates on the *Canterbury Tales* and Watts on *Troilus*.

Payne traces the progress of the poet's self-representation from layman-observer of the action in the *Book of the Duchess* to poet at the very center in the *Prologue to the Legend of Good Women*. David takes a similar view of the early works in his opening chapter; his final two chapters view the *Canterbury Tales* as a progression in which "dramatic illusion" gives way to the "authority" of the poet as maker and breaker of illusion.

Studying the role of assumed audience-reader, Mehl stresses

the "sociable" nature of narrative and Chaucer's awareness of and conscious exploitation of narrative's inevitable "incompleteness;" Chaucer deliberately draws the reader's attention to "gaps" in the rendering of "reality" (p. 183). See also Miskimin's chapter, "The Imaginary Audience," as well as David, Howard, and Burlin, *passim*.

The structure of narrative, the order of words which is the poetic text, is the focus of Gradon's study of early English literature in general, which suggests that the unifying principle is one of "richness and multiplicity of form, a musical technique which has nothing to do with organic unity" (p. 151). Moore also re-examines "unity." Delany finds that in the *House of Fame* "meaning" resides not in "unity...of subject matter and plot development" or "explicit content," but in the method of "structural repetition" (p. 49). A similar "Gothic" view is defined by Brewer, Ryding, and Vinaver and is applied to Chaucerian narratives by Herzman, Jordan, and Joyner. Dwyer proposes that these structural characteristics are related to scribal practices.

Chaucer's overtly structured, rhetorical fiction invites such rigorous analyses of narrative parts as have been undertaken by Provost, Ullmann, and Anderson. Howard's treatment of structure is more speculative (pp. 159-209 and chapter 5) and seeks models in the visual arts, as do Leyerle and Kolve.

BIBLIOGRAPHY

Anderson, Jens K. "An Analysis of the Framework Structure of Chaucer's *Canterbury Tales.*" *OL*, 27 (1972), 179-201.

Auerbach, Erich. *Mimesis: The Representation of Reality in Western Literature.* Trans. W.R. Trask. Princeton: Princeton Univ. Press, 1953.

Baldwin, Ralph. *The Unity of the 'Canterbury Tales'.* Anglistica, 5. Copenhagen: Rosenkilde og Bagger, 1955.

Baltzell, Jane. "Rhetorical 'Amplification' and the Structure of Medieval Narrative." *PCP*, 2 (1967), 32-39.

Bloomfield, Morton W. "Distance and Predestination in *Troilus and Criseyde.*" *PMLA*, 72 (1957), 14-26.

———. "Authenticating Realism and the Realism of Chaucer." *Thought*, 39 (1964), 335-58.

Booth, Wayne C. *The Rhetoric of Fiction.* Chicago: Univ. of Chicago Press, 1961.

Brenner, Gerry. "Narrative Structure in Chaucer's *Troilus and Criseyde.*" *AnM*, 6 (1965), 5-18.

Brewer, D.S. "Gothic Chaucer." In *Geoffrey Chaucer.* Ed. D.S. Brewer. London: Bell, 1974, pp. 1-32

Bronson, Bertrand H. "Chaucer's Art in Relation to His Audience." In *Five Studies in Literature.* Univ. of California Pub. in English, 8. Berkeley, 1940, p. 1-53.

———. *In Search of Chaucer.* Toronto: Univ. of Toronto Press, 1960.

Bruyne, Edgar de. *Études d'esthétique médiévale.* 3 vols. 1946. Rpt. Trans. Eileen B. Hennesy. New York: Ungar Press, 1969.

Bryan, W.F., and Germaine Dempster, eds. *Sources and Analogues of Chaucer's Canterbury Tales.* 1941. Rpt. New York: Humanities Press, 1958.

Burlin, Robert B. *Chaucerian Fiction.* Princeton: Princeton Univ. Press, 1977.

Burrow, J.A. *Ricardian Poetry: Chaucer, Gower, Langland and the Gawain Poet.* London: Routledge, 1971.

Clemen, Wolfgang. *Der junge Chaucer.* Kölner anglistiche Arbeiten, 33. Bochum-Langendreer, 1938.

———. *Chaucer's Early Poetry.* Trans. C.A.M. Sym. London: Methuen, 1963.

Crosby, Ruth. "Chaucer and the Custom of Oral Delivery." *Speculum*, 13 (1938), 413-32.

Cunningham, J.V. "The Literary Form of the Prologue to the *Canterbury Tales.*" *MP*, 49 (1952), 172-81.

———. "Ideal Fiction: *The Clerk's Tale.*" *Shenandoah*, 19 (1968), 38-41.

Curtius, E.R. *European Literature and the Latin Middle Ages*. Trans. W.R. Trask. New York: Pantheon, 1953.

David, Alfred. *The Strumpet Muse: Art and Morals in Chaucer's Poetry*. Bloomington, Ind.: Indiana Univ. Press, 1976.

Delany, Sheila. *Chaucer's House of Fame: The Poetics of Skeptical Fideism*. Chicago: Chicago Univ. Press, 1972.

Deligiorgis, S. "Structuralism and the Study of Poetry: A Parametric Analysis of Chaucer's *Shipman's Tale* and *Parliament of Fowls*." *NM*, 70 (1969), 297-306.

Donaldson, E. Talbot. "Chaucer the Pilgrim." *PMLA*, 49 (1954), 928-36.

————. "The Ending of Chaucer's *Troilus*." In *Early English and Norse Studies Presented to Hugh Smith in Honour of His Sixtieth Birthday*. Ed. Arthur Brown and Peter Foote. London: Methuen, 1963, p. 26-45.

Donner, Morton. "Chaucer and His Narrators: The Poet's Place in His Poems." *WHR*, 27 (1973), 189-95.

Dwyer, Richard A. "The Appreciation of Handmade Literature." *ChauR*, 8 (1974), 221-40.

Everett, Dorothy. "Some Reflections on Chaucer's 'Art Poetical'." *PBA*, 36 (1950). Rpt. In *Essays on Middle English Literature*. Ed. P. M. Kean. Oxford: Clarendon Press, 1955, pp. 149-74.

Frank, R.W. Jr. *Chaucer and the Legend of Good Women*. Cambridge, Mass.: Harvard Univ. Press, 1972.

Frye, Northrop. *Anatomy of Criticism*. Princeton: Princeton Univ. Press, 1957.

Garbáty, Thomas J. "The Degradation of Chaucer's 'Geffrey'." *PMLA*, 89 (1974), 97-104.

Giffin, Mary. *Studies on Chaucer and His Audience*. Hull, Québec: Les Éditions 'L'Éclair,' 1956.

Gombrich, E.H. *Art and Illusion: A Study in the Psychology of Pictorial Representation*. 1960. 2nd ed., rev. New York: Pantheon Books, 1965.

Gradon, Pamela. *Form and Style in Early English Literature*. London: Methuen, 1971.

Hanning, Robert W. "The Theme of Art and Life in Chaucer's Poetry." In *Geoffrey Chaucer*. Ed. G.D. Economou. New York: McGraw-Hill, 1975, pp. 15-36.

Harwood, Britton J. "Language and the Real: Chaucer's Manciple." *ChauR*, 6 (1972), 268-79.

Hatzfeld, Helmut A. "Esthetic Criticism Applied to Medieval Romance Literature." *RPh*, 1 (1948), 304-27.

————. *A Critical Bibliography of the New Stylistics Applied to the Romance Literatures, 1953-1965*. Univ. of North Carolina Studies in Comparative Literature, 37. Chapel Hill, 1966.

Hauser, Arnold. *The Social History of Art*. 2 vols. New York: Knopf, 1951.

Herzman, Ronald B. "The Paradox of Form: *The Knight's Tale* and Chaucerian Aesthetics." *PLL*, 10 (1974), 339-52.

Howard, Donald R. "Chaucer the Man." *PMLA*, 80 (1965), 337-43.

————. *The Idea of the Canterbury Tales*. Berkeley: Univ. of California Press, 1976.

Jordan, Robert M. *Chaucer and the Shape of Creation: The Aesthetic Possibilities of Inorganic Structure*. Cambridge, Mass.: Harvard Univ. Press, 1967.

————. "The Compositional Structure of the *Book of the Duchess*." *ChauR*, 9 (1975), 99-117.

————. "The Question of Genre: Five Chaucerian Romances." In *Chaucer at Albany*. Ed. Rossell Hope Robbins. New York: Burt Franklin, 1975, pp. 77-104.

Joselyn, Sister M. "Aspects of Form in *The Nun's Priest's Tale*." *CE*, 25 (1964), 566-71.

Josipovici, Gabriel. *The World and the Book*. London: Macmillan, 1971.

Joyner, William. "Parallel Journeys in Chaucer's *House of Fame*." *PLL*, 12 (1976), 3-19.

Kittredge, G.L. *Chaucer and His Poetry*. Cambridge, Mass.: Harvard Univ. Press, 1915.

Kolve, V.A. "Chaucer and the Visual Arts." In *Geoffrey Chaucer*. Ed. D.S. Brewer. London: Bell, 1974, pp. 290-320.

Lanham, R.A. "Game, Play, and High Seriousness in Chaucer's Poetry." *ES*, 48 (1967), 1-24.

Leyerle, John. "Thematic Interlace in *The Canterbury Tales*." *E&S*, 29 (1976), pp. 107-121.

Lowes, John L. *Geoffrey Chaucer*. 1934. Rpt. Bloomington, Ind.: Indiana Univ. Press, 1958.

Lüdeke, H. *Die Funktionen des Erzählers in Chaucers epischer Dichtung*. Studien zur englischen Philologie, 72. Halle, 1928.

McCall, John P. "The Trojan Scene in Chaucer's *Troilus*." *ELH*, 29 (1962), 263-75.

Mann, Jill. *Chaucer and Medieval Estates Satire: The Literature of Social Classes and the General Prologue to the Canterbury Tales*. London: Cambridge Univ. Press, 1973.

Mehl, Dieter. "The Audience of Chaucer's *Troilus and Criseyde*." In *Chaucer and Middle English Studies in Honour of Rossell Hope Robbins*. Ed. Beryl Rowland. London: Allen & Unwin, 1974. Kent State Univ. Press, 1974, pp. 173-89.

Miskimin, Alice S. *The Renaissance Chaucer*. New Haven: Yale Univ. Press, 1975.

Moore, Arthur K. "Medieval English Literature and the Question of Unity." *MP*, 65 (1968), 285-300.

Muscatine, Charles. *Chaucer and the French Tradition: A Study in Style and Meaning*. Berkeley: Univ. of California Press, 1957.

Nykrog, Per. *Les Fabliaux: étude d'histoire littéraire et de stylistique médiévale*. 1957. Nouv. éd. Genève: Droz, 1973.

Panofsky, Erwin. *Gothic Architecture and Scholasticism*. 1951. Rpt. New York: Meridian Books, 1957.

Payne, Robert O. *The Key of Remembrance: A Study of Chaucer's Poetics*. 1963. Rpt. Westport, Conn.: Greenwood Press, 1973.

———. "Making His Own Myth: The Prologue to Chaucer's *Legend of Good Women*." *ChauR*, 9 (1975), 197-211.

Provost, William. *The Structure of Chaucer's Troilus and Criseyde.* Anglistica, 20. Copenhagen: Rosenkilde og Bagger, 1974.

Robertson, D.W., Jr. *A Preface to Chaucer: Studies in Medieval Perspectives.* Princeton: Princeton Univ. Press, 1962.

Ruggiers, Paul G. *The Art of the Canterbury Tales.* Madison: Univ. of Wisconsin Press, 1965.

Ryding, William W. *Structure in Medieval Narrative.* The Hague: Mouton, 1971.

Scholes, Robert, and Robert Kellogg. *The Nature of Narrative.* New York: Oxford Univ. Press, 1966.

Shumaker, Wayne. "Alisoun in Wander-Land: A Study in Chaucer's Mind and Literary Method." *ELH,* 18 (1951), 77-89.

Simson, Otto von. *The Gothic Cathedral.* 2nd ed. New York: Pantheon Books, 1962.

Singleton, Charles S. *Dante Studies 1.* Cambridge, Mass.: Harvard Univ. Press, 1954.

Stevens, Martin. "Chaucer and Modernism: An Essay in Criticism." In *Chaucer at Albany.* Ed. Rossell Hope Robbins. New York: Burt Franklin, 1975, pp. 193-216.

Strohm, Paul. "Some Generic Distinctions in the Canterbury Tales." *MP,* 68 (1971), 321-28.

Ullmann, Ingeborg M. *Der Erzähler der Canterbury Tales: Das literarische Werk in seiner kommunikativen Funktion.* European Univ. Papers, ser. 14, vol. 15. Bern, Switzerland, 1973.

Vinaver, Eugène. *Form and Meaning in Medieval Romance.* The *MHRA* Presidential Address, 1966.

————. *The Rise of Romance.* Oxford: Clarendon Press, 1971.

Watts, Ann C. "Chaucerian Selves—Especially two Serious Ones." *ChauR,* 4 (1970), 229-41.

Wölfflin, Heinrich. *Principles of Art History.* Trans. M.D. Hottinger. New York: Dover Pub., 1950.

SIX

BERYL ROWLAND

Chaucer's Imagery

Imagery appears to derive its vitality from a quality of analogy, an analogy, which, however expressed, is usually complex, unifying disparate areas of knowledge in a startling way. It may involve the use of images which seem primarily tactile, visual, auditory, gustatory or olfactory, but it stands for something "inner," and something which means different things to different people. It is most commonly expressed in metaphor or simile. When it is recurring and persistent, it is called symbolic; in a wider sense than we shall be considering here, when it is the parabolic basis of an entire work, it becomes myth.

As used by recent critics the word has many meanings, and Preminger's *Encyclopedia of Poetry and Poetics* or standard works such as those by Tuve, Frye, or Wellek and Warren should be consulted. Important in our discussion is the need to distinguish between imagery, as a modern term, and the tropes described in the treatises of *artes poeticae* which Chaucer studied. Imagery is something organic, sustaining in diverse ways—not all of them the conscious intent of the poet—the aesthetic experience which is the heart of the poem; the tropes or figures of speech recommended by the rhetoricians, while they may illustrate some central truth, are ornamental devices, arranged and patterned to a formal prescription in language traditionally regarded as most suited to the subject.

The study of Chaucer's imagery is recent. Despite Coleridge's recognition of the function of metaphor and his own brief but perceptive readings, there was, indeed, little detailed consideration of the language of poetry until the second decade of this century. In 1924, I. A. Richards' *Practical Criticism*—the title is from the fifteenth chapter of the *Biographia Literaria*—heralded a new method of close textual analysis whereby the poem was examined for itself with scant reference to its context, historical, biographical or philosophical. In this intense study of the poem, particularly of its verbal texture, imagery assumed immediate significance. To Chaucerian scholars, however, the practice of minimizing the relevance of the work's cultural milieu did not recommend it, and even in 1964 one critic could observe somewhat sweepingly that "medievalists have generally steered clear of close reading."

In 1893, Klaeber's *Das Bild bei Chaucer* classified all the metaphors and similes and commented on obvious surface meanings. The implied concept of Chaucer's figurative language as local verbal arrangement was not substantially modified when Edmond Faral's edition of major thirteenth-century treatises on poetics, published in 1924, prompted a number of scholars to examine the poet's practices in relation to the conventions of his age. It is true that Manly's article, developing the thesis (mistaken, as we now believe) that the poet gradually emancipated himself from the rhetoricians, stressed that Chaucer's figures were not merely decorative. But Manly's own definition of imagery in *Some New Light on Chaucer* (p. 284) seems inadequate. Dorothy Everett gave some consideration to what we would call imagery when she examined the descriptive phrases in the opening stanza of the *Parliament of Fowls*. But she was concerned with structure, not with word values and their effect, and her observations were designed to show that Chaucer's organization of rhetorical devices was compatible with rhetorical theory stemming from Quintilian and still followed in the fourteenth century. Chaucer's obvious knowledge of the sort of precepts taught by rhetoricians such as Geoffroi de Vinsauf and Matthieu de Vendôme made it seem desirable to discuss his practice in terms of such devices as he would have regarded as part of his craft. This approach, while it led to more than forty studies, failed to result in any full examination of Chaucer's poetic language.

The year 1950 appears to have been the *terminus a quo* for a closer and more detailed study of Chaucer's imagery. At least four papers, three of which were later included in full-length works, indicated a new area of critical concern: style as a concomitant of meaning. Imagery, being an element of style, received new attention. Recent analyses of imagery in a passage or single work of Chaucer usually begin with assumptions about narrative and meaning and show how the imagery in recurrent, episodic or single units may function both centripetally and in isolable constituents such as dialogue and characterization; stylistic investigation seeks to establish levels of meaning, aesthetic intention and effect by considering choice of words, patterns of imagery, surface arrangement, structure, syntax, sound, rhythm, devices of point of view and tone—in short, it examines all those elements, shaped by literary strategy, which are pertinent to the study of imagery also.

At the English Institute Sanford B. Meech showed how Chaucer's figurative language illustrated the complexities of characterization in *Troilus and Criseyde*, and he subsequently expanded this paper in *Design in Chaucer's Troilus*, a close textual examination of the poem in relation to its principal source. Devoting one quarter of his book to a qualitative and quantitative analysis of imagery, Meech divides the figurative associations into seven areas, Religion and Mythology, Subjugation and Feudal Relationship, Acquired Skills and their Products, Corporeal Existence, the Brute Creation, Insentient Nature, and Fire and Heat and Cold. Chaucer used less than one fifth of Boccaccio's figures but added so many of his own that associatively his poem is far richer than that of the Italian poet. In all areas the figurative patterns underline contrasts in behavior, appearance, character, modes of thought and thematic action, often with ironic effect, and contribute towards what Meech believes to be Chaucer's structural ideal for *Troilus*: "artistic unity emergent from life-like diversity" (p. 15).

Reliance on a close textual reading is also the approach of E. T. Donaldson in "Idiom of Popular Poetry in the *Miller's Tale*" where he examines the ironic effect of certain expressions taken from the vernacular poetic tradition of lyric and romance. A constant epithet given to Nicholas is "hende." Originally meaning "handy" and then applied in the sense of "nice" to almost every good guy in English popular poetry, the word became too déclassé to be eligible for serious employment and could be used by Chaucer to describe a young man who was handy or adept in a particular way:

> In short, the coupling of word and character suggests in Nicholas nothing more than a large measure of physical charm that is skillful at recognizing its opportunities and putting itself to practical sexual use. (p. 125)

Equally illuminating are Donaldson's suspicions regarding Alisoun's white apron which lies "upon her lendes, ful of many a goore" (*MillT*, 3267). We might assume that the triangular insertions of material simply gave the apron a generously seductive flounce. But, as Donaldson observes, Chaucer takes pains to mention "lendes," the loins, which are subsequently to be heartily "thakked" by Nicholas in amorous embrace; the fact that phrases such as "geynest vnder gore" or "glad vnder gore" were applied to numerous heroines in romantic situations suggests that Chaucer may have been using the word evocatively as well as technically (p. 131). The *Middle English Dictionary* (G, 2), published in 1963, attributes only beauty or kindness to such ladies, but its interpretation of idioms such as "gropen vnder gore" and "stingen vnder gore" certainly supports Donaldson's contention. Donaldson concludes that Chaucer's use of words or phrases which have correspondences in popular poetry contributes directly to the rich humor of the tale.

An examination of the imagery assists Charles Muscatine in

reaching the thematic meaning of the *Knight's Tale*. He sees the tale as a "poetic pageant" with all its materials functioning in a complex design expressing the nature of the noble life. Rich description and "sub-surface" images of disorder combine in the texture to become a metaphor for the theme: the necessity for preserving from the forces of chaos the order which is inherent in Chaucer's conception of the truly noble life. The most striking quality of Chaucer's imagery, as Muscatine notes in a later essay, is its range. What characterizes similes such as "his brydel . . . gynglen . . . as dooth the chapel belle," "his eyen . . . stemed as a forneys of a leed," "as leene was his hors as is a rake," "lewed as gees," "as thikke as is a branched ook," as well as things that are not worth "an oystre," "a pulled hen," "a bene," is their conventional rural familiarity. Subject matter places no restriction on choice of image: ploughing oxen, drunken mice, buckets in the well occur even in most elevated contexts. Such language is a native characteristic:

> Some Continental critics have found Chaucer irreducibly "middle class" on account of this language; but that is to be too pure as regards decorum. It is, rather, a great part of his delightful "Englishness," which must be acknowledged however much we may discover of his debt to the Continent in style, subject and genre. And it is even more a source of easy geniality and of an appearance of artless spontaneity. At times . . . it is transformed into a powerful medieval realism, and it enters into overtly comic and ironic combinations. *"The Canterbury Tales . . . ,"* p. 93)

In *Chaucer and the French Tradition*, p. 10, Muscatine remarks that we have a new tolerance of convention and that the contemporary critical atmosphere is propitious for rediscovering "poetry lost and poetic meanings inappreciable to older generations." Neither he nor Donaldson lay claim to a definitive criticism of Chaucer. Muscatine remarks that his study will provide data toward the theory that the perennial significance of great poems depends on the multiplicity of meanings they interrelate; Donaldson observes that his criticism in general is based firmly on the text. In 1950 the studies of both showed that an imaginative examination of Chaucer's imagery was possible without violating linguistic or cultural probabilities.

But there was also another approach, based on a new and enlightened historicism, and first formulated by D. W. Robertson, Jr., in his paper given at the English Institute in 1950, which has been far-reaching in its interpretation of imagery. It emphasizes the medieval poetic based on a premise found in St. Augustine and other writers that all art is ultimately concerned with promoting the doctrine of *caritas*. According to this approach—the "patristic" or "allegorical" approach—medieval literature was figurative and allegorical in the sense that it had a "lying cortex" —a fictional surface covering moral truth. Chaucer, as a Christian poet, expressed through figure and fable the doctrine which the priest might present directly. His message of charity had to be "glosed" from a brilliant and often enigmatic tapestry. His ideas, figures and allusions were derivative and bore traditional relevances or meanings intended to reinforce the *sententia*. To discover the underlying nucleus of truth, the modern reader needed a knowledge of medieval literary and visual arts and of the aesthetic, religious and philosophic principles of the period:

> The poet wished to make his message vivid and memorable, and at the same time he did not want to cast pearls before swine, so that his normal office was to construct obscure and puzzling combinations of events, frequently involving tantalizing surface inconsistencies, in order to stimulate his audience to intellectual effort. ("Historical Criticism," p. 15)

Other critics, not associated with Robertson and his group, have analyzed certain features of Chaucer's imagery for their iconographical value. But Robertson's examination in his *Preface to Chaucer* is more detailed and far-reaching in its implication. With respect to the pilgrims, he finds that Chaucer is not concerned with delineating character but with stressing abstractions which may manifest themselves in human thought and action (p. 248). The Miller is the very picture of *discordia*; the Prioress is an iconographic portrait of false courtesy; the Wife is "a literary personification of rampant 'femininity' or carnality."

The lively and erudite *Preface* with its numerous examples

from art as well as from literature convinces us of the importance of the allegorical mode, and its analysis of ideas, traditions and techniques gives a vital impression of the *sensibility* which undoubtedly lay behind much medieval art and poetry. But our approach to Chaucer's imagery depends on our understanding of his own artistic intentions. Doctrinal and didactic elements may be more prevalent in his works than some of us would wish to believe but the Retraction of "the book of Troilus . . . the tales of Caunterbury, thilke that sownen into synne . . . " seems to suggest that Chaucer was aware that, as a great artist, he could not impose upon his work the limitations of Augustinian aesthetics. As Robert M. Jordan observes: "Chaucer had to find a way of living with the impossible paradox that to be true to his art was to be false to his convictions" (p. 33). Paul G. Ruggiers' comment on the great burden placed upon the practitioner by "the lying art of literature" (p. 40) is equally illuminating.

The design of *A Preface to Chaucer* precludes systematic exposition of Chaucer's poems, but since the figurative element is deemed to exist for the sake of the *sentence*, the work is much concerned with the elucidation of Chaucer's imagery. An application of the same aesthetic to entire poems is reserved for *Fruyt and Chaf*, written jointly by Bernard F. Huppé and Robertson—which examines the *Book of the Duchess* and the *Parliament of Fowls*—Huppé's *A Reading of the Canterbury Tales*, and B. G. Koonce's *Chaucer and the Tradition of Fame*.

The use of Scriptural exegesis is rewarding in R. E. Kaske's analysis of the verbal echoes of the *Song of Songs* in the *Miller's Tale*: a series of correspondences give humor and "a moral edge" —"an implicit orientation toward a controlling set of values" (p. 497). Even a direct image may be figurative, with a basis in Biblical exposition. The Summoner's garlic, onions and leeks, Kaske suggests in another essay, were not only medically significant as notorious irritants of leprosy; to the exegete commenting on Numbers xi, 5, they were linked with moral depravity ("Patristic Exegesis: the Defense," p. 49).

Arthur Hoffman emphasizes the serious intention of the Chris-

tian poet when he examines the imagery in the *General Prologue*.
He finds that a metaphoric unity in the portraits enforces the
external unity arising from the realistic and symbolic device of
the pilgrimage. The description of spring prepares us for the
double view: regeneration and love in the physical world are
paralleled by a supernatural kind of restoration arising from the
Love which all pilgrims acknowledge and which is symbolized in
"the hooly blisful martir." The pilgrims are metaphors for the
dual compulsion motivating humanity: "Go, go, go," of the bird
is the major impulse of the Squire; the Knight's pilgrimage is
more nearly a response to the voice of a Saint. Devices of
sequence, pairing and contrasting of portraits enhance the relative
values. Consanguinity itself may have metaphorical effect, as in
the Christian ideal of brotherly love expressed by the Parson and
the Plowman. In the case of another fraternal pair, the Pardoner
and the Summoner, the theme of love is darkly distorted. The
song "Com hider, love, to me" is "both a promiscuous and perverted invitation and an unconscious symbolic acknowledgement
of the absence of and the need for love" (p. 12).

There are also several recent full-length works such as those
by Claes Schaar and Paull F. Baum, as well as articles, which
make valuable comments *passim* regarding Chaucer's imagery.
J. A. W. Bennett tells us a great deal about the origin, nature and
function of the imagery in the *Parliament of Fowls*:

> These trees, for instance, that at first glance seemed to show
> Chaucer as a nurseryman, and at second glance to be variations
> on a theme of Statius, at a third view are seen to belong to and
> be reminders of the world of actuality, the world of peace and
> war, in which ash trees furnish arrows, palms the victors' wreath;
> in which there is grief and death, elms become coffins, holm-oaks
> whip-handles, and cypresses symbols of mourning. So in the
> midst of the forest, when our sense of its paradisal air is keenest,
> we do not entirely lose awareness of the human world. (p. 79)

Bennett notes a similar lack of concern with "inscape," with the
anatomy of animal, tree or flower, later in the poem. Only one
of the birds, the goshawk "with his fethres dunne and grey"
is given color:

The rest are characterized by their qualities, and in the language of the Bestiaries; and it is the Bestiaries' insistence on *significacio*, and indifference to zoological categories or probability that we must bear in mind as we scan Chaucer's assembly. . . . But the Bestiaries did not sum up all medieval bird-lore. Besides them there was "al this new science that men lere"; and Chaucer, as always, blends old and new . . . . (p. 149)

Studies in irony have given rise to the most sensitive examinations of Chaucer's imagery. Charles Owen shows how a complex ironic unity is achieved through use of symbol. The black rocks in the *Franklin's Tale,* the garden, the blindness and the tree in the *Merchant's Tale,* the old hag's request for love in the *Wife of Bath's Tale,* the gold in the *Pardoner's Tale* and Chaunticleer's smug mistranslation of "In principio, / mulier est hominis confusio" in the *Nun's Priest's Tale* have symbolic values which give an added and unifying dimension, illuminating motivation in both teller and tale, and adumbrating the reversal. The papers of Earle Birney are outstanding for their sound and imaginative perceptions, bringing into play psychological insights, ideas and terms compatible with modern concepts, while recognizing the importance of fourteenth-century poetic conventions. In the *Miller's Tale* "symbolic detail, sly image and verbal play" are interwoven with ironic effect. In the *Summoner's Tale* patterns of irony are elaborately developed through the imagery. Simile and metaphor are related to the hunter-prey theme to achieve a perfect figurative unity.

Must a study of imagery involve considerations of rhetoric? Meech candidly admits his neglect of "the presumed effect upon Chaucer of rhetorical theory" (p. vii). To Ralph Baldwin, Chaucer's technique of discontinuity and incongruity constitutes "the loudest kind of objection to the method of his days": the jump from the Cook's shinbone to his cookery must have seemed to his contemporaries "a delirious garbling of detail" (p. 51). In his analysis of Chaucer's technique of characterization he notes Chaucer's conscientious use of hyperbole—"worthy" five times for the Knight, "ful" ten times for the Prioress, along with such superlatives as "Seint Julian he was in his contree" and "it snewed in his hous . . . / Of alle deyntees." Equally distinctive is what Baldwin calls the *radix trait*, a single capital characteristic with connotative values, such as the "worthynesse" of the Knight and the "wantonnesse" of the Friar, and descriptive phrases, particularly those which give a quick glance at the interior man and those using disparate detail.

Robert Payne, on the other hand, considers that Chaucer's works are experimental answers to questions raised by the manuals of the rhetoricians. Poetry for Chaucer is "a process of manipulating language so that the wisdom evolved in the past will become available, applicable and operative in the present." But if the poet adheres to tradition, the critic can apply modern methods to the results. Thus the *Book of the Duchess* which, except for its latent ironies, might have been written directly from John de Garlande's structural formulae, has a thematic thread, the "lawe of kynde," worked out in plain terms and elaborate figures (pp. 128-9).

Janet Richardson recognizes the importance of rhetoric but feels that neither Chaucer's peculiar kind of irony nor his imagery owe much to medieval rhetorical precepts. Examining six fabliaux, she collates what has been said of the function of their imagery and adds new insights to show how the extended significance of various rhetorical figures and image clusters gives complexity and unity to the whole. A readiness to see moral precept as a dominating motif in the fabliaux leads to some straining in her analysis of the *Shipman's Tale*, but the same chapter also contains admirable perceptions which amplify Silverman's distinction of four image clusters concerned with wild animals, diet, trade and sex. Her thesis is that in the fabliaux Chaucer gave his imagery ironic ramifications which extend their significance beyond their immediate points of reference, causing them to operate organically within the aesthetic whole of the narrative. The imagery functions either in relation to the action, particularly as an adumbrating device, or in reference to specific details found elsewhere in the tale, such as those illustrating character traits.

We may conclude from this survey of recent scholarship that however much our concern with a poem is internal, involving examination of the poetic texture and organic interplay of imagery within the unity of the whole, our overall purpose—which is to find the means whereby the work achieves its effect on the reader —demands that we bring to our study a body of knowledge which would not be required, say, for a poem by Robert Frost. Even our understanding of a contemporary poem is assisted by our awareness of the milieu which produced it. Chaucer wrote for all time but he comes from a world so alien to ours that we need to familiarize ourselves with all aspects of his culture in order to enjoy his poetry.

One of the most obvious problems confronting us in our examination of Chaucer's imagery is that of language. As a starting point for the meaning we must have the value of individual words in contemporary usage as well as a correct grasp of the syntax of the passage. Although incomplete, the new *Middle English Dictionary* is invaluable, each word being amply documented in Middle English usage in all kinds of texts with regional and chronological variants. *The Oxford Dictionary* contains only limited examples of usage, and Stratman's *Middle English Dictionary* cites the locations of other uses, not the contexts. *The Chaucer Concordance* will provide us with all instances of Chaucer's use of a word, and A. C. Baugh's fine glossary in *Chaucer's Major Poetry* may serve a similar purpose as well as assisting in translation. But lexicography can help us little with words which are used so rarely as to have no apparent connotations. In the *Book of the Duchess* we have difficulty in interpreting "the ferses twelve" because, while we know that *fers* is a chess term from the Arabic meaning "queen" or "pawn," there cannot be twelve *ferses* on a regular size chessboard, eight squares by eight. A more common problem is that, despite usage, we still cannot assess the nuances of association which gave the words their full meaning to those listening to the poems. For we must never forget that most medieval poetry was intended to be read aloud to a group, and that Chaucer read his to a sophisticated court audience. Such a procedure inevitably entailed the adoption of a style to suit the peculiar conditions of oral delivery. As D. S. Brewer remarks:

> No poet could stand up in his pulpit before the audience, as medieval poets did, if he was not prepared to use a poetic language with which his audience was reasonably familiar, and which it could be expected to understand and even to like. (p. 1)

Medieval listeners required the familiar phrase. They could not go back over something which they failed to comprehend. They needed a surface simplicity, a texture which was thin or, if full and ornate, was mostly in language in common use, interspersed with formulae and synonymous doublets. They enjoyed repetition, alliteration, onomatopoeia, and all the rhythmic effects of dramatic speech. If they were to respond to a single reading, the poetry had to have a certain diffuseness.

Some of Chaucer's most powerful imagery involves associations unlikely to be made by the listener. It can be organic: its significance extends beyond the immediate passage to function through a series of interrelationships which can enhance or determine theme, illustrate complexities of character or action, or create an ironic substructure. The works of Birney, Donaldson, Owen and Richardson, which I have cited, particularly illustrate such findings.

But Chaucer also fulfilled the demands of his audience. His imagery largely consists of small conventional phrases which his audience could readily understand and appreciate. We are not surprised to find numerous proverbs and proverbial expressions, formulaic groups of words employed to express an essential, accepted idea. Whiting notes that in the Chaucer canon there are 186 proverbs, 630 proverbial phrases of which 372 are comparisons, and 421 sententious remarks. In a series of studies on Chaucer's animal imagery, I found that while Chaucer frequently compares animals to people, his allusions show little interest in or knowledge of wild life. He uses stereotyped traits, conventional ideas about animals which had accrued at his time. Similarly his flowers are usually white and red and his fish are silver because they are not real daisies or trout but flourish in iconographic gardens and streams. Of course there are exceptions: Chaucer's emblematic daisy in the *Prologue to the Legend of Good Women* is so aptly compared for its smell to "gomme, or herbe, or tre," that it must also be the genuine field variety, the *bellis perennis*. In the *Nun's Priest's Tale* we have a contemporary allusion to "Jakke Straw and his meynee" (3394) and in the *Cook's Tale* we learn that Perkyn "sometyme lad with revel to Newegate" (4402). But this kind of particularization is rare. Chaucer's refusal to number the streaks of a tulip gives his imagery a general quality and is importantly related to time. The absence of localization to the specific gives a temporal perspective which can be lengthened or shortened at will. In the *Tale of Constance*, the heroine is accused of murder. The Man of Law continues:

> Have ye nat seyn somtyme a pale face,
> Among a prees, of hym that hath be lad
> Toward his deeth, wher as hym gat no grace,
> And swich a colour in his face hath had,
> Men myghte knowe his face that was bistad,
> Amonges alle the faces in that route?
>
> (645-50)

Appropriate as the simile is to the teller who might have witnessed many such spectacles, nothing in the passage links it specifically to Chaucer's day. The experience is general and for this reason we are able to engage in it more fully. Had it been fixed in time, the emotional shock of the rhetorical approach, deliberately evoking personal memory, would be less. The juxtaposition of two incompatible ideas further extends thought and feeling. Inasmuch as the owner of the pale face is a convicted man being led towards his death, he is separated from the crowd and easily identifiable on that account. In these circumstances the corollary is absurd: it implies a situation that will make a distinction between accused and spectators when there can be no occasion for it. But its effect is to heighten the pity and a feeling of the hopelessness of the heroine's position. Constance is wrongly accused. The phrases describing the doomed man—"as hym gat no grace" and "that was bistad"—are equivocal, but guilty or not, he is being led to his death. The accompanying idea that even in a crowd such a man could be picked out heightens the feeling that the accused is a quarry, a victim who is trapped. Equally general and timeless are briefer similes such as "the smylere with the knyf under the cloke" (*KnT*, 1999) or that applied to a horseman rolling under his mount "as dooth a bal" (*KnT*, 2614)—a practice observed by jockeys today.

What of the effect of this imagery? It may evoke stock responses, stimulating interest by appealing to eye or ear. Despite the simplicity of the analogies, Alisoun's eyebrows are the blacker for being compared to a sloe (*MillT*, 3246), Chaunticleer's comb is the more handsomely crenellated for being "batailled as it were a castel wal" (*NPT*, 2860), and the abbot's salt tears for the "litel clergeon" are all the more poignant because they trickle down "as reyn" (*PrT*, 674). Sound and image may combine to give an immediate emotional effect: "narwe in cage" (*MillT*, 3224), which is how old John tries to keep his gamey young wife, suggests both the stifling oppressiveness and the unnaturalness of such constriction. The harsh sounds even direct point of view: we are not supposed to like what old John is doing. A similar effect can be achieved by brief metonymy. Troilus looks at the places which are full of memories of Criseyde, of her dancing, looking, playing, speaking, singing. The imagery is sparse and what we would term commonplace; but the simple inadequacy of "dere herte" conveys grief just as certainly as the natural pause in the line necessitates a catch in the voice:

> And yonder have I herd ful lustyly
> My dere herte laugh; and yonder pleye
> Saugh ich hire ones ek ful blisfully . . .
>
> (v, 568-70)

Here our response is intensified by our awareness of the paradox: memories of laughter bring sorrow, and we find that there are many such instances when more is demanded from the listener than a stock response: when he is required to make a complex association dependent on context. The allusion to Malkyn's maidenhead in the *Introduction to the Man of Law's Tale*, 30-1, is of a down-to-earth kind suited to its user, the Host: like so many of Chaucer's most vigorous images, it seems to be part of the fabliau cosmos, and catches the rhythms of colloquial speech. It becomes comic because it rounds off the Host's lofty if inaccurate quotation from Seneca and because the mishap of the village prostitute has only a tenuous connection with the Host's profound theme, which is the irrecoverable nature of Time. Our appreciation may depend on the inappropriateness or incongruity of a simple phrase: Diomede "fressh as braunche in May" (*Tr*, v, 844), coming to woo Criseyde, is not our idea of a springtime lover. In the *Nun's Priest's Tale*, 2840, "the goute lette hire nothyng for to daunce" evokes the picture of a poor widow "somdeel stape in age" dancing simply because, as a result of a temperate diet, she is not afflicted by gout. In the *Wife of Bath's Tale*, 1243-4, we perceive the irony of the old hag's promise to be "good and trewe / As evere was wyf, syn that the world was newe" because of our knowledge of the teller.

Full appreciation may depend on something not said but implied in the vehicle. The uproar of the hens when the fox grabs Chaunticleer is compared to that of the Trojan ladies when Pyrrhus seized King Priam "by the berd." The comparison is obviously amusing in that it equates a chicken-run disaster with the destruction of Troy. But the effect is intensified by a familiarity with the passage in the second book of *The Aeneid*. In one of the most tragic scenes in all epic poetry, the trembling, aged King is dragged out by the hair, slipping in the blood of his son just slain, while his daughters-in-law cower together—*praecipites atra ceu tempestate columbae*—"like doves driven downward in a black tempest" (ii, 516). In addition to conveying the noise and confusion of the barnyard, Chaucer's inaccurate and irreverent simile enables us to see the tremulous white feathers of Chaunticleer's fluttering relatives.

But Chaucer's imagery is not primarily intended to make us see. The figures are emotional or intellectual accessories, not representations of life in concrete, accurate detail. Nicholas' door in the *Miller's Tale* remains vividly in the memory because of the cat-hole at the bottom of it. That it should be heaved off its hinges in line 3470, yet be back in its place and shut fast by line 3499 seems irrelevant. What is important is the mental assessment which most of Chaucer's figures require us to make. If we see the Prioress with her lapdogs, an accompanying idea is pervasive: the inappropriateness of her affections to her vocation. There is no visual significance to the line "I trowe he were a geldyng or a mare" (*Gen Prol*, 691). It is Chaucer's explanation for someone whom he recognizes as a sexual deviate and we are left to make the judgment. The Pardoner is either a castrate or he has the traditional qualities of the mare—he is effeminate and extremely lascivious. If the Pardoner were a eunuch he would be forbidden to preach "in chirches" and as a *eunuchus ex nativitate* he would not have the *libido* necessary for his relationship with the Summoner. Since he not only seems to partner the Summoner sexually but contemplates marriage and boasts that he has a jolly wench in every town, the Pardoner, however inadequately so, is obviously bisexual: from the full implications of the line we deduce that the Pardoner is, what in fact his behavior and appearance suggest, a hermaphrodite.

In the *Franklin's Tale* the grisly black rocks which terrify Dorigen are felt rather than seen; she does not even check on Aurelius' story that they have vanished, and Aurelius himself relies on hearsay. Whatever may be the ultimate significance of the birds singing in heavenly harmony in the *Book of the Duchess*, the startling "ther was noon of hem that feyned / To synge" (317-18) tells of the subterfuges of the choristers who have missed rehearsals or of the inexperienced violinists in the last row of the amateur symphony orchestra. But, if the experience comes from life, the image is neither visual nor auditory: it enhances the iconographical intention.

Chaucer wrote for the living voice and ear, and his imagery

gives an impression of particularity and relevance which is strengthened by the familiarity of the image and the colloquial vigor of the language. But, as a conscious artist, he saw beyond his own age and the immediate audience. At times his imagery has a hyper-relevance which creates patterns. The method is antiphonal: the figures set up a series of responses, related by contrast or similarity, which are crucial to the poetic meaning of the whole. The imagery may seem simple but it demands a kind of intellectual response which is not simple at all. Even when the imagery has no organic, unifying function and is significant only in the immediate line or passage, it may have a stimulating complexity. The figurative language is, for the most part, traditional, but the effect transcends the essential forms.

*   *   *   *   *

In the last decade the study of Chaucer's imagery has increased dramatically. In addition to numerous articles investigating convention and innovation, the significance of clusters, recurring patterns, and central images, there have been three specific studies, Janet Richardson's on Chaucer's fabliaux, Chauncey Wood's on astrological imagery, and my own on animal imagery; illuminating analyses in several full-length assessments of Chaucer's poetry, dissertations by J. S. Hatcher, L. B. Fulwiler, Sister M. L. Harig, B. Scrivner; incidental observations in works that principally consider vocabulary, idiom, syntax, and structure, such as those by Norman E. Eliason and Ralph W. V. Elliott.

Studies of particular kinds of imagery are stimulating. Strains of religious imagery are considered by Rodney Delasanta, Paul M. Clogan, David E. Lampe, James I. Wimsatt, Joseph R. Millichap, Kenneth A. Bleeth, and Roy J. Pearcy; musical imagery by David L. Higdon, Jesse M. Gellrich and others; medical and scientific imagery by Joseph E. Grennen and Stephan Kohl. Imagery of various kinds is considered mostly in relation to the *Canterbury Tales* by Christopher Dean, Edmund Reiss, R. E. Kaske, Ann S. Haskell, Emerson Brown Jr., John Block Friedman, John Leyerle, George D. Economou, and others. In *Troilus*, imagery relating to bondage, the eyes, recurrent circular figures, cosmic and eschatological iconography, is profitably explored by Stephen R. Barney, Donald R. Howard, Sam Schuman, and Michael E. Cotton. Sexual imagery has come in for attention in a book by Thomas W. Ross and in articles. At the *MLA* convention in 1976 a session on "Thwarted Sexuality in Chaucer's Works," with Donaldson, Howard, Ridley, and Rowland as speakers, gave some consideration to such imagery. Ross's contention that secondary bawdy meanings are often confirmed by clusters of associated words is illustrated in the findings of Haldeen Braddy, John Bugge, Stephen Manning, and Paula Neuss, and the imagery of the mill, a subject which I first discussed in 1965 in connection with the Wife's proverb, has given rise to several articles. In considerations more peripheral to our subject, solutions to long-standing cruxes are offered by Heiner Gillmeister, Alfred David, Ross and others.

Although many have explored the complex sophistication of Chaucer's imagery in relation to the total meaning and artistic effect, critics making general observations on Chaucer's figurative language tend to stress its commonplaceness, usually relating it, as Spearing does, to the exigencies of oral delivery. Nevill Coghill would deny Chaucer much trade in "ambivalence and play of words . . . it is his custom to use language clearly and decisively rather than suggestively and by opalescence" (p. 117). On the other hand, Charles Muscatine who, in common with J. A. W. Bennett (p. 116), draws attention to similes of rural familiarity in Chaucer, finds the simplicity less than skin deep. However, while John Burrow in 1971 said that we were still waiting for the inquiry into the art and language of Chaucer originally proposed by F. R. Leavis (p. 4), and Akio Oizumi calls for a closer analysis of imagery, Muscatine feels that New Criticism applied to medieval poetry has in itself "reached a dead end." He would subsume the study of imagery in stylistic analysis which "can describe a text, from its syntax and imagery through its narrative form and total structure (not to speak of many other possible stylistic categories), with a new position and concreteness" (*Poetry and Crisis*, p. 4).

Yet it seems to me that interpretations of imagery crucial to the understanding of the work are still capable of reassessment and that, in some instances, the meaning of even a single figurative expression can be crucial to our understanding. For example, despite the lack of philological support, editors assume that "bacoun" (*WB Prol* D418) means "old meat and therefore old men," and that the Wife is declaring that she takes no pleasure in her three elderly spouses. However, in the fabliau of *Le Meunier et Les .II. Clers*, the clerk, when urging his companion to go to bed with the Miller's daughter, says "pren du bacon ta part" (265). If Chaucer is using this very old, established metaphor, the portrayal of the Wife becomes more complex than most critics have allowed.

In different ways and to varying degrees, recent studies such as those by Donald R. Howard and Robert B. Burlin offer proof of the continuing vitality of the study of imagery. As one critic remarks, "Reading a poem intelligently is . . . one of the hardest things on earth to do." Imagery is not necessarily integrating, but in Chaucer's poems a sensitive understanding of the imagery is important to our interpretation of the whole work.

BIBLIOGRAPHY

Baldwin, Ralph. *The Unity of the 'Canterbury Tales'*. Anglistica, 5. Copenhagen: Rosenkilde og Bagger, 1955.

Barney, Stephen R. "Troilus Bound." *Speculum*, 47 (1972), 445-58.

Baugh, Albert C., ed. *Chaucer's Major Poetry*. New York: Appleton-Century-Crofts, 1963.

Baum, Paull F. "Chaucer's Nautical Metaphors." *SAQ*, 49 (1950), 67-73.

———. *Chaucer: A Critical Appreciation*. Durham, N.C.: Duke Univ. Press, 1958.

Bennett, J.A.W. *The Parlement of Foules: An Interpretation*. Oxford: Clarendon, 1957.

————. *Chaucer at Oxford and Cambridge.* Toronto: Univ. of Toronto Press, 1974.

Birney, Earle. " 'After his Ymage': The Central Ironies of the 'Friar's Tale'." *MS*, 21 (1959), 17-35.

————. "Chaucer's 'Gentil' Manciple and His 'Gentil' Tale." *NM*, 61 (1960), 257-67.

————. "The Inhibited and the Uninhibited: Ironic Structure in the 'Miller's Tale'." *Neophil*, 44 (1960), 333-38.

————. "Structural Irony Within the *Summoner's Tale*." *Anglia*, 78 (1960), 204-18.

Bleeth, Kenneth A. "The Image of Paradise in the *Merchant's Tale*." In *The Learned and the Lewed*. Studies in Chaucer and Medieval Literature. Harvard English Studies 5. Cambridge, Mass.: Harvard Univ. Press, 1974, pp. 45-60.

Braddy, Haldeen. "Chaucer's Bawdy Tongue." *SFQ*, 30 (1966), 214-22.

————. "Chaucer's Bilingual Idiom." *SFQ*, 32 (1968), 1-6.

Brewer, D.S. "The Relationship of Chaucer to the English and European Traditions." In *Chaucer and Chaucerians: Critical Studies in Middle English Literature*. Ed. D.S. Brewer. London: Nelson, 1966, pp. 1-38.

Brown, Emerson, Jr. "*The Merchant's Tale: Januarie's 'Unlikely Elde'*." *NM*, 74 (1973), 92-106.

Bugge, John. "Damyan's Wanton *Clyket* and an Ironic New *Twiste* to the *Merchant's Tale*." *AnM*, 14 (1973), 53-62.

Burlin, Robert B. *Chaucerian Fiction.* Princeton, N.J.: Princeton Univ. Press, 1977.

Burrow, J.A. "Chaucer." In *English Poetry: Select Bibliographical Guide*. Ed. A.E. Dyson. London: Oxford Univ. Press, 1971, pp. 1-14.

Clemen, Wolfgang. *Chaucer's Early Poetry.* Trans. C.A.M. Sym. London: Methuen, 1963.

Clogan, Paul M. "The Figural Style and Meaning of *The Second Nun's Prologue and Tale*." *M&H*, 3 (1972), 213-40.

Coghill, Nevill. "Chaucer's Narrative Art in *The Canterbury Tales*." In *Chaucer and Chaucerians*. Ed. D.S. Brewer. London: Nelson: 1966, pp. 114-39.

Cotton, Michael E. "The Artistic Integrity of Chaucer's *Troilus and Criseyde*." *ChauR*, 7 (1972), 37-43.

David, Alfred. "Literary Satire in the *House of Fame*." *PMLA*, 75 (1960), 333-39.

Dean, Christopher. "Imagery in the *Knight's Tale* and the *Miller's Tale*." *MS*, 31 (1969), 149-63.

Delasanta, Rodney. "Christian Affirmation in *The Book of the Duchess*." *PMLA*, 84 (1969), 245-51.

Donaldson, E. Talbot. "Idiom of Popular Poetry in the *Miller's Tale*." In *Speaking of Chaucer*. New York: Norton, 1972, pp. 13-29.

Economou, George D. "Chaucer's use of the Bird in the Cage Image in the *Canterbury Tales*." *PQ* (1975), 679-84.

Eliason, Norman E. *The Language of Chaucer's Poetry: An Appraisal of the Verse, Style, and Structure*. Anglistica, 17. Copenhagen: Rosenkilde og Bagger, 1972.

Elliott, Ralph W.V. *The World of Chaucer's Idiom: Chaucer's English*. London: Deutsch, 1974.

Everett, Dorothy. "Some Reflections on Chaucer's 'Art poetical'." *PBA*, 36 (1950). Rpt. In *Essays on Middle English Literature*. Ed. P.M. Kean. Oxford: Clarendon Press, 1955, pp. 149-74.

Faral, Edmond. *Les arts poétiques du XIIe et du XIIIe siècle*. 1924. Rpt. Paris: E. Champion, 1958.

Friedman, John Block. "The *Nun's Priest's Tale*: The Preacher and the Mermaid's Song." *ChauR*, 7 (1973), 250-66.

Frye, Northrop. *Anatomy of Criticism*. Princeton: Princeton Univ. Press, 1957.

Fulwiler, Lavon Buster. "Image Progressions in Chaucer's Poetry: Exposition of a Theory of Creativity." Diss. Michigan State Univ., 1971.

Gellrich, Jesse M. "The Parody of Medieval Music in the *Miller's Tale*." *JEGP*, 73 (1974), 176-88.

Gillmeister, Heiner. "The Origin of Imperative Constructions and Chaucer's Nonce-words, *viritoot, virytrate,* and *phislyas.*" *Poetica,* 4 (1975), 24-49.

Grennen, Joseph E. "Chaucerian Portraiture: Medicine and the Monk." *NM,* 69 (1968), 569-74.

Hallissy, Margaret Mary Duggan. "Poison Imagery and Theme in Chaucer's *Canterbury Tales.*" Diss. Fordham Univ., 1974.

Harig, Sister Mary Labouré. "The Study of the Literary Garden Tradition and Chaucer." Diss. Case Western Reserve Univ., 1971.

Haskell, Ann S. "The Golden Ambiguity of the *Canterbury Tales.*" *Erasmus Review,* 1 (1971), 1-9.

Hatcher, John Southall. "Chaucer's Imagery." Diss. Univ. of Georgia, 1968.

Higdon, David L. "Diverse Melodies in Chaucer's 'General Prologue'." *Criticism,* 14 (1972), 97-108.

Hoffman, Arthur W. "Chaucer's Prologue to Pilgrimage: The Two Voices." *ELH,* 21 (1954), 1-16.

Howard, Donald R. "Introduction." In *Troilus and Criseyde and Selected Short Poems.* Ed. Donald R. Howard and James Dean. New York: Signet, New American Library (1976), pp. xxxi-xxxiii.

———. *The Idea of the Canterbury Tales.* Berkeley: Univ. of California Press, 1976.

Huppé, Bernard F. *A Reading of the Canterbury Tales.* Albany, N.Y.: State Univ. of New York, 1964.

———, and D. W. Robertson, Jr. *Fruyt and Chaf: Studies in Chaucer's Allegories.* Princeton: Princeton Univ. Press, 1963.

Jordan, Robert M. "Chaucer's Sense of Illusion: Roadside Drama Reconsidered." *ELH,* 29 (1962), 19-33.

Kaske, R.E. "Patristic Exegesis: The Defense." In *Critical Approaches to Medieval Literature.* Ed. Dorothy Bethurum. New York: Columbia Univ. Press, 1960, pp. 27-60.

———. "The *Canticum Canticorum* in the *Miller's Tale.*" *SP,* 59 (1962), 479-500.

———. "Horn and Ivory in the *Summoner's Tale.*" *NM,* 73 (1972), 122-26.

Klaeber, Friedrich. *Das Bild bei Chaucer*. Berlin: R. Heinrich, 1893.

Kohl, Stephan. *Wissenschaft und Dichtung bei Chaucer. Dargestellt hauptsächlich am Beispiel der Medizin.* Studienreihe Humanitas. Frankfurt am Main: Akademische Verlagsgesellschaft, 1973.

Koonce, B.G. *Chaucer and the Tradition of Fame: Symbolism in the House of Fame.* Princeton: Princeton Univ. Press, 1966.

Lampe, David E. "The Truth of a 'Vache': The Homely Homily of Chaucer's 'Truth'." *PLL*, 9 (1973), 311-14.

Lewis, C.S. *The Allegory of Love: A Study in Medieval Tradition.* 1936. Rpt. New York: Oxford Univ. Press, 1958.

Leyerle, John. "The Heart and the Chain." In *The Learned and the Lewed: Studies in Chaucer and Medieval Literature.* Ed. Larry D. Benson, Cambridge, Mass.: Harvard Univ. Press, 1974, pp. 113-45.

Manly, John Matthews. "Chaucer and the Rhetoricians." *PBA,* 12 (1926). Rpt. In *Chaucer Criticism I; The Canterbury Tales.* Ed. R.J. Shoeck and J. Taylor. Notre Dame, Ind.: Univ. of Notre Dame Press, 1960.

———. *Some New Light on Chaucer.* 1926. Rpt. New York: P. Smith, 1952.

Manning, Stephen. "Chaucer's Pardoner: Sex and Non-sex." *SAB,* 39 (1974), 17-26.

Meech, Sanford B. "Figurative Contrasts in Chaucer's *Troilus and Criseyde*." *EIE, 1950.* Ed. A.S. Downer. New York: Columbia Univ. Press, 1951, pp. 57-88.

———. *Design in Chaucer's Troilus.* 1959. Rpt. New York: Greenwood Press, 1970.

Middle English Dictionary, Ed. Hans Kurath and Sherman M. Kuhn. Ann Arbor: Univ. of Michigan Press, 1952-.

Millichap, Joseph R. "Transubstantiation in the *Pardoner's Tale*." *BRMMLA,* 28 (1974), 102-8.

Muscatine, Charles. "Form, Texture and Meaning in Chaucer's *Knight's Tale*." *PMLA,* 65 (1950), 911-29.

———. *Chaucer and the French Tradition: A Study in Style and Meaning.* Berkeley: Univ. of California Press, 1957.

———. "*The Canterbury Tales:* Style of the Man and Style of the Work." In *Chaucer and Chaucerians: Critical Studies in Middle English Literature.* Ed. D.S. Brewer. London: Nelson, 1966, pp. 88-113.

———. *Poetry and Crisis in the Age of Chaucer.* Notre Dame, Ind.: Univ. of Notre Dame Press, 1972.

Neuss, Paula. "Double Meanings: 1. *Double Entendre* in the *Miller's Tale.*" *EIC,* 24 (1974), 325-40.

Oizumi, Akio. "The World of Chaucer's Idiom." [Review Article.] *Poetica,* 5 (1976), 74-81.

Owen, Charles A., Jr. "The Crucial Passages in Five of the *Canterbury Tales*: A Study in Irony and Symbol." *JEGP,* 52 (1953), 294-311.

Payne, Robert O. *The Key of Remembrance: A Study of Chaucer's Poetics.* 1963. Rpt. Westport, Conn.: Greenwood Press, 1973.

Pearcy, Roy J. "Does the Manciple's Prologue Contain a Reference to Hell's Mouth?" *ELN,* 11 (1974), 167-75.

Peltola, Niilo. "Chaucer's Summoner: Fyr-reed Cherubynnes Face." *NM,* 69 (1968), 560-68.

Preminger, Alex, Frank J. Warnke, and O.B. Hardison, Jr., eds. *Encyclopedia of Poetry and Poetics.* Princeton: Princeton Univ. Press, 1965.

Reiss, Edmund. "The Symbolic Surface of the *Canterbury Tales*: The Monk's Portrait." *ChauR,* 2 (1968), 254-72; 3 (1968), 12-28.

Richardson, Janette. *Blameth Nat Me: A Study of Imagery in Chaucer's Fabliaux* .The Hague: Mouton, 1970.

Robertson, D.W., Jr. "Historical Criticism." *EIE, 1950.* Ed. A.S. Downer. New York: Columbia Univ. Press, 1951, pp. 3-31.

———. *A Preface to Chaucer: Studies in Medieval Perspectives.* Princeton: Princeton Univ. Press, 1962.

———. See under Huppé, Bernard F.

Ross, Thomas W. *Dictionary of Chaucer's Bawdy.* New York: Dutton, 1972.

———. "Chaucer's *Friar's Tale*, D 1377 and 1573." *Expl*, 34 (1975), 17.

Rowland, Beryl. "The Wife of Bath's Prologue, D.389." *Explicator*, 24 (1965), 14.

———. "Chaucers She-Ape (*The Parson's Tale*, 424)." *ChauR*, 2 (1968), 159-65.

———. *Blind Beasts: Chaucer's Animal World*. Kent, Ohio: Kent State Univ. Press, 1971.

———. "Chaucer's Dame Alys: Critics in Blunderland?" In *Studies Presented to Tauno F. Mustanoja on the Occasion of His Sixtieth Birthday*. NM, 73 (1972), 381-95.

———. "The Wife of Bath's "Unlawfull Philtrum'," *Neophil*, 56 (1972), 201-06.

———. "Chaucer's Idea of the Pardoner." *ChauR*, forthcoming.

Ruggiers, Paul G. *The Art of the Canterbury Tales*. Madison: Univ. of Wisconsin Press, 1965.

Saito, Mother Masako. R.S.C.J. "The Archetype of Bondage: Five Clusters of Imagery in the *Canterbury Tales*." Diss. Fordham Univ., 1964.

Schaar, Claes. *The Golden Mirror: Studies in Chaucer's Descriptive Technique and Its Literary Background*. Lund: Gleerup, 1955.

Schuman, Samuel. "The Circle of Nature: Patterns of Imagery in Chaucer's *Troilus and Criseyde*." *ChauR*, 10 (1975), 99-112.

Scrivner, Buford, Jr. "Chaucer's Early Poetry: A Study of Imagery in Relation to Theme and Structure." Diss. Florida State Univ., 1972.

Silverman, Albert H. "Sex and Money in Chaucer's *Shipman's Tale*." *PQ*, 32 (1953), 329-36.

Spearing, A.C. *Criticism and Medieval Poetry*. 1964. 2nd ed. London: Arnold, 1972.

Tatlock, J.S.P., and Arthur G. Kennedy. *A Concordance to the Complete Works of Geoffrey Chaucer and to the Romaunt of the Rose*. 1927. Rpt. Gloucester, Mass.: P. Smith, 1963.

Tuve, Rosemond. *Elizabethan and Metaphysical Imagery: Renaissance Poetic and Twentieth-Century Critics.* Chicago: Univ. of Chicago Press, 1947.

———. *Allegorical Imagery: Some Mediaeval Books and Their Posterity.* Princeton: Princeton Univ. Press, 1966.

Wellek, René, and Austin Warren. *Theory of Literature.* 1942. Rpt. New York: Harcourt Brace, 1956.

Whiting, B.J. *Chaucer's Use of Proverbs.* 1934. Rpt. New York: AMS Press, 1973.

Wimsatt, James I. "Chaucer and the Canticle of Canticles." In *Chaucer the Love Poet.* Ed. J. Mitchell and W. Provost. Athens: Univ. of Georgia Press, 1973, pp. 66-90.

Wood, Chauncey. *Chaucer and the Country of the Stars: Poetic Uses of Astrological Imagery.* Princeton: Princeton Univ. Press, 1970.

SEVEN

HALDEEN BRADDY

The French Influence
on Chaucer

From early youth Londoner Chaucer lived amid a royal company of dukes like Lionel of Antwerp and John of Gaunt (Ghent) and their duchesses Elizabeth of Ulster and Blanche of Lancaster who admired the love-vision poetry originating in twelfth-century France. John Gower wrote in both English and French, and Chaucer's close friend Sir Richard Stury also prized Continental literature since he owned a copy of the popular *Roman de la rose*. It was this famous thirteenth-century French work, initiated by Guillaume de Lorris and later continued by Jean de Meun, which Chaucer began to anglicize as the *Romaunt of the Rose*, a work which influenced such diverse pieces as the *Book of the Duchess*, the *Legend of Good Women*, *Troilus and Criseyde*, and the *Canterbury Tales*. Muscatine, concerned more with style and manner than verbal echo, discussed Chaucer's dependence on Lorris for courtly lyricism and Meun for bourgeois and comic realism (pp. 41-57, 67-71). In Jones's anthology Eustache Deschamps' well-known *Ballade* (*A Geffroy Chaucier*) extols the contemporary Chaucer as "Grant translateur" and lauds his translation of "*la Rose*" (pp. 22-3).

Deschamps' reference in the *Ballade* to "Pandras," a name hitherto connected with the legendary Greek king Pandrasus,

Lerch construed as a variant spelling of Chaucer's Pandarus (pp. 67-8). Now in "The Story of Troilus" Lumiansky showed that Boccaccio's *Il Filostrato* was not the sole generator of the English *Troilus* (pp. 727-33). Pratt's additional proofs are of prime importance. In demonstrating that the Londoner utilized a French prose rendering of the Italian masterpiece, Pratt declared that *Le roman de Troilus* (as he wrote the present author that he would now entitle it) "gave Chaucer a wealth of additional material to consider . . ." and that "Chaucer clearly benefited from the lushness, variety, and delicacy of the translator's reworking of Boccaccio" (p. 539). All this rather enhances the plausibility of Lerch's arresting identification inasmuch as Deschamps would more readily link French than Italian with Chaucer, who never mentions Boccaccio. In eulogizing "Chaucier" as a "grant translateur," Deschamps must have had in mind English reshapings of French manuscripts besides the *Roman de la rose*.

For yet another similar reshaping, Dédeck-Héry established in two articles on "Jean de Meun et Chaucer" and "Le Boèce de Chaucer" that the English prose text often leans more heavily on the French than the original Latin of *De consolatione philosophiae* by Boethius (pp. 967-91; pp. 18-25). Dédeck-Héry's discoveries relate importantly to the French influence on Chaucer, whose major and minor works borrowed almost as extensively from Meun's *Consolation* as from his *Roman*. Boethian ideas on predestination or free will and on the mutability of world and time appear in *Troilus and Criseyde* (Book IV), the *Nun's Priest's Tale* (Chauntecleer's discussion), and the *Knight's Tale* (Theseus' final speech); and similarly derived sentiments on various topics occur in *The Former Age*, *Truth*, and *Fortune*. In fact, when both Latin and French texts existed, the Englishman as a rule exhibited a preference for French, as is likewise evident with his handling of Ovid and Lucan. Three decades ago Meech recognized Chaucer's reliance on the *Ovide moralisé* (pp. 182-204), and Robinson noted that the poet in the *Man of Law's Tale* (400) and the *Monk's Tale* (2671) had recourse for Lucan to Jehan de Tuim's *Li hystore de Julius Cesar* (pp. 694, 710, 750). Though the ratio between all borrowings from Latin and Italian authors and all those from their French translators has not yet been investigated, Chaucer's dependence on French appears somewhat more widespread than generally believed. In his chapter in Bryan and Dempster's *Sources and Analogues* Severs underlined this point when he showed that Chaucer in the *Clerk's Tale*, traditionally linked with Petrarch's Latin version of Boccaccio's Italian plot, drew the larger quotient of his phrasing from an hitherto unknown French manuscript (pp. 288-331).

With the *Book of the Duchess,* Chaucer developed from a translator into an author, albeit a highly derivative one. Still under the spell of the *Roman,* he now read such other contemporaries as Deschamps, Machaut, Jean Froissart, and Oton de Graunson, all of whom he probably knew personally, the first two from his numerous journeys across the Channel and the other two both on the Continent and in England. For the episode of Seys and Alcyone (48 ff.), which once may have existed independently, the ultimate source was Ovid's *Metamorphoses* (XI, 410 ff.), but Chaucer also may have read Deschamps' *ballade* no. 35 on "Ceix et Alcione." Braddy observed in "Three Chaucer Notes" that Ovid and Deschamps alike describe the storm and shipwreck, whereas Machaut, whom Chaucer principally follows, does not mention them (p. 96). In "The Sources of 'The Book of the Duchess'," Severs reviewed Chaucer's heavy debt to the anonymous vision *Le songe vert* and some dozen pieces by Machaut: *Le dit de la fontaine amoureuse, Le dit dou lyon, Le dit dou vergier, Le lay de confort, Le remède de fortune,* the third, eighth, and ninth *Motets,* the first *Complainte, Le jugement dou roy de Navarre,* and especially *Le jugement dou roy de Behaingne* (p. 355). Severs added that Froissart's *L'espinette amoureuse* comments like the *Duchess* on lovers too sick with yearning to know what is wrong with them (p. 357). This new link was worth making since Froissart, who mentions Chaucer in his prose *Chroniques,* visited England and, as Anderson recalled in "Blanche, Duchess of Lancaster," mourned her death in his own

Le joli buisson de jonece (p. 159). Although mindful that Graunson wrote two complaints foreshadowing the theme of the *Duchess*, Severs concluded his survey with the observation that *Le songe vert* explains all such specific essentials as a dream-vision involving a lost lady, a knight clad in black, and a mourner bent on self-destruction until dissuaded from his folly (p. 362). French influences are nowhere stronger than in Chaucer's elegy on Blanche.

The *Parliament of Fowls,* though deeply affected by French, Italian, and Latin literature, is a much more original dream-vision than the derivative *Duchess.* The poet no longer lifts long passages or crucial details from French masters as he had earlier. His allegorical abstractions represent the conventions of the *Roman;* his complimentary language, a commonplace of the English court. The council of birds, with ultimate origins in the Orient, had many medieval counterparts in French poetry. Braddy pointed out in *Chaucer and the French Poet Graunson* that a handy example of the Saint Valentine's Day setting, a less hackneyed mechanism, existed in *Le songe saint Valentin* by Graunson, a French devotee of the Cult, who long sojourned in London (pp. 65-6). Since Graunson was a close friend, Chaucer would naturally be interested in reading *Le songe.* Like Chaucer's bird allegory, *Le songe* features a dream-vision, a convocation of birds, the selection of mates for Valentine, and the failure of one female bird to choose a lover —all the primary machinery, in other words, not already familiar to Chaucer in the sources underlying the *Duchess.* As Braddy further remarked, the veiled allegory suspected in the *Parliament,* though not as patent as the personal application of the *Duchess* to Blanche, had a French antecedent in Graunson's unmistakable direction of *Le souhait de saint Valentin* to his *amie* Isabel, whose name he spells acrostically (p. 73). No similar acrostic decorates the *Parliament,* but its English author may mean that the locale of his allegory is France by a double entendre in "The note, I trowe, imaked was in Fraunce" (677). The matter can not be fully explicated by identifying the "note" with the words "*Quien bien aime a tard oublie,*" written in several manuscripts, since the French verse agrees with Machaut's octosyllabic lines but does not match with Chaucer pentameter verses. The English roundel, "Now welcome, somer, with thy sonne softe" (680), follows, as Moore said in "Chaucer's Use of Lyric," the precedent of Machaut's terminal roundel in *La fontaine amoureuse* (p. 41). It would be short-sighted to picture Chaucer as unimaginatively perusing French authors, copying and paraphrasing them, and picking a word and phrase here or there without at the same time being impressed by the occasion for which they wrote. The *Duchess*, it is clear, was meant for Duke John; the lost *Book of the Lion*, as Dear suggested, possibly for Duke Lionel, whom Froissart called "monseigneur Lion" (p. 105); and the *Parliament*, as Braddy claimed, probably for King Richard and Princess Marie, whose betrothal Chaucer went to France in 1377 to negotiate (p. 85).

Love-visions *à la française* still lodged in Chaucer's mind when he composed the Italianate *House of Fame*, but here one finds the author handling with increasing freedom dream-lore evolving from the authority of the *Roman*. With Chaucer's likely obligations to his early *maîtres* (together with such newer ones as Renaud de Beaujeu and Nicole de Margival) already known, Estrich advanced the proposition that Dido's complaint about the integrity of men, especially the division of men's interests into fame, friendship, and harlotry came to Chaucer from Provençal *via* the poet Daude de Pradas (pp. 344-5). This new proposal about Provençal material can not be lightly dismissed on geographical grounds since it is now known that the English ambassador in 1366 traveled through the Midi en route to Spain. The total content of these proposed pilferings still looms less impressive as literary influence than the simple form of the dream-vision which Chaucer introduced from France. Clemen considered the fragmentary *House of Fame* as a typical work of the Londoner's transitional period, as a poem with new content presented within an old framework (p. 114).

The *Legend of Good Women*, last of the four chief love-visions, may employ Graunson slightly in one or two legends, but the

Prologue itself adopts from Machaut, Deschamps, and Froissart the cult of the *marguerite* (daisy). Chaucer's *Prologue* (in F and G versions) introduces for its central theme a discussion between the two orders of the Leaf and the Flower, in which extravagant fiction the God of Love condemns Chaucer for defaming women in his translation of the *Roman* as well as in *Troilus*. As an act of contrition, he now must indite a legendry of Cupid's heroines who were "good" because they observed the religion of Love. The Middle Ages, Pearsall recalled, esteemed the daisy as the symbol of true womanhood in its humility, its purity, and its following the light of the sun (pp. 20-1). To the *marguerite* pieces by Deschamps, Froissart, and Machaut, Smith added that the English ballade on Absolon (249) has its basis in Froissart's *ballade* no. 6 (p. 30). In a judicious survey, Tatlock counted more borrowings from the three French poets in Chaucer's F *Prologue* than in the G (p. 73); and Galway conjectured that the G *Prologue* was revised to compliment Richard II's child queen, Isabel of France, for May, 1397 (p. 280). Beyond these observations, there has been no proposal as to when Chaucer gained access to the French poems on the daisy nor new proof that such pieces were included in the material Deschamps sent to Chaucer by Sir Lewis Clifford.

In the *Legend* itself, the problem of measuring French elements is complicated once more by the fact that several sources, including Latin and Italian, were available to Chaucer. Most of the vignettes betray their Ovidian heredity, but Chaucer had access to an anonymous French redaction of the Latin *Metamorphoses* known as *Ovide moralisé*. In investigations by Huppé and Robertson (p. 41, n. 12) and by Meech (pp. 183, 188-9, 204), one encounters hints that several works by Chaucer may have been influenced by the frenchified Ovid. With it, one may compare descriptions of the cave and streams in Alcyone's dream in the *Duchess*, a passage anent Theseus and Ariadne in the *House of Fame* (405-26), the dawn song of Ninus' daughter in Book v of the *Troilus*, as well as the legends themselves of Ariadne, Philomela, and possibly Thisbe. Finally, Chaucer's favorable attitude toward Medea and his championing of Lucrece may have been prompted, as Braddy suggested, by Graunson's two ballades in praise of Medea and in defense of Lucrece (pp. 66-7). All of Chaucer's four principal love-visions must be characterized as predominantly French in manner and only somewhat less so in subject matter.

In the unfinished *Anelida and Arcite*, a perplexing exercise at best, French strains intersperse plot matter based otherwise on Italian and Latin precursors. The interspersions comprise a proverb found in the thirteenth-century poem *La pleurechante*, two references to the ubiquitous *Roman*, the device of internal rhyme *à la française*, and a complaint similar to Machaut's *Le lay de plour*. The further presence of symbolic colors after the usage of Machaut's *Le remède de fortune* (white for joyful, red for ardent, and green for disloyal) composes another aspect of the poet's French manner. In "Three Chaucer Notes" Braddy pointed out that when Arcite "falsed fair Anelida the quene" the Theban knight "cladde him in her hewe—/Wot I not whethir in white, rede, or grene?" (*Anel*, 145 ff.), by which passage the poet symbolized Arcite's disloyalty, associating his "hewe" with colors other than blue for faithful (p. 92). It has become traditional to dismiss *Anelida* as a composition in the French manner with a setting from Boccaccio, which is an honest summation of what little is presently known about the fragment.

In turning now to Chaucer's shorter pieces, an assortment of such French forms as ballades, complaints, envoys, and roundels, echoes from France again ring clear. *An A B C* freely renders a hymn to the Virgin from Guillaume de Deguileville's *Le pèlerinage de la vie humaine*; *Against Women Unconstant* reproduces the fads of Machaut; the two complaints to Pity and to his Lady, the apostrophes *To Rosemounde* and to *Womanly Noblesse*, and *Lenvoy a Scogan* exhibit Chaucer as a master of the French style, without disclosing which exact Continental originals he imported. But in *A Complaint to his Lady* Chaucer calls his mistress "swete fo" (37), which is the same phrase, Braddy discovered (p. 67), that Graunson wrote in a ballade, namely, "tresdoulce ennemye."

Although the authorship of *Complaynt D'Amours* remains contested, its title is French enough. In addition Chaucer wrote, his Retraction says, "many a song and many a leccherous lay" (1086). These too, according to Moore in "Chaucer's Lost Songs," no doubt imitated the fashions of France, especially the lyrics of Deschamps (p. 208). Two short valentines also belong here. No source has been proposed for *The Complaint of Mars*, which Stillwell found to resemble Graunson's *Songe saint Valentin* in form and mood (p. 79). In a companionate complaint on Venus, Chaucer praises his valentine inspirer, Graunson, as "flour of hem that make in Fraunce" (*Ven*, 82). But Graunson's three ballades, as Braddy observed, speak from a man's point of view; Chaucer's complaint, from a lady's (p. 64). *The Complaint of Venus*, which reproduces the French passage on jealousy and paraphrases the others, retains Graunson's triple theme of the lover's worthiness, jealousy, and constancy. Although Chaucer refers to the scarcity of rhyme in English and the "curiosite" of Graunson (*Ven*, 81), the ten-line English envoy outshines Sir Oton by limiting itself to only two rhymes.

Three of the four remaining shorter pieces involve the possibility of multiple origins. Deschamps' *ballade* no. 823 ("*contre ceux qui se remarient*") bids fittingly as partial inspiration for *Lenvoy de Chaucer a Bukton*, but *The Complaint of Chaucer to his Purse*, whose conclusion Smith compared with Froissart's *ballade* no. 21 (pp. 31-2), could be based on either Machaut's begging poem to John II of France or Deschamps' later petition to Charles VI. Braddy noted in the triple roundel *Merciles Beaute* (which includes verses reminiscent of a roundel by Guillaume d'Amiens, a ballade by the Duc de Berry, and *ballade* no. 570 by Deschamps) that Chaucer's remarks on Daunger and Pitee (16, 20) and the opening verse, "Your yen two wol slee me sodenly," are matched by Graunson's terms Dangier and Pitie and his chanson opening with "*Mon cueur est sailly par mes yeulx*" (p. 67). Although the shorter poems have received slight notice in recent scholarship, Braddy in "The Date of Chaucer's *Lak of Steadfastnesse*," interpreted the English protest as a remonstrance against Richard II's loose governorship and linked it with the Boethian pessimism of Deschamps, counseller of princes, who wrote admonitory ballades to Charles VI of France (pp. 483-7). All the miscellaneous shorter pieces testify, like the translations and the love-visions, to the pervasiveness of French influences in Chaucer's minor poetry.

To trace French influences in Chaucer's masterpiece, the *Canterbury Tales*, one has Bryan and Dempster's compilation of chapters by various scholars, *Sources and Analogues*. In this volume, one finds that the *General Prologue* has a framework similar to Sercambi's Italian *Novelle*. In addition, H. S. V. Jones earlier noted in "The Plan of the *Canterbury Tales*" that Chaucer opens with a pilgrimage which may have been suggested partly from *Le pèlerinage* by Deguileville (p. 46), whom the Englishman freely translated in *An A B C*. But Clawson observed that Chaucer, who resided in Kent for some time after 1385-6, hardly required literary suggestions for the idea of stories told by pilgrims on the road to Canterbury (p. 145). As for the types of pilgrims themselves, a popular French antecedent existed in *Le roman de Troie* by Benoît de Sainte-Maure. The question arose, however, of the degree of Chaucer's reliance on this source as a working pattern, with Pratt and Young holding the portrayals by Benoît and his successors to be "much too limited in social variety and in realistic detail" (*Sources and Analogues*, p. 5). In "Benoît's Portraits" Lumiansky thereupon reasserted the connections between *Le roman de Troie* and Chaucer, declaring that this authority on Troy afforded Chaucer such touches as structural grouping of characters by family and sex, the juxtaposition of personages to point up contrasts, and the interspersions amid the sketches of direct personal comments by the narrator himself (pp. 433-4, 436). Moreover, as Jones observed, some thirty different classes of people (approximately Chaucer's number) appear as gamblers, parasites, tavern keepers, and so on in *Le livre de l'example du riche homme et du ladre*. As for Chaucer's penchant to criticize, his technique may be equated, Jones continued, with the style of the French character books, because the acid Canterbury vignettes

link with a form of Continental social satire readily accessible in
Deschamps' *Estas du monde* and in Jean de Condé's *Dis des estas
du monde*, which attacks justices, knights, prelates, princes,
squires, and (possibly in anticipation of the Wife of Bath) the
estate of married folk. Jones stated in conclusion that Chaucer
accompanied his pilgrims to Becket's shrine in the fashion of the
Renclus de Moiliens' travel book, *Le roman de carité* (pp. 45-6).
The patent contrast in the *Canterbury Tales* between lower and
upper societies resembles contrasts made by French poets, from
whom Chaucer garnered many of his stylistic mannerisms.

To move to the gallery of English pilgrims, Brewer speculated
that the Knight represents King John of France (p. 156), and
Mitchell, following Bowden (p. 55), held out for Pierre de Lusig-
nan, King of Cyprus (pp. 68-9). Historical identifications are
possible, but so are literary ones. Lumiansky accordingly con-
tended in "Benoît's Portraits" that the Knight-Squire descriptions
came from the Frenchman's Hector-Troilus sketches (p. 437), just
as the Squire, the Wife of Bath, and the Pardoner sketches derived
from Meun's depiction in the *Roman* of the debonair lover, La
Vieille, and Faux-Semblant. In many details and special usages of
style, the *Roman* served as a quenchless reservoir, namely the
Yeoman's "takel," the Prioress's dainty manners, the Monk's
oyster equation, the Friar's hypocrisy, the Clerk's "courtepy," the
Sergeant of Law's "ceint of silk," and the Doctor of Physic's
"Pers." Slaughter even revived and reinforced the old notion that
Chaucer conceived Pandarus in terms of the Friend in Meun's
Roman (p. 194). French parallels have been urged for numerous
other Chaucerian ideas, words, and passages; but the *General
Prologue*, interlaced as it is with literary echoes from many languages, stands out as perhaps the most original of all Chaucer's
compositions, certainly more so than the majority of the stories it
introduces.

In discussing foreign influences on the twenty-four entries com-
prising the *Canterbury Tales*, one becomes aware that French
culture had mingled so much with English that Chaucer now
tended to reshape his manuscript materials to his own original

ends and no longer rested content to imitate Continental fashions as obviously as he had in the *Book of the Duchess*. Nonetheless twenty-one of the twenty-four have literary associations with France. The *Manciple's Tale* has a tie with Machaut's *Le Livre du voir dit*. The *Franklin's Tale* in part recalls the Breton *lay*. The *Man of Law's Tale* bases its saga of Constance on an Anglo-Norman version by Nicholas Trivet but probably depended as well on certain passages in Gower's *Confessio Amantis* (II, 587 ff.). Elsewhere Chaucer handles his source materials more freely. Debts to French literature in his individualized types of narratives are nevertheless readily detectable and impressive when given in a mathematical proportion. Eighteen more tales show some reliance on writers from across the Channel. Of these eighteen, eight reveal moderate influence and ten, slight. The eight with marked indebtedness cover tales or their prologues by the Wife of Bath, Summoner, Clerk, Merchant, Physician, Monk, Nun's Priest, and Melibee; the ten with small or theoretical dependence, tales by the Friar, Squire, Pardoner, Sir Thopas, Manciple, Parson, Miller, Reeve, Cook, and Shipman.

To begin with the first group, the *Roman* and Deschamps' *Le miroir de mariage* account for the discussion of marriage sovereignty in the *Wife of Bath's Prologue*, and Lumiansky in "Aspects of the Relationship" speculated that the bedroom lecture on *gentilesse* in her tale (1113-23) came from Benoît *via* Boccaccio's *Filostrato* (pp. 5-6). The Summoner, whom Williams called a Carmelite (p. 510), ridicules friars after the manner of Jacques de Basieux' *fabliau*, *Li dis de le vescie à prestre*. The Clerk, as earlier stated, retells the trials of Griselda from a French redaction of Petrarch's Latin original. Economou compared Januarie's discussion of sin with the *Roman* (pp. 254-6); but the *Merchant's Tale's* weightier first section on the dangers of marrying a young wife and its second on a husband's disbelieving his own eyes parallel, as McGalliard recalled, situations more reminiscent of Deschamps' *Le miroir de mariage* than Julien Macho's *Esope* (pp. 193-220). The Physician's version of Appius and Virginia derives from Livy and the *Roman*. The Monk's collection rehandles the two tragedies of Nero and Croesus according to the *Roman*, and, as Braddy proposed in "Chaucer's Don Pedro" (p. 5), resorts to the unhistorical account of Peter of Cyprus in Machaut's *Prise d'Alexandrie* to emphasize the theme of treason in the "Modern Instances" (p. 5). The Nun's Priest recounts the parable of a cock and fox most often classified with a folk genre like, say, some unknown oral version of the anonymous *Le roman de Renart*. Melibee's recital manifests pronounced French influence, Chaucer shunning the Latin text of Albertane de Brescia to paraphrase its French adaptation, Renaud de Louens' *Le livre de Mellibee et Prudence*.

To pass to the second group, the French ingredient in the ten remaining tales is often slight or impossible to determine. For example, a common oral tradition in England or on the Continent may afford the basis of the *Friar's Tale*, with which Archer Taylor in *Sources and Analogues* compares a modern French folktale (p. 274). The fragmentary *Squire's Tale* contains a few passages that call Froissart to mind. The properties of Canacee's mirror, as H. S. V. Jones remarked in "Some Observations" (pp. 356-8), are the same as those in *L'espinette amoureuse* (2623-6, 2661-6); and prototypes of Canacee's falcon and her father's steed, as Braddy added in "Cambyuskan's Flying Horse," occur in Froissart's account in his prose *Chroniques* of King Charles VI's dream of losing his falcon and recapturing the bird with the aid of his flying stag (pp. 42-3). The public confession in the *Pardoner's Prologue*, as Robinson noted, may have been inspired by the self-interested speeches of Faux-Semblant in the *Roman*, which source less probably explains the "coillons" reference (925 ff.) in the *Pardoner's Tale* itself (pp. 730, 732). The name of the knight, Sir Thopas, whose *Tale* satirizes French romance conventions may come, as mentioned in *Sources and Analogues*, from a long poem by Watriquet de Couvin (p. 493, n. 3). In "Is the *Manciple's Tale* a Success?" Severs recounted Chaucerian retracings from the *Roman*, the *Ovide moralisé*, and Machaut's *Le livre du voir dit* (pp. 1-3). Adjectival phrasings in the *Parson's Tale* prompted Robinson to believe that Chaucer worked from a French rather than a Latin source (p. 766). The final four tales, those by the

Miller, Reeve, Shipman, and Cook, belong to the French *fabliaux*, a type recently discussed by Nykrog (p. 262); but their originals are either lost or unknown, though *Sources and Analogues* printed a French analogue (*Le meunier et les clercs*) for the *Reeve's Tale* (pp. 126-47). The French influence on Chaucer's fabliaux as a whole is discussed in a later chapter in this present volume.

During the Hundred Years War England claimed the Atlantic ports on the Continent, and Chaucer's friend, Sir Peter de Bukton, served twice as mayor of Bordeaux. Kings Edward III and Richard II were of course bilingual, and the poet himself naturally spoke the *langue française* as an emissary abroad. French writing had already gained by then considerable renown as polite literature; but Chaucer, who in 1386 reported his age in French as "quarante ans *et* plus," never wrote, as far as is known, a single original line in that tongue. Nevertheless, the bicultural nature of the English court probably induced the poet to go beyond mere regional events in his native England for the occasions of his historical allegories. Perhaps, also, French culture left its stamp on his liberal cast of mind.

To assess fully the monumental influence French had on Chaucer's *Canterbury Tales* and his other works would be *un travail de recherche magnifique*. But it is altogether clear that he had no single French period that began and ended with his lesser compositions. All one can say here is that lyric strains and narrative incidents from one French author or another haunted his memory as long as he wrote.

*   *   *   *   *

Although broad outlines of dependence remain the same, Chaucerians since 1968 have continued to direct attention to French influences on Chaucer. In 1968 Braddy derived the poet's idiom from both Anglo-Saxon and Old French. In 1968 Foster questioned if the oath "Seynt Loy" were not an Anglo-French pun. Between 1968 and 1970 longer essays or dissertations dealt principally with literary importations from France. The most ambitious investigation of this period, on the *Book of the Duchess*, was completed by Wimsatt, who focussed his research on French love poems.

In 1970 McClintock related the *Shipman's Tale* to Old French fabliaux. In 1972 Pratt importantly discussed three Romance forerunners of the *Nun's Priest's Tale*. During the early seventies less pretentious articles linked Chaucer anew with Deschamps, Froissart, and Machaut. In 1974 Palomo exhibited Chaucer's reworkings of the French *Melibee*. Investigations in the early seventies involved critical evaluations rather than new disclosures about fresh sources, but a dissertation of 1975, by Margaret J. Ehrhart, carefully examined as Chaucer's models four *Dits Amoureux* by Machaut, to which poet Chaucer often turned for guidance. Chaucer's major inspiration was of course French, a fact which Ginsberg in 1975 drove home afresh in his dissertation on poet Chaucer and his chief poetical originals. Also in 1975 Calin, in a volume of essays, paid homage to Machaut and the French courtier's narrative skill.

During 1976 a flurry of papers centered on minor French pilferings. Chaucer's titles which attracted scholars included *Troilus and Criseyde*, the *Man of Law's Tale*, and the *Merchant's Tale*. Robbins's reference to Chaucer as "*poète français,* Father of English poetry*" sums up a good deal. My own idea about the world famous poet from London is that his vocabulary, ideas, and plots stemmed ultimately from France, and that in expressing these in the East Midland dialect he fathered English poetry no less than the English tongue.

BIBLIOGRAPHY

Anderson, Marjorie. "Blanche, Duchess of Lancaster." *MP*, 45 (1948), 152-59.

Bowden, Muriel. *A Commentary on the General Prologue to the Canterbury Tales*. New York: Macmillan, 1948.

Braddy, Haldeen. "The Date of Chaucer's *Lak of Steadfastnesse*." *JEGP*, 36 (1937), 481-90.

———. "Cambyuskan's Flying Horse and Charles VI's '*Cerf Volant*'." *MLR*, 33 (1938), 41-44.

————. "Three Chaucer Notes." In *Essays and Studies in Honor of Carleton Brown.* New York: New York Univ. Press, 1940, pp. 91-99.

————. *Chaucer and the French Poet Graunson.* 1947. Rpt. Port Washington, N.Y.: Kennikat Press, 1968.

————. "Chaucer's Don Pedro and the Purpose of the *Monk's Tale.*" *MLQ,* 13 (1952), 3-5.

————. "Chaucer's Bilingual Idiom." *SFQ,* 32 (1968), 1-6.

————. *Geoffrey Chaucer: Literary and Historical Studies.* Port Washington, N.Y.: Kennikat Press, 1971.

Brewer, D.S. *Chaucer in His Time.* London: Nelson, 1963.

Bryan, W.F., and Germaine Dempster, eds. *Sources and Analogues of the Canterbury Tales.* 1941. Rpt. New York: Humanities Press, 1958.

Calin, William. *A Poet at the Fountain: Essays on the Narrative Verse of Guillaume de Machaut.* Lexington: Univ. of Kentucky Press, 1974.

Clawson, W.H. "The Framework of *The Canterbury Tales.*" *UTQ,* 20 (1951), 137-54.

Clemen, Wolfgang. *Chaucer's Early Poetry.* Trans. C.A.M. Sym. London: Methuen, 1963.

Dear, F.M. "Chaucer's *Book of the Lion.*" *MÆ,* 7 (1938), 105-12.

Dédeck-Héry, V. L. "Jean de Meun et Chaucer, traducteurs de la Consolation de Boèce." *PMLA,* 52 (1937), 967-91.

————. "Le Boèce de Chaucer et les manuscrits français de la *Consolatio* de Jean de Meun." *PMLA,* 59 (1944), 18-25.

Economou, George D. "Januarie's Sin against Nature: The *Merchant's Tale* and the *Roman de la Rose.*" *CL,* 17 (1965), 251-57.

Estrich, Robert M. "A Possible Provençal Source for Chaucer's *Hous of Fame.*" *MLN,* 55 (1940), 342-49.

Foster, Brian. "Chaucer's 'Seynt Loy': An Anglo-French Pun?" *N&Q,* 15 (1968), 244-45.

Galway, Margaret. "Chaucer, Graunson, and Isabel of France." *RES,* 24 (1948), 273-80.

Ginsberg, Warren. " 'Li Grant Translateur': Chaucer and His Sources." *DAI*, 36 (1975), 2843A-44A.

Huppé, Bernard F., and D.W. Robertson, Jr. *Fruyt and Chaf: Studies in Chaucer's Allegories.* Princeton: Princeton Univ. Press, 1963.

Jones, H.S.V. "Some Observations upon the *Squire's Tale*." *PMLA*, 20 (1905), 346-59.

———. "The Plan of the *Canterbury Tales*." *MP*, 13 (1915), 45-48.

Jones, P. Mansell, ed. *The Oxford Book of French Verse*. Oxford: Clarendon Press, 1957.

Lerch, Eugen. "Zu einer Stelle bei Eustache Deschamps." *RF*, 62 (1950), 67-68.

Lumiansky, R.M. "Aspects of the Relationship of Boccaccio's 'Il Filostrato' with Benoit's 'Roman de Troie' and Chaucer's, 'Wife of Bath's Tale'." *Italica*, 31 (1954), 1-6.

———. "The Story of Troilus and Briseida According to Benoit and Guido." *Speculum*, 29 (1954), 727-33.

———. "Benoit's Portraits and Chaucer's General Prologue." *JEGP*, 55 (1956), 431-38.

McClintock, Michael W. "Games and the Players of Games: Old French Fabliaux and the *Shipman's Tale*." *ChauR*, 5 (1970), 112-36.

McGalliard, John C. "Chaucer's *Merchant's Tale* and Deschamps' *Miroir de Mariage*." *PQ*, 25 (1946), 193-220.

Meech, Sanford B. "Chaucer and the *Ovide Moralisé*: A Further Study." *PMLA*, 46 (1931), 182-204.

Mitchell, Charles. "The Worthiness of Chaucer's Knight." *MLQ*, 25 (1964), 66-75.

Moore, Arthur K. "Chaucer's Lost Songs." *JEGP*, 48 (1949), 196-208.

———. "Chaucer's Use of Lyric as an Ornament of Style.' *CL*, 3 (1951), 33-46.

Muscatine, Charles. *Chaucer and the French Tradition: A Study in Style and Meaning.* Berkeley: Univ. of California Press, 1957.

Nykrog, Per. *Les Fabliaux: étude d'histoire littéraire et de stylistique médiévale.* 1957. Nouv. éd. Genève: Droz, 1973.

Palomo, Dolores. "What Chaucer Really Did to *Le Livre de Melli-bee*." *PQ*, 53 (1974), 304-20.

Pearsall, Dererk, ed. *The Floure and the Leafe and The Assembly of Ladies*. London: Nelson, 1962.

Pratt, R.A. "Chaucer and *Le Roman de Troyle et de Criseida*." *SP*, 53 (1956), 509-39.

―――. "Three Old French Sources of the *Nonnes Preestes Tale*." *Speculum*, 47 (1972), 422-44, 646-68.

Robbins, Rossell Hope. "*Geoffroi Chaucier, poète français*, Father of English Poetry." *ChauR*, 13 (1978), 93–115.

Robinson, F.N., ed. *The Works of Geoffrey Chaucer*. 1933. 2nd ed. Boston: Houghton Mifflin, 1957.

Severs, J. Burke. "Chaucer's Originality in the *Nun's Priest's Tale*." *SP*, 43 (1946), 22-41.

―――. "Is the *Manciple's Tale* a Success?" *JEGP*, 51 (1952), 1-16.

―――. "The Sources of *The Book of the Duchess*." *MS*, 25 (1963), 355-62.

Slaughter, Eugene E. "Chaucer's Pandarus: Virtuous Uncle and Friend." *JEGP*, 48 (1949), 186-95.

Smith, Roland M. "Five Notes on Chaucer and Froissart." *MLN*, 46 (1951), 27-32.

Stillwell, Gardiner. "Convention and Individuality in Chaucer's *Complaint of Mars*." *PQ*, 35 (1956), 69-89.

Tatlock, J.S.P. *The Mind and Art of Chaucer*. 1950. Rpt. New York: Gordian Press, 1966.

Williams, Arnold. "Chaucer and the Friars." *Speculum*, 28 (1953), 499-513.

Wimsatt, James I. *Chaucer and the French Love Poets: The Literary Background of the Book of the Duchess*. Chapel Hill, N.C.: Univ. of North Carolina Press, 1968.

―――. "Machaut's *Lay de Confort* and Chaucer's *Book of the Duchess*." In *Chaucer at Albany*. Ed. Rossell Hope Robbins. New York: Burt Franklin, 1975, pp. 11-26.

EIGHT

PAUL G. RUGGIERS

The Italian Influence on Chaucer

This survey of the influence of Italy upon Chaucer addresses itself necessarily to a limited number of questions. After a brief glance at the divisions into which it has been customary to divide Chaucer's artistic development, attention is given to his travels in Italy, and then to his reading and absorption of the writings of Dante and Boccaccio, with a statement of his tenuous relation to Petrarch. I have left out of this account works in Latin, like Pope Innocent III's *De miseria conditionis humanae* which, while "Italian," is representative of another class of literature that was the international possession of western Europe.

I

There is no particular value in addressing ourselves at length to the old question of three periods of Chaucer's artistic development. As proposed, supported and contested by scholars at the end of the nineteenth century, the theory is no longer under serious discussion. There is, however, an insistent notion that, owing to the presence of Italians in many walks of English life, Chaucer may have known their language prior to 1372. But Chaucer's early knowledge of Italian remains a conjecture.

It is clear that the exposure to Italian literature, whenever it occurred, worked a vitalizing alchemy upon Chaucer's artistry. Tatlock, in "Boccaccio and the Plan of the *Canterbury Tales*," wrote in a fanciful vein:

> It is becoming more and more evident that the influence of France and Italy ran along side by side until the day of his [Chaucer's] death . . . . The soundest way of regarding his later career is as a putting farther and farther to sea in *la navicella del suo ingegno*, to the sound of the psalm *In exitu Israel de Egypto* (but he had French and Italian hands in his crew). (p. 116)

And Kittredge, in *Chaucer and his Poetry*, offered a warning against excessively neat divisions into French, Italian and English periods of development. It was his view that the Italians had liberated Chaucer and enabled him at the height of his powers to write with confidence. But his demurral is wise: "The whole process of Chaucer's career . . . was cumulative. Chaucer did not forget French when he studied Italian, and he took with him into the English period all the lessons he had ever learned" (p. 27). With these two views we must concur.

The shift in attitude has been largely the result of a new awareness of the cultural relations of England with the continent, of the emergence of the various vernacular literatures in nations still under the sway of a yet vital universal language and religion. In a world thus both unified and divided Chaucer's habitual pose of the unreflective, somewhat wide-eyed observer conceals a self-preserving, virtually impenetrable sophistication which, it is now reasonable to assume, grew out of his diplomatic and civil duties both in England and the continent. Furthermore, what his way of life as civil servant demanded and what he therefore acquired were languages: French first and foremost, but also Latin and Italian, the possession and use of which mark him as an early example of the international man.

The centrality of the French tradition in medieval culture has a felicitous statement in the opening chapter of Charles Muscatine's *Chaucer and the French Tradition*; it is salutary to know that "in a large sense . . . twelfth-century French (with Provençal) was the seminal vernacular literature of the high Middle Ages. It is behind

Dante and Petrarch, Boccaccio and Machaut, the *dolce stil Nuovo*, *Minnesang*, and English and German romance" (p. 6). Whenever Chaucer encountered the vernacular writers of fourteenth-century Italy, he found there both in style and content, though not execution, many matters which had been assimilated from a French past common to their culture, matters which were in some way already a part of his intellectual equipment, and which he must have recognized as native to Romance literatures.

And since the character of medieval genius is eclectic and absorptive, Chaucer's use of the Italian writers available to him was a natural reaching out for materials essential to his own inward growth: new stimuli towards lyrical utterance, a store of images and ornaments, large bodies of narrative; in brief, examples of successful writing. His gravitation to Dante and Boccaccio must be seen, too, as a move towards possessing in greater measure a tradition which he had grasped in part in the *Romance of the Rose,* and before that in Ovid, Virgil, Statius, and which he now saw in a new complexion in Italian literature. Having served a rewarding apprenticeship Chaucer now finds vital reinforcements for his own genius in the richer stores of Italy, bringing himself to his finest intellectual edge in the *Troilus.* There, with the aid of Boccaccio's *Filostrato* and the sublimating power of Dante's *Divine Comedy*, along with the shaping philosophical genius of the earlier Roman, Boethius, he achieved a comprehensive view of experience which, while peculiarly his own, is replete with echoes of the great tradition to which he has allied himself.

II

For the documents on Chaucer's travels in Italy, the student may consult the recent *Chaucer Life-Records* edited by Martin Michael Crow and Clair C. Olson, which replace the old *Life-Records* compiled for the Chaucer Society (1875-1900). There is a persistent tradition recorded by Speght that Chaucer, along with Petrarch, attended the wedding of Prince Lionel to Violante Visconti, May 28, 1368, in Milan. Chaucer was in fact abroad that year on the

first of many missions (see Haldeen Braddy). Edith Rickert estimated that the sums advanced Chaucer "were sufficient to carry
him to Italy," and she has had recent support from Margaret
Galway in a note to the *Times Literary Supplement* in 1958.

If Chaucer did go to Italy as early as 1368, important questions
are raised as to chronology and dating of those of his works that
reflect Italian influence. As Manly remarked, Chaucer had every
opportunity to be exposed to the Italian language in England
where emissaries of various Italian banks, as well as other professions having to do with commerce or military affairs, were in
residence. Firmly authenticated, however, is Chaucer's journey to
Genoa and Florence in 1372-3.

On December 1, 1372, Chaucer was dispatched on the King's
business to Genoa, to establish an advantageous trading port for
Genoese merchants on the English coast. During this first duty, he
was also charged with conducting business in Florence, in all
likelihood negotiating a loan with one of the banking firms, in the
opinion of A. S. Cook. He returned to England on May 23, 1373,
after an absence of 174 days, or just under six months.

George B. Parks, in *The English Traveller to Italy*, discussing
the routes that Chaucer may have taken, offers the opinion that
he proceeded through the Low Countries and Germany to Basel,
thence over the Mont Cenis route or the Great St. Bernard to
Turin, and thence to Genoa (p. 512). After his visit to Florence
he returned to Genoa possibly by way of Bologna and Verona.
During this time, Chaucer might have had occasion to browse in
Italian private libraries, might have visited Petrarch at either
Arquà or Padua, might have heard talk of Boccaccio at Certaldo
and his approaching lectures on Dante at the University of Florence; might, finally, have had his first contact with the work of
both Dante and Boccaccio. It is fairly obvious that most of these
are suppositions of the scholarly community; real evidence is
lacking.

Chaucer was in Italy once again five years later, between May
28 and September 19, 1378. On this occasion he was sent to

negotiate with Bernabò Visconti of Milan and with his son-in-law, the famous mercenary soldier, Sir John Hawkwood, on matters financial and military pertaining to expediting the King's war with France. The purpose of this visit has been discussed by E. P. Kuhl.

What could have been the first impact of Italy upon Chaucer? H. S. Bennett writes in *Chaucer and the Fifteenth Century*: "To enter Italy for the first time is still a land-mark in a man's life, and it certainly was not less so in Chaucer's day" (p. 41). Scholars are naturally curious to know how Chaucer responded to the topography and people of Italy. Unfortunately Chaucer says almost nothing about Italian landscape, art, or the personality of the Italians, as he is silent on the subject of plagues during his lifetime, his own misfortunes, or the death of friends. No English poet has been so immune to those aspects of Italian life which are usually fervently praised.

Tatlock, in "The Duration of Chaucer's Visits to Italy," offers the view that the four-to-five months of Chaucer's stays in Italy must have given him greater familiarity with the language, must have exposed him to the changing seasons, must have provided him with new perspectives of his own English life (p. 121). And Mario Praz in his essay on the Italians and Chaucer is of the opinion that in addition to much else, what Italy offered Chaucer, besides literature, was the lively vigor of the Italian people and a sharpening of his dramatic sense (p. 84). But we must accept, however ruefully and with whatever cavilling, the dry observation of Sir Mungo MacCallum, that Chaucer was primarily a reader of books, primarily a writer (*Chaucer's Debt to Italy*, p. 7).

Various writers have speculated on aspects of Chaucer's sojourns in Italy. Among the more interesting of these is an early piece of Robert A. Pratt, "Chaucer and the Visconti Libraries," noting the influence of the *Divine Comedy* upon poems completed between 1373 and 1378, and assuming, in the absence of signs of the *Convivio* and various works by Boccaccio and Petrarch, that these must have become known to him during the second journey to Italy. "Most of Chaucer's poems indebted to Italy came after 1378; . . . the earlier poems derive chiefly from one Italian writing,

Dante's *Commedia*. It is only after the second journey that Chaucer would seem definitely to have used Dante's *Convivio*, and works of Boccaccio and Petrarch" (p. 192).

III

The uses of Petrarch in Chaucer's work are few; scholarship has been balked by little evidence. Chaucer names Petrarch twice, once at the head of the *Clerk's Tale*, where he is referred to as "Fraunceys Petrak, the lauriat poete, . . . whos rethorike sweete/ Enlumyned al Ytaille of poetrie . . ." and in the middle of the tale of Cenobia in the Monk's performance (2325), where Petrarch is called "my maister," (though Boccaccio is the source). And of course, the *Cantus Troili* in the first book of Troilus and Criseyde, well discussed by Patricia Thomson, provides the surest instance of a Petrarchan text in Chaucer.

The problem of Petrarchan influence is vexed. It is doubtful that Chaucer ever met Petrarch. Where, when, or how he encountered Petrarch's Latin version of the last tale of Boccaccio's *Decameron* or one of a pair of French versions of it, where or how he encountered Petrarch's *Rime* and in what form and with what variants, we do not know.

A further complication is that Chaucer, who has no hesitation in naming both Petrarch and Dante as his sources, does not mention Boccaccio. He seems either not to know, or to have some private motive for omitting to mention, that Boccaccio is his source for the main plot of the *Knight's Tale*, for the *Troilus*, and for countless images and ideas strewn throughout his poetry, that Boccaccio is the source of the Griselda story (see Severs), and that he did not write the lyric which Troilus utters in his initial agony of love.

It is always tempting to assume that Chaucer actually met and talked with Petrarch; and according to Parks in "The Route of Chaucer's First Journey to Italy," he could have, either at Arquà or Padua sometime between February and April of 1373 (p. 185). Nonetheless, though it appears an unnecessarily lost opportunity, Chaucer seems never to have sought out Petrarch. In the absence of evidence in the voluminous letter-writers like Coluccio Salutati, a leading statesman and intellectual, or Petrarch himself, both of whom would presumably have mentioned so exotic a visitor in their correspondence, to use a phrase of Ernest H. Wilkins, we say only that it remains possible though not probable that Chaucer met or corresponded with leaders of Italy's intellectual community.

IV

The debt to Dante has been the subject of doctoral dissertations by Bethel (Harvard, 1927), and Schless (University of Pennsylvania, 1956). Both of these must remain our most valuable sources for the kind and degree of influence exerted by Dante upon Chaucer. Schless has also expressed some of his differences with John Livingston Lowes' pre-1920 formulations, in an essay "Chaucer and Dante," in *Critical Approaches to Medieval Literature*.

In all, Schless and Bethel give their attention to some 250 *loci* in Dante which may have exerted some sway over almost as many passages in Chaucer's poems. There are many, of course, in which Dante serves as a model, or a source, or a corroborating memory. There are many others, however, which are demonstrable as being in the mind, so to speak, of the Middle Ages as a common intellectual heritage, which it is necessary to cull out of the relationship between Dante and Chaucer.

Some of these relationships demand a kind of subtlety in the demonstration. Others, in which the use of Dante is forthright and obvious, are: the imitation of the inscription over Dante's Hell-gate in the *Parliament of Fowls*; the invocation to Mary in *Paradiso* XXXIII, in the *Prologues* to both the Prioress's and Second Nun's tales; the discussion of nobility in the *Wife of Bath's Tale*, borrowed from the *Convivio*; a version of the story of Count Ugolino, drawn from the *Inferno*, in the *Monk's Tale*; an ecstatic hymn drawn from the familiar praise of Mary in *Paradiso* XXXIII, used as a sublimating factor in the consummation of Troilus and Criseyde's love (Book III, 1261 ff.); and Dante's praise of the Trinity in *Paradiso* XIV, used in the last lines of that great poem.

And it must be recalled that Chaucer is the first experimenter in English with *terza rima*, in lines 15-43 of the *Complaint to his Lady*, which Lowes (p. 725) and Robinson (p. 856) date as "very early in Chaucer's Italian period."

Among the works which treat incidentally of Dante's influence upon Chaucer, it is good to have translated into English the revised version of Wolfgang Clemen's *Der Junge Chaucer* (1938) under the title *Chaucer's Early Poetry*, with its sane approach to the relation of the *House of Fame* to Dante's *Divine Comedy*. In pointing out the similarities between the journeys in the two poems, Clemen does not neglect to note the reversal of tone from Dante's sublimity and nobility to Chaucer's comedy and irony. In dealing with the flight of the eagle he writes:

> Surely Dante's influence must underlie this description at once so precise, so realistic and yet so truly a part of experience. What influenced Chaucer in the *Divine Comedy* was not the basic conception, the thoughts, the "content"; it was Dante's method of presentation, the intensity, precision and perception with which he reproduced sensuous detail, visual impressions of movement and light for the most part, but also of sounds. Chaucer must have been impressed at discovering a poet who portrayed marvels and visions as if they belonged to reality, yet expressed his own reactions so vividly that everything seemed to be happening at that very moment and to himself. This in particular must have been what Chaucer was looking for, to further his own art. (pp. 90-1)

We have come a long way, it is clear, from the assumptions of a hundred years ago that Chaucer was writing a parodic version of Dante's great poem in a comic vein. In our own century the notion has appeared under various guises; when Chiarini offered it at the turn of the century, Robinson, in a now famous review, pointed out that the Dantean reminiscences, quotations and allusions are incidental, not organic or essential to the subject matter of the poem.

The subject is now before us again in the most elaborate form that we have seen up to this time, in B.G. Koonce's *Chaucer and the Tradition of Fame*. Koonce writes:

Structurally the most conspicuous parallel is the division into three books, a parallel reinforced by Chaucer's use of two of Dante's invocations and by a network of details equating the stages of the poets' journeys. Among the more obvious images suggesting the *Comedy* are the desert of Venus in Book I, the flight with Jupiter's eagle in Book II, and the mountain of Fame in Book III, paralleling the "gran deserto" of Hell, the flight with the golden eagle of Purgatory, and the purgatorial mountain whose ascent leads to the beatific visions of Paradise. While these parallels leave little doubt as to Chaucer's deliberate imitation of Dante's pilgrimage, Dante's Scriptural-exegetical symbolism and Chaucer's pagan fiction reveal little outward correspondence in either purpose or meaning. Viewed allegorically, however, these similarities reflect a common body of Christian doctrine connecting Chaucer's imagery with the spiritual meanings of Dante's pilgrimage. (p. 81)

The method revealed by this passage is rich in its ability to increase our knowledge of what may be called the collective mind of the Middle Ages as it informs, however fragmentarily, now here, now there, the minds of individual poets and yields reminiscences in the poems they write. Koonce's essay ranges widely through the intellectual stores of Chaucer's past and present, notably Boethius, who, after Dante, supplies the major elements directing us to the Christian "sentence" beneath the pagan fictions of the allegory. I experienced personally a remoteness of the theory from the poem itself when I reread it, feeling that the statement that the poem makes is its own, however ambiguous and incomplete, and that its meanings must still be sought in it *qua* poem.

A surer indication of the relationship of Chaucer to Dante, one where we can compare the genius of two very different poets, is to be found in their respective treatments of Ugolino, a notable example of Chaucer's power to translate the horrors and grandeur of Dante into his own idiom, that of heart-wringing pity for the young, the gentle, the helpless. It is an account in which, as in the *Prioress's Tale* and the *Physician's Tale*, the horror is overridden by the note of poignancy in the personal relationships expressed. (Theodore Spencer's comparison made in 1934 is still useful.)

Chaucer's tale of Ugolino (*MkT*, 2407-62) is marked by differences in attitude and theological context which serve to indicate the range and perhaps the limitations of Chaucer's tragic view. Dante's Ugolino is in Hell, among the treacherous, one example among many of offense against moral law which sees man as "liable to the reward or punishment of Justice, according as through the freedom of the will he is deserving or undeserving." In the depiction of Ugolino's terrible punishment and in the poetical handling of his suffering, God's now inescapable law lends a moving terror to the scene; our purely human sensibilities, however, yield to the desperate grief of a father watching the death of his children and to the insatiable appetite for revenge upon the enemy, Roger, who has brought them to this plight.

Dante refrains from saying anything of Ugolino's guilt; his position in Hell is sufficient. He refrains from lavishing sympathy upon him; it is sufficient to invest in him that heart-wringing paternalism which forever restores him to human fellowship. However, he takes care to provide an emotional release in an outcry of a deeply felt contempt for Pisa, the modern Thebes, which has countenanced this crime against children. It is this diversion of our emotion into plaintive outcry which provided Chaucer with the clue for his own treatment of the story.

Chaucer's version, then, while still affecting, is a less powerful performance owing to the omission of a larger moral context and judgment. It is capricious Fortune rather than human error which is crucial to the tragic experience here. And so, by omitting the horror, the implications of guilt, the system of just retribution, Chaucer has also omitted the interrelation of character and action, fault and desert, and allows what Dante's system will not finally tolerate: the exoneration of Ugolino at the expense of Roger.

Chaucer's intention, then, is more obviously circumscribed; what he easily achieves is sympathy and pathos, that sense of undeserved suffering of father and children. By omitting in his version that dream in which Ugolino sees foreshadowed their approaching doom, Chaucer also averts any consideration of a destinal order or a suspenseful horror. By such omission, he retreats to a general and diffuse pity which sees the plight of good and bad alike as the work of Fortune, a view which tends to imply that suffering has no meaning beyond its own manifestation. In effect, we face broad limitations in formal intention at which Chaucer himself hints in his closing lines:

> Of this tragedie it oghte ynough suffise;
> Whoso wol here it in a lenger wise,
> Redeth the grete poete of Ytaille
> That highte Dant, for he kan al devyse
> Fro point to point, nat o word wol he faille.
>
>   (MkT, 2458-62)

v

Edward Hutton has remarked that "all the mature work of Chaucer is riddled with Boccaccio." This fact is nowhere better demonstrated than in the evaluation by Robert A. Pratt in "Chaucer's Use of the *Teseida*":

> . . . of all Italian writings except Dante's *Commedia*, the *Teseida* served Chaucer the most widely. It formed the basic material out of which he created the *Knight's Tale,* and was the source of passages in *Anelida and Arcite,* the *Parliament of Fowls, Troilus and Criseyde,* the *Legend of Good Women,* the *Franklin's Tale,* and possibly the *House of Fame.* (p. 598)

It should be noted that Dante's *Commedia,* by its presence in all of the poems that Pratt adduces, assumes a prior status for Chaucer, both in time of encounter and in terms of its importance to him as a repository. But Boccaccio's presence at first as a source for classical ornament in the *House of Fame,* as a stimulus in the abortive *Anelida and Arcite,* as a means of enriching the texture of the *Parliament* where Chaucer adapts or translates some sixteen of Boccaccio's stanzas, and particularly in the substantial support provided (by the *Teseida*) in the *Knight's Tale* and (by the *Filostrato*) in *Troilus and Criseyde,* is for Chaucer more than that of a quarry from which to mine various riches. Boccaccio is the model of style, an example of the ability to carry long narrative structures in stanzaic patterns, a teacher of that special decorum of style with subject matter, as well as the source for classical allusions and epic forms. He is, furthermore, after the *Romance of the Rose*, the successful exemplar of that difficult fusion of erotic love with larger destinal forces, a subject which informs two of Chaucer's most ambitious projects; in this regard, English and American scholarship has a tendency to elevate Chaucer at the expense of Boccaccio. It is chastening to know that to Italians Chaucer is an imitator of—to them—the more sophisticated Boccaccio, and a reading of Boccaccio will make clear that he is not devoid of higher values.

The fact that the *Knight's Tale* and the *Troilus* are derivative of Boccaccio should not blind us, however, to their uniqueness. They are Chaucer's own, not merely in the exercise that the one affords in reducing materials or the other in expansion, but rather in the filtering of their subjects through the mind of a developing genius with its own artistic goals.

Modern criticism of the *Knight's Tale* has directed itself largely to the questions: what has Chaucer done to the *Teseida*? and as a consequence of this, what, on its own terms, is the *Knight's Tale*? Hulbert's early article provides an answer. Other critics have dealt more specifically with comparisons of Boccaccio and Chaucer's texts, with the changes of meaning brought about by the Boethian additions; French, Lloyd and others have considered the characters of Palamon and Arcite, and Bennett has examined the role of Theseus in the poem. Perhaps the most significant group of articles, from the point of view of theme and meaning have been those that in one way or another follow the lead opened up by Frost in 1949, using the Boethian concept of order or love as the unifying thematic element in the tale. The studies of Wilson in 1949 and that of Muscatine in 1950 merit our special attention. (See also Halverson, Lumiansky and Ruggiers.) Lately there have been subtle attempts by Neuse, Underwood, Westlund, Herz and others to read back through the tale to the knight and to formulations of the way in which the story implies facets of his character; this last impulse is natural, considering that the *Knight's Tale* functions as a part of the pilgrimage plan. While we recognize that the tale is well enough suited to the knight, our interpretation of his character in the light of his tale must face the problem, according to Dorothy Everett in "Some Reflections on Chaucer's 'Art Poetical'," that the tale, in all likelihood, was written before the *General Prologue*.

The influence of Boethius upon the *Knight's Tale*, with such large emphases, is but one of the factors that make the tale Chaucer's own; the problem of evil is raised in a tone of high seriousness somewhat at odds with a comic tone elsewhere in the tale. But it is treated here with as much directness as in the *Franklin's Tale* (in all likelihood drawn principally from the story of Menedon in Boccaccio's *Filocolo*) and in the *Troilus*. Something in Boccaccio's romantic narratives gives Chaucer the license to deepen their tone by dealing more directly with universal human concerns. In the opinion of some the *Teseida* is not the most successful of Boccaccio's poems; it wants a unity of effects, and it allows the story of Teseo to become, after the first two of his twelve books, the story of Emily and her wooers; that is to say, Boccaccio's literary motive to write an epic in the grand style is submerged by his passion to recover the love of Maria. There lurks in Chaucer's version, too, an ambiguity in artistic intention. John Speirs has pointed out, in *Chaucer the Maker*, that as a version of courtly romance, the poem contains an "inner tendency towards a completer reality" of comedy or tragedy (p. 123). Paull Baum, furthermore, sensing an excess of enthusiasm among critics in their zeal for stating the power of Chaucer's execution, calls attention to various lapses of control in the poem, and this response of a mature critic should give us pause (*Chaucer: A Critical Appreciation*, pp. 84-104).

We are enabled to see Chaucer at work on a problem of a very different sort in the vast amplification of materials in *Troilus and Criseyde*. Always useful, perhaps even essential to the student of the poem is R. K. Root's fine edition of the poem, reprinted for the third time in 1945, Thomas A. Kirby's *Chaucer's Troilus: A Study in Courtly Love*, 1940, reissued in 1960, Herbert G.

Wright's *Boccaccio in England from Chaucer to Tennyson*, 1957, and Sanford Brown Meech's *Design in Chaucer's Troilus*, 1959. Recent papers by Bloomfield and Jordan have considered the complex vision of the narrator, while Charles Muscatine's chapter on the poem in *Chaucer and the French Tradition* addresses itself to the cultural differences between Chaucer and his sources, whether French or Italian, and to what is unique in Chaucer's handling of the subject. Muscatine, in reminding us that the strains of realism and idealism reflected in Chaucer were both conventional aspects of his intellectual inheritance, makes an advance upon the positions established by C. S. Lewis.

C. S. Lewis had reminded us, in 1932 and 1936, that Chaucer succeeds in fusing love-religion with real religion, thus increasing the degree of seriousness in his poem. But Lewis has a tendency to read Chaucer as a corrector of a subtle, cynical unorthodoxy in Boccaccio, claiming that Chaucer's great contribution is to restore to the story of *Troilus* "those elements in the medieval consciousness which survive in our own." He avers too, in *The Allegory of Love*, p. 176, that "Chaucer was working with 'ful devout corage'; while Boccaccio, for all his epic circumstance, feels in his heart of hearts that all this stuff about gardens and gods of love is 'only poetry'." Lewis' heart, as we all know from his extensive writings, was anchored securely to a "high" and orthodox tradition, and his apologetic writings are designed to call attention to what he deemed perennial in the Christian tradition; but stated in excess, with regard to Chaucer, it leads him to brand the *Canterbury Tales* as sterile in influence. Muscatine's view provides a corrective on the side of naturalism, and more recently Roger Sharrock has provided a salutary second look at Lewis' position.

The differences between Chaucer and Boccaccio in the treatment of *Troilus and Criseyde* are profound and many. Chaucer is older and more settled when he writes his version. He is not driven by so intensely personal a motive as Boccaccio's anguish over his terminated love affair. There is a more overt sense of religion in his nature; with the philosophical inspiration provided by Boethius and Dante, he is more thoughtful and detached. His objective air as historian and reporter enables the reader to enter both into the action empathically and yet to remain outside of it with some sense of judgment. It is necessary to have read Boccaccio first to appreciate how Chaucer has worked not only to deepen the tone of the poem by using Dante and Boethius, but also to change it radically in the direction of dramatically convincing dialogue. In the process of expansion, Chaucer's comment upon human love, to be sure, becomes linked up with a transcendental idealism and holds a romantic eros in delicate balance with the highest aspirations of the human soul. But the hard quality of argument, debate and persuasion links it to an equally persistent strain of realism which is one of the great merits of the poem.

It is no surprise that many of the articles of the past quarter century have devoted their attention to the Palinode in which an episode drawn from the *Teseida* dealing with the soul of Arcite is brilliantly utilized to complete the fate of Troilus. This subject has been discussed by Clark, Cope, Donaldson, Dronke, Kean, Kellogg, Nagarajan and Scott, among others. It should also be noted that virtually all of the new books on Chaucer included in the bibliography have made assessments of the moral and religious implications of Chaucer's conclusion to the poem.

One consideration still with us is the possible influence of the *Decameron* upon the *Canterbury Tales*. Cummings doubted, not only that Chaucer even knew of the existence of a person named Boccaccio, but that the *Decameron* was of any help "whatsoever to Chaucer in the inception, or in the composition of either the frame-work of the *Canterbury Tales* or of the *Tales* themselves" (p. 198). More recently Richard S. Guerin in an unpublished doctoral dissertation at the University of Colorado has reexamined the possible relationships between the *Decameron* and the *Canterbury Tales*. He argues that since there are evidences in Chaucer's works of *Il Filostrato, Il Filocolo, Il Teseida, De casibus virorum, De claris mulieribus,* and *De genealogia deorum,* it seems highly unlikely that he would have known so many of Boccaccio's other works without gaining some knowledge of his masterpiece, *Il Decamerone* (p. 272). He examines similarities and possible borrowings in the *Miller's Tale*, the *Reeve's Tale*, the *Man of Law's Tale*, the *Clerk's Tale*, the *Franklin's Tale*, the *Shipman's Tale*, and in the apologies.

Ranged against this view is that expressed by Robert A. Pratt and Karl Young in *Sources and Analogues*:

> . . . no one acquainted with Chaucer's literary powers and practice would dare to deny that he could have transformed the polished orderliness and elegance of the *Decameron* into the varied realism and humanity of the *Canterbury Tales*, if he had known the Italian collection, and if he had chosen to undertake the transformation. The fundamental reason for doubting Chaucer's indebtedness to the *Decameron*, therefore, is not that it lacks suggestiveness, but that we have no decisive evidence that Chaucer was acquainted with it. Although his thorough knowledge and use of certain other works of Boccaccio is well known, his acquaintance with the most famous of them all cannot be established. Chaucer does not mention the *Decameron*, he borrows no stories directly from it, and no copy or translation of it can be traced in England during the period of his life. (p. 20)

It is a judicious statement, but Tatlock in his last utterance on the subject published in 1950 in *The Mind and Art of Chaucer* (p. 90), refused to relinquish the possibility: "In view of his taste for reading and inexhaustible curiosity, it is incredible that he had not heard of the *Decameron*, and indeed seen it. If he never bought a copy, that may have been because it was a very large and expensive book and he was not an affluent man . . . ."

A possible close link that has been advanced several times is the defense offered by both poets of comic realism, Boccaccio's in *The Proem, The Introduction to the Fourth Day*, and in the conclusion to the *Decameron*, Chaucer in the *General Prologue*, and in the *Prologue to the Miller's Tale*. Both of them are defenses of plain speech and disavowals of responsibility for the morality of audiences; both claim that they are true to their materials and observe a decorum of style and subject matter; both exonerate themselves from charges of immorality. (These sentiments in one form or another appear also in the *Roman*, as Root showed in

1912.) The treatment by the two poets, however, is vastly different. Boccaccio makes the defenses function throughout the collection; later, in a famous letter to Mainardo, he condemned the tales as indecent trifles; and in the *Genealogy of the Gentile Gods* he condemned most comic writing as the dregs of poetry, though he exempted Plautus and Terence. Had Chaucer read the condemnation with its strong insistence that comic writers, because of their ability to subvert the state, should be exterminated? Tatlock and Farnham make interesting conjectures on the availability of the *Decameron*.

Chaucer handles the matter differently: his comic defenses stand at the head of his collection; they function as part of a larger statement about the human condition, absorbed through the process of juxtapositions with other attitudes towards experience. At the close, the spirit of rejection elicits a new evaluation of the role which the comic and ironic has played in the plan of pilgrimage to the extent of implying the moral norms of the whole poem.

VI

But if Chaucer made prudent use of the Italian writers, he cannot be said merely to have imitated them. His eclectic handling of the literature of Italy, like his handling of the French and the Latin sources available to him, is the fulfillment of his genius. Something in his nature as a poet refuses mere emulation of other writers. His largely middle-ground approach to his art precludes both the determined moralism of Dante and his grandeur. While he recognized and revered Dante's greatness, the use he makes of him indicates his own very different powers. Aside from the translations he makes of specific passages in Dante, his debt to him is in the wide range of images he was able to revert to, combining them with reminiscences of images in other poets. Schless and others offer the view that Chaucer clearly knows the whole *Commedia* (although there are concentrations of borrowings from the beginnings and ends of the individual *cantiche*). Yet nothing in Chaucer reflects Dante's systematic and consistent allegory or his habit of writing personal biography in long lyric outbursts.

Aside from the Ugolino story, which, in the opinion of Praz and Baum, Chaucer botched, Chaucer is not inclined to pick materials out of the many dramas that make up Dante's poem. The qualities which according to Longinus comprise greatness—a great soul, great ideas, and skill in diction—demand different definition in Chaucer. In reserving the title of poet for Dante and Petrarch he makes a generous statement about the past; we are not deceived by it, however, into forgetting his own substantial gifts: his interest in the human drama, his power of apt expression, his developing architectonic strength.

His uses of Boccaccio are much like his uses of Dante with regard to individual passages and varied images strewn through all of his major poems. More substantially he offered Chaucer what the fabliaux, in another dimension, were to give him in briefer compass: the successful narratives out of which something new could be fashioned. This in addition to the collateral benefits of repositories of classical allusion, rich description, bold experiments in the long form. Cummings (p. 199) may be right in his view that Boccaccio owes to Chaucer the debt of being made part and parcel of English Literature, admission to which he calls "no slight privilege," but it may be preferable to recall Tatlock's final sympathetic judgment (*The Mind and Art of Chaucer*, p. 35) in 1950 of a congeniality between their two spirits. Reverence Dante though he might, admire his wisdom, power, beauty, it was to Boccaccio's work that he turned, not merely for inspiration and stimulus, but for two of the poems on the bases of which he may himself be called great.

* * * * *

As Larry Benson observes, there is still no work on the Italian traditions in Chaucer comparable to the works on the French tradition in Chaucer. During the last decade, however, J. A. W. Bennett's closely packed book on the *House of Fame* has further revealed Chaucer's transmutation of classical and Italian sources and provided much evidence to support Lydgate's designation

"Dante in Inglissh." Italian as well as classical influences are also emphasized by Paul Clogan who reminds us that it was under their inspiration that Chaucer attained "full imaginative freedom." Cowgill finds Dante's influence in the *Parlement of Fowls* with echoes of the temporary paradise of Dante's *Purgatorio,* and Charles Muscatine comments on the effect of the Italian epic style on Chaucer. Jeffrey Helterman considers both the influence of Dantean love and Petrarchan style in relation to *Troilus.*

There have been many interpretations of Chaucer's use of his Boccaccian models. Helen Corsa, Elizabeth Hatcher and Chauncey Wood make illuminating comparisons between passages in *Il Filostrato* and *Troilus,* and the treatment of Criseyde and Cresseida is explored by Robert apRoberts and John Maguire. Other studies concerned with Italian influences include approaches as different as F. L. Utley who draws attention to the common folklore background of Chaucer and Boccaccio, and Beryl Rowland who points out that the *Physician's Tale* not only reflects the longstanding feud between physicians and lawyers in Italy, but uses the incident which led to the introduction of Italian Law, *mos italicus.* These and other treatments indicate that there was an internationally available reservoir of ideas, symbols, tales upon which Chaucer was able to draw, and that the Italian writers were a part of that reservoir. The specific matter of a clearly demonstrable use of the *Decameron* by Chaucer in the *Canterbury Tales,* though under continuous re-examination by Peter Beidler, Svetko Tedeschi and others, remains an unresolved question.

BIBLIOGRAPHY

I. GENERAL STUDIES

Baum, Paull F. *Chaucer: A Critical Appreciation.* Durham, N.C.: Duke Univ. Press, 1958.

Bennett, H.S. *Chaucer and the Fifteenth Century.* Oxford History of English Literature, 2, pt. 1. Oxford: Oxford Univ. Press, 1947.

Bennett, J.A.W. *Chaucer's Book of Fame: An Exposition of The House of Fame*. Oxford: Clarendon Press, 1968.

Benson, L. D. "A Reader's Guide to Writings on Chaucer." In *Writers and Their Background: Geoffrey Chaucer*. Ed. D.S. Brewer. London: Bell, 1974, pp. 322-72.

Clemen, Wolfgang. *Chaucer's Early Poetry*. Trans. C.A.M. Sym. London: Methuen, 1963.

Coghill, Nevill. *The Poet Chaucer*. 1949. Rpt. 2nd ed., London: Oxford Univ. Press, 1967.

Everett, Dorothy. "Some Reflections on Chaucer's 'Art Poetical'." *PBA*, 36 (1950). Rpt. In *Essays on Middle English Literature*. Ed. P.M. Kean. Oxford: Clarendon Press, 1955, pp. 149-74.

Kittredge, G.L. *Chaucer and his Poetry*. Cambridge, Mass.: Harvard Univ. Press, 1915.

Lewis, C.S. *The Allegory of Love: A Study in Medieval Tradition*. 1936. Rpt. New York: Oxford Univ. Press, 1958.

Muscatine, Charles. *Chaucer and the French Tradition: A Study in Style and Meaning*. Berkeley: Univ. of California Press, 1957.

Payne, Robert O. *The Key of Remembrance: A Study of Chaucer's Poetics*. 1963. Rpt. Westport, Conn.: Greenwood Press, 1973.

Preston, Raymond. *Chaucer*. 1952. Rpt. Westport, Conn.: Greenwood Press, 1969.

Robertson, D.W., Jr. *A Preface to Chaucer: Studies in Medieval Perspectives*. Princeton: Princeton Univ. Press, 1962.

Ruggiers, Paul G. "Notes towards a Theory of Tragedy in Chaucer." *ChauR*, 8 (1973), 181-97.

Shelly, Percy Van Dyke. *The Living Chaucer*. 1940. Rpt. New York: Russell & Russell, 1968.

Speirs, John. *Chaucer the Maker*. 1951. Rev. 2nd ed. London: Faber, 1960.

Tatlock, J.S.P. *The Mind and Art of Chaucer*. 1950. Rpt. New York: Gordian Press, 1966.

II. CHAUCER IN ITALY

Braddy, Haldeen. "New Documentary Evidence Concerning Chaucer's Mission to Lombardy." *MLN*, 48 (1933), 507-11.

Cook, A.S. "Chaucerian Papers." *Trans. of the Conn. Acad. of Arts and Sciences*, 23 (1919), 39-44.

Galway, Margaret. "Chaucer's Journeys in 1368." *TLS*, April 4, 1958, p. 183.

Kuhl, E.P. "Why Was Chaucer Sent to Milan in 1378?" *MLN*, 62 (1947), 42-44.

Manly, John Matthews. "Chaucer's Mission to Lombardy." *MLN*, 49 (1934), 209-16.

Parks, George B ."The Route of Chaucer's First Journey to Italy." *ELH*, 16 (1949), 174-87.

———. *The English Traveller to Italy, 1. The Middle Ages*. Stanford: Stanford Univ. Press, 1954.

Pratt, R.A. "Geoffrey Chaucer, Esq. and Sir John Hawkwood." *ELH*, 16 (1949), 188-93.

Rickert, Edith. "Chaucer Abroad in 1368." *MP*, 25 (1928), 511-12.

Tatlock, J.S.P. "The Duration of Chaucer's Visits to Italy." *JEGP*, 12 (1913), 118-21.

III. DANTE, BOCCACCIO, AND PETRARCH

Bethel, John Perceval. "The Influence of Dante on Chaucer's Thought and Expression." Diss. Harvard, 1927.

Cummings, Hubertis M. *The Indebtedness of Chaucer's Works to the Italian Works of Boccaccio*. Univ. of Cincinnati Studies, 10, pt. 2. 1916. Rpt. New York: Haskell House, 1965.

Farnham, W.E. "England's Discovery of the *Decameron*." *PMLA*, 39 (1924), 123-39.

Guerin, Richard S. "The Canterbury Tales and *Il Decamerone*." Diss. Colorado, 1966.

Koonce, B.G. *Chaucer and the Tradition of Fame: Symbolism in The House of Fame*. Princeton: Princeton Univ. Press, 1966.

MacCallum, Sir Mungo W. *Chaucer's Debt to Italy*. Sydney, Australia: Angus & Robertson, 1931.

Muscatine, Charles. *Poetry and Crisis in the Age of Chaucer*. Notre Dame, Ind.: Univ. of Notre Dame, 1972.

Pratt, R.A. "Chaucer and the Visconti Libraries." *ELH*, 6 (1939), 191-99.

———. "Chaucer's Use of the *Teseida*." *PMLA*, 62 (1947), 598-621.

———. "A Note on Chaucer's Lollius." *MLN*, 65 (1950), 183-87.

Praz, Mario. "Chaucer and the Great Italian Writers of the Trecento." *The Monthly Criterion*, 6 (1927), 18-39, 131-57, 238-42. Rpt. in *The Flaming Heart*. Garden City: Doubleday, 1958.

Root, R.K. "Chaucer and the *Decameron*." *ESt*, 44 (1912), 1-7.

Ruggiers, Paul G. *The Art of the Canterbury Tales*. Madison: Univ of Wisconsin Press, 1965.

Schless, Howard H. "Chaucer and Dante: A Revaluation." Diss. Pennsylvania, 1956.

———. "Transformations: Chaucer's Use of Italian." In *Writer's and Their Background: Geoffrey Chaucer*. Ed. D.S. Brewer. London: Bell, 1974, pp. 184-223.

———. "Chaucer and Dante." In *Critical Approaches to Medieval Literature*. Ed. Dorothy Bethurum. New York: Columbia Univ. Press, 1960, pp. 134-54.

Severs, J. Burke. *The Literary Relationships of Chaucer's Clerk's Tale*. Yale Studies in English, 96. 1942. Rpt. Hamden, Conn.: Archon, 1972.

Sharrock, Roger. "Second Thoughts: C.S. Lewis on Chaucer's *Troilus*." *EIC*, 8 (1958), 123-37.

Spencer, Theodore. "The Story of Ugolino in Dante and Chaucer." *Speculum*, 9 (1934), 295-301.

Tatlock, J.S.P. "Boccaccio and the Plan of the *Canterbury Tales*." *Anglia*, 37 (1913), 69-117.

Tedeschi, Svetko. "Some Recent Opinions about the Possible Influence of Boccaccio's *Decameron* on Chaucer's *Canterbury Tales*." *SRAZ*, 33-36 (1972-73), 849-72.

Thomson, Patricia. "The 'Canticus Troili': Chaucer and Petrarch." *CL*, 9 (1959), 313-28.

Utley, Francis L. "Boccaccio, Chaucer and the International Popular Tale." *WF*, 33 (1974), 181-201.

Wilkins, Ernest Hatch. "*Cantus Troili.*" *ELH*, 16 (1949), 167-73.

Wright, Herbert G. *Boccaccio in England From Chaucer to Tennyson.* London: Athlone Press, 1957.

IV. THE KNIGHT'S TALE

Bennett, J.A.W., ed. *The Knight's Tale.* 1954. Rev. 2nd ed., London: Harrap, 1958.

French, W.H. "Lovers in the *Knight's Tale.*" *JEGP*, 48 (1949), 320-28.

Frost, William. "An Interpretation of Chaucer's Knight's Tale." *RES*, 25 (1949), 289-304.

Halverson, John. "Aspects of Order in the 'Knight's Tale'." *SP*, 57 (1960), 606-21.

Herz, Judith S. "Chaucer's Elegiac Knight." *Criticism*, 6 (1964), 212-24.

Hulbert, J.R. "What was Chaucer's Aim in the *Knight's Tale*?" *SP*, 26 (1929), 375-85.

Lloyd, Michael. "A Defense of Arcite." *EM*, 10 (1959), 11-25.

Lumiansky, R.M. "Chaucer's Philosophical Knight." *TSE*, 3 (1952), 47-68.

Muscatine, Charles. "Form, Texture and Meaning in Chaucer's *Knight's Tale.*" *PMLA*, 65 (1950), 911-29.

Neuse, Richard. "The Knight: The First Mover in Chaucer's Human Comedy." *UTQ*, 31 (1962), 299-315.

Ruggiers, Paul G. "Some Philosophical Aspects of *The Knight's Tale.*" *CE*, 19 (1958), 296-302.

Underwood, Dale. "The First of *The Canterbury Tales.*" *ELH*, 26 (1959), 455-69.

Westlund, Joseph. "*The Knight Tale* as an Impetus for Pilgrimage." *PQ*, 43 (1964), 526-37.

Wilson, H.S. "*The Knight's Tale* and the *Teseida* Again." *UTQ*, 18 (1949), 131-46.

V. TROILUS AND CRISEYDE

apRoberts, Robert P. "The Boethian God and the Audience of the *Troilus*." *JEGP*, 69 (1970), 425-36.

————. "Love in the *Filostrato*." *ChauR*, 7 (1972), 1-26.

Bloomfield, Morton W. "Distance and Predestination in *Troilus and Criseyde*." *PMLA*, 72 (1957), 14-26.

Clark, John W. "Dante and the Epilogue of the *Troilus*." *JEGP*, 50 (1951), 1-10.

Clogan, Paul M. "Chaucer's Use of the *Thebaid*." *EM*, 18 (1967), 9-31.

Cope, Jackson I. "Chaucer, Venus and the 'Seventhe Spere'." *MLN*, 67 (1952), 245-46.

Corsa, Helen Storm. "Dreams in *Troilus and Criseyde*." *AI*, 27 (1970), 52-65.

Donaldson, E. Talbot. "The Ending of Chaucer's *Troilus*." In *Early English and Norse Studies Presented to Hugh Smith in Honour of His Sixtieth Birthday*. Ed. Arthur Brown and Peter Foote. London: Methuen, 1963, pp. 26-45.

Dronke, Peter. "The Conclusion of *Troilus and Criseyde*." *MÆ*, 33 (1964), 47-52.

Everett, Dorothy. "Troilus and Criseyde." In *Essays on Middle English Literature*. Ed. P.M. Kean. Oxford: Clarendon Press, 1955, pp. 115-38.

Hatcher, Elizabeth R. "Chaucer and the Psychology of Fear: Troilus in Book V." *ELH*, 40 (1973), 307-24.

Helterman, Jeffrey. "Mask of Love in *Troilus and Criseyde*." *CL*, 26 (1974), 14-31.

Jordan, Robert M. "The Narrator in Chaucer's *Troilus*." *ELH*, 25 (1958), 237-57.

Kean, P.M. "Chaucer's Dealings with a Stanza of *Il Filostrato* and the Epilogue of *Troilus and Criseyde*." *MÆ*, 33 (1964), 36-46.

Kellogg, Alfred L. "On the Tradition of Troilus's Vision of the Little Earth." *MS*, 22 (1960), 204-13.

Kirby, T.A. *Chaucer's Troilus: A Study in Courtly Love.* 1940. Rpt. Gloucester, Mass.: P. Smith, 1959.

Lewis, C.S. "What Chaucer Really Did to *Il Filostrato.*" *E&S,* **17** (1932), 56-75.

Maguire, John B. "The Clandestine Marriage of Troilus and Criseyde." *ChauR,* 8 (1974), 262-78.

Meech, Sanford B. *Design in Chaucer's Troilus.* 1959. Rpt. New York: Greenwood Press, 1970.

Nagarajan, S. "The Conclusion of Chaucer's *Troilus and Criseyde.*" *EIC,* 13 (1963), 1-8.

Owen, Charles A., Jr. "Mimetic Form in the Central Love Scene of *Troilus and Criseyde.*" *MP,* 67 (1969), 125-32.

Root, R.K. *The Book of Troilus and Criseyde.* Princeton: Princeton Univ. Press, 1926.

Ross, Thomas W. "*Troilus and Criseyde,* II. 582-87: A Note." *ChauR,* 5 (1970), 137-39.

Scott, Forrest S. "The Seventh Sphere: A Note on *Troilus and Criseyde.*" *MLR,* 51 (1956), 2-5.

Walker, Ian C. "Chaucer and *Il Filostrato.*" *ES,* 49 (1968), 318-26.

Wood, Chauncey. "On Translating Chaucer's *Troilus and Criseyde,* Book III, lines 12-14." *ELN,* 11 (1973), 9-14.

VI. OTHER WORKS

Beidler, Peter G. "Chaucer's *Merchant's Tale* and the *Decameron.*" *Italica,* 50 (1973), 266-84.

Cottino-Jones, Marga, "Another Interpretation of the Griselda Story." *Italica,* 50 (1973), 38-52.

Cowgill, Bruce Kent. "The *Parlement of Foules* and the Body Politic." *JEGP,* 74 (1975), 315-35.

Guerin, Richard S. "The *Shipman's Tale:* The Italian Analogues." *ES,* 52 (1971), 412-19.

Rowland, Beryl. "The Physician's 'Historial Thyng Notable' and the Man of Law." *ELH,* 40 (1973), 165-78.

NINE

RICHARD L. HOFFMAN

The Influence of the Classics on Chaucer

By "the Classics," we mean, of course, the Latin Classics, for there is, unfortunately, no real possibility that Chaucer read Greek in any meaningful way. And even of the Roman writers, the list of those whom he knew well and used significantly is not so long as Chaucerians sometimes pretend.

Since at least the time of Dryden, no one has attempted to deny the inescapable fact that Chaucer's favorite Roman *auctoritee* was Ovid. As Shannon remarks, at the very beginning of his conclusion to *Chaucer and the Roman Poets*, "the one dominant idea that emerges from the consideration of Chaucer's relation to the Roman poets is his intimate knowledge of even the details of Ovid's poetry" (p. 371).

Naturally, the only possible second is Virgil, and, as we should expect, the *Aeneid* was rather familiar to Chaucer. Gilbert Highet points to Books I, II, and IV as his favorites, but cautions at the same time (1) that the only real indication of his acquaintance with *Aeneid* VII-XII is a very brief summary in the *House of Fame*, 451-67 and (2) that he probably did not know the *Eclogues* and *Georgics* (p. 592). Even the motto on the Prioress' brooch— "Amor vincit omnia"—cannot serve as evidence to the contrary, for it could as easily have come from the *Speculum historiale* of

Vincent of Beauvais (Chaucer mentions Vincent's "Estoryal Myr-
our" in the *Legend of Good Women*, G, 307) as from *Eclogue*
x, 69.

Chaucer's knowledge of Statius, especially the *Thebaid*, was
well authenticated more than a half-century ago by B. A. Wise;
and, much more recently, R. A. Pratt has shown us "Chaucer's
Claudian."

For the other poets, there has been, frankly, much more wish-
ful thinking than proof. Chaucer may have read some Horace. He
knew at least the title and basic theme of Valerius Flaccus' *Argonautica*. And apparently he knew enough of Lucan's *Pharsalia* to
realize that there was little enough in it for a poet like him to
mine. We may be certain that he read somewhere a part of
Juvenal's *Tenth Satire* ("The Vanity of Human Wishes"), for he
paraphrases lines 2-4 in *Troilus and Criseyde*, IV, 197-201 and
line 22 in the *Wife of Bath's Tale*, 1192-4. It would be pleasant
to know that he read Persius and Catullus, but positive proof
seems lacking. No one has proposed Martial or Propertius.

Among Latin prose authors, Chaucer knew, in some form and
in varying degrees, Cicero, Livy, Seneca, Valerius Maximus, and
"Cato" (supposed author of the *Dionysii Catonis disticha de
moribus ad filium*, written probably in the third or fourth century A.D. but incorrectly assigned in the Middle Ages to Cato
the Elder). Finally, if we count Macrobius and Boethius as classical authors, we should recall that he found useful the *Commentary on the Dream of Scipio* and that he gave us the second
English translation of *The Consolation of Philosophy*.

A complete list of the Latin writings which Chaucer used may
be found in Hammond's *Bibliographical Manual*, pp. 84-105; and
Lounsbury's famous chapter on "The Learning of Chaucer" (II,
ch. 5) contains a very useful discussion of Latin authors (pp. 249-
88). Koch's lengthy article on Chaucer's reading in the Roman
Classics is still a convenient survey, but should be read calmly
and used cautiously; for while Koch's admirable skepticism about
the extent of Chaucer's classical learning provides a healthful
antidote to the enthusiasm of many more devoted Chaucerians,

it leads him to raise some doubts which are not entirely necessary or reasonable. Magoun has given us a very helpful dictionary of "the geographical and ethnic names of the ancient and biblical world" as reflected in Chaucer's writings. The list includes names relating to "the geography of Greek mythology" and "may be taken as representative of his [Chaucer's] knowledge of the subject" (p. 107).

Virtually all of the direct classical influences on Chaucer, including instances of verbal parallelism and recasting of classical originals, are pointed out by Skeat and Robinson in the notes to their great editions of Chaucer's works and by Root in the notes to his text of the *Troilus*. In the case of entire tales which Chaucer borrowed, directly or indirectly, from classical sources (notably, the Physician's from Livy, the Manciple's and the Monk's Tale of Hercules from Ovid), *Sources and Analogues* is an indispensable tool, providing both the text of the original and a full discussion of the sometimes very complex literary relationships.

Rather curiously, only three full-length studies of Chaucer's debt to Rome have been published: Wise's book on the influence of Statius and Shannon's on the Roman poets are both mentioned above. My own study, *Ovid* and the *Canterbury Tales*, attempts at once to support Shannon's conclusion that Chaucer's greatest debt was to Ovid and to correct his impression that "the very nature of the classical influence upon Chaucer . . . meant that the direct borrowings from the Latin should decrease as he advanced into the extensive field of contemporary life" (p. 302). Shannon, believing that Ovid's dominant influence upon Chaucer ceased with completion of the *Legend of Good Women* (which is based upon the *Heroides*), devoted only twenty-four pages of his book to a consideration of Ovidian *and* Virgilian materials in the *Tales*. Since my study tries to reopen this important case by presenting some new evidence concerning both the nature and the extent of Ovid's influence on the *Tales*, and since the book includes material from eleven of my published notes and articles on this subject, I may be permitted to offer here a summary of my procedure and conclusions.

The first part of my study explores the possibility that Chaucer may have learned from the *Metamorphoses* much of his own verse narrative technique and then, postulating the theory that love is the unifying theme of the *Tales*, considers the thematic significance of Ovid's invocation to Venus as "mother of the twin Loves" in *Fasti* IV, 1. Part II is divided into fifteen chapters arranged for convenience according to the order of the prologues and tales in which Ovidian allusions have been noted. For every allusion, the entire relevant passage in Ovid is both quoted and translated, together with its Chaucerian derivative or parallel. Moreover, in an effort to explain *how* Chaucer read Ovid and *why* he borrowed from him, the standard medieval interpretations of Ovid, as developed by Arnulf of Orléans, John of Garland, Giovanni del Vergilio, and Petrus Berchorius, are examined.

The general results of my study, as summarized in Part III, are (1) that Ovid's influence upon Chaucer certainly did not wane after composition of the *Legend of Good Women*, for the *Tales* are filled with Ovidian materials of various kinds—entire tales, mythological and iconographic details, proverbs and other ethical *dicta*—drawn largely from the *Metamorphoses*, the *Ars amatoria*, the *Heroides*, and the *Fasti*; (2) that Chaucer customarily used the *Metamorphoses* as a handbook of mythology; (3) that Chaucer considered Ovid an ethical philosopher and not merely a teller of tales; (4) that Chaucer was concerned with the *sentence* or moral lessons of Ovid's fables as well as with their *sense* or surface meaning, and that the standard moral commentaries on Ovid produced in the high Middle Ages, providing an index to the way Chaucer read Ovid, offer valuable assistance in interpreting the significance of Ovidian material in its Chaucerian context; and finally (5) that Chaucer, fully recognizing this manifold dependence upon his favorite Roman poet, seems to have enjoyed representing himself as an English Ovid.

It is not surprising that most other scholarship of the last half-century on Chaucer's indebtedness to Ovid has focused upon the *Legend of Good Women*, which— as Shannon and all the editors make clear—is Chaucer's most patently and thoroughly Ovidian piece. In a brilliant but necessarily inconclusive article written in 1918, Lowes demonstrated that Chaucer made use of the *Ovide moralisé* in writing his *Legend of Philomela* and gave us some reason to believe that there are traces of the same work in the *Legend of Ariadne* and in the account of Theseus and Ariadne in the *House of Fame*, 405-26. By 1931, de Boer had published his edition of that part of the *Ovide moralisé* which Lowes had needed, and Sanford Meech was able in that year to affirm "the impress of the moralized Ovid" (p. 183) on the legends of Philomela and Ariadne. Concerning the passage on Theseus and Ariadne in the *House of Fame*, however, Meech noted that, while Chaucer "gives several circumstances not found in the eighth book of the *Metamorphoses* nor in the tenth epistle of the *Heroides*," it is impossible to determine whether he derived them from the *Ovide moralisé* or from Machaut's *Jugement dou roy de Navarre* (p. 183).

No less important than his study of Chaucer and the *Ovide moralisé* is Meech's discovery of an Italian translation of the *Heroides*, written probably between 1320 and 1330 by one Filippo "Ceffi." The conclusion of his persuasive essay on Chaucer's knowledge of this work is that "in quoting or paraphrasing the *Heroides* in the Legends of Hypermnestra, Phyllis, Medea, and Dido and in the first book of the *Troilus*, Chaucer, lacking an English translation of them, sought the assistance of Filippo 'Ceffi' in construing the Latin text quite as naturally as an intelligent modern author might avail himself of the Loeb Library" (p. 128).

Norman Callan compares the treatments of Ovid's legend of Thisbe by Chaucer and Gower and judges Chaucer's version preferable, "not so much because he is closer to Ovid and altogether fuller, as by reason of his felicitous re-creations of individual words and lines" (p. 274). And Marvin La Hood, in "an attempt to show how Chaucer Christianized his sources in the *Legend of Good Women*" (p. 274), contrasts the *Legend of Lucrece* with

Ovid's account in the *Fasti*. Finally, the recent dissertation on the *Heroides* and the *Legend of Good Women* by Eleanor Winsor Leach is refreshing in its concern with rhetoric.

Since Virgil's influence on Chaucer is most clearly discernible in *The House of Fame* and *The Legend of Dido*, these works, quite naturally, have attracted the attention of most Virgilian source-hunters, ancient and modern. Without seeking to deny the direct influence of Virgil, Albert C. Friend calls attention to the similarities between Chaucer's treatment of Aeneas in the *House of Fame* and the *Ilias* of Simon Aurea Capra—"a French clerk who entered the house of Saint Victor in Paris in the time of Abbot Gilduin (d. 1155)" (p. 317). Friend's study presents a detailed comparison of Simon's *Ilias* (which was well-known and highly regarded as a commentary on the *Aeneid*) and eleven passages of the *House of Fame*, occurring between lines 151 and 465. While the question "remains whether Chaucer had Simon's work at hand as he wrote," Friend suggests that the *Ilias* belongs with the *Aeneid* "in the background of Chaucer's reading" (p. 323).

D. R. Bradley, challenging a much earlier article by E. B. Atwood on *The Legend of Dido*, 1114-24 (Dido's gifts to Aeneas) and 1326-9 (Aeneas' departure from Dido by night), shows that these passages are not "entirely products of Chaucer's invention" (p. 122), but rather that Chaucer seems to have read carefully the relevant passages of both the *Aeneid* and the Rawlinson *Excidium Troie* and to have integrated his source materials very closely (p. 125).

A most interesting approach to Chaucer's adaptations of the *Aeneid* in both the *House of Fame* and the *Legend of Dido* is that taken by Louis B. Hall, who compares Chaucer's two versions not only with each other but with five representative examples of "medieval tradition in redacting the *Aeneid*" (p. 149). He concludes that "the approach taken by Shannon as well as by those who searched for a unique source ignores the fact that during the entire Middle Ages a tradition of Virgilian adaptation had developed," and that "Chaucer's adaptations should be evaluated in their relation to this tradition as a whole and not in their relation to only one representative of it" (pp. 148-9). The statement is interesting, not only in the specific context of Hall's study, but as an indication of a new direction in recent Chaucerian source studies—namely, the attempt to establish a tradition or convention rather than "discover" a single source.

There have been only two very important studies of Statius and Chaucer since the publication of Wise's seminal book in 1911, but both of these are of such major significance that it will be necessary to discuss them in some considerable detail. The first is F. P. Magoun's essay, "Chaucer's Summary of Statius' *Thebaid* II-XII." Near the end of the *Troilus* (v, 1457-1533), Cassandra interprets for Troilus his dream of seeing Criseyde (v, 1233-41) in the arms of a boar. Chaucer includes in stanzas 213-16 a twenty-six-line summary of *Thebaid* II-XII. In all but two manuscripts of the *Troilus* there is inserted between stanzas 214 and 215 a Latin *Argument* (possibly by Lactantius), consisting of twelve hexameter lines, outlining sketchily the twelve books of the *Thebaid* at the rate of one hexameter per book. Magoun prints stanzas 213-16 of *Troilus and Criseyde*, v, together with the *Argument*, placed between stanzas 214 and 215; and, on the grounds that Chaucer himself and not a scribe first inserted the *Argument* here, he argues that in all editions of the *Troilus*, "the Latin should stay where the manuscripts have it and an English translation should for general convenience be given as a foot-note or end-note" (p. 419).

Magoun maintains, moreover, that Chaucer's summary of the *Thebaid* in his *Troilus* depends not only on these twelve lines but also upon a series of eleven other twelve-line Latin arguments, each devoted to one of the last eleven books of Statius' poem. Magoun gives all eleven arguments, together with translations, and concludes, after a book-by-book analysis (pp. 419-20), that, in outlining the earlier books of the *Thebaid*, Chaucer drew more upon the eleven arguments and, in outlining the later books, more upon the *Argument* which appears in the manuscripts. He seems to have gone to Statius directly for Books VIII and x.

Finally, Magoun notes that there is no surviving Latin argument for *Thebaid* 1 and that Cassandra, significantly, takes no cognizance of Statius' first Book—even though the whole cause of the war against Thebes is there set forth.

Paul M. Clogan has also been concerned with commentaries on Statius. His excellent essay, "Chaucer and the *Thebaid* Scholia," is an outgrowth of his dissertation, "Chaucer and the Medieval Statius" (containing, pp. 25-75, a revision of Wise). Clogan's published article deals specifically with "the extensive glosses and commentaries found in most manuscripts of the *Thebaid* of Chaucer's time" (p. 599). Believing that "the form in which the *Thebaid* was read and enjoyed in the fourteenth century may best be learned through a study of the medieval manuscripts" (p. 601), which can thus help us "to re-evaluate the extent and the nature of Statius' influence upon Chaucer" (p. 603), Clogan examined eighteen of the extant seventy-five manuscripts—those containing the fullest *scholia*. The results of his investigation are contained in the second part of his essay (pp. 603-14), dealing with the specific influence of these glosses. His conclusion is that "Chaucer may have been influenced by the *Thebaid* glosses in the *House of Fame, Anelida and Arcite, Troilus and Criseyde*, and the *Knight's Tale*" and that he may be even more generally and extensively indebted to "the rich font of classical and mythological lore in the glosses and commentaries on Statius" (p. 615).

Clogan's very sound approach to Statius reflects the methodology of Karl Young, R. A. Pratt, J. Burke Severs, and a number of other Chaucerians who, like them, have labored long to establish "The Chaucer Library" and to examine "Chaucer's learning." Specifically, Clogan's work bears the imprint of his teacher, Pratt, whose study of "Chaucer's Claudian" in 1947 gave direction to some of the most distinguished Chaucerian source studies of the last two decades; for Pratt's admitted aim there was "to redirect attention to the importance of studying Chaucer's sources as they appear in mediaeval manuscripts" (p. 429).

Pratt begins his article by reminding us that it was Karl Young who first suspected that Chaucer must have known the standard medieval school reader called *Liber Catonianus*, containing works by "Cato," Theodulus, Avianus Maximianus, Statius, and Claudian (p. 419). Significantly, Pratt reports that Claudian's *De raptu Proserpinae* (sometimes with glosses) is included in most thirteenth-century manuscripts of the *Liber Catonianus* and demonstrates how these manuscripts of the *Liber* make it possible "to reappraise both the extent and the nature of Claudian's influence upon Chaucer" (p. 420). In an effort to determine "the form in which Chaucer may have known Claudian's poetry" (p. 419), Pratt first presents the group of medieval manuscripts containing the *De raptu Proserpinae* and then considers, *seriatim*, those passages in Chaucer which show Claudian's impress. He concludes that, although scholars have found parallels to four of Claudian's poems in Chaucer, the number must, in fact, be reduced to two; for while Chaucer knew, unmistakably, the *De raptu* and *Laus Serenae*, there is no clear evidence that he used the *In Rufinum* or the *Panegyricus de sexto consulatu Honorii Augusti* (p. 420).

Unhappily, there is still no real agreement about the extent of Chaucer's acquaintance with Horace. More than fifty years ago Harriet Seibert pointed out that of the eight passages usually noted by scholars where Chaucer "apparently had lines from Horace in mind," "convenient second-hand sources" exist for five (p. 304). Seibert managed to suggest such "second-hand sources" for two of the remaining three passages and then dismissed the last as merely proverbial. Seven years later, C. L. Wrenn reexamined the evidence and concluded that "Chaucer—though he cannot be said to have been familiar with Horace, or to have known him at all completely—was directly acquainted with his *Epistola ad Pisones de arte poetica*, and with at least one (perhaps two) of his Odes" (p. 292). And, in a fascinating but not entirely convincing article, George R. Coffman sought to associate Chaucer's several discussions of old age with Horace's description in *Ars poetica*, 169-74.

At least one Horatian ghost, however, does seem at long last to have been laid. Apparently Chaucer's references in the *Troilus* and the *House of Fame* to "myn auctour called Lollius" as an authority on the Trojan War is the result—as Latham, Kittredge, and Ten Brink suggested—of his misunderstanding of Horace's *Epistola* I, ii, 1-2. But, as Pratt implies in his note on "Chaucer's Lollius," Chaucer probably read—or rather misread—Horace's lines not in a manuscript of Horace but in a copy of John of Salisbury's *Policraticus*, where they are quoted—or rather misquoted—in the context of a discussion of Troy.

For Lucan, Shannon's early statement—made ten years before the publication of his book—has been allowed to stand: Chaucer read "the grete poete, daun Lucan," but made very little use of him in his own poetry because "Lucan's subject-matter and style in the *Pharsalia* were not such as to make an appeal to our English story-teller poet" (p. 614).

The judgment on Catullus is even more severe. As McPeek observes: "However much we might like to believe that Chaucer had read Catullus, since Chaucer mentions him nowhere, and since no passages in his work may be traced beyond peradventure to the *Carmina*, we must conclude that he never knew the great pre-Augustan lyrist" (p. 301).

Among the handful of "classical" prose writers whom Chaucer knew familiarly, only "Cato" has received close attention in recent years. Richard Hazelton's dissertation, "Two Texts of the 'Disticha Catonis' and Its Commentary," has yielded a fine article on "Chaucer and Cato," which—once again—reveals the influence of Pratt's work on Claudian. On the basis of twenty-three manuscripts of the *Liber Catonis* which he examined carefully, Hazelton concludes that this famous medieval book provided Chaucer "as it did all other literate men of his era, not only with training in Latin but with an introduction to ethics. For the *ethica Catonis*, like other grammar school texts, served a purpose beyond mere language training. The material of the book, as all the glossators point out, is the four cardinal virtues" (pp. 357-8). Commentaries on "Cato's" distichs grew by accretion from the ninth century, when Remigius of Auxerre glossed them, to the sixteenth, when Erasmus produced an edition of "Cato" together with *Scholia perbrevia*. "It is," Hazelton reports, "in the context of these pedagogical materials—the 'scole-matere' that clustered around the *Liber Catonis*—that I have studied Chaucer's knowledge of Cato" (p. 359).

The results of this study are interesting and rather surprising, for it appears that Chaucer was indebted to "the Cato-book" for a good deal more than is usually assumed from "the mere citation of his borrowings from the distichs." Unlike most of his contemporaries—for example, Deschamps, Langland, and Gower, who all regard "Cato" with sober respect—Chaucer did not "utilize Cato honorifically as a traditional source of ethical doctrine, but rather . . . turned Catonian doctrine to the uses of parody" (p. 360). In fact, "Chaucer's most extensive and most striking uses of Cato are openly irreverent and at times even mocking." The most notable instances of this parodic and heterodox use of "Cato" occur in the tales of the Nun's Priest, the Miller, the Reeve, the Merchant, and the Manciple.

Finally, and most recently, Pratt has challenged Chaucer's direct acquaintance with Seneca and Valerius Maximus. His article, "Chaucer and the Hand that Fed Him," explores the strong possibility that Chaucer used instead John of Wales' *Communiloquium*—a late thirteenth-century "mosaic of several thousand quotations, chiefly from the Bible and such classical, patristic, and medieval writers as Cicero, Horace, Trogus Pompeius, Valerius Maximus, Seneca, Ambrose, Jerome, Augustine, Boethius, Isidore, Gregory the Great, John of Salisbury, Anselm, Alexander Neckam, and Innocent III" (pp. 619-20). The major poems in which Pratt finds traces of this work are the *Prologue* and *Tale of the Wife of Bath*, the *Summoner's Tale*, and the *Pardoner's Tale* (p. 620). The most important conclusion of his study for our purposes is that "some writings as such are hereby completely eliminated from Chaucer's shelves": these include the *opera* of Seneca and the *De factis dictisque* of Valerius Maximus (p. 638).

Naturally, this rapid survey of scholarship on Chaucer's use of the Classics must not be considered exhaustive. I have offered merely a sampling of what seems to me, and to others, most significant on the subject, especially from the last twenty years.

A considerable amount of material—and very much of it worthy —has had to be omitted. The student who wishes to pursue the matter further may complete his picture by consulting Hammond, Griffith, Crawford, and the annual bibliography in *PMLA*. Finally, there are, of course, a number of substantial books on Chaucer which are concerned, *passim*, with classical materials, and these, too, I have had to ignore here. Even to suggest, for example, the wealth of absorbing information on Chaucer's relationship to classical tradition contained in John McCall's dissertation on classical myth in the *Troilus* or D. W. Robertson's *Preface to Chaucer*—to name only two such studies—would require more space than I have had.

If such a survey as this permits us to reach any conclusion—or, perhaps, to form any impression—it is, surely, that those of us who love Chaucer and the Latin Classics and enjoy practicing the time-honored sport of source-hunting have come, rather recently, upon some new preserves. Quite clearly, it is no longer deemed sufficient simply to point out, by citations of verbal parallelism, that Chaucer knew Claudian or "Cato", Ovid or Statius. We have begun to open up just such manuscripts of the Classics as Chaucer himself must have read—and we are coming increasingly to realize that we should examine the glosses and commentaries as well as the texts.

The results of this active concern are some fresh questions concerning—these words appear so often in the recent scholarship—the *nature* as well as the *extent* of classical influence. In what form did Chaucer read this author? How did he understand him? Why does he quote this passage here? What did he glean from the commentaries and glosses on this work? How does all this illuminate Chaucer's own poetry? In short, what place do the Latin Classics occupy in the development of Chaucer's genius and the creation of his art?

A rather staggering amount of work must still be done before we can presume to answer these questions, but if we may judge from what has already been accomplished, the search will be stimulating and the fruits of such labor, good.

* * * * *

Research in Chaucer's much Latin and no Greek has been quite vigorous during the past decade, with studies ranging from the rather general to the very specific. Among notable examples of the former are Bruce Harbert's essay, "Chaucer and the Latin Classics," Georgene M. Bertolotti's dissertation on "Chaucer's Use of Classical Story," and two unpublished dictionaries of classical, mythological, and astrological names in Chaucer. Noteworthy among very specific source studies are John W. Carr's proposal that Chaucer's first line in the *House of Fame*, "God turne us every drem to goode!," may be derived from Tibullus III.iv.95 ("haec deus in melius crudelia somnia vertat") and Chandler B. Beall's observation that Seneca's "et . . . gaudeo discere, ut doceam" may have prompted Chaucer to say of his Clerk, "And gladly wolde he lerne and gladly teche."

A remarkable amount of attention has been given recently (both in publications and in doctoral dissertations) to individual mythological figures and to the medieval traditions that funneled them to Chaucer. Examples are Judson B. Allen and Patrick Gallacher on Midas, Emerson Brown on Priapus and Pyramus and Thisbe, Joseph B. Martin on Ceyx and Alcyone, Joyce E. Potter on Jove, Melvin G. Storm on Mars, McKay Sundwall on Deiphobus and Helen, Raymond P. Tripp on Dido, and Alan T. Gaylord on Saturn (as god and star). Gaylord's essay, like Robert S. Haller's article on epic tradition, deals specifically with that apparently inexhaustible mythographical masterpiece, the *Knight's Tale*. Predictably enough, many of these studies focus (as the bibliography will show) upon Chaucer's two favorite Roman authors, Ovid and Vergil, and upon the rich corpus of medieval allegorical commentary on them—including, of course, the *Ovide moralisé*.

Finally, and most significantly, the last decade has seen the birth and healthy growth of a *Chaucer Variorum*. Among the innumerable benefits to be derived from the same should be the identification of *all* of Chaucer's classical sources, large and small —until more are discovered later.

BIBLIOGRAPHY

Allen, Judson B., and Patrick Gallacher. "Alisoun through the Looking Glass: or Everyman His Own Midas." *ChauR*, 4 (1970), 99-105.

Atwood, E.B. "Two Alterations of Virgil in Chaucer's *Dido*." *Speculum*, 13 (1938), 454-57.

Beall, Chandler B. "And Gladly Teche." *ELN*, 13 (1975), 85-86.

Bertolotti, Georgene M. "Chaucer's Use of Classical Story." Diss. Brown, 1973.

Bradley, D.R. "Fals Eneas and Sely Dido." *PQ*, 39 (1960), 122-25.

Brown, Emerson, Jr. "Hortus Inconclusus: The Significance of Priapus and Pyramus and Thisbe in the *Merchant's Tale*." *ChauR*, 4 (1970), 31-40.

————. "Priapus and the *Parlement of Foulys*." *SP*, 72 (1975), 258-74.

Bryan, W.F., and Germaine Dempster, eds. *Sources and Analogues of Chaucer's Canterbury Tales*. 1941. Rpt. New York: Humanities Press, 1958.

Callan, Norman. "Thyn Owne Book: A Note on Chaucer, Gower and Ovid." *RES*, 22 (1946), 269-81.

Carr, John W. "A Borrowing from Tibullus in Chaucer's *House of Fame*." *ChauR*, 8 (1974), 191-97.

Clogan, Paul M. "Chaucer and the Medieval Statius." Diss. Illinois, 1961.

————. "Chaucer and the *Thebaid* Scholia." *SP*, 61 (1964), 599-615.

Coffman, George R. "Old Age from Horace to Chaucer: Some Literary Affinities and Adventures of an Idea." *Speculum*, 9 (1934), 249-77.

Crawford, William R. *Bibliography of Chaucer, 1954-63*. Seattle: Univ. of Washington Press, 1967.

Delany, Sheila. "Chaucer's House of Fame and the *Ovide Moralisé*." *CL*, 20 (1968), 254-64.

De Weever, Jacqueline E. "A Dictionary of Classical, Mythological and Sidereal Names in the Works of Geoffrey Chaucer." Diss. Pennsylvania, 1972.

Dillon, Bert. "A Dictionary of Personal, Mythological, Allegorical and Astrological Proper Names and Allusions in the Work of Geoffrey Chaucer." Diss. Duke, 1973.

Dronke, Peter, and Jill Mann. "Chaucer and the Medieval Latin Poets." In *Geoffrey Chaucer*. Ed. D.S. Brewer. London: Bell, 1974, pp. 154-83.

Friend, Albert C. "Chaucer's Version of the Aeneid." *Speculum*, 28 (1953), 317-23.

Gaylord, Alan T. "The Role of Saturn in the *Knight's Tale*." *ChauR*, 8 (1974), 171-90.

Griffith, Dudley D. *Bibliography of Chaucer, 1908-1953*. Seattle: Univ. of Washington Press, 1955.

Hall, Louis B. "Chaucer and the Dido-and-Aeneas Story." *MS*, 25 (1963), 148-59.

Haller, Robert S. "The *Knight's Tale* and the Epic Tradition." *ChauR*, 1 (1966), 67-84.

Hammond, Eleanor P. *Chaucer: A Bibliographical Manual*. 1908. Rpt. New York: P. Smith, 1933.

Harbert, Bruce. "Chaucer and the Latin Classics." In *Geoffrey Chaucer*. Ed. D.S. Brewer. London: Bell, 1974, pp. 137-53.

Hazelton, Richard. "Two Texts of the 'Disticha Catonis' and Its Commentary, with Special Reference to Chaucer, Langland, and Gower." Diss. Rutgers, 1956.

———. "Chaucer and Cato." *Speculum*, 35 (1960), 357-80.

Highet, Gilbert. *The Classical Tradition: Greek and Roman Influences on Western Literature*. New York: Oxford Univ. Press, 1957.

Hoffman, Richard L. *Ovid and the Canterbury Tales*. Philadelphia: Univ. of Pennsylvania Press, 1967.

Koch, John. "Chaucers Belesenheit in den römischen Klassikern." *ESt*, 57 (1923), 8-84.

LaHood, Marvin J. "Chaucer's The Legend of *Lucrece*." *PQ*, 43 (1964), 274-76.

Leach, Eleanor Jane Winsor. "The Sources and Rhetoric of Chaucer's 'Legend of Good Women' and Ovid's 'Heroides'." Diss. Yale, 1963.

Lounsbury, T.R. *Studies in Chaucer: His Life and Writings.* 3 vols. 1892. Rpt. Princeton: Princeton Univ. Press, 1965.

Lowes, John L. "Chaucer and the *Ovide Moralisé.*" *PMLA*, 33 (1918), 302-25.

McCall, John P. "Classical Myth in Chaucer's *Troilus and Criseyde*: An Aspect of the Classical Tradition in the Middle Ages." Diss. Princeton, 1955.

McPeek, James A.S. "Did Chaucer Know Catullus?" *MLN*, 46 (1931), 293-301.

Magoun, Francis P., Jr. "Chaucer's Ancient and Biblical World." *MS*, 15 (1953), 107-36; "Addenda," *MS*, 16 (1954), 152-56.

———. "Chaucer's Summary of Statius' *Thebaid* II-XII." *Traditio*, 11 (1955), 409-20.

Martin, Joseph B., III. "The Medieval Ceyx and Alcyone: Ovid's *Metamorphoses* XI, 407-750, and Chaucer's *Book of the Duchess.*" Diss. Duke, 1973.

Meech, Sanford B. "Chaucer and an Italian Translation of the *Heroides.*" *PMLA*, 45 (1930), 110-28.

———. "Chaucer and the *Ovide Moralisé*: A Further Study." *PMLA*, 46 (1931), 182-204.

Potter, Joyce E. "Chaucer's Use of the Pagan God Jove." Diss. Duke, 1972.

Pratt, R.A. "Chaucer's Claudian." *Speculum*, 22 (1947), 419-29.

———. "A Note on Chaucer's Lollius." *MLN*, 65 (1950), 183-87.

———. "Chaucer and the Hand that Fed Him." *Speculum*, 41 (1966), 619-42. [Cf. Harry M. Ayres, "Chaucer and Seneca." *RR*, 10 (1919), 1-15.]

Robertson, D.W., Jr. *A Preface to Chaucer: Studies in Medieval Perspectives.* Princeton: Princeton Univ. Press, 1962.

Rowland, Beryl. "The Physician's 'Historial Thyng Notable' and the Man of Law." *EHL*, 40 (1973), 165-78.

Seibert, Harriet. "Chaucer and Horace." *MLN*, 31 (1916), 304-7.

Shannon, E.F. "Chaucer and Lucan's *Pharsalia*." *MP*, 16 (1919), 609-14.

————. *Chaucer and the Roman Poets.* Cambridge, Mass.: Harvard Univ. Press, 1929.

Storm, Melvin G., Jr. "Chaucer's Poetic Treatment of the Figure of Mars." Diss. Illinois, 1973.

Sundwall, McKay. "Deiphobus and Helen: A Tantalizing Hint." *MP*, 73 (1975), 151-56.

Tisdale, Charles P. "The *House of Fame*: Virgilian Reason and Boethian Wisdom." *CL*, 25 (1973), 247-61.

Tripp, Raymond P., Jr. "Chaucer's Psychologizing of Vergil's Dido." *BRMMLA*, 24 (1970), 51-59.

Wise, B.A. *The Influence of Statius upon Chaucer.* 1911. Rpt. New York: Phaeton Press, 1967.

Witlieb, Bernard L. "Chaucer and the *Ovide Moralisé*." *N&Q*, 17 (1970), 202-7.

Wrenn, C.L. "Chaucer's Knowledge of Horace." *MLR*, 18 (1923), 286-92.

TEN

CHAUNCEY WOOD

Chaucer and Astrology

As Robinson has observed in his introduction to Chaucer's *Treatise on the Astrolabe*, Chaucer's "references to astronomy and astrology are so numerous and important that their elucidation has been a principal part of the work of his commentators" (p. 541). It is certainly true that Chaucer's references are important and that they have attracted a good deal of scholarship, but at the present there is no book-length study of Chaucer and astrology such as exists for Dante and even for Gower. The many scholarly excursions on Chaucer's astrology are fragmentary and are usually confined to an examination of the technical aspects of the astrology and ignore its function in the poetry.

Even in the technical area of astrology, which might be considered a rather matter-of-fact business, a consensus on Chaucer's meaning cannot be found for even the most frequently discussed passages. The cause of this curious situation is that astrology itself is a vast, sometimes obscure, and occasionally self-contradictory science. As D. C. Allen says, "the literature of astrology is as vast as the history of man. No one scholar can possibly hope to untangle all of its intricately woven strands; in the course of his life, he cannot read the extant works on the subject, let alone resolve its intricate patterns of thought" (p. v). Indeed, if

the scholar *did* read everything, he might still find himself perplexed, for as Skeat remarks in the notes to his edition of the
Works: "The old astrologers used to alter their predictions almost
at pleasure, by stating that their results depended on several
causes, which partly counteracted one another; an arrangement
of which the convenience is obvious" (v, 151).

Because of the nature of the primary materials of astrology it
is fortunate that there are various aids available to the scholar.
There are several general histories of science that are useful for
orientation, the most substantial of which is George Sarton's
Introduction to the History of Science. Somewhat more particularly concerned with astrology is a massive work often cited by
Chaucerian scholars, Lynn Thorndike's *A History of Magic and
Experimental Science*. It should be noted, however, that Professor Thorndike maintains a partisanship for astrology in its
various dialogues with the medieval church that is often intrusive.
Other works that deserve particular mention are Pierre Duhem's
Le système du monde and *Sternglaube und Sterndeutung* by Boll
and Bezold. A very clear and well-illustrated volume addressed
to a general audience is Louis MacNeice's *Astrology*.

Beyond the broad histories of science and of astrology there
are numerous specialized volumes that are indispensable to those
who wish to work closely with astrological materials. Chief
among these is Francis Carmody's bibliography of *Arabic Astronomical and Astrological Sciences in Latin Translation*. This is an
immensely helpful research tool; it even discusses in detail the
various anonymous compilations. The only flaw in the work is
that the author is sometimes too much of a purist; the scholar
who searches for Albohazen Haly will search in vain unless he
knows that the better Westernization of the Arabic name is Haly
Abenragel. Another excellent scholarly aid that has not been
much used by literary scholars is the remarkable compilation by
Saxl and Meier of the illuminations of English and European
astrological and mythological manuscripts. When the scholar
wishes to work with secondary materials on Chaucer and astrology, the bibliography in W. C. Curry's *Chaucer and the Mediaeval*

Sciences is useful even though it covers more sciences than just astrology. The bibliographies of Griffith and Crawford have sections on Chaucer's scientific backgrounds, thereby providing coverage of scholarship on Chaucer and astrology up to the early 1960's.

Oftentimes what is needed by the scholar or student is not a history of astrology or analysis of its impact, but something that in a more practical way explicates the terminology of the subject and explains the basic phenomena. For this purpose the best work is Florence Grimm's *Astronomical Lore in Chaucer*, the usefulness of which is attested by its customary unavailability in libraries around the country. Another work on astrology that has good diagrams illustrating the various celestial motions is M. A. Orr's *Dante and the Early Astronomers*. There are also sophisticated outlines of the subject in Derek Price's edition of the *Equatorie of the Planetis*, a work ascribed by some to Chaucer, and in Price's article "Chaucer's Astronomy." In spite of these various aids the neophyte will often be puzzled by the workings of astrology even after studying it for some time, and some introduction to the introductions is in order. At the heart of the matter is the fact that the old cosmology is clear once understood, but it is difficult to understand certain parts of the theory. While the several expositions tell what is needed, they do not sufficiently emphasize what it means when we say that a planet is "in" a sign, and how a planet both progresses daily from east to west around the earth and yet simultaneously proceeds along the zodiac at a much slower rate in the opposite direction. For Chaucerian scholars it is quite permissable to be vague about epicycles, deferents, and eccentrics, but the two motions of the heavens *must* be understood if any sense at all is to be made out of poems such as *The Complaint of Mars*. Perhaps the basic difficulty is that while it is easy enough to envision a planet such as Mars rising in the east like the sun once every twenty-four hours and moving from east to west across the heavens to return to rise again twenty-four hours later, the motion through the zodiac runs, as it were, against the grain, and it is not insignificant that in the Middle Ages this motion was always characterized as being "irrational." If we envision a sign of the zodiac over our heads, our natural impulse is to number the degrees in the sign from 1 through 30 from left to right, but the planet moves through the sign from our right to our left over a period of days or years, depending on the planet, and it is extremely awkward to visualize numbers running "backwards." But it helps. Once the rudiments of the system have been investigated the intrinsic beauty of the old cosmology and its particular appeal to the medieval imagination should be explored, and here C. S. Lewis' series of lectures on *The Discarded Image* is invaluable.

Curry argues that "it is both a futile and a useless procedure" (p. xv) to attempt to determine Chaucer's personal attitude toward astrology, but surely this is wrong on both counts. However difficult it may be we must attempt to determine both Chaucer's attitude and the customary attitude of his audience, for otherwise we simply cannot determine the meaning of certain passages. When the Wife of Bath tells us that she followed the path the stars *inclined* her toward, it makes all the difference in the world whether Chaucer and his audience believed that she was irrevocably compelled to follow this way or not compelled at all. Therefore, determining Chaucer's attitude is certainly not useless, but is it futile? One would think not, in view of the fact that speaking *in propria persona* in the *Treatise on the Astrolabe* Chaucer flatly disclaims belief in the cornerstones of judicial astrology—that part of the science having to do with horoscopes, and elections of favorable times (p. 551). However, astonishingly enough, Robinson's note to this passage says that for Chaucer's *own* attitude we must look further afield. One wonders, if this passage does not express Chaucer's *own* attitude, whose view it does set forth. Unfortunately, when one investigates the various analyses of Chaucer's attitude, one finds in both of the works by Tatlock and in T. O. Wedel's study of the medieval attitude toward astrology, that there is a tendency to downgrade Chaucer's own statement on astrology on the one hand and a tendency to let Chaucer's literary characters speak for Chaucer the man on the other. Consequently these essays grant more belief to Chaucer than is warranted, and possibly grant more to his epoch than they should.

It is somewhat astonishing to discover that there are more than a half-dozen editions of Chaucer's *Treatise on the Astrolabe*, which is a work of rather limited appeal. For the Chaucerian student many of these editions are of interest more for their peripheral material than for their texts. For example, A. E. Brae's edition contains essays on astrology in the *General Prologue* and on the vexatious astrological imagery in the *Parson's Prologue*, as well as on other astrological topics and related matters such as the meaning of the word "prime." Skeat's edition has copious notes on astrological imagery in Chaucer's poetical works, and these are interesting to compare with the notes he wrote twenty years later in his edition of the complete works. He several times changes his arguments. Gunther's edition prints a translation of the basic source by Messahalla, and Pintelon's edition has a bibliography of previous editions, which unaccountably omits Gunther's. That the *Treatise* owes at least a partial debt to Sacrobosco has been argued on very flimsy evidence by Veazie. However, there is a good deal of indirect evidence that Chaucer would have known the work.

The astrological description of the time of the year in the *General Prologue* is part of one of the most famous passages in all English literature, and yet after 600 years scholars are still not in agreement about what is intended by the figure. Chaucer tells us that the showers of April have pierced the drought of March, and that the sun has run its "half-course" in the Ram, and this has elicited numerous interpretations. In the eighteenth century Tyrwhitt was all for emending "Ram" to "Bull" (I, 75), but Brae and Skeat urged that we interpret the "half-course" in the Ram as the *second* half course, the one the sun traverses in April (pp. 81-4, *Works*, V, 2-3). Robinson adopted Brae's and Skeat's solution but not everyone has concurred. Baldwin has stated that the sun was only halfway through the Ram (p. 54), and James Winny has remarked that the pilgrims set out "soon" after the sun entered the

Ram, rather than more than a month afterwards (pp. 169-70). D. W. Robertson, Jr. has suggested that the pilgrims leave when the sun is in Taurus because that is the astrological house of Venus, who represents the love of God or of the world that may motivate different pilgrims (p. 373). Bernard F. Huppé has noted that a four-teenth-century encyclopedist, Pierre Bersuire, likened the sun's passage through the signs of the zodiac in spring to Christ's "passage" through the three parts of penitence: contrition, confession, and satisfaction (p. 19). Finally, Chauncey Wood has argued that the specific time of year would suggest to Chaucer's audience a parallel between the April showers and Noah's Flood, which was traditionally interpreted as a figure of Baptism—thus creating a norm against which the characters in the *General Prologue* can be measured (pp. 263-9). Outside of the imagery of the zodiac in the opening lines there is little astrology in the *General Prologue*, but Winny, in a bold critical maneuver, has named the governing planets of the horoscopes of the Prioress, the Host, the Miller, and the Reeve, from an analysis of their characters.

The abundance of astrological imagery in the *Knight's Tale* has elicited a good deal of critical comment, but while the literal machinations of astrology in this tale are easy enough to expli-cate, the artistic function of the astrological images is much more difficult to grasp, because the *tone* of the tale as a whole is slip-pery. Thus, Curry writes that "the real conflict behind the sur-face action of the story is a conflict between the planets, Saturn and Mars" (p. 120), and yet in the same chapter he makes the remark that Chaucer "is not interested chiefly in astrology; the *Knight's Tale* is in no sense presented to illustrate the influence of Saturn and Mars in the affairs of two heroes" (p. 153). While these statements are not at all contradictory, one feels neverthe-less that the *place* of the astrological machinations has not been fixed with adequate nicety.

A similar problem arises with the larger issue of the extent to which the astrological gods cause and to what extent they reflect or echo the action of the earthly story. Curry has argued that Chaucer used "as a motivating force that formative and impelling influence of stars in which his age believed" (p. 119), and yet this view is perhaps too broad. Within the tale itself there is not one view of destiny but two, and Arcite's fatalistic determinism ("We moste endure it . . . ," *KnT*, 1091), echoed by Palamon, is contradicted by Theseus, whose remarks on destiny in terms of Providence (*KnT*, 1663ff.) embody a Boethian distinction much in line with his other expressions. In any event, the matter is not a closed issue.

More detailed astrological matters in the *Knight's Tale* have also come in for their share of elucidation and obfuscation. As long ago as 1908 W. H. Browne observed that the planetary hours were important in the tale, and that by calculation one could determine that Saturn's reversal of the apparent victory of Mars' knight Arcite occurs in Saturn's hour (pp. 53-4). P. E. Dustoor attempted a similar computation in order to demonstrate that Palamon's escape from prison occurred in the hour of Mercury, who therefore helps both Arcite and Palamon (p. 318), but his calculations do not work out as neatly, and in contrast with the situation involving Saturn's hour, no mention is made of Mercury in this spot in the text.

A more ambitious interpretation of an astrological detail has been advanced by Johnstone Parr, who argues that Saturn's statement "I do vengeance and pleyn correccioun, / Whil I dwelle in the signe of the leoun" (*KnT*, 2461-2), is to be seen as historical allegory. Because Saturn was in Leo from July 1, 1387 to August 15, 1389, Parr argues that "vengeance" refers to the Duke of Gloucester's persecution of young Richard II and his friends after Richard had been forced to submit to a regency the previous year, while "pleyn correccioun" would refer to Richard's turnabout in forcing the Privy Council to dissolve the regency in May of 1389 (pp. 307-14). For those who admire historical allegory this interpretation is quite attractive on the whole, although one may speculate as to whether its inclusion in a list of traditional Saturnine influences might not have been intrusive and even jarring in the midst of the *Knight's Tale*. There is also some doubt whether Chaucer would use *one* astrological image to describe *both* sides of a contemporary political battle. Walter E. Weese objected that Saturn is merely describing activities that are legitimately his (p. 333) and it is worthwhile to note in this regard that elsewhere Parr himself has argued that a reference in the *Knight's Tale* to the "cherles rebellyng" (*KnT*, 2459), which many have seen as an allusion to an event of history—namely to the Peasants' Revolt—is in fact an astrological tradition (pp. 393-4). Weese's second objection is that Chaucer would not describe Gloucester's usurpation as "vengeance" (p. 333), but this is less well taken, since Parr is talking about the *persecution* not the *usurpation* as vengeance. With this noted, however, doubt still remains as to the propriety of describing the persecution as vengeance.

A thoroughly admirable treatment of Chaucer's uses of astrology and astrological tradition is to be found in John J. O'Connor's study of the astrological background of the *Miller's Tale*. O'Connor skillfully recreates the tradition that envisioned Noah as an astrologer who abetted divine revelation with astrological calculation, and then shows us with equal adeptness how Nicholas plays upon this association to gull old John, who is normally suspicious of astrology. For a linking of the *Miller's Tale* to the astrologically determined date in the *General Prologue*, see Wood's article already cited (pp. 269-70).

Constance's horoscope in the *Man of Law's Tale* is presented in rather obscure language, and it is not surprising that the technical aspects of the astrology have been debated. Critics have not, however, convincingly refuted Skeat's explication of the astrology in the notes to his edition (v, 148-52). Both Curtiss and Browne offer objections, but Browne offers no evidence in support of his statements and Curtiss' principal argument—that Mars cannot be the powerful Lord of the Ascendant because he is fallen helpless—imposes a condition on the Lord of the Ascendant not to be found in the astrologers. It may also be observed in passing that Curry's diagram showing the moon in "quartile aspect" (p. 175) is in error—the correct designation would be "triune aspect." The poetic functions of the horoscope and of a passage on the deterministic power of the stars are also difficult to determine, for the tale as a whole has mystified critics because of its peculiar tone. Curry, for example, argues that Chaucer here rationalizes a character by giving her a nativity that seems to "govern and direct the prescribed action" (p. 164). But this seems somewhat at odds with Curry's later remark that in this tale the stars are powerful but are still subject to the will of God (p. 189). While it is not impossible to reconcile these two positions, such a reconciliation has not been made, and we must still remain perplexed at the tone of a tale that seems simultaneously to endorse astral determinism and divine intervention. Perhaps the solution lies in separating the astrological interpolations of the story's teller, the Man of Law, from the less worldly story he takes as his raw material.

The Wife of Bath's plangent cry, "Myn ascendent was Taur, and Mars therinne. / Allas! allas! that evere love was synne!" (*WB Prol*, 613-14) is perhaps the most famous horoscope in English literature, but it has attracted astonishingly little critical comment. The reason for this is perhaps that the astrological facts, even as interpreted by the Wife herself, do not wholly jibe with scholars' ideas of what the Wife *ought* to be like. She herself says simply that she was influenced by two planets, Mars and Venus, and that the latter gave her her "likerousnesse" and the former her "hardynesse" (*WB Prol*, 611-12). Curry, however, would credit Venus with causing a kind of poetic impulse which was subsequently warped by the influence of Mars (p. 115). This view, of course, must overlook the Wife's own less flattering interpretation. Because some scholars have recently made much of the fact that the Wife of Bath abuses her Biblical references in her *apologia*, it is worth noting that both Flügel and Steele long ago observed that her quotations from Ptolemy's *Almagest* are in fact citations from a later introduction to that work.

There is a useful introduction to astrology in general and to the particular problems of the *Franklin's Tale* in Phyllis Hodgson's edition of the poem, and of course Tatlock's article on astrology and magic in the tale and his book *The Scene of the Franklin's Tale Visited* are the proper starting points for any discussion of these issues. Much of Tatlock's work is given over to discussions of Chaucer's attitude toward astrology, and it is unfortunate that these are vitiated by a willingness to let Chaucer's characters speak for their creator.

An attractive article by Standish Henning on the astrology in the *Nun's Priest's Tale* observes that Chauntecleer is fittingly caught by the throat while the sun is in Taurus—the sign governing the neck and throat in one branch of astrology—and this action represents the culmination of a whole series of throat images in the tale. The article is one of the rare attempts to analyze the poetic function of an astrological image in Chaucer.

There are numerous other observations on astrological images within and without the *Canterbury Tales*, but the most important discussions are those on *Troilus and Criseyde* and *The Complaint of Mars*. In the *Troilus* two images have come in for a good deal of discussion: the sphere to which Troilus' soul is removed, and the conjunction of Saturn and Jupiter which causes the rain that keeps Criseyde in her uncle's house.

Root and Russell in an early article pointed out that the conjunction of Saturn and Jupiter in Cancer is a very rare phenomenon that actually occurred in 1385 after a lapse of many centuries. From this they argue that the date of composition should be fixed at no earlier than 1385—the year in which Chaucer would have observed the conjunction. Not all scholars have been convinced, however, that Chaucer might not have envisioned rather than observed the spectacle, and O'Connor's article on the subject argues that the astrological situation was a famous portent that could have been adopted from traditional astrological writings as well as or better than from fourteenth-century life. With fine sensitivity O'Connor further suggests that because the conjunction of these two superior planets is commonly associated with the fall of kingdoms, there is a nice irony in Troilus' achieving his desires under the influence of the conjunction that will bring down his city (p. 562). To which one might add that there may well be a comic element in such awesome celestial workings for such an evanescent earthly event.

A number of articles have been devoted to the question of Troilus' exact position at the end of the poem. He is either in the seventh or the eighth sphere according to the manuscripts, but since it is possible to count the spheres either from the earth outwards or vice versa, Troilus could be discovered in the sphere of the moon, Mercury, Saturn, or the fixed stars, or his position could be deliberately ambiguous. While the various arguments cannot be examined here in detail, Jackson I. Cope's observation that Chaucer elsewhere in the same poem numbers from the inside to the outside (p. 245) is convincing evidence that we ought to discover Troilus in the sphere of Saturn or of the fixed stars. Morton W. Bloomfield's arguments for Troilus' return to the ogdoad, the sphere of the fixed stars where virtuous pagans were rewarded, is more convincing than Cope's argument for the seventh sphere of Saturn because of a supposed parallel between Troilus' and Dante's souls who were given wholly to divine devotion (p. 246). Even so, a completely satisfactory analysis of the situation would investigate why the details of the view from the last sphere are so similar in Chaucer to Dante's *Paradiso* in spite of the fact that the two "lovers" in those poems are so different from one another. As Robertson once observed, we should note that it is Mercury, not Beatrice, who guides Troilus.

Troilus' apostrophe to the "paleys desolat" (*Tr*, v, 540) has been interpreted by John F. Adams as a metaphor involving a house or palace of the zodiac which has lost its planet. With the poetic appropriateness of this there can be little argument, for, as Adams says, Chaucer is "applying the celestial and figurative as a metaphor for the mundane and literal" (p. 62), but not everyone will be willing to see that the metaphor in fact is warranted.

Because the fifteenth-century copyist Shirley wrote that *The Complaint of Mars* was written at the instigation of John of Gaunt concerning the liaison between the Duchess of York (John of Gaunt's sister-in-law) and John Holland, the Earl of Huntingdon (who married John of Gaunt's daughter), the poem has become a cynosure for the historical allegorists of Chaucer. The problem, however, is why John of Gaunt would request such a commemoration, and what the tone of the commemoration is. Thus Cowling finds it "incredible" that Chaucer could mock the lovers' discovery without exacting retribution from the lady's husband, and he consequently proposes that the lady is the *daughter* of John of Gaunt, and Chaucer's aim "was not to mock, but to congratulate, and to apologize for the sin" (p. 407). Williams also sees the poem as "essentially a plea for tolerance of Mars' illicit love" (p. 169), but he too changes the characters and makes Mars John of Gaunt and Venus Katherine Swynford, Chaucer's sister-in-law. A more judicious view is that of Gardiner Stillwell who points out that "Chaucer's fun is that of telling the lovers exactly the opposite of what they . . . hope to be told . . ." (p. 72). Therefore, he concludes, Shirley was having a little joke of his own. Stillwell also calls attention to a hitherto unnoticed analogue in the *Ovide moralisé* (p. 75), and criticism of the poem would surely profit from more attention to the fact that the adultery of Mars and Venus was a common motif on into the Renaissance, and that nowhere is the adultery praised or congratulated: from Ovid on the lovers are caught and humiliated. Those who would discover Chaucer apologizing for the affair of Mars and Venus overlook the fact that in the poem Venus leaves Mars for Mercury. It may also be noted that Manly, correcting Koch's earlier calculations, showed that at no time during Chaucer's adult life were the astrological conditions of the poem fulfilled in actuality, which may indicate that Chaucer had a general and not a specific purpose in mind.

The pattern of the criticism recounted here is significant for Chaucerian studies. Almost every astrological and astronomical problem in the Chaucer canon has attracted some critical attention, and many such problems have given rise to whole series of arguments, rebuttals, rejoinders, and new departures. Numerous cruces remain unresolved and others are only apparently settled, all of which invites further critical speculation and, perhaps, final elucidation.

*   *   *   *   *

Since 1968 studies have appeared on all aspects of this topic, ranging from technical works on the medieval astrolabe to very broad discussions of Chaucer's attitude toward and employment of astrology. Among the latter the most comprehensive is Chauncey Wood's *Chaucer and the Country of the Stars: Poetic Uses of Astrological Imagery*. As its title implies, it is an attempt to analyze Chaucer's astrological passages in terms of his uses of poetic images generally; an approach prompted by Chaucer's disavowal of belief in judicial astrology in his *Treatise on the Astrolabe*. A very different approach has been taken by J. D. North, who argues that Chaucer referred the action of his tales to celestial "configurations subsisting within his lifetime" (p. 129). Hamilton Smyser has raised some objections to North's analyses, but it should be noted that Smyser differs from Wood as well, for he argues that Chaucer makes "an avowal of faith" (p. 372) in astrology in the *Man of Law's Tale*. Another broad study, of Chaucer and science by Mahmoud Manzalaoui, takes frequent exception to Wood's book, which Manzalaoui calls a "tangle of technicalities" (p. 233).

Of the studies devoted to specific problems the most comprehensive is John M. Steadman's erudite treatment of Troilus' position in the spheres. There are also fine essays by Neil Hultin and Rodney Merrill on Chaucer's astrological poem *The Complaint of Mars* and a chapter on the subject by John Norton-Smith which takes exception to Wood's "wayward" (p. 25) interpretation. Chaucer's Physician's use of astrological medicine has been examined in detail by Huling Ussery and Stephan Kohl, and numerous other articles have appeared on the many astrological cruxes in Chaucer's canon.

In December, 1976, a session on Chaucer and astrology was held at the MLA meetings, featuring Professors Masi, Eisner, Laird, and Wood as speakers. This event, the several doctoral dissertations of recent years on the subject, and the many works that have appeared since 1968 combine to suggest that the stars are favorable for even more activity in this sphere in the years to come.

BIBLIOGRAPHY

Adams, John F. "Irony in Troilus' Apostrophe to the Vacant House of Criseyde." *MLQ*, 24 (1963), 61-65.

Allen, Don Cameron. *The Star-Crossed Renaissance: The Quarrel about Astrology and Its Influence in England.* 1941. Rpt. New York: Octagon Books, 1966.

Baldwin, Ralph. *The Unity of the 'Canterbury Tales'.* Anglistica, 5. Copenhagen: Rosenkilde og Bagger, 1955.

Bloomfield, Morton W. "The Eighth Sphere: A Note on Chaucer's *Troilus and Criseyde*, v, 1809." *MLR*, 53 (1958), 408-10.

Boll, Franz, and Carl Bezold. *Sternglaube und Sterndeutung.* Rev. by W. Gundel. Leipzig: Teubner, 1931.

Brae, Andrew Edmund. *The Treatise on the Astrolabe of Geoffrey Chaucer.* London, 1870.

Brewer, D.S. "Chaucer's 'Complaint of Mars'." *N&Q*, NS 1 (1954), 462-63.

Browne, William Hand. "Notes on Chaucer's Astrology." *MLN*, 23 (1908), 53-54.

Carmody, Francis J. *Arabic Astronomical and Astrological Sciences in Latin Translation: A Critical Bibliography.* Berkeley: Univ. of California Press, 1956.

Chaucer, Geoffrey. *The Canterbury Tales of Chaucer.* Ed. Thomas Tyrwhitt. 2 vols. Oxford, 1798.

―――. *The Complete Works of Geoffrey Chaucer.* Ed. W.W. Skeat. 7 vols. 1894-97. Rpt. London: Oxford Univ. Press, 1960.

―――. *The Works of Geoffrey Chaucer.* Ed. F.N. Robinson, 1933. 2nd ed. Boston: Houghton Mifflin, 1957.

Clark, John W. "Dante and the Epilogue of *Troilus*." *JEGP*, 50 (1951), 1-10.

Conlee, John W. "The Meaning of Troilus' Ascension to the Eighth Sphere." *ChauR*, 7 (1972), 27-36.

Cope, Jackson I. "Chaucer, Venus, and the 'Seventhe Spere'." *MLN*, 67 (1952), 245-46.

Cowling, G.H. "Chaucer's *Complaintes of Mars and of Venus.*" *RES*, 2 (1926), 405-10.

Crawford, William R. *Bibliography of Chaucer, 1954-1963.* Seattle: Univ. of Washington Press, 1967.

Curry, Walter Clyde. " 'Fortuna Major'." *MLN*, 38 (1923), 94-96.

————. *Chaucer and the Mediaeval Sciences.* 1926. Rev. and enl. ed. 1960. Rpt. New York: Barnes & Noble, 1962.

Curtiss, Joseph T. "The Horoscope in Chaucer's *Man of Law's Tale.*" *JEGP*, 26 (1927), 24-32.

Dobson, E.J. "Some Notes on Middle English Texts." *English and Germanic Studies*, 1 (1947-8), 56-62. (Title varies: *English Philological Studies.*)

Drake, Gertrude C. "The Moon and Venus: Troilus's Havens in Eternity." *PLL*, 11 (1975), 3-17.

Dronke, Peter. "The Conclusion of *Troilus and Criseyde.*" *MÆ*, 33 (1964), 47-52.

Duhem, Pierre. *Le système du monde.* 10 vols. Paris: A. Hermann, 1913-59.

Dustoor, P.E. "Chaucer's Astrology in 'The Knight's Tale'." *TLS*, May 5, 1927, p. 318.

Eisner, Sigmund. "Building Chaucer's Astrolabe." *JBAA*, 86 (1975), 18-29; 125-32; 219-27.

————. "Chaucer's Use of Nicholas of Lynn's Calendar." *E&S*, 29 (1976), 1-22.

Emerson, O.F. "Some Notes on Chaucer and Some Conjectures." *PQ*, 2 (1923), 81-96.

Farnham, W.E. "The Dayes of the Mone." *SP*, 20 (1923), 70-82.

Flügel, Ewald. "Ueber einige Stellen aus dem Almagestum Cl. Ptolemei bei Chaucer und im Rosenroman." *Anglia*, 18 (1896), 133-40.

Griffith, Dudley D. *Bibliography of Chaucer, 1908-1953.* Seattle: Univ. of Washington Press, 1955.

Grimm, Florence Marie. *Astronomical Lore in Chaucer.* Univ. of Nebraska Studies in Language, Literature, and Criticism, 2. 1919. Rpt. New York: AMS Press, 1970.

Gunther, R.T. *Chaucer and Messahalla on the Astrolabe.* Early Science in Oxford, v. Oxford: Oxford Univ. Press, 1929.

Hamlin, B.F. "Astrology and the Wife of Bath: A Reinterpretation." *ChauR,* 9 (1974), 153-65.

Harvey, S.W. "Chaucer's Debt to Sacrobosco." *JEGP,* 34 (1935), 34-38.

Heather, P.J. "The Seven Planets." *Folklore,* 54 (1943), 338-61.

Henning, Standish. "Chauntecleer and Taurus." *ELN,* 3 (1965), 1-4.

Hodgson, Phyllis, ed. *The Franklin's Tale.* London: Athlone Press, 1960.

Hultin, Neil C. "Anti-Courtly Elements in Chaucer's *Complaint of Mars.*" *AnM,* 9 (1968), 58-75.

Huppé, Bernard F. *A Reading of the Canterbury Tales.* Albany, N.Y.: State Univ. of New York, 1964.

Koch, John. "Das Datum von Chaucer's 'Mars and Venus'." *Anglia,* 9 (1886), 582-84.

Kohl, Stephan. *Wissenschaft und Dichtung bei Chaucer: Dargestellt hauptsächlich am Beispiel der Medizin.* Frankfurt am Main: Akademische Verlagsgesellschaft, 1973.

Laird, Edgar S. "Astrology and Irony in Chaucer's *Complaint of Mars.*" *ChauR,* 6 (1972), 229-31.

———. "Chaucer's *Complaint of Mars,* line 145: 'Venus valaunse'." *PQ,* 51 (1972), 486-89.

Lee, Dwight A. "Chaucer's Prioress and St. Venus." *Mankato Studies in English,* 3 (1968), 69-75.

Lewis, C.S. *The Discarded Image.* Cambridge: Cambridge Univ. Press, 1964.

MacNeice, Louis. *Astrology.* New York: Doubleday, 1964.

Manly, John Matthews. "On the Date and Interpretation of Chaucer's *Complaint of Mars.*" *Harvard Studies and Notes in Philology and Literature,* 5 (1896), 107-26.

Manzalaoui, Mahmoud. "Roger Bacon's 'In Convexitate' and Chaucer's 'In Convers' (*Troilus and Criseyde,* v. 1810)." *N&Q,* 209 (1964), 165-66.

———. "Chaucer and Science." In *Geoffrey Chaucer*. Ed. D.S. Brewer. London: Bell, 1974, pp. 224-61.

Masi, Michael. "Chaucer, Messahala and Bodleian Selden Supra 78." *Manuscripta*, 19 (1975), 36-47.

Merrill, Rodney. "Chaucer's *Broche of Thebes*: The Unity of *The Complaint of Mars* and *The Complaint of Venus*." *Literary Monographs*, 5 (1973), 3-61.

Miller, Amanda H. "Chaucer's 'Secte Saturnyn'." *MLN*, 47 (1932), 99-102.

North, J.D. "Kalenderes Enlumyned Ben They: Some Astronomical Themes in Chaucer." *RES*, 20 (1969), 129-54: 257-83; 418-44.

Norton-Smith, John. "The Complaint: *Venus, Pity* and *Mars*." In John Norton-Smith, *Geoffrey Chaucer*. London: Routledge and Kegan Paul, 1974, pp. 16-34.

O'Connor, John J. "The Astrological Background of the *Miller's Tale*." *Speculum*, 31 (1956), 120-25.

———. "The Astronomical Dating of Chaucer's *Troilus*." *JEGP*, 55 (1956), 556-62.

Orr, M.A. (Mrs. John Evershed). *Dante and the Early Astronomers*. London: Wingate, 1956.

Parr, Johnstone. "The Date and Revision of Chaucer's *Knight's Tale*." *PMLA*, 60 (1945), 307-24.

———. "Chaucer's *Cherles Rebellyng*." *MLN*, 69 (1954), 393-94.

Pintelon, P. *Chaucer's Treatise on the Astrolabe*. Antwerp: De Sikkel, 1940.

Price, Derek J. "Chaucer's Astronomy." *Nature*, 170 (1952), 474-75.

———. ed. *The Equatorie of the Planetis*. Cambridge: Cambridge Univ. Press, 1955.

Prins, A.A. "The Dating of the *Canterbury Tales*." In *Chaucer and Middle English Studies in Honour of Rossell Hope Robbins*. Ed. Beryl Rowland. London: Allen & Unwin, 1974. Kent, Ohio: Kent State Univ. Press, 1974, pp. 342-47.

Robertson, D.W., Jr. *A Preface to Chaucer: Studies in Medieval Perspectives*. Princeton: Princeton Univ. Press, 1962.

Root, R.K., and Henry Norris Russell. "A Planetary Date for Chaucer's *Troilus.*" *PMLA,* 39 (1924), 48-63.

Sarton, George. *Introduction to the History of Science.* 3 vols. in 5. Washington: Baltimore Pub. for the Carnegie Institute, 1927-48.

Saxl, Fritz, and Hans Meier. *Verzeichnis Astrologischer und Mythologischer illustrierter Handschriften des lateinischen Mittelalters.* 3 vols. in 4. Heidelberg: C. Winter, 1915-53.

Scott, Forrest S. "The Seventh Sphere: A Note on *Troilus and Criseyde.*" *MLR,* 51 (1956), 2-5.

Skeat, Walter W., ed. *A Treatise on the Astrolabe.* Chaucer Soc. 1st ser., No. 29 and EETS, extra ser., No. 16. London: Trübner, 1872.

Smyser, Hamilton M. "A View of Chaucer's Astronomy." *Speculum,* 45 (1970), 359-73.

Spencer, William. "Are Chaucer's Pilgrims Keyed to the Zodiac?" *ChauR,* 4 (1970), 147-70.

Steadman, John M. *Disembodied Laughter: Troilus and the Apotheosis Tradition.* Berkeley: Univ. of California Press, 1972.

Steele, R. "Chaucer and the 'Almagest'." *Library,* ser. 3, 10 (1919), 243-47.

Stillwell, Gardiner. "Convention and Individuality in Chaucer's *Complaint of Mars.*" *PQ,* 35 (1956), 69-89.

Tatlock, J.S.P. "Astrology and Magic in Chaucer's *Franklin's Tale.*" In *Anniversary Papers by Colleagues and Pupils of George Lyman Kittredge.* 1913. Rpt. New York: Russell & Russell, 1967, pp. 339-50.

―――. *The Scene of the Franklin's Tale Visited.* Chaucer Soc., 2nd ser., No. 51. London: Trübner, 1914.

Thorndike, Lynn. *A History of Magic and Experimental Science.* 8 vols. New York: Columbia Univ. Press, 1923-58.

Tupper, Frederick. "Saint Venus and the Canterbury Pilgrims." *The Nation,* 97 (1913), 354-56.

Ussery, Huling E. *Chaucer's Physician: Medicine and Literature in Fourteenth-Century England.* New Orleans: Tulane Univ. Dept. of English, 1971.

Veazie, Walter B. "Chaucer's Text-book of Astronomy. Johannes de Sacrobosco." *Univ. of Colorado Studies, ser. B, Studies in the Humanities*, 1 (1939-40), 169-82.

Wedel, Theodore Otto. *The Medieval Attitude Toward Astrology.* 1920. Rpt. Hamden, Conn.: Anchor Books, 1968.

Weese, Walter E. " 'Vengeance and Pleyn Correccioun; *Knt* 2461." *MLN*, 63 (1948), 331-33.

Williams, George. "What is the Meaning of Chaucer's *Complaint of Mars?*" *JEGP*, 57 (1958), 167-76.

Winny, James. "Chaucer's Science." In *An Introduction to Chaucer.* By M. Hussey, A.C. Spearing, and J. Winny. Cambridge: Cambridge Univ. Press, 1965, pp. 153-84.

Wood, Chauncey "The April Date as a Structural Device in the *Canterbury Tales.*" *MLQ*, 25 (1964), 259-71.

————. *Chaucer and the Country of the Stars: Poetic Uses of Astrological Imagery.* Princeton: Princeton Univ. Press, 1970.

————. "Medieval Astronomy and Astrology." In *The Literature of Medieval England.* Ed. D.W. Robertson, Jr. New York: McGraw-Hill, 1970, pp. 10-23.

ELEVEN

CHARLES A. OWEN, JR.

The Design of
the Canterbury Tales

One of the very first readers of the collected *Canterbury Tales* has left a record of his understanding of the basic design of the work, the relationship between the portraits of the *Prologue* and the tales told by the pilgrims. The man for whom the Ellesmere manuscript was made not only restored the links to their original readings and devised a tale order consistent with the pilgrims named in the links but also had each tale illustrated, not with a scene or figure from the story, but with a portrait of the pilgrim telling the tale. These portraits show that the illuminators were familiar with details from the descriptions in the *Prologue* and were not merely depicting stereotypes of the professions and trades represented. An anonymous contemporary, writing a continuation of the *Canterbury Tales,* introduced *The Tale of Beryn* with a lively description of the conduct of the pilgrims in Canterbury and of their departure on the homeward journey. Lydgate in a similar effort, *The Siege of Thebes*, describes for us his joining the pilgrims at their inn in Canterbury, the early start they make the next morning "fully in purpoos to come to dynere/Unto Osspryng and breke ther oure faste," (154-5), and the host's calling on him for the first story of the homeward journey. In his summary of the tales which Chaucer had already written, Lydgate

mentions the churls in particular, accounting for their performance by station and by the stimulation of drink, and in the case
of the Pardoner, whom he conflates with the Summoner, "beerd-
lees al his Chyn/Glasy-eyed and face of Cherubyn" (33-4), by
his anger at the Friar.

This early understanding of the pilgrimage as in some sense
dramatic seems to have given way to an appreciation of the work
as a collection of stories. Criticism of the *Canterbury Tales* was
primarily general, a recognition of Chaucer as the "father" of
English poetry, honored by all, but read only by those willing to
make an effort with the difficulties of his language and of a somewhat mangled text. Dryden's famous dictum points to the richly
peopled world Chaucer presents us, and his practise, in "fortify-
ing" the portrait of the Parson as well as some of the tales, is
unique in the poetic translations of parts of the *Canterbury Tales*
up to the second half of the nineteenth century. Blake and Stot-
hard with their engravings of the company (the former also with
some of his comments on the pilgrims) are further exceptions.
But Arnold's appreciation of Chaucer, perceptive and partial at
the same time, concentrated on style and overlooked the variety
and strength of Chaucer's characterizations. To the second half
of the nineteenth century belongs the first systematic study of
Chaucer, to which we owe not only the establishment of a satisfactory text and of the facts about Chaucer's life and his works,
but also the clarification of his metrics and his meanings, on
which all interpretive criticism depends. The emphasis on the
Canterbury Tales as a collection of stories received support in
this period and in the early years of the present century from the
study of sources and analogues.

At the same time the question of the proper ordering of the
fragments was receiving attention. Furnivall, the editor for the
Chaucer Society texts, worked out a tale-order that eliminated
the geographical inconsistency of the Ellesmere order and took
account of the progress of the pilgrims along the road to Canterbury, while Henry Bradshaw suggested a less drastic revision of
the order, later to be adopted by R. A. Pratt. (See W. W. Law-

rence, *Chaucer*, pp. 90 ff., for a lively history of the tale-order controversy.) Until the thorough study of the manuscripts by the Chicago editors, Manly and Rickert, and the important contributions of J. S. P. Tatlock and Germaine Dempster, however, this aspect of the study of design was hampered by the assumed authority of the manuscripts. The opinion expressed by Manly (*Text*, II, 475, 489) that the manuscript orders are without authority has found support in the brilliant series of articles by Dempster on the development of the different groups of manuscripts and seems likely to stand up despite Pratt's efforts to revive their authority in support of the order he favors (*PMLA*, LXVI, 1165 ff.).

The explanations G. L. Kittredge gave in his *Atlantic Monthly* article (1893) of what had been considered gross violations of dramatic propriety in the performances of the Physician and the Pardoner and his proposal in an article in *MP* (1912) that the Wife of Bath initiated in her prologue and tale a discussion on sovereignty in marriage have had a most stimulating effect on the study of design. In his subsequent work on the *Canterbury Tales*, best illustrated in *Chaucer and his Poetry*, Kittredge extended and developed his view of the *Canterbury Tales* as a "Human Comedy," with the pilgrims as the *dramatis personae* and their stories "long speeches expressing, directly or indirectly, the characters of the several persons . . . ." But they "are not mere monologues, for each is addressed to all the other personages, and evokes reply and comment, being thus, in a real sense, a part of the conversation" (p. 155). Kittredge's view, occasionally challenged in whole or in part (see the articles by H. B. Hinckley, C. P. Lyons, J. R. Hulbert, and Kemp Malone, *Chapters on Chaucer*, pp. 210 ff.), has been generally accepted. Several critics have suggested an earlier start for the marriage group in the tales of Fragment B^2 (W. W. Lawrence, pp. 121 ff. and R. A. Pratt, *PMLA*, LXVI, 1158), pointing out the relevance of the *Melibeus*, of the Host's account of his relations with Goodelief, and of the *Nun's Priest's Tale* to the issues raised by the Wife of Bath. Pratt has extended this relevance to what he considers the antifeminism of the Monk (*PMLA*, LXVI, 1158, and *Selections*, p. xl), borne out in the tragedies of Samson and (very mildly) Hercules, but strangely absent from that of Adam and actually contradicted in the tragedy of Cenobia. Dempster has shown that Chaucer was at work on the B^2 fragment and the marriage group during the same period (c. 1396). He could easily have effected the close connection postulated between the two groups of tales by having the Wife of Bath break in at the end of the *Nun's Priest's Epilogue*. He preferred, it would seem, to separate the two groups and to mark the thematic reprise after an interval by the Host's amusing references to his difficult wife.

Design in series of tales other than the marriage group has been the subject of recent critical concern. William Frost pointed out in the final section of his article on the *Knight's Tale* the relationship between the first two tales of Fragment A with their contrasting accounts of rivalry for the love of a woman. Two other articles explored further elements of design in the fragment. William C. Stokoe, Jr. found Chaucer's overall purpose in the series of tales a contrast in moral and aesthetic preferences between the gentils and the churls. "If Chaucer arrays himself on the side of the *gentils* at last, he will do so only after an examination of the merits of the case" (p. 123). To the contrasting rivalries in love between the *Knight's Tale* and the *Miller's Tale* Stokoe adds a number of other parallel elements, notably the use of astrology and the supernatural, the importance of a fall in the denouements, the balanced fates of the lovers. He then points out that the Reeve is only superficially successful in avenging himself on what he takes to be insult from the Miller. His tale puts greater emphasis on the "impropriety," exhibits malice against a number of its characters and reveals its narrator not just as ill-mannered but as ill-natured. The Cook in awarding the decision to the wrong wrangler simply compounds the moral anarchy stimulated by the Miller's cynicism about love. Many of Stokoe's conclusions receive support in my article on the stories of the first day in *English Studies*. This article emphasizes elements of design that emerge, many of them unintentionally, from the divergent purposes and ideals of the narrators. For instance John the Carpenter's and Symkin the Miller's comments on learning are seen not only as foreshadowing ironically their own fates but as reflecting the general points of view of the two narrators. The paradoxical outcome of the narrators' quarrel repeats on a different plane the pattern first established by the rivalry of Palamon and Arcite in the *Knight's Tale*. The *Cook's Tale* promises new emergent patterns, a third warning on the dangers of harboring strangers and the completion of a realistic triptych on contemporary life in town, country and city. The three fabliaux come into being in defiance of the Host's control, but in their contrast with the Knight's chivalric idealism they project a meaning more important than any the Host had in mind. The first four stories in fact set some of the thematic limits for the work as a whole, they confirm the groundwork of character as the basic reality of the *Canterbury Tales*, they reveal the limitations of the Knight's views at the same time that they expose the different qualities of a parcel of churls.

The Tales of Fragment B² have long been seen as affording in a series of six "tales" (the Monk's performance of course is stopped after seventeen of his tragedies) examples of as many different medieval genres. Paull F. Baum in *Chaucer: A Critical Appreciation*, pp. 74 ff., suggested as a title for the series of tales "The Surprise Group," pointing out the way in which each pilgrim surprises us in the story he chooses to tell and the plausible motivation that preserves verisimilitude. The interruptions by Host and Knight and the marital confession by the virile Host in response to the *Melibeus* confirm the pattern. In addition to the series of surprises, which certainly occur, the series might also be seen as reinforcing the literary interest of the pilgrimage. What the Host sets up in the *Prologue* is a storytelling *contest*. In none of the fragments are so many critical questions raised. Chaucer and the Nun's Priest show a sophisticated concern in their tales for the uses and abuses of style and form, while the Monk reveals what insensitive and literal acceptance of medieval principles can mean. The Host's critical opinions ring with a confident absurdity at the very moment he reminds the pilgrims of his role as judge and reporter of the tales. His exclusive assumption of the second function—"And wel I woot the substance is in me, / If any thyng shal wel reported be" (B²3993-4)—underlines his unwitting rivalry with the pilgrim whose tale he had earlier with some rudeness interrupted and whose account of the pilgrimage has survived.

The G fragment was clearly intended for the morning the pilgrims reach Canterbury with its references to the inn at Ospring and to Boughton under Blee, approximately the half-way point of the nine-mile stage. It suggests in its contrasting tales (the *Second Nun's* and the *Canon's Yeoman's*) the distractions from their religious purpose which beset the pilgrims throughout their journey and from contemporary accounts (see especially *The Tale of Beryn*) were to be expected at the Cathedral itself (see Owen, *PMLA*, LXVI, 825). An interesting article by Wayne Shumaker discusses H-I as a connected pair of stories, planned by Chaucer to bring his work to an end. Pratt's otherwise systematic testing of the possible positions for the unordered fragments also assumes a connection between H and I (*PMLA*, LXVI, 1144). Even if the doubtful reading "Manciple" is allowed to stand in the first line of I, the evidence against the connection of the two tales is overwhelming. The time and place references forbid it. Even more decisive is the fact that the Cook has not told his story in H, but in I the Host repeatedly states that the only pilgrim still to tell his story is the Parson.

The most systematic application of Kittredge's dramatic principle occurs in R. M. Lumiansky's *Of Sondry Folk*. Without at all discounting the importance of the stories as stories, Lumiansky finds in the performances of the pilgrims "three stages of dramatic development." The first of these, "the simple suiting of tale and teller," applies to the following: the Second Nun, Squire, Prioress, Knight, Franklin, Physician, Man of Law, Shipman, and the Cook. What Lumiansky calls "an externally motivated dramatic situation" in addition to the suiting of tale and teller occurs in the *Manciple's Tale*, the *Monk's Tale*, the *Parson's Tale*, the *Nun's*

Priest's Tale, Melibee, the *Clerk's Tale,* and in the quarrels of Miller and Reeve, Friar and Summoner. Finally, there is a third group which adds to the qualifications of the other two an "internally motivated and extended self-revelation of which the teller is not fully aware": The Merchant, Canon's Yeoman, Wife of Bath and Pardoner (Lumiansky, pp. 7 ff., 247 ff.). The implications of Lumiansky's categories are important. We must not expect to find in each performance the complete revelation a few of the pilgrims make. Some of the pilgrims aim at a plausible concealment. The variety in the performances adds to the interest and to the verisimilitude. In some instances, such as the Nun's Priest and the Pardoner, Lumiansky's interpretations create a drama that the text hardly supports. In both of these cases, however, his systematic treatment of all the evidence is stimulating. In the case of the Wife of Bath he emphasizes three important areas of inadvertent revelation, and he shows the relevance of January's theories of marriage to the Merchant's bitterness. For some of the less startling performances, such as the Man of Law's, the Monk's, the Physician's, he provides a plausible motivation.

A number of recent critics have found a more sophisticated religious design in the *Canterbury Tales* than the one set forward by Frederick Tupper. His effort to interpret the work as structured on the basis of the seven deadly sins survived the attack of J. L. Lowes only in the general acceptance of a tavern as the scene of the *Pardoner's Prologue and Tale.* Gerould in *Chaucerian Essays,* pp. 55 ff., gave important reasons for rejecting even this suggestion, finding the Pardoner's "ale-stake" to be no actual tavern-sign but the garland referred to in the *Prologue* as adorning the head of the Summoner (A 666-7). Ralph Baldwin's *The Unity of the Canterbury Tales* concentrates on the beginning and the end of the work and finds in pilgrimage the image that successfully unifies and controls the dramatic particulars. His analysis of the roles played by the Host, by the Parson, and by Chaucer as poet and pilgrim (pp. 71 ff., 92 ff.) brings support to his thesis from an imaginative reading of the text and from a richly informed knowledge of the medieval background. The *Canterbury*

Tales begins in the spring as the season of renewal both physical and spiritual, suggests by the literal pilgrimage the wayfaring life experienced by all humanity, and has as its goal the "Jerusalem celestial" of salvation. This goal, to be reached only through penitence, receives its definition in the Parson's sermon which corrects the errors of previous speakers and justifies their willingness "to enden in som vertuous sentence" (I 63). "That the tale and the scene it involves are not without drama is brought out most poignantly, because it even excites a public confession from Chaucer himself. . . . Chaucer's immediate recantation is the denouement of the pilgrim-drama. Its very suddenness, without preparation, without explanations, except those latent in the drama, would be a turn of event quite understandable to the medieval mind" (p. 99). "Chaucer knew, with uncomfortable sensitivity, perhaps as only a mediaeval Christian could, the insuppressible arrogance, defiance, and libertinism that lurked in the artist. Though that part of his nature showed an admirable technical discipline, still any moral trespass must be acknowledged and repented for" (p. 108).

The Art of the Canterbury Tales by Paul Ruggiers accepts the encompassing form postulated in Baldwin's book and proceeds to an examination of the "Great Middle," the stories and their narrators. Ruggiers divides the tales into those prevailingly comic and those prevailingly romantic, seeing in the former the "views of a stable community . . . set over against the folly or willfulness of the individual" (p. 146), and in the latter a "purgatorial world in which the heroes become undeceived, tutored, resigned . . ." (p. 238), in which the possibilities of choice are faced. The "middle" is thus a field of conflict:

> In short Chaucer's view of humanity produces the whole range of comic and romantic experience, a range so comprehensive as to make tragedy a mere episode and so inclusive as to admit the presence even of the vile Pardoner and the intrusion of the Canon's Yeoman, trembling on the brink of momentous conviction. (p. 252)

From the whole work emerge not only Chaucer's final commitment to virtue in the Retraction, but also the experience of varieties of truth juxtaposed and a "sense of the mystery, a sense of charity towards the human beings involved . . ." (p. 257).

Bernard F. Huppé in *A Reading of the Canterbury Tales* shows an awareness of the development of Chaucer's plan as an important element in the consideration of design and suggests that the connection between *The Man of Law's Epilogue* and *The Wife of Bath's Prologue* (first pointed out by Owen, JEGP, LVII, 452, MS, XXI, 209, and by Pratt, "The Development of the Wife of Bath," p. 56) may have persisted through the composition of the D fragment and the marriage group. He finds in the *Constance* a presentation of marriage that aroused the Wife's opposition and inspired her autobiographical revelations and her tale. He also suggests that the quarrel between Friar and Summoner comes when it does because each sees in the Wife a profitable victim. His acceptance of the religious emphasis finds reinforcement in the exegetical approach to all medieval literature which he and D. W. Robertson, Jr. have proposed. Thus he frequently uses the *Parson's Tale* as a means of pointing up the doctrinal "sentence" inherent in earlier stories. He proposes as a dramatic motif in the B^2 fragment the Host's desire to repeat the "myrthe" of the *Shipman's Tale* but finds in the refusal of the clergy to oblige a sign that though the Prioress and the Monk do not embody the monastic ideal, "they are not ready to betray it" (p. 231). Chaucer's *Melibeus* gives in its allegorical meaning a foreshadowing of the *Parson's Tale* and the Retraction. "In short the Tale of Melibeus is an allegory of Penance, and of the inward meaning of the words of the Lord's Prayer: forgive us our sins as we forgive those who have sinned against us" (p. 239). His approach to the *Canterbury Tales* is more moderate than that of Robertson who in *A Preface to Chaucer* finds the poet "concerned primarily with ideas rather than with the affective values of the concrete" (p. 279) and speaks of the Wife of Bath as "not a character in the modern sense at all, but an elaborate iconographic figure designed to show the manifold implications of an attitude" (p. 330). For Robertson the tales are "significant in an exemplary fashion"; not expressions of character, they function as "developments in a conceptual realm" (p. 272). Both Robertson and Huppé read "tretys" in B²2147 and 2153 as referring to the *Canterbury Tales* rather than the work Chaucer is translating, and Robertson uses this reading (misreading, in my view) as proof the *Melibeus* has the same "sentence" as all of the stories (p. 369).

The question posed by Baldwin's book and the others that adopt the same general attitude is one of degree. Religion plays an important role in the pilgrimage. For some of the pilgrims it is a dominant one. Whether Chaucer planned finally to bring his pilgrims back to the Tabard for a dinner at which the Host would announce his verdict on the best story or whether he planned to end the *Canterbury Tales* with the surprise of his own Retraction will no doubt continue to puzzle critics and readers. My own study of the development of Chaucer's plans (*JEGP*, LVII and *MS*, XXI) has led me to conclude that the religious emphasis belongs to a relatively early stage of the work and that the Retraction with its reference to "this litel tretys" and its mention of the "tales of Caunterbury, thilke that sownen into synne," along with other poems, belongs with the treatise on penitence but not with the *Canterbury Tales*. After Chaucer's death his literary executors were only too glad to find a suitable prose piece for the Parson and an ending for the whole work so much in keeping with the conventional thought of the period. The Chaucerian qualities that make the work unique, the author's interest in character, his humor, his wide-ranging sympathy, his firm grasp of the distinction between the respectable and the virtuous, his growing appreciation of the limits of didacticism, encompass without in any way contradicting the religious ideals of his characters and contemporaries. To the dictum so often cited—"Al that is writen is writen for oure doctrine" (I 1083)—should be added "And eek men shal nat maken ernest of game" (A 3186), and to that again "But 'sooth pley, quaad pley,' as the Flemyng seith" (A 4357).

Most recent critics of the *Canterbury Tales* have assumed that the fragments take the pilgrims to Canterbury. They are satisfied with an order that does no violence to the geography of their route (see Pratt, *Selections*, pp. xxxix f.). In fact, however, no arrangement taking account of references to both time and place can fit all the fragments into such a one-way journey. Tatlock (*PMLA*, XXI, 481) pointed out that contemporary travelers to Canterbury could find overnight accommodations at Dartford, Rochester, and Ospring. The location of these places on the road from Southwark to Canterbury as well as the others named in the links can be seen from the following diagram.

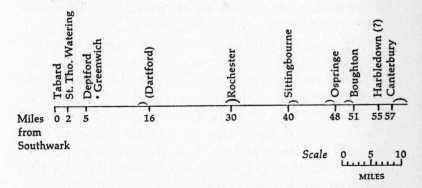

The A fragment is firmly in place. The B fragments could be assigned to the second day with a stop at Rochester (though, as Tatlock pointed out, the pilgrims seem to be passing Rochester in the *Monk's Prologue*). The D fragment mentions Sittingbourne, ten miles beyond Rochester, and could constitute a nucleus for the stories of the third day, bringing the pilgrims to Ospring. The G fragment like the A is firmly fixed to the morning they leave Ospring and arrive in Canterbury only nine miles away. C with no reference to time or place and H with its reference to the Blee forest near Canterbury could presumably be fitted into the scheme. But E-F with its repeated mentions of the Wife of Bath and with the Squire's "I wol nat taryen yow, for it is pryme" (F 73), and the *Parson's Prologue* with its "foure of the clokke" will simply not fit. Even the assignment of H and I to the homeward journey (Root, *MLN*, XLIV; Manly, *SP*, XXVIII) still leaves the E-F fragment out of account. The conclusion, so often drawn, that the inconsistencies are another evidence of incompleteness or even of carelessness is not a necessary one. Not only will all the fragments fit if one assumes the two-way journey proposed by the *Prologue*, but some reason for the existence of the fragments themselves can also be deduced. The text provides evidence for three important changes in Chaucer's plan for the work. The first occurred when Chaucer assigned to the Man of Law the *Constance* to replace the tale in prose (the *Melibeus*?) that was originally his. The second occurred when he shifted to the Shipman the tale originally written for the Wife of Bath and made it the first of the six linked stories that carry the pilgrims past Rochester. The third was the change in the number of tales each pilgrim was to tell from one to four or from four to one. The reasons for preferring the first of these alternatives are too complicated to enumerate here but are covered in my article, "The Development of the *Canterbury Tales*."

For a reading of the *Canterbury Tales* the second of these changes is the most significant. Dempster has shown (*PMLA*, LXVIII, 1142 ff.) that work on the B² fragment and on the D, E-F, and C fragments was being done at the same time (with the year 1396 as an approximate date). Why did Chaucer break the *Wife's Prologue* from its connection with the *Man of Law's Epilogue* (Owen, *JEGP*, LVII, 452 and Pratt, "The Development of the Wife of Bath," p. 56) at the very moment when he was creating the sequence of tales that take the pilgrims past Rochester? The answer I think most plausible is that he saw in her performance and in the repercussions it was to have on other pilgrims a dramatic interest sufficient to prevent the homeward journey from being anti-climactic. The Host's reticence about his wife at the end of the *Merchant's Tale,* in such contrast to the volubility he displayed after the *Melibeus*, finds its explanation then not only in his awareness of the Wife of Bath but also in the diminishing distance from his Goodelief at the Tabard.

The *Canterbury Tales* can best be read in the following order:

FIRST DAY: A   The pilgrims leave Southwark, pass Deptford and Greenwich and spend the night presumably at Dartford. (The plan is for four tales from each pilgrim.)

[B¹ An abandoned start for the story telling, not yet revised and fitted into the sequence. It probably once contained the *Melibeus* as the prose tale indicated in B 96 and introduced the Wife of Bath with part of her prologue and the *Shipman's Tale*.]

SECOND DAY: B² The pilgrims pass Rochester and spend the night at Ospring. (The plan here and for the rest of the fragments is for one tale from each pilgrim, with the possibility of more than one mooted in G 597 and F 698.)

THIRD DAY: G The pilgrims arrive in Canterbury in the morning, visit the shrine of St. Thomas in the afternoon and spend the night in Canterbury.

FOURTH DAY: H D C The pilgrims start the homeward journey, arriving at Sittingbourne at the end of D and spending the night in Rochester.

FIFTH DAY: E-F I The pilgrims return to the Tabard for the prize-awarding supper.

The *Parson's Tale* may well have been among Chaucer's Canterbury material, awaiting adaptation to the pilgrim, and with the Retraction, written when Chaucer translated it, attached. If Chaucer had intended the Retraction to end the *Canterbury Tales*, I cannot believe that he would have referred to the work as he did. "The tales of Caunterbury, thilke that sownen into synne" is a reference to something separate from the work in hand. Fortunately those who wrote the rubrics did not tamper with the text. The Parson himself certainly thought of the pilgrimage as a figure for "thilke parfit glorious pilgrymage / That highte Jerusalem celestial" (I 50). Chaucer, if he could have seen the work completed, would have stated the controlling theme in slightly different terms, I think:

> For certeinly, oure appetites heer,
> Be it of werre, or pees, or hate, or love,
> Al is this reuled by the sighte above.
>
> (A 1670-2)

The freedom he gave his pilgrims, including the Host, was parallel to the freedom he felt he had himself. They could quarrel, argue, seek to impose themselves and their visions, or hide behind a facade of respectability; they could admire, love, reflect their piety in their actions and utterances; they could reveal their virtues and vices and be themselves. He would report them as they were, whatever they said or did, enjoying to the full the variety and the plenitude, secure in the knowledge that if he were true enough to the Great Creation in his own, the pattern and the meaning would emerge.

* * * * *

A great deal of work on the design of the *Canterbury Tales* has been done since the first edition of the *Companion*. Most of those who have written have accepted the Ellesmere order (see articles in favor by Lee S. Cox, John Gardner, and E. T. Donaldson), have envisaged the pilgrimage as not reaching Canterbury, and have found in the *Parson's Tale* and the *Retraction* an appropriately religious ending for the pilgrimage and the tales. Russell Peck, Rodney Delasanta, and Edmund Reiss use numerology, as applied especially to the *General Prologue* and the *Parson's Prologue*, to reinforce a religious reading of the frame story; Chauncey Wood finds similar meaning in the dating and zodiacal references; and Esther Quinn, in a measured review of the religious element throughout the *Canterbury Tales*, reaches the conclusion that it is not primarily a religious work, though by a Christian poet. Ann S. Haskell follows the imagistic associations of gold and love in prologue and tales and finds gold reinforcing the range of meaning from the *caritas* in the Parson's image of himself to the basest *cupiditas* of the Pardoner's revellers and the Canon's Yeoman's alchemists; Barbara Page sees the Host as embodying the bourgeois secular world, a foil at the end for the Parson, while Cynthia Richardson sees him as representing forces external to the artist that press him to be creative

—the needs of society, the confrontation with time, death, and his own mortality; Gerhard Joseph in a highly original approach shows a relationship between the ernest-game opposition and the handling of time and space, especially in Fragment A and the *Nun's Priest's Tale*, and he sees the movement in the sequence of tales from "game" to "ernest" countered in the judgment of the Host, who would see all the tales at once. Going against the tide of religious emphasis, Norman T. Harrington points to the importance of the links in providing the normative, "a kind of gauge by which we can test the validity of those truths that have been conveyed to us by the 'olde wyse' through the medium of literature" (p. 199); and Daniel Knapp views the probable reference to St. Thomas's "olde breech" in the words of the Host to the Pardoner as modifying the pilgrimage motif and throwing light on the probable ending.

Design within sections of the tales has also come in for comment. Noteworthy are Penn R. Szittya on the parallel development of tales in Fragments A and D, with the *Friar's Tale* and the *Miller's Tale* performing similar functions; Claire C. Olson, Michael Cherniss, D. S. Silvia, and Daniel Murtaugh on the structural and thematic elements in the marriage group, especially Murtaugh's emphasis on anti-feminism and courtly love (the cloister and the garden) as the mutually supporting fantasies the marriage group explores and transcends; Alan Gaylord on the Host's critical ideas and the art of storytelling as the controlling thematic concerns of Fragment B^2 with the Host-Chaucer contrast especially important; Gerhard Joseph and R. Michael Haines on the gifts of nature, fortune, and grace in Fragment C; Russell Peck, K. Michael Olmert, and Bruce Rosenberg on the different alchemies of the *Second Nun's* and *Canon's Yeoman's Tales* with their reverberations in other parts of the *Canterbury Tales*.

Two scholars, Robert Jordan and Norman Eliason, have called in question the dramatic reading of the tales. Both would keep the frame and the stories as separate entities in what Jordan calls the "multiple unity," inorganic in nature, typical of late medieval or gothic form. A third, Martin Stevens, finds an exaggerated realism in the emphasis on "roadside drama" and calls for a "modernist" approach with more attention to conscious "dehumanized" artistry and to the image of the artist's "centrality within his created universe" (p. 210). In an undoctrinaire but rigorous examination, P. M. Kean posits a very limited thematic organization, with recurring but unsystematic emphasis on fortune and free will, on marriage in relation to order and disorder, and on the nobleness of man. "The frame and tales grow together," according to Kean, with the characters revealing themselves through their actions and stories (p. 75). A view of the basic structure of the *Canterbury Tales* is shared, remarkably, by a number of important books—Jordan's *Chaucer and the Shape of Creation* (despite its special views on unity), Christian Zacher's *Curiosity and Pilgrimage*, Alfred David's *The Strumpet Muse*, Donald Howard's *The Idea of the Canterbury Tales*, and John Gardner's *The Poetry of Chaucer*. As the tales (in the Ellesmere order) approach their end, the activity of storytelling itself comes in question. The *Manciple's Tale*, as Howard puts it, ends with the "empty blah-blah of too much talk and the flapping of an empty mouth" (p. 304). With the *Parson's Tale* and the *Retraction* we leave the world of fiction altogether.

Though my own book, *Pilgrimage and Storytelling in the Canterbury Tales*, sees a quite different direction of development (with Chaucer turning away from the conventional toward the values experienced and tested in fiction, as he worked on the *Canterbury Tales*), it shares with all but Jordan the emphasis on drama as important to a full understanding of the stories, and the idea of a complex dialectic at the heart of the work. Howard and Gardner both emphasize the historical and cultural background in their rejection of the Robertsonian attitude toward medieval literature. Gardner sees rival points of view in each of the blocks—on the nature of justice, the idea of authority, the basis of power in the world—a "flawed" dialectic, since every one of the pilgrims is subtly wrong (p. 223), as "opposing points of view zero in on the unknowable truth" (p. 225). Howard finds a number of ideas inherent in the work, the pilgrimage as a one-way journey, the idea of "bookness," the search for the world, the performance of the poet, the pilgrimage in retrospect (memory), the flower (which relates to the powerful *rosa-rota* image represented in rose windows), the recurring juxtaposition of knightly and religious ideals (Knight-Man of Law, Prioress-Thopas, Melibeus-Parson), shifting pairs of tales within groups of tales, the retrospective structure imposed by the *Parson's Tale* "comparable to what the *General Prologue* imposes sequentially" (p. 216). He finds in the interlace and possibly in the labyrinth or *domus dedaly* models for the kind of structure to be found in the *Canterbury Tales*.

BIBLIOGRAPHY

Baker, Donald C. "The Bradshaw Order of *The Canterbury Tales*: A Dissent." *NM*, 63 (1962), 245-61.

Baldwin, Ralph. *The Unity of the 'Canterbury Tales'*. Anglistica, 5. Copenhagen: Rosenkilde og Bagger, 1955.

Baum, Paull F. *Chaucer: A Critical Appreciation*. Durham, N.C.: Duke Univ. Press, 1958.

Beryn, The Tale of. See under Furnivall.

Cherniss, Michael D. "The *Clerk's Tale* and *Envoy*, the Wife of Bath's Purgatory, and the *Merchant's Tale*." *ChauR*, 6 (1972), 235-54.

Cox, Lee S. "A Question of Order in the *Canterbury Tales*." *ChauR*, 1 (1967), 228-52.

David, Alfred. *The Strumpet Muse: Art and Morals in Chaucer's Poetry*. Bloomington: Indiana Univ. Press, 1976.

Delasanta, Rodney. "The Theme of Judgement in the *Canterbury Tales*." *MLQ*, 31 (1970), 298-307.

Dempster, Germaine. "Manly's Conception of the Early History of the *Canterbury Tales*." *PMLA*, 61 (1946), 379-415.

———. "A Chapter in the Manuscript History of the *Canterbury Tales*: The Ancestor of Group *d*; the Origin of Its Texts, Tale-order, and Spurious Links." *PMLA*, 63 (1948), 456-84.

————. "The Fifteenth-Century Editors of the *Canterbury Tales* and the Problem of Tale Order." *PMLA*, 64 (1949), 1123-42.

————. "A Period in the Development of the *Canterbury Tales* Marriage Group and of Blocks B^2 and C." *PMLA*, 68 (1953), 1142-59.

Donaldson, E. Talbot. "The Ordering of the *Canterbury Tales*." In *Medieval Literature and Folklore Studies: Essays in Honor of Francis Lee Utley*. Ed. J. Mandel and B. Rosenberg. New Brunswick, N.J.: Rutgers Univ. Press, 1970, pp 193-204.

Eliason, Norman E. *The Language of Chaucer's Poetry*. Anglistica, 17. Copenhagen: Rosenkilde og Bagger, 1972, pp. 214-44.

Fisher, John H. "Chaucer's Last Revision of the *Canterbury Tales*." *MLR*, 67 (1972), 241-51.

Frost, William. "An Interpretation of Chaucer's Knight's Tale." *RES*, 25 (1949), 289-304.

————. "What Is a Canterbury Tale?" *WHR*, 27 (1973), 39-59.

Furnivall, F.J. *Temporary Preface*. Chaucer Soc., 2nd ser., No. 3. London: Trübner, 1868.

————, and W.B. Stone, eds. *The Tale of Beryn*. Chaucer Soc., 2nd ser., Nos. 17, 24. London: Trübner, 1887.

Garbáty, Thomas J. "The Monk and the *Merchant's Tale*: An Aspect of Chaucer's Building Process in the *Canterbury Tales*." *MP*, 67 (1969), 18-24.

Gardner, John. "The Case Against the 'Bradshaw Shift'; or the Mystery of the Manuscript in the Trunk." *PLL*, 3 (1967), Supplement, 80-106.

————. *The Poetry of Chaucer*. Carbondale: Southern Illinois Univ. Press, 1977.

Gaylord, Alan T. "*Sentence* and *Solaas* in Fragment VII of the *Canterbury Tales*: Harry Bailly as Horseback Editor." *PMLA*, 82 (1967), 226-35.

Gerould, G.H. *Chaucerian Essays*. Princeton: Princeton Univ. Press, 1952.

Haines, R. Michael. "Fortune, Nature and Grace in Fragment C." *ChauR*, 10 (1976), 220-35.

Harrington, Norman T. "Experience, Art and the Framing of the *Canterbury Tales.*" *ChauR*, 10 (1976), 187-200.

Haskell, Ann S. "The Golden Ambiguity of the *Canterbury Tales.*" *Erasmus Review*, 1 (1971), 1-9.

Hinckley, H.B. "The Debate on Marriage in the *Canterbury Tales.*" PMLA, 32 (1917), 292-305.

Howard, Donald R. *The Idea of the Canterbury Tales.* Berkeley: Univ. of California Press, 1976.

Hulbert, J.R. "The *Canterbury Tales* and Their Narrators." *SP*, 45 (1948), 565-77.

Huppé, Bernard F. *A Reading of the Canterbury Tales.* Albany, N.Y.: State Univ. of New York, 1964.

Jordan, Robert M. *Chaucer and the Shape of Creation: The Aesthetic Possibilities of Inorganic Structure.* Cambridge, Mass.: Harvard Univ. Press, 1967.

Joseph, Gerhard. "Chaucerian 'Game'—'Ernest' and the 'Argument of Herbergage' in *The Canterbury Tales.*" *ChauR*, 5 (1970), 83-96.

————. "The Gifts of Nature, Fortune and Grace in the *Physician's, Pardoner's* and *Parson's Tales.*" *ChauR*, 9 (1975), 237-45.

Kean, P.M. *Chaucer and the Making of English Poetry.* Vol. 2. London: Routledge, 1972.

Kittredge, G.L. "Chaucer's Pardoner." *Atlantic Monthly*, 72 (1893), 829-33.

————. "Chaucer's Discussion of Marriage." *MP*, 9 (1912), 435-67.

————. *Chaucer and His Poetry.* Cambridge, Mass.: Harvard Univ. Press, 1915.

Knapp, Daniel. "The Relyk of a Seint: A Gloss on Chaucer's Pilgrimage." *ELH*, 39 (1972), 1-26.

Lawrence, William Witherle. *Chaucer and the Canterbury Tales.* New York: Columbia Univ. Press, 1950.

Lowes, John L. "Chaucer and the Seven Deadly Sins." *PMLA*, 30 (1915), 237-371.

Lumiansky, R.M. *Of Sondry Folk: The Dramatic Principle in the Canterbury Tales.* Austin: Univ. of Texas Press, 1955.

Lydgate, John. *Seige of Thebes*. Ed. Axel Erdmann. EETS, Extra Series, 108. London: Oxford Univ. Press, 1911.

Lyons, Clifford P. "The Marriage Debate in the *Canterbury Tales*." *ELH*, 2 (1935), 252-62.

Malone, Kemp. *Chapters on Chaucer*. Baltimore: Johns Hopkins Univ. Press, 1951.

Manly, John Matthews. "Tales of the Homeward Journey." *SP*, 28 (1931), 613-17.

———, and Edith Rickert, eds. *The Text of the Canterbury Tales*. 8 vols. Chicago: Univ. of Chicago Press, 1940.

Murtaugh, Daniel. "Women and Geoffrey Chaucer." *ELH*, 38 (1971), 473-92.

Olmert, K. Michael. "*The Canon's Yeoman's Tale*: An Interpretation." *AnM*, 8 (1967), 70-94.

Olson, Clair C. "The Interludes of the Marriage Group in the *Canterbury Tales*." In *Chaucer and Middle English Studies in Honour of Rossell Hope Robbins*. Ed. Beryl Rowland. London: Allen & Unwin, 1974. Kent, Ohio: Kent State Univ. Press, 1974, pp. 164-72.

Owen, Charles A., Jr. "The Plan of the Canterbury Pilgrimage." *PMLA*, 66 (1951), 820-26.

———. "Chaucer's *Canterbury Tales*: Aesthetic Design in Stories of the First Day." *ES*, 35 (1954), 49-56.

———. "The Development of the *Canterbury Tales*." *JEGP*, 57 (1958), 449-76.

———. "The Earliest Plan of the *Canterbury Tales*." *MS*, 21 (1959), 202-10.

———. "The Twenty-Nine Pilgrims and the Three Priests." *MLN*, 76 (1961), 392-97.

———. "The Transformation of a Frame Story: The Dynamics of Fiction." In *Chaucer at Albany*. Ed. Rossell Hope Robbins. New York: Burt Franklin, 1975, pp. 125-146.

———. *Pilgrimage and Storytelling in the Canterbury Tales: The Dialectic of "Ernest" and "Game"*. Norman: Univ. of Oklahoma Press, 1977.

Page, Barbara. "Concerning the Host." *ChauR,* 4 (1970), 1-13.

Peck, Russell. "The Ideas of 'Entente' and Translation in Chaucer's *Second Nun's Tale.*" *AnM,* 8 (1967), 17-37.

Pratt, R.A. "The Order of the *Canterbury Tales.*" *PMLA,* 66 (1951), 1141-67.

————. "The Development of the Wife of Bath." In *Studies in Medieval Literature in Honor of Professor Albert Croll Baugh.* Ed. MacEdward Leach. Philadelphia: Univ. of Pennsylvania Press, 1961, pp. 45-79.

————, ed. *Selections from the Tales of Canterbury.* Boston: Houghton Mifflin, 1966.

Quinn, Esther C. "Religion in Chaucer's *Canterbury Tales*: A Study in Language and Structure." In *Geoffrey Chaucer: A Collection of Original Articles.* Ed. George Economou. New York: McGraw-Hill, 1975, pp. 55-73.

Reiss, Edmund. "The Pilgrimage Narrative and the *Canterbury Tales.*" *SP,* 67 (1970), 295-305.

Richardson, Cynthia. "The Function of the Host in *The Canterbury Tales.*" *TSLL,* 12 (1970), 325-44.

Robertson, D.W., Jr. *A Preface to Chaucer: Studies in Medieval Perspectives.* Princeton: Princeton Univ. Press, 1962.

Root, R.K. "The Manciple's Prologue." *MLN,* 44 (1929), 493-96.

Rosenberg, Bruce A. "The Contrary Tales of the Second Nun and the Canon's Yeoman." *ChauR,* 2 (1968), 278-91.

Ruggiers, Paul G. *The Art of the Canterbury Tales.* Madison: Univ. of Wisconsin Press, 1965.

Schulz, Herbert C. *The Ellesmere Manuscript of Chaucer's Canterbury Tales.* San Marino, Calif.: Huntington Lib., 1966.

Shumaker, Wayne. "Chaucer's *Manciple's Tale* as Part of a Canterbury Group." *UTQ,* 22 (1953), 147-56.

Silvia, D.S. "Geoffrey Chaucer on the Subject of Men, Women, Marriage and Gentilesse." *Revue des Langues Vivantes,* 33 (1967), 227-36.

Stevens, Martin. " 'And Venus laugheth': An Interpretation of the *Merchant's Tale.*" *ChauR,* 7 (1972), 118-31. See especially pp. 129-31.

————. "Chaucer and Modernism: An Essay in Criticism." In *Chaucer at Albany.* Ed. Rossell Hope Robbins. New York: Burt Franklin, 1975, pp. 193-216.

Stokoe, William C., Jr. "Structure and Intention in the First Fragment of *The Canterbury Tales.*" *UTQ,* 21 (1952), 120-27.

Szittya, Penn R. "The Green Yeoman as Loathly Lady: The Friar's Parody of the Wife of Bath's Tale." *PMLA,* 90 (1975), 386-94.

Tatlock, J.S.P. "The Duration of the Canterbury Pilgrimage." *PMLA,* 21 (1906), 478-85.

————. "The Canterbury Tales in 1400." *PMLA,* 50 (1935), 100-39.

Tupper, Frederick. "Chaucer and the Seven Deadly Sins." *PMLA,* 29 (1914), 93-128.

Wood, Chauncey. *Chaucer and the Country of the Stars: Poetic Uses of Astrological Imagery.* Princeton: Princeton Univ. Press, 1970.

Zacher, Christian K. *Curiosity and Pilgrimage: The Literature of Discovery in Fourteenth-Century England.* Baltimore; Johns Hopkins Univ. Press, 1976.

TWELVE

THOMAS A. KIRBY

The General Prologue

To describe the *General Prologue to the Canterbury Tales* as the greatest portrait gallery in English literature—if not in all literature—is a cliché of literary history, sufficiently accurate as a reminder that it is largely composed of a series of sketches differing widely in length and in method and blending the individual and the typical in varying degrees. Like all clichés, however, terms such as "portrait gallery" and "historical record" are both vague and inaccurate as applied to the *Prologue*, for it is much more than a collection of character sketches: it reveals the author's intention in bringing together a heterogeneous assortment of people and narrative materials, sets the tone for the storytelling, makes clear the plan for the *Tales*, helps to motivate the telling of several of them, and acquaints the reader with some of the author's attitudes toward both literature and life.

The *General Prologue* opens with an eighteen-line sentence which utilizes much conventional detail to describe the springtime setting and to show the serious objective of the pilgrims:

> Whan that Aprill with his shoures soote
> The droghte of March hath perced to the roote,
> And bathed every veyne in swich licour
> Of which vertu engendred is the flour;

Whan Zephirus eek with his sweete breeth
Inspired hath in every holt and heeth
The tendre croppes, and the yonge sonne
Hath in the Ram his halve cours yronne,
And smale foweles maken melodye,
That slepen al the nyght with open ye
(So priketh hem nature in hir corages);
Thanne longen folk to goon on pilgrimages,
And palmeres for to seken straunge strondes,
To ferne halwes, kowthe in sondry londes;
And specially from every shires ende
Of Engelond to Caunterbury they wende,
The hooly blisful martir for to seke,
That hem hath holpen whan that they were seeke.

"April is the cruelest month, breeding / Lilacs out of the dead land" is Eliot's reflection of his time, just as "Whan that Aprill ..." is Chaucer's mirroring of his.

Taken literally, this verse paragraph states merely that it is now spring, that nature (perhaps *Nature*; cf. Magoun, p. 399) has inspired small birds to make music, and that people wish to make a pilgrimage to Canterbury. Very much more, however, is implied in these lines. The showers of April have done away with the drought of March, but here the poet is offering us a paradox, for an English March is anything but a dry month. As E. T. Donaldson has remarked (*Chaucer's Poetry*, p. 876): "It is a comment on Chaucer's 'naturalism' that England suffers no drought in March; Chaucer's drought is a metaphorical one taken from a rhetorical tradition that goes back to classic literature, and to the Mediterranean countries where March is a dry month." Zephyrus, the west wind of classical mythology, has brought nature back to life, and the young sun (so called because with the vernal equinox it was believed to start on its annual journey once again) has passed half way through the Ram (Aries, one of the signs of the Zodiac), all of which is the poet's beautifully elaborate way of saying that it is mid-April. Even the little birds experience the regenerative powers of Spring, "so priketh hem nature in hir corages." All these details lead up to the main statement of the sentence: then (i.e., at this season) people long to go on pilgrimages. However, Chaucer momentarily removes the stress from *pilgrimages* by reminding us of those professionals, the palmers, who were more interested in travel than in the practice of religion, and it is only after this aside that the reader is told definitely that the shrine of "the hooly blisful martir" (St. Thomas à Becket) at Canterbury is the objective of folk who wish "to goon on pilgrimages."

"In these opening lines," Ralph Baldwin writes (p. 30), "Chaucer covers the ground with remarkable economy and a telling factuality. It is a model of narrative compression. The first eighteen lines—one periodic sentence, one verse paragraph, with a subordinate clause (1-11) of seventy-nine words and a highly figured statement of time, and a main clause (12-18) of forty-nine words, depicting habitual pilgrim action concomitant with and, as it were, released by the spring of the year—all this is achieved along with a diminuendo to the familiar, straightforward, low-style presentation. Chaucer has thrown out the contemporary narrative hook and artfully drawn his readers into the story without either the discontinuousness or the magniloquence we might expect from most of his contemporaries."

Chaucer's world is a real world, but there are frequent hints of the ideal world as well. Most readers will probably agree with Raymond Preston (p. 168) that the "*Prologue* gives us a 'real' England, and rather more than we should get in a fourteenth-century group. We can also see, in a glimpse, an ideal England, not so people could dream about it after dinner, but in order that they might desire it." Then, quoting lines 15-16 ("And specially from every shires ende . . ."), he concludes:

> The consciousness of nationality was new and exciting; . . . I cannot read these two lines without a certain emphasis. They have their relation to the contemporary preaching about St. Thomas of Canterbury, St. Thomas of *yngelonde*. And if we desire this Yngelonde, the Engelond that is always "Now and in England," then the opening of Chaucer's *Prologue* contains even more than

Englishmen going towards Augustine's Canterbury, and trying to find, in the art of *felaweshipe*, the good life: it contains also the water of life quenching the drought, it contains death and resurrection, Lent and Easter, a new Spring that may come to all pilgrims. (pp. 168-9)

Hoffman's commentary on nature and supernature is also illuminating (pp. 1-16).

Chaucer's first reference to himself comes in line 20, "In Southwerk at the Tabard as I lay," but the voice of Chaucer the poet (and, by indirection, that of the pilgrim as well) is clearly heard in the opening lines. The parenthetic statement ("So priketh . . .") is clearly an author's aside to the reader (and, we must always remember, to his audience as well), just as the preceding line (10), "That slepen al the nyght with open ye," with its reflection of a popular folk belief, also suggests the presence of the poet. In this fashion he reminds the reader that he too is a part of the springtime regeneration, a detail made much more specific in the second verse paragraph (19-34), in which he identifies himself clearly with the pilgrims and agrees to join them on pilgrimage. These few lines introduce a problem of some importance: Who is the "I" of the *General Prologue* and some of the linking passages? Chaucer the man? Chaucer the poet? Chaucer the pilgrim? A fictitious *persona* created by the poet? This is, of course, a problem by no means peculiar to Chaucer, and readers will vary in their reactions to it. One critic, Ben Kimpel, for example, does not accept the notion of a friendly and sociable narrator as an essential part of Chaucer's scheme ("Indeed, the narrator in the *Canterbury Tales* is not a definite enough personality to prove anything," p. 80), and B. H. Bronson dismisses what he calls "the schizoid notion of two Chaucers" (p. 28) in no uncertain terms. Others have argued strongly in favor of a *persona*-narrator. One of the most convincing presentations is that by E. T. Donaldson (in his edition of Chaucer, pp. 877-81, and more elaborately in an earlier article, "Chaucer the Pilgrim"). E. H. Duncan provides an elaborate examination of the narrator's point of view in the portrait-sketches. How is Chaucer's narrator, "limited to his own observation by a group of chance-encountered folk," able to "report intimate details of their past lives and experiences?" (p. 91). Duncan believes that Chaucer resolved the difficulty through the use of two devices: "First, he involved his Narrator equally with the pilgrims in the immediate situation and gave him an opportunity to speak to each one before he described them. Secondly, he left the Narrator, as a personality, so vague and undeveloped that the reader's interest is at once centered not on him or the sources of his knowledge but on the matters the Narrator himself is interested in: the situation and the other pilgrims" (p. 92). Most readers will probably share P. G. Ruggiers' view that the *persona* is ". . . useful in the *General Prologue* when the persistent innocence of the narrator leads to a simpleton's appreciation of the pilgrims without regard to a common standard of morality, a yielding to the essential humanity of his companions, a sense of being overwhelmed by their worth, and success, and obvious talents. Praise and appreciation fall easily from his lips, sometimes for reasons we ourselves corroborate, but often with the feeling that the narrator's personality has led him to equate their worth with their capacity to interest him" (p. 17). *Piers Plowman*, the *Confessio Amantis*, and *Pearl* are all contemporary works utilizing the same device, and the *Divine Comedy* is the supreme example of the creation of a *persona* to speak for the poet and, at the same time, to represent man in general.

The eight lines (35-42) introducing the portraits appear to be only a rather casual declaration of intention to describe each pilgrim—who he is, his rank, his condition, his dress:

> But nathelees, whil I have tyme and space,
> Er that I ferther in this tale pace,
> Me thynketh it acordaunt to resoun
> To telle yow al the condicioun
> Of ech of hem, so as it semed me,
> And whiche they weren, and of what degree,
> And eek in what array that they were inne;
> And at a knyght than wol I first bigynne.

Actually, however, the poet is explaining his method and suggesting that he is going to observe the precepts of the rhetoricians.
"What Chaucer is doing primarily, in his *descriptiones*, is bracket-
ing the rhetorical *notatio* [moral description] with his *condicioun*, and the standardized *effictio* [physical description] with
his *whiche*. In that way he portrays the person, the inner man,
the *character* (*condicioun*), as well as the physical attributes, the
outer man, appearance (*whiche*), though he does not severely
separate, but rather mixes the two phases of the description quite
indiscriminately" (Baldwin, p. 37). The major portion of the
General Prologue, 43-714, is devoted to these descriptions, which,
however, are presented so casually and colloquially (note, for
example, the use of such expressions as "I gesse," "I seyde," "I
telle," "I woot," and so on) that one is hardly aware of the
rhetorical tradition that was so important a factor in Chaucer's
writing, the art that conceals art. A short but illuminating discussion of Chaucer's use of the tradition may be found in Nevill
Coghill's comments on the Wife of Bath and the Prioress (*Geoffrey
Chaucer*, pp. 50-3).

The idea of a framework device for enclosing a series of stories
was by no means original with Chaucer. What was original was
the plan of associating the tales with a variety of narrators engaged in a common endeavor, "to unite the diversity of his tales
by allotting them to a diversity of tellers joined in some likely
common purpose. This, analytically speaking, is the root-principle
of the *Canterbury Tales*" (N. Coghill, *The Poet Chaucer*, p. 115).
Chaucer found his characters in the world about him and in the
world of books and brought them eternally alive through his own
creative powers. He "presented his characters in the jumble and
haphazardy of life, with a mild apology for his neglect of rank.
All was to seem fortuitous, and yet all the ranks and vocations,
the trades and the professions were there. What Shakespeare
would have called 'degree' was omnipresent, though in a deliberately disordered chain, and the historian can rebuild out of the
Prologue the twin ladders of Church and State as they then were,
with scarcely a rung missing" (Coghill, p. 116). This statement is

essentially correct, though one might quarrel with one or two points: certainly not *all* ranks (the higher aristocracy, for example) are included nor are *all* trades, and the choice of the word *jumble* is unhappy. Let us turn to the portraits and see if any organizing principles may be discerned.

The descriptions fall naturally into two parts, the first (43-541) about three times the length of the second (545-714). Lines 542-4 mark the transition and serve to let the reader know that what has begun to seem like an interminably long series is about to come to a conclusion:

> There was also a REVE, and a MILLERE,
> A SOMNOUR, and a PARDONER also,
> A MAUNCIPLE, and myself—ther were namo.

It is interesting to note that Chaucer includes himself with those toughies, the Miller and the Reeve; the most unsavory pair on the pilgrimage, the Summoner and the Pardoner; and that crafty cost accountant, the Manciple. The reasons for the author's listing himself with these five swindlers I leave to the reader's conjecture.

In spite of the fact that the poet declares his intention of giving an account of each of the pilgrims (38-9) he does not really do so. Actually, only twenty-six are described, and since five of these, the Gildsmen (361-78), are lumped together in a group portrait, there are only twenty-two sketches for twenty-six pilgrims. I omit the nun and the three priests (if indeed there were three; cf. M. P. Hamilton, pp. 189-90); the Second Nun is merely named here and is not described in the prologue to her tale, as one might expect, and there is no further reference to the three priests. The poet may very well have intended *three* in line 164, but it is *the* Nun's Priest (not *one* of the nun's priests) who is assigned the tale of Chauntecleer and Pertelote and who is described sufficiently in the prologue to that tale and more briefly in its cancelled epilogue. Very probably the reason for our not being told anything about these figures is the poet's carefully avoiding descriptions of more than one representative for each vocation; there is *one* knight, *one* squire, *one* yeoman, etc., and five full-length portraits of two nuns and three priests would have done violence to this part of the plan. Although statistics do not normally enhance literary appreciation, the varying lengths of the sketches suggest something of the importance, or at least the interest, which the author attaches to each. The longest portrait, for example, is that of the Friar (62 lines); the shortest, the Cook (9 lines). More suggestive perhaps is the way in which the pilgrims may be grouped into two main divisions, the ecclesiastical and the secular. A total of 320 lines is devoted to the seven religious figures (Friar, Parson, Pardoner, Summoner, Monk, Prioress, Clerk), but only slightly more, 349 lines, to the other nineteen (Knight, Reeve, Doctor, Wife of Bath, Franklin, Shipman, Man of Law, Miller, Squire, Manciple, Gildsmen, Yeoman, Merchant, Plowman, Cook). Within each of these groups the pilgrims are listed in descending order according to the length of each portrait. These two almost equal divisions suggest that Chaucer must have had a special interest in the religious figures (whose actual number, with the addition of the Second Nun and the three priests, is eleven rather than seven), for he not only devotes almost half of his space to them but also accords the final position to the Pardoner, his way of calling special attention to that particular individual; see K. Malone, pp. 155-6, who cites Schütte's law to the effect that the last place in a traditional list goes to the person or group in whom the author is most interested. If this is true, then it is also relevant to point out that the series constituting Part I of the descriptions concludes with the accounts of the Parson and his brother, the Plowman, which fact may well reflect Chaucer's desire to put special emphasis on these two characters, so good, so perfect in every respect that they contrast sharply with all the rest of the pilgrims, whether worldly or ecclesiastical.

There are other natural pairs or groups in the series: (1) Knight, Squire, Yeoman; (2) Prioress and attendants; (3) Monk and Friar; (4) Merchant, Clerk, Lawyer, Franklin; (5) Gildsmen and Cook; (6) Miller, Manciple, Reeve; (7) Summoner and Pardoner; groups (2) and (3) might be combined. Groups (4) and (6) are not cohesive, but these figures are appropriately brought together. At first glance it may seem that Merchant, Clerk, Man of Law and Franklin hardly form a unit, but the Clerk is placed between the Merchant and the Lawyer as an obvious contrast to the worldliness and material success of these two, and the Franklin follows along naturally enough after the Sergeant of the Law; for a Sergeant was a much more imposing figure, both socially and professionally, than the Epicurean country gentleman typified by the Franklin. Additionally, one may note that the excessive stress on the delights of the table in contrast with the sobriety of the Clerk sharpens further the difference between the latter and the other three in this group. One may theorize in much the same fashion that although Chaucer keeps the Miller, the Manciple, and the Reeve well separated physically, these three constitute another group, with the wily and coldly efficient Manciple inserted by way of contrast between the Miller and the Reeve, those likable churls cut from the same cloth. If one chooses, he may feel that all five of these pilgrims in the second part of the series constitute a single unit because all of them devote their lives to cheating and deception in one form or another.

Several of the pilgrims do not seem to fall into any sort of grouping: Shipman, Doctor, Wife of Bath, Parson, Plowman. O. F. Emerson (p. 90) labels these a "provincial" group, but this is rather forced. They are not joined by any common bond, as is the case with the others, and certainly the Parson and the Plowman are intended as a pair.

For the most part, the medieval requirements regarding rank and order are met. (One of the most informative analyses of the grouping of the pilgrims is that by John Reidy, pp. 595-603.) The fact that the Knight comes first in his group of Knight-Squire-Yeoman is, of course, as it should be, and that he is the first in the series of pilgrims should surprise no one; this is simply another illustration of Schütte's law (see above, p. 250), i.e. first place is accorded to the person most worthy of respect. The Prioress is presented next because she outranks the Monk, who in turn comes properly before the Friar, the monastic orders taking precedence over the mendicants. The sequence of Merchant-Clerk-Lawyer (commerce-learning-law) follows logically at this point, with the Franklin next, a public official of sorts—"At sessiouns ther was he lord and sire; / Ful ofte tyme he was knyght of the shire" (355-6)—and hence not unrelated to the Man of Law. The Five Gildsmen, workers who have been so successful that they are now qualified to hold public office, provide the transition to the solid citizens remaining in Part I who represent the essential day-to-day activities of cooking, sailing, doctoring, weaving, preaching, and plowing. The appropriateness of bringing Miller, Manciple, Reeve, Summoner, and Pardoner together has already been commented on, as has also the reason for placing the Pardoner at the end. It is only natural that his companion, the Summoner, be placed next to him and that the trio of Miller-Manciple-Reeve precede these two. Thus, although Chaucer apologizes to the reader for not having presented everyone according to rank—". . . foryeve it me / Al have I nat set folk in hir degree / . . . as that they sholde stonde" (743-5)—he has nevertheless paid sufficient attention to the fondness for order described by the rhetoricians of the day, but at the same time he has not hesitated to modify a tradition demanding a rigorous and highly schematized pattern of presentation. The apology is not so much apology as explanation that he, the author, knows perfectly well what is expected but that he has not been completely conventional in the way in which he has ordered his materials. The explanation he offers—"My wit is short, ye may wel understonde" (746)—of course has very little to do with the apology. The poet, through his *persona*, enjoyed throwing in these little quips from time to time; they are an element in establishing the personal and colloquial tone so important in maintaining the vitality of the *General Prologue*.

How did the poet create so varied an assemblage of living people? This is the question we ask not only about Chaucer but also about any other creative artist, and the greater his achievement, the more elusive the answer. However, although we cannot really explain Chaucer's success, we can point out certain things that he did to make his characters come alive. To do this with reference to each pilgrim is obviously impossible in the space available, but such detailed analysis is hardly essential for our purposes here.

One may note, first of all, that each description constitutes a verse paragraph and that the poet thereby has limited his presentation severely. The paragraph as a rhetorical unit has, admittedly, no prescribed length, but the author has been careful to make the descriptions relatively short; as already mentioned (p. 250), they range in length from nine to sixty-two lines; the average is slightly more than thirty. Eleven sketches have less than thirty lines each—Manciple, Squire, Miller, Man of Law, Shipman, and Clerk range from twenty to twenty-four; Plowman, Merchant, Yeoman, and Gildsmen, thirteen to eighteen; Cook, nine. These portraits, half of the total of twenty-two, run to 205 lines or approximately a third of the whole, 669. Quite obviously, then, there is bound to be wide variation in the amount of detail employed and in the effect resulting in each instance.

Several devices are used to develop the twenty-six pilgrims who are described: (1) the use of conglomerate detail; (2) exaggeration; (3) focus on a single quality; (4) the sudden thrust. All these do not enter into every description nor are they used to the same extent or with the same result—fortunately, for to have done so would have been to destroy the lifelikeness of the *Prologue.* How much Chaucer's art had developed with respect to portraiture is made clear by comparing the description of almost any of the pilgrims with the highly stylized, thoroughly conventional account of the lady in the *Book of the Duchess,* 817-1040, where, in spite of the richness of detail so systematically presented, the end effect is one of almost total artificiality. The tradition, of course, was slow to disappear. Witness Olivia's words in *Twelfth Night,* I, v, 252-7: "I will give out divers schedules of my beauty. It shall be inventoried, and every particle and utensil labeled to my will—as, item, two lips, indifferent red; item, two gray eyes, with lids to them; item, one neck, one chin, and so forth."

The account of the Monk illustrates strikingly our author's use of heterogeneous detail. The people of the late fourteenth century knew what a Monk should be, and so did Chaucer. He chose, however, instead of idealizing this figure, to do quite the contrary; for nearly everything about him is quite the opposite of what a good Monk ought to be. To convey this conception the author tells us at the very start that the Monk was an outrider (i.e., an inspector of monastic properties) who enjoyed hunting, *venerie*. However, there is some ambiguity here since this word may also mean "indulgence in sexual pleasure"; hence "a manly man, to been an abbot able" (167) has overtones which are not immediately apparent at first reading. We are then told about the Monk's fine horses and his indifference to the narrowness of monastic rules, for he is a modern man—"and heeld after the newe world the space" (176)—and contemptuous of those who say that monks are not holy men. Lines 183-8 constitute an editorial aside: "Chaucer ironically asks how these valuable services [secular jobs held by clergy] are to be rendered if the clergy confine themselves to their religious duties and manual labor" (F. N. Robinson, p. 656). The next four lines mention the Monk's greyhounds and his willingness to spare no expense for either riding or hunting. After this we are told briefly of his dress: his sleeves trimmed with fur (not just any fur, however, but "the fyneste of a lond") and his hood fastened under his chin with a "ful curious pyne," i.e., an artfully designed brooch, with a love-knot (looped design) at the larger end of it. Mention is first made of his physical condition in lines 199-200—his bald head and greasy complexion ("as he hadde been enoynt")—and similar details might be expected to follow. Instead, however, the author makes another general statement, "now certeinly he was a fair prelaat," following which the description is brought to an end with three lines of completely unrelated detail (205-7): he was not pale like a tormented spirit, a fat swan was his favorite dish, and his horse was brown as a berry.

"Here," Kemp Malone observes (p. 175), "is a perfect picture of a successful man." It is difficult to conceive how it might be improved upon—surely not by rearranging the lines so that all related items are put together in a series of compartments (riding, hunting, physical appearance, dress, general observations, author's comment) and neatly rounding them off with a concluding statement of some sort. The effectiveness of this portrait is almost entirely dependent upon the disordered piling up of detail that results in the worldly figure Chaucer has provided. "The monastic ideal," Donaldson notes (p. 885), "is specifically a rejection of the world in favor of eternity, but the Monk is described entirely in terms of this world. He is a fine figure of a man, whose flesh no monastic fasting or vigil have mortified. Indeed, he has a superabundant vitality that reminds one of the fine horses he owns and the fine fat beasts he loves to hunt. His masterful personality quite overwhelms the narrator, just as, in a different way, the Prioress' charming femininity had done." The details Chaucer employs to produce this effect are all the sort that might arise from direct personal observation and from chatting with his fellow pilgrims. It is all very much as if the poet made his own notes, then talked with his companions and learned about their past lives, found out what they thought about some of their associates on pilgrimage, and finally went back to his room, sifted the information he had collected, omitted, expanded, revised as the spirit and his purpose in each instance moved him, and then concluded by putting it all together in the planned disorder illustrated in the description of the Monk.

There has been so much talk of the *General Prologue* as an historical record, its verisimilitude, etc., that readers are sometimes prone to think of the Canterbury pilgrims as actual persons. To do so is arrant nonsense. They are fictions, they belong to literature, and they reflect the literary conventions of the time. They are not ordinary folk; each is a superior specimen of its type. It is here that the element of exaggeration plays an important role. The Knight, for example, was a *worthy* man, but he was also very *worthy* in his lord's war and ever honored for his *worthiness*. This same *worthy* knight had fought against the heathen in Turkey and, finally, "though that he were worthy, he was wys" (68). Thus the adjective and its cognate are used five times in the course of twenty-five lines, an average of once for every five verses. The Knight's "worth" is further emphasized by the observation that in his whole life he never spoke rudely to anyone and finally by that oft-quoted statement: "He was a verray, parfit gentil Knyght" (72). This latter is a reminder of the use of the same type of hyperbole in a number of other instances: "Ther nas no man nowher so vertuous" (251)—Friar; "So greet a purchasour was nowher noon" (318)—Man of Law; "Ther nas noon swich from Hulle to Cartage" (404)—Shipman; "In al this world ne was ther noon hym lik" (412)—Physician; "A bettre preest I trowe that nowher noon ys" (524)—Parson; "And yet this Manciple sette hir aller cappe" (587). The description of the Franklin (331-60) provides the most elaborate illustration of this technique. To live in delight was "evere his wone"; "Seint Julian he was in his contree"; his bread and ale were "always after oon"; in his house it snowed of food and drink and all the delicacies that men could think of; finally, "was nowher swich a worthy vavasour."

Chaucer frequently focuses on a single quality or characteristic and relates details to it. His doing so does not mean that other traits are omitted, but simply that there is a dominant element that provides a center of reference. In the case of the Pardoner, for example, it is hypocrisy; the Friar, "wantonnesse"; the Knight, "worthynesse"; the Squire, youth; the Parson, priestliness. There are usually two kinds of description or statement employed for the portraits: the sort that helps build up the figure into a model type or ideal exemplar and the kind that serves to mark him as an individual and bears witness to his essential humanity. The two together help call attention to the dominant trait. In the case of the Knight, for example, a large part of the description is devoted to presenting him as a paragon of what a proper knight should be, the very essence of "worthynesse"; at the same time there is sufficient mention of his manner, his horses, his dress, and of his having joined the pilgrimage directly without having taken time to change his attire to remind us that he was a man as well as a type of ideal knighthood.

What I have called "the sudden thrust" is used less frequently than the other devices but is one of the most effective, all the more so because it gives the impression of being a thought that just struck the author, who proceeded at once to insert it immediately into the description and then went on to something else or resumed a train of thought already begun. The most effective example of this device, in my opinion, is the observation about the Man of Law: "Nowher so bisy a man as he ther nas, / And yet he seemed bisier than he was" (321-2). This couplet has no connection with anything that precedes or follows, and yet it belongs exactly where it is; it could not have been introduced appropriately any earlier, and to have added it at the end after the lines describing the Lawyer's clothes would have given the impression of a bright afterthought loosely tacked on. It stands where it is as a flash of intuition that illuminates the character of the Sergeant of the Law and heightens the satire in significant fashion. Another example of the same sort of thing is the couplet occurring in the portrait of the Physician: "For gold in phisik is a cordial, / Therefore he lovede gold in special" (443-4). A third illustration is the line on the Pardoner (691), "I trowe he were a geldyng or a mare," though it is so well prepared for by the preceding lines that it does not have quite the same effect.

Twentieth-century scholars have devoted much attention to the possibility of Chaucer's having drawn some of his characters from life. Impetus to this type of investigation has been provided by the fact that the Host's name is Harry Bailly and that there was a late fourteenth-century Southwark innkeeper named Harry Bailly. If Chaucer drew the name from actual life, then is it not reasonable to assume that many of the details about the Host also come from the same source? If *pynche* in line 326 is a pun on *Pynchbek*, was not Chaucer probably indebted to Thomas Pynchbek for the general conception presented in the portrait of the Lawyer? There was a Thomas Pynchbek in Chaucer's day who was a sergeant of the law and who died toward the end of the century; Chaucer must almost certainly have known, or known of, him. The fact that Pynchbek once signed a writ for Chaucer's arrest could even explain the satire that is done so pointedly in this case. There are other instances that might be adduced, but space precludes even a cursory review of this aspect of Chaucer's creativity; others have already spent far too much time on the topic. Did Chaucer draw from life? Of course he did; he was not a character writer; he did not start with abstractions. His public career put him in the position of being able to see and meet all types and conditions of people, and he was undoubtedly acquainted with more than one knight and one prioress and one merchant and one pardoner. He was, however, not a photographer and did not merely reproduce; he was an artist, and artists create. The most distinguished scholar to devote attention to this aspect of Chaucer's work is John M. Manly, who spent much time in going through a great variety of documentary materials in an effort to throw light on possible sources for some of the pilgrims. However, in summarizing his position even he wisely observes (p. 263): ". . . I also am as far from believing that Chaucer merely photographed his friends and acquaintances as I am from believing that more abhorrent doctrine that he built up his matchless pictures of human life entirely by piecing together scraps from old books, horoscopes, astrological and physiological generalizations, bits from Ovid and Jean de Meun and Machaut and the treatises on vices and virtues. His method of character drawing was, I believe, the method of all good artists. From the experiences and observations of his life, his imagination derived the materials for its creative processes." (The reference to horoscopes and astrological and physiological generalizations is to the work of Walter Clyde Curry, a learnedly provocative and informative proponent of the notion that Chaucer was indebted to such materials for the development of some of his characters; yet even he stresses that "Chaucer was in his poetical works first an artist and secondarily a philosopher or a scientist," p. xii.)

Lines 715-858 bring the *General Prologue* to a conclusion and constitute a kind of epilogue, just as lines 1-42 may be regarded as a prologue. This final portion of the *Prologue* falls into five parts: (1) an address to the reader, lines 715-24; (2) the author's apology, lines 725-46; (3) introduction of the Host, lines 747-60; (4) the plan for the storytelling, lines 761-821; (5) the start of the pilgrimage, lines 822-58. The fourth line of the *Parson's Prologue* reports that the altitude of the sun at that time was twenty-nine degrees. It is difficult to believe that Chaucer, reaching the end of the *Canterbury Tales*, did not intend this as a verbal echo of the "Wel nyne and twenty in a compaignye" near the beginning of the *Prologue* (24). In similar fashion, lines 715-24 recall the passage in which the author announced at the start precisely what he intended to do (35-42). He now tells the reader in much the same fashion (direct address; easy, colloquial style) that the job is finished and, further, that he may expect to hear about the activities that night at the Tabard and about the rest of "our viage" and "our pilgrimage." Before proceeding, however, he gives us the twenty-two lines of apology for the manner in which he has dealt with his material; the last four have already been dealt with (see p. 252). The other eighteen lines are justification for having spoken so frankly and broadly: he cannot help it; an author must not take liberties with his material, or he will tell his tale untruly, pretend something, or supply new words; he must be literal—"He moot as wel seye o word as another" (738). Chaucer offers a comparable apology in the *Miller's Prologue*, 3171-86; it is much the same type and makes the same points but is phrased with special reference to the *Miller's Tale*. Both disclaimers were obviously written with tongue in cheek. No doubt there were certain taboos in the fourteenth century as there are today, but it is worth noting, as Lawrence phrases it (p. 81), that "never in Chaucer's formal apologies is there any suggestion that the loose tales may give offense as being immoral in the modern sense."

The few lines devoted to the Host sketch him in broad outline. He was a proper man to be a marshal in a hall—no small compliment (Bowden, pp. 292-3)—large, bold in speech, well taught (in the ways of the world, presumably), a merry fellow. Two details remind us of the Monk: both had "eyen stepe," and each is virile: "And of manhod hym lakkede right naught" (756) and "A manly man" (167). Short though the description is, there is room for the usual hyperbole: "A fairer burgeys is ther noon in Chepe" (754). This general outline is filled in through details supplied in the many linking passages in which the Host appears in the course of the journey, not so much through descriptive detail as through his own words and what others say to him. The end product is an impressive figure even though the method of presenting him is quite different from that employed for the other descriptions. It is probably unnecessary to note that the Host is the key figure in the unfolding of the tales. It is he who gets things going and keeps them moving from the time that he announces the plan and supervises the drawing of the lots for the first speaker until the *Parson's Prologue,* where he calls upon the Parson to tell what he says will be the final tale. Furthermore, through his varied roles of innkeeper, master of ceremonies, literary critic, social commentator, etc., through the comments evoked in these several capacities his place in the Canterbury series is much like that of the Chorus in Greek tragedy. "The Host stands," as Charles Muscatine comments (p. 171), "as mediator between the two processions [i.e., of travelers and tales], director of both. He is made apt for the job by his trade, by his magnificent presence, and by his choric activity, which, though sometimes imperfectly, links the larger world with the local one."

The rest of the epilogue is devoted to making clear the plan for the storytelling and getting it under way. How many tales should there have been? Four times the number of pilgrims. How many were they? Chaucer says twenty-nine, but thirty are named in the *Prologue,* and if the poet is included, as he must be, the number is thirty-one. If, however, the three priests are taken as one, then the total would be twenty-nine, including Chaucer. Later on, the Canon's Yeoman joins the group, and hence the total would be thirty (assuming that he continued with the travelers and did not ride off, as did his master). At any rate, thirty is a good round number (it also has symbolic significance in the medieval exegetical tradition; cf. Steadman, p. 224), and simple arithmetic tells us that had the plan been fully implemented, there would have been one hundred and twenty stories. However, Chaucer obviously changed his intention as he went along. In the link at the end of the *Squire's Tale*, 697-8, the Host tells the Franklin that he knows "that ech of yow moot tellen atte leste / A tale or two, or breken his biheste," and from the comment of the Host in the *Parson's Prologue*, 16-17, it is clear that only one tale per person is the final pattern: "Now lakketh us no tales mo than oon. / Fulfilled is my sentence and my decree." In actuality, of course, "mo than oon" story is lacking, for only twenty-four were written and of these, twenty alone are complete. Why Chaucer abandoned the original plan we shall never know. Perhaps it was because of ill health in later years, or possibly he was afraid that he could not maintain himself at a reasonably high level of accomplishment through one hundred and twenty stories; he may even have got bored with the whole project and simply have abandoned it. Whatever the cause, English poetry is the less rich, for in general the *Canterbury Tales* reveals a progressive development of literary power; the less esteemed tales are generally the earlier ones.

The pilgrims were quick to accept the plan for the storytelling, which included accepting the Host as umpire and master of ceremonies, agreeing to provide as prize for the winner a supper at the cost of all the others, and consenting without even mild protest to the outrageous fine proposed by the Host to be inflicted on anyone going against his judgment: "And whoso wole my juggement withseye / Shal paye al that we spenden by the weye" (805-6). The next morning lots were drawn and, as was both socially and artistically proper, the Knight was selected as teller of the first tale. The average reader might well expect that, the pattern having been established, all other speakers would also be chosen in this fashion. Such, however, is not the case, and it is the Host who normally selects the speaker, either directly or through adroit maneuvers that determine who shall tell the next tale.

Such, then, is the *General Prologue* to the *Canterbury Tales.* John Livingston Lowes sums up the matter rather well when he writes: "There had never before . . . been the like of that super-latively *modern* thing—to use our most complacent form of approbation—the Prologue" (p. 198), and a little later on he notes: "But the Prologue is more than a Prologue. It is an integral part of the plan as a whole. And that plan is unique in that the tales are part and parcel of a largely conceived and organically unified structure" (p. 202). Theoretically, the *Canterbury Tales* could have been composed without the *General Prologue,* but it would necessarily have been a rather different poem; and the *Prologue* might well have been written as an independent piece, though it is difficult to imagine it without the introduction and conclusion as they now stand. "The *Prologue* is great in itself," as Percy Van Dyke Shelly says (p. 204), "considered as a self-contained work of art. But it is greater still as a part of the larger whole, the *Canterbury Tales,* than it is by itself. The *Prologue* is static. The portraits are still-life. And it gains its chief interest and importance from what follows, from the tales and links which put the pilgrims in action."

Chaucer normally concluded a tale with a short prayer or pious ejaculation. For having given the world the *General Prologue* he may be thanked in words which he wrote in a very different context: "Thonked be God that is eterne on lyve" (*WB Prol,* 5).

* * * * *

During the last several years Chaucer criticism and research on the *General Prologue* have continued in unrestrained fashion (see, *inter alia,* the annual bibliographies published by the Modern Language Association and the *Chaucer Review*), and hence this commentary must be highly selective. One may begin by mentioning the most basic of all problems, the text itself. Aside from the inevitable school editions (here one thinks, for example, of Phyllis Hodgson's admirable edition of the *General Prologue*), probably the most important attempt to establish a new text is that made by R. A. Pratt, first in 1966 in a paperback of selections from the *Canterbury Tales* and short poems and then in 1976 with a complete edition of the *Tales of Canterbury* (which, on the basis of the internal evidence, the editor considers the only correct title). Although no new text of Chaucer is really going to revolutionize our thinking about the poet and his work, any attempt to establish a new text is invariably of interest. To cite only one problem, what of the three priests in line 164? Pratt solves it neatly enough by omitting "and preestes thre", something that should have been done years ago since there is well nigh unanimous agreement that these words were not written by the author. Thus scholars may stop debating this bit of trivia and get on to more important items.

Perhaps the most important scholarly book devoted exclusively to the *General Prologue* published to date during this decade is Jill Mann's *Chaucer and Medieval Estates Satire:*

> In contrast to the usual view that Chaucer took typical figures as a point of departure and added new details which transformed them into individuals, I have suggested that Chaucer deliberately invented new material which reinforced the impression of the type. Yet I do not wish to dissent from the general critical consensus that the Canterbury pilgrims give us an extraordinarily vivid *impression* of their existence as individuals. (pp. 15-16)

Most of the book is devoted to an analysis of the following seven groups of pilgrims.

"The Anti-Clerical Tradition in Estates Satire," Monk and Friar;
"Estates Ideals," Ploughman, Clerk;
"The Omission of the Victim," Sergeant of the Law, Doctor of Physic, Merchant, and Guildsmen;
"Independent Traditions: Chivalry and Anti-Feminism," Knight, Squire, and Wife of Bath;
"Descriptive Traditions: Beauty and the Beast," Prioress and Summoner;
" 'Scientific' Portraits," Pardoner, Franklin, Miller, and Reeve;
"New Creations," Cook, Shipman, Yeoman and Manciple.

To summarize the evidence for these groupings is impossible here, but the author's reiteration of her position should be noted:

"...I have tried to show that our strong impression of the figures in the *Prologue* is due to the fact that Chaucer encourages us to *respond* to them as individuals," and she also observes that "Chaucer forces us to feel that we are dealing with real people because we cannot apply to them the absolute responses appropriate to the abstractions of moralistic satire" (p. 189).

P. M. Farina argues briefly that Chaucer arranges the pilgrims in dependence groups, the dependence "being the result of ties of blood or of social and domestic hierarchy," an ingenious if not especially convincing suggestion. Donald R. Howard's *The Idea of the Canterbury Tales,* a brilliant reassessment of our poet's major work, contains much of interest on the *General Prologue:* see especially pages 94-109 and 139-58 for the analysis of the pilgrims and the suggestion that they are arranged in three groups of seven each with each group headed by an ideal portrait; the Guildsmen with the Cook and the Prioress with her companions are thought of as two pilgrims rather than the eleven we would otherwise have. Alfred David in *The Strumpet Muse* (Chapter 4) suggests a rather less formalized series of groups beginning with Knight, Parson, and Plowman and ending at the other end of the spectrum with Summoner and Friar as last of several pairs and groups.

During the last several years many studies devoted to individual portraits have appeared. I shall merely list some of the pilgrims together with the last names of authors of items appearing in the supplementary bibliography. Clerk (Ussery); Franklin (Frankis, Pearcy); Knight (Beidler, Hatton); Monk (Gillmeister, Reiss, Ussery, White); Pardoner (Halverson); Physician (O'Neill, Ussery); Prioress (Foster, Knight, Knoepflmacher, Simons); Summoner (Peltola, Tashiro); Wife of Bath (Reid); Host (Page, Williams). More general matters are discussed in the items by Daley ("droughte of March"), Rogers (names of the pilgrims), and Spencer (the pilgrims and the signs of the Zodiac).

Just as D. W. Robertson, Jr.'s *A Preface to Chaucer* has caused a major rethinking of many aspects of the study of Chaucer's poetry, so also has the same author's *Chaucer's Lon-*

don provided a non-traditional history of the last half of the fourteenth century. Only incidentally concerned with Chaucer's poetry, it nevertheless is indispensable for an understanding of the milieu in which the poet wrote and hence is especially helpful for an appreciation of the *General Prologue*. More recently, Robertson has published a stimulating article entitled "Some Disputed Chaucerian Terminology," in which he points out the need for more extensive studies of the pilgrims and the groups they represent in order to gain a more complete understanding, especially of the humbler members of society. Robertson's history may be profitably supplemented by consulting Christian K. Zacher's *Curiosity and Pilgrimage: The Literature of Discovery in Fourteenth-Century England*. Another recent publication, *Chaucer: Sources and Backgrounds* (R. P. Miller, ed.), also provides highly illuminating reading by making available materials from a wide variety of sources (the foreign items are all translated) that Chaucer surely used as well as others that reflect attitudes, ideas, and beliefs that contributed to his development. There are many selections in it that are of direct relevance to the *General Prologue*.

Finally, mention should be made of John Gardner's two contributions to Chaucer studies, *The Life and Times of Geoffrey Chaucer* and *The Poetry of Chaucer*. Since the author is a popular novelist as well as a medievalist of some standing, these books will doubtless attract a good deal of attention, especially since the biography is published by one of our most respected commercial publishers and the critical study has been brought out by one of the better university presses. However, a word of caution is in order. The books complement each other and will provide useful and interesting information, especially to the reader making his first acquaintance with the *General Prologue*. It should be kept in mind, nevertheless, that *The Life of Chaucer* is basically speculative biography (with speculation considerably abetted by imagination) and that *The Poetry of Chaucer*, though replete with the usual scholarly apparatus, is essentially personal criticism that as often as not takes positions which are not convincingly supported. Yet surely there is at least something to be said for the writer who is sometimes brightly wrong rather than always dully right.

Those unwilling or unable to become familiar with any of the vast amount of writing and research that has been done on the *General Prologue* may take pleasure in thumbing through the handsome little edition of the Ellesmere miniatures in color under the editorship of Theo Stemmler.

BIBLIOGRAPHY

Baldwin, Ralph. *The Unity of the 'Canterbury Tales'.* Anglistica, 5. Copenhagen: Rosenkilde og Bagger, 1955.

Beidler, Peter G. "Chaucer's *Knight's Tale* and Its Teller." *The English Record*, 18 (1968), 54-60.

Bowden, Muriel. *A Commentary on the General Prologue to the Canterbury Tales.* 1948. 2nd ed. New York: Macmillan, 1967.

Bronson, Bertrand H. *In Search of Chaucer.* Toronto: Univ. of Toronto Press, 1960.

Coghill, Nevill. *The Poet Chaucer.* 1949. 2nd ed. London: Oxford Univ. Press, 1967.

————. *Geoffrey Chaucer.* Writers and Their Work, No. 79. London: Longmans, Green, 1956.

Curry, Walter Clyde. *Chaucer and the Mediaeval Sciences.* 1926. Rev. and enl. ed. 1960. Rpt. New York: Barnes & Noble, 1962.

Daley, A. Stuart. "Chaucer's 'Droghte of March' in Medieval Farm Lore." *ChauR*, 4 (1970), 171-79.

David, Alfred. *The Strumpet Muse: Art and Morals in Chaucer's Poetry.* Bloomington: Indiana Univ. Press, 1976.

Donaldson, E Talbot. "Chaucer the Pilgrim." *PMLA*, 69 (1954), 928-36.

————, ed. *Chaucer's Poetry: An Anthology for the Modern Reader.* 1958. 2nd ed. New York: Ronald Press, 1975.

Duncan, Edgar H. "Narrator's Points of View in the Portrait-sketches, Prologue to the *Canterbury Tales.*" In *Essays in Honor of Walter Clyde Curry.* Foreword by Hardin Craig. Nashville, Tenn.: Vanderbilt Univ. Press, 1955, pp. 77-101.

Emerson, O.F. "Some Notes on Chaucer and Some Conjectures." *PQ*, 2 (1923), 81-96.

Farina, Peter M. "The Twenty-nine Again: Another Count of Chaucer's Pilgrims." *LangQ*, 9 (1971), 29-32.

Foster, Brian. "Chaucer's 'Seynt Loy': An Anglo-French Pun?" *N&Q*, 15 (1968), 244-45.

Frankis, P.J. "Chaucer's 'Vavasour' and Chrétien de Troyes." *N&Q*, (1968), 47-48.

Gardner, John. *The Life and Times of Chaucer*. New York: Knopf, 1977.

————. *The Poetry of Chaucer.* Carbondale: Southern Illinois Univ. Press, 1977, chapters 7-8.

Gillmeister, Heiner. "Chaucer's Mönch und die 'Reule of Seint Maure or of Seint Beneit'." *NM*, 69 (1968), 222-32.

Halverson, John. "Chaucer's Pardoner and the Progress of Criticism." *ChauR*, 4 (1970), 184-202.

Hamilton, Marie P. "The Convent of Chaucer's Prioress and Her Priests." In *Philologica: The Malone Anniversary Studies*. Ed. Thomas A. Kirby and Henry Bosley Woolf. Baltimore: Johns Hopkins Univ. Press, 1949, pp. 179-90.

Hatton, Thomas J. "Chaucer's Crusading Knight, A Slanted Ideal." *ChauR*, 3 (1968), 72-87.

Hodgson, Phyllis, ed. *General Prologue to the Canterbury Tales*. London: Athlone Press, 1969.

Hoffman, Arthur W. "Chaucer's Prologue to Pilgrimage: The Two Voices." *ELH*, 21 (1954), 1-16.

Howard, Donald R. *The Idea of the Canterbury Tales*. Berkeley: Univ. of California Press, 1976.

Kimpel, Ben. "The Narrator of the *Canterbury Tales*." *ELH*, 20 (1953), 77-86.

Knight, S.T. " 'Almoost a Spanne Brood'." *Neophil*, 52 (1968), 178-80.

Knoepflmacher, U.C. "Irony through Scriptural Allusion: A Note on Chaucer's Prioresse." *ChauR*, 4 (1970), 180-83.

Lawrence, William Witherle. *Chaucer and the Canterbury Tales*. New York: Columbia Univ. Press, 1950.

Lowes, John L. *Geoffrey Chaucer and the Development of His Genius*. 1934. Rpt. *Geoffrey Chaucer*. Bloomington: Indiana Univ. Press, 1958.

Magoun, Francis P., Jr. "*Canterbury Tales* A 11." *MLN*, 70 (1955), 399.

Malone, Kemp. *Chapters on Chaucer*. Baltimore: Johns Hopkins Univ. Press, 1951.

Manly, John Matthews. *Some New Light on Chaucer*. 1926. Rpt. New York: P. Smith, 1952.

Mann, Jill. *Chaucer and the Medieval Estates Satire: The Literature of Social Classes and the General Prologue to the Canterbury Tales*. London: Cambridge Univ. Press, 1973.

Miller, Robert P., ed. *Chaucer: Sources and Backgrounds*. New York: Oxford Univ. Press, 1977.

Muscatine, Charles. *Chaucer and the French Tradition: A Study in Style and Meaning*. Berkeley: Univ. of California Press, 1957.

O'Neill, Ynez Violé. "Chaucer and Medicine." *JAMA*, 208 (1969), 78-82.

Page, Barbara. "Concerning the Host." *ChauR*, 4 (1970), 1-13.

Pearcy, Roy J. "Chaucer's Franklin and the Literary Vavasour." *ChauR*, 8 (1973), 33-59.

Peltola, Niilo. "Chaucer's Summoner: 'Fry-reed Cherubynnes Face'." *NM*, 69 (1968), 560-68.

Pratt, R.A., ed. *Selections from the Tales of Canterbury and Short Poems*. Boston: Houghton Mifflin, 1966.

———, ed. *The Tales of Canterbury*. Boston: Houghton Mifflin, 1974.

Preston, Raymond. *Chaucer*. 1952. Rpt. Westport, Conn.: Greenwood Press, 1969.

Reid, David S. "Crocodilian Humor: A Discussion of Chaucer's Wife of Bath." *ChauR*, 4 (1970), 73-89.

Reidy, John. "Grouping of Pilgrims in the General Prologue to *The Canterbury Tales.*" *PMASAL*, 47 (1962), 595-603.

Reiss, Edmund. "The Symbolic Surface of the *Canterbury Tales*: The Monk's Portrait." *ChauR*, 2 (1968), 254-72; 3 (1969), 12-28.

Robertson, D.W., Jr. *Chaucer's London.* New York: John Wiley & Sons, 1968.

———. "Some Disputed Chaucerian Terminology." *Speculum*, 52 (1977), 571-81.

Robinson, F.N., ed. *The Works of Geoffrey Chaucer.* 2nd ed. Boston: Houghton Mifflin, 1957.

Rogers, P. Burwell. "The Names of the Canterbury Pilgrims." *Names*, 16 (1968), 339-46.

Ruggiers, Paul G. *The Art of the Canterbury Tales.* Madison: Univ. of Wisconsin Press, 1965.

Shelly, Percy Van Dyke. *The Living Chaucer.* 1940. Rpt. New York: Russell & Russell, 1968.

Simons, Rita D. "The Prioress's Disobedience of the Benedictine Rule." *CLAJ*, 12 (1968), 77-83.

Spencer, William. "Are Chaucer's Pilgrims Keyed to the Zodiac?" *ChauR*, 4 (1970), 147-70.

Steadman, John M. "Chaucer's Thirty Pilgrims and *Activa Vita.*" *Neophil*, 45 (1961), 224-30.

Stemmler, Theo, ed. *The Ellesmere Miniatures of the Canterbury Pilgrims.* Mannheim: Univ. of Mannheim, English Dept., 1977.

Tashiro, Tom T. "English Poets, Egyptian Onions and the Protestant View of the Eucharist." *JHI*, 30 (1969), 563-78.

Ussery, Huling E. "The Status of Chaucer's Monk: Clerical, Official, Social, Moral." *TSE*, 17 (1969), 1-30.

——— ."Fourteenth-Century English Logicians: Possible Models for Chaucer's Clerk." *TSE*, 18 (1970), 1-15.

———. *Chaucer's Physician: Medicine and Literature in Fourteenth-Century England.* New Orleans: Tulane Univ. Dept of English, 1971.

White, Robert B., Jr. "Chaucer's Daun Piers and the Rule of St. Benedict: The Failure of an Ideal." *JEGP*, 70 (1971), 13-30.

Williams, Celia A. "The Host—England's First Tour Director." *EJ*, 57 (1968), 1149-50; 1214.

Zacher, Christian K. *Curiosity and Pilgrimage: The Literature of Discovery in Fourteenth-Century England.* Baltimore: Johns Hopkins Univ. Press, 1976.

THIRTEEN

J. BURKE SEVERS

The Tales of Romance

Because of the great variety of medieval narratives which have traditionally been embraced by the term "romance," it is very difficult to define the genre. Basically, it is "a story of adventure, fictitious and frequently marvelous or supernatural" (Baugh, p. 173) with medievalized background; most often, it reflects the ideals of chivalry, of knights dedicated to lord, to lady, and to Church—hence the emphasis upon bravery and honor, or themes of love, or religious faith. Of Chaucer's works, obviously the *Knight's Tale*, the *Squire's Tale*, the *Wife of Bath's Tale*, the *Franklin's Tale*, *Sir Thopas*, and *Troilus and Criseyde* all deal with knightly life and love, and clearly qualify as romances. But the *Man of Law's Tale* and the *Clerk's Tale* are also stories which fall into an accepted category of romances: the so-called "Eustace-Constance-Florence-Griselda Legends" (see Hornstein in Severs, *A Manual*, pp. 120ff.): stories of Job-like sufferers sustained by religious faith. These tales, however, are very much like Saints' Legends, indeed would qualify as such under Gordon H. Gerould's latitudinous definition of that genre (p. 5). Even Margaret Schlauch, who has studied the *Man of Law's Tale* and its literary relationships in depth (*Chaucer's Constance and Accused Queens*), discusses the *Man of Law's Tale* in her *English*

Medieval Literature (pp. 260-5) under her category "Saints' Lives and Pious Tales" rather than under her category "Romances"; and Robert O. Payne in his recent study of Chaucer's poetics, *The Key of Remembrance* (p. 157), classifies both the *Man of Law's Tale* and the *Clerk's Tale* as "Saints' Legends" rather than as "Romances." Surely the *Knight's Tale*, the *Squire's Tale*, the *Wife of Bath's Tale*, the *Franklin's Tale*, and *Troilus and Criseyde* share chivalric conventions, including Chaucer's conception of courtly love, which are foreign to the *Man of Law's Tale* and the *Clerk's Tale*. For this reason, though in a broad definition one might well include the latter two tales as romances, they will be excluded in the present chapter. *Troilus* also will be excluded, not because it is not a chivalric romance (indeed, it shares with the anonymous *Sir Gawain and the Green Knight* the honor of being the very best of the genre produced in our English literature), but because it is being dealt with in a separate chapter. I should add further that these tales of romance are being discussed in this chapter as romances; hence some studies dealing with other aspects of the tales may not be mentioned here, though it should be borne in mind, as George Kane observes (p. 100), that "the qualities of permanent appeal and permanent artistic success [in the romances] are, broadly speaking, those of all narrative fiction."

Chaucer's first tale of romance, both in date of composition and in order of telling on the pilgrimage to Canterbury, was the *Knight's Tale*. For it his major source was Boccaccio's *Teseida*, which he transformed from epic to romance, and medievalized by merging the mythological gods with the astrological planets, introducing the motif of violated sworn brotherhood and creating a *demande d'amours*, and investing all with a Boethian philosophy which changed Boccaccio's fate into Christian Providence (Pratt on the *Teseida*, Wilson; but see Haller and Westlund for epic and pagan emphases).

Writing in 1906, R. K. Root said, "If we are to read the *Knight's Tale* in the spirit in which Chaucer conceived it ... we must ... not ask too many questions" (p. 169). Criticism has asked far too many questions, and many more since Root wrote than before. For since Root wrote, criticism of the *Knight's Tale* has passed through two phases, the first (ending about mid-century) debating chiefly characterization in the tale (Fairchild, Hulbert, Baker, Baum, Marckwardt, Webb, French), the second (after mid-century) chiefly its philosophy; and if E. B. Ham, writing at the end of the first of these phases, could decry the critical "clouds of obscurity and latter-day mystifications" (p. 252), one can only exclaim now that these clouds have deepened and darkened in the second phase.

In the best general study of the tale that had yet appeared by mid-century, Frost stressed Theseus' role as "the ideal conquering governor" (p. 299), non-partisan, dominant, the executant of destiny, who in his climactic "cheyne of love" speech (2987-3066), despite the apparently chaotic and hideous vicissitudes of life, justifies the ways of God to man. (Robertson, incidentally, finds that Theseus is traditionally the man of wisdom.) The theological interest in the tale (to continue with Frost) is paralleled by the human interest of love-rivalry between two knights and the ethical interest of a conflict between love and sworn brotherhood. Wilson finds that the controlling interest of the poem is the overruling power of love in the affairs of men.

Since mid-century, greater emphasis has been put upon the philosophical content of the poem: the Boethian concept that despite the vicissitudes of life, with their apparent unconcern or even injustice, there is a Divine Providence guiding all things to a beneficent end. Finding a relationship between the philosophy of the poem and its form, Muscatine conceived that the symmetry of the poem's design reflects the order of the noble life, and the poem's central theme is this noble life, which embraces both love and chivalry and leads to the perception of the order behind the chaos. Lumiansky and Kaske have stressed the dramatic suitability of this philosophy to the Knight, who tells the story of Palamon and Arcite and who interrupts the Monk's un-Boethian bewailing of Fortune's strokes. Ruggiers observes that the pagan gods are instrumentalities by which the Boethian

God works out his Providence, and that Theseus' final description of a universe held in bounds by love and directed by Providence answers both Arcite's and Palamon's earlier complaints about their evil fortune. Using these same latter materials to arrive at similar conclusions, Underwood notes that, after Arcite questions the order and wisdom of men and Palamon questions the order and wisdom of the divine, Egeus accepts rather than questions the human situation and Theseus finally accepts both the human situation and the order of the divine; and Halverson suggests that Palamon and Arcite in their early speeches reflect the benighted and desperate state of Boethius early in the *Consolatio*, whereas Theseus reflects Philosophy's conclusions, showing "that misfortune is part of providential order" (p. 619). Even Arcite's misfortune, as Pratt shows, ends in "joye after wo" (2841) in that he is released at the height of honor out of the "foule prisoun of this lyfe" (3061). Westlund finds that the tension between man's predicament and the notion that there is a transcendent order makes the tale especially appropriate at the beginning of a spiritual quest.

Most recent critics offer objections and qualifications to a serious philosophical interpretation of the poem. Underwood finds Theseus an imperfect and incomplete Boethian expositor: the Duke fails to see that his own will and attempt at order have contributed to Arcite's death—though the poem (Underwood claims, in what seems to me a questionable distinction) does see this. From the first, the somewhat incongruous presence of humorous touches in this tragedy has been noted (by Tatlock, Patch, Baum in his *Chaucer: A Critical Appreciation*); Robertson, and Huppé (in his *Reading*) find Chaucer's treatment of the lovers mocking and comic; and Preston, Neuse, and Penninger believe that the poem has been taken far too seriously. Neuse, with disproportionate emphases, unconvincingly argues that "the Knight's approach is basically comic and ironic" (p. 300), and, *contra* Muscatine, maintains that the "geometric design of the *Knight's Tale* functions more as a comic 'mechanism' than as a means for expressing a concept of order" (p. 306). According to Penninger, despite the presence of chivalric ideals and Boethian philosophy, Chaucer did not intend the *Knight's Tale* "to be read as profound" (p. 399); and the Knight himself, in his view of tragedy, shows "deficiency of wisdom" and a failure to "come to terms with reality" (pp. 404-5). To these charges of a lack of high seriousness, one may oppose Wilson's early comment on the levity in the piece: "This is ever Chaucer's way, and one would not deny the play of his comic irony over all his work . . . He sees the comic ironies of life even in its moments of tragedy" (pp. 145-6). Huppé similarly seeks to reconcile "the disparate elements of the philosophical and the comic" by viewing the *Knight's Tale* as "high comedy" (*A Reading*, p. 54).

It is not surprising that the Knight's son, the Squire, also tells a tale of romance. In writing the *Squire's Tale* Chaucer apparently had no one source before him but worked freely with elements from the legends of Prester John, the *Cléomadès* of Adenès li Rois, and *The Arabian Nights*. It is possible, too, that *Gawain and the Green Knight* was in his mind as he wrote (Whiting and Chapman). Braddy has suggested that the story would have developed as a framing tale, on the analogy of an Oriental type, with the exploits which are summarized at the end of Part II to be presented as intercalary episodes.

The presence of the incest motif in the Oriental cycle which may have influenced Chaucer has led Braddy to speculate that the explanation for Chaucer's breaking off his tale may have been his belated discovery, after he had written two parts of the tale, that the plot contained incest. It is hard to believe that an artist like Chaucer could have embarked upon a tale without having envisaged its ending, or if he had that he could not have altered the offending plot as he had done so often in working with other inherited tales. Root earlier had suggested that Chaucer broke off because he was at a loss as to how to complete the tale, and Furnivall had suggested boredom as the reason. More recently, Stillwell has argued that the intellectual, realistic, humorous Chaucer discontinued what he was finding to be an insupportably romantic narrative.

Marie Neville rejects Kittredge's argument that the *Squire's Tale*, coming as it does between the Merchant's and Franklin's, forms an interlude in the Marriage Group; rather, she believes that it constitutes a bridge, for the ideals of love and *gentilesse* in the *Squire's Tale* are the same as those in the *Franklin's Tale* and contrast with those in the Wife of Bath's and Merchant's tales; and the Squire continues the fairy tale machinery of the Wife's and Merchant's tales. Neville and Pearsall both point to the youth and immaturity of the Squire as a storyteller. Neville finds the Squire imitating his father by "doubling or trebling the romantic elements" (p. 170); following Coghill's and Preston's lead, Pearsall, in an exaggerated and unconvincing argument, describes the Squire as a nervous, bungling storyteller whom the Franklin, for the sake of the listening pilgrims and the foundering Squire himself, interrupts with the pretense that he thought the story complete. Similarly critical of the Squire (and also unconvincingly), Haller argues that Chaucer is satirizing the young man for a defective knowledge of the art of rhetoric.

The matter of the *Knight's Tale* was drawn from classical Thebes, and that of his son, the Squire, from the exotic East. Although Chaucer alludes to Lancelot in the *Nun's Priest's Tale* (3212) and to both Lancelot and Gawain in the *Squire's Tale* (95, 287), his only telling of a tale drawn from the Arthurian cycle is the Wife of Bath's. Eisner's *Tale of Wonder* interestingly shows the antecedent combining and altering processes which go into the developing of an Arthurian romance like the *Wife of Bath's Tale*. Notable in this tale is Chaucer's improvement in the arrangement of the plot materials (our learning the true answer to the question "What do women most desire?" for the first time in full court, and our learning of the hag's marriage-demand for the first time after the knight has been exonerated) to achieve greater suspense and more arresting climax (Sumner). Chaucer also modified the choice which the hag-bride gives her new husband from fair-by-day and foul-by-night or vice versa, to foul-and-virtuous or fair-and-doubtful, thus posing a subtler, more significant choice from patristic literature (Schlauch in "The

Marital Dilemma") which has to do with character as well as external beauty and links the tale more meaningfully to the subsequent tales dealing with the husband-wife relationship (*MerchT*, *ClT*, *FranklT*). Further, Chaucer substituted rape for murder as the knight's transgression at the opening of the story, thus changing his hero's relation to the plot from a testing of his knightly word, as in the analogue, to a developing realization of the meaning of the Queen's question and, through the lecture on *gentilesse*, an understanding of the proper treatment of sovereign ladies (Huppé in "Rape and Woman's Sovereignty," Roppolo, Salter, Silverstein, and Miller, who finds the tale a comic inversion of a common motif in medieval exempla). Those who believe that Chaucer found rape in his source (Eisner, Malone) can offer no substantiation and fail to see how this alteration is an integral part of Chaucer's altered conception of character and theme. Most of these alterations, though playing their several parts in the development of the story itself, and necessary for this reason, also adapt the story to the character of the Wife of Bath as teller and to her thesis in her *Prologue*: that is, the tale becomes an instrument to convey her anti-antifeministic view (compare also her opening comment on *incubi* and her characteristic digression on incorrect responses to the Queen's question; also the arguments by Townsend, Owen, and Steinberg that the tale is her wish-fulfillment, and by Haller that she is imposing her bourgeois ethic on all three estates—the commons and a clerk in her own husbands, a knight in the husband of her tale).

The *Franklin's Tale*, as that worthy tells us himself (709-15), is a Breton lay, a specialized kind of romance. According to the Franklin's understanding, Breton lays were old stories of various adventures written by noble Bretons in their own language in rhymed verse either to be sung with instrumental accompaniment or to be read. Chaucer derived his understanding of the form from his reading in an early fourteenth-century manuscript anthology of verse (the Auchinleck MS.: see Loomis) where he found three English exemplars of the lay—*Sir Degare*, *Le Freine*, and *Sir Orfeo*—the latter two opening with definitions of the genre much like Chaucer's own, though he could have learned from them additionally that the lays often dealt with the supernatural and most often with love. As he read *Sir Orfeo*, he would have identified the theme of married lovers with the Breton lay, and he would have come upon a devoted wife and husband whose happy marriage was threatened by a suitor associated with the supernatural, a Maytime garden, and a pivotal rash promise which had to be kept. Though it is possible that Chaucer's source for the *Franklin's Tale* may have been a now lost Breton lay, it is more likely that he derived his tale from the similar story in Boccaccio's *Filocolo*, and that when he found in the *Filocolo* story elements like those mentioned above in *Sir Orfeo*, he associated Boccaccio's tale with the Breton lay and in his own telling of the story pretended, as a natural literary artifice, to be following a lay.

The *Franklin's Tale* is a story of an ideal marriage in which the husband promises not to assert sovereignty over his wife, not to be jealous, and to exercise understanding and forebearance at all times. It is a tale in praise of *gentilesse*, the highest conception of chivalric honor, the keeping of one's word at whatever personal cost, and the contagious influence of a noble deed passing from knight, to squire, to clerk.

Kittredge early proposed that the views on marriage expressed in the tale constituted Chaucer's own solution to the problem of marital sovereignty previously dealt with in the *Wife of Bath's Tale*, the *Clerk's Tale*, and the *Merchant's Tale*. Many recent critics have questioned this, maintaining that the views are the Franklin's, not Chaucer's (Lumiansky, Holman, Howard, Gaylord, Huppé in *A Reading*, David, Hodge, Joseph). Some of these critics have found the tale, on analysis, to be critical of courtly love (Lumiansky, Holman) or *gentilesse* (Owen). The most severe of them, annoyed by an idealistic philosophy which they feel is untenable, maintain that the tale is full of moral absurdities (unethical disregard of a prior marriage vow, a rash promise not real in intent taken to be binding, an ostensibly honorable courtly lover forcing himself by deception on a loving wife who did not want him), that the Franklin does not understand the implications of his own tale, and that Chaucer is presenting him and his shallow ideal of *gentilesse* ironically (Gaylord, Huppé, Hodge); too often these critics ignore the obvious meaning of the tale in order to read into it private views unsanctioned by the tale itself either at the level of the Franklin or of his creator. Some critics, following Benjamin's perception of the disruption caused by Dorigen's questioning of God's order, have offered a religious interpretation (Kee, analyzing the pagan-Christian garden of lust and sin; Huppé and Robertson, observing that forgoing of husbandly sovereignty is a violation of God's moral order; Joseph, maintaining that the natural apparent evil of the rocks and Dorigen's human error serve an ultimately redemptive purpose; and Howard, suggesting that the *Physician's Tale*, stressing virginity, and the *Second Nun's Tale*, stressing marital chastity and martyrdom, are more likely to be Chaucer's final word on marriage than the *Franklin's Tale*, stressing temporal, worldly happiness).

In contrast to those of the preceding critics who find the Franklin's characters fatuous or unscrupulous and their ideals ludicrous, another group of critics have been carrying forward their analyses of the tale in a framework more sympathetic to the Franklin's characters and ideals. Kittredge was mentioned above. Dempster, Sledd, and Baker have discussed Dorigen's complaint in the tale, the latter two finding it artistically functional. Benjamin has shown how Arveragus' moral sureness and self-sacrifice have restored a disrupted order. David reads the tale as a sentimental comedy, presenting a love under the control of reason to bring about a happy ending, in contrast to the Knight's necessitarian tragedy with its overpowering unreasoning love leading to limited happiness. Severs has demonstrated that Arveragus' unconventional, idealistic concept of the marriage relationship, which Kittredge took to be Chaucer's final view, serves a necessary and integral function in the tale itself, preparing for Arveragus' unconventional, idealistic act at the climax of the story. And finally Mann, in one of the soundest recent studies, offers a thorough analysis of the medieval concept of *gentilesse* and a detailed application of its elements to the *Franklin's Tale*, proving that the poem "dramatizes the triumph of the ideal of a high 'gentilesse,' of virtue, the power of a fused chivalric and Christian ideal firmly and rationally embraced to overcome and transform selfishness and evil" (p. 25).

Even though Chaucer took the romances seriously enough to write a goodly number of them, we have seen that on occasion he could not suppress a smile here and there at the extravagances of the form. In *Sir Thopas* his earlier, occasional smiles turned into concentrated, hearty laughter. His burlesque is not limited to any particular "school" of romances, nor is it limited to late, decadent romances; rather he makes fun of the absurdities and excesses of the genre in whatever exemplar he found them, whether tail-rhyme or couplet, whether early or late (Trounce, Loomis in *Sources and Analogues*). Of course he is not attacking the genre as a whole, nor is all his fun to be taken as satire. In short space he skilfully laughs at the loose-knit, repetitious, long-winded narrative, the crudities of style such as stereotyped diction and stock phrases and extreme exaggerations, the chopped-up stanzas with their tagrag rhymes and jolting movement (for analysis, see Manly in *MP*, and Green), the ludicrous representation of knight and knight-errantry, suggested no doubt by the bourgeois authors' ignorance of courtly manners but developed into rollicking fun by Chaucer's predilection for exaggerated contrast in the portrait of the diminutive, effeminate, cowardly, yeomanly, tradesmanlike, unknightly gem of a knight, Sir Thopas. No doubt Chaucer also was poking fun at the minstrels who retailed the romances with their crude and impolite addresses to their gentle audiences (Moore). It is possible that in developing the humorous contrasts inherent in his incongruous plebeian knight he may also have had Flemish bourgeois knighthood in mind (Manly, in *E&S*, Winstanley; but see Lawrence for a strong dissent on this score).

Chaucer's knowledge of the romances came probably from hearing minstrels recite them and certainly from reading them in one or more manuscript anthologies. Just as he learned of the Breton lay from exemplars of that form in the Auchinleck MS.

(see above under the *Franklin's Tale*), so he became acquainted with three of the romances which he mentions in *Sir Thopas* from reading them in that same MS. *Horn Child*, *Bevis of Hampton*, and *Guy of Warwick*, mentioned in two consecutive lines in *Sir Thopas* (2088-9), are found together only in the Auchinleck MS.; *Horn Child* exists only there and Chaucer's allusion to it is the only one known in all our early literature; and echoes of *Guy of Warwick* in its unique form in the Auchinleck MS. are more frequent in *Sir Thopas* than echoes from any other extant romance (Loomis, *Essays and Studies*).

There are few treatments of Chaucer's romances as a whole, historical or critical (see Schlauch, *English Medieval Literature*, pp. 260-4, and Kane, who puts the romances in their place with the whole body of romances). Patch surveys appreciatively the elements of romance in Chaucer's works, but also observes that Chaucer's realism, humor, interest in character all tend to transform his romances into something beyond what one usually finds in the genre. Some critics see Chaucer growing away from romance, in certain limited ways, as he developed: A. K. Getty, studying Chaucer's attitude toward the courtly lover, finds that the *Squire's Tale* is entirely conventional but that the *Knight's Tale* and *Franklin's Tale* "contain striking instances of Chaucer's impatience" (p. 216; but see also Muscatine, p. 923; and compare Schlauch, *ELH*, iv, 201 ff.); and Moorman, studying all the chivalric romances and *Thopas*, finds that Chaucer's treatment of knighthood reveals a growing "dissatisfaction with chivalry— not, of course, with its vows and ideals, but with its poses and mannerisms" (p. 99). Stillwell, going further and speaking more generally of the literary genre, argues that basically romance is uncongenial to Chaucer; Preston agrees; and Herz opines that Chaucer fails in at least one romance (the *Knight's Tale*) because the genre is unsuited to his purposes.

Certain it is that Chaucer has modified the romance genre by making it reflect the idiosyncrasies of his tellers of romances; and sometimes these modifications (in the view of some critics, at least) have detracted from the effectiveness of his stories as romances, however much they may have contributed to a complex and otherwise admirable art. In varying degrees this is the judgment of Herz (*KnT*), Neville, Pearsall, and Berger (*SqT*), Kane (*WBT*); and of course it is true of Chaucer's own burlesque of romance, *Sir Thopas*. Other critics, demanding what they consider more realistic character portrayal, seem to condemn the tales for being too romantic (romance-like), though they do not state their objections in these terms: for instance, Gaylord and Hodge (*FranklT*).

This survey of the scholarship and criticism on the tales of romance may conclude with a generalization which, though it is true of the criticism of Chaucer's non-romantic works as well as the romantic, has been borne in upon the present writer by his recent rereading of the criticism on the romantic tales. Briefly it is this: the duty of the critic to keep his eye on the poem and to seek to understand and appreciate it as in itself it *is*, is no longer recognized by many modern critics. They do not hesitate to falsify the emphases in a poem, to impart into their reading foreign and external considerations, to allow modern attitudes to displace medieval and to impose irrelevant medieval attitudes, to permit private, idiosyncratic, super-subtle interpretations to replace the natural and obvious. This has led to absurd and perverse judgments. Accordingly, much of what is being written these days in Chaucer criticism is invalid: the sufficient answer to most of it is simply to reread the poem carefully. Hence, a caveat. The student is always under the obligation to go back to the poem and test all judgments (sometimes widely conflicting judgments) by *it*; thus at least one benefit accrues to him from the current critical chaos—he may (if he will) learn the discipline and the delight of an attentive, receptive, and sympathetic reading of Chaucer's poetry.

* * * * *

Of the five tales of romance, more studies have been devoted to the *Knight's Tale* than to any other. In these, most interest has been evinced in some aspect of the philosophy of the poem, especially the theme of order versus disorder—the disorder of life, man's futile attempt to impose order upon it, and the divine underlying order of the cosmos (Cameron, Cozart, Van in "Imprisoning," Elbow, Blake, Fichte, Thundy). Considerable interest continues in reconciling the poem's humor and satire with its romantic idealism (Foster, Thurston, Beidler, demonstrating that the humor befits the aging, battle-experienced Knight—see also Meier; Gunn, finding that the humor and idealism are but two of a dozen aspects in a complex tale). Special attention has been given to some of the characters: Fifield and Van in "Theseus" to Theseus, Loomis to Saturn, Schmidt to Arcite, Delasanta to Palamon and Arcite, Tatelbaum to Venus, and Meier to the Knight as narrating *persona*. Some studies relate the tale to history (Benson, Cowgill) or to medieval science (Brooks and Fowler, Gaylord), or explore its imagery (Dean, Helterman) or, more importantly, its formal qualities (Herzman, Turner).

The poor Squire, the Knight's son, continues to be castigated for his ineptitude as a story-teller and his deficiencies of character (Duncan, Peterson, Kahrl). These views are usually accompanied by the gratuitous latter-day heresy that the Franklin interrupts the tale to rescue a suffering audience (although Spenser and Milton—fit audience, though few!—would gladly have suffered the Squire to continue)—a heresy which should be effectually silenced by Clark's sensible and convincing two-page rebuttal. Some additional attention has been given to the origins of the tale (Friend, Finkelstein), and Moseley has posited an intended Northern audience for it.

Though much has been written on the Wife of Bath, little has been written on her tale, and much of that little is linked to the Wife's character (Levy, Harwood, Colmer, Oberembt, Rowland briefly toward the end); and Reid asserts that the tale, under the Wife's values, becomes a mock-romance, a burlesque. It has been subjected to both the psychoanalytic (Holland) and the Jungian (Brown) approach. Koban believes that Chaucer is preaching persuasively against willfulness, Cary that he is creating a unified tale dominated by feminine values, and Verdonk that he is portraying the knight as a static character congruent with, not changed by, the incidents of the plot (contra Huppé, 1948, et al.).

The *Franklin's Tale* has been fortunate in having recent expositors who have corrected the vagaries of previous critics: White has brought criticism back to the centrality in the poem of the moral ideal of *gentilesse* (see also Golding), and Hume in "The Pagan Setting" has demonstrated the inappropriateness of Christian censure of the protagonists. But new critical twists continue: Tripp argues that the Franklin's solution to the marriage debate is the non-solution of non-consummation of their marriage; and Robertson would have the teller and tale a humorous criticism of the administrators of royal justice in England. Two studies deal with the tale as a Breton lay (Donovan and Hume in "Why Chaucer"), one with its rhetoric (Knight).

Most studies of *Sir Thopas* have dealt, in one way or another, with the diction of the poem (Burrow's "worly" and "listeth"; Cullen's "drasty"; Conley's "Thopas"; Van Arsdale's "prike," etc., to disprove alleged homosexual implications); and Haskell suggests, largely by examining the diction, that Sir Thopas, Chaucer the pilgrim, and Chaucer the real person are all puppets, each manipulated by the next—Chaucer the real person being manipulated by the gods. Stanley examines the bob-lines in the poem; and Burrow in "Sir Thopas" argues very plausibly, by MS evidence, stanzaic forms, and phraseology, that the poem should be divided into three fits.

General comment on the romances confirms earlier judgments that Chaucer's attraction to romances and courtly love was early, to be later qualified by his realism (Brewer, Reiss); and Lenaghan explores the social complexity of the role of Chaucer the clerk telling romances of *gentilesse* in the court. Of influences upon Chaucer's romances, Brewer finds some slight evidence that Chaucer knew Chrétien, and Haymes demonstrates that Chaucer retained some of the formulaic expressions of the metrical romances; but Blake finds no evidence that Chaucer's use of alliteration was influenced by the alliterative romances. Jordan, to end on a negative note, argues that since Chaucerian romance cannot be satisfactorily defined either by subject-matter or by compositional technique, actually no such genre exists in the Chaucer canon.

BIBLIOGRAPHY

I. GENERAL STUDIES

Baugh, Albert C., ed. *A Literary History of England*. 1948. 2nd ed. New York: Appleton-Century-Crofts, 1967.

Blake, N.F. "Chaucer and the Alliterative Romances." *ChauR*, 3 (1969), 163-69.

Brewer, D.S. "Chaucer and Chrétien and Arthurian Romance." In *Chaucer and Middle English Studies in Honour of Rossell Hope Robbins*. Ed. Beryl Rowland. London: Allen & Unwin, 1974. Kent, Ohio: Kent State Univ. Press, 1974, pp. 255-59.

Coghill, Nevill. *The Poet Chaucer*. 1949. 2nd ed. London: Oxford Univ. Press, 1967.

Gerould, G.H. *Saints' Legends*. 1916. Rpt. Folcroft, Pa.: Folcroft Press, 1969.

Getty, Agnes K. "Chaucer's Changing Conceptions of the Humble Lover" *PMLA*, 44 (1929), 202-16.

Haymes, Edward R. "Chaucer and the Romance Tradition." *SAB*, 37 (1972), 35-43.

Hornstein, L.H. "Eustace-Constance-Florence-Griselda Legends." In *A Manual of the Writings in Middle English*, pp. 120-32, 278-91. See under Severs.

Huppé, Bernard F. *A Reading of the Canterbury Tales*. Albany, N.Y.: State Univ. of New York, 1964.

Jordan, Robert M. "Chaucerian Romance?" *YFS*, 51 (1974), 223-24.

Kane, George. *Middle English Literature: A Critical Study of the Romances, the Religious Lyrics, Piers Plowman*. 1951. Rpt. Folcroft, Pa.: Folcroft Press, 1969.

Kittredge, G.L. *Chaucer and His Poetry*. Cambridge, Mass.: Harvard Univ. Press, 1915.

Lenaghan, R.T. "The Clerk of Venus: Chaucer and Medieval Romance." In *The Learned and the Lewed: Studies in Chaucer and Medieval Literature.* Ed. Larry D. Benson. Harvard English Studies, No. 5. Cambridge, Mass.: Harvard Univ. Press, 1974, pp. 31-43.

Moorman, Charles. "The Philosophical Knights of the *Canterbury Tales.*" *SAQ,* 64 (1965), 87-99.

Owen, Charles A., Jr. "The Crucial Passages in Five of the *Canterbury Tales*: A Study in Irony and Symbol." *JEGP,* 52 (1953), 294-311.

Patch, Howard Rollin. "Chaucer and Medieval Romance." In *Essays in Honor of Barrett Wendell.* Cambridge, Mass.: Harvard Univ. Press, 1926, pp. 93-108.

Payne, Robert O. *The Key of Remembrance: A Study of Chaucer's Poetics.* 1963. Rpt. Westport, Conn.: Greenwood Press, 1973.

Preston, Raymond. *Chaucer.* 1952. Rpt. Westport, Conn.: Greenwood Press, 1969.

Reiss, Edmund. "Chaucer's Courtly Love." In *The Learned and the Lewed.* Ed. Larry D. Benson. pp. 95-111.

Robertson, D.W., Jr. *A Preface to Chaucer: Studies in Medieval Perspectives.* Princeton: Princeton Univ. Press, 1962.

Root, R.K. *The Poetry of Chaucer: A Guide to Its Study and Appreciation.* Boston, 1906 (ed. cit). Rev. ed. 1922. Rpt. Gloucester, Mass.: P. Smith, 1957.

Schlauch, Margaret. *Chaucer's Constance and Accused Queens.* New York: New York Univ. Press, 1927.

————. *English Medieval Literature and Its Social Foundations.* 1956. Rpt. Warsaw: Pánstwöwe Wydawnictwo Naukowe. London: Oxford Univ. Press, 1967.

Severs, J. Burke, ed. *A Manual of the Writings in Middle English 1050-1500: The Romances.* New Haven: Conn. Academy of Arts and Sciences, 1967.

Tatlock, J.S.P. *The Mind and Art of Chaucer.* 1950. Rpt. New York: Gordion Press, 1966.

II. THE KNIGHT'S TALE

Baker, Courtland D. "A Note on Chaucer's *Knight's Tale*." *MLN*, 45 (1930), 460-62.

Baum, Paull F. "Characterization in the 'Knight's Tale'." *MLN*, 46 (1931), 302-4.

————. *Chaucer: A Critical Appreciation*. Durham, N.C.: Duke Univ. Press, 1958.

Beidler, Peter G. "Chaucer's *Knight's Tale* and Its Teller." *EngR*, 18 (1968), 54-60.

Benson, C. David. "The *Knight's Tale* as History." *ChauR*, 3 (1968), 107-23.

Blake, Kathleen A. "Order and the Noble Life in Chaucer's *Knight's Tale*?" *MLQ*, 34 (1973), 3-19.

Brooks, Douglas, and Alastair Fowler. "The Meaning of Chaucer's *Knight's Tale*." *MÆ*, 39 (1970), 123-46.

Cameron, Allen B. "The Heroine in the *Knight's Tale*." *SSF*, 5 (1968), 119-27.

Cowgill, Bruce Kent. "The *Knight's Tale* and the Hundred Years' War." *PQ*, 54 (1975), 670-79.

Cozart, William R. "Chaucer's *Knight's Tale*: A Philosophical Reappraisal of a Medieval Romance." In *Medieval Epic to the "Epic Theater" of Brecht*. Ed. Rosario P. Armato and John M. Spalek. Univ. of Southern California Studies in Comparative Literature, No. 1. Los Angeles, 1968, pp. 25-34.

Dean, Christopher. "Imagery in the *Knight's Tale* and the *Miller's Tale*." *MS*, 31 (1969), 149-63.

Delasanta, Rodney. "Uncommon Commonplaces in the *Knight's Tale*." *NM*, 70 (1969), 683-90.

Elbow, Peter H. "How Chaucer Transcends Oppositions in the *Knight's. Tale*." *ChauR*, 7 (1972), 97-112.

Fairchild, Hoxie N. "Active Arcite, Contemplative Palamon." *JEGP*, 26 (1927), 285-93.

Fichte, Joerg O. "Man's Free Will and the Poet's Choice: The Creation of Artistic Order in Chaucer's *Knight's Tale*." *Anglia*, 93 (1975), 335-60.

Fifield, Merle. "The Knight's Tale: Incident, Idea, Incorporation." *ChauR*, 3 (1968), 95-106.

Foster, Edward E. "Humor in the *Knight's Tale*." *ChauR*, 3 (1968), 88-94.

French, W.H. "The Lovers in the *Knight's Tale*." *JEGP*, 48 (1949), 320-28.

Frost, William. "An Interpretation of Chaucer's Knight's Tale." *RES*, 25 (1949), 289-304.

Gaylord, Alan T. "The Role of Saturn in the *Knight's Tale*." *ChauR*, 8 (1974), 172-90.

Gunn, Alan M.F. "Polylithic Romance: With Pages of Illustration." In *Studies in Medieval, Renaissance, American Literature: A Festschrift* [Honoring Troy C. Crenshaw, Lorraine Sherley, and Ruth Speer Angell]. Ed. Betsy F. Colquitt. Fort Worth: Texas Christian Univ. Press, 1971, pp. 1-18.

Haller, Robert S. "The *Knight's Tale* and the Epic Tradition." *ChauR*, 1 (1966), 67-84.

Halverson, John. "Aspects of Order in the 'Knight's Tale'." *SP*, 57 (1960), 606-21.

Ham, Edward B ."Knight's Tale 38." *ELH*, 17 (1950), 252-61.

Helterman, Jeffrey. "The Dehumanizing Metamorphoses of the *Knight's Tale*." *ELH*, 38 (1971), 493-511.

Herz, Judith S. "Chaucer's Elegiac Knight." *Criticism*, 6 (1964), 212-24.

Herzman, Ronald B. "The Paradox of Form: The *Knight's Tale* and Chaucerian Aesthetics." *PLL*, 10 (1974), 339-52.

Hulbert, J.R. "What Was Chaucer's Aim in the *Knight's Tale*?" *SP*, 26 (1929), 375-85.

Kaske, R.E. "The Knight's Interruption of the *Monk's Tale*." *ELH*, 24 (1957), 249-68.

Loomis, Dorothy B. "Saturn in Chaucer's *Knight's Tale*." In *Chaucer und seine Zeit: Symposion für Walter F. Schirmer*. Ed. Arno Esch. Buchreihe der *Anglia, Zeitschrift für englische Philologie*, No. 14. Tübingen: M. Niemeyer, 1968, pp. 149-61.

Lumiansky, R.M. "Chaucer's Philosophical Knight." *TSE*, 3 (1952), 47-68.

Marckwardt, Albert H. "Characterization in Chaucer's *Knight's Tale*." *UMCMP*, 5 (1947), 1-23.

Meier, T.K. "Chaucer's Knight as 'Persona': Narration as Control." *EM*, 20 (1969), 11-21.

Muscatine, Charles. "Form, Texture, and Meaning in Chaucer's *Knight's Tale*." *PMLA*, 65 (1950), 911-29.

Neuse, Richard. "The Knight: The First Mover in Chaucer's Human Comedy." *UTQ*, 31 (1962), 299-315.

Penninger, F. Elaine. "Chaucer's *Knight's Tale* and the Theme of Appearance and Reality in *The Canterbury Tales*." *SAQ*, 63 (1964), 398-405.

Pratt, R.A. "Chaucer's Use of the *Teseida*." *PMLA*, 62 (1947), 598-621.

————. "'Joye after Wo' in the *Knight's Tale*." *JEGP*, 57 (1958), 416-23.

Ruggiers, Paul G. "Some Philosophical Aspects of *The Knight's Tale*." *CE*, 19 (1958), 298-302.

Schmidt, A.V.C. "The Tragedy of Arcite: A Reconsideration of the *Knight's Tale*." *EIC*, 29 (1969), 107-16.

Tatelbaum, Linda. "Venus' Citole and the Restoration of Harmony in Chaucer's *Knight's Tale*." *NM*, 74 (1973), 649-64.

Thundy, Zacharias. "Chaucer's Quest for Wisdom in the *Canterbury Tales*." *NM*, 77 (1976), 582-98.

Thurston, Paul T. *Artistic Ambivalence in Chaucer's Knight's Tale*. Gainesville, Fla.: Univ. of Florida Press, 1968.

Turner, Frederick. "A Structuralist Analysis of the *Knight's Tale*." *ChauR*, 8 (1974), 279-96.

Underwood, Dale. "The First of *The Canterbury Tales*." *ELH*, 26 (1959), 455-69.

Van, Thomas A. "Imprisoning and Ensnarement in *Troilus* and the *Knight's Tale*." *PLL*, 7 (1971), 3-12.

————. "Theseus and the 'Right Way' of the *Knight's Tale*." *SLitI*, 4 (1971), 83-100.

Webb, Henry J. "A Reinterpretation of Chaucer's Theseus." *RES*, 23 (1947), 289-96.

Westlund, Joseph. "The *Knight's Tale* as an Impetus for Pilgrimage." *PQ*, 43 (1964), 526-37.

Wilson, H.S. "*The Knight's Tale* and the *Teseida* Again." *UTQ*, 18 (1949), 131-46.

III. THE SQUIRE'S TALE

Berger, Harry, Jr. "The F-Fragment of the *Canterbury Tales*." *ChauR*, 1 (1966), 88-102.

Braddy, Haldeen. "The Genre of Chaucer's *Squire's Tale*." *JEGP*, 41 (1942), 279-90.

Chapman, C.O. "Chaucer and the *Gawain*-Poet: A Conjecture." *MLN*, 68 (1953), 521-24.

Clark, John W. "*Does* the Franklin Interrupt the Squire?" *ChauR*, 7 (1972), 160-61.

Duncan, Charles F., Jr. " 'Straw for Youre Gentilesse': The Gentle Franklin's Interruption of the Squire." *ChauR*, 5 (1970), 161-64.

Finkelstein, Dorothee. "The Celestial Origin of Elpheta and Algarsyf in Chaucer's *Squire's Tale*." *Euroasiatica* (Napoli), 4 (1971), 3-13.

Friend, Albert C. "The Tale of the Captive Bird and the Traveler: Nequam, Berechiah, and Chaucer's *Squire's Tale*." *M&H*, NS, 1 (1970), 57-65.

Furnivall, F.J. "Forewords" to *John Lane's Continuation of Chaucer's "Squire's Tale*." Chaucer Soc., 2nd ser., No. 23. London: Trübner, 1888.

Haller, Robert S. "Chaucer's *Squire's Tale* and the Uses of Rhetoric." *MP*, 62 (1965), 285-95.

Kahrl, Stanley J. "Chaucer's *Squire's Tale* and the Decline of Chivalry." *ChauR*, 7 (1973), 194-209.

Moseley, C.W.R.D. "Some Suggestions about the Writing of the *Squire's Tale*." *Archiv*, 212 (1975), 124-27.

Neville, Marie. "The Function of the *Squire's Tale* in the Canterbury Scheme." *JEGP*, 50 (1951), 167-79.

Pearsall, Derek. "The Squire as Story-Teller." *UTQ*, 34 (1965), 82-92.

Peterson, Joyce E. "The Finished Fragment: A Reassessment of the *Squire's Tale.*" *ChauR*, 5 (1970), 62-74.

Stillwell, Gardiner. "Chaucer in Tartary." *RES*, 24 (1948), 177-88.

Whiting, B.J. "Gawain: His Reputation, His Courtesy and His Appearance in Chaucer's *Squire's Tale.*" *MS*, 9 (1947), 189-234.

IV. THE WIFE OF BATH'S TALE

Brown, Eric D. "Transformation and the Wife of Bath: A Jungian Discussion." *ChauR*, 10 (1976), 303-15.

Cary, Meredith. "Sovereignty and Old Wife." *PLL*, 5 (1969), 375-88.

Colmer, Dorothy. "Character and Class in the *Wife of Bath's Tale.*" *JEGP*, 72 (1973), 329-39.

Eisner, Sigmund. *A Tale of Wonder: A Source Study of The Wife of Bath's Tale.* 1957. Rpt. Folcroft, Pa.: Folcroft Press, 1970.

Haller, Robert S. "The Wife of Bath and the Three Estates." *AnM*, 6 (1965), 47-64.

Harwood, Britton J. "The Wife of Bath and the Dream of Innocence." *MLQ*, 33 (1972), 257-73.

Holland, Norman N. "Meaning as Transformation: The *Wife of Bath's Tale.*" *CE*, 28 (1967), 279-90.

Huppé, Bernard F. "Rape and Woman's Sovereignty in the *Wife of Bath's Tale.*" *MLN*, 63 (1948), 378-81.

Koban, Charles. "Hearing Chaucer Out: The Art of Persuasion in the *Wife of Bath's Tale.*" *ChauR*, 5 (1971), 225-39.

Levy, Bernard S. "The Wife of Bath's *Queynte Fantasye.*" *ChauR*, 4 (1970), 106-22.

Malone, Kemp. "The Wife of Bath's Tale." *MLR*, 57 (1962), 481-91.

Miller, Robert P. "*The Wife of Bath's Tale* and Mediaeval Exempla." *ELH*, 32 (1965), 442-56.

Oberembt, Kenneth J. "Chaucer's Anti-misogynist Wife of Bath." *ChauR*, 10 (1976), 287-302.

Reid, David S. "Crocodilian Humor: A Discussion of Chaucer's Wife of Bath." *ChauR*, 4 (1970), 73-89.

Roppolo, Joseph P. "The Converted Knight in Chaucer's *Wife of Bath's Tale*." *CE*, 12 (1951), 263-69.

Rowland, Beryl. "Chaucer's Dame Alys: Critics in Blunderland?" *NM*, 73 (1972), 381-95.

Salter, F.M. "The Tragic Figure of the Wyf of Bath." *PTRSC*, 3rd Ser., 48 (1954), 1-13.

Schlauch, Margaret. "The Marital Dilemma in the *Wife of Bath's Tale*." *PMLA*, 61 (1946), 416-30.

Silverstein, Theodore. "Wife of Bath and the Rhetoric of Enchantment; or, How to Make a Hero See in the Dark." *MP*, 58 (1961), 153-73.

Steinberg, Aaron. "The Wife of Bath's Tale and Her Fantasy of Fulfillment." *CE*, 26 (1964), 187-91.

Sumner, Laura, ed. *The Weddynge of Sir Gawen and Dame Ragnell*. Smith College Studies in Modern Languages, 5, No. 4. Northampton, Mass., 1924.

Townsend, Francis G. "Chaucer's Nameless Knight." *MLR*, 49 (1954), 1-4.

Verdonk, P. " 'Sire Knyght, Heer Forth Ne Lith No Wey': A Reading of Chaucer's *The Wife of Bath's Tale*." *Neophil*, 60 (1976), 297-308.

V. THE FRANKLIN'S TALE

Baker, Donald C. "A Crux in Chaucer's *Franklin's Tale*: Dorigen's Complaint." *JEGP*, 60 (1961), 56-64.

Benjamin, Edwin B. "The Concept of Order in the *Franklin's Tale*." *PQ*, 38 (1959), 119-24.

David, Alfred. "Sentimental Comedy in the *Franklin's Tale*." *AnM*, 6 (1965), 19-27.

Dempster, Germaine. "Chaucer at Work on the Complaint in the *Franklin's Tale*." *MLN*, 52 (1937), 16-23.

Donovan, M.J. *The Breton Lay: A Guide to Varieties.* Notre Dame, Ind.: Univ. of Notre Dame Press, 1969, pp. 173-89.

Gaylord, Alan T. "The Promises in *The Franklin's Tale.*" *ELH,* 31 (1964), 331-65.

Hodge, James L. "The Marriage Group: Precarious Equilibrium." *ES,* 46 (1965), 289-300.

Holman, C. Hugh. "Courtly Love in the Merchant's and the Franklin's Tales." *ELH,* 18 (1951), 241-52.

Howard, Donald R. "The Conclusion of the Marriage Group: Chaucer and the Human Condition." *MP,* 57 (1960), 223-32.

Hume, Kathryn. "The Pagan Setting of the *Franklin's Tale* and the Sources of Dorigen's Cosmology." *SN,* 44 (1972), 289-94.

———. "Why Chaucer Calls the *Franklin's Tale* a Breton Lai." *PQ,* 51 (1972), 365-79.

Joseph, Gerhard. "The *Franklin's Tale*: Chaucer's Theodicy." *ChauR,* 1 (1966), 20-32.

Kee, Kenneth. "Two Chaucerian Gardens." *MS,* 23 (1961), 154-62.

Knight, Stephen. "Rhetoric and Poetry in the *Franklin's Tale.*" *ChauR,* 4 (1970), 14-30.

Loomis, Laura Hibbard. "Chaucer and the Breton Lays of the Auchinleck MS." *SP,* 38 (1941), 14-33.

Lumiansky, R.M. "The Character and Performance of Chaucer's Franklin." *UTQ,* 20 (1951), 344-56.

Mann, Lindsay A. " 'Gentilesse' and the *Franklin's Tale.*" *SP,* 63 (1966), 10-29.

Robertson, D.W., Jr. "Chaucer's Franklin and His Tale." *Costerus,* NS 1 (1974), 1-26.

Severs, J. Burke. "Appropriateness of Character to Plot in the *Franklin's Tale.*" In *Studies in Language and Literature in Honour of Margaret Schlauch.* Ed. M. Brahmer, Helsztyński, and J. Krźyanowski. Warsaw: Pánstwöwe, 1966, pp. 385-96.

Sledd, James. "Dorigen's Complaint." *MP,* 45 (1947), 36-45.

Tripp, Raymond P., Jr. "The Franklin's Solution to the Marriage Debate." In *New Views on Chaucer: Essays in Generative Criticism.* Ed. W.C. Johnson, Jr., and Lauren C. Gruber. Denver: Society of New Language Study, 1973, pp. 35-41.

White, Gertrude M. "The *Franklin's Tale*: Chaucer or the Critics." *PMLA*, 89 (1974), 454-62.

VI. SIR THOPAS

Burrow, J.A. " 'Listeth, Lordes': *Sir Thopas*, 712 and 833." *N&Q*, 15 (1968), 326-27.

————. " 'Worly under Wede' in *Sir Thopas*." *ChauR*, 3 (1969), 170-73.

————. " 'Sir Thopas': An Agony in Three Fits." *RES*, 22 (1971), 54-58.

Conley, John. "Peculiar Name Thopas." *SP*, 73 (1976), 42-61.

Cullen, Dolores L. "Chaucer's *The Tale of Sir Thopas*." *Expl*, 32 (1974), Item 35.

Green, A. Wigfall. "Chaucer's 'Sir Thopas': Meter, Rhyme, and Contrast." *UMSE*, 1 (1960), 1-11.

Haskell, Ann S. "Sir Thopas: The Puppet's Puppet." *ChauR*, 9 (1975), 253-61.

Lawrence, William Witherle. "Satire in *Sir Thopas*." *PMLA*, 50 (1935), 81-91.

Loomis, Laura Hibbard. "Chaucer and the Auchinleck MS: *Thopas* and *Guy of Warwick*." In *Essays and Studies in Honor of Carleton Brown.* New York: New York Univ. Press, 1940, pp. 111-28.

————. "Sir Thopas." In *Sources and Analogues of Chaucer's Canterbury Tales.* Ed. W.F. Bryan and Germaine Dempster. 1941. Rpt. New York: Humanities Press, 1958, pp. 486-559.

Manly, John Matthews. "The Stanza Forms of *Sir Thopas*." *MP*, 8 (1910), 141-44.

————. "Sir Thopas, A Satire." *E&S*, 13 (1928), 52-73.

Moore, Arthur K. "*Sir Thopas* as Criticism of Fourteenth-Century Minstrelsy." *JEGP*, 53 (1954), 532-45.

Stanley, E.G. "The Use of Bob-Lines in *Sir Thopas*." *NM*, 73 (1972), 417-26.

Trounce, A.M. "The English Tail-Rhyme Romances." *MÆ*, 1 (1932), 87-108, 168-82; 2 (1933), 34-57, 189-98; 3 (1934), 30-50.

Van Arsdale, Ruth. "The Chaste Sir Thopas." *AN&Q*, 13 (1975), 146-48.

Winstanley, Lilian, ed. *The Prioress's Tale, The Tale of Sir Thopas*. Cambridge: Cambridge Univ. Press, 1922.

FOURTEEN

D. S. BREWER

The Fabliaux

The *Canterbury Tales* is among other things remarkable for the way in which Chaucer shows his virtuosity in every vernacular literary genre of the time except lyric and drama. In all this variety, the fabliau-genre bulks far the largest. There are plenty of paradoxes here. Astonishingly, there are practically no other fabliaux in English, yet Chaucer's own handling of the genre shows both his deep understanding of it, in its original French form, and his transformation of it. It has been reasonably suggested that these indecent anecdotes were Chaucer's greatest interest in his maturity. Indecent as they are, their fundamental morality has also been emphasized. Furthermore, they are now accepted as among Chaucer's highest achievement, yet only in the twentieth century have they begun to receive adequate criticism.

It will be most convenient to begin the present discussion with some consideration of what a fabliau is, especially among the French, then follow in outline the progress of twentieth-century criticism and scholarship of the fabliau, before turning finally to brief notes on the individual poems.

The mechanical basis of definition of the fabliau is simple. It is a versified short story designed to make you laugh, and its subject matter is most often indecent, concerned either with sexual or excretory functions. The plot is usually in the form of a practical joke carried out for love or revenge. This strict definition excludes a number of poems, by Chaucer and others, such as the *Friar's Tale*, and the *Wife of Bath's Prologue*, which are obviously more or less close in form and spirit, but which do not fully accord. It would be absurd to worry about too precise a grouping. Literary kinds are like families, to take Wittgenstein's famous image in *Philosophical Investigations* (tr. G. E. M. Anscombe, Oxford, 1953), paragraphs 65-7. The generic name covers a range of individuals who are linked in a common network of characteristics, but who do not necessarily all have any single one or two characteristics in common. Chaucer's fabliaux are the grandchildren of the originals, and must be expected to differ. However, the tales of Chaucer which are traditionally called fabliaux are the Miller's, Reeve's, Cook's (though being incomplete and so short it will not be discussed here), the Friar's, Summoner's, Merchant's, and Shipman's. They are called fabliaux from the name of the French genre, for the French invented this form of literature, which for all the apparently universal appeal of the subject matter is characteristic of thirteenth-century French literature.

It is essential to grasp the apparent contradictions here to understand Chaucer's achievement: first, a subject matter of apparently universal appeal, set out in a form which persisted in French little more than a century; secondly, an English author succeeding supremely with a French literary form effectively dead before he was born.

The medieval French fabliaux were first edited and studied in the eighteenth century; collections began to be made, and the standard collection of Montaiglon and Raynaud was published 1872-90. The basic modern study, whereby the distinguished French scholar J. Bédier made his reputation, appeared in 1893. Its elegance and power are such that his essay may count as a work of art in its own right, independent of the acceptance of its conclusions. His thesis, *Les Fabliaux*, is one of the many fine flowers of French bourgeois scholarship of the nineteenth century. No brief summary can give more than a hint of its contents. Bédier's long section on the problem of "where the stories come from," notable for its elegant contempt of other scholars, emphasized, and indeed over-emphasized, the universality of the themes. Europe was shown to be capable of inventing its own dirty stories, even if these stories did coincide with those of the East. Furthermore, Bédier enunciated the important principle that each age is responsible for the stories with which it amuses itself, whatever the ultimate possible origin and date of the story. Bédier showed clearly that the fabliau was the invention of the thirteenth century in France and did not long persist in the fourteenth. He also conceived of the refined and idealizing romance as a courtly genre, with the coarse and realistic fabliau as a bourgeois genre. He saw well enough much interpenetration of genres, much evidence for some courtly authorship and much courtly enjoyment of fabliaux, but these important modifications of his thesis were largely ignored. The post-Romantic anti-bourgeois movement of late nineteenth- and twentieth-century literary culture (sustained almost entirely by bourgeois authors, scholars, and teachers!) has insisted on the coarseness of the fabliau as a bourgeois characteristic.

One of the paradoxes of which literary history is full is that only now, in the middle of the twentieth century, when contemporary bourgeois literary culture, especially in the United States, has developed a coarseness of thought and language undreamt-of even by the nobility in the Middle Ages, do we realize that the fabliau is as courtly a genre as the romance—is indeed the comic and realistic side of the coin of serious and idealizing romance. The courtliness of the fabliau has been made clear by the magisterial work of P. Nykrog whose study corrects Bédier's in this and several other respects, and which must now be taken as the foundation of any general and historical commentary on fabliaux. Nykrog, while still accepting Bédier's general literary description of the fabliaux' realism, impersonality, lack of rhetorical adornment and of characterization, and rapidity of narration, shows very conclusively their predominantly courtly origin, their quality as *written* poems, and their emphasis on erotic themes, on satire of the bourgeoisie and of certain clergy (e.g. parish-priests). The fabliaux have a typical French brilliance and harshness. They are aristocratic burlesques, contemptuously holding up to amusement the coarse buffooneries of lower classes and some clergy. The European tradition of libertine literature has always been designed for the educated upper classes. Nevertheless, the fabliaux have well-marked limits of indecency: the subject matter is low, and gross words are sometimes used for their shock effect, but there is no erotic elaboration, no pornography, no perversion.

The most easily available collection of texts in French, with valuable introduction, notes and glossary in English, is perhaps that by Johnston and Owen. Hellman and O'Gorman offer a representative selection of fabliaux in translation with an excellent introduction and short bibliography. The close parallel of the fabliau *La veuve* by the fascinating Gautier le Leu (who is discussed at some length by Nykrog) with the *Wife of Bath's Prologue* has since been noticed. Bryan and Dempster offer some untranslated fabliaux as sources and analogues of the appropriate tales, together with English summaries.

The relationship between Chaucer's fabliaux and the French, or, in some cases, the Italian analogues, is paradoxical. Chaucer's poems are both very close to and very far from the fabliau form. Their indecency of plot and event which is characteristic of the fabliau caused mostly amusement in the first five centuries of reading Chaucer, as I have shown in a general way in "Images of Chaucer." Wordsworth's memory of laughing with Chaucer in *The Prelude* (1850), III, 278-9, is fairly representative. But some dissident notes in the earlier centuries herald the embarrassment found in those books of criticism which begin to appear in the early twentieth century, when, perhaps, it was felt necessary to spare the blush on the cheek of that very hypothetical Young Person cherished by Mr. Podsnap. Those giants of Chaucerian scholarship and criticism who preferred to avert their eyes include Manly, Root, Kittredge, Lowes, and Patch. Manly omitted the fabliaux from his edition of the *Canterbury Tales*. Root was not much interested in them; he refers a little disdainfully to "those who wish to go farther with this not very profitable theme" (p. 175). He points out the extreme indecency of the Miller's and Reeve's tales. Root is eminently calm and sensible about the morality or lack of morality of these poems, but he is divided in his judgment. On the one hand they provide "merely a diverting interlude," and thus appear to him to be low in artistic value; on the other hand he comments on how in, for example, the *Miller's Tale*, attention is diverted from the lustful and nasty features of the story to the brilliant characterization and consummate narrative skill. Later criticism has followed this second judgment, showing how Chaucer has enriched the spare, direct, impersonal fabliau—in itself a process somewhat contradictory to the essential nature of the French fabliau.

A notable impetus to the general study of Chaucer's fabliaux was provided by Germaine Dempster's work on *Dramatic Irony in Chaucer* (1932). Dempster saw two main influences in the development of Chaucer's sense of dramatic irony: *Il Filostrato* and the fabliaux. The former is part of the Italian influence on Chaucer, and the concern of another chapter, (and the fabliaux are also, naturally, a part of the general French influence); but in her book, effectively for the first time, the fabliaux are shown to be an artistic center of Chaucer's poetry. Dempster remarks that the French fabliaux are full of ironies of circumstance and action, especially of the kind where a dupe runs into a snare laid by his own hands, but that even so Chaucer reveals his own taste by choosing the more ironical of the fabliaux to rewrite. In her view, the qualities which Chaucer particularly learnt from the fabliaux were consistent objectivity and impersonality of style, quickness and lightness of touch, and pervading realism. Dempster also comments on what Chaucer added to the basic anecdote by way of description and characterization. She notes the cruelty and fierce irony of some of the tales. She observes, however, that in the pear tree episode in the *Merchant's Tale*, Chaucer not only makes the irony more definite, but also lamentably pathetic, "seizing the opportunity to make the poor blind man express his helpless devotion to young May" (p. 56). Regarding "poetic justice," a term much used by later critics, she remarks:

> There is something like it in the punishment of the miller. But shall we "make ernest of game?" The phrase "poetic justice" ssems to put moral values too much in the foreground. . . . The dramatic irony of our fabliau and of the *Reeve's Tale* is pure, un-adulterated fun. (p. 34).

The vivid realism, the attractive merriment, and especially the lively characterization of the fabliaux are well illustrated by Shelly (1940), who also finds some kind words to say of January's generosity and pathos. He comes out clearly in favor of the artistry and delight in the fabliau, as indeed did Lowes, though very briefly, in his famous book. Shelly notes the neglect of the fabliaux by critics.

The next generation of general books to survey more or less fully either Chaucer's life and works or at least the *Canterbury Tales* were those appearing in the late forties and early fifties, by Bennett, Brewer, Coghill, Preston, Lawrence, Lumiansky, Speirs. These all clearly emphasize the greatness of the fabliau as poetry. Coghill, one of the empirics, shows his enjoyment, and contrasts the fantasy of the plots with the realism of description and character. Lawrence deals briskly and sensibly with many problems. In particular, he considers the question of the inter-relationships of the *Tales*, a general topic which has since re-ceived further discussion in terms of thematic and organic unities, but which is not yet exhausted. Lawrence thinks that Chaucer became particularly interested in the fabliau-genre as he grew older, and that he may indeed have chosen a pilgrimage in order to introduce fabliaux with dramatic plausibility. One can hardly gauge Chaucer's intentions now (though too many Chaucer critics still fall into the Intentionalist Fallacy), but certainly there are more fabliaux amongst the *Tales* than other kinds of poem, and Lawrence's point is important. Lumiansky, in a cheerful and en-thusiastic book, develops with energy another important question on which "diverse folk, diversely they said"—that is, the question of dramatic appropriateness of tale to speaker. Clearly there is some appropriateness, some decorum in relation of tale to speaker, for almost all, perhaps all, the *Tales*; but that this appropriateness is a naturalistic, psychologically dramatic expressiveness has been questioned by Bronson (another empirical critic), Brewer, Craik, and others.

Speirs was one of the earlier critics to suggest, besides the usual items of enrichment such as characterization and description, that allegorical or symbolic dimension in the poems which has become an important topic of late (pp. 25-6). He points also to Chaucer's imagery and remarks that Chaucer's cultivated English "is rooted in the speech—concrete, figurative, proverbial—of the agricultural English folk" (p. 21). We must not forget, of course, that if ever there was a literary and courtly intellectual, Chaucer is he. But the way in which he *spans* the range from farmyard to court is certainly remarkable and has recently been developed by Muscatine in his essay in *Chaucer and Chaucerians*.

The fabliaux are fundamental to Muscatine's thesis in what is still the best critical book on Chaucer, *Chaucer and the French Tradition*. Muscatine uses the tension between the idealistic style and the realistic style to articulate his presentation of the range and variety of Chaucer's work. He was unable to make use of Nykrog's book (which appeared in the same year) and so still sometimes associates the realistic with the bourgeois, but this doubtful liaison does not invalidate his extremely successful exposition. The fabliaux represent the extreme of realism, that is, "naturalism." "Naturalism," with its nineteenth-century French philosophical overtones of materialism, evolution, and symbolism, is an awkward term to use with Chaucer, as Muscatine knows very well. Chaucer's fundamental attitudes were of historical necessity mentalist; that is, they were almost entirely opposed to the materialist and positivist values of naturalism and symbolism, and of twentieth-century literature in general. Yet naturalism historically arose out of realism, as René Wellek has shown, and Chaucer in his fabliaux especially is extremely realistic. Muscatine sees the fabliau-genre as the most naturalistic of medieval forms, and the *Miller's Tale* as fabliau at its stage of richest elaboration, "the genre virtually made philosophical. . . . a self-assertive vehicle for the purest fabliau doctrine, the sovereignty of animal nature" (p. 224). There is obviously a potential conflict, or contradiction here, in Chaucer, between the *general* "idealism" of his world-view, and his realism-naturalism. The poems maintain the conflict in some sort of equilibrium, a part of Gothic duality and tension, which gives dynamic form to the conflicting variety of experience. This duality is in part rendered by the "mixed style," and Muscatine sees the mixed style of the *Miller's Tale* as itself a part of the meaning of the poem. Other poems too, notably the *Merchant's Tale*, are seen to be similarly dualistic, a mixture of courtliness and naturalism.

With Muscatine we have moved into a subtlety of stylistic analysis which earlier criticism had never conceptualized, whatever its responsiveness and enjoyment. This new subtlety, much indebted to the New Criticism, is also represented by E. T. Donaldson, who introduced into general Chaucer criticism the notion of the narrator of the poem, Chaucer the Pilgrim, who is, and is not, the poet himself. (This notion is to some extent in conflict with the simpler one of the "dramatic" narrator of each tale, whose character is expressed by his tale.) Donaldson also led the way in stylistic analysis with his essay on the language of the *Miller's Tale*, where he shows how the poem mocks old-fashioned provincial poetic diction, such as that found in *The Harley Lyrics*. Donaldson's very subtle and sensitive criticism, discriminating between levels of narration and kinds of style, along with many fresh and witty observations, may be found gathered in the Commentary of his *Chaucer's Poetry: An Anthology for the Modern Reader*. Not everybody has been convinced by the narrator. He has been argued against by Major and Bronson in general terms, and also by T. W. Craik in his book on *The Comic Tales of Chaucer*. Craik is another empiric, like most Englishmen, perhaps, who resists generalized notions and themes. The strength of his book lies in its fresh and sensitive detailed commentary, a specific examination and appreciation of "the thing in itself as it really is," written in knowledge of current discussion, but without invoking it, or using any historical considerations. He includes more than the fabliaux in his account, but the subject of his book shows how the fabliaux have arrived.

Finally, in this brief survey of general treatments, we move away again from the empirical to the conceptual and thematic. The important and controversial work of D. W. Robertson, Jr., *A Preface to Chaucer*, covers many topics and only incidentally treats the fabliaux, which are, indeed, somewhat recalcitrant to his general line of treatment. Robertson, like Muscatine, is a philosophical critic, who takes "style" as his point of entry into the poems. But where Muscatine emphasizes a Symbolist Chaucer, with particular reference to that realism inherent in Symbolism, Robertson emphasizes the allegorical and conceptual elements, with particular reference to "idealism." (The similarities and differences, like those between allegory and symbol, are complex and a brief account necessarily oversimplifies.) Robertson rightly questions any simple notion that the fabliaux are generally "like life." In detecting a conceptual basis he sees, for example, the *Miller's Tale*, as having a framework of three basic temptations or sins, and maintains that the humorous as opposed to the merely farcical element "is due entirely to its theological background." Robertson has also emphasized the conceptual or allegorical elements in the garden of the *Merchant's Tale*, and he affirms that the grotesque characters and the characters who are described in terms of iconographic attributes "call attention to abstract concepts" (p. 257).

Other philosophical critics are Helen Corsa and Paul G. Ruggiers. Corsa's general view of Chaucer as poet of mirth and morality is expressed in the title of her book, and she sees the fabliaux as particularly concerned with justice of several kinds. Ruggiers, in his thoughtful and interesting book, is deeply concerned with the nature of artistic unity. He sees the informing principle of the *Canterbury Tales* as "one central theme" of "ceaseless debate" between the concept of destiny, or Providence, with which goes the wish-fulfillment of spiritual notions of the nature of man, on the one hand; and on the other hand, "the fatiguing promise of moral responsibility," "freedom of the will," "persistent claims of natural appetite," and the "realistic" claims of the "all-too-real world." Like others he sees Chaucer as more and more sympathetic to the secular and profane as he grew older, and so particularly interested in the fabliaux. Ruggiers also emphasizes Chaucer's concern with morality and considers that the so-called non-serious tales imply the "moral norms" of the whole *Canterbury Tales*; the pilgrimage symbolizes, as other critics have claimed, some Christian scheme, and all the tales, even if bitter or indecent, thus contribute to some moral end; Chaucer achieves "a reconciliation of art with prudence" (p. 39). Ruggiers concedes that the moral intentions which he, Robertson and others attribute to Chaucer in writing the fabliaux make the Retraction, at the end of the *Tales*, of those tales which "sownen unto sin," very puzzling; nevertheless, Ruggiers' emphasis on morality does some justice to the humane optimism and sanity which prevent Chaucer's fabliaux from corrupting the reader. Ruggiers also sees the tales very much as expressions of the characters of the tellers.

To sum up so far, it is clear that from a lowly position, regarded with contempt or neglect, however modified by amusement, in the earlier part of this century, Chaucer's fabliaux have rocketed into a position of central importance for most critics of Chaucer. This has been due to several causes. The Romantic notion of poetry as concerned only with matters of high and solemn seriousness has faded (though it persists in some suggestions that the fabliaux are *really* serious); satire and humor are now seen to be fully capable of poetic expression; modern literature has become so very indecent and immoral that it is in every way laughable to hesitate at Chaucer's indecency. Moreover, the subject matter of the fabliaux is nowadays not merely less objectionable: it is regarded by some critics as, in various ways, *truer* to life than that of other tales; our modern pessimism relishes the "naturalism" of the fabliaux. Paradoxically, critics seem to take less interest in the sheer comedy caused by reversal of order, perhaps because we no longer believe in any fundamental order; having lost our sense of Providential justice, we are inclined to emphasize poetic justice; the universe no longer appearing to have a moral structure, we seek morality in, of all places, fabliaux.

However this may be, such changes in outlook have encouraged critics to realize the rich poetic texture which Chaucer has draped over the originally bare and simple fabliaux-form. The liveliness of characterization and its relationships within and without the tales have been constantly praised. The structure of plots (almost certainly improved and elaborated on by Chaucer from his models) has been shown to be beautifully ironic, and many have commented on their poetic justice. The allegorical, symbolic, thematic implications of the tales have been explored, along with the relationships between tales, and also between tales and historical real life. The poetic language and imagery have received some attention. The narrative point-of-view has been much debated. A number of studies of individual poems have been made bringing out special points and defining individual quality, and to a very brief summary of these we now turn.

The *Miller's Tale* has received much the greatest attention. Donaldson's comment on the quality of its language as a parody of popular romance (and perhaps of lyric) has already been noted, and Stillwell has continued this. Muscatine and others point out Freudian symbolism in the action and style. There has also been much work done on the characterization and its relationships; Alison is a parody of a courtly lady, in the rhetorical tradition, whereby Alison is mocked, not the ideal. But the vivid country images in which Alison is described do full justice to her allure. Absalom has also been placed in the rhetorical tradition, greatly to his enrichment, by Beichner. He has further been accused of having a babyish oral orientation by Birney and others. P. A. Olson, while emphasizing poetic justice, believes that the action arises from the characters, though of course, this cannot be the *historical* truth, since the elements of the action were widespread in other versions with different characters in Europe in Chaucer's day. The poem has also been seen, apart from its moral structuring, as burlesquing the Seven Liberal Arts and the Miracle Plays, as having references to astrological learning, and, by Kaske, as alluding to the Song of Songs, with Absalom a comic parallel to the Divine Lover and Alison to the Divine Beloved. Here is a rich mixture indeed! And all in a poem of some six hundred lines. It is justly summed up by Bolton, who emphasizes the Biblical associations: "The organization and success of the tale depend on the juxtaposition of courtly and common, sacred and profane, realistic and fantastic, in a single ironic statement." Perhaps there is a risk of forgetting that the poem is, at its heart, a delightful comedy of sex, as Brewer once suggested, full of heartless injustice, and quite immoral.

By contrast, the *Reeve's Tale* is a comedy of social pride, only less rich than the *Miller's Tale*. Hart long ago established the lines on which criticism would develop, emphasizing poetic justice and comic morality. He made useful comparisons with the French fabliaux to show how Chaucer enriches the bare structure of the plot. The language of the *Reeve's Tale* has been little examined, with the striking exception of Tolkien's analysis of the Northern dialect of the two clerks. Although Tolkien has an unwarrantably low opinion of the literary quality of the fabliau he shows how good a philologist Chaucer was. This article deserves to be followed up with other linguistic and stylistic studies. The relation of the tale to the character of the elderly, choleric Reeve has been much discussed; and there has even been some confusion between the miller in the *Reeve's Tale*, and the pilgrim-Miller. Kaske has detected literary parody of the dawn-song in the clerk's parting from the miller's daughter, but far less density of texture has been discovered in this poem as yet than in the *Miller's Tale*. Copland, in the fullest and subtlest examination of the poem so far, calls it a "gray" tale, in which the Reeve's "respectability" is ironically enacted, and whose implicit severity criticizes the jolly animality of the *Miller's Tale*.

The Friar's and Summoner's tales obviously make another interrelated pair, and the satirical cross-references to the pilgrim-Friar and pilgrim-Summoner have been well-explored by Beichner,

Birney, Bonjour and others. Apart from a valuable note by Nathan on pronouns of address in the *Friar's Tale,* in which he demonstrates subtle nuances of tone, there has been little linguistic or stylistic analysis. Cawley, however, in his valuable article (which also summarizes scholarship on the subject) has shown that the tale is full of echoes of excommunication; but he concludes that realism is sacrificed to irony. Irony has indeed been generally seen as the central quality of the tale, emphasized by the poetic justice of the biter bit. Greed and coarse sexuality dig their own pits to fall into. The historical situation of friars and summoners, and other references give these two tales an unusually topical flavor for Chaucer.

On the whole the *Summoner's Tale* has been found the richer, though the more unsavory, of the two. Ruggiers describes it as psychologically one of Chaucer's richest. Baum has discussed the puns, and others have commented on verbal allusions. Adams has found in the language "suggestive patterns of anal wordplay" which perhaps makes the poem sound nastier than it is. The characterization of the Friar in the tale through his odiously "smarmy" speech has of course drawn attention, as have the irony and poetic justice of the plot. Williams has put the conventional satire of friars into historical perspective, and similar aspects have been discussed by Haselmayer and Mroczkowski. But no one seems to have commented on scholastic elements, nor found local references, though Chapman touched on the preaching a long time ago.

The *Shipman's Tale* is nearer to the pure fabliau-type, and to the harsh brilliant simplicity of Boccaccio, than is any of Chaucer's other fabliaux; in consequence, as Lawrence and Copland point out, it is "harder" than the others. There has been discussion of the *double-entendres* at the end—particularly (by Caldwell and Jones) of the ambiguity of *taillynge*—but it is still not agreed whether the poem was originally meant for a woman speaker. There has, however, been general agreement that the tale explores the close relationship between sex and money (see Silverman). Chaucer altered the plot as it reached him in order to let the wife escape (as she does in the Miller's and the Merchant's tales).

If the *Shipman's Tale* is closest to the fabliau-type, the *Merchant's Tale* is by general agreement furthest away; it has attracted much interest, though it is a difficult tale to handle. It does not fit into any simple category, its mood is hard to assess, and the daring dislocations of narrative structure (of which the most striking is the allusion to the Wife of Bath by the semi-allegorical character, Justinus, *within* the tale, line 1685) have puzzled and sometimes annoyed critics. Linguistic and stylistic comment has mostly been directed to the obvious ironic references to the *Song of Songs*, though this has necessarily merged into discussion of the allegorical-symbolic implications, especially of the garden. The physical and moral blindness of January offer another, more Freudian layer of symbolism. The views expressed on marriage create other relationships within the so-called Marriage Group, while the general parody-relationship to what medieval authors called *fine amour* (which bears some similarity to what modern critics call "courtly love") has been investigated by Holman. The structure of plot is clearly ironical, but the levels of narration, the degree to which the tale is to be attached to the Merchant's own experience, and how fully dramatic the tale really is, are all still matters of argument. Some critics have felt that the Merchant's disillusionment and the low moral quality of the chief characters implies a bitterness of tone in the narration. Others have denied this, and Burrow, for example, in his excellent article sees a moral seriousness and an impulse to understand, leading to generalization, evidenced in passages of generosity and lyricism in the poem. The wit and learning, and also the courtly secularism of Pluto and Proserpine—whom Chaucer has substituted for the representation of God and St. Peter, or of two saints, in other versions—have been felt to emphasize the bitterness, as well, of course, as greatly enriching the poem (see Donovan and Wentersdorf). Poetic justice has been claimed for the poem, even when it has been felt to be bitter. Nothing illustrates the life and liveliness of the poem more than these persisting and fruitful disagreements among scholars and critics. (See, for example, Bronson, Jordan, Olson, Robertson and White.)

The rapid advance in the criticism of Chaucer's fabliaux, and the extraordinary jump in critical estimation, is perhaps the major twentieth-century development in Chaucer criticism. Yet although much has been accomplished, there is still much to be done. We need not seek total critical agreement—when that arrives the poetry will be dead—but we might seek to follow further some explorations, and to discuss some questions at a different level, as well as to acquire more knowledge. There is still room for examination of the differences from and similarities to the traditional fabliau in Chaucer's work. For example, the traditional fabliaux are anti-feminist and anti-clerical; Chaucer's are not. In technical matters the differences may be summed up thus: the French fabliaux have minimal rhetoric effects, Chaucer's maximal. We still need more understanding of Chaucer's philological, linguistic and stylistic resources, here as elsewhere in his work, though some of the valuable general work, such as that by Baum on puns, has already been done. The levels of narration and the *kind* of characterization deserve more consideration, both within the poems, and in the poems' relationships to the dramatic speaker and to Chaucer-the-poet. A mist of nineteenth-century literary psychologizing hangs about some discussions, and the *variety* of Chaucer's devices has perhaps not been sufficiently recognized. Again, Gothic form is more dislocated, less confined by the frame, less realistic overall, than nineteenth-century *genre*-pictures, and Chaucer's structures, like much medieval visual art, may be found to have more in common with modern fragmented art and literature than with the smooth illusoriness of the art of the late nineteenth century. A nineteenth-century expectation of organic form may well be disappointed. Chaucer challenges our *contemporary* sensibility. This is well seen in the case of irony, which is often, by modern critics and theorists, equated with poetry itself. Chaucer's irony is essentially a modern discovery, and this aspect of his genius has been plentifully illustrated. The emphasis on Chaucer's poetic justice has been valuable, but it is perhaps time to insist that there is also an important element of poetic *in*justice inherent in the fabliau-genre. Injustice is, after all, very lifelike. The assertion, too, of Chaucer's fundamental morality, which means his humanity, his life-enhancing power, has been valuable: but let us not blind ourselves to the *real* indecency and immorality of the fabliaux, not, indeed to reprobate them, for literature is fortunately not life, but in order to see the truth, and to recognize the quite proper imaginative release they offer from the even more proper tension of moral aspiration. Finally, to come back to the beginning, let us pay full attention to Chaucer's words, that "eek men shal nat maken ernest of game" (*Prol MillT*, 3186). I do not mean that we should deny the fabliaux our serious thought. It is a fallacy to suppose that literary cheerfulness, optimism and comedy are less deserving our study, less important, less significant, less true to life, than gloom and tragedy. But we should see the fabliaux for what they are, as comedies, fantasies full of fun and enjoyment, both like and unlike life. They do not offer total expressions of a philosophy on their own; they contribute their own characteristic delight to the Gothic splendor and variety of a larger whole.

* * * * *

The last ten years have seen an enormous increase in the study of the fabliaux, both generally and those so called, somewhat approximately, which were written by Chaucer. The bibliography notes only a representative few of many studies of the European fabliaux. In the study of Chaucer's bawdy poems the *Miller's Tale* has yielded first place in popularity to the *Merchant's Tale*, and the *Cook's Tale* has at last had a substantial and important article devoted to it. There has been a greater readiness to examine Chaucer's poems as examples of the International Comic Popular Tale. Both their learned and their folktale elements have been considered in the light of European sources and analogues, and religious backgrounds and implications have been explored. There has been some tendency to argue that Chaucer knew Boccaccio's *Decameron*.

General critical directions have remained much as in previous years. The fabliaux are still normally assumed to be bourgeois. Muscatine has argued (bibliography, section one) that at least they are bourgeois in spirit and that Chaucer witnesses to this by placing them in the mouths of "low" characters. Almost all critics take them to be expressive of their speaker's character, a view strongly and judiciously argued most recently by Burlin. Moral judgments, poetic justice, and realism are still going strong, though there are still those who in various ways, like Whittock, claim that Chaucer has elevated the fabliaux to the status of religious fable. Others continue to find depths of bitterness and disgust (though apparently very attractive) especially in the *Merchant's Tale*, where Stevens' robust commonsense represents a minority to which this writer also belongs.

There has been a certain amount of exploration of wordplay, imagery (Ross, Rowland, and Richardson) and of the detail of actual historical physical setting, of which last J.A.W. Bennett's book is a notable example (bibliography, section two).

BIBLIOGRAPHY

I. FRENCH FABLIAUX

Bédier, J. *Les Fabliaux*. Bibl. de l'école des hautes études, fasc. 98. Paris: Emile Bouillon, 1893.

Benson, Larry D., and T.M. Andersson. *The Literary Context of Chaucer's Fabliaux: Texts and Translations*. New York: Bobbs-Merrill, 1971.

Cooke, Thomas D., and B.L. Honeycutt. *The Humor of the Fabliaux*. Columbia: Univ. of Missouri Press, 1974.

Dronke, Peter. "The Rise of the Medieval Fabliau. Latin and Vernacular Evidence." *RF*, 85 (1973), 275-97.

Hellman, Robert, and Richard O'Gorman, eds. and trans. *Fabliaux*. London: Arthur Barker, 1965.

Johnston, R.C., and D.D.R. Owen, eds. *Fabliaux*. 2nd ed. Oxford: Blackwell, 1965.

Medieval Comic Tales. Trans. P. Rickard, A. Deyermond, D.S. Brewer, David Blamires, Peter King and Michael Lapidge. With Afterword, by D.S. Brewer, "Notes toward a Theory of Medieval Comedy." pp. 140-49. Cambridge: Brewer, 1973.

Montaiglon, Anatole de, and Gaston Raynaud, eds. *Recueil général et complet des fabliaux des XIIIe et XIVe siècles, imprimés ou inédits, publiés avec notes et variantes d'après les manuscrits*. 6 vols. Paris, 1872-90.

Muscatine, Charles. "The Social Background of the Old French Fabliaux." *Genre*, 9 (1976), 1-20.

Nykrog, Per. *Les Fabliaux: étude d'histoire littéraire et de stylistique médiévale*. 1957. New ed. Genève: Librairie Droz, 1973.

Pearcy, Roy J. "Investigation of the Principles of Fabliau Structure." *Genre*, 9 (1976), 345-78.

Proceedings of First Beast Epic, Fable and Fabliau Colloquium. Glasgow, 1977. Ed. Kenneth Varty. Glasgow: Varty, 1976. (Papers by Richard Spencer and Anne Ladd.)

Proceedings of Second Beast Epic, Fable and Fabliau Colloquium. Amsterdam, 1977. Ed. N.H.J. van den Boogaard and J. de Caluwé. (Papers by P. Bennett, N.H.J. van den Boogaard, K. MacGillavry, J. van Os, Beryl Rowland, M.-J. Stearns Schenck, R. Spencer, E. Schulze-Busacker, H. Verhulsdonck.) Forthcoming in *Marche Romane*, 29, 3-4, 1979.

Prospettive sui Fabliaux. Premessa di A. Limentani. Padua: Liviana Editrice, 1976.

II. SOME GENERAL DISCUSSIONS

Baum, Paull F. "Chaucer's Puns." *PMLA*, 71 (1956), 225-46.

———. "Chaucer's Puns: A Supplementary List." *PMLA*, 73 (1958), 167-70.

Bennett, H.S. *Chaucer and the Fifteenth Century*. Oxford History of English Literature, II, pt. 1. Oxford: Oxford Univ. Press, 1947.

Bennett, J.A.W. *Chaucer at Oxford and at Cambridge*. Toronto: Univ. of Toronto Press, 1974.

Braddy, Haldeen. "Chaucer's Bawdy Tongue." *SFQ,* 30 (1966), 214-22. Rpt. In *Geoffrey Chaucer Literary and Historical Studies.* Port Washington, N.Y.: Kennikat Press, 1971, pp. 131-39. See also, "Chaucer—Realism or Obscenity?" pp. 146-58.

Brewer, D.S. "The Ideal of Feminine Beauty in Medieval Literature, especially 'Harley Lyrics,' Chaucer and Some Elizabethans." *MLR,* 50 (1955), 257-69.

————. "Images of Chaucer 1386-1900." In *Chaucer and Chaucerians: Critical Studies in Middle English Literature.* London: Nelson, 1966, pp. 240-70.

————. *Chaucer.* 1953. 3rd ed., rev. and supplemented. London: Longmans, 1973.

————. "Towards a Chaucerian Poetic." Gollancz Memorial Lecture. *PBA,* 60 (1974), 219-52.

————. "Structures and Character-types of Chaucer's Popular Comic Tales." In *Estudios Sobre Los Generos Literarios.* Ed. J. Coy y J. De Hoz. Universidad de Salamanca, Spain, 1975, pp. 107-18.

————, ed. *Chaucer and Chaucerians: Critical Studies in Middle English Literature.* London: Nelson, 1966.

Brody, Saul N. "The Comic Rejection of Courtly Love." In *In Pursuit of Perfection.* Port Washington, N.Y.: Kennikat Press, 1975, pp. 221-61.

Bronson, Bertrand H. *In Search of Chaucer.* 1960. 2nd ed. Toronto: Univ. of Toronto Press, 1965.

Bryan, W.F., and Germaine Dempster, eds. *Sources and Analogues of Chaucer's Canterbury Tales.* 1941. Rpt. New York: Humanities Press, 1958.

Burlin, Robert B. *Chaucerian Fiction.* Princeton: Princeton Univ. Press, 1977.

Coghill, Nevill. *The Poet Chaucer.* London: Oxford Univ. Press, 1949.

Corsa, Helen Storm. *Chaucer: Poet of Mirth and Morality.* Notre Dame, Ind.: Univ. of Notre Dame Press, 1964.

Craik, T.W. *The Comic Tales of Chaucer.* London: Methuen, 1964.

Dempster, Germaine. *Dramatic Irony in Chaucer.* 1932. Rpt. New York: Humanities Press, 1959.

Donaldson, E. Talbot. "Chaucer the Pilgrim." *PMLA*, 69 (1954), 928-36.

————, ed. *Chaucer's Poetry: An Anthology for the Modern Reader*. 1958. 2nd ed. New York: Ronald Press, 1975.

Howard, Donald R. *The Idea of the Canterbury Tales*. Berkeley: Univ. of California Press, 1976.

Hussey, S.S. *Chaucer: An Introduction*. London: Methuen, 1971.

Kean, P.M. *Chaucer and the Making of English Poetry*. 2 vols. London: Routledge, 1972.

Kittredge, G.L. *Chaucer and His Poetry*. Cambridge, Mass.: Harvard Univ. Press, 1915.

Lawrence, William Witherle. *Chaucer and the Canterbury Tales*. New York: Columbia Univ. Press, 1950.

Lowes, John L. *Geoffrey Chaucer and the Development of His Genius*. 1934. Rpt. *Geoffrey Chaucer*. Bloomington: Indiana Univ. Press, 1958.

Lumiansky, R.M. *Of Sondry Folk: The Dramatic Principle in The Canterbury Tales*. Austin: Univ. of Texas Press, 1955.

McDonald, Donald. "Proverbs, *Sententiae*, and *Exempla* in Chaucer's Comic Tales: The Function of Comic Misapplication." *Speculum*, 41 (1966), 453-65.

Major, John M. "The Personality of Chaucer the Pilgrim." *PMLA*, 75 (1960), 160-62.

Manly, John Matthews, ed. *The Canterbury Tales*. New York: Holt, 1928.

Muscatine, Charles. *Chaucer and the French Tradition: A Study in Style and Meaning*. Berkeley: Univ. of California Press, 1957.

————. "*The Canterbury Tales*: Style of the Man and Style of the Work." In *Chaucer and Chaucerians*. Ed. D.S. Brewer, pp. 88-113.

Nathan, N. "Pronouns of Address in the *Canterbury Tales*." *MS*, 21 (1959), 193-201.

Olson, Clair C. "The Interludes of the Marriage Group in the *Canterbury Tales*." In *Chaucer and Middle English Studies in Honour of Rossell Hope Robbins*. Ed. Beryl Rowland. London: Allen & Unwin, 1974. Kent, Ohio: Kent State Univ. Press, 1974, pp. 164-72.

Olson, Glending L. "The Medieval Theory of Literature for Refreshment and Its Use in the Fabliau Tradition." *SP*, 71 (1974), 291-313.

Owen, Charles A., Jr. "Chaucer's *Canterbury Tales*: Aesthetic Design in Stories of the First Day." *ES*, 35 (1954), 49-56.

Patch, Howard Rollin. *On Rereading Chaucer*. Cambridge, Mass.: Harvard Univ. Press, 1939.

Preston, Raymond. *Chaucer*. 1952. Rpt. Westport, Conn.: Greenwood Press, 1969.

Richardson, Janette. *Blameth Nat Me: A Study of Imagery in Chaucer's Fabliaux*. The Hague: Mouton, 1970.

Robertson, D.W., Jr. *A Preface to Chaucer: Studies in Medieval Perspectives*. Princeton: Princeton Univ. Press, 1962.

Robinson, Ian. *Chaucer and the English Tradition*. Cambridge: Cambridge Univ. Press, 1972.

Root, R.K. *The Poetry of Chaucer: A Guide to Its Study and Appreciation*. 1906. Rev. ed. 1922. Rpt. Gloucester, Mass.: P. Smith, 1957.

Ross, Thomas W. *Chaucer's Bawdy*. New York: Dutton, 1972.

Rowland, Beryl. *Blind Beasts: Chaucer's Animal World*. Kent, Ohio: Kent State Univ. Press, 1971.

Ruggiers, Paul G. *The Art of the Canterbury Tales*. Madison: Univ. of Wisconsin Press, 1965.

Shelly, Percy Van Dyke. *The Living Chaucer*. Philadelphia: Univ. of Pennsylvania Press, 1940.

Speirs, John. *Chaucer the Maker*. 1951. Rev. 2d ed. London: Faber, 1960.

Utley, Francis L. "Boccaccio, Chaucer, and the International Popular Tale." *WF*, 33 (1974), 181-201.

Weissman, Hope P. "Antifeminism and Chaucer's Characterization of Women." In *Geoffrey Chaucer*. Ed. George D. Economou. New York: McGraw-Hill, 1975, pp. 93-110.

Wellek, René. "The Concept of Realism in Literary Scholarship." *Neophil*, 44 (1960), 1-20. Rpt. in *Concepts of Criticism*. New Haven: Yale Univ. Press, 1963, pp. 222-55.

Whittock, T. *A Reading of the Canterbury Tales*. Cambridge: Cambridge Univ. Press, 1968.

III. THE MILLER'S TALE

The Miller's Tale. Ed. C.B. Hieatt. New York: Odyssey Press, 1970.

The Miller's Prologue and Tale. Ed. James Winny. Cambridge: Cambridge Univ. Press, 1971.

Beichner, Paul E. "Absolon's Hair." *MS*, 12 (1950), 222-23.

Biggins, Dennis. "Sym(e)kyn/*simia*: The Ape in Chaucer's Millers." *SP*, 65 (1968), 44-50.

Birney, Earle. "The Inhibited and the Uninhibited: Ironic Structure in the *Miller's Tale*." *Neophil*, 44 (1960), 333-38.

Bloomfield, Morton W. "The Miller's Tale—An UnBoethian Interpretation." In *Medieval Literature and Folklore Studies: Essays in Honor of Francis Lee Utley*. Ed. J. Mandel and B.A. Rosenberg. New Brunswick, N.J.: Rutgers Univ. Press, 1971, pp. 205-11.

Bolton, W.F. "The *Miller's Tale*: An Interpretation." *MS*, 34 (1962), 83-94.

Bowker, Alvin W. "Comic Illusion and Dark Reality in *The Miller's Tale*." *MLS*, 4 (1974), 27-34.

Bratcher, James T., and Nicolai von Kreisler. "The Popularity of the *Miller's Tale*." *SFQ*, 35 (1971), 325-35.

Clark, Roy Peter. "Squeamishness and Exorcism in Chaucer's *Miller's Tale*." *Thoth*, 14 (1974), 37-43.

Donaldson, E. Talbot. "Idiom of Popular Poetry in the *Miller's Tale*." In *Speaking of Chaucer*. New York: Norton, 1970, pp. 13-29.

Gellrich, Jesse M. "The Parody of Medieval Music in the *Miller's Tale*." *JEGP*, 73 (1974), 176-88.

Hill, Betty. "Chaucer: *The Miller's* and *Reeve's Tales.*" *NM*, 74, (1973), 665-75.

Hirsch, John C. "Why does the *Miller's Tale* Take Place on Monday?" *ELN*, 13 (1975), 86-90.

Kaske, R.E. "The *Canticum Canticorum* in the *Miller's Tale.*" *SP*, 59 (1962), 479-500.

Kiernan, Kevin S. "The Art of the Descending Catalogue and a Fresh Look at Alysoun." *ChauR*, 10 (1975), 1-16.

Miller, Robert P. "The *Miller's Tale* as a Complaint." *ChauR*, 5 (1971), 147-60.

Mogan, J.J. "The Mutability Motif in the *Miller's Tale.*" *AN&Q*, 8 (1969), 19.

Neuss, Paula. "*Double entendre* in The *Miller's Tale.*" *EIC*, 24 (1974), 325-40.

Novelli, Cornelius. "Absolon's 'Freend So Deere': A Pivotal Point in the *Miller's Tale.*" *Neophil*, 52 (1968), 65-69.

Olson, Paul A. "Poetic Justice in the *Miller's Tale.*" *MLQ*, 24 (1963), 227-36.

Reiss, Edmund. "Daun Gervase in the *Miller's Tale.*" *PLL*, 6 (1970), 115-24.

Richards, Mary P. "The *Miller's Tale*: 'By seinte Note'." *ChauR*, 9 (1975), 212-15.

Rowland, Beryl. "The Play of the *Miller's Tale*: A Game within a Game." *ChauR*, 5 (1971), 140-46.

————. "Chaucer's Blasphemous Churl: A New Interpretation of the *Miller's Tale.*" In *Chaucer and Middle English Studies in Honour of Rossell Hope Robbins.* Ed. Beryl Rowland, pp. 43-55.

Stillwell, Gardiner. "The Language of Love in Chaucer's Miller's and Reeve's Tales and in the Old French Fabliaux." *JEGP*, 54 (1955), 693-99.

Thro, A. Booker. "Chaucer's Creative Comedy: A Study of the *Miller's Tale* and the *Shipman's Tale.*" *ChauR*, 5 (1971), 97-111.

IV. THE REEVE'S TALE

Brewer, D.S. "The Reeve's Tale and the King's Hall, Cambridge." *ChauR*, 5 (1971), 311-37.

Burbridge, R.T. "Chaucer's *Reeve's Tale* and the Fabliau 'Le Meunier et les .II. clers'." *AnM*, 12 (1971), 30-36.

Copland, Murray. "*The Reeve's Tale*: Harlotrie or Sermonyng?" *MÆ*, 31 (1962), 14-32.

Correale, Robert M. "Chaucer's Parody of Compline in the *Reeve's Tale*." *ChauR*, 1 (1967), 102-12.

Delany, Sheila. "Clerks and Quiting in the *Reeve's Tale*." *MS*, 29 (1967), 351-56.

Frank, R.W., Jr. "The *Reeve's Tale* and the Comedy of Limitation." In *Directions in Literary Criticism*. Ed. S. Weintraub and P. Young. Pennsylvania: Pennsylvania Univ. Press, 1973, pp. 53-69.

Friedman, John B. "A Reading of Chaucer's *Reeve's Tale*." *ChauR*, 2 (1967), 8-19.

Garbáty, Thomas J. "Satire and Regionalism: The Reeve and His Tale." *ChauR*, 8 (1973), 1-8.

Hart, Walter Morris. "The Reeve's Tale: A Comparative Study of Chaucer's Narrative Art." *PMLA*, 23 (1908), 1-44.

Kaske, R.E. "An Aube in the 'Reeve's Tale'." *ELH*, 26 (1959), 295-310.

Kirby, T.A. "An Analogue(?) to the *Reeve's Tale*." In *Chaucer and Middle English Studies in Honour of Rossell Hope Robbins*. Ed. Beryl Rowland, pp. 381-83.

O'Keefe, Timothy J. "Meanings of 'Malyne' in *The Reeve's Tale*." *AN&Q*, 12 (1973), 5-7.

Olson, Glending L. " 'The Reeve's Tale' and 'Gombert'." *MLR*, 64 (1969), 721-25.

————. "The *Reeve's Tale* as a Fabliau." *MLQ*, 35 (1974), 219-30.

Tolkien, J.R.R. "Chaucer as a Philologist: *The Reeve's Tale*." *TPS*, (1934), pp. 1-70.

V. THE COOK'S TALE

Stanley, E.G. "Of This Cokes Tale Maked Chaucer Na Moore." *Poetica*, 5 (1976), 36-59.

VI. THE FRIAR'S TALE

The Friar's, Summoner's and Pardoner's Tales. Ed. N.R. Havely. London: Univ. of London Press, 1974.

The Friar's Tale. Ed. A.C. and J.E. Spearing. In *Poetry of the Age of Chaucer.* London: Edward Arnold, 1974, pp. 169-93.

Beichner, Paul E. "Baiting the Summoner." *MLQ*, 22 (1961), 367-76.

Birney, Earle. " 'After his Ymage': The Central Ironies of the 'Friar's Tale'." *MS*, 21 (1959), 17-35.

Bonjour, Adrien. "Aspects of Chaucer's Irony in 'The Friar's Tale'." *EIC*, 11 (1961), 121-27.

Cawley, A.C. "Chaucer's Summoner, the Friar's Summoner, and the Friar's Tale." *Leeds*, 8 (1957), 173-80.

Haselmayer, Louis A. "The Apparitor and Chaucer's Summoner." *Speculum*, 12 (1937), 43-57.

Hennedy, Hugh L. "The Friar's Summoner's Dilemma." *ChauR*, 5 (1971), 213-17.

Lenaghan, R.T. "The Irony of the *Friar's Tale*." *ChauR*, 7 (1973), 281-94.

Mroczkowski, Przemyslaw. "*The Friar's Tale* and Its Pulpit Background." In *English Studies Today.* Ed. G.A. Bonnard, 2 (1961), 107-20.

Nathan, N. "Pronouns of Address in the *Friar's Tale*." *MLR*, 17 (1956), 39-42.

Passon, R.H. " 'Entente' in Chaucer's *Friar's Tale*." *ChauR*, 2 (1968), 166-71.

Richardson, Janette. "Friar and Summoner, the Art of Balance." *ChauR*, 9 (1975), 227-36.

Stroud, T.A. "Chaucer's Friar as Narrator." *ChauR*, 8 (1973), 65-69.

Szittya, Penn R. "The Green Yeoman as Loathly Lady: The Friar's Parody of the *Wife of Bath's Tale*." *PMLA*, 90 (1975), 386-94.

VII. THE SUMMONER'S TALE

Adams, John F. "The Structure of Irony in *The Summoner's Tale*." *EIC*, 12 (1962), 126-32.

Beichner, Paul E. "*Non Alleluia Ructare*." *MS*, 18 (1956), 134-44.

Birney, Earle. "Structural Irony Within the *Summoner's Tale*." *Anglia*, 78 (1960), 204-18.

Chapman, C.O. "Chaucer on Preachers and Preaching." *PMLA*, 44 (1929), 178-85.

Clark, Roy Peter. "Doubting Thomas in Chaucer's *Summoner's Tale*." *ChauR*, 11 (1976), 164-78.

Fleming, John V. "The Antifraternalism of the *Summoner's Tale*." *JEGP*, 45 (1966), 688-700.

———. "The Summoner's Prologue: An Iconographic Adjustment." *ChauR*, 2 (1967), 95-107.

Hartung, Albert E ."Two Notes on the *Summoner's Tale*: Hosts and Swans." *ELN*, 4 (1967), 175-80.

Kaske, R.E. "Horn and Ivory in the *Summoner's Tale*." *NM*, 73 (1972), 122-26.

Levitan, A. "The Parody of Pentecost in Chaucer's *Summoner's Tale*." *UTQ*, 40 (1971), 236-46.

Levy, Bernard S. "Biblical Parody in the *Summoner's Tale*." *TSL*, 11 (1966), 45-60.

Williams, Arnold. "Chaucer and the Friars." *Speculum*, 28 (1953), 499-513.

VIII. THE SHIPMAN'S TALE

The Shipman's Tale. In *English Verse 1300-1500*. Ed. John Burrow. London: Longmans, 1977, pp. 201-20.

Caldwell, Robert A. "Chaucer's *taillynge ynough, Canterbury Tales*, B² 1624." *MLN*, 55 (1940), 262-65.

Copland, Murray. "*The Shipman's Tale*: Chaucer and Boccaccio." *MÆ*, 35 (1966), 11-28.

Guerin, Richard S. "The *Shipman's Tale*: the Italian Analogues." *ES*, 52 (1971), 412-49.

Hogan, Moreland H., Jr. "A New Analogue of the *Shipman's Tale*." *ChauR*, 5 (1971), 245-46.

Jones, C. "Chaucer's *Taillynge Ynough*." *MLN*, 52 (1937), 570.

Lawrence, William Witherle. "Chaucer's *Shipman's Tale*." *Speculum*, 33 (1958), 56-58.

Levy, Bernard S. "The Quaint World of *The Shipman's Tale*." *SSF*, 4 (1967), 112-18.

McClintock, Michael W. "Games and the Players of Games: Old French Fabliaux and the *Shipman's Tale*." *ChauR*, 5 (1971), 112-36.

Silverman, Albert H. "Sex and Money in Chaucer's *Shipman's Tale*." *PQ*, 32 (1953), 329-36.

Stillwell, Gardiner. "Chaucer's 'Sad' Merchant." *RES*, 20 (1944), 1-18.

IX. THE MERCHANT'S TALE

The Merchant's Prologue and Tale. Ed. Maurice Hussey. Cambridge: Cambridge Univ. Press, 1966.

Beidler, Peter G. "January, Knight of Lombardy." *NM*, 72 (1971), 735-38.

————. "The Climax in the *Merchant's Tale*." *ChauR*, 6 (1972), 38-43.

————. "Chaucer's Merchant and the Tale of January." *Costerus*, 5 (1972), 1-25.

————. "Chaucer's *Merchant's Tale* and the *Decameron*." *Italica*, 50 (1973), 266-84.

Blanch, Robert J. "Irony in Chaucer's *Merchant's Tale*." *LHR*, 8 (1966), 8-15.

Bleeth, Kenneth A. "The Image of Paradise in the *Merchant's Tale*." In *The Learned and the Lewed*. Ed. Larry D. Benson. Cambridge, Mass.: Harvard Univ. Press, 1974, pp. 45-60.

Bronson, Bertrand H. "Afterthoughts on *The Merchant's Tale*." *SP*, 58 (1961), 583-96.

Brown, Emerson, Jr. "*The Merchant's Tale*: Why is May called 'Mayus'?" *ChauR*, 2 (1968), 273-77.

————. *Hortus Inconclusus*: The Significance of Priapus and Pyramus and Thisbe in the *Merchant's Tale*." *ChauR*, 4 (1970), 31-40.

————. "*The Merchant's Tale*: Why was Januarie Born 'of Pavye'?" *NM*, 71 (1970), 654-58.

————. "Biblical Women in the *Merchant's Tale*: Feminism, Antifeminism, and Beyond." *Viator*, 5 (1974), 387-412.

Bugge, John. "Damyan's Wanton *Clyket* and an Ironic New *Twiste* to the *Merchant's Tale*." *AnM*, 14 (1973), 53-62.

Burrow, J.A. "Irony in *The Merchant's Tale*." *Anglia*, 75 (1957), 199-208.

Dalbey, Marcia A. "The Devil in the Garden: Pluto and Proserpine in Chaucer's 'Merchant's Tale'." *NM*, 75 (1974), 408-15.

Donaldson, E. Talbot. "The Effect of the Merchant's Tale." In *Speaking of Chaucer*. New York: Norton, 1970, pp. 30-45. See also "The Masculine Narrator and Four Women of Style." pp. 46-64.

Donovan, M.J. "The Image of Pluto and Proserpine in the *Merchant's Tale*." *PQ*, 36 (1957), 49-60.

Garbáty, Thomas J. "The Monk and the *Merchant's Tale*. An Aspect of Chaucer's Building Process in the *Canterbury Tales*." *MP*, 67 (1969), 18-24.

Gates, Barbara T. " 'A Temple of False Goddis': Cupidity and Mercantile Values in Chaucer's Fruit-tree Episode." *NM*, 77 (1976), 369-75.

Grennen, Joseph E. "Another French Source for *The Merchant's Tale*." *RomN*, 8 (1966), 109-12.

Harrington, Norman T. "Chaucer's *Merchant's Tale*: Another Swing of the Pendulum." *PMLA*, 86 (1971), 25-31.

Hartung, Albert E. "The Non-Comic *Merchant's Tale*, Maximianus, and the Sources." *MS*, 29 (1967), 1-25.

Hoffman, Richard L. "Ovid's Priapus in the *Merchant's Tale*." *ELN*, 3 (1966), 169-72.

Holman, C. Hugh. "Courtly Love in the Merchant's and the Franklin's Tales." *ELH*, 18 (1951), 241-52.

Jordan, Robert M. "The Non-dramatic Disunity of the *Merchant's Tale*." *PMLA*, 78 (1963), 293-99.

von Kreisler, Nicolai. "An Aesopic Allusion in the *Merchant's Tale*." *ChauR*, 6 (1972), 30-37.

Olson, Paul A. "Chaucer's Merchant and January's 'Hevene in erthe heere'." *ELH*, 28 (1961), 203-14.

Otten, Charlotte F. "Proserpine: *Liberatrix suae Gentis*." *ChauR*, 5 (1971), 271-87.

Pittock, Malcolm. "The Merchant's Tale." *EIC*, 17 (1967), 26-40.

Robertson, D.W., Jr. "The Doctrine of Charity in Medieval Literary Gardens: A Topical Approach through Symbolism and Allegory." *Speculum*, 26 (1951), 24-49.

Rosenberg, Bruce A. "The 'Cherry-Tree Carol' and the *Merchant's Tale*." *ChauR*, 5 (1971), 264-76.

Schroeder, Mary C. "Fantasy in the 'Merchant's Tale'." *Criticism*, 12 (1970), 167-79.

Shores, David L. "*The Merchant's Tale*: Some Lay Observations." *NM*, 71 (1970), 119-33.

Stevens, Martin. "'And Venus laugheth': An Interpretation of the *Merchant's Tale*." *ChauR*, 7 (1972), 118-31.

Turner, W. Arthur. "Biblical Women in the *Merchant's Tale* and the *Tale of Melibee*." *ELN*, 3 (1965), 92-95.

Wentersdorf, Karl P. "Theme and Structure in the *Merchant's Tale*: The Function of the Pluto Episode." *PMLA*, 80 (1965), 522-27.

———. "Chaucer's Merchant's Tale and Its Irish Analogues." *SP*, 63 (1966), 604-29.

White, Gertrude M. "'Hoolynesse or Dotage'; The Merchant's January." *PQ*, 44 (1965), 397-404.

X. THE WIFE OF BATH'S PROLOGUE

Matthews, William. "The Wife of Bath and All her Sect." *Viator*, 5 (1974), 413-43.

Muscatine, Charles. "The Wife of Bath and Gautier's *La Veuve*." In *Romance Studies in Memory of Edward Billings Ham*. Ed. Urban

T. Holmes, Hayward. Calif.: California State College, 1967, pp. 109-14.

Reid, David S. "Crocodilian Humor: A Discussion of Chaucer's Wife of Bath." *ChauR*, 4 (1970), 73-89.

Rowland, Beryl. "On the Timely Death of the Wife of Bath's Fourth Husband." *Archiv*, 209 (1972), 273-82.

Sands, Donald B. "The Non-Comic, Non-Tragic Wife: Chaucer's Dame Alys as Sociopath." *ChauR*, 12 (1978), 171-82.

FIFTEEN

ROBERT P. MILLER

Allegory in the Canterbury Tales

The first session of the English Institute of 1958-9 was devoted to the question of the allegorical interpretation of medieval literature. In *Critical Approaches to Medieval Literature* Dorothy Bethurum prefaced the papers of the session by observing:

> The [critical] method that has aroused the most disputatious comment recently is ... the application of patristic exegesis to the study of medieval literature. It arose, doubtless, from an attempt to fill out the intellectual background of various authors by discovering and recalling to a secular age commonly accepted religious beliefs as defined by orthodox authority. Since the method of the Fathers in explicating scriptural texts is usually what we loosely call allegorical, ... those who apply this exegesis to literature have become known in current critical jargon as the "allegorists." (pp. v-vi)

Concerted interest in allegory as a critical tool which might be applied to the *Canterbury Tales* is thus a comparatively recent phenomenon. Though Morton W. Bloomfield (p. 74) traces this interest to the appearance in 1929 of Harry Caplan's "The Four Senses of Scriptural Interpretation," and H. Flanders Dunbar's *Symbolism in Medieval Thought*, effects in criticism of the *Canterbury Tales* are not felt until much later. In *The Allegory of*

Love (1936) C. S. Lewis found the *Canterbury Tales* irrelevant to his study of allegory (p. 161) and in fact concluded: "Nowhere in Chaucer do we find what can be called a radically allegorical poem" (p. 166)—that is, a poem presenting an action involving personified passions or "mental facts" which can be "translated" point for point into a "literal" statement of meaning. Lewis' rigid distinction between symbolism and allegory (pp. 45-6), brought under question in such articles as Bertrand Bronson's "Personification Reconsidered" and R. W. Frank's "The Art of Reading Medieval Personification-Allegory," has largely given way to the more inclusive sense of "allegory" assumed in the following discussion. The most influential presentation of this sense is to be found in *A Preface to Chaucer* (1962) by D. W. Robertson, Jr., although review articles of this book prove that the question remains disputatious.

As an approach to the *Canterbury Tales* "exegetical criticism" participates in a critical movement whose application to medieval studies has been rather late in occurring. A. O. Lovejoy's *The Great Chain of Being* (1936) and E. M. W. Tillyard's *The Elizabethan World Picture* (1943) directed attention to the critical value of the "intellectual background of various authors." For the medieval period the intellectual background is of necessity preserved in a clerical format; the examination of these sources has produced the recent interest in "patristic"—or more accurately, "clerical"—interpretation. It is true that as early as 1914 Frederick Tupper attempted to pattern the *Canterbury Tales* around the scheme of the Seven Deadly Sins, but the critical temper of the times is better exemplified in the genial literalism of such standard authorities as R. K. Root's *The Poetry of Chaucer* (1906, 1922) and G. L. Kittredge's *Chaucer and His Poetry* (1915). The conviction that Christian allusion and the concerns of the Church were organically relevant to Chaucer's art is really felt in the fifties. In 1953 Charles A. Owen, Jr. was willing to entertain ironies arising from an "Adam-and-Eve parallel" to the action of the *Nun's Priest's Tale* (p. 307). In the same year M. J. Donovan pushed the parallel into doctrinal allegory by observing that "the key to the *moralite* is hidden in the identification of Chauntecleer as any holy man and Daun Russell as heretic and devil"—and, in addition, the *povre wydwe* as the Church. In 1954 C. R. Dahlberg sought to restrict the allegory even further, again by recourse to clerical sources. He saw Chauntecleer as a priest (i.e., the secular clergy), Daun Russell as a Franciscan friar, and offered a point for point allegorical reading of the tale. More recently B. F. Huppé, in *A Reading of the Canterbury Tales*, has claimed that the tale shows "that marriage must be seen in the light of biblical revelation, specifically in the light of the first married pair, Adam and Eve, and of Adam's sin" (p. 177). (Huppé's book is by far the best extended expression of this critical approach.)

Other tales have been similarly vested with allegorical meaning. The technique, however, remains very much a matter for dispute. Thus Ralph Baldwin's view of the pilgrimage as figuring a popular Christian trope for the life of man, set in the symbolic context of the liturgical year, is politely but firmly declined by Muriel Bowden (p. 76). The following pages are not intended to contribute to the dispute, only to outline the assumptions of the "allegorist" and to provide some illustrations of an allegorical approach to the *Canterbury Tales*.

Medieval allegory is better regarded as a habit of mind than as any rigid system of artistic composition. Inherited from late classical antiquity, the allegorical habit, particularly as it contributed to methods employed for the interpretation of Scripture, was fostered in the medieval schools, where the development of a complex but highly coherent library of "authority" provided what became its characteristic "language." Allegorical imagery—that is, language carrying correspondences and associations codified or standardized within this tradition—may be managed in a variety of ways. Thus allegorical expression in the *Canterbury Tales* need not be exclusively dogmatic or doctrinal, as has sometimes been held.

When we speak of the literary allegory employed by Chaucer, we assume a habit of mind which attaches to ideas, events, qualities, and things, a series of standard "meanings," primarily those developed and conventionalized within the system of clerical authority. The classes of these extended meanings, insofar as they apply to the Church (society thought of as the communion of the faithful), to the moral life of the individual, or to the mysteries of Christian faith, can be roughly equated with the three "levels" of allegorical significance that had become standard in the exposition of Scripture by Chaucer's day. Although Dante in his *Convivio* and in his letter to Can Grande distinguished between the allegory of the theologian and that of the poet, his distinction rests, according to R. H. Green (p. 125), upon the fact that poetic meanings are generated by a fiction of the human imagination, whereas the subject of theological exegesis rests upon divinely ordained fact. The same habit of mind, however, controls both types of allegory. Divine utterance, whether in Nature or Scripture, is in itself true, although it may adumbrate further truths; a medieval poet sought to reaffirm such truths by composing an artificial *integumentum* ("covering") out of traditional materials. Thus, in the view of Isidore of Seville, "the function of the poet is in this, that by the aid of a figurative and indirect mode of speech he gracefully changes and transforms to a different aspect what has really taken place" (*Etym.* VIII, vii, 10). The Christian poet differed from the pagan poet in that he drew for his *alieniloquium* (the word Isidore used to translate *allegoria* : *Etym.* I, xxxvii, 22) upon figures which had been schematically related to the truth of Christian revelation, whereas the pagan could use only the flawed or false philosophies of the "heathens."

The systematization of what I have called the language of clerkly authority has recently been extensively discussed by Robertson (*Preface*, ch. iv), who also provides lists of medieval sources as helpful to the modern student as they no doubt were to the medieval preacher and poet. In what is necessarily a simplification, we can identify three interrelated activities which contribute to a unified "literary vocabulary." These are the analysis of what was called the Book of Nature, the exposition of the

Scriptures, and the allegorization of the pagan classics. Essentially the same habit of mind characterizes all three activities: each is in its own way an "allegorization" of its subject matter, as an educative endeavor to seek out a more perfect truth "to oure doctrine." That individual scholars such as Isidore of Seville, Rabanus Maurus, or Peter Berchorius could freely engage in all three suggests not only that these studies were not exclusive, but also that they could be harmonized with relative ease.

As an expression of the Will of God, Nature was regarded as a kind of artistic fact, a *pictura* by the divine Artist (Curtius, Excursus xxi). Our main consideration here is with the iconographical character ascribed to the created universe. The nature of things could be studied (where possible in connection with their appearance in Scriptural contexts) to elucidate the deeper intents of the Artist; properly understood, they were signs of moral principles useful to human life, or of divine mysteries. The catalogue of signs with their extended significances grew throughout the middle ages: Nature's iconography became exceedingly elaborate. The higher meanings for natural signs absent in Isidore's *Etymologiae*, which he considered incomplete, appear in his *De natura rerum*, are extended by his follower Rabanus Maurus in the *De universo*, and reach truly encyclopedic dimensions in the *Repertorium morale* of Peter Berchorius. The tradition is perhaps best known in the form of specialized popular handbooks, "chapters" in the Book of Nature: bestiaries, herbals, lapidaries, physiognomies, and such. The camel is a sign of humility; sunrise represents the enlightenment of reason after the darkness of ignorance or heresy; the fox signifies the hypocrite, to secular (as opposed to fraternal) writers a friar, and mystically the Devil. To the student of the Book of Nature the world about him must have appeared to be a tapestry of signs. Itself a kind of poetry, it could be assimilated into the vocabulary of Christian poets who sought to transform reality "to a different aspect."

The reading of Scripture was the end of a literate education, and a knowledge of natural signs was primarily useful as an aid in Scriptural exposition: for, as independent expressions of the unchanging divine Will, Creation and Scripture could not stand in contradiction. Smalley, Spicq, and de Lubac provide detailed summaries of the development of the traditions of Scriptural allegory, the main function of which was to seek the "spirit" beneath the veil of the "letter" (see 2 Cor. iii, 6; Gal. iv, 24). Powerful commentators such as Jerome and Augustine at an early date made possible such compilations as the *Allegoriae in sacram scripturam*; authoritative exegesis was collected in the *Glossa ordinaria*, which accompanied the Bible as a kind of critical *variorum*; the main lines of figuration were visually popularized in works like the *Biblia pauperum*, not to mention the great medieval cathedrals and monuments. The techniques of Scriptural allegory eventually crystallized about the "four-fold" method, which classified supra-literal meanings in terms of their field of reference: "allegorical" if the referent concerned the Church Militant; "tropological" if it had to do with moral principles; "anagogical" or mystical when mysteries of faith are the subject. The expositor might use a number of widely separated citations as an aid in the interpretation of a text, to elucidate the figurative meanings of "eunuchry," for instance (see Miller, "Chaucer's Pardoner"). In "The Doctrine of Charity in Mediaeval Literary Gardens" Robertson has explored the developed implications of the Scriptural image of the "garden." This image appears literally in Genesis (ii-iii), tropologically in the Song of Songs (as in iv, 12-16) where the Bride is described as a kind of "paradise," and by extension anagogically in the Apocalypse (xxi, 2) where the holy city appears mystically as a "bride adorned for her husband." Such expressions direct the allegorical reading of the "garden" in Genesis. A popular tropological understanding of the Fall, for example, appears in the *Parson's Tale* (330 ff.): Eve is identified as (not with) "flessh," Adam as "reson," and the event becomes a sign of the moral conflict described in Gal. v, 17 (*ParsT*, 341). In this case the garden is thought of as *anima humana*, the terrain of the conflict.

The effect of such commentary was to establish for the reading of the Bible a vast, interrelated figurative context whose associations seem to us now often arbitrary, as when the worm is seen as a sign of Christ (Psa. xxi, 7), or incoherent, as in the tropology of the Fall (since the garden as *anima humana* can itself be seen as a "bride"). Sometimes meanings seem to be multiplied beyond any possible literary use. For example, Rabanus Maurus gives six allegorical values for the figure of the "bed" in different Scriptural contexts: "According to the allegory a bed [*lectus*] signifies either repose in Christ, or the contemplative life, or fleshly infirmity, or a life of opulence, or deception of heretics, or tribulation of the life to come" (*De universo, PL*, CXI, 607). Berchorius warns us that the meaning is *multiplex*, and lists more than twenty distinctions (*Dictionarium*, III, 902-3). Some principles governing the erection of the allegorical system, however, can help us to appreciate its spirit.

1. It is customary to view any figure either *in bono* or *in malo*, depending on whether the meaning is considered in connection with an ideal existence governed by charity, or with an evil existence governed by the antithetical love, cupidity. "Generally speaking," says Berchorius, "there is a good bed and a bad bed." The principle of opposites, philosophically affiliated with the Boethian view of evil as a denial of good, powerfully affects the allegorical habit of mind. In effect, charity builds one world, while the denial of charity builds its antithesis. One consequence of the principle is the proliferation of antitypes within the figurative system—Adam seen in opposition to Christ, Eve to Mary, the Fall to the Passion, *Ecclesia* to the "Church of Satan," and so on.

2. The *levels* of allegory operate both *in bono* and *in malo*. Rabanus balances and inverts the order of these levels in the example above, proceeding from anagogy to tropology to allegory, and then back from allegory to anagogy. We have, then, a fundamental meaning seen in six aspects, according to the typical allegorical structure.

3. An allegorical reading possesses an inner coherence distinct from that of the letter. The worm can be a sign of something to do with Christ, but Christ does not help to explain the worm's

nature. The tropological account of the Fall is meaningful in itself; however, it cannot be expected to correspond to all the human implications of the historical event. For this reason personified abstractions like Prudence and Griselda do not make good "characters."

For literature the tradition of Scriptural allegory like the allied study of Nature is of semantic significance in that it codified meanings and associations within the language of literate men. The principle of contraries, furthermore, provided a language ready-made for ironies based on ambiguity and wit arising from paradox. Thus the figure of "woman" involves us in the ambiguities resting on the prototypes of Eve and Mary and their conventional allegorical extensions. In a literary context the figure can reflect her prototype obviously in a character like Prudence, or less obviously in someone like May, who after all provides a "revelation" for her husband. And what of the "wise wife" who quotes Scripture to preach her "doctrine"? The comedy here is fully available only in the extended context of the allegorical system. When, in addition, we find a "wise wife" placed "in bed" (as in the conclusion to the *Wife of Bath's Tale*), we have a *conjunctura* of significant figures which makes for a situation of complex allegorical potential.

While the study of Nature and Scripture involved the "allegory of the theologian," early allegorization of the pagan classics made use, at least in principle, of the "allegory of the poet." The classical predecessors of the medieval literary tradition were regarded as historically deprived of the benefits of Revelation, though possessing a kind of natural wisdom "transformed to a different aspect" in their poetry. Pseudo-Fulgentius prefaced his commentary on Statius' *Thebaid* by commending the "prudence of poets" who have usefully implanted a variety (*seriem*) of moral principles "beneath the seductive covering [*tegumento*] of poetic fiction." Consequently, "not only do entertaining and pleasing things lie in the easiness of their literal and historical sense, but in the mystical exposition of figures lie things useful for the improvement of the *mores* of human life" (ed. Helm, p.

180). To this exposition of figures the commentator brought tools similar to those familiar in theological expositions: etymology, typology, and preconceived allegorical possibilities where the Christian vocabulary coincided with that of the pagan author. Commentaries such as those of Fulgentius and Bernard Silvestris on the *Aeneid*, or those of Arnulf of Orléans and Berchorius on Ovid's *Metamorphoses*, undoubtedly reflect the kind of critical apparatus that accompanied these works in the schools. The *Ovide moralisé*, a truly monumental compilation of allegorical interpretations, reflects as well the fact that the expositor soon abandoned any restriction to natural (as opposed to revealed) wisdom among the ancients, but could gloss Orpheus, for example, as a type of Christ. It was inevitable that standard interpretations should be compiled in mythographic manuals like Boccaccio's *De genealogia deorum gentilium*, of which Books xiv and xv present an eloquent justification of the interpretive method. Natalis Comes and Vincenzo Cartari testify in the sixteenth century to the continuing power of what amounts to the "conversion" of the pagan classics.

Mythographic exegesis thus served to adapt the pantheon of pagan gods and fables of the ancients so that they could operate consistently as figures in connection with the Christian language drawn from Nature and Scripture. Isidore (*Etym.* viii, xi, 80) defined Cupid as the *daemon fornicationis* and explained his traditional attributes in this connection. Pseudo-Fulgentius linked Theseus etymologically with *theos* ("God"), and saw his combat with Creon as a figure for the victory of humility over pride, by which Thebes (*anima humana*) is "freed" (ed. Helm, p. 186). Bernard Silvestris' twofold interpretation of Venus accords with the principle of opposites: "We read that there are two Venuses, a legitimate goddess and a goddess of lechery. We say that the legitimate Venus is *mundana musica*, that is, the equal proportion of worldly things, which some call Astrea and others 'natural justice.' For she is in the elements, in the stars, in times, in animate things [for whom cf. *Cons. Phil.* ii, m. 8]. But the shameful Venus, the goddess of sensuality, we call concupiscence of the flesh, which is the mother of all fornication" (ed. Riedel, p. 9).

Such terms as *mater fornicationis* relate the figure firmly to the system of clerical authority. Venus' passport into the "language" of Christendom is thus allegory. As a result, Theseus and Venus could operate significantly as figures in a literary context expressing the concerns of a model Christian Knight.

The allegorical mode within which Chaucer worked naturally depended upon a reservoir of established meanings shared by the poet and his audience. In *Literature and Pulpit in Medieval England* (see especially ch. ii) Owst has shown how the pulpit popularized some standard allegorical figures, but competence in Christian allusion and symbolism—even in doctrine—was, it is clear, far from universal. Chaucer's pilgrims themselves exhibit a wide range of literacy which probably reflects that of his own audience, capable of misapplying or of being ignorant of conventional doctrinal and allegorical materials. Chaucer's response to this situation was to make a virtue of necessity by turning a seeming liability to artistic advantage. Each pilgrim tells his tale from his own point of view, but this point of view is finally to be measured in the perspective afforded by the allegorical system. Thus the very basis of Chaucer's dramatic technique is that reservoir of established meanings which permits us to evaluate the special deviations of different pilgrims. Their success or failure in exploiting the language at their disposal is an important measure of their identities. The technique in a simplified form can be seen in the *Melibeus*, where Melibeus' view of the *sentence* of several matters is shown to be wrong by Prudence, who explains the true *sentence*, drawing upon authority. More subtly, but nonetheless obviously, the Miller's ignorance is perfectly captured in Nicholas' climactic call for "water" (3815). Especially in the narrative context, the extended meanings of "water" are obvious, the Flood being a familiar prefiguration of baptism (1 Pet. iii, 20-1) and consequently of purification in many senses. In any sense this is precisely what is lacking in the Miller's world; the extended meanings of Nicholas' call constitute a reflexive comment on the teller, particularly because he is personally blind to them. We understand the Prioress better because of her limited sense of *gentillesse*. Here the expected sense of spiritual *gentillesse* (as in *Bo.* III, pr. and m. 3; and *ParsT*, 460-73), properly due to the nun as a "bride of Christ," is played against her worldly concern "to countrefete cheere / Of court" (*Gen Prol*, 139-40)— a limited notion which corresponds to the treatment of the idea of "mercy" in her tale. Characters such as the Wife of Bath are made to invert clerical standards to state their views, as in her *Prologue*, 93-4 (for which cf. *PhysT*, 77-82):

> Freletee clepe I, but if that he and she
> Wolde leden al hir lyf in chastitee.

In her lexicon moral strength (*virtus*) has simply been replaced by sexual prowess, a contrary, with comic effect, as one demonstration of her consistent antipathy to apostolic values.

Chaucer undoubtedly recognized ignorance, vanity, and "experiential wisdom" in his audience. To them the truths of life's "pilgrimage" were necessarily distorted or obscure. His literate pilgrims, on the other hand, employ a language consistent with the system of clerical authority, whether they be clerics—as the Parson, Clerk, Nun's Priest, Second Nun—or not. The Knight draws his language appropriately from the tradition of historical romance, a fashionable genre, modulated to his own perspective and heightened by a thorough (and correct) assimilation of Boethius; but where his figures or actions permit allegorical extension we can count on established values for help. Where the Parson, who is immediately concerned with doctrinal principles, illustrates these with conventional figures (as in his discussion of marriage —325 ff.), he is generating allegorical imagery which we find used —and often misused—in other tales. For their fictions the Nun's Priest and the Clerk explicitly require allegorical explication:

> But ye that holden this tale a folye,
> As of a fox, or of a cok and hen,
> Taketh the moralite, goode men.
> For seint Paul seith that al that writen is,
> To oure doctrine it is ywrite, ywis;
> Taketh the fruyt, and lat the chaf be stille.
>
> (*NPT*, 3438-43; cf. *CIT*, 1142-8)

The language in which the *moralite* is couched is undoubtedly that standardized by clerical authority.

In the tales themselves Chaucer used allegorical language and forms as literary tools which could operate in a great variety of ways, not necessarily doctrinal in their immediate intent. His Merchant suggests for us a secular and middle-class respectability for allegorical expression, by presenting (along with an abundance of conventional images) the figures of Justinus and Placebo, hardly more than personified abstractions. Any *equation* of allegory with the expression of Christian doctrine can only obscure the wit with which Chaucer employs the system. We can observe something of the range of this wit by thinking of the tales as either "formally" or "informally" allegorical. I do not suggest this as an official distinction, only that some of the *Canterbury Tales* make deliberate, traditional use of the conventions, and that others use allegorical materials in less formal ways.

Formal allegory is illustrated most obviously in the *Melibeus*; less obviously, though certainly intended, in romantic narratives such as the *Clerk's Tale* and the *Man of Law's Tale*. The allegorical framework of the *Melibeus* is rigid and traditional: its elements, though utterly commonplace, are yet relentlessly explicated on a tropological level:

> Thy name is Melibee, this is to seyn, "a man that drynketh hony."/ Thou hast ydronke so muchel hony of sweete temporeel richesses, and delices and honours of this world, / that thou art dronken, and hast forgeten Jhesu Crist thy creatour. / . . . for certes, the three enemys of mankynde, that is to seyn, the flessh, the feend, and the world, / thou hast suffred hem entre in to thyn herte wilfully by the wyndowes of thy body, / and hast nat defended thyself suffisantly agayns hire assautes and hire temptaciouns, so that they han wounded thy soule in fyve places; / this is to seyn, the deedly synnes that been entred into thyn herte by thy fyve wittes.
>
> (*Mel*, 1409-24)

Such as it is, narrative here exists solely for the sake of these standard, virtually literalistic correspondences. However ennobling its doctrinal content, we may suspect that the pedestrian technique of the *Melibeus* ran counter to Chaucer's artistic tastes, especially if we feel that this allegory is a joke on himself, like the *Thopas*. If so, however, it is merely the extreme rigidity of formal didactic allegory which he found unsuitable.

A more poetically suitable formal allegory can be traced in the *Clerk's Tale*. A higher version of allegorical art, its correspondences challenge the reader's ability to distinguish between objective principle and subjective experience—a fact which poses problems for the literal-minded reader, and pleasure for the reader who can see the spirit beneath the letter. This is a principle of allegorical expression not performed by the *Melibeus*. Griselda does not betray her true nature by etymology; Walter's inexplicable determination to try his wife is, literally speaking, an awful abuse of marital *maistrie*. But the Clerk explicitly denies an application at this level of response (1142-7):

> This storie is seyd, nat for that wyves sholde
> Folwen Grisilde as in humylitee,
> For it were inportable, though they wolde;
> But for that every wight, in his degree,
> Sholde be constant in adversitee
> As was Grisilde ....

On this basis we can develop an "allegorical" significance for the surface details of the narrative. Griselda now represents the individual soul ("every wight"), and her experience is meaningful only in this light. As an allegorical figure for God, the controller of *adversitee*, Walter deprives her of the life of her two children (Death as God's "sergeant" being an allegorical commonplace, as we can judge from its perpetuation in Hamlet's reference to "this fell sergeant, Death" [v, ii, 347]), and subjects her to the trial of separation from him. Her performance is emblematic of the truly faithful soul's devotion to its "heavenly bridegroom," in fulfillment of her initial identification. Like Rebecca (Gen. xxiv, 15 ff.),

> ... she set doun hir water pot anon,
> Biside the thresshfold, in an oxes stalle,
> And doun upon hir knes she gan to falle,

> And with sad continance kneleth stille,
> Til she had herd what was the lordes wille.
>
> (*ClT*, 290-4)

It is a composite portrait, for the *oxes stalle* of course involves us in associations with the Nativity, reinforced by analogies with the Annunciation (as also in lines 319-20: cf. Luke i, 38). Such allusions identify her not with Rebecca and Mary (both exemplars of the "good woman"), but with the standard exegetical values of these historical ladies. Chief among these is *anima pura*, the holy soul, submissive to God's will. Griselda's nature and her devotion to her lord and master are meaningful *only* in these terms; thus she goes through her trial unscathed, and is rewarded with reclamation and reunion in what is, on the level of the Merchant's literalistic understanding, undoubtedly an improbably romanticized conclusion.

There can be no real correlation between such spiritual truth and the human terms employed by the Clerk to represent it. Consequently, if we regard Griselda as a person we may find her repellent as both a wife and a mother, since what is appropriate to the relationship between the soul and its God is not appropriate to a human marriage. As for Walter, his tyranny is a model of unhusbandly behavior, artistically calculated to frustrate the literal mind of the Wife of Bath, whose last clerkly husband exhibited similar intemperance. Walter can illustrate God's powers, but he cannot appropriate God's powers as a human being; though the husband is supposed to love his wife "as Christ also loved the church" (Eph. v, 25), the injunction does not grant him the absolute authority of Godhead. This discrepancy between the human and divine permits the *Clerk's Tale* to fulfill the traditional ends of allegory, that is, to reveal to the worthy, and to conceal from the unworthy.

Chaucer's informal allegories do not represent a rejection of the allegorical system. In them, rather, he has found ways of adapting the principles and potentials of his literary tradition to qualify seemingly coherent surface meanings or, as in the *Knight's Tale*, to strengthen and enrich a theme implied by the action.

Although the *Knight's Tale* has a *sentence,* or "inner meaning," it does not present an explicit or continuous allegorical structure. The *sentence* is the advice "to maken vertu of necessitee" (3042), an appropriately secular principle exemplified positively in the person of Theseus and negatively in the frivolous exploits of Palamon and Arcite. But numerous allegorical elements support and elaborate this central concern. Theseus, Athens, the pantheon of gods and goddesses along with their respective temples, are all the subject of traditional mythographic interpretation. Theseus' conquest of *Femenye* and the terms of his marriage to Hippolyta are, as Robertson says (*Preface,* pp. 264-5), emblematic of the proper order between "man" and "woman" in their extended meanings; as such they form an idealized backdrop against which to measure the aberrant antics of Palamon and Arcite. The young lovers themselves suggest in their dedication to Venus and Mars (or to their versions of these "deities") the concupiscible and irascible passions with which Boccaccio himself associated them—though it must be stressed that arbitrary distinctions between the two are not rigidly maintained. That these passions are imperfectly realized versions of the chivalric ideals of justice and mercy, however, suggests that Chaucer thought of his Knight as using his Boccaccian materials in an exemplary fashion for the benefit of young Squires aspiring to knighthood. Palamon's victory, insofar as he illustrates a love tempered in time, may involve a generalized allegorical significance.

We can read the Knight "straight," because we assume him to be dedicated to the highest chivalric ideals. As a secular man he carefully avoids theological argumentation, but where his figures permit theological extension they do so appropriately. The Merchant, on the other hand, is an embittered husband ironically pinched by his "marriage debt," who is made to employ standard figures for perverse ends. The allegorical "content" of his tale comically clashes with the traditional implications of his materials. We are presented with allegorical characters, Placebo and Justinus, and are to imagine Januarie allegorically tossed between the counsel of flattery (see *ParsT*, 616) and justice. Yet the speeches of Justinus do not offer a legitimate alternative; rather they express a stereotyped antifeminism which permits no marriage at all—"justice" only insofar as it duplicates the sour prejudices of the teller. The Merchant betrays similar "blindness" to the symbolic potential of such standard figures as that of the paradisaic garden. Because he is personally unable to understand the ideal by which "paradis" may be an image for the good wife or the state of marriage, his Januarie is cheated in his "garden of delights" only in the sense that it represents a condition of sensual indulgence. No awareness of the clerically defined "model" of marriage enters into his personal attack on the state of matrimony. Yet this failure on the part of the teller does not prevent the reader from entertaining standard clerical associations. This is especially true of the climactic action. Here we recognize elements which compose an allegorical pattern central to Christian awareness: the lord and lady in a paradisaic garden, the traitor in the fruit-tree, and an action which states that by the "plucking of the fruit" the eyes of the husband were opened. It is a revelation episode, to which the Merchant intends us to understand that Januarie foolishly committed himself by marrying, and in which he learns a truth which might have saved him. What is ironic is that he arrives at this "wisdom" by a kind of reenactment of Adam's fall which defines it in a way not intended by the Merchant. Since this moment of revelation duplicates his own experience (as well as that of his surrogate Justinus), it becomes clear, on an allegorical basis, that the Merchant is offering a corrupt "knowledge of good and evil" to the Canterbury company.

The cast of characters in the *Franklin's Tale* do not have allegorical names but are nonetheless patterned in such a way as to reflect a principle infinitely more significant than the simply social principle (i.e., the classes of Knight, Squire, and Clerk) to which the speaker apparently refers. Like the Knight, whom he emulates, the Franklin turns to Boccaccio for his materials, but without the Knight's sense of understanding. Fortunately for today's critics Boccaccio appended a critical analysis of the "Tale of Menedon" in his *Filocolo,* so that we have an insight into the medieval perspective on the action—an allegorist's view of his own work, —and even an authorized solution to the *questione d'amore* in the conclusion. It becomes apparent immediately that Boccaccio constructed his characters to represent the three motives of "the World" described in 1 John ii, 16 as "concupiscence of the flesh, and the concupiscence of the eyes, and the pride of life, which is not of the Father, but is of the world." In medieval theory these motives are elaborately equated with sensuality, avarice, and pride, as well as with "the flessh, the feend, and the world." In his *Confessions* (x, xxxv, 55) and elsewhere St. Augustine further described the concupiscence of the eyes as "unlawful curiosity" and cited the practice of magic as an example. (Hence the Franklin can describe magic in line 1120 as "artes that been curious.") Pride is typified by the man who exalts himself in empty honors. Boccaccio's solution to the *questione* ingeniously underlines the correspondence between his characters and this pattern of worldly motives. To decide who was the most generous, we are asked to consider what each gave up. The lover gave up his "libidinous will," the magician gave up the wealth he had gained, and the husband gave up his honor. Of all these surely the most precious is honor (especially when one's very salvation depends upon preserving it, as Boccaccio indicates). The conclusion is a medieval clerical joke which can hardly have failed to appeal to Chaucer. The husband wins the generosity-contest, but only because he has sinned most gravely.

In adapting this tale for his Franklin, Chaucer reinforces, specifies, and enriches the allegorical framework he found in Boccaccio, so that the three main characters, taken together, comprise the "worldliness" appropriate to "Epicurus owene sone." Arveragus is shown in innumerable ways to be the man who exalts himself in empty honors, concerned only with the "name of soveraynetee" (751). As a "courtly lover" Aurelius pursues sensual gratification much as a Christian soul might seek Grace. The curious arts of the businesslike Clerk reflect at every turn their perversions of the ideals of clerical behavior. Allegorical imagery and allusions richly reinforce the theme of deception, an "Epicurean" rationalizing of unpleasant truths in the interests of temporal "ese." Thus the artificial improvements upon nature in the garden, while certainly to the Franklin's tastes, symbolize the efforts of Dorigen's "frendes" to substitute human pleasures for the dark reality symbolized by the black rocks. But here, where

> . . . craft of mannes hand so curiously
> Arrayed hadde this gardyn, trewely,
> That nevere was ther gardyn of swich prys,
> But if it were the verray paradys,
>
> (*FranklT*, 909-12)

Dorigen becomes involved with Aurelius. A Boethian context (865 ff.) provides the philosophical "model" which establishes the allegorical function of the rocks; they represent adversity within the providential scheme, so that the desire to remove them, as well as their "magical" disappearance, are both emblematic of the Epicurean imagination. Their disappearance is, in fact, only an "apparence," like Arveragus' dilemma itself, but it creates troublesome consequences for those who live according to worldly illusions. We are probably to date this magical "apparence," ironically, on Epiphany.

Unlike the Merchant, the Franklin does not conspicuously employ the methods of allegory. The allegorical pattern and imagery are Chaucer's means of commenting delightfully on the Epicurean values of this "man of the world." In his approval of such a Knight, Squire, and Clerk, he expresses his own illusory values. When we see this, we see that the fictional world of his tale is an apt allegorical extension of the mind of one who, by loving "all that is in this world," inverts the injunction of John.

In such tales the allegorical dimension deepens the dramatic relationship between teller and tale. As the different pilgrims use or misuse the language of clerkly authority they tend to establish themselves personally within the scheme of that authority, and we begin to see them as spokesmen for recognizable viewpoints. One might propose that the controlling theme of the *Canterbury Tales* is the pursuit of wisdom—the "pilgrimage" itself being an allegorical image of it—and that Chaucer gives each pilgrim the opportunity to prove a point, using his tale in an exemplary fashion to illustrate something which he considers a mark of wisdom. In the tales mentioned here, the particular visions represented are controlled by medieval stereotypes— the secular *sapientia et fortitudo* of the chivalric man, the fallen vision of the betrayed husband, the pleasant Epicureanism of the "worldly wiseman," and we may add the Wife of Bath's "doctrine" of *sovereynetee*.

These attitudes can be duplicated in medieval discussions of chivalry, the Fall of Adam, Epicureanism, and antifeminism. Such standard interests in the different tales are a reflection of standard elements in the characters themselves, and to the degree that these attitudes correlate with one of the categorical systems of medieval authority, the pilgrims are also allegorically conceived abstracts of their time. To this degree as well, Chaucer's conception of his characters is built upon allegorical—or allegorized— models. Thus the description of the Knight is based on fortitude and sapience ("thogh that he were *worthy*, he was *wys*"—*Gen Prol*, 68) which are the established ideals of his Estate, and which also make him an inheritor of literary traditions of chivalric or "heroic virtue" reaching back to the mythological Aeneas, "quo *iustior* alter / Nec *pietate* fuit . . . maior" (*Aen*. 1, 544-5; see Curtius, p. 173). The lineage of the Merchant can be traced to le Jaloux in the *Roman de la rose*, modified by Scripturally sanctioned meanings attached to "merchantry." A composite of mutually correspondent prototypes, the Franklin contains recognizable elements of "the Epicure," of Ami—the "false friend" in the *Roman de la rose*—and of clerical platitudes concerning "worldly wisdom." Perhaps the consummate composite is the Wife of Bath, in whom we can detect the stereotyped *mulier* of antifeminist literature, particularly that crystallized, according to Jerome ("Against Jovinian"), by Theophrastus. From classical precedent she inherits characteristics of a standard figure, the *vetula* ("old woman," wise in years) exemplified by Ovid's Dipsas (*Amores* 1, viii) whose medieval literary descendents culminate in Jean de

Meun's la Vieille. Some details of the composite can be traced back to the *mulier fortis* of the Bible (Prov. xxxi, 10 ff.), as well as to the Samaritan woman (John iv, 7 ff.). In this case, as in the others to be mentioned, the models point up the Wife's failure to fulfill the ideals of Christian "wifehood." The clerical commonplace that in marriage the good wife will exert a beneficial moral influence upon her husband (a trope reflected in Constance, Prudence, Cecilia—cf. *Mel*, 1093 ff. and such inversions as *MerchT*, 1356-74), provides the aspect by which the Wife appears as a "schoolmistress" (an aspect shared with her French predecessors), and as a "cleric" promulgating doctrine. In her determination to offer armor against adversity ("wo in mariage") she often resembles another "cloth-weaver" (*Bo.* I, pr. 1, 20 ff.) of great repute, Dame Philosophy.

As a final example of informal allegory, the *Wife of Bath's Tale* may be read as an extension of her allegorical character. I have elsewhere suggested that the materials of this tale may be thought of as a reworking of some convential motifs in medieval *exempla*, as an apt reflection of her "clerical" pose. According to this view the tale employs figures conventional to *exempla* of conversion, particularly that of a miraculously transformed Loathly Hag. In the idiom of clerical authority a visionary lady (or *succuba*), who occupies the minds of men tempted by sensual indulgence, is "revealed" to be truly "foul" to a will purified by Obedience. In *exempla* she is glossed as the "spirit of fornication," fair to the sensual will, but truly repugnant when revealed to the reason. This allegorical pattern is employed by the Wife to exemplify her own, antithetical "doctrine." When the reason submits in Obedience to the sensual will the Foul Lady is revealed to be "as fair as any lady, emperice, or queene" (1246). The Wife's "sermon" in favor of sensual indulgence is thus attractively illustrated by an allegorical *exemplum* which inverts conventional clerical meanings. In other words, we can imagine a clerkly original, perhaps something related by one of her clerk-husbands, which she reworks by substituting the values of experience for those of *auctoritee*.

To see this is not to deny the immediate appeals of the *Wife of Bath's Tale*. In the *Canterbury Tales* allegory never *replaces* the human, surface meaning; Chaucer delighted in his "chaf" as well as in his "fruyt." Even though the formal allegories are to be read according to the "language" of clerkly authority, a literal reading of them raises dramatically relevant questions. In such informal allegories as the *Wife of Bath's Tale* we are simply asked to remember the perspectives afforded by the system of medieval authority. To the extent that we are able to do so are we rewarded by the deeper reaches of Chaucer's comic spirit.

* * * * *

Applications of clerical authorities to an interpretation of the *Canterbury Tales* in the last ten years have proliferated almost beyond count. The Fourth Alabama Symposium on English and American Literature, held at the University of Alabama in October, 1977, was dedicated to "Signs and Symbols in Chaucer's Poetry." Selected papers from this symposium, to be published in 1978, will illustrate the vital ways in which historical scholarship continues to compete with criticism which seeks to promote modern predispositions at the expense of medieval meanings as a means of understanding Chaucer's art.

Yet serious use of medieval clerical authority as a critical criterion has been disparaged in some recent major books on Chaucer's art, when they deal with "allegory." Robert M. Jordan rejects "sophisticated efforts to read Chaucer as though he were practicing allegorical expression" (p. 33), emphasizes rhetorical structure at the expense of the elements "structured," and arrives at a new kind of literalism. Donald R. Howard's oversimplified view of historical criticism is almost emotional: "Those critics who see in Chaucer only the doctrine of *caritas* preached over and over again in a hundred allegories...have to resort to nonsense" (p. 50); their attempt to reclaim medieval assumptions which differ from contemporary interests "is all very dreary" (p. 51). Such attitudes simply distort the contributions of "allegorical" critics to an honest understanding of Chaucer's work. For response to individual *Canterbury Tales* Howard falls back on a presumptive medieval audience interested in tidings rather than truth, for which, however, he is himself a norm. The same readership can be seen as an implicit critical and aesthetic standard in Alfred David's analyses, especially of those tales in which, he claims, Chaucer worked from "experience" rather than from "authority." Chaucer's experience remarkably resembles the critic's. Thus "The Wife of Bath is in a profound sense a persona of Chaucer the artist" (p.135; cp. Jordan, p. 214); Chaucer "identifies with the Wife" (p. 157). This begins to sound like a fifth level of allegory. A sad victim of neglecting clerical authorities has been Chaucer's use of irony. Happily, the wit with which Chaucer treats these materials has a place in John Gardner's account of his poetry, which often sees Chaucer as funny.

A clear exposition of the tradition which makes "allegory" in the *Canterbury Tales* possible is provided by James I. Wimsatt, with bibliography, in his *Allegory and Mirror*. Judson Boyce Allen's *The Friar as Critic* organizes more technical materials in exemplary fashion. Actual major texts of the tradition, in translation, are anthologized with annotations to the tradition and Chaucer's text, in R. P. Miller's *Chaucer: Sources and Backgrounds*. Chaucer's ironic use of such texts has been well illustrated in the studies of scholars like Hoffman, Peterson, Delasanta, Levy, and many others. John V. Fleming's study of the *Roman de la rose* provides a most valuable context for Chaucer's understanding and use of this central work.

A special application of authority, stemming perhaps from Harder's 1956 essay, has led to a number of studies exploring patterns of Scriptural story in Chaucer's tales. For example, Bruce A. Rosenberg hears "parodic" echoes of Joseph and Mary in the Merchant's Januarie and May. Roy Peter Clark sees Doubting Thomas' probing the wounds of Christ comically distorted in the *Summoner's Tale*. The Annunciation is shown by Beryl Rowland to account for much of the situation, action, and imagery in the *Miller's Tale*. At the Alabama Symposium Gail Gibson brilliantly argued that the *Shipman's Tale* involves a parody of the risen Christ's appearance to Mary Magdalene. The accumulation of such studies seems to reveal a fundamental moral aspect of Chaucer's fabliaux: men's lives are seen as burlesque reenactments of sacred prototypes in which "the ephemeral world of trivial lust and vulgar jest is set against the cosmic and timeless background of divine ordinance" (Rowland, "Chaucer's Blasphemous Churl...," p. 51).

This is what Chaucer would have regarded a primary value of "allegory" to a significant art.

BIBLIOGRAPHY

Allen, Judson B. *The Friar as Critic: Literary Attitudes in the Later Middle Ages*. Nashville: Vanderbilt Univ. Press, 1971.

Baldwin, Ralph. *The Unity of the 'Canterbury Tales'*. Anglistica, 5. Copenhagen: Rosenkilde og Bagger, 1955.

Berchorius, Petrus. *Opera Omnia*. 3 vols. Mainz, 1609.

Bethurum, Dorothy, ed. *Critical Approaches to Medieval Literature: Selected Papers from the English Institute, 1958-1959*. New York: Columbia Univ. Press, 1960.

Bloomfield, Morton W. "Symbolism in Medieval Literature." *MP*, 56 (1958), 73-81.

Bowden, Muriel. *A Reader's Guide to Geoffrey Chaucer*. New York: Farrar, 1964.

Bronson, Bertrand H. "Personification Reconsidered." *ELH*, 14 (1947), 163-77.

Caplan, Harry. "The Four Senses of Scriptural Interpretation and the Mediaeval Theory of Preaching." *Speculum*, 4 (1929), 282-90.

Clark, Roy Peter. "Doubting Thomas in Chaucer's *Summoner's Tale*." *ChauR*, 11 (1976), 164-78.

Curtius, E.R. *European Literature and the Latin Middle Ages*. Trans. W.R. Trask. New York: Pantheon, 1953.

Dahlberg, Charles R. "Chaucer's Cock and Fox." *JEGP*, 53 (1954), 277-90.

David, Alfred. *The Strumpet Muse: Art and Morals in Chaucer's Poetry*. Bloomington: Indiana Univ. Press, 1976.

Delasanta, Rodney. "And of Great Reverence: Chaucer's Man of Law." *ChauR*, 5 (1971), 288-310.

———. "Chaucer and the Exegetes." *SLitI*, 4 (1971), 1-10.

———. "Penance and Poetry in the *Canterbury Tales*." *PMLA*, 93 (1978), 240-47.

Donovan, M.J. "The *Moralite* of the Nun's Priest's Sermon." *JEGP*, 52 (1953), 498-508.

Dunbar, H. Flanders. *Symbolism in Medieval Thought*. 1929. Rpt. New York: Russell & Russell, 1961.

Fleming, John V. *The Roman de la Rose: A Study in Allegory and Iconography*. Princeton: Princeton Univ. Press, 1969.

Frank, R.W., Jr. "The Art of Reading Medieval Personification-Allegory." *ELH*, 20 (1953), 237-50.

Fulgentius, Fabius Planciades. *Opera*. Ed. R. Helm. Leipzig: Teubner, 1898.

Gardner, John. *The Poetry of Chaucer*. Carbondale: Southern Illinois Univ. Press, 1977.

Gibson, Gail McMurray. "Resurrection as Dramatic Icon in Chaucer's *Shipman's Tale*." (forthcoming).

Green, R.H. "Dante's 'Allegory of Poets' and the Mediaeval Theory of Poetic Fiction." *CL*, 9 (1957), 118-28.

Harder, Kelsie B. "Chaucer's Use of the Mystery Plays in the *Miller's Tale*." *MLQ*, 17 (1956), 193-98.

Hoffman, Richard L. *Ovid and the Canterbury Tales*. Philadelphia: Univ. of Pennsylvania Press, 1967.

Howard, Donald R. *The Idea of the Canterbury Tales*. Berkeley: Univ. of California Press, 1976.

Huppé, Bernard F. *A Reading of the Canterbury Tales*. Albany, N.Y.: State Univ. of New York, 1964.

Isidore of Seville. *Etymologiarum sive originum, libri XX*. Ed. W.M. Lindsay. 2 vols. 1911. Rpt. Oxford: Clarendon, 1962.

Jordan, Robert M. *Chaucer and the Shape of Creation*. Cambridge, Mass.: Harvard Univ. Press, 1967.

Kittredge, G.L. *Chaucer and His Poetry*. Cambridge, Mass.: Harvard Univ. Press, 1915.

Levy, Bernard S. "The Wife of Bath's *Queynte Fantasye*." *ChauR*, 4 (1969), 106-22.

————. "*Gentilesse* in Chaucer's *Clerk's* and *Merchant's Tales*." *ChauR*, 11 (1977), 306-18.

Lewis, C.S. *The Allegory of Love: A Study in Medieval Tradition*. 1936. Rpt. New York: Oxford Univ. Press, 1958.

Lubac, Henri de. *Exégèse médiévale: Les quatre sens de l'Écriture*. 2 vols. Paris: Aubier, 1959-64.

Miller, Robert P. "Chaucer's Pardoner, the Scriptural Eunuch, and the Pardoner's Tale." *Speculum*, 30 (1955), 180-99.

————. "*The Wife of Bath's Tale* and Medieval Exempla." *ELH*, 32 (1965), 442-56.

————. *Chaucer: Sources and Backgrounds*. New York: Oxford Univ. Press, 1977.

Osgood, C.G. *Boccaccio on Poetry*. 1930. Rpt. New York: Liberal Arts Press, 1956.

Owen, Charles A., Jr. "The Crucial Passages in Five of the *Canterbury Tales*: A Study in Irony and Symbol." *JEGP*, 52 (1953), 294-311.

Owst, G.R. *Literature and Pulpit in Medieval England*. 1933. Rev. 2nd ed. Oxford: Blackwell, 1961.

Peterson, Joyce E. "The Finished Fragment: A Reassessment of the *Squire's Tale*." *ChauR*, 5 (1970), 62-74.

Robertson, D.W., Jr. "Historical Criticism." *EIE, 1950*. Ed. A.S. Downer, New York: Columbia Univ. Press, 1951, pp. 3-31.

————. "The Doctrine of Charity in Mediaeval Literary Gardens: A Topical Approach through Symbolism and Allegory." *Speculum*, 26 (1951), 24-49.

————. *A Preface to Chaucer: Studies in Medieval Perspectives*. Princeton: Princeton Univ. Press, 1962.

Root, R.K. *The Poetry of Chaucer: A Guide to Its Study and Appreciation.* 1906. Rev. ed. 1922. Rpt. Gloucester, Mass.: P. Smith, 1957.

Rosenberg, Bruce A. "The 'Cherry-Tree Carol' and the *Merchant's Tale.*" *ChauR,* 5 (1971), 264-76.

Rowland, Beryl. "The Play of the *Miller's Tale*: A Game within a Game." *ChauR,* 5 (1971), 140-46.

——. "Chaucer's Blasphemous Churl: A New Interpretation of the *Miller's Tale.*" In *Chaucer and Middle English Studies in Honour of Rossell Hope Robbins.* Ed. Beryl Rowland. London: Allen & Unwin, 1974. Kent, Ohio: Kent State Univ. Press, 1974, pp. 43-55.

Silvestris, Bernard. *Comm. super sex libros Eneidos Virg.* Ed. G. Riedel. Greifswald, 1924.

Smalley, Beryl. *The Study of the Bible in the Middle Ages.* 1952. Rpt. Notre Dame, Ind.: Univ. of Notre Dame Press, 1964.

Spicq, V.C. *Esquisse d'une histoire de l'exégèse latine au moyen âge.* Paris: Bibliothèque thomiste, 1944.

Tupper, Frederick. "Chaucer and the Seven Deadly Sins." *PMLA,* 29 (1914), 93-128.

Tuve, Rosemond. *Allegorical Imagery: Some Mediaeval Books and Their Posterity.* Princeton: Princeton Univ. Press, 1966.

Wimsatt, James I. *Allegory and Mirror: Tradition and Structure in Middle English Literature.* New York: Pegasus, 1970.

SIXTEEN

VANCE RAMSEY

Modes of Irony in the Canterbury Tales

Irony in Chaucer's work has been recognized from the beginning (see Birney, "Is Chaucer's Irony a Modern Discovery?"). Perhaps no age, however, has made so much of Chaucer's irony as the present one. Beginning with this century and especially with discussions of the relations of the tales and tellers, criticism has discerned not only such local instances as were recognized earlier but also the broader operations and implications of Chaucer's irony. Hoffman, for example, has shown how in the beginning of the *General Prologue* natural and supernatural forces are at work simultaneously, not in opposition or separately but in such close conjunction as to make it difficult at times to say which predominates (as in the portrait of the Prioress). These two forces operate through the remainder of the *Canterbury Tales*, sometimes separately but often simultaneously, and from their interaction come many of the larger ironies in the work.

The first of the tales will serve as an example. Volumes about the late medieval tournament are expressed in the exclamation by the narrator of the *Knight's Tale*, 2115-16; "To fighte for a lady, *benedicitee*! / It were a lusty sighte for to see." Yet at another crucial moment in the tale's career, quite another point is also made feelingly: "This world nys but a thurghfare ful of wo, / And we been pilgrymes, passynge to and fro" (*KnT*, 2847-8). Earlier in this century, there was a tendency among scholars to minimize the importance of passages like the second of these; there is now some tendency to ignore the implications of the first.

Most definitions of irony point to a "double audience," one understanding fully, the other in the dark (see Fowler, p. 305). Certainly this distinction fits many instances of irony, but not such a form as sarcasm which is usually meant to be understood by both victim and bystander. More frequently there is at work in irony some form of "withholding." It may be knowledge which is withheld, as in dramatic irony, or a withholding of direct abuse, as in sarcasm and some other kinds of verbal irony (cf. certain portraits in the *General Prologue*), or some other form of withholding, such as refusing to comment directly on the juxtaposition of tale and answering tale. This withholding is akin to the style of many writers who are primarily artists rather than preachers or propagandists, and this kinship has caused some modern critics to use the term so broadly as almost to equal style. Wimsatt and Brooks, for example, call irony "the slight warping of signification continually made by the poet as he shades the word to its precise meaning in his context" (p. 674).

In this chapter the term *irony* will be more strictly limited to deliberately developed cases of opposition, or at least countercurrents, operating in the use of a word, or in larger elements of a work, including its form and the narrator's manner. Kenneth Burke is illuminating in describing irony as interaction without negation:

> Irony arises when one tries, by the interaction of terms upon one another, to produce a development which uses all the terms. Hence from the standpoint of this total form (this "perspective of perspectives"), none of the participating "sub-perspectives" can be treated as either precisely right or precisely wrong. They are all voices or personalities, or positions, integrally affecting one another. (p. 512)

Defined only so far, however, irony might be identified with certain types of allegory (Knox notes, p. 6, that several medieval

rhetoricians did identify the two). Though there is a need for clarification of the relationship of the two, it seems that a major difference is that allegory emphasizes likenesses between the "outer"
expression and "inner" signification, whereas irony lays its emphasis on oppositions. Burrow has touched on the relationship
of the two in a further way which is suggestive for the *General
Prologue* and other works by Chaucer, saying that a "generalizing impulse (characteristic of allegory) exists side by side in Chaucer with the ironic or satiric impulse (characteristic of fabliau)
which tends to isolate its object and particularize it" (p. 208).

I

In the *Art of Satire* David Worcester provides a systematic and
illuminating classification of the modes of irony which, with
modifications, will serve as the basis for the discussion of modes
of irony in the *Canterbury Tales*. In this study he describes four
modes of operation of irony, three of them having very roughly
to do with the *mythos*, *ethos*, and *dianoia* of the work (dramatic,
cosmic and verbal irony) and a fourth involving the relation of a
narrator or other speaker to what is said (irony of manner). Not
the least of Professor Birney's many achievements in studying
Chaucer's irony is the light which he has shed on the operation
of a fifth mode of irony in the *Canterbury Tales*, which, like
dramatic irony, has to do primarily with the *mythos*—structural
irony.

Most familiar and pervasive of modes of irony in the *Canterbury Tales* is the irony of the mode of expression (*verbal irony*).
Of this type is the comment of the narrator of the *Merchant's
Tale*, 1268-9, concerning the marriage of January and May: "To
take a wyf it is a glorious thyng, / And namely whan a man is
oold and hoor; . . ." This example involves the simplest kind of
verbal irony, simple inversion. That there are other kinds of
verbal irony (and more prevalent ones) in the *Canterbury Tales*
many studies have demonstrated.

The Oxford English Dictionary, standard glosses such as
Skeat's, and the *Middle English Dictionary* should prove very

valuable aids in the understanding of verbal irony. Certainly Griffith had a point in protesting that only when the most usual meaning of a word is known can the critic appreciate deviations and their purposes. At the word level, the studies by Baum and others of Chaucer's puns are applicable—as is Baum's *caveat* concerning the dubiousness of some of the suggested puns. The discussions, pro and con, of the suggested puns at the end of the *Shipman's Tale* are instructive of the difficulties (see Caldwell, Copland, Jones and Silverman; other good discussions of the tale are by Lawrence and Stillwell).

Several studies have explored religious, literary, social and rhetorical influences on Chaucer's use of irony, verbal and otherwise. Concerning sermons of "satire and complaint" which Chaucer would have heard regularly, Owst, alluding particularly to the Wife of Bath and to the Pardoner and his "sermon," says it is "quite impossible" to imagine that Chaucer "should fail to draw inspiration from these past-masters of vivid Realism and incisive portraiture" (p. 230). The influence of the rhetorical tradition is the subject of another chapter in this volume, but Kökeritz's article on "rhetorical word-play" should be mentioned (cf. Eliason and Beichner, "*Non Alleluia Ructare*").

Several articles have demonstrated the value of background studies in illuminating the comic irony of the *Miller's Tale*, and their techniques would seem to be applicable to other tales. Beichner's three studies have demonstrated Chaucer's use of the religious background for purposes of ironic portraiture; Kaske has discussed the ironic use of echoes of the Song of Songs (cf. Siegel); Harder has noted the possible influence of the drama; O'Connor has explored the astrological background; Coffman has shown the use Chaucer makes of Nicholas' education in the seven liberal arts for purposes of burlesque. Donaldson and Stillwell have made interesting studies of the ironic use of courtly vocabulary. Irony in the structure of the tale has been variously discussed by Birney, Bolton, and Olson.

The claim that Chaucer's increasingly more realistic and ironic style is attributable to Italian influence has been countered by dis-

cussions of the various types of French literature which may have
been known to him (see Birney, "The Beginnings of Chaucer's
Irony"). Hart's articles on the fabliaux are still illuminating but
should be supplemented by such studies as Haselmayer's and
especially Muscatine's discussion of the "bourgeois tradition."
Hart's comparison of the *Reeve's Tale* with French fabliaux is
still of great value; Kaske's discussion of the "aube" in the tale
is another instance of the illumination which the proper application of background information may afford. Other interesting
recent studies are by Copland, Forehand, and Olson. Muscatine's
discussion of the influence of the "courtly tradition" on Chaucer
is also valuable (cf. Lewis). Though exact classical influences on
Chaucer's irony are difficult to be sure of, Shannon's study may
be mentioned (see also McPeek's suggestion of possible Goliard
influence).

The native traditions have received increasing attention since
Whiting noted Chaucer's occasionally ironic use of proverbs, both
native and foreign, and especially since Birney's "English Irony
before Chaucer." Utley has provided a valuable study of the
native antifeminist tradition; various studies of the *Miller's Tale*
may be recalled; and, though not specifically on irony, Mroczkowski has made suggestive comments on the possible influence of
medieval art (see also the discussions of form in the books by
Muscatine and Ruggiers; all of these discussions have a more
direct bearing on the mode of structural irony). There is a great
need for a comprehensive treatment of the subject of irony both
in the Middle Ages generally and in Middle English in particular,
of the kind begun by Birney in his excellent dissertation, "Chaucer's Irony."

A second mode of irony exists in the way a narrator or speaker
presents himself (*irony of manner*). These categories are not, of
course, mutually exclusive, but involve a kind of continuum; as
verbal irony becomes not an occasional gambit but a customary
strategy and mode of communication, it is clear that the speaker
has adopted a manner which informs the seemingly most innocent of his remarks. More often than not, irony of manner in-

volves the adoption of the guise of an ignorant but earnest and well-meaning innocent (in the manner of Socrates, but not necessarily for the purposes implied in the term *Socratic irony*); often there is also false or exaggerated praise of another (in the manner of the *eiron* with the *alazon* in classical comedy). This guise of the earnest innocent is familiar in the *House of Fame* and other early works and has been attributed to the overall narrator of the *Canterbury Tales* (see Worcester, pp. 95-102, on Chaucer's irony of manner in several works; Meech has a useful list of other studies, pp. 372-3).

Several other chapters take up the subject of the overall narrator of the *Canterbury Tales;* however, this example of irony of manner is too important to be left without some notice. The comments have ranged from assertions that the narrator is Chaucer himself (Woolf, Lawrence in *Chaucer and the Canterbury Tales,* and Howard in "Chaucer the Man"), that the narrator "is not a definite enough personality to prove anything" (Kimpel, p. 86), or that there is an inconsistent and shifting point of view (Duncan, Major), to Donaldson's contention that the narrator's irony of manner is complete enough to give a designation of "persona" to the guise adopted ("Chaucer the Pilgrim"). Howard's discussion of Chaucer's position as a bourgeois poet writing for an aristocratic audience as an explanation of the ironic manner recalls the thesis of Birney's "Chaucer's Irony"; perhaps implied, though not stated, in Howard's study is the very good point that the habit of oral delivery actually affords many opportunities for irony of manner, rather than inhibiting it as Bronson seems to think (*In Search of Chaucer*, pp. 26-8). In his book Ruggiers devotes an excellent chapter to the broader implications of irony and the narrator (pp. 16-41).

Irony of manner usually implies a consciousness of disparity by the principal. Certainly this is true of Socratic irony as well as that of Chaucer the pilgrim-poet. At a second remove from the poet, however, are other principals—the pilgrims and narrators of the tales. With them the ignorance which is assumed by the overall narrator at times may be partially or wholly genuine (like

that of a Gulliver or Candide), so that there are disparities between conscious and unconscious motive, between the self presented by the pilgrim and the self perceived by the reader.

By now virtually every portrait has been claimed to have ironic
features (see, for example, Mitchell's introductory remarks and
his reading of the Knight's portrait); however, at least a few of
the portraits have usually been accepted as having no important
ironies—those of the Knight, Yeoman, Clerk, Parson, and Plowman. With the exception of the Clerk's envoy, the relations of
these pilgrims to the others and to their own tales have likewise
been taken as lacking in irony. Aside from the portraits, the possibilities of irony of manner are generally explored in the relation
of the pilgrim to his tale (e.g. the Monk), the pilgrim to other
pilgrims (e.g. Friar and Summoner), and of the narrator to one
or more characters in his tale (e.g. the Merchant and January).
The ironies in the portraits tend to fall most heavily on the ecclesiastical figures. As Speirs says: "The art is in seeing exactly
what each is in relation to what each ought to be" (p. 103). These
ironies tend to be more biting—closer to sarcasm, as that word's
etymology implies—when the narrator reveals clearly his own
awareness of them, as in the portraits of the Summoner and
Pardoner, than when he seems relatively unaware, as in the portraits of the Monk, Friar, and Prioress. About this last pilgrim,
however, there is considerable disagreement. Earlier studies usually regarded the ironies in her portrait as comparatively light,
but recent studies have tended to take them more seriously,
especially in conjunction with Chaucer's alleged satire on anti-
Semitism in the *Prioress's Tale*, reaching a kind of climax in
Schoeck's article. Florence Ridley has given a convenient résumé
and a balanced assessment of various critical pronouncements on
the Prioress and her tale. The irony in the secular portraits tends
to turn on questions of money (cf. Nevo) as with the Merchant,
Physician, Manciple, and Reeve, physical violence as with the
Miller and Shipman, love of luxury (Franklin, Man of Law, and
the five Gildsmen), personal appearance (Cook and Wife of
Bath), and amatory habits (Squire). These are often used in com-

bination, of course, as in the portrait of the violent Miller with his "thumb of gold."

Though objected to (e.g. Jordan), the Kittredge theory of the tales as dramatic speeches has led to some valuable discussions of the relations of the pilgrims to the tales they tell. Chaucer assigns to himself, for example, the wretched *Sir Thopas* as the "beste rym" he knows (*Thop*, 2118), then switches to prose at the request of the appalled Host (see Winstanley, Lawrence, and Manly). Irony has been shown in the Monk's disappointment of the Host's expectations and the discrepancy between his personality and his tale (see Tatlock, Kuhl, Frank, and Baum's *Chaucer*). The Merchant's portrait and tale have been the subjects of some excellent recent studies, including those of Burrow, Holman, Muscatine, Schlauch, and G. G. Sedgewick. The prologue to this tale serves particularly to heighten the irony with parallels between his own marital experience and the speeches and experience of the tale. On various aspects of the tale, see the studies of Blanch, Bronson, Kaske, Park, and Tatlock. The Clerk's portrait is usually accepted as straightforward, its contrast to the preceding one being sometimes noted (Malone, Bronson). But some recent critical comment has raised the question of satiric intent in the *Clerk's Tale* (e.g. Reiman); an excellent review of discussions and critique of matters pertaining to the tale is provided in Sledd's article (on the structure and Chaucer's additions to Petrarch, see Heninger). Considerable comment has been caused by the question of whether the envoy really fits the Clerk (Kittredge, Preston, Donaldson's *Chaucer's Poetry*) or is simply Chaucer's own (Malone). The relation of the Franklin's portrait to the tale assigned to him has elicited much comment. Although the wealth and influence attributed to him have been questioned, the historical accuracy seems well established (see Gerould, pp. 33-54). Donaldson, in *Chaucer's Poetry*, has denied any satire in the portrait, saying that the Franklin is "one of the relatively few pilgrims capable of disinterested conduct" (p. 891). The ironies of the tale itself have been discussed in very different ways by Gaylord and by Baum. Though ironies connected with the Man of Law have usually been thought to be confined to his portrait, Baum, in answer to Duffey, asserts ("Man of Law's Tale," p. 12) that Chaucer was aware of the absurdities of the tale and dealt with it "in a spirit midway between what you might call low seriousness and levity."

Both of the great confessions, the Wife of Bath's and the Pardoner's, are made with conscious irony, but in both there are larger ironies of which each speaker is unaware. The Pardoner, for example, is conscious of the irony of his practicing the very sin he preaches against and of feeding his own sin in the act of attacking it; he is largely unconscious of other ironies such as the larger one of his serving as the living example and warning of the final truth of his sermon (for an opposite view, compare Reiss). There are many open questions about the Pardoner's portrait and tale. Many have followed Curry's lead (pp. 54-70) in taking him to be *eunuchus ex nativitate* (cf. Ethel and Miller); yet both Gerould (p. 59) and Elliott (pp. 62-3) point out that Chaucer leaves the question open. Some recent critics have found the Pardoner's greatest sin to be pride rather than avarice (see Stockton; Ethel says he has all the sins); on the question of his drunkenness, Elliott notes: "Nowhere does Chaucer say or even suggest that the Pardoner is drunk" (p. 63; but compare Swart). Several have noted a tendency toward allegory in the tale itself; Miller's reading is the most categorical (compare Steadman's assessment of the allegory and irony in the tale). Valuable reviews of scholarship may be found in Baum's *Chaucer* (pp. 44-59) and Sedgewick; in addition the studies of Beichner and Evanoff should be noted. Scholarship threatens to inundate the Wife of Bath with a flood of the clerkish literature which elicited her ironic scorn. Among the most valuable background studies and criticism of her prologue and tale are the studies by Pratt and the discussions in Muscatine's book (pp. 77-88, 204-13); also valuable are Preston's remarks and Malone's article.

Though Worcester does not list it, Birney ("Structural Irony Within the *Summoner's Tale*") and others have demonstrated a mode of irony in the structure of certain tales. Furthermore, the implication of studies of the relations of certain tales seems to be that there are ironic relationships in the larger structure of the *Canterbury Tales* (compare Muscatine's comment, p. 162, on the *Troilus* that "the greatest source of irony, for the first four Books, is in the narrative structure, the pattern of characters, and the contrast of styles . . ."). The fundamental methods of structural irony are arrangement and juxtaposition (cf. recent studies of the portraits in the *General Prologue*).

The most famous theory of the relations of certain tales is certainly that of the Marriage Group, put forward by Hammond (p. 256) and elaborated by Kittredge and others. Although the neatness of the group (with assertion, comment and counter-comment, leading to a solution in the *Franklin's Tale*) has been rendered suspect, Germaine Dempster has demonstrated manuscript authority for such a discussion (cf. Pratt, "The Order of the *Canterbury Tales*"). Also Lawrence, Dempster and others have suggested links with the *Nun's Priest's Tale*, the *Monk's Tale*, and the *Melibeus*, with the Wife's *Prologue* following. Howard has rather tentatively proposed the addition of the tales of the Physician and Second Nun at the end of the group. Within the group Holman has amply demonstrated ironic relations between the tales of the Merchant and Franklin.

The complex and ironic relations among the tales of the first day have been explored by Frost, Owen and Stokoe. Frost has also demonstrated structural ironies within the *Knight's Tale* itself. Ironies relating variously to structure have been discussed by Owen in five tales ("The Crucial Passages in Five of the *Canterbury Tales*"). The ironies growing out of the pairing of the Summoner's and Friar's tales and connected with their quarrel have long been noticed. In addition Birney has demonstrated the artistic function of irony within the tales themselves (for rather different readings, compare Bonjour and Mroczkowski on the *Friar's Tale* and Adams on the *Summoner's Tale*). Shumaker has suggested that the tales of the Manciple and Parson and the Retraction "constitute a natural and consciously intended group" (p. 147; on the first of these, see Birney, "Chaucer's 'Gentil' Manciple and his 'Gentil' Tale," and Hazelton).

In the *Nun's Priest's Tale,* Chaucer makes perhaps his most finished use of structural irony in conjunction with modes of irony already noted. Muscatine has said that Chaucer wrote the tale "in an aura at once . . . cosmic and . . . comic" (p. 238), and adds that the tale "does not so much make true and solemn assertions about life as it tests truths and tries out solemnities" (p. 242). As Manning notes, some critics have responded to the solemnities without due allowance for the "trying out" and have themselves been found too solemn. Lenaghan has duly noted the twin dangers of reading the tale as a simple joke or as simply serious and has found two "voices" speaking in the tale (cf. Severs).

Although the fourth mode, *dramatic irony,* is, as the name suggests, probably more common in drama, particularly tragedy, than in narrative poetry, Germaine Dempster has convincingly demonstrated the importance of Chaucer's use of the mode, defining it thus: "Dramatic irony is the irony resulting from a strong contrast, unperceived by a character in a story, between the surface meaning of his words or deeds and something else happening in the same story" (p. 7). Dempster's study is fundamental and illuminating, but a curious addition to her list of "narratives with little or no dramatic irony" is the *Knight's Tale.* Two very telling and important instances are the promise by Mars of "victory" for Arcite and Mercury's promise to him that in Athens "is thee shapen of thy wo an ende" (*KnT,* 1392). The difference between Arcite's understanding of these promises and their further meanings makes for irony in keeping with the larger context of the tale, as discussed by Frost and Ruggiers. A comic instance of dramatic irony comes from the lips of Absolon in the following tale when he says, "My mouth hath icched al this longe day; / That is a signe of kissyng atte leeste" (*MillT,* 3682-3).

As may be seen from this example, dramatic irony in comedy or tragi-comedy is often clear only in hindsight. Foreknowledge of the end of a well-known story can make for instantaneous, remarkable results in the performance of a tragedy such as *Oedipus.* Because of the lesser-known story of comedy, and because its conclusion is better hidden, dramatic irony often requires a second reading for detection. This fact raises some important questions concerning the relation of composition for oral delivery and Chaucer's use of dramatic irony.

Studies in the last twenty years have increasingly demonstrated the existence of the fifth mode, *philosophic irony*, in the *Canterbury Tales*. Studies of the *Knight's Tale*, such as those of Frost and Ruggiers, have emphasized the philosophical dimension and multiple perspectives of the tale. Similarly Owen says of the comic tales, "The fabliau as it took new form under Chaucer's compelling interest in characterization, brought him up against problems of morality that were to become basic in the developed *Canterbury Tales*" ("Morality as a Comic Motif," p. 226). Studies of the Retraction which assert its genuineness and its relevance to the overall form also involve a philosophical dimension (Gordon provides a useful review of earlier discussions; in addition see the books of Baldwin and Ruggiers).

Philosophic irony involves two basic perspectives (cf. Burke), one earthly, time-bound and limited, the other celestial, timeless and limitless. Hoffman's study of the two loves at work in the *General Prologue*, Donaldson's contrast of the limited vision of the pilgrim with the larger vision of the poet, and Frost's demonstration of the "three concentric circles" of interest in the *Knight's Tale* have variously discerned the co-existence of the very limited and the larger vision within the *Canterbury Tales*. The earthly vision discerns such various forces as fortune and destiny and the stars, then struggles helplessly to relate them to free will and the "purveiaunce" of God. From the "otherworldly" perspective, the larger vision directs the ironies down to man and his merely natural activities (e.g. Troilus' laughter from the eighth sphere and the theme of the palinode generally). The ironies from this perspective tend to be objective rather than self-directed and turn on the difference between ignorance and knowledge, false love and true love—the general conflict between the apparent and the real.

Philosophic irony makes the greatest demands on all the information and powers which a reader of another time can bring to bear. It calls upon the poet and reader at least temporarily to share certain assumptions and feelings and also to entertain certain doubts and uncertainties. If they do not share certain assumptions at least for the time (cf. Coleridge's "willing suspension of disbelief"), the one is likely to be presenting straightforwardly from within an intellectual context what the other is viewing ironically from without (cf. Robertson). Conversely, the writer may be presenting with an obliqueness and skepticism what the other receives as direct (cf. earlier assertions of Chaucer's "modernity").

II

There are few topics with more vexed questions or broader implications than that of Chaucer's irony. While there has been in this century general recognition of the many ironies in Chaucer's works, there has been little agreement about the implications or even about various instances of it. This is not surprising, because the very nature of irony forgoes "either-or" in favor of "both-and." The irony, complexity, and finally the integrity of vision in Chaucer's best work lies in his own refusal to employ the simplistic and easy. If modern scholarship has long since rejected a naive or artless Chaucer, it has at times shown a strange longing to substitute a simple Chaucer of its own. The work of an ironist of any subtlety will scarcely yield much fruit to such a desire, however the simpler answer may satisfy for a time.

Of no author is it truer than of Chaucer that the meaning of his work must be sought in the whole of it rather than in any single part. This is partially due to the variety of his forms and subjects; it is due in part to the kaleidoscope of moods and tones; a great part of the reason lies in his continual use of irony. The first warning which an understanding of his irony gives is to be suspicious of any claim that a passage or poem or theme is Chaucer's "final answer" on any subject. The palinode to *Troilus and Criseyde* and the Retraction at the end of the *Canterbury Tales* are final in a structural sense, but in a very real sense each gives only part of the whole meaning just as each is only a part of the whole work.

Chaucer's was an age nourished on paradox and irony (see, for example, Lovejoy, pp. 67-98). The very religion which some have looked to for simple solutions to problems of interpretation helped in this; consider, for example, the simultaneous glory and guilt of the phrase *felix culpa* or such a familiar paradox as "In the midst of life, we are in death"—remembering that both death *and* life are present. Ruggiers has said that

> the very core of Chaucer's artistic vision is that ceaseless debate, which ultimately produces the contemplative ironist, between the concept of destiny and divine Providence and the fatiguing promise of moral responsibility and the freedom of the will, between the persistent claims of the appetites of the natural man and the higher claims of the spiritual man . . . . (p. 252)

In Burke's words there are many competing "voices" or "sub-perspectives" (p. 512) in the *Canterbury Tales*: The Wife of Bath sets experience against "auctoritee"; the Miller sets natural instinct and cunning against idealizations of human conduct; the pilgrims are brought forth both by spring and the call of the martyr; the author himself sets the demands of his art against the demands of his religion, yet makes no apparent attempt to destroy what he seems to retract. It is quite possible that the mode of structural irony is the most instructive of all because the competition of voices, the variation of perspectives, is the least deniable. The *Miller's Tale* does not negate the *Knight's Tale*; nor is the *Miller's Tale* simply an appendage or comic footnote. Each is excellent in its own kind. Each is undeniably *there*. Both are voices whose comment and counter-comment add to a harmony which is larger than either.

The extent to which irony has become a literary habit for the poet of the *Canterbury Tales* is indicated by the *Merchant's Tale*, an example of his maturest art. That he can write affectingly of love the *Franklin's Tale* and *Troilus and Criseyde* are clearest examples; that the words *gentil* and *gentilesse* represent an ideal of conduct which is very close to him seems likewise manifest; yet after depicting May's easy yielding to Damian's note in a privy, Chaucer allows the Merchant to use his own favorite line for a bitterly ironic comment: "Lo, pitee renneth soone in gentil herte" (*MerchT*, 1986).

* * * * *

Although space limitations and the great outpouring of articles in the last decade prevent anything like a full listing, some of the better articles on the subject of irony in the *Canterbury Tales* (as well as a representative sampling of others) are listed in the appended bibliography. Writings on irony in the last decade have seemed characterized by three traits: (1) a rather general acceptance of the pervasiveness of irony in many parts of the *Canterbury Tales*; (2) a less pervasive yet significant unease about the uncritical resort to irony as a "universal solvent," as one critic called it; and (3) some significant attempts to gain a larger perspective on Chaucer the man and especially on the direction of his life's work.

Near the end of a chapter representative of the third trait ("What kind of poet is Chaucer?"), Brewer alludes to the presence of the first: "What haunts this discussion is the fact of Chaucer's irony" (p. 217). This could serve as motto for much Chaucer criticism of the last decade whose subject was ostensibly removed from such considerations. Donaldson termed this quality "the elusion of clarity" and explained his coinage as pointing to a Chaucerian clarity which is both "often more apparent than real" and "a means by which he evades, for the sake of poetic complexity, the laws and obligations of logical simplicity" (p. 23; compare Miskimin, pp. 30-1).

Still, if all agree that the irony is there in many places, warnings about finding ironies, like the Wife's friars, under every bush have never been so germane. A constant danger has been the temptation to evade the context by claiming that in a particular locus an ironic reversal is operative which only Chaucer's contemporaries could have understood (without the aid of the scholar at hand). Foremost among those finding thematic countercurrents and narrator positions the reverse of appearances have been those applying some version of the exegetical tradition. Of the *Miller's Tale* Bowker tells us of a "dark spirit beneath action too often construed as solely comic," while Reiss finds the Gerveys of the inappropriate teasing of Absolon "a parody of God the Creator," and Clark sees Absolon "in the symbolic role of a squeamish devil." Attempts to return to more traditional responses have often centered on such favorite exegetical targets as the Wife of Bath by variously comparing fourteenth- and twentieth-century realities and ways of perceiving: such critics as Parker, Reid, and Rowland finding more points of contact than the exegetes have admitted.

Two accomplishments of the "exegetical approach" which perhaps all would recognize are the increased attention to the cultural milieu of the fourteenth century and a heightened sense of the seriousness and complexity of Chaucer's work generally. Particularly the latter effect seems involved in recent significant attempts to attain a larger perspective on Chaucer's career as a whole. Garbáty, for example, has made an important attempt to come to terms with the problem of the narrator in all of Chaucer's work ("Degradation"), arguing, "If the controlling feature of Chaucer's work is comic irony, then the central force of that irony is the Chaucerian pose" (pp. 103-4). In another attempt to take a larger look at Chaucer's work, Bloomfield examines and rejects recent exegetical readings of the Wife of Bath, calling them "Jansenist, Puritan, and Manichean," arguing that "the Chaucerian negative capability demands a negative capability from us" (p. 68) and, like Garbáty, finding "the essence of Chaucerian humor" appearing "in Chaucer's portrayal of himself." Similarly Brewer ("Towards") examines the image of Chaucer within his works and, much like Garbáty, finds that "the older he grows the less he suggests even those hints of personal expressivity found in earlier poems,... and the more he poses as an old-fashioned traditional storyteller, the climax being his own telling of that drasty rhyme 'Sir Thopas'..." ("Towards," p. 247). In addition to the shifting image of a poet who "eludes clarity" identified by other studies, Brewer attends to the other important concerns of recent studies of Chaucerian irony, to finding the limits of its presence, and to attempting an overview of Chaucer's *œuvre*. In the course of his study, Brewer presents a test of ironic (and/or allegorical) readings: "Unless there is explicit, internal evidence to the contrary, the face value of a 'naked text' should be accepted, whether secular or devotional" ("Towards," p. 223).

BIBLIOGRAPHY

Adams, John F. "The Structure of Irony in *The Summoner's Tale*." *EIC*, 12 (1962), 126-32.

Allen, Judson B. "The Ironic Fruyt: Chauntecleer as Figura." *SP*, 66 (1969), 25-35.

———. "The Old Way and the Parson's Way: An Ironic Reading of the Parson's Tale." *JMRS*, 3 (1973), 255-71.

———, and Patrick Gallacher. "Alisoun Through the Looking Glass: Or Every Man His Own Midas." *ChauR*, 4 (1970), 99-105.

Baldwin, Ralph. *The Unity of the 'Canterbury Tales'*. Anglistica, 5. Copenhagen: Rosenkilde og Bagger, 1955.

Baum, Paull F. "*The Man of Law's Tale*." *MLN*, 64 (1949), 12-14.

———. "Chaucer's Puns." *PMLA*, 71 (1956), 225-46.

———. *Chaucer: A Critical Appreciation*. Durham, N.C.: Duke Univ. Press, 1958.

———. "Chaucer's Puns: A Supplementary List." *PMLA*, 73 (1958), 167-70.

Beichner, Paul E. "Absolon's Hair." *MS*, 12 (1950), 222-33.

———. "Chaucer's Hende Nicholas." *MS*, 14 (1952), 151-53.

———. "*Non Alleluia Ructare*." *MS*, 18 (1956), 135-44.

———. "Characterization in *The Miller's Tale*." In *Chaucer Criticism I: The Canterbury Tales*. Ed. R.J. Schoeck and J. Taylor. Notre Dame, Ind.: Univ. of Notre Dame Press, 1960, pp. 117-29.

———. "Chaucer's Pardoner as Entertainer." *MS*, 25 (1963), 160-72.

Birney, Earle. "Chaucer's Irony." Diss. Toronto, 1936.

———. "English Irony before Chaucer." *UTQ*, 6 (1937), 538-57.

———. "The Beginnings of Chaucer's Irony." *PMLA*, 54 (1939), 637-55.

————. "Is Chaucer's Irony a Modern Discovery?" *JEGP*, 41 (1942), 303-19.

————. " 'After His Ymage': The Central Ironies of the 'Friar's Tale'." *MS*, 21 (1959), 17-35.

————. "Chaucer's 'Gentil' Manciple and His 'Gentil' Tale." *NM*, 61 (1960), 257-67.

————. "The Inhibited and the Uninhibited: Ironic Structure in the 'Miller's Tale'." *Neophil*, 44 (1960), 333-38.

————. "Structural Irony Within the *Summoner's Tale*." *Anglia*, 78 (1960), 204-18.

Blanch, Robert J. "Irony in Chaucer's *Merchant's Tale*." *LHR*, 8 (1966), 8-15.

Bloomfield, Morton W. "The Gloomy Chaucer." In *Veins of Humor*. Ed. H. Levin. Cambridge, Mass.: Harvard Univ. Press, 1972, pp. 57-68.

Bolton, W.F. "The *Miller's Tale*: An Interpretation." *MS*, 24 (1962), 83-94.

Bonjour, Adrien. "Aspects of Chaucer's Irony in the *Friar's Tale*." *EIC*, 11 (1961), 121-27.

Bowker, Alvin W. "Comic Illusion and Dark Reality in the *Miller's Tale*." MLS, 4 (1974), 27-34.

Brewer, D.S. *Chaucer*. 1953. 3rd rev. ed. London: Longmans, 1973.

————. "Towards a Chaucerian Poetic." *PBA*, 60 (1974), 219-54.

Bronson, Bertrand H. *In Search of Chaucer*. Toronto: Univ. of Toronto Press, 1960.

————. "Afterthoughts on *The Merchant's Tale*." *SP*, 58 (1961), 583-96.

Burke, Kenneth. *A Grammar of Motives*. 1945. Rpt. New York: Prentice Hall, 1952.

Burrow, J.A. "Irony in the *Merchant's Tale*." *Anglia*, 75 (1957), 199-208.

Caldwell, Robert A. "Chaucer's *taillynge ynough, Canterbury Tales*, B² 1624." *MLN*, 55 (1940), 262-65.

Carruthers, Mary. "Letter and Gloss in the Friar's and Summoner's Tales." *JNT*, 2 (1972), 208-14.

Clark, Roy Peter. "Squeamishness and Exorcism in Chaucer's *Miller's Tale*." *Thoth*, 14 (1973), 37-43.

Coffman, George R. "*The Miller's Tale*: 3187-215: Chaucer and the Seven Liberal Arts in Burlesque Vein." *MLN*, 67 (1952), 329-31.

Copland, Murray. "*The Reeve's Tale*: Harlotrie or Sermonyng?" *MÆ*, 31 (1962), 14-32.

———. "*The Shipman's Tale*: Chaucer and Boccaccio." *MÆ*, 35 (1966), 11-28.

Curry, Walter Clyde. *Chaucer and the Mediaeval Sciences*. Rev. and enl. ed. 1960. Rpt. New York: Barnes & Noble, 1962.

Delany, Sheila. "Clerks and Quiting in the *Reeve's Tale*." *MS*, 29 (1967), 351-56.

Dempster, Germaine. *Dramatic Irony in Chaucer*. 1932. Rpt. New York: Humanities Press, 1959.

———. "A Period in the Development of the *Canterbury Tales* Marriage Group and of Blocks B² and C." *PMLA*, 68 (1953), 1142-59.

De Neef, A. Leigh. "Chaucer's *Pardoner's Tale* and the Irony of Misinterpretation." *JNT*, 3 (1973), 85-96.

Donaldson, E. Talbot. "Chaucer the Pilgrim." *PMLA*, 69 (1954), 928-36.

———. "Idiom of Popular Poetry in the *Miller's Tale*." In *Speaking of Chaucer*. London: Athlone Press. New York: Norton, 1970, pp. 13-29.

———. "Chaucer and the Elusion of Clarity." *E&S*, 25 (1972), 23-44.

———, ed. *Chaucer's Poetry: An Anthology for the Modern Reader*. 1958. 2nd ed. New York: Ronald Press, 1975.

Duffey, B.I. "The Intention and Art of *The Man of Law's Tale*." *ELH*, 14 (1947), 181-93.

Duncan, Edgar H. "Narrator's Point of View in the Portrait-sketches, Prologue to the *Canterbury Tales*." In *Essays in Honor of Walter Clyde Curry*. Foreword by Hardin Craig. Nashville, Tenn.: Vanderbilt Univ. Press, 1955, pp. 77-101.

Eliason, Norman E. "Some Word-Play in Chaucer's Reeve's Tale." *MLN*, 71 (1956), 162-64.

Elliott, Ralph W.V. "Our Host's 'Triacle': Some Observations on Chaucer's 'Pardoner's Tale'." *REL*, 7 (1966), 61-73.

Ethel, Garland. "Chaucer's Worste Shrewe: The Pardoner." *MLQ*, 20 (1959), 211-27.

Evanoff, Alexander. "The Pardoner as Huckster: A Dissent from Kittredge." *BYUS*, 4 (1962), 209-17.

Finlayson, John. "The Satiric Mode and the *Parson's Tale*." *ChauR*, 6 (1971), 94-116.

Forehand, Brooks. "Old Age and Chaucer's Reeve." *PMLA*, 69 (1954), 984-89.

Fowler, H.W. *A Dictionary of Modern English Usage*. 2nd ed. Oxford: Clarendon Press, 1965.

Frank, Grace. "Chaucer's Monk." *MLN*, 55 (1940), 780-81.

Frost, William. "An Interpretation of Chaucer's Knight's Tale." *RES*, 25 (1949), 289-304.

Garbáty, Thomas J. "Satire and Regionalism: The Reeve and His Tale." *ChauR*, 8 (1973), 1-8.

―――. "The Degradation of Chaucer's 'Geffrey'." *PMLA*, 89 (1974), 97-104.

Gaylord, Alan T. "The Promises in *The Franklin's Tale*." *ELH*, 31 (1964), 331-65.

Gerould, G.H. *Chaucerian Essays*. Princeton: Princeton Univ. Press, 1952.

Gordon, James D. "Chaucer's Retraction: A Review of Opinion." In *Studies in Medieval Literature in Honor of Professor Albert Croll Baugh*. Ed. MacEdward Leach. Philadelphia: Univ. of Pennsylvania Press, 1961, pp. 81-96.

Griffith, Dudley D. "On Word Studies in Chaucer." In *Philologica: The Malone Anniversary Studies*. Ed. Thomas A. Kirby and Henry Bosley Woolf. Baltimore: Johns Hopkins Univ. Press, 1949, pp. 195-99.

Halverson, John. "Chaucer's Pardoner and the Progress of Criticism." *ChauR*, 4 (1970), 184-202.

Hamilton, Alice. "Helowys and the Burning of Jankyn's Book." *MS*, 34 (1972), 196-207.

Hammond, Eleanor P. *Chaucer: A Bibliographical Manual*. 1908. Rpt. New York: P. Smith, 1933.

Harder, Kelsie B. "Chaucer's Use of the Mystery Plays in the *Miller's Tale*." *MLQ*, 17 (1956), 193-98.

Harrington, David V. "Dramatic Irony in the *Canon's Yeoman's Tale*." *NM*, 66 (1965), 160-66.

Hart, Walter Morris. "The Fabliau and Popular Literature." *PMLA*, 23, (1908), 329-74.

———. "The *Reeve's Tale*: A Comparative Study of Chaucer's Narrative Art." *PMLA*, 23 (1908), 1-44.

———. "The Narrative Art of the Old French Fabliaux." In *Anniversary Papers by Colleagues and Pupils of George Lyman Kittredge*. 1913. Rpt. New York: Russell & Russell, 1967, pp. 209-16.

Haselmayer, Louis A. "The Portraits in Chaucer's Fabliaux." *RES*, 14 (1938), 310-14.

Hazelton, Richard. "The *Manciple's Tale*: Parody and Critique." *JEGP*, 62 (1963), 1-31.

Heninger, S.K. "The Concept of Order in Chaucer's *Clerk's Tale*." *JEGP*, 56 (1957), 382-95.

Hennedy, Hugh L. "The Friar's Summoner's Dilemma." *ChauR*, 5 (1971), 213-17.

Hoffman, Arthur W. "Chaucer's Prologue to Pilgrimage: The Two Voices." *ELH*, 21 (1954), 1-16.

Holman, C. Hugh. "Courtly Love in the Merchant's and the Franklin's Tales." *ELH*, 18 (1951), 241-52.

Howard, Donald R. "The Conclusion of the Marriage Group: Chaucer and the Human Condition." *MP*, 57 (1960), 223-32.

———. "Chaucer the Man." *PMLA*, 80 (1965), 337-43.

———. *The Idea of the Canterbury Tales*. Berkeley: Univ. of California Press, 1976.

Jones, C. "Chaucer's *Taillynge Ynough.*" *MLN,* 52 (1937), 570.

Jordan, Robert M. "Chaucer's Sense of Illusion: Roadside Drama Reconsidered." *ELH,* 29 (1962), 19-33.

Kaske, R.E. "An Aube in the 'Reeve's Tale'." *ELH,* 26 (1959), 295-310.

———. "January's 'Aube'." *MLN,* 75 (1960), 1-4.

———. "The *Canticum Canticorum* in the *Miller's Tale.*" *SP,* 59 (1962), 479-500.

Kauffman, Corinne E. "Dame Pertelote's Parlous Parle." *ChauR,* 4 (1970), 41-48.

Kimpel, Ben. "The Narrator of the *Canterbury Tales.*" *ELH,* 20 (1953), 77-86.

Kittredge, G.L. *Chaucer and his Poetry.* Cambridge, Mass.: Harvard Univ. Press, 1915.

Knoepflmacher, U.C. "Irony Through Scriptural Allusion: A Note on Chaucer's Prioresse." *ChauR,* 4 (1970), 180-83.

Knox, Norman. *The Word Irony and Its Context, 1500-1755.* Durham, N.C.: Duke Univ. Press, 1961.

Kökeritz, Helge. "Rhetorical Word-play in Chaucer." *PMLA,* 69 (1954), 937-52.

Kuhl, E.P. "Chaucer's Monk," *MLN,* 55 (1940), 480.

Lawrence, William Witherle. "Satire in *Sir Thopas.*" *PMLA,* 50 (1935), 81-91.

———. *Chaucer and the Canterbury Tales.* New York: Columbia Univ. Press, 1950.

———. "Chaucer's *Shipman's Tale.*" *Speculum,* 33 (1958), 56-68.

Lenaghan, R.T. "The Nun's Priest's Fable." *PMLA,* 78 (1963), 300-7.

———. "The Irony of the *Friar's Tale.*" *ChauR,* 7 (1973), 281-94.

Lewis, C.S. *The Allegory of Love: A Study in Medieval Tradition.* 1936. Rpt. New York: Oxford Univ. Press, 1958.

Lovejoy, Arthur O. *The Great Chain of Being.* 1936. Rpt. Cambridge, Mass.: Harvard Univ. Press, 1964.

McPeek, James A.S. "Chaucer and the Goliards." *Speculum*, 26 (1951), 332-36.

Major, John M. "The Personality of Chaucer the Pilgrim." *PMLA*, 75 (1960), 160-62.

Malone, Kemp. *Chapters on Chaucer*. Baltimore: Johns Hopkins Univ. Press, 1951.

———. "The Wife of Bath's Tale." *MLR*, 57 (1962), 481-91.

Manly, John Matthews. *Some New Light on Chaucer*. 1926. Rpt. New York: P. Smith, 1952.

———. "*Sir Thopas*: A Satire." *E&S*, 13 (1928), 52-73.

Mann, Jill. *Chaucer and Medieval Estates Satire: The Literature of Social Classes and the General Prologue to the Canterbury Tales*. New York and London: Cambridge Univ. Press, pp. 194-98 *et passim*.

———. "*Speculum Stultorum* and the *Nun's Priest's Tale*." *ChauR*, 9 (1975), 262-82.

Manning, Stephen. "The Nun's Priest's Morality and the Medieval Attitude Toward Fables." *JEGP*, 59 (1960), 403-16.

Meech, Sanford B. *Design in Chaucer's Troilus*. Syracuse, N.Y.: Syracuse Univ. Press, 1959.

Mehl, Dieter. "The Audience of Chaucer's *Troilus and Criseyde*." In *Chaucer and Middle English Studies in Honour of Rossell Hope Robbins*. Ed. Beryl Rowland. London: Allen & Unwin, 1974. Kent, Ohio: Kent State Univ. Press, pp. 173-89.

Miller, Robert P. "Chaucer's Pardoner, the Scriptural Eunuch, and the Pardoner's Tale." *Speculum*, 30 (1955), 180-99.

Millns, T. "Chaucer's Suspended Judgments." *EIC*, 27 (1977), 1-19.

Miskimin, Alice S. *The Renaissance Chaucer*. New Haven: Yale Univ. Press, 1975.

Mitchell, Charles. "The Worthiness of Chaucer's Knight." *MLQ*, 25 (1964), 66-75.

Mroczkowski, Przemyslaw. "Medieval Art and Aesthetics in *The Canterbury Tales*." Speculum, 33 (1958), 204-21.

————. "*The Friar's Tale* and Its Pulpit Background." In *English Studies Today*. Ed. G.A. Bonnard, 2 (1961), 107-20.

Muscatine, Charles. *Chaucer and the French Tradition: A Study in Style and Meaning*. Berkeley: Univ. of California Press, 1957.

————. "*The Canterbury Tales*: Style of the Man and Style of the Work." In *Chaucer and Chaucerians: Critical Studies in Middle English Literature*. Ed. D.S. Brewer. London: Nelson, 1966, pp. 88-113.

————. *Poetry and Crisis in the Age of Chaucer*. Notre Dame, Ind.: Univ. of Notre Dame Press, 1972. [See pp. 111-45.]

Nevo, Ruth. "Chaucer: Motive and Mask in the *General Prologue*." *MLR*, 58 (1963), 1-9.

O'Connor, John J. "The Astrological Background of the *Miller's Tale*." *Speculum*, 31 (1956), 120-25.

Olson, Paul A. "The *Reeve's Tale*: Chaucer's *Measure for Measure*." *SP*, 59 (1962), 1-17.

————. "Poetic Justice in the *Miller's Tale*." *MLQ*, 24 (1963), 227-36.

O'Reilly, William M., Jr. "Irony in the *Canon's Yeoman's Tale*." *Greyfriar*, 10 (1968), 23-39.

Owen, Charles A., Jr. "The Crucial Passages in Five of the *Canterbury Tales*: A Study in Irony and Symbol." *JEGP*, 52 (1953), 294-311.

————. "Chaucer's *Canterbury Tales*: Aesthetic Design in Stories of the First Day." *ES*, 35 (1954), 49-56.

————. "Morality as a Comic Motif in the *Canterbury Tales*." *CE*, 16 (1955), 226-32.

Owst, G.R. *Literature and Pulpit in Medieval England*. 1933. Rev. 2nd ed. Oxford: Blackwell, 1961.

Page, Barbara. "Concerning the Host." *ChauR*, 4 (1970), 1-13.

Park, B.A. "The Character of Chaucer's Merchant." *ELN*, 1 (1964), 167-75.

Parker, David. "Can We Trust the Wife of Bath?" *ChauR*, 4 (1970), 90-98.

Patch, Howard Rollin. *On Rereading Chaucer*. Cambridge, Mass.: Harvard Univ. Press, 1939.

Pratt, R.A. "The Order of the *Canterbury Tales*." *PMLA*, 66 (1951), 1141-67.

————. "The Development of the Wife of Bath." In *Studies in Medieval Literature in Honor of Professor Albert Croll Baugh*. Ed. MacEdward Leach. Philadelphia: Univ. of Pennsylvania Press, 1961, pp. 45-79.

Preston, Raymond. *Chaucer*. 1952. Rpt. Westport, Conn.: Greenwood Press, 1969.

Reid, David S. "Crocodilian Humor: A Discussion of Chaucer's Wife of Bath." *ChauR*, 4 (1970), 73-89.

Reiman, Donald. "The Real *Clerk's Tale*; or, Patient Griselda Exposed." *TSLL*, 5 (1963), 356-73.

Reiss, Edmund. "The Final Irony of the *Pardoner's Tale*." *CE*, 25 (1964), 260-66.

————. "Daun Gerveys in the *Miller's Tale*." *PLL*, 6 (1970), 115-24.

Richardson, Cynthia C. "The Function of the Host in the *Canterbury Tales*." *TSLL*, 12 (1970), 325-44.

Richardson, Janette. "Friar and Summoner, the Art of Balance." *ChauR*, 9 (1975), 227-36.

Ridley, Florence H. *The Prioress and the Critics*. *UCPES*, 30. Berkeley: Univ. of California Press, 1965.

Robertson, D.W., Jr. *A Preface to Chaucer: Studies in Medieval Perspectives*. Princeton: Princeton Univ. Press, 1962.

Ross, Thomas W. *Chaucer's Bawdy*. New York: Dutton, 1972.

Rothman, Irving N. "Humility and Obedience in the *Clerk's Tale*, with the Envoy Considered as an Ironic Affirmation." *PLL*, 9 (1973), 115-27.

Rowland, Beryl. "Chaucer's Dame Alys: Critics in Blunderland?" *NM*, 73 (1972), 381-95.

————. "The Play of the *Miller's Tale*: A Game within a Game." *ChauR*, 5 (1971), 140-46.

Ruggiers, Paul G. "The Form of *The Canterbury Tales: Respice Fines.*" *CE*, 17 (1956), 439-44.

———. "Some Philosophical Aspects of *The Knight's Tale.*" *CE*, 19 (1958), 296-302.

———. *The Art of the Canterbury Tales.* Madison: Univ. of Wisconsin Press, 1965.

Schlauch, Margaret. "Chaucers *Merchant's Tale* and Courtly Love." *ELH*, 4 (1937), 201-12.

Schoeck, R.J. "Chaucer's Prioress: Mercy and Tender Heart." In *The Bridge, A Yearbook of Judaeo-Christian Studies.* II. New York: Pantheon, 1956, pp. 239-55.

Sedgewick, G.G. "The Structure of *The Merchant's Tale.*" *UTQ*, 17 (1948), 337-45.

———. "The Progress of Chaucer's Pardoner." *TSE*, 1 (1949), 1-29.

Severs, J. Burke. "Chaucer's Originality in the *Nun's Priest's Tale.*" *SP*, 43 (1946), 22-41.

Shallers, A. Paul. "The *Nun's Priest's Tale*: An Ironic Exemplum." *ELN*, 42 (1975), 319-37.

Shannon, E.F. *Chaucer and the Roman Poets.* Cambridge, Mass.: Harvard Univ. Press, 1929.

Shumaker, Wayne. "Chaucer's *Manciple's Tale* as Part of a Canterbury Group." *UTQ*, 22 (1953), 147-56.

Siegel, Paul N. "Comic Irony in *The Miller's Tale.*" *BUSE*, 4 (1960), 114-20.

Silverman, Albert H. "Sex and Money in Chaucer's *Shipman's Tale.*" *PQ*, 32 (1953), 329-36.

Slade, Tony. "Irony in the *Wife of Bath's Tale.*" *MLR*, 64 (1969), 241-47.

Sledd, James. "*The Clerk's Tale*: The Monsters and the Critics." *MP*, 51 (1953), 73-82.

Speirs, John. *Chaucer the Maker.* 1951. Rev. 2nd ed. London: Faber, 1960.

Steadman, John M. "Old Age and *Contemptus Mundi* in *The Par-doner's Tale*." *MÆ*, 33 (1964), 121-30.

Stillwell, Gardiner. "Chaucer's 'Sad Merchant'." *RES*, 20 (1944), 1-18.

———. "The Language of Love in Chaucer's Miller's and Reeve's Tales and in the Old French Fabliaux." *JEGP*, 54 (1955), 693-99.

Stockton, Eric W. "The Deadliest Sin in *The Pardoner's Tale*." *TSL*, 6 (1961), 47-59.

Stokoe, William C., Jr. "Structures and Intention in the First Fragment of the *Canterbury Tales*." *UTQ*, 21 (1952), 120-27.

Swart, J. "Chaucer's Pardoner." *Neophil*, 36 (1952), 45-50.

Tatlock, J.S.P. "Chaucer's *Merchant's Tale*." *MP*, 33 (1936), 367-81.

———. "Chaucer's Monk." *MLN*, 55 (1940), 350-54.

Taylor, Willene P. "Chaucer's Technique in Handling Anti-Feminist Material in 'The Merchant's Tale': An Ironic Portrayal of the *Senex-Amans* and Jealous Husband." *CLAJ*, 13 (1969), 153-62.

Thurston, Paul T. *Artistic Ambivalence in Chaucer's Knight's Tale*. Gainesville: Univ. of Florida Press, 1968.

Toole, William B., III. "Chaucer's Christian Irony: The Relationship of Character and Action in the *Pardoner's Tale*." *ChauR*, 3 (1968), 37-43.

Utley, Francis L. *The Crooked Rib: An Analytical Index to the Argument about Women in English and Scots Literature to the End of the Year 1568*. Columbus, Ohio: Ohio State Univ. Press, 1944.

———. "Stylistic Ambivalence in Chaucer, Yeats and Lucretius—The Cresting Wave and Its Undertow." *UR*, 37 (1971), 174-98.

Whiting, B.J. *Chaucer's Use of Proverbs*. 1934. Rpt. New York: AMS Press, 1973.

Wimsatt, W.K., and Cleanth Brooks. *Literary Criticism: A Short History*. 1957. Rpt. New York: Knopf, 1962.

Winstanley, Lilian, ed. *The Prioress's Tale, The Tale of Sir Thopas*. Cambridge: Cambridge Univ. Press, 1922.

Wood, Chauncey. "Chaucer and *Sir Thopas*: Irony and Concupiscence." *TSLL*, 14 (1972), 389-403.

Woolf, Rosemary. "Chaucer as Satirist in the General Prologue to the *Canterbury Tales.*" *CritQ,* 1 (1959), 150-57.

Worcester, David. *The Art of Satire.* 1940. Rpt. New York: Russell & Russell, 1960.

SEVENTEEN

ROSSELL HOPE ROBBINS

The Lyrics

Chaucer's lyrics are minor not only in comparison with his great works; they're just minor poems. His love lyrics, like the *Complaynt d'Amours* and the intercalated lyrics, are strictly occasional, not significantly different from similar court poetry in the following century. Yet Chaucer's major influence on the fifteenth century was not through the *Canterbury Tales*, but through these formal, conventional lyrics (and his early dream visions) derived from contemporary French verse. As models, the least of the minor turns out major.

Study of the lyrics is limited too: three editions (Nicolas 1846, Skeat 1888 and 1896, Koch 1928), one chapter of one critical study (Clemen 1963), and from 1954 to 1967, fifteen articles. Earlier commentary concerned itself with authentication of the poems, textual criticism, establishment of a canon, sources and parallels in French court verse, and attempts at historical identification.

Few of Chaucer's lyrics remain. He said he wrote lyrics (*LGW*, G, 411, *HF*, 621-2), and in his Retraction (1086) he abjured "*many* a song and *many* a leccherous lay" (emphasis mine). His disciples confirmed his fecundity: Lydgate in *The Fall of Princes* (I, 352-3); Gower in the *Confessio Amantis* (VIII, 2943-7) has

Venus say that with Chaucer's "ditees...the lond fulfild is overal." Brusendorff, however, dismissed such catalogues as a literary device, like Froissart's "rondeaus, balades, virelais, / Grant foisson de dis et de lays" (p. 432).

What one hopes for is a collection of love lyrics like that in MS. Fairfax 16; unfortunately these nineteen ballades, complaints, supplications, and letters are fostered on Chaucer's grandson-in-law, the Duke of Suffolk. The group of fifteen lyrics in Harley MS. 7578 comes close, but only six are Chaucer's. Considering that major poems like *The Book of the Leoun* and *Origines upon the Maudeleyne* could disappear, loss of lyrics is not surprising.

Preservation is variable, ranging from extensive repetition of moralizing poems to unique copies of love lyrics: *Truth* in twenty-three manuscripts, *The Complaint unto Pity* in nine manuscripts, *To Rosemounde* in a single manuscript. As a corpus, Chaucer's lyrics were unknown until 1532, when Thynne printed ten of them. Stow in 1561 reprinted Thynne, with "diuers addicions" including *Against Women Unconstant, A Complaint to his Lady,* and *Adam Scriveyne.* Thereafter, new lyrics came into the canon one by one: *An A B C* was first (Stow 1598), *Womanly Noblesse* was last (Skeat 1894).

Lounsbury (I, 362), Payne (p. 185) and Moore would augment Chaucer's surviving lyrics with passages from his longer poems. "There is no valid reason for denying the intercalated lyrics a place beside the other short pieces," urged Moore (p. 198).

The following extracts are isolable (for religious examples see p. 395). The first three differ in form from the host text and may have circulated independently:

(1) "I have of sorwe so gret won" (*BD,* 475-86). A "com-playnte," two stanzas, *aabba, ccdccd.* Many editors ignore the poetic form: Thynne made a couplet out of line 479 by adding "And thus in sorowe lefte me alone." The poem is based on Machaut's *Jugement du roy de Behaingne* (193-200) and on Machaut's *motet* no. 3.

(2) "Lord, hyt maketh myn herte lyght" (*BD,* 1175-80). Lyric, *aabbaa.* No known source.

(3) "Now welcome, somer, with thy sonne softe" (*PF*, 680-92). A valentine (to Bennett, p. 182, an epithalamium), rondel, *ABBabABabbABB*, in three of the fourteen manuscripts, written out fully in one only. Source not established.

(4) "Hyd, Absolon, thy gilte tresses clere" (*LGW*, F, 249-69, G, 203-23). Ballade, three stanzas rhyme royal with refrain, common-rhymes throughout, parallels several poems by Machaut, Deschamps, and Froissart (Smith, p. 30).

(5) "If no love is, O God what fele I so" (*Tr*, I, 400-20). *Canticus Troili*, a complaint, ballade in three stanzas rhyme royal. A "fairly close rendering" of Petrarch's sonnet 88 from *In Vita* (Wilkins, p. 169; Thomson, p. 316).

Moore and Payne would add further passages from *Troilus and Criseyde* like Antigone's song (II, 827-75), the aubes (III, 1422-42, 1450-70, 1472-91, 1493-1518, 1702-8), Troilus' hymn to Love (III, 1744-71), Troilus' *Ubi sunt* complaint (v, 218-45), the second *Canticus Troili* (v, 638-44), and the *Litera Troili* (v, 1317-1421). But all these lyrical extracts, if not dramatic, are bound to the longer poem by specific references, like "hiest out of Troie" and "coming into Troye" in the aubes. Only one developed a separate life: the (first) *Canticus Troili*, found independently in two manuscripts.

These and other lyric clusters make *Troilus and Criseyde* a vast "sonnet" sequence, to which court poets of the fifteenth century, and even of the sixteenth, could turn for inspiration and even plunder. *Troilus and Criseyde* was fair game.

Notwithstanding the topicality of the *Litera Troili* ("youre comyng hom ageyn to Troie"), the opening stanza (v, 1317-23) could surely be divorced from its context. In genre, this stanza is no whit different from the "Letter Protesting his Devotion" (Robbins, *Sec. Lyrics*, No. 142), or from the "Lettyr" in MS. Fairfax 16 (MacCracken, p. 159):

> Ryght goodly floure, to whom I owe seruyse
> Wyth alle myn hert, and to non othir wyght,
> To yow I wryte, my lady, in thys wyse,

As her that I owe fayth of verry ryght,
As ofte as I haue wysshed me in your syght
And flours of Apryle bygynne for to sprede,
I recomaunde me to your womanhede.

In the mid-sixteenth-century Devonshire MS., lyrical passages in *Troilus and Criseyde* were uprooted to make new poems (Nos. 50-4, *Tr*, II, 337-43, 344-50, 778-91, 855-61). Another lyric (No. 14, signed T. H.) is a blatant redeployment of four stanzas (IV, 288-308, 323-9) with a couplet heading (IV, 13-14); references to Criseyde (IV, 292, 307) are expunged. In his edition, Muir overlooked their filiation and attributed the extracts to Lord Thomas Howard (p. 281); actually, as Southall observed (p. 144), they were copied from Chaucer by Mary Shelton.

Nor was this the only borrowing. Among the love lyrics in MS. Rawlinson C. 813 is a love letter to a mistress, using nine stanzas from various books of *Troilus and Criseyde*. And Howell in his *Devises* (1581) incorporated lines from this poem.

No matter how many or how few of Chaucer's lyrics survive, their importance is incontestable.

Despite the achievements of the poets of the late thirteenth and early fourteenth century that culminated in the superlative anthology of English and French (and Latin) poetry in Harley MS. 2253, their lyrics had no influence. Chaucer started all over again, as if there had never been an English tradition. Chaucer's are— after 1340—the *first* sophisticated lyrics in English, introducing from France new metrical and stanzaic forms and new themes that were to dominate court verse in the following centuries. Chaucer's lyrics are not only the pacemakers; they are the *only* specimens. In the second half of the fourteenth century, the Middle English secular lyric had no other existence. Not until the second quarter of the fifteenth century do secular lyrics proliferate —in the styles developed by Chaucer.

Of the fashionable French forms, Chaucer favored the ballade and the rondel. Complaints are a genre rather than a form, and most of Chaucer's secular ballades are thematically complaints.

The ballade was popularized by Machaut in his *Remède de fortune* (about 1340). In the thirteenth century a musical form, with Machaut (himself a musician) the ballade had become a literary pattern: three common-rhymed stanzas of uniform length —seven, eight, or more lines—each with a refrain. Machaut's disciple, Deschamps, introduced the envoy. Chaucer paraphrased ballades from both (*Against Women Unconstant*, *Merciles Beaute*). A third French influence on Chaucer's lyrics was Froissart, whose ballades patterned Chaucer's "Hyde, Absolon, thy gilte tresses clere." In addition, from Graunson, Chaucer translated three ballades for *The Complaint of Venus*.

If the ballade form is followed *strictly*, nine or even twelve common-rhyming words are needed, and, as Friedman observed (p. 100), "the easy way out . . . was to use rime words with Latin or French suffixes (-ate, -ation, -tye, -esse, -ure, -te, etc.)." Since "rym in Englissh hath such skarsyte" (*Ven* 80), English ballades generally demand only a common refrain. Unlike the French poets, who used a variety of stanza patterns up to fourteen lines, Chaucer stabilized the English ballade in rhyme royal (*ababbcc*) or monk's stanza (*ababbcbc*)—both schemes taken over from the French.

Under Machaut, the rondel too became a literary form. As he had for the ballade, Deschamps formulated three variations for the rondel, but Chaucer used only one, *ABBabABabbABB*, probably the form, too, of his fragment in the *Knight's Tale* (1510-12).

None of Chaucer's virelais has survived. Robinson's suggestion (p. 790) that the rhymes in Anelida's strophe (*Anel* 256-71) "approach the arrangement of a virelai" lacks precision—no interlocking rhymes (as correctly in stanzas 8 and 18 of *The Lay of Sorrow*). Stanza 6 shows a closer virelai pattern and should be printed as short lines.

For love lyrics like Chaucer's in *formes fixes*, literary and social conventions form the underpinning and must be accepted without deviation. Making and reading such lyrics was one of the games people played, and provided sophisticated fun for poet and a knowledgeable audience. Court verse explored the rules of social ritual: how should a lady and gentleman behave toward each other? The "Ten Commandments of Love," for example, told the lady to "pointe by discretion youre houre, tyme and place, / Conueniently mething with armes to embrace" (Robbins, *Sec. Lyrics*, No. 177).

This other-world of courtly dalliance existed primarily in the mind. Its justification lay in its unreality; it was an escape from the pressures and tensions of the work-a-day life that stifled the niceties of love-making. Any discussion of real social problems, like those of adulterous relationships, was taboo.

The staple literary expression of the game was the complaint. It was described in the englished *Roman de la rose* (1865-71): the God of Love wounded the poet so he "sighede sore in compleyning." Similar accounts occur in *Troilus and Criseyde* (I, 540-5) and, in the fifteenth century, in *The Complaint of the Black Knight*, *Supplicacio Amantis*, *The Temple of Glas*, and *The Flower of Courtesy*.

The complaint conventions, originally French, structure Chaucer's earlier lyrics. They are variations on a single theme: stanzas from one poem are interchangeable with stanzas from another. Love is dearly bought (*Bal Compl* 7, *Lady* 39, *Lodesterre* 3). The lady lacks the quality of mercy (*Compl d'Am* 55, *Lady* 101, *Pity* 90), albeit she possesses all the other virtues, like beauty (*Bal Compl* 5, *Compl d'Am* 51, *Wom Nob* 2) and goodness (*Compl d'Am* 53, *Lady* 24, *Pity* 58, *Wom Nob* 3). Once the love experience has started, the lover must go on loving (*Bal Compl* 21, *Compl d'Am* 82, *Lady* 22, 91, *Lodesterre* 40, *Mortal Foe* 2-3, *Pity* 115). Though unworthy (*Compl d'Am* 19, *Lady* 67), the lover will die innocent of any offense (*Compl d'Am* 30, *Lady* 60). It is unjust (*Lady* 48, *Mortal Foe* 11-14), but inevitable (*Compl d'Am* 23). The lady alone can effect a cure (*Compl d'Am* 45, *Lady* 126, *Lodesterre* 8, *Mortal Foe* 24), but the lady is obdurate (*Compl d'Am* 59, *Lady* 17, *Lodesterre* 7, *Pity* 110). The only person who could help will not listen to his complaint (*Compl d'Am* 10, *Lady* 95, *Pity* 25).

Womanly Noblesse is an early metrical experiment in the diffi-

cult strict ballade form of nine-line stanzas (used in *Anel* 211 ff.),
with envoy. The theme is conventional: praise of his lady's beauty
and nobility, his unswerving devotion, and plea "my peynes for
to redresse." The last line of the envoy picks up the second line
of the complaint (compare *Anel* 211, 350, *Pity* 2, 119).

A Balade of Complaint ("doubtful" in Robinson, p. 524) may
have started as a strict ballade (*-ere* rhymes in all three stanzas);
there is no refrain. Basically, the lyric (an epistle like the *Complaynt d'Amours*) is a series of simple apostrophes to "my hertes
lady," "my worldes joy," "myn heven hool, and al my suffi-
saunce."

A Complaint to his Lady, another early work (1373-4), is a
series of four metrical experiments in the complaint genre, fragments or drafts, some lines being reused in the *Complaynt
d'Amours* (29, 131 = *Compl d'Am* 7, 31), *The Complaint unto
Pity* (3, 47-9, 51-2 = *Pity* 81, 99-100, 110), and *Anelida and
Arcite* (see p. 323). Thematically, the pieces are uncomplicated
and adhere to the rules; metrically, they are notable for introducing *terza rima* (Fragment III, not again until Wyatt and Surrey),
a decasyllabic ten-line stanza, *aabaabcddc* (Fragment IV). Rhyme
royal was used more extensively in the early companion piece,
The Complaint unto Pity, and in *A Balade of Complaint* and
Complaynt d'Amours. No direct French models have been found.

The *Complaynt d'Amours* or *An Amorous Complaint* (about
1374) consists of a proem introducing "the sorwefulleste man,"
two terns of direct address to his lady (stanzas 2-4, 10-12), and
five parenthetic stanzas generalizing on her lack of pity. This
theme, "It is hir pley to laughen when men syketh," is thrice
repeated (10, 48-9, 61). A final envoy-like stanza, paralleling the
proem, brings the complaint into the valentine tradition. Braddy
noted parallels with Graunson's *La complainte amoureuse de
seint Valentin*, and thought "the French and English poems are to
be regarded as companion pieces" (p. 56, disputed by Bennett in
his review, p. 37).

"In sory tyme I spende / My lyf" (*Compl d'Am* 24-5) is the
title of a song. Part of the complete text has been discovered by

Stanley; it shows the informal complaint before Chaucer refined it:

> In sory tyme my lyf is y-spent
> and euer so lengur more and more
> and ӡut wel more but hyt amende
> y may not liue y nam but lore
> hure loue to lenun and y ne may
> for sykurlyche y wot hyt wel

Complaint to my Mortal Foe, a modified ballade, begs his "mortal fo, which I best loue and serue" to "mercy have and routhe." Sandwiched between the direct petitions to his lady are prayers to St. Valentine, Cupid, and Venus to intercede "that to her grace my lady shulde me take." This and the next lyric, not included by Robinson, are printed by Skeat (IV, xxvii-xxxi).

Verbal echoes of this lyric are found in the *Complaint to my Lodesterre* (39, 40 = *Mortal Foe* 29, 31). As in the *Complaynt d'Amours* and *The Complaint of Mars*, the lover justifies his right to bewail: "no wight has greater cause." The cause is nothing new: she who should be his "hertes leche" gives him no remedy. His lodestar has become his mortal foe. The final (seventh) stanza serves as an envoy to "noble seint Valentyne," closing with a homely proverb on his frustrations:

> For yet wiste I never noon, of my lyue,
> So litel hony in so fayre hyve.

What techniques can deepen simple complaints like the foregoing, give them a perspective and relate them to people? The simplest device is a narrative frame, which of necessity introduces a second character, the poet, who overhears the complainant. On the other hand, if the lover meets his lady, she might then explain why she is cruel and the complaint would break down and turn into a debate (like *De Clerico et Puella* or *The Notbrowne Mayde*).

The narrative may include a temple of Venus, lists of disconsolate lovers and obdurate mistresses, protestations of humility,

and scientific accounts of Nature. An author so minded may keep
the kernel of his complaint and, as in the *Book of the Duchess* or
The Isle of Ladies, evolve a full-scale dream vision. At this stage
the complaint shrinks to an interpolated lyric.

Chaucer wrote four extended complaints.

A Complaint unto Pity is simple polite verse: narrative does
not overwhelm complaint, and biographical allusions are absent.
"A scaffolding of abstraction is erected; and a process of analysis
into conventional patterns brings to an end any personal emotion," summarized Clemen (p. 182). Pittock, on the other hand,
sees Chaucer "exploring the nature and importance of compas-
sion" (p. 161). Rather is Chaucer exploring the genre to see how
far he can stretch it without breaking. That he succeeded can be
gauged from its fifteenth-century imitations.

Nor is the poem ambiguous. The first clue comes in Stanza 5:
the action is all in the lover's mind, the allegory mirrors his own
worst fears: "But yet encreseth me this wonder newe, / That no
wight wot that she is ded, but I." The second clue is in the Pity-
Grace equation, the same "pitee, mercy . . . grace" syndrome
(*Lady* 17) writ large, for example, in "The All Virtuous She"
(Robbins, *Sec. Lyrics*, No. 131), *The Complaint of the Black
Knight* (477-83), or *The Temple of Glas* (1132-7), where Venus
explicitly orders the young lady:

> Vnto ȝour grace fulli hym receyue,
> In my presence, bicause he haþ so long
> Holli ben ȝoures, as ȝe may conceyue
> That, from ȝoure merci nov if ȝe him weyue,
> I wil my self recorden cruelte
> In ȝoure persone, and gret lak of pite.

Two extended complaints present the woman's side.

The Complaint of Venus—which isn't about Venus—para-
phrases or translates three ballades (Skeat, 1, 400-4; Piaget, pp.
411-16) by Graunson, lauded as "flour of hem that make in
Fraunce." Graunson had written lyrics to Isabella, Duchess of
York, and both Skeat (1, 87) and Braddy (p. 83) believe that
Chaucer too was writing (about 1385) to this "Princesse."

Although termed "compleynt," the three ballades (in strict form) are conventional praises. The first tells how "every wight preiseth his gentilesse." The second describes the symptoms of love (anticipating Troilus) and the troubles caused by Jelosie:

> Ther doth no wyght nothing so resonable
> That al nys harm in her ymagenyng.

The third affirms "To love hym best ne shal I never repente."

In Graunson, a man addresses his "douce et plaisant dame." In Chaucer, a woman speaks. Yet court-courtly expressions of love are so interchangeable that no reorientation was necessary. The second ballade could serve either sex; all the first and third need is a change of pronoun. "Il a en li bonté, beauté, et grace" becomes "In him is bountee, wisdom, gouernaunce." "Honneur la vuelt sur toutes honnores" is neutral: "Honour honoureth him for his noblesse." *The Complaint of Venus* underscores better than most love lyrics the complete artificiality and unreality of the game of love, by its disregard of the distinctive psychology of the sexes.

"The Compleynt of Anelida the quene upon fals Arcite" is found in eight manuscripts as part of *Anelida and Arcite*, and separately in five others—not surprisingly, for the epic invocation and the early story of Thebes are inharmonious with the tender complaint. Using mythological figures, however, this story presents a more credible motivation than obduracy: a devoted mistress jilted by her lover. The situation may be credible, but it need not be factual. Are Arcite and Anelida the Earl of Oxford and Philippa de Coucy or the Count and Countess of Ormonde? Robinson gives all the arguments (p. 788).

The metrical virtuosity of this poem, inspired by Machaut's *Le lai de la souscie*, has received much praise from Ker (p. 237) and Clemen (p. 198). The last stanza of each strophe has twenty-seven short lines, two- and single-stress, with two uniting tail-rhymes (Fabin, p. 271).

The major reason for the success of Anelida's complaint is that Chaucer created a character reacting spontaneously and colloquially to her grief; she is not a talking doll with three inches of pre-recorded tape in her sawdust. Anelida admits, for example, that Arcite will never be capable of remaining faithful:

> For thogh I hadde yow to-morrowe ageyn,
> I myght as wel holde Aperill fro reyn
> As holde yow, to make yow be stidfast.

How can she be such a fool as to want him back? "And yet desireth that myn harm be more." Nevertheless her diction is thoroughly conventional: "I wil non other medecyne," "sleen me with the peyne." How lifeless do these same expressions become when spoken by a puppet, for example, the *man* in the earlier *A Complaint to his Lady* (*Lady* 17, 31, 46, 51, 101-2 = *Anel* 216, 222, 236, 214, 247).

Does *The Complaint of Mars* covertly allude to a court scandal? Many critics have dug up liaisons. If not a *roman à clef*, then may it not be a *jeu d'esprit* to entertain the court? "Chaucer's fun is that of telling lovers exactly the opposite of what they ought to be told or hope to be told on St. Valentine's Day," wrote Stillwell (p. 73). Stillwell should be complemented by Clemen, who similarly contrasted "the convention and the break-through of the unconventional touches that shatter its dignity" (p. 194).

The Complaint of Mars opens with a clichéd but not ungraceful valentine. Then come eighteen stanzas of narrative which, with churl's speech ("unto bed thei go") balancing lord's apostrophes ("myn hertes lady swete"), turn the gentility of a night visit into a backdoor escapade. On top of all this, presented as dawn songs (*Mars* 25-6), follow five complaints which so completely reject conventions as to form anti-complaints, leading to "a climax of increasing originality and wit, of increasing breadth of generalization, of increasing directness in addressing his audience" (Stillwell, p. 85):

(1) Essentially conventional: "For this day in her servise shal I dye."

(2) Conventional opening: "To whom shal I than pleyne?" to introduce a problem in situational ethics: should the faithful suitor of an obdurate lady remain chaste? "But he be fals, no

lover hath his ese"—a far remove from the courtly rules.

(3) Philosophical probing on the nature of love: why does God let people fall in love, when love's joy "ne lasteth not the tweynkelyng of an ye"? "The lament is obviously moving away from the sphere of the French *Complainte* and approaching that of the middle-Latin *planctus*" (Clemen, p. 196).

(4) Another anti-conventional tern: the lady is not responsible for provoking love, "but he that wroghte hit" (the Brooch of Thebes analogy). Not the God of Love but the God of Divine Justice is here criticized.

(5) An appeal to the courtly audience: this could happen to you. If Venus cannot help herself, how can she help you in your affairs? "Ye oghte have some compassioun / Of my disese."

The complaint, by definition, ignores serious problems. *A Complaint unto Pity* treats conventionally a non-serious problem: a lady is obdurate. *The Complaint of Mars* treats realistically a serious problem: what happens to illicit lovers who are caught in the act? When characterization becomes more complex, frame more elaborate, problems more immediate, then the complaint breaks down. The way out leads to *Troilus and Criseyde*.

Later, Chaucer wrote several short poems disrespectful of the game of love, seemingly continuing the genuine skepticism of Mars.

To Rosemounde is a romp, full of fun-poking at the computer-match praise of a mistress—who might even be a little girl. Seven-year-old Princess Isabel, perchance? (Rickert, "A Letter," p. 255). Though his lady with her "chekes rounde" does him "no daliaunce"—at this, the lover should be dying—yet seeing her dance is "an oynement unto my wounde." So in love, he is like a "pyk walwed in galauntyne" (a phallic pike, according to Reiss, p. 64). The chattiness is deceptive; the poetry is artificial: the form rigid, the style rhetorical—in the first four lines examples of *exclamatio, translatio, imago,* and *expolitio* (Davies, p. 328).

Against Women Unconstant or *Newfangelnesse* is another strict ballade; it exposes the nether parts of courtly love, a fickle mistress: "In stede of blew, thus may ye were al grene." For this lyric, Chaucer went to several French poets, especially to Machaut, for the refrain, "Qu'en lieu de bleu, Dame, vous vestez vert."

Merciles Beaute is a fine example of a triple rondel. The catchy first line was quoted verbatim in a pseudo-Lydgate poem (Skeat, VII, 281). The first two rondels are conventional: the lover wounded by his mistress' piercing beauty; the lover dying since Beauty has exiled Pity (cf. *Pity* 22). The third rondel is a reversal: the lover giving thanks for not falling in love.

The first rondel is a fairly close rendering of a virelai by Des-champs, with its "Ne les douls regars endurer / De voz biaux yeux." The conceit, however, is common, as in Graunson: "Mon cueur est sailly par mes yeux." The third rondel resembles another poem by Deschamps, a rondel, "Puis qu'Amour ay servi trestout mon temps," and a ballade by the Duc de Berry, "Puiz qu'a Amours suis si gras eschapé."

Chaucer's obverted love lyrics, however, were just as conven-tional (and as influenced by the French) as the direct complaints; and the fifteenth century saw the spread of this sub-genre (Rob-bins, *Sec. Lyrics*, Nos. 207-12).

Chaucer's five moralizing and four biographical lyrics may be dismissed more briefly, though they have sparked numerous articles, no doubt because of their historical overtones. To whom did Chaucer present *Truth*? Who was Bukton?

The theme of *Gentilesse* was discussed in the *Wife of Bath's Tale* (1109-70) and summarized in the *Clerk's Tale* (1570-8): "Bountee cometh al of God, not of the streen / Of which they been engendered and ybore." As well as Boethius (III, pr. 6), Chaucer drew on Dante and the *Roman de la rose*.

Truth or *Balade de bon conseyl* shows only general influence from Boethius. In fact, Brusendorff found a French ballade similar to *Truth* in the same manuscript (pp. 151-2). Comment has con-centrated on the envoy's "Thou Vache"—in one manuscript only out of the twenty-three, and probably tagged on later (though "beste" may anticipate "Vache"). No one has contested Rickert's identification of Sir Philip de la Vache, a friend of Chaucer's, in disfavor with the king from 1386 to 1389. The ballade may consequently have been written "to bring him encouragement or consolation in misfortune" (Robinson, p. 861, following Rickert, p. 224).

In one manuscript (Cambridge Univ. Ii. 3. 21), the triple ballade *Fortune* (and *The Former Age*) are added under the text of Chaucer's translation of Boethius at Book II, m. 5. *Fortune* also resembles several of Deschamps' ballades (Patch, p. 381). The concluding stanza of the third ballade forms the envoy, and consequently cannot be an afterthought (as the envoys to *Truth*, *Lak of Stedfastnesse*, and *Purse* might well be). Presumably it addresses the Dukes of Lancaster, York, and Gloucester, after 1390 sole dispensers ("three of you or tweyne") of royal grants.

Lak of Stedfastnesse, with Boethius (II, m. 8) as a starting point, diverges from the Boethian stress on love and presents the *un*-natural order of society: "Trouthe is put doun." The refrain is imitated from Deschamps' *ballade* no. 234: "Tout se destruit et par defaute de garde." Estimates of the date vary: Robinson (p. 862) favors 1386-9; Brusendorff (p. 174), Braddy (p. 67), and Norton-Smith (p. 123) a date nearer 1399.

The poem approximates the evils-of-the-age tradition; one could almost rewrite Chaucer from single lines of other jeremiads. The envoy is similarly traditional: poets advised kings ("Goo forth kyng reule the by sapience" or "rule the be reson and vpritte sitte"). It was so conventional, in fact, that Lydgate incorporated this envoy in his "Prayer for England," where "it satisfactorily dovetails into the whole poem" (Robbins, *Hist. Poems*, p. 389).

The first half of *The Former Age* paraphrases Boethius (II, m. 5); the last, Ovid, *Roman de la rose*, Machaut. Norton-Smith sees a personal feeling (especially in the last stanza) of an immediate breakdown of society into "manslauhtre and mordre" (p. 120). Yet it too resembles other lyrics which likewise decry "Ielesye, doubleness, and tresoun."

What of the four biographical lyrics?

Adam Scriveyn (about 1386) is a squib. Scholarly debate has raged on the scribe's identity (best bet: Brusendorff's Adam Pinckhurst, p. 57). "The very person to whom Chaucer's *Lenvoy a Scogan* was addressed," according to Skeat (1, 83), was Henry, tutor to the four sons of Henry IV, in whose "morale balade" (about 1410) *Gentilesse* was inserted complete. Chaucer's letter is usually dated about 1391, the year of the great floods (*Scogan* 14), amusingly depicted as Venus' tears at Scogan's defection from her worship. French minimizes any suggestion of a plea for assistance (p. 292). A second letter, the *Envoy to Bukton*, is another near-ballade. Kuhl's suggested addressee, Sir Peter Bukton, has displaced Tatlock's and Hulbert's candidate, Sir Robert (Robinson, p. 864). Chaucer takes a typical theme, and jokingly warns his friend against "the sorwe and wo that is in mariage." Then he advises Bukton to read all about it from the "Wyf of Bathe." Kittredge, Lowes, and Brusendorff have produced various ballades of Deschamps which satirize marriage, especially nos. 823 and 929, which latter uses the slavery of marriage imagery: "J'ay demouré entre les Sarrasins, / Esclave esté en pays de Surie."

A bouleversement of the love complaint, *Purse* has Chaucer begging money from his "Queen of confort" (an epithet from *A B C* 77)—his empty purse! Chaucer presented his petition with the envoy to the new King Henry IV about February, 1400, and was speedily rewarded. Legge (pp. 18-21), Giffin (pp. 89-105), and Ferris give historical documentation; Scott thinks the promptitude due to the political usefulness of Chaucer's son and nephew as henchmen to the new king (p. 85). Chaucer's models may have been Deschamps' *ballade* no. 247, requesting help in 1381 from Charles V, or Froissart's *ballade* no. 31 (Smith, p. 31). But these, and Hoccleve's rondel, "Compleynt to Lady Moneye," all forgo the witty money-mistress personification.

An A B C (about 1380), a paraphrase of a French ornamental devotion in Deguileville's lengthy *Pèlerinage de l'ame* (about 1340), is highly praised by Clemen (pp. 175-9), and even more highly by Reiss (pp. 57-62). Chaucer's version is not that of a "grant translateur:"

> Fleeing, I flee for socour to thy tente
> Me for to hyde from tempest ful of drede,
> Biseching you that ye you not absente,
> Though I be wikke. O help yit at this nede!

It is a close copy of the French (both texts from Skeat, i, 263):

> Fuiant m'en viens a ta tente
> Moy mucier pour la tormente
> Qui ou monde me tempeste.
> Pour mon pechié ne t'absente,
> A moy garder met t'entente,
> A mon besoing soiez preste.

To read into this copy an "often frantic movement" is to read too much between the lines. Compared with the religious lyrics of the fourteenth century, *An A B C* is novel—in Brown's anthology there is nothing like it. By the fifteenth century, it is one of the many polished devotional pieces. This was not Chaucer's only venture into religious verse. He included two isolable prayers in the prologues to the *Second Nun's Tale* (29-77) and to the *Prioress's Tale* (467-80).

Chaucer's lyric reputation depends on his being "first with the mostest." Without Chaucer there could not have been a Hoccleve or a Lydgate, and—in that case—fifteenth-century court poets would have been imitating Gower's *Cinquante Balades*—in French! From Chaucer the English court poets learned what the international French set were saying and how they were saying it. Hence in the following century the dominant forms were rhyme royal and monk's stanza, the dominant theme court-courtly love, and the dominant genres dream vision and lyric. This was Chaucer's bequest to the Chaucerians.

* * * * *

The past decade has seen some twenty-two articles and notes on Chaucer's lyrics, but none, despite five papers on *The Com-*

plaint of Mars and three on *Scogan,* has affected the conclusions originally presented in this chapter in 1967. Of a few lyrics, new texts (all previously known) have been printed, but only one hitherto unrecorded text (of *Purse,* in the Mellish MS. now at Nottingham University) has turned up. Among critical papers, one might note Wimsatt's, which has reinforced the parallels between Chaucer's *Anelida and Arcite* and Machaut and Frois-sart; Hultin's belief that a "conventional Valentine poem has become in Chaucer's hands an ironic commentary on the nature of that behaviour celebrated in courtly poetry" (p. 74); and Cherniss's discovery of unity in the juxtaposed elements of *The Complaint of Mars* and *The Complaint of Venus,* and linking Isabel Langeley (if one can accept John Holland as the lover) to an "ironic" reapplication of Graunson.

Articles about the lyrics will routinely continue to appear, but I doubt any kind of critical approach will elevate these little poems into the masterpieces of the criticasters. They happen to be minor poems because (as I have said) they are indeed minor —occasional, ephemeral, run-of-the-mill. *Purse* is fun and a true Chaucerian *jeu d'esprit,* but *Gentilesse* and *Truth* are merely exemplars of technically adequate platitudes, written for the moment and circulated among a few friends at court.

One speculative comment about Chaucer's love lyrics might be offered here in conclusion.

Given the social conditions, it was inevitable that Chaucer, a young French-speaking valet de chambre in a French-speaking royal court, wrote his earliest poems in French. That none of these French lyrics remain is certainly not surprising. For who would preserve little exercises by an unknown, undistinguished commoner, who had yet to profit from his family ties with the mistress of England's most powerful magnate? Rarely would any such vers de société be preserved. Two early fifteenth-century rondeaux added to a flyleaf of Honoré Bonet's *L'Arbre des Batailles* (in MS. Royal 20. c. viii) are exceptional. But they suggest the sort of verse Chaucer (and the other squires in royal service) would have been writing. Here is one of them:

Je nay pouoir de viure en joye
Et si ne puis mourir de deul.
Je ne puis hair ne ne veul
Celle qui ces dolours menuoye.
Ellas et coment gueriroye
De la doleur dont je me deul.
[Je nay pouoir de viure en joye
Et si ne puis mourir de deul.]
Sun jour amours abandonnoye,
Je scay gun gracieux acuel
Mi ratroyroit par vn doulx eul,
Et puis je recomenceroye.
Je nay pouoir [de viure en joye].

This rondeau, it will be noted, is reminiscent of lines in the *Complaynt D'Amours*, attributed (perhaps erroneously) to Chaucer:

And in this wyse and in dispayr I live
In love; nay, but in dispayr I dye!
But shal I thus yow my deth foryive,
That causeles doth me this sorwe drye?

But French lyrics of this type, whether by Chaucer or any other court writer, did not set the pattern for English love lyrics. For the next 150 years, such poems derive from the few specimens that have been preserved in the English of Geoffrey Chaucer. The full impact of Chaucer on the English lyric will ultimately be demonstrated through the English Chaucerians, and the Father's part will be clarified through his Children's imitations. That chapter in literary history, however, has still to be written.

BIBLIOGRAPHY

Bennett, J.A.W., "*Chaucer and the French Poet Graunson* by Haldeen Braddy" [Review]. *MÆ*, 18 (1949), 35-37.

————. *The Parlement of Foules: An Interpretation*. Oxford: Clarendon Press, 1957.

Braddy, Haldeen. *Chaucer and the French Poet Graunson*. 1947. Rpt. Port Washington, N.Y.: Kennikat Press, 1968.

Brown, Carleton, ed. *Religious Lyrics of the XIVth Century*. 1924. 2nd ed. 1952. Rpt. Oxford: Clarendon Press, 1957.

Brusendorff, Aage. *The Chaucer Tradition*. London: Oxford Univ. Press, 1925.

Cherniss, Michael D. "Chaucer's *Anelida and Arcite*: Some Conjectures." *ChauR*, 5 (1970), 9-21.

Clemen, Wolfgang. *Chaucer's Early Poetry*. Trans. C.A.M. Sym. London: Methuen, 1963.

Clogan, Paul M. "The Textual Reliability of Chaucer's Lyrics: *A Complaint to His Lady*." *M&H*, 5 (1974), 183-89.

David, Alfred. "Chaucer's Good Counsel to Scogan." *ChauR*, 3 (1969), 265-74.

Davies, R.T. *Medieval English Lyrics*. London: Faber and Faber, 1963. Evanston, Ill.: Northwestern Univ. Press, 1964.

Davis, Norman. "Chaucer's *Gentilesse*: A Forgotten Manuscript with Some Proverbs." *RES*, 20 (1969), 43-50.

Dean, Nancy. "Chaucer's Complaint: A Genre Descended from the *Heroides*." *CL*, 19 (1967), 1-27.

Doyle, A.I., and George B. Pace. "A New Chaucer Manuscript." *PMLA*, 83 (1968), 22-34.

————. "Further Texts of Chaucer's Minor Poems." *SB*, 28 (1975), 41-61.

Fabin, Madeleine. "On Chaucer's 'Anelida and Arcite'." *MLN*, 34 (1919), 266-72.

Ferris, Sumner. "The Date of Chaucer's Final Annuity and of the 'Complaint to his Empty Purse'." *MP*, 65 (1967), 45-52.

Finnel, Andrew J. "The Poet as Sunday Man: 'The Complaint of Chaucer to his Purse'." *ChauR*, 8 (1973), 147-58.

French, W.H. "The Meaning of Chaucer's *Envoy to Scogan*." *PMLA*, 48 (1933), 289-92.

Friedman, Albert B. "The Late Mediaeval Ballade and the Origin of Broadside Ballades." *MÆ*, 27 (1958), 95-110.

Giffin, Mary. *Studies on Chaucer and His Audience*. Hull, Québec: Les Éditions 'L'Éclair', 1956.

Haskell, Ann S. "Lyrics and Lyrical in the Works of Chaucer: The Poet in His Literary Context." *English Symposium Papers*, III. Ed. Douglas Shepard. Fredonia, N.Y.: SUNY College at Fredonia, 1972, pp. 1-45.

Hultin, Neil C. "Anti-Courtly Elements in Chaucer's *Complaint of Mars*." *AnM*, 19 (1968), 58-75.

Ker, W.P. *English Literature Medieval*. London: Williams and Norgate, 1905.

Kittredge, G.L. "Chaucer's 'Envoy to Bukton'." *MLN*, 24 (1909), 14-15.

Koch, John. *Geoffrey Chaucer: Kleinere Dichtungen*. Heidelberg: Winter, 1928.

Kuhl, E.P. "Chaucer's 'My Maistre Bukton'." *PMLA*, 38 (1923), 115-32.

Laird, Edgar S. "Astrology and Irony in Chaucer's *Complaint of Mars*." *ChauR*, 6 (1972), 229-31.

Lampe, David. "The Truth of A 'Vache': The Homely Homily of Chaucer's 'Truth'." *PLL*, 9 (1973), 311-13.

Legge, M. Dominica. " 'The Gracious Conqueror'." *MLN*, 68 (1953), 18-21.

Lenaghan, R.T. "Chaucer's *Envoy to Scogan*: The Uses of Literary Convention." *ChauR*, 10 (1975), 46-61.

Lounsbury, T.R. *Studies in Chaucer: His Life and Writings*. 3 vols. 1892. Rpt. New York: Russell & Russell, 1962.

Lowes, John L. "The Chaucerian 'Merciles Beaute' and Three Poems of Deschamps." *MLR*, 5 (1910), 33-39.

———. "The Date of the 'Envoy to Bukton'." *MLN*, 27 (1912), 45-48.

Ludlum, Charles D. "Heavenly Word-Play in Chaucer's *Complaint to his Purse*." *N&Q*, 23 (1976), 391-92.

MacCracken, Henry Noble. "An English Friend of Charles d'Orleans." *PMLA*, 26 (1911), 142-80.

Merrill, Rodney. "Chaucer's Brooch of Thebes: The Unity of 'The Complaint of Mars,' and 'The Complaint of Venus'." *Literary Monographs*, 5. Ed. Eric Rothstein. Madison: Univ. of Wisconsin, 1973, pp. 1-61.

Moore, Arthur K. "Chaucer's Lost Songs." *JEGP*, 48 (1949), 196-208.

―――. "Chaucer's Use of the Lyric as an Ornament of Style." *CL*, 3 (1951), 33-46.

Muir, Kenneth. "Unpublished Poems in the Devonshire MS." *Leeds*, 6 (1944-45), 235-83.

Nicolas, Sir Harris (intro. memoir). *Pickering's Aldine Poets*, VI. 1845. For further bibliographical detail, see Eleanor Prescott Hammond. *Chaucer: A Bibliographical Memoir*. 1908. Rpt. New York: P. Smith, 1933, pp. 140-41.

Nichols, Robert E. "Chaucer's *Fortune, Truth,* and *Gentilesse*: The 'Last' Unpublished Manuscript Transcriptions." *Speculum*, 44 (1969), 46-50.

North, J.D. "Kalenderes Enlumyned Ben They: Some Astronomical Themes in Chaucer." *RES*, 20 (1969), 129-54, 257-83, 418-44.

Norton-Smith, John. "Chaucer's *Etas Prima*." *MÆ*, 32 (1963), 117-24.

―――. "Chaucer's Epistolary Style." In *Essays on Style and Language: Linguistic and Critical Approaches to Literary Style*. Ed. Roger Fowler. London: Routledge and Kegan Paul, 1966, pp. 157-65.

―――. "The Complaint: Venus, Pity and Mars." In John Norton-Smith, *Geoffrey Chaucer*. London: Routledge and Kegan Paul, 1974, pp. 16-34.

Owen, Charles A., Jr. "Thy Drasty Rhyming. . . ." *SP*, 63 (1966), 533-64.

Patch, Howard Rollin. "Chaucer and Lady Fortune." *MLR*, 22 (1927), 377-88.

Payne, Robert O. *The Key of Remembrance: A Study of Chaucer's Poetics*. 1963. Rpt. Westport, Conn.: Greenwood Press, 1973.

Piaget, Arthur. "Oton de Graunson et ses poésies." *Romania*, 19 (1890), 237-59, 403-48.

Pittock, Malcolm. "Chaucer: 'The Complaint unto Pity'." *Criticism*, 1 (1959), 160-68.

Polzella, Marion L. " 'The Craft So Long to Lerne': Poet and Lover in Chaucer's 'Envoy to Scogan' and *Parliament of Fowls*." *ChauR*, 10 (1976), 279-86.

Reiss, Edmund. "Dusting Off the Cobwebs: A New Look at Chaucer's Lyrics." *ChauR*, 1 (1966), 55-65.

Rickert, Edith. " 'Thou Vache'." *MP*, 11 (1913), 209-25.

———. "A Leaf from a Fourteenth-Century Letter Book." *MP*, 25 (1928), 249-55.

Robbins, Rossell Hope, ed. *Secular Lyrics of the XIVth and XVth Centuries*. 1952. Rev. ed. Oxford: Clarendon, 1955.

———, ed. *Historical Poems of the XIVth and XVth Centuries*. New York: Columbia Univ. Press, 1959.

———. "Chaucer's 'To Rosemounde'." *SLitI*, 4 (1971), 73-81.

———. "The Chaucerian Apocrypha." In *A Manual of the Writings in Middle English 1050-1500*. Gen. ed. Albert E. Hartung. New Haven: Connecticut Academy, 1973, vol. 4, chapter 11, pp. 1061-1101, 1286-1303.

———. "The Vintner's Son: French Wine in English Bottles." In *Eleanor of Aquitaine: Patron and Politician*. Ed. William W. Kibler. Austin: Univ. of Texas Press, 1976, pp. 147-72.

Robinson, F.N., ed. *The Works of Geoffrey Chaucer*. 1933. 2nd ed. Boston: Houghton-Mifflin, 1957.

Rogers, William E. *Image and Abstraction: Six Middle English Religious Lyrics*. Anglistica 18. Copenhagen: Rosenkilde og Bagger, 1972, pp. 82-106.

Scott, Florence R. "A New Look at 'The Complaint of Chaucer to his Empty Purse'." *ELN*, 2 (1964), 81-87.

Skeat, Walter W., ed. *The Complete Works of Geoffrey Chaucer*. 6 vols. Oxford: Clarendon, 1894. Vol. 7, *Chaucerian and Other Pieces*. Oxford: Clarendon, 1978, Rpt. 1960.

———, ed. *The Minor Poems*. 1888. Rev. 2nd ed. Oxford: Clarendon, 1896.

Smith, J.Norton. See under Norton-Smith, John.

Smith, Roland M. "Five Notes on Chaucer and Froissart." *MLN*, 66 (1951), 27-32.

Southall, Raymond. "The Devonshire Manuscript Collection of Early Tudor Poetry, 1532-41." *RES*, 15 (1964), 142-50.

Stanley, E.G. "An Inedited Scrap of ME Verse from the West Midlands." *NM*, 60 (1959), 287-88.

Stillwell, Gardiner. "Convention and Individuality in Chaucer's *Complaint of Mars*." *PQ*, 35 (1956), 69-89.

Thomson, Patricia. "The 'Canticus Troili': Chaucer and Petrarch." *CL*, 11 (1959), 313-28.

Wilkins, Ernest Hatch. " 'Cantus Troili'." *ELH*, 16 (1949), 167-73.

Wimsatt, James I. *"Anelida and Arcite*: A Narrative of Complaint and Comfort." *ChauR*, 5 (1970), 1-8.

EIGHTEEN

D. W. ROBERTSON, JR.

The Book of the Duchess

The *Book of the Duchess* is an elegy for Blanche, Duchess of Lancaster, who died of the plague on September 12, 1369. At that time her husband the Duke, John of Gaunt, was campaigning on the continent, whence he did not return until November 3. He established an annual memorial service to be held each year at St. Paul's, London, arranged for a tomb for Blanche and for himself to be erected there, and endowed two chantry priests to sing masses daily. As we learn from Froissart, Blanche was an extremely attractive young woman, and at the time of her death she was among the highest ranking ladies at the English court. Chaucer's poem was probably (although not certainly) used in connection with one of the annual services, perhaps in 1374, when the Duke was able to attend for the first time. In any event, the poem should be thought of as a part of a ceremony of considerable dignity and national importance held for members of the royal and Lancastrian households and great men of London.

Briefly, as the poem opens, the speaker, echoing the words of Froissart, describes himself as being overcome by "sorwful ymaginacioun" and unable to sleep. After reading the Ovidian tale of Seys and Alcyone (somewhat altered to suit the purposes of the poem), he is enabled to fall asleep. In a dream he awakens at dawn to hear birds singing a "solempne servise." His chamber is decorated with scenes from the story of Troy, which appears in the windows, and the "text and glose" of the *Roman de la rose*, which appears on the walls. Riding out, he witnesses the beginning of a hunt, led by "th'emperour Octovyen." After being led by a whelp through an earthly paradise, he finds a beardless Black Knight under an oak. The Knight sings a tuneless lament for his deceased beloved that the dreamer apparently overhears. But the dreamer, feigning ignorance, questions him at length. He discovers that the Knight has lost his "bliss" in a chess game with Fortune. In youth he gave himself up to love and idleness, saw his lady, and was overcome by her beauties and virtues. These are described at length in what has sometimes been called the "elegy proper." When he approached her first, awkward and ashamed, she would have nothing to do with him. "Another yere," when she realized his good intentions, he was granted mercy and thereafter lived under her "governaunce." On further questioning, he admits that his lady is dead. The "hert-huntyng" is over, the king rides to a "long castel" on a rich hill wherein a bell strikes twelve, and the dreamer awakens. The poem contains many echoes of fashionable French poetry, and is enlivened by touches of humor.

Modern discussions of the poem usually follow, in general outline, the account of G. L. Kittredge (1915), wherein the Knight, identified as the bereaved John of Gaunt, is described as being a "finished gentleman," whereas the dreamer is naive, full of "child-like wonder," and "stupefied by long suffering." Kittredge regarded love as "the only life that became the gently nurtured" so that "submission to the god [of Love] was their natural duty" (p. 63). He felt that the dream itself was "near to the actual phenomena of dream life." Following this general outline, H. R. Patch (1939) called the dreamer a "poor dolt" (p. 29) and described the poem in colorful terms, saying that it is "full of the high frivolity of Courtly Love." Kittredge's views were repeated by H. S. Bennett (1947), but he also expressed some dissatisfaction with the poem. It is, he said, structurally faulty, containing much that is "derivative and crude," and lacking in "profound emotion or any piercing thought" (p. 36). Adverse criticism also appeared in the discussion of J. S. P. Tatlock (1950), where the poem is said to be repetitious and dilatory, and the dreamer, who is here not Chaucer, indifferent to "human reality" (p. 30). The dreamer continued to suffer in the discussion of Kemp Malone (1951), where his lack of awareness is said to be an inconsistency on Chaucer's part. Malone also asserted that Chaucer was forced to turn the marriage of John of Gaunt (the Black Knight) into "an extra-marital love affair for the sake of the conventions of courtly love" (p. 40). The dream, he said, is "realistic."

Kittredge's "naive" dreamer has not lacked defenders, however, and the integrity of the poem has been vigorously supported. James R. Kreuzer (1951) denied the dreamer's naiveté altogether, refusing to identify the dreamer and the speaker (pp. 544-5). The dreamer's lack of awareness, he explained, was "consciously contrived" to enable him to administer a cathartic remedy. In a long and carefully wrought article, B. H. Bronson (1952) elaborated the idea of the dreamer's "tact," at the same time describing the Knight and Blanche as ideal "courtly lovers." Here the Knight acts as a "surrogate" for the dreamer. His description of Blanche is both his own (i.e., the Duke's) and Chaucer's. However, D. S. Brewer (1953), calling attention to the public presentation of the poem and to its "conventionality," warned that it was not "a private outcry of grief nor a private consolation" (pp. 44-5). Brewer considered the humor of the poem to be largely unintentional and the portrait of Blanche to be archetypal. With some similar misgivings about Chaucer's own participation, Donald C. Baker (1955) made the description of the lady the work of a "peer" (John of Gaunt) rather than of the poet, since the expression of such noble grief was, he asserted, beyond the comprehension of the poet-dreamer. The poet's inadequacy as a personal eulogist was also emphasized by Stephen Manning (1956), but at the expense of the dreamer once more, who is said to be characterized by "nonpareil dullwittedness." In a later article (1958) Manning's dreamer still displays "customary stupidity," and the

portrait of Blanche is said to show the influence of the trouba-
dours and of the traditions of "courtly love."

Professor Malone's observations on extra-marital "courtly
love" were answered elaborately by John Lawlor (1956), who
maintained that such love, stemming from the traditions of the
Roman de la rose, could exist between married persons, especially
in England, and that Chaucer halted his account of the love affair
at its highest point, which is not marriage but the acceptance of
the lover (p. 631). This is, Lawlor assures us, the "highest earthly
good," a good that the Knight has enjoyed but that the dreamer,
whose love is unrequited, has not. In a briefer and more recent
statement of his thesis (1966), the same author, using a hint from
Bronson, makes the poet a "substitute figure for the real
mourner." The dreamer is further exculpated by W. H. French
(1957), for, it is said, the song he overheard might well be taken
simply as a conventional lyric without specific personal application. In Charles Muscatine's treatment of the poem's style (1957),
the dreamer is a lover, but the realism or "factualism" of the
dream itself is seriously questioned. R. M. Lumiansky (1959)
maintained, however, that the narrator in the poem suffered from
bereavement, not love-longing, and that he, Alcyone, and the
Knight are united in grief. An extended argument is presented to
show that the poem consoles both the dreamer and the Knight.
But the dreamer was severely criticized once more by Dorothy
Bethurum (1959), who found him obtuse, a failure as a lover,
and ignorant of currently fashionable classical lore. He was de-
fended once more by Joseph E. Grennen (1964) for his deft
"psychological maneuvering" that reflects conventional treatments of *cardiaca passio*. Finally, in a carefully reasoned article,
J. Burke Severs (1964) maintained that the speaker's condition at
the opening was not due to unrequited love, and that the dreamer
never speaks as a lover. He, speaking for Chaucer, keeps the
Black Knight talking until he can face his sorrow "in plain
utterance."

These are the principal variations on the pattern of interpretation established by Professor Kittredge. The questions that have

concerned scholars most are (1) whether the speaker at the open-ing suffers from unrequited love or from grief as a result of bereavement; (2) whether the dreamer is naive, or even awkward, or, on the other hand, courteous and considerate; and (3) whether the consolation is well applied, and if so how it is applied. Some of the works mentioned above, especially those of Bronson, Lawlor, Lumiansky, and Severs, contain elaborate treatments of the third question that cannot be summarized adequately in a few words. In addition to the works mentioned above, there have been at least two extensive critical appreciations of the poem in recent years, one by Donald C. Baker (1958), using "archetypal imagery," and one by Georgia Ronan Crampton (1963). These read a little like pleasant afternoon lectures on abstract paintings, although the tendency to treat Chaucer's poem as a work of modern expressionism is by no means confined to these two essays.

There have been a number of efforts to explain specific details in the poem. John M. Steadman (1956) suggested that the "whelp" might be a symbol of marital fidelity, calling attention to dogs in Alciati's *Emblemata*, in Pierius' *Hieroglyphica*, and on late medieval funerary monuments. Beryl Rowland (1962) sug-gested that the "twelve ferses" may constitute a reference to the signs of the Zodiac, and that the chess game in the poem might be a variant of the standard game. She also suggested (1963) that the "round tour of yvoyre" used in the description of the lady might refer to an ivory chess piece. Turning to the "whelp," the same author (1965) found that Chaucer never commends dogs, and that the whelp may be a kind of nightmare feature of the dream hunt that acts to split the dreamer into two parts (Black Knight and interrogator). James I. Wimsatt (1967), in a careful and detailed article, has shown that the description of Blanche contains definite suggestions of the Blessed Virgin Mary.

The general formulation established by Professor Kittredge was abandoned altogether by D. W. Robertson, Jr. (1962), who considered the "courtly love" that plays such a large part in the usual discussions to be, as it is there used, an irrelevant modern

fantasy. In this account, the Black Knight is said to be no literal
reflection of John of Gaunt, but the erring will of the speaker that
sees the loss of the lady as the loss of a gift of Fortune, while
the dreamer represents the reason. The dream thus contains a
dialogue between what may be considered as two parts of the
same person (pp. 463-5) who represents the mourners for Blanche.
B. F. Huppé and Robertson (1963) sought to interpret the entire
poem in the light of medieval literary theory, offering interpretations of many of its details on the basis of traditional iconography. Here the Knight is not the Duke but a kind of alter-ego
of the dreamer, expressive of grief over the loss of Blanche as a
merely physical object of desire. The details in the description of
Blanche are said to reflect conventional imagery, chiefly Scriptural
in origin, and to point to her spiritual virtues. Some features of
this explanation were elaborated in an essay by Robertson (1965)
in an attempt to place the poem in its historical setting. Chaucer's
poem is here said to be consistent with the conventional themes
of funerary consolation as they are implicit in *The Consolation
of Philosophy* and explicit in the Mass for the Burial of the Dead.
Its surface humor is attributed to the chivalric character of the
audience and to the underlying idea that Chaucer had no desire
to cultivate grief on an occasion of hope and inspiration. The
speaker typifies the initial sorrow of all of the mourners for
Blanche. The Knight and the dreamer are not "characters" but
exemplifications of attitudes, so that the Knight may be dismissed
as soon as the theme of the poem becomes clear. That is, "if the
virtues of the Duchess were an inspiration to reasonable and
noble conduct in life, her memory should continue to inspire
such conduct," not the helpless sorrow of the speaker at the
opening, nor the bitter grief of Alcyone, who has no hope, nor
the sloth of the Man in Black, who has lost his "bliss" to Fortune
and does not understand the implications of the lady's virtue,
even after he has described them in his own words.

It is obvious that further contributions to our knowledge of
the poem must rest on an intensive study of primary materials.
We have hardly begun to understand the French sources. As the

late Rosemond Tuve demonstrated in her study of *Allegorical Imagery* (1966), we may need to revise considerably our general estimate of even such well-known works as the *Roman de la rose*, which is mentioned explicitly in Chaucer's poem. Again, we know very little about the meaning of the dream vision as a poetic form; it is, in any event, certainly not conducive to dream "realism" of the kind envisaged by Kittredge and Malone. Again, we are largely ignorant of the conventions of Gothic iconography as they were manifested in fourteenth-century England. Finally, there are many traits of style, attitude, and demeanor in the England of Edward III that remain obscure. Simple readjustments of the ideas set forth in the secondary sources above without careful attention to primary materials may fatten our bibliographies, but they will not contribute substantially to our knowledge of Chaucer's work, nor to any real appreciation for it.

* * * * *

During the years since the above was written over thirty notes, articles, and chapters in books have been devoted to the *Book of the Duchess*, only a few of which can be mentioned here to illustrate variety of opinion. "Courtly love" has been less popular, although John Gardner (1977) seeks to revive it, praising Chaucer for his "psychological realism" and calling the poem a "celebration of earthly love." The character of the dreamer still causes difficulty. Perhaps we should remember that Chaucer was well-known to his audience, some of whom were his superiors, so that, not being a pompous man, he avoided taking himself too seriously, although he had important things to say. The serious side of the dreamer is emphasized in two Boethian interpretations. The first, by Michael D. Cherniss (1969), shows parallels between the dialogue in the poem and the first two books of the *Consolation*. Cherniss maintains, however, that the Knight is not consoled (See lines 566, 1301). Charles P. R. Tisdale (1973) compares the relation between the dreamer and the Knight with the "two parts of the same person" ascribed by

Jean de Meun to the speakers in the *Consolation,* and discusses the significance of Boethian "imagination." However, "comic," "stupid," or "foolish" dreamers still abound.

In an article reflecting current interest in number symbolism Russell A. Peck (1970) says that the Knight is led to recount acts of "memory, intellect, and love," and that his likeness (the Trinity within) is restored in his "marriage." He discusses other numbers as well. A rhetorical interpretation by Robert M. Jordan (1974) explains that the poem is discontinuous rather than "organic," so that consistent characters are not to be expected. There have been "psychological" interpretations, although these are usually remote from the poem and from fourteenth-century life and thought, notably by John Norton-Smith (1974), who discusses the curative effects of objectified dreams. John M. Fyler (1977) adopts the views of Amis in the *Roman de la rose* to show that the Knight and Blanche represent Golden Age innocence.

Edward I. Condren (1971) on the basis of the eight years' malady seeks to date the poem in 1377, and John H. Palmer (1974) presents evidence to show that Blanche died in 1368.

BIBLIOGRAPHY

Baker, Donald C. "The Dreamer again in *The Book of the Duchess*." *PMLA,* 70 (1955), 279-82.

———. "Imagery and Structure in Chaucer's *Book of the Duchess*." *SN,* 30 (1958), 17-26.

Bennett, H.S. *Chaucer and the Fifteenth Century.* Oxford History of English Literature, II, pt. 1. Oxford: Oxford Univ. Press, 1947.

Bethurum, Dorothy. "Chaucer's Point of View in the Love Poems." *PMLA,* 74 (1959), 511-20.

Brewer, D.S. *Chaucer.* 1953. Rev. 3rd ed. London: Longmans, 1973.

Bronson, Bertrand H. "*The Book of the Duchess* Re-opened." *PMLA,* 67 (1952), 863-81.

Cherniss, Michael D. "The Boethian Dialogue in Chaucer's *Book of the Duchess*." *JEGP,* 68 (1969), 655-65.

Condren, Edward I. "The Historical Context of the *Book of the Duchess*." *ChauR*, 5 (1971), 195-212.

Crampton, Georgia Ronan. "Transitions and Meanings in *The Book of the Duchess*." *JEGP*, 62 (1963), 486-500.

French, W.H. "The Man in Black's Lyric." *JEGP*, 66 (1957), 231-41.

Fyler, John M. "Irony and the Age of Gold in the *Book of the Duchess*." *Speculum*, 52 (1977), 314-328.

Gardner, John. *The Poetry of Chaucer*. Carbondale: Southern Illinois Univ. Press, 1977.

Grennen, Joseph E. "*Hert-Huntyng* in the *Book of the Duchess*." *MLQ*, 25 (1964), 131-39.

Huppé, Bernard F., and D.W. Robertson, Jr. *Fruyt and Chaf: Studies in Chaucer's Allegories*. Princeton: Princeton Univ. Press, 1963.

Jordan, Robert M. "The Compositional Structure of the *Book of the Duchess*." *ChauR*, 9 (1974), 99-117.

Kittredge, G.L. *Chaucer and His Poetry*. Cambridge, Mass.: Harvard Univ. Press, 1915.

Kreuzer, James R. "The Dreamer in the *Book of the Duchess*." *PMLA*, 66 (1951), 543-47.

Lawlor, John. "The Pattern of Consolation in *The Book of the Duchess*." *Speculum*, 31 (1956), 626-48.

———. "The Earlier Poems." In *Chaucer and Chaucerians: Critical Studies in Middle English Literature*. Ed. D.S. Brewer. London: Nelson, 1966, pp. 39-64.

Lumiansky, R.M. "The Bereaved Narrator in Chaucer's *The Book of the Duchess*." *TSE*, 9 (1959), 5-17.

Malone, Kemp. *Chapters on Chaucer*. Baltimore: Johns Hopkins Univ. Press, 1951.

Manning, Stephen. "That Dreamer Once More." *PMLA*, 71 (1956), 540-41.

———. "Chaucer's Good Fair White: Woman and Symbol." *CL*, 10 (1958), 97-105.

Muscatine, Charles. *Chaucer and the French Tradition: A Study in Style and Meaning*. Berkeley: Univ. of California Press, 1957.

Palmer, John H. "The Historical Context of the *Book of the Duchess*: A Revision." *ChauR*, 8 (1974), 253-61.

Patch, Howard Rollin. *On Rereading Chaucer*. Cambridge, Mass.: Harvard Univ. Press, 1939.

Peck, Russell A. "Theme and Number in Chaucer's *Book of the Duchess*." In *Silent Poetry*. Ed. A. Fowler. New York: Barnes & Noble, 1970, pp. 73-115.

Robertson, D.W., Jr. *A Preface to Chaucer: Studies in Medieval Perspectives*. Princeton: Princeton Univ. Press, 1962.

——. "The Historical Setting of Chaucer's *Book of the Duchess*." In *Mediaeval Studies in Honor of Urban Tigner Holmes, Jr.* Ed. J. Mahoney and J.E. Keller. 1965. Rpt. New York: Russell & Russell, 1976, pp. 169-195.

——. See under Huppé, Bernard F.

Rowland, Beryl. "The Chess Problem in Chaucer's *Book of the Duchess*." *Anglia*, 80 (1962), 384-89.

——. " 'A Round Tour of Yvoyre'." *N&Q*, 10 (1963), 9.

——. "The Whelp in Chaucer's *Book of the Duchess*." *NM*, 66 (1965), 148-60.

——. *Blind Beasts: Chaucer's Animal World*. Kent, Ohio: Kent State Univ. Press, 1971, pp. 161-65.

Severs, J. Burke. "The Sources of *The Book of the Duchess*." *MS*, 25 (1963), 355-62.

——. "Chaucer's Self-Portrait in the *Book of the Duchess*." *PQ*, 43 (1964), 27-39.

Steadman, John M. "Chaucer's 'Whelp': A Symbol of Marital Fidelity?" *N&Q*, 3 (1956), 374-75.

Tatlock, J.S.P. *The Mind and Art of Chaucer*. 1950. Rpt. New York: Gordian Press, 1966.

Tisdale, Charles P. "Boethian 'Hert-Huntyng': The Elegiac Pattern of the *Book of the Duchess*." *ABR*, 24 (1973), 356-80.

Tuve, Rosemond. *Allegorical Imagery: Some Mediaeval Books and their Posterity*. Princeton: Princenton Univ. Press, 1966.

Wimsatt, James I. "The Apotheosis of Blanche in *The Book of the Duchess*." *JEGP*, 66 (1967), 26-44.

————. "Machaut's *Lay de Confort* and Chaucer's *Book of the Duchess*." In *Chaucer at Albany*. Ed. Rossell Hope Robbins. New York: Burt Franklin, 1975, pp. 11-26.

NINETEEN

LAURENCE K. SHOOK

The House of Fame

There are many poems which are properly described only as informal arts of poetry and which, although they were not composed to be such, were more or less consciously so in the awareness of the fashioning poet. The *House of Fame* is such a poem. Dorothy Everett's view of the poem seems to have been similar when she developed the theme in her important British Academy lecture, "Some Reflections on Chaucer's 'Art Poetical'," given in 1950. She never came to grips with the central critical issue, however, but worked at the periphery, choosing to deal with poetic craftsmanship as encountered in the medieval *artes* and manuals. This is understandable in that John M. Manly's extravagant claims for the influence of the rhetoricians on poetics were still being widely listened to.

The great critical studies of the past also strike through to truth or to an approximation of it. Still indispensable among these is William O. Sypherd's *Studies in Chaucer's Hous of Fame* published by the Chaucer Society in 1908. Sypherd reads the text of the poem surely, assesses judiciously its intellectual depth where such depth is present, and revels in those parts of the poem in which its high humor is achieved. He not only assembles the best criticism which preceded him, but evaluates its contribution and rejects what he finds wanting in it. Thus Sypherd has great confidence that the poem is a love-vision in the French tradition, a series of serious judgments in the tradition of Boethius, and a genuine search, in Book III, for tidings (in the form of discords, jealousies, murmurs, novelties) of love. In all this he makes forthright judgments: all talk about imitation of the *Divine Comedy* must be forgotten; there is no symbolic representation of some personal plight; there is above all no moralizing about worldly fame or hateful rumor. Such things, for him, are "not the state of the case" (p 171). Sypherd's work, in raising all the issues, makes an excellent point of departure for a study of the poem.

Since Sypherd's time, Howard R. Patch and Nevill Coghill have made the best use of his leads. Patch places the poem, especially the first part, squarely in the Ovidian and conventional medieval traditions of love, and fortune, which he regards as convertible, and in the fine tradition of Boethian philosophy (pp. 40-5). Coghill is perhaps more challenging. Although he finds the *House of Fame* the poorest of Chaucer's "longer poems," and lacking in unity of tone and theme, yet it is finely marked by "moments of new greatness" (p. 49). Recent studies have focused upon Coghill's affront to the integrity of the structure of the poem, or on insights specifying what may conceivably be "new" about it.

In 1953 Paul G. Ruggiers published his important paper on "The Unity of Chaucer's *House of Fame*," a paper which was subsequently discussed, together with that of Robert J. Allen, by Donald C. Baker. Taking his cue from Patch, Ruggiers finds Fame also to be convertible with Love and Fortune, and to be the factor binding the three books of the poem together: Fame as Love in Book I, as Order in Book II and as Wisdom in Book III. Fame moving outward to the increasingly universal attains at last a Boethian wisdom. In such a pattern it is hardly surprising that Boethius should be the "man of gret auctorite."

Although the practicalities of Ruggiers' solution are, it seems to me, doubtful, I find one of his suggestions highly pertinent in the context of the view which I am putting forward: "The steadily expanding compass of the successive books of the *House of Fame* demonstrates in small Chaucer's whole development as an artist as he masters a literary type, absorbs a new and liberating philosophy from Boethius, and creates a new form."

The work of Wolfgang Clemen belongs in this tradition. He first published *Der junge Chaucer* in the *Kölner anglistische Arbeiten* in 1938. He republished it enlarged and revised in a new definitive English version, translated by C. A. M. Sym, *Chaucer's Early Poetry* (1963). A comparison of the two versions shows how Clemen's stature as a critic improved during the interim when the influence of Patch, Coghill and others was strong. Clemen now emphasizes strongly the "new path" which Chaucer takes in this poem, and he is also aware that "there is more emphasis on himself and his work as a poet" (p. 69). Although overly inclined to see Chaucer reducing everything to a farce, Clemen grasps the importance of seeing the *House of Fame* as an "allegorical or heavenward journey" which conforms at no point to any known type. In concluding that this poem has some extraordinary poetic moments—the desert at the end of Book I, and the entire heavenward journey in Book II, Clemen can only suggest that what is really "new" about it is a concept of Fame vacillating between "glory" and "rumour." But he had his finger on the key to the poem at the end of the section headed "A General Appraisal" when he spoke of the conflict "between what is handed down and a man's personal experience," of material "presented in a spirit directly contrary to convention," and of the postulate "a new critical attitude to poetry" (pp. 113-14).

B. G. Koonce, in *Chaucer and the Tradition of Fame* (1966), tries something altogether different. Turning to the early suggestion (dismissed by Sypherd as a "pertinacious obsession") that there is a parallel between the *House of Fame* and Dante's *Divine Comedy*, he retraces in a brilliant manner the process by which the symbols and figures of the *House of Fame* have accumulated their widely-ranging significance. He then interprets these figures and symbols in the light of medieval scriptural exegesis and the allegorical modes attaching to it. The validity of Koonce's analysis of the *House of Fame* depends largely upon that of the related current assumption that Chaucer invariably composed under the influence of exegesis and that he was consistently oriented toward Christian charity.

My own view is that, despite an ostensible concern with "tydynges of Love's folk," the subject of the *House of Fame* is the art of poetry itself. Many medieval poets spoke of themselves as "lovers" because they felt that to be a lover was in some way to be a poet. Certain classical writers, such as Plato and Ovid, seem to have been of the same opinion. If one wished to be a poet, one became a lover, and an Art of Love was in a real sense an Art of Poetry. "In the first place . . . ," said Plato, in the *Symposium* "the god [of Love] is so clever a poet that he can make others poets as well. At any rate, anyone whom love touches becomes a poet 'although a stranger to the muse before.' We should accept this as evidence that, broadly speaking, love excels in any kind of artistic creation" (196, D-E). Although Ovid said that he was composing an *Ars amatoria*, he was in fact writing an Art of Poetry. He was conscious that making poems was an art, and he presented his love material in such a way that it could be, and still can be, read as though it really were a poetic. He was read in this way during the twelfth century. A Berlin manuscript (*Berlin Latin Folio 34*, f.27 r.) contains an *accessus Ovidii sine titulo*, that is, an introductory comment on Ovid's *Amores*, which states that "the final cause, that is, the *utilitas* of this work is the embellishing of language (*ornatus verborum*) and the becoming acquainted herein with lovely themes (*et pulchras hic cognoscere positiones*)." To read about love in Ovid was to learn about poetic composition.

The troubadour poets and others can be similarly interpreted. Peire Vidal attributed his art to love: "The merit for anything I am able to create or compose belongs to her because she has given me the poetic skill (*sciensa*) and the poetic knowledge (*conoissensa*) to be a pleasing poet." ("*Abl'alen tir vas me l'aire*," 23-4.) Guillaume de Lorris' part of the *Roman de la Rose* may be

termed an *Ars amatoria aut poetica.* Love there is to be identified with the poetic art. Many fourteenth-century poets were
really writing on the same subject when they composed the
poems which we used to call works of courtly love. The *Book
of the Duchess* includes some reflections on the nature and
origins of poetic composition; the *House of Fame* deals with no
other subject and is only properly understood as an *Ars poetica*
of the kind which I have been discussing.

Throughout Book 1 of the *House of Fame,* Chaucer is effectively writing on the poetic art. His total interest is the making
of the poem, but he has a structural objective here. He is preparing the stage for a dramatic escape from what may be called
the temple of love tradition, that is, the tradition which holds
that poems are made out of the experience of love.

Both the proem and the invocation show a preoccupation with
the making of the poem. Twice he prays: "Turne us every
dreme to goode" (1, 58). He asks the inspirer of poets to turn
his love-vision into a poem. Having had a dream, as the convention wants him to put it, his poet's task is to *tell* it: "I wol yow
tellen everydel" (65).

The list of various kinds of dreams has been elucidated by
Newman and Giaccherini. Newman considers that the catalogue
implied a competent technical knowledge of dream theory on the
part of the narrator, despite his confession of confusion. But the
one thing not suggested as the cause of the dream is love. Indeed,
Bethurum, David, and Bevington find a parody of conventions
here. If the poem was not specially composed for a Christmas
festival of the Inner Temple as Schoeck proposed, the December
tenth date seems to have been selected in deliberate opposition
to the customary May of the dream-vision love poems.

The invocation is a strange double prayer to Morpheus and
the Holy Trinity: to Morpheus the god of dreams asking for the
gift to tell the dream aright, to the Trinity that the listening
audience and the critics will hear the poem (when it is finished
and read aloud) with gracious charity. I feel sure that Chaucer
has the Trinity in mind: although he speaks of the Mover of All,

he does so in the words of the second part of the *gloria patri*, as he who "is and was and ever shall be."

Because the poem is a discussion or treatise on poetry, Chaucer takes a story from Virgil, the poet's poet, and focuses upon the love of Dido for Aeneas. Love, after all, provides the experiences (emotions, passions, feelings) out of which poems are made. Such was the temple of love thesis from which Chaucer departs in Book II when he makes his own new House of Fame proposal.

The dream opens in a "temple ymad of glas" (120), later a "chirche" (473), some variant of the temple of love in which poems are born. This glass temple is more than likely a temple of mirrors, that is, a temple which is, like poetry, filled with images or fictions: "Yet sawgh I never such noblesse / Of ymages" (471-2). The "ymages" in the temple are emphasized. These had been mentioned earlier (121). Why they receive such emphasis is not clear for the moment. The story, of course, is a sort of prolonged image. The full significance of the images appears at the end of Book II.

The main function of the Dido-Aeneas story is directed toward the Art of Poetry. Dido's intriguing soliloquy dwells on the real object of a man's love. Does he really love a woman to the exclusion of everything else? He does not, says Dido. He has to have a new woman every year. Or to be more accurate, she says, he has to have three women at once (305-10). This triune goddess whom man seeks is not from Virgil, not from any writer at all. She is from Chaucer himself: "Non other auctour alegge I" (314). And what does the statement mean? A man has to love not one woman, but a goddess, a trinity of fame, friendship, and personal pleasure or gain—a sort of deification of that love which the informal *artes* have long been identifying with poetry, with poetry in the temple of love tradition.

Another critical question to arise in the story is the poet's subject matter. Where does he go for the "matter" of his poetry? If he wants to "tell" about hell, he has to "know" about hell. Where does he find out? "He moste rede many a rowe / On

Virgile or on Claudian, / on Daunte" who really know about hell, and who "hit telle kan" (448-50).

Such are the reflections of the creative poet on his own work in the old temple of love tradition. Now, however, new inspiration comes to Chaucer in the form of the golden eagle. The eagle may well have come right out of Dante, as most say, or out of Ovid, but he belongs to a very old tradition. The eagle appears in Pindar as a sign of poetic inspiration (see W. W. Jaeger, *Paideia*, tr. Gilbert Highet, I, 220). In addition to various other significances, the eagle also symbolized clear vision, acute perception, and insight, as Steadman shows. Certainly this eagle which came to Chaucer brought a new vision of the whole art of poetry, one in which Chaucer was to set aside the temple of love in favor of the House of Fame as the basis of his Art of Poetry.

Book II provides a whole new approach to the subject. Jove, speaking through the eagle, in effect tells Chaucer for his "lore" and for his "prow" (579) that the workshop of poetry is not in the temple of love but in Fame's House: poems are made not out of love but out of sound. The allusions to love are "robustly realistic," according to Winny. No wonder that, as Grennen remarks, the poet displays the symptoms of an apoplectic seizure!

Through his messenger, Jove tells Chaucer that to try to make love poems without a basis in practical experience is absurd. It is not the experiencing of erotic love that turns a man into a poet; it is hearing the sounds that rise from created things. The poet ought to be preoccupied with sound as experienced in things, particularly with those sounds which have been given the order attached to human speech (765-81). The poet's privilege is to control sound, and especially the speech of men (959).

Jove then through the eagle makes his first two startling revelations. Poetry is:

> "The grete soun,"
> Quod he, "that rumbleth up and doun
> In Fames Hous, full of tydynges,
> Bothe of feir speche and chidynges,
> And of fals and soth compouned."
> (1025-9)

Secondly, men and women come to life in the images which are created out of sounds—"and ys not this a wonder thyng?" (1083).

The invocation to Book III makes clear that "art poetical" is now to be demonstrated. In adding that it is to be demonstrated "pleasantly," Chaucer seems to suggest that this book will not be a handbook of the rules of versification and composition but will itself be a story. The "plot" of the poem as a whole will now be related in the general context of the new theory on poetry which is in process of being expounded.

So what we have in Book III is the main story of the imaginary visit to the House of Fame where we find explained, in the presence of that Goddess of Fame who presides over the destiny of the meaningful sounds that come from men, not only how these meaningful sounds get into poetry, but how they take on their fictional or feigned partly-true-and-partly-false character. This explanation is in line with the definition of poetry, the "grete soun" or the "grete swogh," of the preceding book.

The dream which is resumed at line 1110 is the central plot or story of the poem as a whole. It is neither a formal nor an informal poetic. It deals in turn with the following: the rock of ice, the appearance of Fame's House, the catalogue of sound-makers (harpers, pipers, trumpeters, magicians), the catalogue of historians and poets (especially of the "Troy poets" and of those classical poets for whom Chaucer seems to have had a special preference), the goddess herself, and her capricious distribution of favors to the nine groups who are related to sound as institutionalized in poetry and who are all potential subjects of important poems. Then comes Chaucer's own contact with Fame, followed by the removal of Chaucer and the eagle to the House of Rumor where an explanation is proposed, in terms of the revolving house—a sort of whipper or mixer—for the false element in poetry. All this is in the imaginative fiction of the poem. It is told for its own sake as a story (not by any means Chaucer's best story even in these early years) and it is only incidentally related to the overall informal Art of Poetry which the *House of Fame* actually is.

Yet even this focal story element of Book III contains two moments of real importance for the overall "new" poetic. The first of these moments arrives in the superb piece of dialogue (1867-1915) where, somewhat unusually, the truly thoughtful lines are in Chaucer's own mouth. Have you, says the friend at Chaucer's back, come here to be written about? No, says Chaucer, I am not a subject for poetry. I write the stuff and will be quite satisfied if I am not victimized by those who talk about poetry and poets. "Sufficeth me, as I were ded, / That no wight have my name in honde" (1876-7). This is an important remark, especially if one refers it back to the invocation of Book I, 81-108, where the same subject is the substance of that part of the invocation addressed, not to Morpheus, but to the First Mover, the triune God, the Jesus God. But after this comment on a practising poet's attitude to fame, Chaucer makes a further comment for the benefit of anyone who might think that a poem really does come from some inspiring spirit as the allegory seems to be saying. In the last and important analysis, a poem is the work (albeit in the medium of sound and with subjects and themes proposed by the recorded history of man in whatever form) of a man who is a poet:

> "I wot myself best how y stonde
> For what I drye, or what I thynke,
> I wil myselven al hyt drynke,
> Certeyn, for the more part,
> As fer forth as I kan myn art."
>   (1878-82)

The remainder of this dialogue, that is, up to 1915, concerns only the plot or story as presented in Book III.

There remains one last significant point to make about the treatment of the "new" poetic in Book III, and this concerns the fictional element of all art wherein "fals and soth" are compounded in every "tiding," every poetic theme or subject. There is no question of praise or blame here; poetry is what it is, or as the eagle had said in Book II: "The grete soun," poetry, is a mixed bag of tidings embracing encomium and satire, truth and falsehood, but forthrightly spoken for all to hear and know. "Herke wel," the eagle had said, "hyt is not rouned." It is precisely because a poet, as poet, has no secrets that he is entitled to a friendly hearing.

* * * * *

When the foregoing hypothesis was presented in 1968, several Chaucer specialists were already deep into their work on the general subject of the "art poetical" in the *House of Fame*. Their results have now appeared: *Chaucer's Book of Fame* by J. A. W. Bennett came out in the same year, 1968; *Chaucer's 'House of Fame'* by Shiela Delany in 1972; in 1973 Patricia Kean gave a short account of the poem in her book. All three scholars subscribe to the general thesis that the basic theme of Chaucer's *House of Fame* is poetry itself. No two of them see the thesis in the same way.

Bennett's book is essentially what its subtitle calls it: "An Exposition of the 'House of Fame'," that is, a running and skipping commentary on the literary sources and backgrounds of Chaucer's text and imagery. Since Bennett is more widely and precisely informed than Chaucer, his book takes the reader far beyond Chaucer's conscious world into that of the poet *par excellence*. Bennett is concerned primarily with artistic representation, and his approach is mainly visual and iconological, focussing on what Chaucer sees rather than on what he hears.

Delany, the subtitle of whose book is "The Poetics of Skeptical Fideism," remains closer than Bennett to the intellectual materials of Chaucer's poem but finds the poet uncertain of the validity of these materials. Her Chaucer takes on the character of a comic, light-hearted Siger of Brabant puzzled by the antinomies of a double truth. Delany handles her backgrounds well. However, relating Chaucer to his more scientific modes of thought is not a simple matter either and tends to distract her from his poetic awareness.

In my view, the most convincing treatment to appear to date is that of Kean's. It is not that her work is more profound than Bennett's or Delany's but that its premise—the poet as maker—is better and more consistently adhered to. "It seems to me," she writes, "that in the *House of Fame*, Chaucer has taken as his main theme the relation of poetry to the traditions which form its material." She rightly maintains that Chaucer felt he was doing something "new." New for Chaucer is this discovery of sound. The poet's words take on his very personality: it is his "speche" that "wexeth lyk the same wight / which that the word in erthe spak." It is his spoken word, much less than his written ("be hyt clothed red or blak") that "hath so verray hys lyknesse / that spak the word" (II, 1076-80).

The importance of this aspect of the *House of Fame* appears in various places as, for example, in the analysis of F. P. Magoun and Tauno Mustanoja, in C. B. Hieatt's study of the poem and in recent articles by John Leyerle and Reginald Berry on the talkative eagle whom Chaucer allowed to introduce his new poetic.

The analysis here attempted does not remove the validity of very different approaches: Cawley, Baker, and others, regarded *fama* as a major motive, and Ann Watts has written on "amor gloriae." In the Albany papers edited by Rossell Hope Robbins, Donald Fry sees the poem as demonstrating metaphorically the unreliability of transmitted secular knowledge; Beryl Rowland as an externalization of the process of the "artificial memory." Like Overbeck and many others they both speculate on the identity of the "man of gret auctorite." The crux of the poem, I suppose, will always lie in what the eagle, also Chaucer's *persona* in the present context meant by "this" when he asked "and ys not this a wonder thyng?"

BIBLIOGRAPHY

Allen, Robert J. "A Recurring Motif in Chaucer's *House of Fame*." *JEGP*, 55 (1956), 393-405.

Baker, Donald C. "Recent Interpretations of Chaucer's *Hous of Fame*." *UMSE*, 1 (1960), 97-104.

Bennett, J.A.W. *Chaucer's Book of Fame: An Exposition of the 'House of Fame'*. Oxford: Clarendon Press, 1968.

Berry, Reginald. "Chaucer's Eagle and the Element Air." *UTQ,* 43 (1974), 285-97.

Bethurum, Dorothy. "Chaucer's Point of View as Narrator in the Love Poems." *PMLA,* 74 (1959), 511-20.

Bevington, David M. "On Translating Ovid in Chaucer's *House of Fame*." *N&Q* 7 (1960), 206-207.

———. "The Obtuse Narrator in Chaucer's *House of Fame*." *Speculum,* 36 (1961), 288-298.

Carr, John W. "A Borrowing from Tibullus in Chaucer's *House of Fame*." *ChauR,* 8 (1974), 191-97.

Cawley, A.C. "Chaucer, Pope and Fame." *REL,* 3 (1962), 9-19.

Clemen, Wolfgang. *Der junge Chaucer*. Kölner anglistische Arbeiten, 33. Bochum-Langendreer, 1938.

———. *Chaucer's Early Poetry*. Trans. C.A.M. Sym. London: Methuen, 1963.

Coghill, Nevill. *The Poet Chaucer*. 1949. 2nd ed. London: Oxford Univ. Press, 1967.

David, Alfred. "Literary Satire in the *House of Fame*." *PMLA,* 75 (1960), 333-39.

Delany, Sheila. *Chaucer's House of Fame: The Poetics of Skeptical Fideism*. Chicago: Univ. of Chicago Press, 1972.

———. " 'Ars Simia Naturae' and Chaucer's *House of Fame*." *ELN* (1973), 1-5.

Everett, Dorothy. "Some Reflections on Chaucer's 'Art Poetical'." *PBA,* 36. 1950. Rpt. In *Essays on Middle English Literature*. Ed. P.M. Kean. Oxford: Clarendon Press, 1955, p. 149-74.

Fry, Donald. "The Ending of the *House of Fame*." In *Chaucer at Albany*. Ed. Rossell Hope Robbins. New York: Burt Franklin, 1975, pp. 27-40.

Grennen, Joseph E. "Science and Poetry in Chaucer's *House of Fame*." *AnM,* 8 (1967), 38-45.

Hieatt, C.B. *The Realism of Dream Vision*. Hague: Mouton, 1967.

Kean, P.M. *Chaucer and the Making of English Poetry*. 2 vols. London: Routledge, 1972.

Kellogg, Alfred L., et al. *Chaucer, Langland, Arthur: Essays in Middle English Literature*. New Brunswick, N.J.: Rutgers Univ. Press, 1972.

Koonce, B.G. *Chaucer and the Tradition of Fame: Symbolism in the House of Fame*. Princeton: Princeton Univ. Press, 1966.

Leyerle, John. "Chaucer's Windy Eagle." *UTQ*, 40 (1971), 285-97.

Magoun, Francis P., Jr., and Tauno Mustanoja. "Chaucer's Chimera: His Proto-Surrealist Portrait of Fame." *Speculum*, 50 (1975), 48-54.

Manly, John Matthews. "Chaucer and the Rhetoricians." *PBA*, 12. 1926.

Newman, F.X. "Chaucer's 'Hous of Fame', 7-12." *ELN*, 6 (1968), 5-12.

Overbeck, P.T. "The 'Man of Gret Auctorite' in Chaucer's *House of Fame*." *MP*, 73 (1975), 157-67.

Patch, Howard Rollin. *The Goddess Fortuna in Medieval Literature*. 1927. Rpt. New York: Octagon Bks., 1967.

Rowland, Beryl. "Bishop Bradwardine, the Artificial Memory, and the *House of Fame*." In *Chaucer at Albany*. Ed. Rossell Hope Robbins. New York: Burt Franklin, 1975, pp. 41-62.

Ruggiers, Paul G. "The Unity of Chaucer's *House of Fame*." *SP*, 50 (1953), 16-29.

————. "Words into Images in Chaucer's *Hous of Fame*: A Third Suggestion." *MLN*, 69 (1954), 34-37.

Schoeck, R.J. "A Legal Reading of Chaucer's *Hous of Fame*." *UTQ*, 23 (1954), 185-92.

Steadman, John M. "Chaucer's Eagle: A Contemplative Symbol." *PMLA*, 75 (1960), 153-59.

————. "Chaucer's 'Desert of Libye', Venus and Jove (The House of Fame, 486-487)." *MLN*, 76 (1961), 196-201.

Sypherd, W.O. *Studies in Chaucer's Hous of Fame*. Chaucer Soc., 2nd ser., No. 39. 1908. Rpt. New York: Haskell House, 1965

Watts, Ann C. " 'Amor Gloriae' in Chaucer's *House of Fame*." *JMRS*, 3 (1973), 87-113.

Wilson, William S. "The Eagle's Speech in Chaucer's *House of Fame*." *QJS*, 50 (1964), 153-58.

———. "Exegetical Grammar in the *House of Fame*." *ELN*, 1 (1964), 244-48.

———. "Scholastic Logic in Chaucer's *House of Fame*." *ChauR*, 1 (1966), 181-84.

Winny, James. *Chaucer's Dream-Poems*. London: Chatto & Windus, 1973.

TWENTY

DONALD C. BAKER

The Parliament of Fowls

The *Parliament of Fowls* combines openness and indirection in a way that epitomizes most of the problems and pleasures that students find in Chaucer, just as it gathers into 699 lines nearly all aspects of Chaucer's art and thought, and phases of his poetic development. It offers the critic, the biographer, and the philosopher what each looks for in Chaucer. As we examine the poem, it changes its form and color—a thing so simple, yet complex; so personal, yet anonymous; so philosophic, yet comic. It establishes Chaucer as having that double vision which allows the poet to see himself, his people, and his art, as foolish but worth their folly. It sums up the elements in Chaucer which were to deny him "high seriousness," but which allowed him in his own way something better.

The contrasted but unified elements of the love-vision can be best seen by examining its structure, which has obvious parallels with both the *Book of the Duchess* and the *House of Fame*. The *Parliament* opens (1-28) with a discussion of the extremes of love, the miracles and cruel ire of the god, followed by Chaucer's usual disclaimer of personal experience. The poet tells us that he knows of love only through reading, and that he encountered a book "write with lettres olde" (19)—Macrobius' commentary on

Cicero's *Somnium Scipionis.* He began to read, "a certeyn thing to lerne" (20). The second part of the poem (29-91) is a summary of the *Somnium,* in which Africanus appears to Scipio in a dream and shows him the universe, both physical and moral. Africanus instructs Scipio to "... know thyself first immortal / And loke ay besyly thow werche and wysse / To commune profit ..." (73-5). Eternal bliss rewards those who obey, and a limbo-like existence awaits breakers of the law and "likerous folk" (79). Chaucer concludes his reading by observing that "... I hadde thyng which that I nolde, / And ek I nadde that thyng that I wolde" (90-1). Chaucer then falls asleep, and the main part of the poem begins (92-693). He dreams, as in the *Book of the Duchess,* and, lo, Africanus appears to *him!* The old Roman explains that he has come to reward Chaucer for diligence in reading his book. The poet pauses to pray to Venus—Cytherea —who has caused the dream, and to ask her help in writing it (113-19). Africanus, like the eagle in the *House of Fame,* then seizes Chaucer and brings him to a gate; on one side is written an invitation to the garden of love inside, and on the other, a warning: "Th' eschewing is only the remedye" (140). Africanus assures Chaucer that neither applies to him, because he is without experience in love, and shoves the hesitant poet into the park. In this commonplace of medieval literature (see Curtius, pp. 183-202) the poet encounters the population of the land of love-allegory: Cupid, Plesaunce, Lust, Curteysie, Rape, Gentilesse, and, in her temple of brass, Venus herself. Further on, Chaucer sees Nature seated on a hill of flowers, surrounded by birds (295 ff.), and the parliament begins. The birds are met on St. Valentine's Day to choose their mates, and the eagles are to choose first, followed by the lesser "foules of ravyne," and the other birds, in order of rank. Each kind of bird is described by its attributes in medieval lore: the "wedded turtil," the "skornynge jay," and the sparrow, "Venus sone." Nature sets the rules and the choosing begins. But trouble quickly arises, for the royal tercel's claim for the formel eagle is challenged by two other tercels, and a debate ensues. The other fowls protest the delay, and a second debate begins, with some birds defending the chivalrous code of the eagles (*fine amour*), and some, like the duck and goose, demanding that they get on without the high-flown nonsense: "Al this nys not worth a flye!" (501). The falcon tercelet proposes solution by combat, but Nature finally leaves the question to the formel herself, who asks a year's respite from deciding. Nature grants the request, the other birds quickly choose, and they all express their gratitude by singing a roundel (680-92) in praise of St. Valentine. The noise wakes Chaucer, and the poet in the last stanza completes the "envelope" of his dream by taking himself to other books, hoping some day "that I shal mète som thyng for to fare / The bet, and thus to rede I nyl nat spare" (698-9).

The *Parliament* has an intricate structure (opening, book-reading, garden of love and parliament of birds, and return to reading) and employs the common vision device of development by link and parallel rather than by straight narrative. Like the *Book of the Duchess* and the *House of Fame*, the *Parliament* deals with more than one kind of experience, and its tone varies.

This very variety has been to some extent responsible for the fragmentary nature of much scholarly comment. Writers have been preoccupied by a part of the poem rather than the whole. Naturally, the most spectacular part, the parliament of birds, attracted the earlier attention. The vision poem "about" choosing a mate was seen as an allegorical compliment to noble personages. The most "popular" identifications of the royal tercel and formel eagle are those of Koch and Emerson, Rickert, and Braddy ("The *Parlement of Foules* in Its Relation to Contemporary Events"). The first two critics argue that the *Parliament* alludes to the betrothal of Richard II to Anne of Bohemia in 1381; the third, that it refers to Richard and Philippa of Lancaster, eldest daughter of John of Gaunt, who hoped for this match in 1381; the fourth suggests that the *Parliament* reflects the negotiations in 1376-7 for the marriage of Richard to Princess Marie of France (for other candidates, see Robinson's notes, p. 791).

Other more generally allegorical interpretations of the debate of the birds have been offered. These see the groups of birds as classes of society or as shadowing the English parliaments of 1376 onwards (see Brewer, ed., *The Parlement of Foulys*, pp. 37-8). Rickert read the *Parliament* as a satire on the lower classes; Patrick, not to be outdone, saw it as a satire on the upper classes, and Thackaberry suggested that the birds' dispute satirizes all classes of society who fail to work together for common profit. This last idea has been found in most criticisms of the poem since.

Much scholarship has centered on the *genre* and tradition of Chaucer's poem. The dream vision itself stems directly from the *Roman de la rose* and many thirteenth- and fourteenth-century French poems (see Neilson for summaries of love visions), as well as from the *Somnium*, and perhaps saints' visions in legendaries, but what of the debate? Farnham argued ("The Contending Lovers") that the poem is a retelling of the contending lovers folk-tale, though there seems little clear folk-tradition in the *Parliament*. Manly ("What Is the *Parlement of Foules*?") decided that it is a *demande d'amour*, a French love-debate, usually unresolved, which presented complex questions of love, such as, which of two lovers was worthier, the ugly but true, or the handsome but faithless? Chaucer used a kind of *demande* in the *Franklin's Tale* and the *Wife of Bath's Tale* (see Brewer, "The Genre of the *Parlement of Foules*," for further discussion, and for the relation of the poems to the Valentine tradition). But Chaucer's *demande* in the *Parliament* is, as usual, with a difference, for the question debated by the birds is in essence the validity of *fine amour*, or "courtly love"! The device of the parliament of creatures is, of course, scattered throughout medieval literature.

Many scholars have given attention to Chaucer's models and borrowings. Most of the candidates for Chaucer's model are very tenuous indeed, but two have commanded some respect. Damon found in Jordanus' *Pavo* a possible source, and Braddy argued in *Chaucer and the French Poet Graunson* that Oton de Graunson's *Le songe saint Valentin* provided the model. But, in any case, Chaucer's tone and attitudes are so different that it would be unprofitable to pursue either very far. Poems by Machaut and Deschamps have been championed as sources, and even an Old Czech poem (see Robinson, p. 792).

But there are innumerable bits of recollection and borrowing from other writers in the *Parliament*. Basically, the influence on the *Parliament* of the *Roman* is pervasive, though as Fansler argues (pp. 134, 179-80), there is little direct imitation; but the ideas, and the psychological allegorization of love, were the result of Chaucer's long apprenticeship to that seminal poem. Apart from the *Somnium*, direct borrowings are from Alanus de Insulis' *De planctu Naturae*, from which the concept of Nature is taken (298 ff.); and Boccaccio's *Teseida*, as Pratt has shown (pp. 605-8), provides much of the description of the temple of Venus. Dante is suggested frequently, particularly as the source of the mottos on the gates of the garden, and Chaucer parallels Dante's use of Virgil in the idea of a guide like Africanus (see Brewer, *The Parlement of Foulys*, pp. 45-6; and Lowes, "Chaucer and Dante," p. 706). Boethius figures in the *Parliament*, directly in 90-1, and generally in the idea of a harmonious universe, an idea also present in the *Somnium*, but one which Chaucer had taken directly from the *Consolatio* in his *House of Fame*. Claudian's *De raptu Proserpinae*, Joseph of Exeter's *Iliad*, Ovid's *Fasti*, Alanus' *Anticlaudianus*, and several other poems probably contributed lines and phrases as a kind of residue in Chaucer's mind (Robinson, pp. 791-6, and Brewer, *The Parlement of Foulys*, pp. 101-27). The critical value of understanding these literary traditions in the poem is brilliantly shown by J. A. W. Bennett's analysis in *The Parlement of Foules: An Interpretation*, which demonstrates the ways in which "influences" reflect Chaucer's thought as he develops his poem. Apart from the strictly literary heritage, the presentation of medieval science and of the lore of dreams in the poem has been discussed by Curry (pp. 195-218).

The rhetoric of the *Parliament* has received attention: Manly's famous lecture "Chaucer and the Rhetoricians" (inclined to be prejudiced against rhetoric as a sign of "formalism"), Everett's two splendid essays, H. S. Bennett's *Chaucer and the Fifteenth Century* (pp. 89-91), Payne's *The Key of Remembrance* (pp. 139-

46), and Schaar's two rambling books *passim* contain some illuminating comments on the rhetorical structures in Chaucer's poetry. Naunin provides a general study of rhetoric in Chaucer, and Curtius, Baldwin and Faral are indispensable for the rhetorical traditions in medieval literature. Chaucer's masterly handling of rhetoric in the *Parliament* has been touched upon by so many critics in recent years that even a brief discussion here is impossible (for a summary, see Brewer, *The Parlement of Foulys*, pp. 47-51).

The role of the narrator in Chaucer's poetry generally has become a popular topic in criticism in the past twenty years, and the *Parliament* has been given its share of scrutiny. Most writers have touched upon the dreamer-narrator-poet as Chaucer himself, a *persona*, or a combination of the two, but the most stimulating discussions are those of Clemen (pp. 126-8), Owen, and Bethurum, "Chaucer's Point of View as Narrator in the Love Poems."

In spite of the effort expended on the poem by scholars in the nineteenth and twentieth centuries, it is not an exaggeration to say that evaluation of the poem as a whole begins with Bronson's 1935 essay "In Appreciation of Chaucer's *Parlement of Foules*." Although he wrote much with which most now disagree, such as dismissing Africanus as irrelevant, and describing the subject and *genre* of the *Parliament* as "radically uncongenial to his [Chaucer's] temper" (p. 197), Bronson dealt with problems that needed solving: the questions of the poem's unity and tone. Bronson concluded that the theme of the poem is the ironic and comic contradictions of man's attitudes toward love (pp. 216-19). A more "philosophical" kind of criticism had its beginnings in Goffin's "Heaven and Earth in the *Parlement of Foules*" which saw the poem as Chaucer's poetic presentation of the choice which he must make, to write of morality or of life, to choose between true and false felicity, the world of the *Somnium* or the garden of love. Lumiansky elaborated this idea and argued that Chaucer is trying to reconcile his service to love with his desire for salvation. Huppé and Robertson followed much the same argument in far greater detail (pp. 101-48). The popularity of this approach is growing, and a recent essay by Selvin suggests that the *Parliament* mirrors Chaucer's desire to make worldly love acceptable to religious convictions, and concludes with a compromise: acceptance of natural *caritas* and eschewal of passion. These interpretations, of course, turn on the contrast of the *Somnium* and the garden of love, on Chaucer's concern with dualities in love in the *Knight's Tale* and *Troilus,* and on the poet's statement in the *Parliament* that he reads to learn something but can't find what he is looking for, thus suggesting a struggle to resolve a conflict.

Other interpretations seeing the poem as a whole and offering worthwhile suggestions are two essays of Stillwell, who reads the poem as a humorous satire on the inability of men to work for common profit, illustrated by their failure to understand even so basic a thing as different customs of love-making. McDonald sees the poem as expressing a conflict between courtly love and natural love for common profit; the parliament of birds is a wry treatment of the extremes of attitudes toward love and life found in society, and all are harmonized in nature. Frank argues that the *Parliament* satirizes the love-vision *genre* as well as exclusive attitudes toward love: the moralistic, the literary, and the realistic, as seen in the three main sections of the poem, the *Somnium,* the temple, and the debate. Owen finds a way of utilizing most of these interpretations by analyzing the poem as a four-level allegory. A provocative essay by Emslie has argued that the *Parliament* contrasts courtly love and natural love as they reflect class distinctions.

Most of the general books on Chaucer have helpful appreciation to add to the burgeoning reputation of the *Parliament.* Of the older books, Lowes (pp. 116-26), Root (pp. 63-8), Patch (pp. 45-55), and Shelly (pp. 70-81) may still be read with profit. Malone (pp. 61-79), Coghill (pp. 55-64), Brewer (*Chaucer,* pp. 78-87), Muscatine (pp. 115-23), Bronson (*In Search of Chaucer,* pp. 42-8), Corsa (pp. 19-29), and Lawlor (in *Chaucer and Chaucerians,* pp. 50-7) are variously helpful and stimulating. Of extensive studies of the poem, we are fortunate to have Brewer's splendid edition (complete with translations of pertinent passages from sources), and J. A. W. Bennett's thorough and sensitive book-length analysis. Perhaps the wisest and most Chaucerian of the commentaries is that of Clemen (pp. 142-69), who in his expanded and revised version of an earlier important book (*Der junge Chaucer*), strikes a tolerant balance among the various interpretations.

I have sketched, as I have seen them, the major scholarly interests in the *Parliament*. Not all views, of course, could have been mentioned. These and others I draw upon in my own comments to follow.

I shall begin by confessing that I am not at all sure what the *Parliament* is about. We must all share Bronson's feeling that "it is too nimble for criticism, which hops always behind" (*In Search of Chaucer*, p. 46). We know very little indeed of what we want to know, and know too much perhaps of what is not necessary, to paraphrase Chaucer's own concern.

We speak, for instance, with reasonable confidence of the poem's date, usually given as c. 1382, though, as Bronson has shown in "The Parlement of Foules Revisited" (pp. 252 ff.), the allusion (*PF*, 117) to Venus as north-north-west is shaky evidence for dating. Few scholars can agree on historical allusion which could help fix the date, though most agree on 1381-2 (see Robinson, p. 791). But, generally, we are, I think, right enough, within three or four years. The springy flexibility of the five-beat line, such an improvement on the octosyllables of the *House of Fame*, the rime royal stanza, the precise and imaginative language (analyzed by Lewis, pp. 171-5)—all would suggest a date in the late 1370's or early 1380's, before the *terminus ad quem* of the first *Prologue to the Legend of Good Women*. Also, Chaucer's mature synthesis of major influences and literary traditions—the French, Italian, philosophic and realistic—suggests a rather late date.

We can also agree on the form: it is a love vision, to which something like a *demande d'amour* has been grafted. The occasion is St. Valentine's Day, and the subject is love. The poem may well have been intended as a compliment, and it would be foolish to deny the possibility; in fact, Braddy's case is very tempting, though 1377 seems a trifle early. But, as Chaucer seems to have done everything with a "twist," it is doubtful that knowing the exact background would be very helpful. We can also see in the *Parliament* what seems to be a real concern with a philosophical theme, the role of love in the universal scheme; clearly, this does not make the poem a moral treatise, but just as clearly moral concern is there. The amused treatment of the headstrong, self-centered birds suggests everywhere satire; Chaucer is no bird-watcher, he is a people-watcher. The birds are society, and it seems sensible to read Chaucer's revelation of folly and intolerance as a reflection of the troubled times in the age of the Peasants' Revolt. But, equally, the *Parliament* does not seem primarily a social criticism. It is clear that Chaucer is a poet of love, and that, nearly all aspects of human existence being in some way bound to love, the *Parliament* necessarily reflects most of them. For such a small poem, it can stand a great deal of interpretation without going under.

Chaucer as the dreamer is his usual bumbling self, inexperienced in love, but a loyal servant to the god and to lovers true. Cytherea, the planet Venus in Chaucer's poetry, who seems to represent all but divine love, is the managing directress of the poem and, as Chaucer tells us, is responsible for his dream. Whether her design includes Chaucer's reading the *Somnium*, with its emphasis on self-sacrifice for the "commune profit," is not clear. At any rate, the juxtaposition of the stern morality of Macrobius and Cicero with the garden of love has always seemed puzzling. It is not wise to push a parallel with Dante too far, but it is certain that Dante influenced Chaucer's thought and poetry on every level, and Dante's use of the pagan Virgil—symbolizing terrestial harmony to medieval man, and especially to Dante—as his guide through the winding paths of the human soul profoundly moved Chaucer, though the English poet expressed himself in his own idiom (witness his use of Dante's eagle as guide and vehicle in the *House of Fame*). Africanus, who has just revealed to Scipio a universal harmony in which all things have their proper places, is, I would suggest, for Chaucer's purpose, a kind of Virgil on a much smaller scale and in a far different tone. Chaucer probably began his poem in the interests of his love poetry, for he opens with a definition of love and his own relation to it. He had hit upon Macrobius' commentary, and continued reading because, not only was he interested in dreams, but this one provided a vision of the universe, man's place, and a hint on the relation of love to that place. Chaucer quotes the *Somnium* at length only once: on man's duty to know himself immortal and to work for "commune profit," eschewing "likerousnes," which distracts man from "commune profit" (73-84). This latter is perhaps the thing "that I nolde"; and the information "that I wolde," I suggest, is the relation of love to common profit. If this is so, then the dream that Cytherea sends would appear to be an explanation. Africanus is to serve as Chaucer's guide, though he doesn't stay to answer questions!

The garden of love to which Africanus leads the poet is, I agree with Dorothy Bethurum ("The Center of the *Parlement of Foules*"), the heart of the poem. It is, as she argues (pp. 41-6), an allegorical setting depicting the psychology of love. All its aspects are there: the disdain, pleasure, beauty, jealousy, courtesy, and "gentilesse." These are effects and causes, the workings of love in man. The language and imagery, borrowed largely from Boccaccio, are from courtly love because, of course, the only tradition of analysis of human love was from the literature of *fine amour*; we should not, however, conclude, as so many have, that only courtly love is intended. Away from the temple of Venus, Chaucer comes in a further part of the garden to a "hil of floures," upon which sits ". . . this noble goddesse Nature" (303). I think that Venus is not a power utterly separate from Nature, but symbolic of a part of Nature (there are not two gardens with two gates, after all). We go from the literary-psychological analysis of love to love in life, which shows remarkable parallels with the allegory of the first part of the garden. Just as the allegory has shown the many sides of love, from "gentilesse" to Priapus, so in the "natural" choosing we find many different aspects. We have not only the noble birds, and the true (the "wedded turtil"), but "likerous" birds, like the sparrow, "Venus sone." The birds, like humans, are motivated by differing concerns, united only in the natural drive to express love in their own ways: the noble birds carry out their courtly dance, and the duck wants to get on with it. The conclusion, of course, is that love is good, although the abuse of love is reprehensible, as expressed in the allegory of both parts of the garden. This is, at any rate, the impression I receive from the *Parliament*, brimming in its conclusion with joy in the birds' roundel in praise of Nature—and of St. Valentine, who has, in a sense, by his auspices, worked a kind of baptism of secular love. So we have Cytherea's response to the stoicism of Cicero: working to common profit does not exclude love. Man has his choice of the way of acceptance or the way of denial, and he has a further choice in the way of acceptance: the use or abuse of love.

But what about Chaucer's reading, his searching for "a thyng," and his concluding statement that he will continue to read "that I shal mete som thyng for to fare / The bet . . ." (698-9)? I suggest that this refers to Chaucer's own role as a poet. That Chaucer was seriously concerned with the role of the secular poet of human love seems clear in his epilogue to *Troilus*, the ideas in the *House of Fame*, and the Retraction to the *Canterbury Tales*. I do not argue that Chaucer wrote the *Parliament* deliberately to expound his concern, but that his interest manifested itself in the direction which the poem took and in the sources upon which he drew. Boethius and Platonic-Christian tradition gave the poet no worthy role in the universal scheme. Dante and Boccaccio, the great literary influences on Chaucer, honored the poet. These influences, it seems to me, contribute a precarious balance in the *Parliament*. The reading of the *Somnium* sets the uncomfortable problem; Cytherea proposes in the dream, dominated by Dante and Boccaccio, a solution: the celebration of human love is the justification of the love poet.

Such an interpretation will doubtless meet the objection that it ignores the humor of the poem, but I do not think that it does.

The fun of the *Parliament* is obvious, and in no way contradicts other implications of the poem. All of Chaucer's love poems are deeply humorous. The humor, the social satire, the *Parliament's* probable purpose as a compliment and likely function in a court festivity, all blend, as the poem's parts blend, in an affirmation of human worth.

But there is a lingering personal doubt. The dream is, of course, Chaucer's own creation. Perhaps he wishes to find something of authority expressing his own hoped-for solution so that he may "fare the bet" as a poet of love. But, for now, this remarkable comic valentine exalting love as a natural force will suffice until, hopefully, Chaucer encounters another "olde bok totorn."

* * * * *

In the years since this essay was published (1968), much has been written about the poem, most of it concerned with the harmonious or inharmonious design and the clear or inconclusive theme. Wilhelm argues that the poem develops in three time progressions, from the religious through the romantic to the realistic. Uphaus distinguishes the narrator as dreamer-poet from Chaucer's actual construction of the poem. Chaucer succeeds, he says, where the narrator does not, and exhibits through the narrator's search for form the ambiguous relationship between life and art. Cawley suggests that the time-schemes in the *Parliament* are arranged so as ". . . to emphasize the worldly aspects of the garden and to strengthen the contrast between the celestial paradise of Scipio and the earthly paradise of Nature" (p. 126). Chaucer thus achieves coherence through the skilfull juxtaposition of Scipio, Venus, and Nature, not by a reconciliation of them. Similar structure and themes among the *Parliament*, the *Book of the Duchess*, and the *House of Fame* are found by Whitman. McCall argues that the harmony of the *Parliament* is derived by the counterpointing of the earthly mysterious harmony against the background of Africanus' report of the heavenly music of the spheres. Pursuing a somewhat similar theme,

Chamberlain emphasizes the use by Chaucer of medieval ideas about music as harmonizing and clarifying agents in the poem, revealed by parallel relations between Cicero's heaven, hell and earth, and the three regions of Chaucer's park.

An interesting investigation of Chaucer's relation to contemporary medieval thought is Eldredge's essay which argues that Chaucer in the poem moves toward a position of moderate realism. The disharmony of the poem is the subject of a long chapter in Winny's book in which he suggests that the inconclusiveness of the *Parliament* reveals the stress between Chaucer's developing comic style and the conventions within the love vision, and which was released in the already-beginning *Canterbury Tales*. Somewhat similarly, Leicester sees the *Parliament* as a statement of the disharmony of the poetic experience and traditional authority, and argues that Chaucer generalizes this disharmony as applied to society. In part of a larger essay, Schless analyzes Chaucer's use of Boccaccio's description of the Temple of Venus in the *Teseide* which in the *Parliament* becomes a temple of *luxuria*—an illuminating instance of the way in which Chaucer's mind worked. Spearing contrasts the dissatisfaction of the dreamer with his dream and the satisfying completeness found by most readers in the poem that contains the dream. He stresses that the ". . . difference is that between the conscious mind, always looking for rational solutions to life's problems on the 'bookish' level of philosophy, and the unconscious mind which achieves mastery over problems by enacting them in the form of concrete images rather than through rational analysis" (p. 99). In the most recent treatment Stephen Knight gives an extended close reading of the poem, paying special attention to its relation to *Anelida and Arcite,* and concentrating on rhyme, repetition, and alliteration.

The criticism has become more sophisticated, but answers are as hard to find as ever.

BIBLIOGRAPHY

Alanus de Insulis. *Opera. Patrologia Latina.* Ed. J.-P. Migne. 210. Paris, 1877.

————. *The Complaint of Nature by Alain de Lille.* Trans. D.M. Moffat. Yale Studies in English, 36. 1908. Rpt. Hamden, Conn.: Archon Bks., 1972.

Baldwin, Charles S. *Medieval Rhetoric and Poetic.* 1928. Rpt. Gloucester, Mass.: P. Smith, 1959.

Bateson, F.W. "Editorial appendix to D.S. Brewer's 'English in the Universities III: Language and Literature'." *EIC,* 11 (1961), 255-63.

Bennett, H.S. *Chaucer and the Fifteenth Century.* Oxford History of English Literature, II, pt. 1. Oxford: Oxford Univ. Press, 1947.

Bennett, J.A.W. *The Parlement of Foules: An Interpretation.* Oxford: Clarendon Press, 1957.

Bethurum, Dorothy. "The Center of the *Parlement of Foules.*" In *Essays in Honor of Walter Clyde Curry.* Foreword by Hardin Craig. Nashville: Vanderbilt Univ. Press, 1955, pp. 39-50.

————. "Chaucer's Point of View as Narrator in the Love Poems." *PMLA,* 74 (1959), 511-20.

Braddy, Haldeen. *Chaucer's Parlement of Foules In Its Relation to Contemporary Events.* New York: Octagon, 1969. (A revised and expanded version of the essay in *Three Chaucerian Studies.*)

————. *Chaucer and the French Poet Graunson.* 1947. Rpt. New York: Kennikat Press, 1968.

Brewer, D.S. "The Genre of the *Parlement of Foules.*" *MLR,* 53 (1958), 321-26.

————. *Chaucer.* 1953. Rev. 3rd ed. London: Longmans, 1973.

————, ed. *The Parlement of Foulys.* London: Nelson, 1960.

Bronson, Bertrand H. "In Appreciation of Chaucer's *Parlement of Foules.*" *University of California Publications in English,* 3 (1935), 193-224.

————. "The *Parlement of Foules* Revisited." *ELH,* 15 (1948), 247-60.

———. *In Search of Chaucer*. Toronto: Univ. of Toronto Press, 1960.

Cawley, A.C. "Chaucer's Valentine: The *Parlement of Foules*." In *Chaucer's Mind and Art*. Ed. A.C. Cawley. Edinburgh: Oliver & Boyd, 1969, pp. 125-39.

Chamberlain, D. "The Music of the Spheres and the *Parlement of Foules*." *ChauR*, 5 (1970), 32-56.

Clemen, Wolfgang. *Chaucer's Early Poetry*. Trans. C.A.M. Sym. London: Methuen, 1963.

Coghill, Nevill. *The Poet Chaucer*. 1949. 2nd ed. London: Oxford Univ. Press, 1967.

Corsa, Helen Storm. *Chaucer: Poet of Mirth and Morality*. Notre Dame, Ind.: Univ. of Notre Dame Press, 1964.

Curry, Walter Clyde. *Chaucer and the Mediaeval Sciences*. 1926. Rev. and enl. ed. 1960. Rpt. New York: Barnes & Noble, 1962.

Curtius, E.R. *European Literature and the Latin Middle Ages*. Trans. W.R. Trask. New York: Pantheon Bks., 1953.

Damon, P.W. "*The Parlement of Foules* and the *Pavo*." *MLN*, 67 (1952), 520-24.

Eldredge, L. "Poetry and Philosophy in *The Parlement of Foules*." *Revue de l'Université d'Ottawa*, 40 (1970), 441-59.

Eliason, Norman E. "Chaucer the Love Poet." In *Chaucer the Love Poet*. Ed. J. Mitchell and W. Provost. Athens, Ga.: Univ. of Georgia Press, 1973, pp. 9-26.

Emerson, O.F. "The Suitors in Chaucer's *Parlement of Foules*" *MP*, 8 (1910), 45-62.

———. "What Is the *Parlement of Foules*?" *JEGP*, 13 (1914), 566-82.

Emslie, M. "Codes of Love and Class Distinctions." *EIC*, 5 (1955), 1-17.

Everett, Dorothy. "Some Reflections on Chaucer's 'Art Poetical'." *PBA*, 36 (1950). Rpt. In *Essays on Middle English Literature*. Ed. P.M. Kean. Oxford: Clarendon Press, 1955, pp. 149-74.

———. "Chaucer's Love Visions, with Particular Reference to the *Parlement of Foules*." In *Essays on Middle English Literature*. London: Oxford Univ. Press, 1955, pp. 97-114.

Fansler, D.S. *Chaucer and the Roman de la Rose.* 1914. Rpt. Gloucester, Mass.: P. Smith, 1965.

Faral, Edmond. *Les arts poétiques du XIIe et du XIIIe siècle.* 1924. Rpt.
Paris: E. Champion, 1958.

Farnham, W.E. "The Contending Lovers." *PMLA,* 35 (1920), 247-323.

Frank, R.W., Jr. "Structure and Meaning in the *Parlement of Foules.*"
PMLA, 71 (1956), 530-39.

Goffin, R.C. "Heaven and Earth in the *Parlement of Foules.*" *MLR,*
31 (1936), 493-99.

Hieatt, C.B. *The Realism of Dream Visions.* The Hague: Mouton,
1967.

Huppé, Bernard F., and D.W. Robertson, Jr. *Fruyt and Chaf: Studies
in Chaucer's Allegories.* Princeton: Princeton Univ. Press, 1962.

Kellogg, Alfred L., and Robert C. Cox. "Chaucer's St. Valentine: A
Conjecture." In *Chaucer, Langland, Arthur: Essays in Middle
English Literature.* New Brunswick, N.J.: Rutgers Univ. Press,
1972, pp. 108-45.

Knight, Stephen. *rymyng craftily: meaning in Chaucer's poetry.* London: Angus & Robertson, 1973.

Koch, John. "The Date and Personages of the 'Parlement of Foules'."
In *Essays on Chaucer, His words and works.* Chaucer Soc., 2nd
ser., No. 18, pt. iv. London: Trübner, 1878, pp. 400-9.

———, ed. *Geoffrey Chaucer: Kleinere Dichtungen.* Heidelberg: Winter, 1928.

Lawlor, John. "The Earlier Poems." In *Chaucer and Chaucerians: Critical Studies in Middle English Literature.* Ed. D.S. Brewer. London: Nelson, 1966, pp. 39-64.

Leicester, H.M., Jr. "The Harmony of Chaucer's *Parlement*: A Dis-
sonant Voice." *ChauR,* 9 (1974), 15-34.

Lewis, C.S. *The Allegory of Love: A Study in Medieval Tradition.*
1936. Rpt. New York: Oxford Univ. Press, 1958.

Lowes, John L. "Chaucer and Dante." *MP,* 14 (1917), 705-35.

———. *Geoffrey Chaucer and the Development of His Genius.* 1934.
Rpt. Bloomington: Indiana Univ. Press, 1958.

Lumiansky, R.M. "Chaucer's *Parlement of Foules:* A Philosophical Interpretation." *RES,* 24 (1948), 81-89.

McCall, John P. "The Harmony of Chaucer's *Parliament.*" *ChauR,* 5 (1970), 22-31.

McDonald, C.O. "An Interpretation of Chaucer's *Parlement of Foules.*" *Speculum,* 30 (1955), 444-57.

Macrobius. *Opera.* Ed. F. Eyssenhardt. Leipzig: Teubner, 1868.

————. *Commentary on the Dream of Scipio.* Trans. W.H. Stahl. New York: Columbia Univ. Press, 1952.

Malone, Kemp. *Chapters on Chaucer.* Baltimore: Johns Hopkins Univ. Press, 1951.

Manly, John Matthews. "What Is the *Parlement of Foules?*" *Studien zur englischen Philologie,* 50 (1913), 279-90.

————. "Chaucer and the Rhetoricians." *PBA,* 12. London, 1926.

Muscantine, Charles. *Chaucer and the French Tradition: A Study in Style and Meaning.* Berkeley: Univ. of California Press, 1957.

Naunin, Traugott. *Der Einfluss der mittelalterlichen Rhetorik auf Chaucers Dichtung.* Diss. Bonn, 1929.

Neilson, William Allen. *Origins and Sources of the Court of Love.* Harvard Studies and Notes in Philology and Literature, 6. 1899. Rpt. New York: Russell & Russell, 1967.

Owen, Charles A., Jr. "The Role of the Narrator in the *Parlement of Foules.*" *CE,* 14 (1953), 264-69.

Patch, Howard Rollin. *On Rereading Chaucer.* Cambridge, Mass.: Harvard Univ. Press, 1939.

Patrick, David. "The Satire in Chaucer's *Parliament of Birds.*" *PQ,* 9 (1930), 61-65.

Payne, Robert O. *The Key of Remembrance: A Study of Chaucer's Poetics.* 1963. Rpt. Westport, Conn.: Greenwood Press, 1973.

Pratt, R.A. "Chaucer's Use of the *Teseida.*" *PMLA,* 62 (1947), 598-621.

Rickert, Edith. "Geoffrey Chaucer: A New Interpretation of the *Parlement of Foules.*" *MP,* 18 (1920), 1-29.

Root, R.K. *The Poetry of Chaucer*. Boston, 1906. Rev. ed. 1922. Rpt. Gloucester, Mass.: P. Smith, 1957.

Rowland, Beryl. *Blind Beasts: Chaucer's Animal World*. Kent, Ohio: Kent State Univ. Press, 1971.

Schaar, Claes. *Some Types of Narrative in Chaucer's Poetry*. Lund Studies in English, 25. Copenhagen, 1954.

————. *The Golden Mirror: Studies in Chaucer's Descriptive Technique and Its Literary Background*. Lund: Gleerup, 1955.

Schless, Howard H. "Transformations: Chaucer's Use of Italian." In *Geoffrey Chaucer*. Ed. D.S. Brewer. London: Bell, 1974, pp. 184-223.

Selvin, R.H. "Shades of Love in the *Parlement of Foules*." *SN*, 37 (1965), 146-60.

Shelly, Percy Van Dyke. *The Living Chaucer*. 1940. Rpt. New York: Russell & Russell, 1968.

Smith, F.J. "Mirth and Marriage in *The Parlement of Foules*." *Ball State University Forum*, 14 (1973), 15-22.

Spearing, A.C. *Medieval Dream-Poetry*. Cambridge: Cambridge Univ. Press, 1976.

Stillwell, Gardiner. "Unity and Comedy in the *Parlement of Foules*." *JEGP*, 49 (1950), 470-95.

————. "Chaucer's Eagles and Their Choice on Feb. 14." *JEGP*, 53 (1954), 546-61.

Thackaberry, R.E. "Chaucer's *Parlement of Foules*: A Reinterpretation." Diss. Iowa, 1937.

Uphaus, R.W. "Chaucer's *Parlement of Foules*: Aesthetic Order and Individual Experience." *TSLL*, 10 (1968), 349-58.

Whitman, Frank H. "Exegesis and Chaucer's Dream Visions." *ChauR*, 3 (1969), 229-38.

Wilhelm, J.J. "The Narrator and His Narrative: Chaucer's *Parlement*." *ChauR*, 1 (1967), 201-6.

Winny, James. *Chaucer's Dream-Poems*. London: Chatto & Windus, 1973.

TWENTY-ONE

JOHN P. McCALL

Troilus and Criseyde

Most students of Chaucer have read in the *Canterbury Tales* before coming to *Troilus and Criseyde*. They are often surprised to discover that the second work is not only the finest long narrative poem in English literature, but Chaucer's masterpiece. The *Tales* sparkle with all the variety that art seems able to muster from life and thought and literary convention: its pilgrims are sketched with swift and striking detail and they are often at odds with each other, with themselves, and with their stories. In the midst of complexity and drama, therefore, a reader soon learns that he must be ready to shift his perspective, change his assumptions—in short, be constantly alert. But *Troilus and Criseyde* asks to be read in an entirely different way. Its movement is leisurely, its texture rich and full, and its structure is broadly and classically symmetric. It is a poem to be savored.

The outlines of the story are simple. Young Prince Troilus, who is second only to Hector among the Trojan warriors, falls in love with Criseyde, a lonely and lovely widow; her father, Calchas the prophet, after divining the future destruction of Troy, flees to the Greeks and abandons his daughter. Troilus' best friend, Pandarus, who is also the uncle and guardian of Criseyde, secretly brings the lovers together in a happy union that lasts for several years until Criseyde is exchanged, like a prisoner of war, for one of Troilus' captured brothers. Despite her promise to return, Criseyde remains in the enemy camp with her father and then gives her love to the Greek warrior, Diomede. Still faithful but in despair, Troilus learns of his beloved's treachery, seeks his death in battle and is finally slain by Achilles. After death Troilus' spirit rises above the earth and scorns with laughter the love and world that he has known.

It is no disservice to the *Troilus* to emphasize the simplicity of its story. In fact, as the poem opens, Chaucer summarizes the whole of Troilus' "aventures" in love ("Fro wo to wele, and after out of joie") in only five lines. Obviously he wants his reader to grasp the complete action immediately and briefly, and this despite the fact that the narrative is long—about three and a half times as long as the *Knight's Tale*.

Moreover, this impression of simplicity is reinforced by the way in which the narrative concentrates on only a few major events that occur in only a few select days. On a day in April Troilus sees Criseyde and suffers the torments of love (I, 148-434); a few days later Pandarus learns of Troilus' plight and agrees to help him (I, 547-1064). On the fourth and fifth of May, then, Pandarus begins to persuade Criseyde to fall in love, carries letters of friendship between his niece and Troilus (II, 64-1323), and soon arranges for them to meet alone while a banquet is going on (II, 1401-757; III, 50-420). On a stormy evening in May Pandarus next brings them together to consummate their love (III, 547-1666).

In Book IV the actions which lead to the separation of Troilus and Criseyde—a Trojan defeat, Calchas' plea for his daughter and the negotiations for exchange—all come suddenly and swiftly; and thereafter most of the narrative until well into the last Book is concentrated in a three-day period during which the Trojan parliament approves the exchange, the lovers lament their plight, spend their last night together (IV, 141-1701) and finally part (V, 15-434). Only toward the end does the narrative move away from this select and clearly defined chronology: we see the reactions of Troilus and Criseyde to their ten days of separation, after which Criseyde has promised to return (v, 435-765, 771-1034, 1100-91); and then an increasingly indefinite period of time elapses during which Criseyde's heart gradually changes and Troilus' fear of her betrayal grows to certainty (v, 766-70, 1035-99, 1192-743). At the close there are constant shifts between the past, present and future until, with Troilus' death, the whole temporal order merges with eternity (v, 1807-69): Troilus' spirit rises above the earth to scorn all worldly vanity in relation to "the pleyn felicite / That is in hevene above"; and the narrator parallels this move by contrasting the ephemeral life of man in the past and present with the uncircumscribed, everlasting life of God.

A glance at the chronology of the *Troilus* discloses something of the symmetry of the poem and suggests as well, if only by inference, that Chaucer has impressed a precision of detail and a richness of amplification upon the story which he received from others. Scholars from Karl Young and N. E. Griffin to Robert A. Pratt and Sanford B. Meech have, of course, confirmed this conclusion by describing in detail the relationship of the *Troilus* to its sources. As far as we know, the story of Troilus and Criseyde had its origin in Benoît de Ste. Maure's *Roman de Troie*, a twelfth-century French romance which was "popularized" in a thirteenth-century Latin prose redaction (*Historia Trojana*) by Guido delle Colonne. These two works describe only the parting of the lovers as an episode in the long battle for Troy; but in the fourteenth century they became the sources for Boccaccio's *Il Filostrato*, which is entirely devoted to the story of the lovers. In addition to the three works mentioned, Chaucer also knew and used a French translation of Boccaccio, *Le roman de Troyle et de Criseida* by Beauveau, Seneschal of Anjou. Although there may be more to learn from the intermediate French source, it is still possible to assume with earlier critics that one of the best ways of appreciating Chaucer's *Troilus* is through a comparison with Boccaccio's work. And recently this task has been made easier by Meech's careful account of Chaucer's changes.

But even when changes are identified, questions continue to be asked as to why they were made and to what effect. Such questions are, in fact, the basis for a large part of the commentary on the *Troilus* and the answers are various. C. S. Lewis, for example, has claimed that Chaucer's rendering of *Il Filostrato* was most influenced by medieval rhetoric and French romance, especially by the *Roman de la rose*. Thus, the historical pose of the narrator, the many sententious expressions, *exempla* and proverbs, and particularly the amplification of Troilus and Criseyde's courtship—all suggest that "*Il Filostrato* underwent at Chaucer's hands . . . first and foremost a process of *medievalization*" (p. 56). The argument is an impressive one. And yet others have found it possible to move in a very different direction and have concluded that Chaucer has "Trojanized" his story and consciously made it more classical and pagan. He has added invocations (to Tisiphone, Clio, Venus, Mars and the Furies), prayers and oaths in the names of pagan deities, references to pagan divination and religious practice, and allusions to the Fates and to such legendary figures as Procne, Philomela, Orpheus, Eurydice, and Nisus' daughter. In summary, G. L. Kittredge observed that Chaucer added about one hundred such details in order "to give the tale an ancient—a Trojan—atmosphere" (pp. 50-1).

Since there is evidence for both views, many critics have concluded that Chaucer purposefully created two perspectives, medieval and ancient, for a double effect: the medievalization of the poem in various ways creates what Morton W. Bloomfield has called "the strong reality and, in a sense, [the] nearness of the past" (p. 17); and the Trojan and pagan allusions create a sense of historical distance which reinforces the "pastness" of the story. Whether such perspectives are at odds, or on different levels of reality, or finally in some way congruent has long been a central issue in the interpretation of the *Troilus*.

In one of the earliest discussions along these lines J. S. P. Tatlock argued that the *Troilus* is a "heartfelt worldly tale" with a pious Christian conclusion that is "sudden and arbitrary": Chaucer "tells the whole story in one mood and ends in another"

(p. 636). Although some critics still basically agree with Tatlock, the tendency in recent years has been to show—one way or another—that Chaucer's poem is consistent and coherent from beginning to end. Some of the courtly love interpretations, for example those of C. S. Lewis, T. A. Kirby and Donald R. Howard, are similar to Tatlock's in that they see a dualism in the poem, but they argue that the dualism grows out of an inherent medieval contradiction: the acceptance, on one hand, of a code of love which upheld secretive, extra-marital and quasi-religious unions, and the simultaneous acceptance of a Christian orthodoxy, which, if applied, would find such love idolatrous, illicit and heretical.

Although the basis of this argument has been shaken by some recent reinterpretations of French romances and of Andreas' *Art of Courtly Love*, a completely sympathetic approach to the beauty of Troilus and Criseyde's love has, nevertheless, been sustained in a number of important studies by such critics as Dorothy Bethurum, E. Talbot Donaldson, Alfred David, T. P. Dunning, Robert P. apRoberts and Siegfried Wenzel. These have argued in various ways that Chaucer idealizes Troilus' love as a natural, pagan devotion which is good in itself—"vertuous in kynde" (I, 254). Within the limits and lights of a pagan world this love ennobles its servant (Troilus) and makes him courteous, gentle, considerate, selfless and even wise. Thus Troilus is converted from his carefree disdain for love by the sight of Criseyde and becomes, through his desire, the best of knights:

> . . . the frendlieste wight,
> The gentilest, and ek the mooste fre,
> The thriftiest and oon the beste knyght,
> That in his tyme was or myghte be.
>
> (I, 1079-82)

Furthermore, Troilus pleads his case humbly, restrains his passion with "goode governaunce" and is completely committed to protect Criseyde's honor and reputation. The consummation of this love, then, is like the bliss of heaven itself and makes Troilus a participant in the harmonious love "that of erthe and se hath governaunce" (III, 1744).

Looked at in this way, Chaucer's love story is marred only by Criseyde's betrayal, but even that is a reflection of the natural transitoriness of things which leads Troilus through suffering to a heightened understanding of the world and finally, in death, to a transcendent vision of the heavenly pattern of all love. As Alfred David observes, "Troilus' tragic error, if such an error can be called tragic, is to have tried to love a human being with an ideal spiritual love" (p. 578); and in his devotion to Criseyde he gains "a glimpse" of the heaven that he finally came to see in all its fullness. In the end this view of the *Troilus* reaches a conclusion, very different from Tatlock's, on the Christian closing of the poem: instead of there being a clash between earthly and heavenly love, these loves really prove to be complementary. The poem as a whole, then, affirms the goodness of earthly love even though it be transitory; and it affirms as well the greater goodness of a Christian love which is now available to men and which reaches beyond the world and time.

The sympathetic and dualistic interpretation of the *Troilus* would assert with Lewis and Howard that this is a poem in praise of love. Still, there are many critics who have found this position incomplete or entirely unacceptable because it fails to account for much that the poem seems to insist on: the frailities of the major characters, their deceptions and self-deceptions; the various kinds of irony—comic, philosophic and dramatic; and finally a medieval Christian view which may be pervasive rather than perfunctory. In essays such as those by H. R. Patch, J. L. Shanley, John Speirs, and Roger Sharrock a reader is encouraged to read the *Troilus* from an objective and critical distance, in something of the same serene, ironic and yet tolerant frame of mind that many readers consider uniquely Chaucerian. From such a position Troilus' falling in love seems marked by an extravagant self-pity which is undercut by his own ironic comments on the folly and instability of blind love (I, 197-203, 330-50), and then magnified by Pandarus' pragmatic and business-like approach to satisfying his friend. Troilus, for example, alludes to his honorable intentions toward Criseyde, but Pandarus simply laughs these off with carefree reassurance (I, 1030-43).

In Book II Pandarus' efforts to bring Criseyde to love are cloaked in smiling lies and rhetorical tricks. He is at once attractive, amusing and suspect: only Criseyde's friendship is being sought (II, 332, 360, 371, 379); some tears on a love letter will help (II, 1027); a feigned sickness may prove helpful (II, 1506-33); and perhaps Criseyde will believe that Troilus thinks she loves another (III, 792-8). And when the gentle approach fails, the more direct path will serve as well: the love letter is thrust down Criseyde's bosom (II, 1154-5), and Troilus, in a faint, must be tossed ingloriously into bed with his beloved and undressed (III, 1090-9). Even the bliss of heaven that Troilus feels he enjoys with Criseyde is, in fact, an uncertain and tormenting joy that cannot satisfy or last.

With the change of fortune and the imminent departure of Criseyde in Book IV, Troilus evolves into a painful, pathetic counterpart of his success. His philosophizing is short-sighted and ignorant, his prayers pathetic and blasphemous by turns, his attempt at suicide rash and defiant. Fortune's favorite has become Fortune's fool, and his sufferings become an exemplar for all who would depend on the fickleness of the world. Thus, at the close of the poem, instead of a clashing or coherent dualism, some critics have found the fulfillment of a single view that has gradually evolved from the beginning of the poem. D. W. Robertson, Jr., who has argued this point of view formally and fully, concludes that there is "a remarkable logic in the events of Chaucer's tragedy, an intellectual coherence that is rooted firmly in Christian doctrine and Boethian philosophy"; specifically, then, he thinks that "the tragedy of Troilus is, in an extreme form, the tragedy of every mortal sinner" (p. 36).

Some critics who are inclined to accept this kind of reading for the *Troilus* have also elaborated on some of its ironies. Alan Gaylord, for example, has discussed the *gentilesse* of the poem in terms of a conflict between a superficial gentility which is personally and socially attractive and a true gentility which is grounded in morally right conduct. And in another essay Gaylord has also suggested that Pandarus is not an ideal friend but an ironic inversion of Boethius' Lady Philosophy who leads his charge into Fortune's snares. In a similar vein I have argued this same point while theorizing that the overall structure of the *Troilus* reflects a formal inversion by Chaucer of the five-book structure of Boethius' *de Consolatione*. Finally, John F. Adams has elaborated on an ironical interpretation of Troilus' apostrophe to Criseyde's vacant house (Book v); and Robert E. Kaske has analyzed the *aube*, or parting lyrics of the lovers in Book III, to show that literary convention has been turned inside-out by Criseyde's assumption of the man's role and Troilus' of the woman's.

Although many recent studies have been concerned with reinforcing either a sympathetic or ironic reading of the *Troilus*, they have also been intimately concerned with formal matters. Some, such as those by Henry W. Sams, Charles A. Owen, Jr. and Sanford B. Meech, make it increasingly clear that Chaucer had a firm grasp of the diverse materials of his long poem and that he consciously created evolving and balanced patterns in such ways that parts of his long poem speak to each other allusively and suggestively. The rising actions of Books I-III, for example, are clearly designed to be recalled in the falling actions of Books IV-V. The opening references to "Tisiphone" and the "aventures" of Fortune prepare for the later allusions to Fortune and the three Furies; the crowded temple scene where Troilus first sees Criseyde is balanced by the hectic Parliament scene where Criseyde's surrender to the Greeks is approved; Hector's early kindness to Criseyde is recalled in his lone and chivalrous appeal on her behalf: "We usen here no wommen for to selle" (IV, 182); and Troilus' tormented laments for love—first alone and then with Pandarus—are paralleled by his later laments—alone and then again with his friend.

In Book v Troilus rereads his old love letters and visits the scenes of his former joy; and Criseyde, wooed again, but by a

suit more direct and bold, finds herself retracing a path of knowing but passive acceptance; even the laughter at love by Troilus
and the prayerful appeal by the narrator echo across the story.
These and many similar parallels no doubt elude a precise interpretation, but they are, perhaps, a reminder of the tragic fact that

> The worste kynde of infortune is this,
> A man to han ben in prosperitee,
> And it remembren, whan it passed is.
>
> (III, 1626-8)

There are, of course, other ways in which criticism has sought
to illuminate Chaucer's art. Since Morton W. Bloomfield's impressive study of the role of the narrator, there have been several very
good discussions by Robert M. Jordan, Dorothy Bethurum, E.
Talbot Donaldson and Robert M. Durling. And although these
are often at odds regarding the fullness or limitation of the narrator's vision, they all agree in seeing the importance of his role
for drawing together various perspectives in the poem. In addition, Charles Muscatine has provided one of the most satisfying
general critiques on the *Troilus* through a stylistic analysis. According to Muscatine, Chaucer has employed two conventional
medieval styles in his poem to help create different perspectives:
a courtly style for Troilus' idealism, a realistic style for Pandarus'
pragmatism, and a mixture of these for Criseyde's ambiguity.
From these perspectives, he contends, a "philosophic third view"
arises which "hovers over every important sequence in the
Troilus" (p. 132).

Finally, in one of the most sensitive readings of the *Troilus*,
Robert O. Payne has disclosed something of the coherence and
integrity of Chaucer's art through a series of observations on the
poem's rhetorical procedures (e.g., its lyrical and atmospheric
amplifications; its humorous and serious digressions). Moreover,
as Payne sees it, the double vision of the *Troilus*—from the pagan
past and Christian present—is not really a problem; in fact, this
"is exactly the aim of poetry in the rhetorical definition: the
double validation of truth by finding it in the past and making it

live in the present" (p. 175). The kind of simultaneity and unity that Payne argues for may be confirmed in various ways. In discussing the Trojan scene in the *Troilus*, for example, I have shown elsewhere that Chaucer has arranged the background of his story so that the history of Troy becomes a corporate analogue of Troilus' own tragic story: from his rise to good fortune in a city that is confident and joyous to his fall in a city that is anxious of its fate and finally doomed. In both the background and foreground, however, we are aware that these events of the past are in fact following a tragic pattern ("fro wo to wele, and after out of joie") which draws its meaning from a moral frame of reference that is Boethian and medieval rather than pagan and classical.

More might be said in the same vein of the ways in which Chaucer has related some of the pagan details of his poem to the Christian world of his audience. The Feast of the Palladion, where Troilus first sees Criseyde, is (as Root has noted, p. 413) a pagan equivalent of medieval Easter, "whan clothed is the mede / With newe grene" (I, 156-7) and when knights and ladies are "ful wel arayed . . . bothe for the seson and the feste" (I, 167-8). Moreover, Criseyde's widowhood puts her under the patronage of Pallas Athena (goddess of wisdom and chastity) who reflects the traditional virtues of the Christian widow described as early as Augustine and Ambrose and as recently as John XXIII. The invocation to Venus in the proem of Book III is couched in language both of pagan myth and of Christian theology; and even the two brief prayers to trinities of pagan deities—one in a humorous and one in a serious context—parallel the traditional Christian distinction between the Persons of the Holy Trinity in terms of Power, Wisdom and Love: Minerva (wisdom), Jupiter (power) and Venus (love) II, 232-4; Jove (power), Apollo (wisdom) and Cupid (love) V, 207. Troilus' "Almyghty Jove in trone" (IV, 1079) is Pandarus' "O myghty God . . . in trone" (IV, 1086), and both are echoes of biblical phraseology; and the allusions to Jove as the "auctour of nature" (III, 1016) and the source of Divine Providence (V, 1-2, 1446) are like the familiar "pagan" colloquialism,

"ther Joves yeve the sorwe!": they are all simple translations of
Christian idioms into pagan terms. Juno, like Mary, is besought
to send her *grace* (IV, 1117), and at the end Mercury (V, 1827),
like a pagan angel, disposes of Troilus' departed spirit. Similarly,
from the very beginning of the *Troilus*, Cupid, the god of love, is
described in a mixed vocabulary of pagan mythology and medieval moral philosophy: Cupid is not only the blind bow-boy of
the ancients who hits Troilus with his arrow; he is also the law
of fallen nature, "the lawe of kynde" (I, 238, 979), long associated
with the irrational and spontaneous movement of the senses or,
as Isidore of Seville expressed it (VIII, xi, 80), "*daemon fornicationis.*" To put it in another way, he is the Cupid from Venus'
temple in the *Parliament of Fowls,* where Troilus is remembered
(*PF,* 211-17, 291), rather than an emblem of the harmonious love
that Lady Nature represents in the same poem (*PF,* 379-92).

In these and other similar allusions Chaucer has not allegorized
the pagan gods—for Juno is not Mary, and Mercury is not an
angel; he has rather adapted myth in such a way that a distant
and unfamiliar pagan world is made to appear much like the
Christian world of fourteenth-century England, even in its religious terminology and practice. It is not a world that benefits from
the redemptive love of Christ; and its forms and usages are different. But it is a world in which life is still very much the same.
In making these adaptations Chaucer has not, of course, blazed
a new path. Beryl Smalley has shown in some detail how "the
parallel between pagan and Christian worship" (p. 104) occurs
again and again in the works of the classicizing friars of fourteenth-century England; her suggestion that these men helped
educate Chaucer and his audience to antiquity (pp. 27, 307) is
nowhere more evident than in the *Troilus.*

What has been said, however, is not meant to imply that all of
the pagan myth in the *Troilus* is of a piece. Some of it, for example, reinforces the idea of treachery or betrayal which Speirs
(p. 96) previously noted as a recurrent theme in the poem.
Criseyde's father, Calchas, breaks his faith at the beginning of
the story; Antenor, for whom Criseyde is exchanged, will betray

Troy in its final defeat; as Criseyde's guardian, Pandarus admits that there is treason involved in his bringing Criseyde to Troilus' love, and even she (though we may wonder how seriously) makes similar observations; Pandarus falsely suggests that Troilus thinks *she* may be false and, of course, Criseyde's final betrayal of her lover is the culminating treachery.

Along with these obvious references, there are others less obtrusive. According to Karl P. Wentersdorf, Pandarus' telling the tale of Wade (III, 614) suggests the abduction of a woman by deceitful means just when Pandarus is in the middle of his plot for bringing Criseyde and Troilus together. A number of mythological allusions follow a similar pattern. When Pandarus awakes on the morning of May 4, the swallow Procne stirs him with the song of how her husband (Tereus) committed rape upon her sister (Philomela), and this awakens him to the memory of "his grete emprise"—to get Criseyde for Troilus (II, 64-73). The narrator intervenes with a prayer for Pandarus to Janus, the two-faced "god of entree," and very soon thereafter Pandarus interrupts Criseyde's reading of a story of betrayal ("how the bisshop, as the book kan telle, / Amphiorax, fil thorugh the ground to helle," II, 104-5) to suggest that there are better things to do. Later, in a lying oath regarding his good intentions, Pandarus calls down on his head the fate of Capaneus, the blasphemer (II, 1145), and in a scene of high irony at Deiphebus' party, Helen, a sweet traitor herself, takes Criseyde by the hand and curses anyone who means her harm, "if that I may, and alle folk be trewe" (II, 1610).

It is perhaps ironic, as Robertson has observed, that Troilus should leave a message that he is at the temple of Apollo (god of wisdom and truth) when he is in fact hidden away at Pandarus' home for his night of bliss. But it is certainly ironic that Pandarus should curse himself to the fate of Tantalus, who served a treacherous meal to the gods and suffered the consequences, just when he is inviting Criseyde to a treacherous meal (III, 554-95). That Criseyde's mother should be named "Argyve" (IV, 762), after the wife of the famous Theban traitor (Polynices), is no more accidental than Criseyde's curse upon herself to suffer the same fate as treacherous "Athamante" (IV, 1539) if she is false to Troilus. Finally, as a bitter reminder of Procne's song, "Nysus doughter" (the lark), who betrayed her father, "song with fressh entente" (V, 1110) on the morning when Troilus and Pandarus wait vainly for Criseyde's promised return.

Although I would suggest that there is a pervading theme of treachery in the *Troilus*—a theme fulfilled in the narrator's final references to the "false worldes brotelnesse" over against "that sothefast Crist" who "nyl falsen no wight" (V, 1832, 1845, 1860) —there is certainly much more to the *Troilus*; more, too, than some of the best criticism, only briefly mentioned here, has been able to show. For all its surface simplicity, this is one of the richest and most challenging poems in the English language, a masterpiece for any time.

* * * * *

Some of the recent commentary on the *Troilus* continues to argue the grand question of love. P. M. Kean and R. P. apRoberts find the union of Troilus and Criseyde to be as perfect as circumstances permit and see the source of Troilus' tragedy in his inability to change from a vain expectation "of permanent fidelity in a human love." In the end, as Heidtman observes, Troilus achieves the pagan equivalent of salvation—the reward of Cupid's martyr. Arguments to the contrary take several forms: for example, raising doubts about the ennobling effects of Troilus' love (Whitman), noting the lack of selflessness in his virtue (Lockhart), and even questioning his understanding when he finally escapes his suffering life (Reiss).

While such differences go on, current criticism now tends to by-pass the snarled dispute between the Flower and the Leaf (to leave it to implication, perhaps) and focuses more on specific issues, particularly of structure. For example, John Steadman provides a learned study of the "Epilog" and its traditions in order to emphasize the links between the conclusion and the rest of the poem; and William Provost outlines the poem's major organizational units while prescinding almost entirely from any interpretation. There are three fine essays on the love scene in Book III which illuminate its atmosphere (Howard), its language (Eliason) and its structure (Owen). And there are divergent analyses of Book v which argue on one side for Chaucer's care and success with his materials (Hatcher) and on the other for his cursory treatment and failure (Hussey). Even the cluster of articles on Pandarus—by Cook, Freiwald, Gaylord and Rowland —say as much about the form of the poem as they do about characterization.

Of all the recent work on the *Troilus*, Ida Gordon's is the most ambitious in its effort to grasp "how the sympathy that the narrative invites is compatible" with its irony and how its irony and comedy "are to be reconciled with the emotional effect of the poetry." Her approach to the ambiguities of the text (like J. N. Ganim's in his fine essay) is particularly sensitive to Chaucer's capacity for creating multiple effects. It may be, as Dieter Mehl suggests, that those effects come primarily from Chaucer's ability to force us (his audience) to decide, infer and evaluate his narrative for ourselves; or perhaps better, from his ability to force us to view his narrative from different perspectives. Indeed, it may be that the study of the "Rose-Wheel Design" in medieval art will ultimately lead us to a clearer formulation of this very complex problem.

BIBLIOGRAPHY

Adams, John F. "Irony in Troilus' Apostrophe to the Vacant House of Criseyde." *MLQ*, 24 (1963), 61-65.

apRoberts, Robert P. "The Central Episode in Chaucer's *Troilus*." *PMLA*, 77 (1962), 373-85.

———. "Criseyde's Infidelity and the Moral of the *Troilus*." *Speculum*, 44 (1969), 383-402.

Bethurum, Dorothy. "Chaucer's Point of View as Narrator in the Love Poems." *PMLA*, 74 (1959), 511-20.

Bloomfield, Morton W. "Distance and Predestination in *Troilus and Criseyde*." *PMLA*, 72 (1957), 14-26.

Cook, Robert. "Chaucer's Pandarus and the Medieval Ideal of Friendship." *JEGP*, 69 (1970), 407-24.

David, Alfred. "The Hero of the *Troilus*." *Speculum*, 37 (1962), 566-81.

Donaldson, E. Talbot, ed. *Chaucer's Poetry: An Anthology for the Modern Reader*. 1958. Rpt. New York: Ronald Press, 1975.

————. "The Ending of Chaucer's *Troilus*." In *Early English and Norse Studies Presented to Hugh Smith in Honour of His Sixtieth Birthday*. Ed. Arthur Brown and Peter Foote. London: Methuen, 1963, pp. 26-45.

Dunning, T.P. "God and Man in *Troilus and Criseyde*." In *English and Medieval Studies Presented to J.R.R. Tolkien*. Ed. N. Davis and C.L. Wrenn. London: Allen & Unwin, 1962, pp. 164-82.

Durling, R.M. "Chaucer." In *The Figure of the Poet in Renaissance Epic*. Cambridge, Mass.: Harvard Univ. Press, 1965, pp. 44-66.

Eliason, Norman E. "Chaucer the Love Poet." In *Chaucer the Love Poet*. Ed. Jerome Mitchell and William Provost. Athens, Ga.: Univ. of Georgia Press, 1973, pp. 9-26.

Freiwald, Leah R. "Swych Love of Frendes: Pandarus and Troilus." *ChauR*, 6 (1971), 120-29.

Ganim, John N. "Tone and Time in Chaucer's *Troilus*." *ELH*, 42 (1976), 141-53.

Gaylord, Alan T. "Uncle Pandarus as Lady Philosophy." *PMASAL*, 47 (1961), 571-95.

————. "*Gentilesse* in Chaucer's *Troilus*." *SP*, 61 (1964), 19-34.

————. "Friendship in Chaucer's *Troilus*." *ChauR*, 3 (1969), 239-64.

Gordon, Ida L. *The Double Sorrow of Troilus: A Study in Ambiguities in Troilus and Criseyde*. Oxford: Clarendon Press, 1970.

Griffin, N.E., and A.B. Myrick, trans. *The Filostrato of Giovanni Boccaccio: A Translation with Parallel Text*. Philadelphia: Univ. of Pennsylvania Press, 1929.

Hatcher, Elizabeth R. "Chaucer and the Psychology of Fear: Troilus in Book v." *ELH*, 40 (1973), 307-24.

Heidtmann, Peter. "Sex and Salvation in *Troilus and Criseyde.*" *ChauR*, 2 (1968), 246-53.

Howard, Donald R. "Courtly Love and the Lust of the Flesh: *Troilus and Criseyde.*" In *The Three Temptations: Medieval Man in Search of the World*. Princenton, N.J.: Princeton Univ. Press, 1966, pp. 77-160.

————. "Literature and Sexuality: Book III of Chaucer's *Troilus.*" *MR*, 8 (1967), 442-56.

Hussey, S.S. "The Difficult Fifth Book of 'Troilus and Criseyde'." *MLR*, 67 (1972), 721-29.

Isidore of Seville. *Etymologiarum sive originum, Iibri XX*. Ed. W.M. Lindsay. Oxford: Clarendon Press, 1911.

Jordan, Robert M. "The Narrator in Chaucer's *Troilus.*" *ELH*, 25 (1958), 237-57.

Kaske, R.E. "The Aube in Chaucer's *Troilus.*" In *Chaucer Criticism II: Troilus and Criseyde and the Minor Poems*. Ed. R.J. Schoeck and J. Taylor. Notre Dame, Ind.: Univ. of Notre Dame Press, 1961, pp 167-79.

Kean, P.M. *Chaucer and the Making of English Poetry*. Vol. 1, Boston: Routledge and Kegan Paul, 1972, pp. 112-78.

Kirby, T.A. *Chaucer's Troilus: A Study in Courtly Love*. Baton Rouge, La.: Louisiana State Univ. Press, 1940.

Kittredge, G.L. "Chaucer's Lollius" *Harvard Studies in Classical Philology*, 28 (1917), 50-55.

Lewis, C.S. "What Chaucer Really Did to *Il Filostrato.*" *E&S*, 17 (1932), 56-75.

————. *The Allegory of Love: A Study in Medieval Tradition*. 1936. Rpt. New York: Oxford Univ. Press, 1958.

Leyerle, John. "The Rose-Wheel Design and Dante's Paradiso." *UTQ*, 46 (1977), 280-308.

Lockhart, Adrienne R. "Semantic, Moral and Aesthetic Degeneration in *Troilus and Criseyde.*" *ChauR*, 8 (1973), 100-18.

McCall, John P. "Five-Book Structure in Chaucer's *Troilus*." *MLQ*, 23 (1962), 297-308.

———. "The Trojan Scene in Chaucer's *Troilus*." *ELH*, 29 (1962), 263-75.

Meech, Sanford B. *Design in Chaucer's Troilus*. 1959. Rpt. New York: Greenwood Press, 1970.

Mehl, Dieter. "The Audience of Chaucer's *Troilus and Criseyde*." In *Chaucer and Middle English Studies in Honour of Rossell Hope Robbins*. Ed. Beryl Rowland. London: Allen & Unwin, 1974. Kent, Ohio: Kent State Univ. Press, 1974, pp. 173-89.

Muscatine, Charles. *Chaucer and the French Tradition: A Study in Style and Meaning*. Berkeley: Univ. of California Press, 1957.

Owen, Charles A., Jr. "The Significance of Chaucer's Revisions of *Troilus and Criseyde*." *MP*, 55 (1958), 1-5.

———. "Significance of a Day in *Troilus and Criseyde*." *MS*, 22 (1960), 366-70.

———. "Mimetic Form in the Central Love Scene of *Troilus and Criseyde*." *MP*, 67 (1969), 125-32.

Patch, Howard Rollin. "Troilus on Determinism." *Speculum* 6 (1931), 225-43.

Payne, Robert O. *The Key of Remembrance: A Study of Chaucer's Poetics*. 1963. Rpt. Westport, Conn.: Greenwood Press, 1973.

Pratt, R.A. "Chaucer and *Le Roman de Troyle et de Criseida*." *SP*, 53 (1956), 509-39.

Provost, William. *The Structure of Chaucer's Troilus and Criseyde*. Anglistica 20. Copenhagen: Rosenkilde og Bagger, 1974.

Reiss, Edmund. "Troilus and the Failure of Understanding." *MLQ*, 29 (1968), 131-44.

Robertson, D.W., Jr. "Chaucerian Tragedy." *ELH*, 19 (1952), 1-37.

Root, R.K., ed. *The Book of Troilus and Criseyde*. Princeton, N.J.: Princeton Univ. Press, 1926.

Rowland, Beryl. "Pandarus and the Fate of Tantalus." *OL*, 24 (1969), 3-15.

Sams, H.W. "The Dual Time-Scheme in Chaucer's *Troilus*." *MLN*, 56 (1941), 94-100.

Shanley, J.L. "The *Troilus* and Christian Love." *ELH*, 6 (1939), 271-81.

Sharrock, Roger. "Second Thoughts: C.S. Lewis on Chaucer's *Troilus*." *EIC*, 8 (1958), 123-37.

Smalley, Beryl. *English Friars and Antiquity in the Early Fourteenth Century*. Oxford: Blackwell, 1960.

Speirs, John. "Chaucer: (1) *Troilus and Criseyde*." *Scrutiny*, 11 (1942), 84-108.

Steadman, John M. *Disembodied Laughter: Troilus and the Apotheosis Tradition*. Berkeley: Univ. of California Press, 1972.

Tatlock, J.S.P. "The Epilog of Chaucer's *Troilus*.' *MP*, 18 (1921), 625-59.

Wentersdorf, Karl P. "Chaucer and the Lost Tale of Wade." *JEGP*, 65 (1966), 274-86.

Wenzel, Siegfried. "Chaucer's Troilus of Book IV." *PMLA*, 79 (1964), 542-47.

Whitman, Frank H. "*Troilus and Criseyde* and Chaucer's Dedication to Gower." *TSL*, 18 (1973), 1-11.

TWENTY-TWO

JOHN H. FISHER

The Legend
of Good Women

No major English poet shows more obvious artistic development than Geoffrey Chaucer. Critics naturally expect this growth to be steadily incremental, from the conventionality of the early poems, through the dramatic splendor of *Troilus,* to the rich humanity of the *Canterbury Tales.* However, the *Legend of Good Women* has always been hard to fit into such a regular pattern. Its place in Chaucer's chronology seems fixed by the list of Chaucer's works given in the prologue (F 417), which includes all of his other poems except the *Canterbury Tales.* Yet the persona in the *Legend* prologue is himself a lover, as he had been only in the earliest poems; the frame of the *Legend* is the love vision, which Chaucer had abandoned by the time of *Troilus*; and the technique of the stories in the *Legend* is inferior to that of the earlier *Troilus* and *Knight's Tale* (*Palamon and Arcite* at F 420). As a result, many critics have regarded the *Legend* as a byway, if not an outright retreat, in the course of Chaucer's artistic development.

A further complication was the discovery by Henry Bradshaw (1864) of a unique variant of the prologue to the *Legend* in Cambridge University Library MS. Gg.4.27. F. J. Furnivall (1872) judged this an early, rejected version of the prologue that had been superseded by the "revised" version found in Bodleian MS. Fairfax 16 and ten other manuscripts. Cambridge Gg Furnivall therefore labeled A, and Fairfax et al. B. These designations were used by most British and American scholars until the time of Robinson's edition (1933), although Ten Brink (1892) and the German scholars very early began to use the designations F (for Fairfax) and G (for Cambridge Gg).

The supposed inconsistency of the *Legend* in the pattern of Chaucer's development, and the existence of the two prologues were originally explained in terms of an occasional motive for its composition. Like the *Book of the Duchess*, this poem refers to a royal patron. At F 496 Alcestis commands, "And whan this book ys maad, yive it to the quene,/ On my byhalf, at Eltham or at Sheene." Perhaps merely on the basis of these lines, or perhaps with additional information, Lydgate in the introduction to the *Fall of Princes* (c. 1435) said that "This poete wrote, at the request of the queene,/ A Legende of perfite holynesse/ Of Good Women, to fynd out nyneteene." Speght (1598) and Tyrwhitt (1775) accepted the identification of Alcestis with Queen Anne, and as the motive for composition the account in the prologue, that the compilation was commanded as a penance for the supposed antifeminism in Chaucer's translation of the *Romaunt of the Rose* and *Troilus and Criseyde*. Ten Brink (1870, 1892) elaborated this explanation by attributing the F version of the prologue to Chaucer's gratitude to the Queen for her good office in allowing him to appoint a permanent deputy at the custom house in 1385 so that he could devote more of his time to writing, and the excision of the reference to the Queen in G to his disappointment at the loss of his court emoluments after 1386. This explanation persisted until Tatlock (1903) showed that the appointment of Chaucer's deputy had no connection with the Queen.

Lounsbury (1892) accepted Ten Brink's explanation, but he joined to it a critical argument that has become more important than the occasional explanation in recent criticism. Lounsbury discussed the *Legend* as a stage in Chaucer's artistic development: "There is nothing more peculiar in the 'Legend of Good Women' than the steadily growing dissatisfaction of the author with his subject which marks its progress. . . . The taste which made collections of stories of this kind popular came to be recognized by Chaucer as essentially vicious in art, and therefore transitory." Discussions of the *Legend* since 1900 have turned upon various combinations and permutations of these two viewpoints: the *Legend* as an occasional poem motivated by royal command, and the *Legend* as a stage in Chaucer's poetic development. Before following these themes through the subsequent decades, let me underscore the obvious by observing that these two interpretations are not mutually exclusive. A poem can be occasional and still be a genuine work of art. The fact that the *Book of the Duchess* is an elegy does not prevent its being an important poem in its own right. *Bukton, Scogan*, and *Lack of Steadfastnesse* are pretty successful balades. It is highly probable that *Pearl* is an elegy as well as a great poem, as are *Lycidas* and *In Memoriam*.

The first question about the occasional interpretation was raised by Kittredge (1903), followed almost immediately by Lowes (1904, 1905). Tyrwhitt had remarked upon the resemblance of the prologue of the *Legend* to the marguerite poems of Machaut and Deschamps. Kittredge and Lowes demonstrated its extensive indebtedness, both verbal and conceptual, to the French court poems. Lowes went so far as to specify Deschamps' *Lay de Franchise* as the principal source for lines 1-196, and Froissart's *Paradys d'Amours* for lines 197 to the end of the prologue. This identification had implications for the date of the prologue, since Deschamps' *Lay* was known to have been composed for Mayday 1385. Accepting Kittredge's suggestion that the prologue of the *Legend* was a response to Deschamps' complimentary balade to Chaucer delivered by Sir Lewis Clifford, Lowes traced the movements of Deschamps, Clifford, and Chaucer and concluded that the balade could not have been delivered to Chaucer before the spring of 1386, so the prologue could not have been written before the summer of 1386. By showing that

F was verbally closer to the French sources, and that the differences in G could best be explained as changes from F, Lowes (1913) demonstrated as conclusively as is possible from internal evidence that G is a revision of F. As a means of dating the revision, he observed that the reference to the queen (F 497) must have been excised after Anne's death in 1394, and that the late date is supported by the introduction into G of references to the author's advanced age.

Brilliant as their perceptions were, Kittredge's and Lowes' articles were curiously schizophrenic. They based their arguments for the relationship to the French court poems and the dates of the two prologues largely on external evidence. At the same time, they argued that the similarity of the daisy allegory to the French sources precluded the identification of the daisy-Alcestis with Queen Anne and the interpretation of the composition as the result of a royal command. This conclusion was at once attacked by J.S.P. Tatlock (1907), in a detailed discussion of the possible relation of the two prologues to Richard and Anne. Tatlock supported the textual analysis by which Lowes had argued for the priority of F. He pointed out, however, that most of the critical discussion, whether in connection with the priority of F or G, advanced the aesthetic superiority of F, and that despite arguments that could be made for the greater concision and lucidity of G, F was undoubtedly the more delightful version to read. The reason for the superiority of F is its more spontaneous, more personal expression. The excision of this sort of expression from G cannot be accounted for on purely aesthetic grounds, but only through supposition of some sort of external influence. The key to this influence Tatlock found in the excision of the Eltham-Sheene reference to the queen. The supposition that the prologue was revised after the death of Queen Anne offers the best explanation for the kinds of changes we find in G: the removal of expressions of personal devotion on the part of the poet, the elimination of suspense as to the identity of the lady of the daisies, the excision of the reference to the queen, and so on.

Tatlock's only suggestion as to Chaucer's reason for revising the prologue after the Queen's death was "consideration for the feelings of Richard after the death of his dearly-beloved wife." H. Lange extended this argument in a series of articles (1915 ff.) suggesting that the change of the description of the God of Love's apparel as "enbrouded ful of grene greves,/ In-with a fret of rede rose-leves,/ The fresshest syn the world was first bygonne" (F 227-29) to "ybrouded ful of greene greves,/ A garlond on his hed of rose-levys,/ Steked al with lylye flourys newe" (G 159-61) reveals that the motivation for the revision was to convert a poem originally written in honor of Queen Anne to one celebrating the 1396 marriage of Richard to Princess Isabella of France. Chaucer's expressions of personal devotion to Queen Anne would have to be removed in the revision, and the reference to the fleur-de-lis introduced. The reason that the G version exists in only one manuscript is that it was intended for a special presentation, and Lydgate and the scribes recognized that F was the official version. (This parallels the situation of Gower's *Confessio Amantis,* whose revised version dedicated to Henry of Lancaster likewise exists in only a limited number of manuscripts; Fisher 1964.)

Lange continued his heraldic defense of the priority of the F prologue against a series of studies by V. Langhans (1917 ff.) arguing that G was the only genuinely Chaucerian version of the prologue, aesthetically far superior to F, which was the work of a monkish reviser—presumably Lydgate—who introduced the religious coloring and expressions of devotion to the queen to curry favor with the court. Between 1915 and 1938, Lange, Langhans, and Koch published twenty items exploring various aspects of this private argument. (In 1926 the editor of *Anglia* announced that he would publish no more on the topic, but to no avail; the articles kept coming, and still in *Anglia.*)

The occasional interpretation of the prologue has been carried forward by Margaret Galway (1938 ff.). Instead of Anne and Richard, Galway proposed Richard's mother, Joan of Kent, and her dead husband, the Black Prince, as Alceste and the God of Love. This proposal obviates the objection of Kittredge (1909) that since Alceste at F 497 commands the poet to give the book to the queen, she cannot herself be the queen, and it is attractive in other ways, although it is difficult to follow Galway in the extent to which she would read the entire Chaucer canon up to the *Canterbury Tales* as dictated by Joan of Kent. In 1948 Galway resurrected and extended Lange's suggestion that the G revision was created in honor of Isabella of France. Loomis (1944), Weese (1948), Huppé (1948), and Ruggiers (1950) have cast doubts on the documentary evidence and the readings by which Galway supported her arguments. Fisher (1964) supported Galway's position, suggesting that the *Legend* and Gower's *Confessio Amantis* are parallel pieces, emanating from the same royal command. As J. Norton-Smith has most recently observed (1974), the occasional interpretation turns upon how one reads medieval court poetry. He feels that modern readers are not nearly sensitive enough to the patron-client relationship. He sees the poet's relation to a patron as the central theme of the prologue, whose original purpose was to create "a poetic image of court culture." This is why the G revision is so profoundly unsatisfactory.

Nevertheless, since the 1930's the occasional interpretation of the prologue has fallen out of favor, and critical analysis of the revision in terms of Chaucer's artistic development has become increasingly popular. An early instance of this sort of criticism was H. C. Goddard's suggestion (1908) that a series of "legends" in which the behavior of manifestly "bad" women was praised as "good" could be understood only as satire and irony, and that the revision of the prologue was intended to sharpen this irony as Chaucer moved toward the style of the *Canterbury Tales*. Lowes (1909) rebutted this interpretation by arguing that Goddard misinterpreted the meaning of "good" and by citing examples from medieval literature which indicated that "good women" were those who were faithful in love. R. M. Garrett (1923) joined the interpretation of the stories as satiric with the argument introduced by Skeat and Lounsbury that the expressions of weariness in the stories revealed Chaucer's growing impatience with the uncongenial task that had been assigned him by the Queen. Humor and satire were the devices by which Chaucer sublimated his annoyance. Like Lounsbury and Goddard, Garrett saw the prologue and legends as a stage in Chaucer's artistic development.

In 1923 D. D. Griffith developed fully an aspect of the revision of the prologue which has been remarked by earlier critics: the elimination in G of the language of devotion to the religion of love found in F. He saw the change as evidence that Chaucer grew more formally religious as he grew older and came to regard the religion of love as blasphemous. This view was seconded by Preston (1953) and LaHood (1964). In 1937 R. M. Estrich moved to eliminate completely the occasional interpretation and argued that the changes between F and G were purely the result of Chaucer's maturing art. Lowes had seen the more distant relationship of G to the French court poems merely as evidence that G was later; Estrich saw it as evidence that G was more independent, more satirical, and more dramatic, moving in the direction of the art of the *Canterbury* prologue. In this and in a later article (1939) Estrich followed the lead of W. Sypherd (1908), who had cast doubt on the immediate indebtedness of the *Legend* prologue to Deschamps' *Lay de Franchise*. This process culminated in Marian Lossing's demonstration (1942) that neither the verbal nor the structural parallels from which Lowes had argued are unique to the *Lay*, and hence that Chaucer's inspiration was more general and less exactly datable than Lowes had imagined.

D. C. Baker and R. O. Payne in 1963 accounted for Chaucer's return to the dream vision frame on the grounds of his aesthetic and spiritual development. Baker sees the prologue as a final exploration of the role of the poet in relation to society that Chaucer had explored progressively through the early vision poems. Particularly after the pagan *Troilus*, Chaucer grew more and more preoccupied with the place of the poet in the Christian universe. The revision of the prologue shows the poet excising the paganism of courtly love and enhancing the role of Christian symbolism and of the poet. Payne also sees the revision as evidence of Chaucer's spiritual-aesthetic development. In his book (1963) he sees the poet being scolded by Alceste for the nature of his poetry. The God of Love likewise accuses him of writing bad poetry. Both of these are critical strictures. To Chaucer, according to Payne, better poetry is more devotional poetry; the revision of the prologue shows courtly love evolving toward Christian love, and Alceste toward the tutelary role of the Virgin Mary. In his article (1975), Payne regards the prologue to the *Legend* as the watershed in Chaucer's poetic career, a valedictory that puts behind him the dream journey and the enchanted garden of love in preparation for a "radically different" view of poetry in the *Canterbury Tales.*

It is interesting to observe that none of the recent interpretations of the *Legend of Good Women* as preparation for the *Canterbury Tales* has mentioned the discussion by Skeat (1889) of the prosody of the *Legend* as preparation for that of the *Tales.* In the *Legend* Chaucer introduced into English verse the iambic pentameter (heroic) couplet, which he used to such effect in the *Canterbury* collection.

All of the scholarship and criticism discussed so far focus on the prologue to the *Legend.* In the period before 1930, the sources and allusions of the legends themselves had been discussed at some length, but there is little point in citing many of the more than forty books and articles that treat the relations of the legends to Ovid, the *Ovide Moralisé*, Virgil, Horace, Claudian, Vincent of Beauvais, Dante, Boccaccio, and other authorities. Bech (1872), Morley (1887), and other early commentators believed that Boccaccio's *De Claris Mulieribus* provided the model for the *Legend.* All of the stories except Ariadne, Philomela, and Phyllis are indeed found in *De Claris Mulieribus*, but there are many differences in detail and scarcely any verbal echoes between the two collections. The problem here is the same as with that of the influence of the *Decameron* upon the *Canterbury Tales.* Given Chaucer's penchant for borrowing, if he had really modeled the *Legend* on *De Claris Mulieribus*, why did he not borrow more heavily from it?

W. Connelly (1924) and Eleanor Leach (1962) attributed the tone and structure of the *Legend* to Ovid's *Heroides*. These and other scholars saw the narrative technique of the legends as training for the short narratives in the *Canterbury Tales*. As E. F. Shannon observed (1926), "Chaucer chose the best of Ovid's stories and by the time he abandoned the *Legend*, he had learned the art of brief narrative." In 1972 R. W. Frank developed these hints in a detailed study of the art of the legends. His analysis of how Chaucer transformed his material reveals that in no case did he merely translate, but always selected and adapted with an eye to establishing the tone of the narrative and the roles of the principal characters. Cleopatra is the first, feeble attempt to break with the chivalric tradition. Thisbe is the most successful of the legends and Chaucer's first successful handling of love outside the courtly conventions. "My guess is," says Frank, "that Ovid's Pyramus and Thisbe taught Chaucer the art of simple poetic narrative." After this, Chaucer-like, the poet strove for variety. Dido is a sort of tragicomedy, in which the character and passion of Dido are delineated with sympathy and the falseness of Aeneas made to seem comic. Hypsipyle and Medea is "an odd combination of the jaunty and comic, with a dash of the bitter." Lucrece is a study of horror and pathos. Ariadne is a parody of the romance form. Philomela is an unsuccessful attempt to turn a narrative of horror into one of pathos. Phyllis is another mocking tale. And the final legend, Hypermnestra, is, like Thisbe, a well-made story showing how completely Chaucer had mastered the technique of the brief narrative. Frank (1965) does not accept the traditional view that Chaucer abandoned the *Legend* because he grew weary of his assignment; he interprets the expressions of impatience and boredom as rhetorical *abbreviatio* and *occupatio* used to punctuate the process by which Chaucer was streamlining his material.

Three recent dissertations have likewise focused on the legends rather than on the prologue. Mary Smagola (1972) follows

Goddard and others in interpreting the legends as "masterpieces of comic irony." The prologue is an ironic warning that the reader should not take seriously what follows. The naive dreamer of the *Book of the Duchess* collects stories that reveal the wickedness of women believing sincerely that they demonstrate women's virtue. In this process, Chaucer is discovering the ironic narrative voice of the *Canterbury Tales* and the uses of the frame story. Mary Shaner (1973) follows Lowes (1909) in asserting that the question of whether the legends are to be understood as idealistic or ironic depends on how contemporaries regarded the heroines. She concludes that the view varied from heroine to heroine, and that Chaucer's method was to contrast one not so bad with one not so good, e.g., Cleopatra with Thisbe, Dido with Lucrece, Medea with Hypsipyle. Virginia Shea (1971) sees the characterizations of the legends as "training" for Chaucer's more complex characterizations in the *Canterbury Tales*. (She does not remark on the complex characterizations that had already appeared in *Troilus and Criseyde*.) She returns to the view that Boccaccio's *De Claris Mulieribus* was the model for the *Legend*, and that the revision of the prologue was to make it more lucid and dramatic, and to heighten the comic coloration in preparation for the *Canterbury Tales*.

We may conclude this survey by observing that the *Legend of Good Women* provides a touchstone for the way that Chaucer has been read. Up to 1940, while it was considered profitable to read him in terms of historical and personal associations, there were 115 articles and sections of books dealing mostly with the two forms of the prologue in their historical context. Since 1940, while Chaucer scholarship and criticism have burgeoned, there have been only 48 articles and books devoted to the *Legend*, the majority focussed on its artistry and its place in Chaucer's artistic and intellectual development. Since 1970 have appeared the first studies—a book and three dissertations—devoted principally to the art of the legends themselves, all four concerned chiefly with Chaucer's world view and the evolution of his art. This history appears to indicate that while interest was in occasion, audience, and external motivation, the *Legend of Good Women* was one of the most intriguing of Chaucer's poems. When attention turned to structure, irony, and moral allegory, the poem declined both in interest and importance in the Chaucer canon.

BIBLIOGRAPHY

Baker, Donald C. "Dreamer and Critic: The Poet in the *Legend of Good Women*." *UCSLL,* 9 (1963), 4-18.

Bech, M. "Quellen und Plan der *Legend of Good Women* und ihr Verhältniss zur *Confessio Amantis*." *Anglia,* 5 (1872), 313-38.

Connelly, Willard. "Imprints of the Heroides in the *Legend of Good Women*." *Classical Weekly,* 17 (1924), 9-13.

Estrich, Robert M. "Chaucer's Maturing Art in the *Legend of Good Women*." *JEGP,* 36 (1937), 326-37.

————. "Chaucer's Prologue to the *Legend of Good Women* and Machaut's *Le Jugement Dou Roy De Navarre*." *SP,* 36 (1939), 20-39.

Fisher, John H. *John Gower, Moral Philosopher and Friend of Chaucer.* New York: New York Univ. Press, 1964.

Frank, R.W., Jr. "The Legend of the *Legend of Good Women*." *ChauR,* 1 (1966), 110-33.

————. *Chaucer and the Legend of Good Women.* Cambridge: Harvard Univ. Press, 1972.

————. "The *Legend of Good Women*: Some Implications." In *Chaucer at Albany.* Ed. Rossell Hope Robbins. New York: Burt Franklin, 1975, pp. 63-76.

Furnivall, F.J. "A Note on the Two Forms of the Prologue to the *Legend of Good Women*." *Athenaeum,* 2 (1872), 528.

Galway, Margaret. "Chaucer's Sovereign Lady: A Study of the Prologue to the *Legend* and Related Poems." *MLR,* 33 (1938), 145-99.

————. "Chaucer, Graunson, and Isabel of France." *RES,* 24 (1948), 273-80.

Garrett, R.M. "Cleopatra the Martyr and Her Sisters." *JEGP,* 22 (1923), 64-74.

Goddard, H.C. "Chaucer's *Legend of Good Women.*" *JEGP*, 7 (1908), 87-129; 8 (1909), 47-112.

Griffith, Dudley D. "An Interpretation of Chaucer's *Legend of Good Women.*" In *Manly Anniversary Studies.* Chicago: Univ. of Chicago Press, 1923, p. 32-41.

Huppé, Bernard F. "Chaucer: A Criticism and A Reply." *MLR*, 43 (1948), 393-99.

Kittredge, G.L. "Chaucer and Some of His Friends." *MP*, 1 (1903), 1-18.

————. "Chaucer's Alceste." *MP*, 6 (1909), 435-39.

LaHood, Marvin J. "Chaucer's *The Legend of Lucrece.*" *PQ*, 43 (1964), 274-76.

Lange, Hugo. "Zur Datierung des GG-Prologs Chaucers Legende von guten Frauen: Eine heraldische Studie." *Anglia*, 39 (1915), 347-55.

Langhans, Viktor. "Der Prolog zu Chaucers Legende von guten Frauen." *Anglia*, 41 (1917), 162-81.

————. "Hugo Lange und die Lösung der Legendenprologfrage bei Chaucer." *Anglia*, 50 (1926), 70-103.

Leach, Eleanor Jane Winsor. "The Sources and Rhetoric of Chaucer's 'Legend of Good Women' and Ovid's 'Heroides'." Diss. Yale, 1963.

Loomis, Roger S. "Chaucer's Eight-Year Sickness." *MLN*, 59 (1944), 178-80.

Lossing, Marian. "The Prologue to the *Legend of Good Women* and the *Lai de Franchise.*" *SP*, 39 (1942), 15-35.

Lowes, John L. "The Prologue to the *Legend of Good Women* as related to the French Marguerite Poems and to the *Filostrato.*" *PMLA*, 19 (1904), 593-683.

————. "The Prologue to the *Legend of Good Women* Considered in Its Chronological Relations." *PMLA*, 20 (1905), 749-864.

————. "Is Chaucer's *Legend of Good Women* a Travesty?" *JEGP*, 8 (1909), 513-69.

————. "The Two Prologues to the *Legend of Good Women*: A New Test." In *Anniversary Papers by Colleagues and Pupils of*

George Lyman Kittredge. 1913. Rpt. New York: Russell & Russell, 1967, pp. 95-104.

Lounsbury, T.R. *Studies in Chaucer: His Life and Writings.* 3 vols. 1892. Rpt. New York: Russell & Russell, 1962.

Norton-Smith, John. *Geoffrey Chaucer.* London: Routledge, 1974.

Payne, Robert O. *The Key of Remembrance: A Study of Chaucer's Poetics.* 1963. Rpt. Westport, Conn.: Greenwood Press, 1973.

————. "Making His Own Myth." *ChauR,* 9 (1975), 197-211.

Preston, Raymond. *Chaucer.* 1952. Rpt. Westport, Conn.: Greenwood Press, 1969.

Ruggiers, Paul G. "Tyrants of Lombardy in Dante and Chaucer." *PQ,* 29 (1950), 445-48.

Shaner, Mary C.E. "An Interpretive Study of Chaucer's *Legend of Good Women.*" Diss. Univ. of Illinois, 1973.

Shannon, E.F. *Chaucer and the Roman Poets.* Cambridge: Harvard Univ. Press, 1926.

Shea, Virginia A. " 'Nat Every Vessel Al of Gold': Studies in Chaucer's *Legend of Good Women.*" Diss Univ. of Connecticut, 1971.

Smagola, Mary P. " 'Spek Wel of Love': The Role of Women in Chaucer's *Legend of Good Women.*" Diss. Case Western Reserve, 1972.

Sypherd, W.O. *Studies in Chaucer's Hous of Fame.* 1908. Rpt. New York: Haskell House, 1965.

Tatlock, J.S.P. "The Dates of Chaucer's *Troilus and Criseyde* and *Legend of Good Women.*" *MP,* 1 (1903), 317-29.

————. *The Development and Chronology of Chaucer's Works.* 1907. Rpt. Gloucester, Mass.: P. Smith, 1963.

Ten Brink, Bernhard. *Chaucer: Studien zur Geschichte seiner Entwicklung und zur Chronologie seiner Schriften.* Münster: Russell, 1870.

————. "Zur Chronologie von Chaucer's Schriften." *ESt,* 12 (1892), 13-23.

Weese, Walter E. "Alceste and Joan of Kent." *MLN,* 63 (1948), 474-77.

Abbreviations

CQ	*Cambridge Quarterly*
DAI	*Dissertation Abstracts International*
EA	*Études Anglaises*
E&S	*Essays and Studies by Members of the English Association*
EIC	*Essays in Criticism*
EIE	*English Institute Essays*
EJ	*English Journal*
ELH	*Journal of English Literary History*
ELN	*English Language Notes* (University of Colorado)
EM	*English Miscellany*
EngR	*English Record*
ES	*English Studies*
ESt	*Englische Studien*
Expl	*Explicator*
JAMA	*Journal of American Medical Association*
JAS	*Journal of the Acoustical Society*
JBAA	*Journal of the British Astronomical Association*
JEGP	*Journal of English and Germanic Philology*
JHI	*Journal of the History of Ideas*
JMRS	*Journal of Medieval and Renaissance Studies*
JNT	*Journal of Narrative Technique*
KR	*Kenyon Review*
Lang&S	*Language and Style*

LangQ	Language Quarterly
Leeds	Proceedings of the Leeds Philosophical and Literary Society (Literary and Historical Section)
LHR	Lock Haven Review
MÆ	Medium Ævum
M&H	Mediavalia and Humanistica
MHRA	Modern Humanities Research Association
MLN	Modern Language Notes
MLQ	Modern Language Quarterly
MLR	Modern Language Review
MLS	Modern Language Studies
MP	Modern Philology
MR	Massachusetts Review
MS	Mediaeval Studies (Toronto)
MSpr	Moderna Språk
N&Q	Notes and Queries
Neophil	Neophilologus (Groningen)
NM	Neuphilologische Mitteilungen
OL	Orbis Litterarum
PBA	Proceedings of the British Academy
PCP	Pacific Coast Philology
PLL	Papers on Language and Literature
PMLA	Publications of the Modern Language Association of America
PMASAL	Papers of the Michigan Academy of Science, Arts, and Letters

PQ	*Philological Quarterly* (Iowa City)
PTRSC	*Proceedings and Transactions of the Royal Society of Canada*
QJS	*Quarterly Journal of Speech*
QR	*Quarterly Review*
REL	*Review of English Literature* (Leeds)
RES	*Review of English Studies*
RF	*Romanische Forschungen*
RomN	*Romance Notes*
RPh	*Romance Philology*
RR	*Romanic Review*
SAB	*South Atlantic Bulletin*
SAQ	*South Atlantic Quarterly*
SatR	*Saturday Review*
SB	*Studies in Bibliography*
SELit	*Studies of English Literature* (Univ. of Tokyo)
SFQ	*Southern Folklore Quarterly*
SLitI	*Studies in the Literary Imagination*
SM	*Speech Monographs*
SN	*Studia Neophilologica*
SP	*Studies in Philology*
SRAZ	*Studia Romanica et Anglica Zagrabiensia*
SSF	*Studies in Short Fiction*
TLS	*Times Literary Supplement* (London)
TPS	*Transactions of the Philological Society* (London)

TSE	*Tulane Studies in English*
TSL	*Tennessee Studies in Literature*
TSLL	*Texas Studies in Literature and Language*
UCPES	*University of California Publications, English Studies*
UCSLL	*University of Colorado Studies in Language and Literature*
UMCMP	*University of Michigan Contributions in Modern Philology*
UMSE	*University of Mississippi Studies in English*
UR	*University Review*
UTQ	*University of Toronto Quarterly*
WF	*Western Folklore*
WHR	*Western Humanities Review*
YFS	*Yale French Studies*

II. CHAUCER'S WORKS

Adam	*Adam Scriveyn*
Anel	*Anelida and Arcite*
Astr	*A Treatise on the Astrolabe*
Bal Compl	*A Balade of Complaint*
BD	*The Book of the Duchess*
Bo	*Boece*
Buk	*Lenvoy de Chaucer a Bukton*
CkT	*The Cook's Tale*
ClT	*The Clerk's Tale*

Compl d'Am	Complaynt d'Amours
CT	The Canterbury Tales
CYT	The Canon's Yeoman's Tale
Form Age	The Former Age
Fort	Fortune
FranklT	The Franklin's Tale
FrT	The Friar's Tale
Gen Prol	The General Prologue
Gent	Gentilesse
HF	The House of Fame
KnT	The Knight's Tale
Lady	A Complaint to his Lady
LGW	The Legend of Good Women
MancT	The Manciple's Tale
Mars	The Complaint of Mars
Mel	The Tale of Melibee
MercB	Merciles Beaute
MerchT	The Merchant's Tale
MillT	The Miller's Tale
MkT	The Monk's Tale
MLT	The Man of Law's Tale
NPT	The Nun's Priest's Tale
PardT	The Pardoner's Tale
ParsT	The Parson's Tale
PF	The Parliament of Fowls

PhysT	The *Physician's Tale*
Pity	*The Complaint unto Pity*
PrT	The *Prioress's Tale*
Purse	*The Complaint of Chaucer to his Purse*
Rom	The *Romaunt of the Rose*
RvT	The *Reeve's Tale*
Scog	*Lenvoy de Chaucer a Scogan*
SecNT	The *Second Nun's Tale*
ShipT	The *Shipman's Tale*
SqT	The *Squire's Tale*
Sted	*Lake of Stedfastnesse*
SumT	The *Summoner's Tale*
Thop	*Sir Thopas*
Tr	*Troilus and Criseyde*
Ven	*The Complaint of Venus*
WBT	The *Wife of Bath's Tale*
Wom Nob	*Womanly Noblesse*
Wom Unc	*Against Women Unconstant*

Contributors

ROBERT W. ACKERMAN, Emeritus Professor of English Philology at Stanford University.

DONALD C. BAKER, Professor of English at Kent University, England.

ALBERT C. BAUGH, Emeritus Schelling Memorial Professor of English at the University of Pennsylvania.

HALDEEN BRADDY, Emeritus Professor of English at the University of Texas at El Paso.

D. S. BREWER, Master of Emmanuel College and Reader in Medieval English at the University of Cambridge, England.

JOHN H. FISHER, John C. Hodges Professor at the University of Tennessee.

RICHARD L. HOFFMAN, Professor of English at Virginia Polytechnic Institute and State University.

ROBERT M. JORDAN, Professor of English and Head of the Department at the University of British Columbia, Vancouver.

THOMAS A. KIRBY, Emeritus Professor of English and Former Head of the Department of English at Louisiana State University.

JOHN P. MCCALL, Professor of English, Senior Vice-President and Provost at the University of Cincinnati.

ROBERT P. MILLER, Professor of English at Queens College, City University of New York.

TAUNO F. MUSTANOJA, Emeritus Professor of English at the University of Helsinki.

CHARLES A. OWEN, JR., Professor of English at the University of Connecticut.

ROBERT O. PAYNE, Professor of English at the Graduate Center, City University of New York.

R. VANCE RAMSEY, Professor of English at Ohio Univerity.

ROSSELL HOPE ROBBINS, International Professor at the State University of New York at Albany.

D. W. ROBERTSON, JR., Professor of English at Princeton University.

BERYL ROWLAND, Professor of English at York University.

PAUL G. RUGGIERS, David Ross Boyd and George Lynn Cross Research Professor of English at the University of Oklahoma.

J. BURKE SEVERS, Emeritus Distinguished Professor of English and Former Chairman of the Department of English at Lehigh University.

LAURENCE K. SHOOK, Emeritus Professor and Past President of the Pontifical Institute of Mediaeval Studies and Emeritus Professor of English at the University of Toronto.

CHAUNCEY WOOD, Professor of English at McMaster University.

Name Index

Subject Index

For this index the editor has revised and expanded an index for the first edition compiled by Linda K. Rambler in 1970.

An ABC, 21, 149, 151, 394–95; early printing of, 381; influence of ballade on, 82

abbreviatio, 45, 46

Absolon, 26, 366; dramatic irony in, 362

acrostics and Chaucer, 146

Adam Scriveyn, 394; early printing of, 381

Adenès li Roi: influence on *SqT*, 275

aesthetics, medieval, 109

Against Women Unconstant, 149, 384, 391–92; early printing of, 381

Alanus de Insulis: influence on *PF*, 432

Alchemy, 32

Alfred, King, 34

Alison, 29, 120, 130

allegoria, 49, 52

allegorical system, principles of, 332–33

allegory: in *CT*, 326–51; classical, 333–35; formal *vs.* informal, 337–44; historical, 212–13; historical, in *BD*, 408; in *CT*, 302; in *KnT*, 208–9; in *Mars*, 408; in *MerchT*, 304; in *MillT*, 304; in *PF*, 429, 434, 437; in *Pity*, 388; imagery of, 328; includes irony, 353–54; medieval definition of, 328; religious, 334–35; types of, 329. *See also* scriptural allegory

Almonry School of St. Paul's, 6

An Amorous Complaint. See Complaynt d'Amours

amplificatio, 45, 46

Anelida and Arcite, 149, 386, 389–90, 396, 440; Boccaccio's influence on, 170; complaint within, 389; metrical structure, 80; *Thebaid* influence on, 192; virelai form in, 384

Anne of Bohemia: in *PF*, 430

anti-antifeminism: by Wife of Bath, 277

anti-feminism, 223; study of tradition, 356

Antigone, 382

anti-Semitism, 358

The Arabian Nights: source of *SqT*, 275

Arcite, 273, 274, 283; astrological destiny of, 208; Boccaccio's influence on, 171

Aristotle, 33

Arnulf of Orléans: critique of *Metamorphoses*, 334

ars dictandi, 42

ars praedicandi, 42

art critics: on reality *vs.* realism, 108–9

Arthurian legend, 276

astrology, 214; in *BD*, 407; Chaucer

the Man of Law, 13, 226, 227, 250, 251, 256, 257; irony in portrait, 359–60

the *Man of Law's Tale*, 129–30, 144, 156, 229, 237, 272; astrology in, 209–10, 214; Boccaccio's influence on, 175; evidence of tale revision, 232; formal allegory in, 337; literary relationships of, 271; romance, 271; saint's legend, 271–72; source of, 153

the Manciple, 249, 250, 251, 252, 256

the *Manciple's Tale*, 226, 236; Cato's influence on, 195; French influence on, 153, 154; Latin influence on, 187; structural irony in, 361; tale-teller relationship, 226

manuscripts: of *Anel*, 389; evidence for Marriage Group, 361; illustrations from, 266; of minor poems, 381; study of, 192, 194–96, 223; Auchinleck, 277–78; Cambridge University Ii., 393; Corpus Christi College, Cambridge, 9, 13, 71; identification of lyrics in, 383; minor poems in, 381; MS. Harley 7578: minor poems in, 381; MS. Harley 2253: anthology of thirteenth- and fourteenth-century poetry in, 383

marguerite: medieval cult of, 148

Marie de France: in *PF*, 147, 430

Marriage Group, 11, 223, 278; manuscript evidence for, 361; relationship of *MerchT* to, 309; solution to in *FranklT*, 361

Matthew de Vendôme, 119

medieval attitudes on astrology, 205

medieval literature: allegory in, 326; exegetical approach to, 229

medieval narrative: study of, 98

medieval rhetorical-poetic doctrine, 44

medieval symbolism, 326

Medievalization: in *Tr*, 449

the Merchant, 227, 250, 251, 252, 277, 358; as ironic figure, 340; self-revelation of, 227; source of, 344

the *Merchant's Tale*: allegory in, 304, 340–341; Cato's influence on, 195; as a fabliaux, 297, 309–10; French influence on, 153; *gentilesse* in, 276; host's reticence about wife, 232; imagery in, 125; irony in, 300–1, 365; naturalism in, 303; scholarship on, 359; sovereignty in, 278; teller *vs.* tale, 359; verbal irony in, 354

Merciles Beaute, 384, 392; influence on Lydgate, 392; sources of, 150; meter: Chaucer as metrical artist, 70; influence of French *decasyllable*, 76; influence of Italian *endecasillabo*, 76; *hendecasyllabic*, 76; Middle English, 69; Old English, 69; rhyme as basis for chronology, 79; rhyme-words, 80

metrical line: experiment in *Lady*, 386; French influence on, 75; use of enjambement, 75

Le meunier et les ii clers, 135

Middle Ages: irony in, 364–65

mill imagery, 134

the Miller, 122, 249, 250, 251, 252; French influence on, 155; governing planets of, 207; paradox in, 365; rival of the Reeve, 224, 227

the *Miller's Prologue*, 259; Boccaccio's influence on, 175; defense of plain speech in, 175

the *Miller's Tale*, 26, 29, 120, 123, 235, 311, 348, 366; allegorical elements in, 304, 335; astrological dating of, 209; astrology in, 209; Biblical associations in, 307; Boccaccio's influence on, 175; a burlesque, 307; Cato's influence on, 195; characters in, 300, 305; comic irony in, 355; fabliaux, 297; imagery in, 125, 130, 132; irony in structure of, 355; language in,

textual revision: in *CT*, 232

Thebaid: influence on Chaucer, 186, 191; influence on *Anel*, *HF*, and *KnT*, 192; study of by Pseudo-Fulgentius, 333; use in *TR*, 191-92. *See also Statius*, Publius Papinius, 273–74

Theseus, 274; allegorical figure, 340

time: in *Tr*, 448

To Rosemounde, 149, 391; manuscripts of, 381

traductio, 50, 52

translatio: in *To Rosemunde*, 391

Trastamara, Henry de, 16

Treatise on the Astrolabe, 202, 214; editions of, 206; Sacrobosco's influence on, 206; use of astrology in, 205

Trivet, Nicholas: influence on Chaucer, 153

trochaic substitution, 77

Troilus and Criseyde, 12, 21, 26, 32–34, 52, 85, 97, 102, 105, 107, 130, 131, 134, 143, 144, 165, 272, 364, 391, 446–63; astrology in, 211–12; Boccaccio's influence, 170, 171; Boethius' influence, 144; Chaucer on love, 365, 438; comment about human love, 174; complaint in, 385; criticism on, 173; Dante's influence, 166, 173–74; foreign influence, 162; Horace's influence, 193–94; imagery, 130; influence on fifteenth century, 382; influence on sixteenth century, 383; irony, 361; Juvenal's influence, 186; Latin influence, 187, 194; narrative style, 98; narrator, 50, 110; outline of story, 446–48; pagan influence, 455–56; Petrarch mentioned in, 165, 178; philosophical tones, 434; portrait of Chaucer in MS., 9; problem of evil, 172; religious implications, 174; rhetoric, 61, 454; rhyme words, 80; a romance, 271; sources, 119, 448–49; Sta-

tius' influence, 191, 192; stylistic analysis, 454; unity of, 453

Truth, 21, 144, 392, 396; manuscripts of, 381

Ugolino, 169, 177; compare Dante and Chaucer on, 168–70

unity: in *CT*, 55, 103, 227–28; in *TR*, 453. *See also* design of the *Canterbury Tales*

Vache, Sir Philip de la, 392–93

valentine tradition, 386, 396; in *Mars*, 390

Valerius Flaccus, Gaius: *Argonautica*, 186

Valerius Maximus: influence on Chaucer, 186, 195

Vergil, 131, 162, 185, 197, 471; influence on Chaucer, 185; influence on *HF*, 419; influence on *PF*, 436–37; Vergilian tradition in Middle Ages, 190–91

versification, 67; source of Middle English, 69

Vincent of Beauvais, 186, 471

virelai, 384; in *MercB*, 392

Virgil. *See* Vergil

Visconti, Bernabò: Chaucer's negotiations with, 163–64

Visconti, Violante: marriage of in 1368, 162

Watriquet de Couvin: influence on *Thop*, 154

the Wife of Bath, 27, 28, 32, 33, 107, 122, 224, 248, 250, 251; allegorical model of, 344–45; alluded to in *MerchT*, 309; astrological influence on, 205; character of, 360; as Dame Philosophy, 345; related to Marriage Group, 223; self-revelation of, 227; sovereignty discussion, 223

the *Wife of Bath's Prologue*: "ba-